An Introduction to Intercultural Communication

Ninth Edition

WITHDRAWN

COVENTRY UNIVERSITY LONDON
University House
109 - 117 Middlesex Street, London. E1 7JF
Tel: 024 7765 1016
www.coventry.ac.uk/london

Sara Miller McCune founded SAGE Publishing in 1965 to support
the dissemination of usable knowledge and educate a global
community. SAGE publishes more than 1000 journals and over
800 new books each year, spanning a wide range of subject areas.
Our growing selection of library products includes archives, data,
case studies and video. SAGE remains majority owned by our
founder and after her lifetime will become owned by a charitable
trust that secures the company's continued independence.

Los Angeles | London | New Delhi | Singapore | Washington DC | Melbourne

An Introduction to Intercultural Communication

Identities in a Global Community

Ninth Edition

Fred E. Jandt

Los Angeles | London | New Delhi
Singapore | Washington DC | Melbourne

FOR INFORMATION:

SAGE Publications, Inc.
2455 Teller Road
Thousand Oaks, California 91320
E-mail: order@sagepub.com

SAGE Publications Ltd.
1 Oliver's Yard
55 City Road
London, EC1Y 1SP
United Kingdom

SAGE Publications India Pvt. Ltd.
B 1/I 1 Mohan Cooperative Industrial Area
Mathura Road, New Delhi 110 044
India

SAGE Publications Asia-Pacific Pte. Ltd.
3 Church Street
#10-04 Samsung Hub
Singapore 049483

Copyright © 2018 by SAGE Publications, Inc.

Printed in the United Kingdom

Library of Congress Cataloging-in-Publication Data

Names: Jandt, Fred Edmund, author.

Title: An introduction to intercultural communication: identities in a global community / Fred E. Jandt.

Description: Ninth Edition. | Thousand Oaks, California: SAGE, [2018] | Previous edition: 2016. | Includes bibliographical references and index.

Identifiers: LCCN 2017029744 | ISBN 9781506390727 (International Student Edition paperback: acid-free paper)

Subjects: LCSH: Intercultural communication. | Intercultural communication–United States. | Communication, International.

Classification: LCC GN345 .J43 2018 | DDC 303.48/2–dc23 LC record available at https://lccn.loc.gov/2017029744

Acquisitions Editors: Karen Omer,
                       Terri Accomazzo
Editorial Assistants: Sarah Dillard, Erik Helton
Content Development Editors: Anna Villaruel,
                             Jennifer Jovin
Production Editor: Tracy Buyan
Copy Editor: Sarah J. Duffy
Typesetter: Cenveo Publisher Services
Proofreader: Jen Grubba
Cover Designer: Scott Van Atta
Marketing Manager: Amy Lammers

This book is printed on acid-free paper.

17 18 19 20 21 10 9 8 7 6 5 4 3 2 1

Brief Contents

PART 4. Cultures Within Cultures

PART 5. Applications

Detailed Contents

©iStockphoto.com/itchySan

PART 2. Communication Variables

CHAPTER 3. Context, Perception, and Competence   74

©iStockphoto.com/
STUDIOGRANDOUEST

CHAPTER 4. Nonverbal Communication   102

©iStockphoto.com/
robyvannucci

CHAPTER 5. Language as a Barrier   130

PART 3. Cultural Values

©iStockphoto.com/
valentinrussanov

CHAPTER 6. Dimensions of Nation-State Cultures 166

©iStockphoto.com/
kreicher

Marco Di Lauro/
Getty Images

CHAPTER 8. Religion and Identity 230

Theo Wargo/
Getty Images

CHAPTER 9. Culture and Gender   256

PART 4. Cultures Within Cultures

SAUL LOEB/
Getty Images

Jonathan Bachman/
Getty Images

©iStockphoto.com/
kali9

PART 5. Applications

© iStockphoto.com/
porcorex

About the Author

Fred E. Jandt was born of second-generation German immigrants in the multicultural south-central region of Texas. After graduating from Texas Lutheran University and Stephen F. Austin State University, he received his doctorate in communication from Bowling Green State University. He has taught and been a student of intercultural communication for more than 40 years, developing his experience through travel and international training and research projects. While professor of communication at The College at Brockport, State University of New York, his reputation as a teacher led to his appointment as SUNY's first director of faculty development. He has retired as professor and branch campus dean after having been named outstanding professor. He has also been a visiting professor at Victoria University of Wellington, in New Zealand. He has extensive experience in the areas of intercultural and international communication, negotiation, mediation, and conflict management. He was one of the first scholars to introduce the study of conflict to the communication discipline with his text *Conflict Resolution Through Communication* (Harper & Row, 1973). He has subsequently published many other titles in this area, including the successful trade book *Win-Win Negotiating: Turning Conflict Into Agreement* (Wiley, 1985), which has been translated into eight languages, and a casebook on international conflict management, *Constructive Conflict Management: Asia-Pacific Cases* (SAGE, 1996) with Paul B. Pedersen. For several years, he conducted the training workshop "Managing Conflict Productively" for major corporations and government agencies throughout the United States. Jandt continues to train volunteers who are learning to become mediators in the California justice system and serves as an elected trustee of the Desert Community College District.

Preface

Why Study Intercultural Communication?

When a student asks, "What is this class about?" I have two answers. If it's a short hallway conversation I say something like "to learn to become a more effective communicator with peoples of diverse cultural backgrounds." If we have time for a sit-down discussion, I start by talking about identities—the identities each of us accepts to be known by in the world. We then discuss what goes with that identity—everything from what we wear, to the language we speak, to the values we use to guide our behavior. It then becomes obvious that diverse identities can be at the root of many communication barriers. At this point students see the broader challenges and raise the issues of immigration, treatment of women, clash of religions and terrorism, corporate influence over local cultures, and countries exerting unwelcome influence over other countries.

In order to live, work, and play in an increasingly interconnected and interdependent world, we all need to communicate effectively with people of diverse cultural backgrounds. We need to be aware of how our language and nonverbal communications might be understood by people whose frame of reference is different than ours. We also need to understand how the historical relationships between cultures inform how they interact today. The aim of this book is to equip students with the knowledge and skills to be competent and confident intercultural communicators. In each chapter the book guides students through key concepts and helps readers connect intercultural competence to their own life experiences in order to increase understanding.

The core objectives of this book have not changed with the ninth edition: We continue to promote the skills of intercultural competence by developing an understanding of cultures to better appreciate the opportunities and challenges each culture presents to its people, developing a better understanding of how people become who they are, becoming less threatened by those of different backgrounds, and becoming better able to select and perform communication behaviors appropriate to various settings.

What I strive to do is to provide information that is balanced and up-to-date in a manner that is accessible and interesting. It has been my objective from the first edition of this book to make it readable, engaging, and thought provoking while at the same time flexible enough to support individual instructors' approaches to the content theories.

After reading this book, students will become effective intercultural communicators by developing the following skills and knowledge:

- expanding the range of verbal and nonverbal communication skills
- becoming able to communicate effectively in unfamiliar settings
- recognizing the influence our own culture has had on the way in which we view ourselves
- expanding knowledge of different cultural traditions

It has been my pleasure to have worked with thousands of students face-to-face and online through the years. I consider this book's readers to be part of that group and have received many questions and comments from them via e-mail that have helped improve each edition. Thank you for reading this book and for participating in this learning community to appreciate and to become more effective in intercultural encounters.

New to the Ninth Edition

The world has changed dramatically in the past few years: Attitudes toward immigration and refugees, attitudes toward gender identifications, awareness of social class identity, and awareness of religious identity are just a few of the changes our society has experienced in recent years. This edition addresses these shifts throughout the text.

As before, the major regulators of human life—religion, nation, class, gender, race, and civilization—are the core themes that run throughout the book. Chapter content is up-to-date with current international developments and communication challenges. Each chapter also includes materials on social media.

Pedagogical Features

Many of the most successful features from previous editions—those that really enhance student engagement and learning—are still here, updated for the new edition. These include the following:

- Focus on Skills boxes that challenge students to apply the key concepts they have learned in each chapter to a "real-life" intercultural communication scenario
- Focus on Technology features that explore contemporary examples of intercultural communication on the Internet, social media, and mobile devices
- Focus on Theory boxes that call students' attention to communication theories
- Focus on Culture features, which help students understand cultural practices within their own and other cultures
- Global Voices boxes that use brief, provocative quotes to introduce students to a range of perspectives on global intercultural communication
- Learning Objectives at the start of each chapter that identify what students should expect to know or be able to do after engaging with the chapter material
- Charts, graphics, and photos that convey information in a visually engaging way

- Maps that help readers better understand the geographical and cultural locales discussed
- Case studies of specific cultures that connect key concepts to real-world examples
- Discussion Questions that spark in-class conversation and encourage students to reflect critically on what they have learned in each chapter
- Glossary with Key Terms highlighted in each chapter
- Readings at the end of each chapter that connect the chapter to resources in *Intercultural Communication: A Global Reader,* which may be used alongside this text

Digital Resources

Additional digital materials further support and enhance the learning goals of this edition.

$SAGE edge™

http://edge.sagepub.com/jandt9e

SAGE edge offers a robust online environment you can access anytime, anywhere, and features an impressive array of free tools and resources to keep you on the cutting edge of your learning experience.

SAGE edge for Students provides a personalized approach to help you accomplish your coursework goals in an easy-to-use learning environment.

- Mobile-friendly eFlashcards strengthen your understanding of key terms and concepts.
- Mobile-friendly practice quizzes allow you to independently assess your mastery of course material.
- Chapter summaries with learning objectives reinforce the most important material.
- Video and multimedia links appeal to students with different learning styles.
- Chapter exercises for both classwork and homework give instructors creative ways to reinforce the chapter material and help students apply the concepts from the text to their lives.
- EXCLUSIVE! You now have access to full-text SAGE journal articles that have been carefully chosen to support and expand on the concepts presented in each chapter.

SAGE edge for Instructors supports your teaching by making it easy to integrate quality content and create a rich learning environment for students.

- Test banks provide a diverse range of prewritten options as well as the opportunity to edit any question and/or insert your own personalized questions to assess students' progress and understanding.
- Sample course syllabi for semester and quarter courses provide suggested models for structuring your courses.
- Editable, chapter-specific PowerPoint® slides offer complete flexibility for creating a multimedia presentation for your course.

- EXCLUSIVE! You now have access to full-text SAGE journal articles that have been carefully selected to support and expand on the concepts presented in each chapter.
- Video and multimedia links appeal to students with different learning styles.
- Lecture notes summarize key concepts by chapter to help you prepare for lectures and class discussions.
- Chapter-specific discussion questions help launch engaging classroom interaction while reinforcing important content.
- Chapter exercises for both classwork and homework give instructors creative ways to reinforce the chapter material and help students apply the concepts from the text to their lives.
- A course cartridge is included for easy LMS integration.

Acknowledgments

Through the years many people have reviewed previous editions, and I have thanked them in each and every edition. That list has grown so that I can only thank previous reviewers collectively and list the new reviewers for this edition. This group of reviewers has provided extensive critical comments that have made this the best possible edition.

Mo Bahk, California State University, San Bernardino

Joseph A. DeVito, Hunter College, City University of New York

Shinsuke Eguchi, University of New Mexico

Catherine Levitt, College of the Desert

Ané Pearman, Tidewater Community College

Aimee L. Richards, Fairmont State University

Ralph Webb, Purdue University

Over the years, the professional staff at SAGE has done so much to make this book such a success. Matthew Byrnie, associate director, guided the revisions for the seventh and eighth editions with sensitivity and foresight. Karen Omer, speech communication acquisitions editor, enthusiastically took over that role for this new edition. Anna Villarruel, associate development editor, provided valuable feedback and acted as a guide for the new edition. Jennifer Jovin, content development editor, shepherded the project through production and supervised the development of the digital materials for this edition. Sarah Dillard provided needed and much-appreciated assistance throughout manuscript development. Thanks to Sarah Duffy, copy editor for this edition, and very special thanks to Tracy Buyan, senior project editor, who guided this manuscript and others for me through the production process with such experience and attention. The team at SAGE has done so much to make this edition the best, and I am deeply appreciative.

Part 1

Culture as Context for Communication

Chapter 1

©iStockphoto.com/FatCamera

Defining Culture and Communication

Have you ever considered why there's not just one human culture rather than many cultures? Biologists Rebecca Cann, Mark Stoneking, and Allan C. Wilson (1987) studied genetic material from women around the world and contend that all humans alive today share genetic material from a woman who lived some 200,000 years ago in sub-Saharan Africa. Their African "Eve" conclusion is supported by linguistic observations. Cavalli-Sforza, Piazza, Menozzi, and Mountain (1988) have shown that considerable similarity exists between Cann's tree of genetic relationships and the tree of language groups, which hypothesizes that all the world's languages can be traced to Africa.

The languages that vary the most from other languages today can be found in Africa. This suggests that these African languages are older. Africa's Khoisan languages, such as that of the !Kung San, use a clicking sound that is denoted in writing with an exclamation point. Such evidence, along with genetic evidence, suggests that all 7 billion of us alive today share ancestry from one group in Africa. Yet among the 7 billion of us there are diverse ways of understanding the world, of languages, of beliefs, and of ways of defining our identities. In this chapter you'll first read about the regulators of human behavior and identify. Then you'll read about the related concepts of culture, subculture, co-culture, subgroup, and microculture. Finally, you'll read about the concept of communication as something that is itself a

3

product of culture, meaning that how communication as a concept is defined and how communication is performed are very much part of each cultural group—so much so that it has been said culture and communication can only be understood together.

Sources of Identity

How, then, did so many distinct human identities develop? Climate changes and other pressures led to migrations out of Africa. The first wave may have been along the coastline of southern Asia through southern India into Australia. The second wave may have traveled to the Middle East, and from there, one branch went to India and a second to China. Those who left the Middle East for Europe may have actually traveled first through Central Asia and then throughout the world to other parts of Asia, Russia, the Americas, and Europe (Wells, 2002). Neuroscientist Antonio Damasio (2010) contends that our world, our environment, is so complex and so varied on the planet that diverse social networks developed to regulate life so that we could survive. Centuries of geographical separation lead to the development of diverse social network regulators of human life. These social network regulators of human life over the history of humanity have been the basis for ways of understanding the world, for beliefs, and for shared individual identities, which at times resulted in confrontations and conflicts between groups. Understanding these identities and the resulting confrontations explains our past, provides insights about the present, and predicts our future. Sir David Cannadine (2013) posits six forms of regulators of human life and identity: religion, nation, class, gender, race, and civilization.

@iStockphoto.com/pushlama

Generational transmission of important cultural rituals provides cultural continuity through the ages.

Religion and Identity

Cannadine (2013) argues that religion is the oldest source of human identity and conflict. Religion can clearly be a regulator of how we live our lives and provide a clear sense of identity. Religious wars are those clearly caused or justified by differences in religious beliefs exclusive of other issues. Even with that restrictive definition, religious wars have resulted in tens of millions of deaths. The Crusades of the 11th through 13th centuries against the Muslims were blessed as a *bellum sacrum* ("holy war") by Pope Urban II. In the 16th century there was a succession of wars between Roman Catholics and Protestants known as the French Wars of Religion. The Nigerian Civil War (1967–1970) pitted Islam against Christianity, as does ongoing violence in the Central African Republic. In the early 1990s, Serbs, Croats, and Bosniaks in the former Yugoslavia were divided along Orthodox, Catholic, and Muslim lines. In Iraq, Muslims are divided between Sunni and Shiite. At other times, of course, religious groups have coexisted without conflict.

Let's look in more detail into Cannadine's remaining five sources of human identity and conflict.

Global Voices

The Hindu faces this way, the Muslim the other. The Hindu writes from left to right, the Muslim from right to left. The Hindu prays to the rising sun, the Muslim faces the setting sun when praying. If the Hindu eats with the right hand, the Muslim with the left. . . . The Hindu worships the cow, the Muslim attains paradise by eating beef. The Hindu keeps a mustache, the Muslim always shaves the upper lip.

—Words of a Hindu nationalist addressing the conflict with Indian Muslims (Jacoby, 2011)

National Identity

The nation-state may be the most significant political creation of modern times. For much of humanity from the 18th century on, national identity has superseded religious identity as a primary identity in many parts of the world. It has become common practice today to equate nation-state identity with cultural identity. In most cases, this is largely true. Ladegaard (2007), for example, demonstrated that in a large global corporation employing some 8,500 people in nearly 40 countries, employees perceive their nation-states as the frame of reference or identity while any conceptualization of a global identity is perceived as a hypothetical construction. An individual born and raised in Spain who has worked for years for the Swedish technology company Ericsson at its service center in India most likely self-identifies as Spanish.

National identity is not descriptive when arbitrarily drawn political boundaries do not reflect peoples' identities. For example, in Europe there are several examples of popular support for secessionist states. In the United Kingdom, a vote for independence for Scotland was held in 2014. In a hotly contested election, nearly 45% voted for independence. While the referendum failed, British Prime Minister David Cameron pledged reforms granting Scotland greater autonomy. Catalonia is a region of about 7.5 million people in northeastern Span with its own culture and language. In late 2014, more than 80% of voters in Spain's Catalan region voted to support secession in an unofficial, nonbinding poll. Against Spain's government's objections, the region's parliament has begun the process of separating from Spain. In Belgium, Dutch-speaking Flemings in the north have pressed for separation from the French- and German-speaking Walloon population in the south.

Just as religious identity has been the basis for conflict, obviously national identity has been the basis for millions and millions of deaths from conflicts. Cultures provide diverse ways of interpreting the environment and the world as well as relating to other peoples. To recognize that other peoples can see the world differently is one thing. To view their interpretations as less perfect than ours is another.

How differences can lead to conflict can be seen in the evolution of the connotative meaning of the word *barbarian* from its initial use in the Greek of Herodotus to its meaning in contemporary English (Cole, 1996). To better understand the origins of hostilities between the Greeks and the Persians, Herodotus visited neighboring non-Greek societies to learn their belief systems, arts, and everyday practices. He called these non-Greek societies *barbarian*, a word in Greek in his time that meant people whose language, religion, ways of life, and customs differed from those of the Greeks. Initially, *barbarian* meant different from what was Greek.

Later, the Greeks began to use the word *barbarian* to mean "outlandish, rude, or brutal." When the word was incorporated into Latin, it came to mean "uncivilized" or "uncultured."

The *Oxford English Dictionary* gives the contemporary definition as "a rude, wild, uncivilized person," but acknowledges the original meaning was "one whose language and customs differ from the speaker's." Conflict between nations often begins with the judgment that how others live their lives is in some ways less perfect than how we live our own.

Class and Identity

Marx and Engels (1850) claimed that identities were not created by religions or countries, but in the relationship to the means of production, that is, the capitalists who own the means of production and the proletariat, or "working class," who must sell their own labor. The opening sentence of *The Communist Manifesto* is "The history of all hitherto existing society is the history of class struggle" (Marx & Engels, 1850). In this understanding of class, conflict is inevitable. The collapse of Communism, though, has demonstrated that this understanding of class is not pervasive nor an all-encompassing source of identity (Cannadine, 2013). Max Weber believed that social class was determined by skill and education rather than by one's relationship to the means of production. Following this, class refers to one's economic position in a society. Basically, this is the basis of today's use of the terms *upper, middle,* and *lower class.*

PBS/Photofest

The drama television series *Downton Abbey* depicted aristocratic and domestic servant life in the post-Edwardian era. British society was characterized by marriage within one's class and hereditary transmission of occupation, social status, and political influence. Today, social status in the United Kingdom is still influenced by social class, with other factors such as education also being significant.

While classes may exist in any society, how clearly defined they are and how much they are a source of identity varies. When asked to identify an example of social classes, some think of British television drama series such as *Upstairs, Downstairs* and *Downton Abbey,* two of the most widely watched television dramas in the world, which depicted the lives of servants and masters. Others identify the Indian Hindu caste system as one of the oldest and most rigid. Based on heredity, castes ranked from the Brahmin to the Kshatriya, to the Vaishya caste of artisans, farmers, and merchants, to the lower castes of Shudra and Ati-shudra laborers. Below these were the Dalits (formerly known as Untouchables), who continue to experience social and economic marginalization 70 years after India's constitution outlawed caste-based discrimination. Additionally, there were a large number of subcastes.

In France, the States-General established in 1302 provided a legislative assembly ranking members by hereditary class. The First Estate were the highborn sons of families who had devoted themselves to religion. The Second Estate were the highborn sons devoted to war. The Third Estate were the richest members of the bourgeoisie. The rigidity of the French hereditary system was one cause of the French Revolution. The United Kingdom's Parliament reflected the European class structure. In the 19th century the term *Fourth Estate* was used to identify the press.

While in many countries it is not popular to accept that class is a regulator of human life and provides identity, a system of social classes that divides people, assigns values to differences, and is a source of identity can lead to conflicts.

Gender and Identity

According to feminists like Germaine Greer, gender identity is more significant than religion, nation, or class. In *The Whole Woman,* Greer (1999) wrote, "Before you are of any race, nationality, religion, party or family, you are a woman" (p. 11). However, Cannadine (2013) contends it is difficult to substantiate that there is a unifying identity solidarity among all women.

For at least the past half-century, various scholars have attempted to demonstrate fundamental differences between the genders. Rather than review that research and argue for separate gender identities, one chapter in this text is devoted to how nations treat genders differently. How a nation deals with gender reveals much about that nation's values. Gender identity may be influenced more by one's national identity and other factors than by one's biology alone.

Race, Skin Color, and Identity

While class and gender may not have the same strength of regulation of human life and of identity creation as national identity, some would argue that race and skin color do. Race has been defined from two perspectives: biological and sociohistorical.

It was popularly believed that differences between peoples were biological or racial. From the popular biological perspective, race refers to a large body of people characterized by similarity of descent (Campbell, 1976). From this biologically based definition, your race is the result of the mating behavior of your ancestors. The biologically based definition is said to derive from Carolus Linnaeus, a Swedish botanist, physician, and taxonomist, who said in 1735 that humans are classified into four types: *Africanus, Americanus, Asiaticus,* and *Europeaeus.* Race became seen as biologically natural and based on visible physical characteristics such as skin color and other facial and bodily features. In the

Global Voices

The one thing my sons are always amazed by when they visit India is the condescension displayed toward entire groups of people. They hate the way people speak to their maids, their drivers, their waiters—anybody Indians consider socially inferior. I try to explain to them that India has been independent for only 60-odd years and the U.S. for more than three times as long and that while India has made great progress in pursuing democracy, it hasn't yet translated into social and economic equality.

—Mehta (2014, p. 37)

©iStockphoto.com/Soubrette

Why are we more aware of skin color than of other variables that distinguish each of us? For example, how aware are you of having detached or attached ear lobes?

19th century the "racial sciences" rank ordered distinct races from the most advanced to the most primitive. Such science became the basis for hospitals segregating blood supplies, Hitler's genocidal Germany, and South Africa's apartheid state.

While some physical traits and genes do occur more frequently in certain human populations than in others, such as some skull and dental features, differences in the processing of alcohol, and inherited diseases such as sickle cell anemia and cystic fibrosis, 20th-century scientists studying genetics found no single race-defining gene. Popular indicators of race, such as skin color and hair texture, were caused by recent adaptations to climate and diet. Jablonski and Chaplin (2000) took global ultraviolet measurements from NASA's Total Ozone Mapping Spectrometer and compared them with published data on skin color in indigenous populations from more than 50 countries. There was an unmistakable correlation: The weaker the ultraviolet light, the fairer the skin. Most scientists today have abandoned the concept of biological race as a meaningful scientific concept (Cavalli-Sforza, Menozzi, & Piazza, 1994; Owens & King, 1999; Paabo, 2001).

The second way to define race is as a sociohistorical concept, which explains how racial categories have varied over time and between cultures. Worldwide, skin color alone does not define race. The meaning of race has been debated in societies, and as a consequence, new categories have been formed and others transformed. Dark-skinned natives of India have been classified as Caucasian. People with moderately dark skin in Egypt are identified as White. Brazil has a history of intermarriage among native peoples, descendants of African slaves, and immigrants from Europe, the Middle East, and Asia, but no history of explicit segregation policies. So in Brazil, with the world's largest Black population after Nigeria, and where half of the population is Black, there are hundreds of words for skin colors (Robinson, 1999), including a census category *parda* for mixed ancestry (see Focus on Culture 1.1).

The biologically based definition establishes race as something fixed; the sociohistorically based definition sees race as unstable and socially determined through constant debate (Omi & Winant, 1986). People may be of the same race but of diverse cultures: Australia and South Africa have very different cultures that include individuals of the same ancestries. People can be of the same culture but of different ancestries: The United States, for example, is a country of people of many ancestries.

Civilization and Identity

Cannadine's (2013) final form of identity is civilization. Oswald Spengler and Arnold Toynbee believed civilizations to be the most significant determinant of identity but also believed that civilizations were largely self-sufficient and sealed off from one another.

In the 19th century, the term *culture* was commonly used as a synonym for Western civilization. The British anthropologist Sir Edward B. Tylor (1871) popularized the idea that all societies pass through developmental stages, beginning with "savagery," progressing to "barbarism," and culminating in Western "civilization." It's easy to see that such a definition assumes that Western nations were considered superior. Both Western nations, beginning with ancient Greece, and Eastern nations, most notably imperial China, believed that their own way of life was superior.

In his 1996 book *The Clash of Civilizations and the Remaking of World Order*, Samuel P. Huntington continued the position that civilizations were the most important form of human identity. In general, Huntington identified the world's civilizations as Western, Latin American, Sub-Saharan African, Eastern Orthodox (including the former Soviet Union), Islamic, Confucian, Hindu, and Japanese.

Focus on Culture 1.1

What is Person 1's race? *Mark* [X] *one or more boxes.*
- ☐ White
- ☐ Black, African Am., or Negro
- ☐ American Indian or Alaska Native — *Print name of enrolled or principal tribe.* ↗

- ☐ Asian Indian ☐ Japanese ☐ Native Hawaiian
- ☐ Chinese ☐ Korean ☐ Guamanian or Chamorro
- ☐ Filipino ☐ Vietnamese ☐ Samoan
- ☐ Other Asian — *Print race, for example, Hmong, Laotian, Thai, Pakistani, Cambodian, and so on.* ↗   ☐ Other Pacific Islander — *Print race, for example, Fijian, Tongan, and so on.* ↗

- ☐ Some other race — *Print race.* ↗

U.S. Census Bureau

Racial categories on the U.S. Census have varied over the years. This question is from the 2010 census.

U.S. Census Bureau Definitions of Race

Information on race has been collected in every U.S. census, beginning with the first in 1790, but what the U.S. Census Bureau considers as a racial category has changed in almost every census.

For example, according to Gibson and Jung (2002), from 1790 to 1850, the only categories used were "White and Black (Negro), with Black designated as free and slave." In 1890 categories included mulatto, quadroon, octoroon, Chinese, and Japanese. The 2010 survey raised some concerns in that it included the term Negro in addition to Black and African-American.

During decades of high immigration, Irish, Italians, and many central European ethnic groups were considered distinct races. "Armenians were classified as white in some decades, but not in others" (Hotz, 1995, p. A14).

In the 1930 census, there was a separate race category for Mexican; later, people of Mexican ancestry were classified as White and today as Hispanic but who could be of any race.

Immigrants from India have gone from Hindu, a religious designation used as a racial category, to Caucasian, to non-White, to White, to Asian Indian.

Michael Omi, an ethnic studies expert at the University of California, Berkeley, described the resulting confusion: "You can be born one race and die another" (quoted in Hotz, 1995, p. A14).

A recent study showed that 9.8 million people in the United States changed their race or ethnicity identity response from the 2000 census to the 2010 census (Lieblier, Rastogi, Fernandez, Noon, & Ennis, 2014).

Huntington predicts that future conflicts would be among civilizations, especially between the West and Islam. There are many critics of Huntington's thesis, including Paul Berman (2003), who argues that distinct civilization boundaries do not exist today, that is, that national identities have become more important than any civilization identities.

Culture

Can each of these sources of identity be considered a "culture"? To answer this question, we need to look at definitions of culture, co-culture, subculture, subgroup, and microculture.

Traditionally, the term culture was used to refer to the following:

- A community or population sufficiently large enough to be self-sustaining, that is, large enough to produce new generations of members without relying on outside people.

- The totality of that group's thought, experiences, and patterns of behavior and its concepts, values, and assumptions about life that guide behavior and how those evolve with contact with other cultures. Hofstede (1994) classified these elements of culture into four categories: symbols, rituals, values, and heroes. Symbols refer to verbal and nonverbal language. Rituals are the socially essential collective activities within a culture. Values are the feelings not open for discussion within a culture about what is good or bad, beautiful or ugly, normal or abnormal, which are present in a majority of the members of a culture, or at least in those who occupy pivotal positions. Heroes are the real or imaginary people who serve as behavior models within a culture. A culture's heroes are expressed in the culture's myths, which can be the subject of novels and other forms of literature (Rushing & Frentz, 1978). Janice Hocker Rushing (1983) has argued, for example, that an enduring myth in U.S. culture is the rugged individualist cowboy of the American West.
- The process of social transmission of these thoughts and behaviors from birth in the family and schools over the course of generations.
- Members who consciously identify themselves with that group. Collier and Thomas (1988) describe this as cultural identity, or the identification with and perceived acceptance into a group that has a shared system of symbols and meanings as well as norms for conduct. What does knowing an individual's cultural identity tell you about that individual? If you assume that the individual is like everyone else in that culture, you have stereotyped all the many, various people in that culture into one mold. You know that you are different from others in your culture. Other cultures are as diverse. The diversity within cultures probably exceeds the

Focus on Skills 1.1

Applying Cultural Concepts

Throughout this book, take note of special boxes marked Focus on Skills that identify intercultural communication skills appropriate to the content of that chapter.

Members of a culture share symbols and behavior norms, and identify as members of the culture. While families are not cultures, we can use that setting to explore the concept of culture.

Assume you have a sister, brother, or very close childhood friend. Think back to your relationship with that sibling or friend as a child. Probably, you remember how natural and spontaneous your relationship was. Your worlds of experience were so similar; you shared problems and pleasures; you disagreed and even fought, but that didn't mean you couldn't put that behind you because you both knew in some way that you belonged together.

Now imagine that your sibling or friend had to leave you for an extended period. Perhaps your brother studied abroad for a year or your sister entered the military and served overseas. For some time, you were separated.

1. Identify some of the experiences your friend or sibling had that may have changed your relationship in some way. For example, during the time your brother studied abroad, he likely acquired new vocabulary, new tastes, and new ideas about values. He uses a foreign-sounding word in casual conversation; he enjoys fast food or hates packaged food; he has strong feelings about politics.
2. Identify the ways that that separation changed how the two of you now communicate.

differences between cultures. So just knowing one person's cultural identity doesn't provide complete or reliable information about that person. Knowing another's cultural identity does, however, help you understand the opportunities and challenges that each individual in that culture has had to deal with.

We can have no direct knowledge of a culture other than our own. Our experience with and knowledge of other cultures is limited by the perceptual bias of our own culture. An adult Canadian will never fully understand the experience of growing up as an Australian. To begin to understand a culture, you need to understand all the experiences that guide its individual members through life. That includes language and gestures; personal appearance and social relationships; religion, philosophy, and values; courtship, marriage, and family customs; food and recreation; work and government; education and communication systems; health, transportation, and government systems; and economic systems. Think of culture as everything you would need to know and do so as not to stand out as a "stranger" in a foreign land. Culture is not a genetic trait. All these cultural elements are learned through interaction with others in the culture.

Focus on Culture 1.2

In Turkey, blue eye beads are said to ward away the "evil eye." These beads are often worn as jewelry or hung in houses, in cars, or even on trees.

©iStockphoto.com/architetta

Superstitions

Some cultural customs are often labeled as superstitions. They are the practices believed to influence the course of events. Whether it is rubbing a rabbit's foot for luck or not numbering the 13th floor in a building, these practices are part of one's cultural identification. We may not follow them, but we recognize them. For example, in Japan you may see a maneki neko, or "beckoning cat" figurine with its front paw raised. The beckoning gesture brings customers into stores and good luck and fortune into homes.

In China, sounds and figures reflect good fortune. The phonetic sound of the number 8, *baat* in Cantonese and between *pa* and *ba* in Mandarin, is similar to *faat*, meaning prosperity. The number 8, then, is the most fortuitous of numbers, portending prosperity. The date and time of the 2008 Olympics opening ceremony had as many eights as possible (8:08:08 p.m., August 8, 2008). In Hong Kong, a license plate with the number 8 is quite valuable. But the number 4 can be read as *shi*, which is a homophone for the word for "death," so the Lucky Dragon Hotel & Casino, the first Las Vegas Asian-themed resort, has no room numbers or phone numbers with a 4. The nine-story hotel has no fourth floor. Superstitions are only a small part of culture but certainly an interesting part. Remember, culture refers to the totality of a people's socially transmitted products of work and thought.

This understanding of the concept of culture is common in popular literature and media in reference to national sources of identity. Thus people commonly think of national citizenship as one's culture. Yet clearly within nations there are small groups that have continuity and that function as cultures in the sense that they regulate human behavior and provide important parts of identity. The terms *subcultures, co-cultures, subgroups,* and *microcultures* have been used to identify these groups.

Subculture

Complex societies are made up of a large number of groups with which people identify and from which are derived distinctive values and rules for behavior. These groups have been labeled *subcultures.* A subculture resembles a culture in that it usually encompasses a relatively large number of people and represents the accumulation of generations of human striving. However, subcultures have some important differences. They exist within dominant cultures and are often based on geographic region, ethnicity, or economic or social class.

Ethnicity

The term ethnicity refers to a group of people of the same descent and heritage who share a common and distinctive culture passed on through generations (Zenner, 1996). For some, *tribes* would be a more understood term. In Afghanistan, for example, people identify by tribes—Tajiks and Pashtuns. According to some estimates, there are 5,000 ethnic groups in the world (Stavenhagen, 1986). Ethnic groups can exhibit such distinguishing features as language or accent, physical features, family names, customs, and religion. Ethnic identity refers to identification with and perceived acceptance into a group with shared heritage and culture (Collier & Thomas, 1988). Sometimes, the word *minority* is used. Technically, of course, the word *minority* is used to describe numerical designations. A group might be a minority, then, if it has a smaller number of people than a majority group with a larger number. In the United States, the word *majority* has political associations, as in the *majority rules,* a term used so commonly in the United States that the two words have almost become synonymous. According to the *Oxford English Dictionary,* the term *minority* was first used to describe ethnic groups in 1921. Since that time, advantage has been associated with the majority and disadvantage has been associated with the minority.

Just as definitions of words such as *culture* have changed, the way words are written has changed. There has been considerable controversy surrounding whether terms such as *Italian American* should be spelled open or hyphenated. It has been argued that immigrants to the United States and their descendants have been called "hyphenated Americans," suggesting that their allegiance is divided. Style manuals such as the *American Heritage Dictionary of the English Language,* 5th edition, suggest omitting the hyphen.

As you read in Focus on Culture 1.1, the U.S. Census Bureau establishes categories of identity. Figure 1.1 shows categories proposed for the 2020 census. The U.S. Office of Management and Budget is considering major revisions in how people report racial and Hispanic identity on census and other federal government forms.

That ethnic identity can be the basis of a cultural identity and affect communication with others outside that group has been demonstrated by D. Taylor, Dubé, and Bellerose (1986). In one study of English and French speakers in Quebec, they found that though interactions between ethnically dissimilar people were perceived to be as agreeable as those between similar people, those same

Figure 1.1   Sample of Possible Questionnaire Revisions for 2020 Census

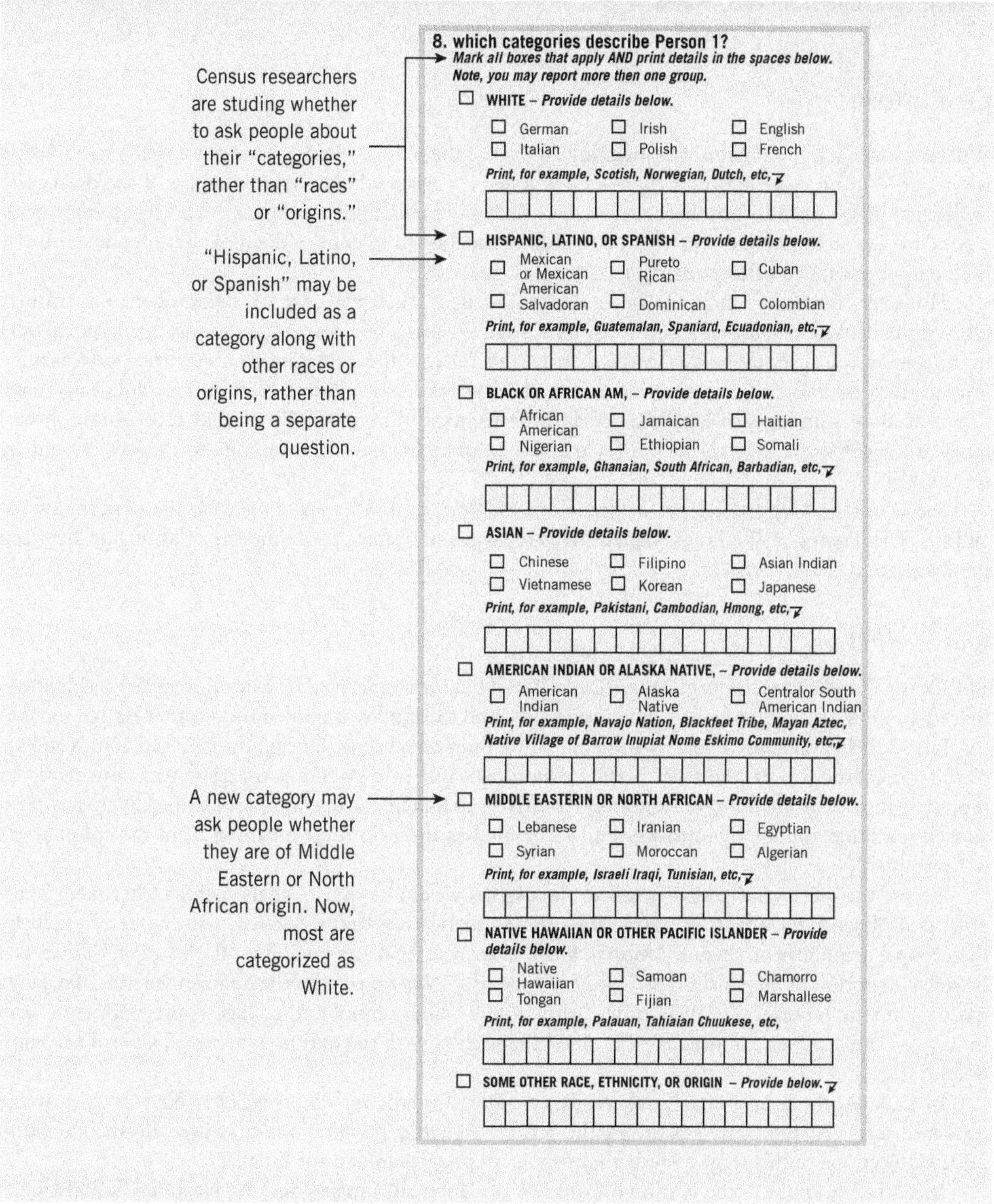

Census researchers are studing whether to ask people about their "categories," rather than "races" or "origins."

"Hispanic, Latino, or Spanish" may be included as a category along with other races or origins, rather than being a separate question.

A new category may ask people whether they are of Middle Eastern or North African origin. Now, most are categorized as White.

8. which categories describe Person 1?
Mark all boxes that apply AND print details in the spaces below. Note, you may report more then one group.

☐ **WHITE** – *Provide details below.*

☐ German   ☐ Irish   ☐ English
☐ Italian   ☐ Polish   ☐ French

Print, for example, Scotish, Norwegian, Dutch, etc,

☐ **HISPANIC, LATINO, OR SPANISH** – *Provide details below.*

☐ Mexican or Mexican American   ☐ Pureto Rican   ☐ Cuban
☐ Salvadoran   ☐ Dominican   ☐ Colombian

Print, for example, Guatemalan, Spaniard, Ecuadonian, etc,

☐ **BLACK OR AFRICAN AM,** – *Provide details below.*

☐ African American   ☐ Jamaican   ☐ Haitian
☐ Nigerian   ☐ Ethiopian   ☐ Somali

Print, for example, Ghanaian, South African, Barbadian, etc,

☐ **ASIAN** – *Provide details below.*

☐ Chinese   ☐ Filipino   ☐ Asian Indian
☐ Vietnamese   ☐ Korean   ☐ Japanese

Print, for example, Pakistani, Cambodian, Hmong, etc,

☐ **AMERICAN INDIAN OR ALASKA NATIVE,** – *Provide details below.*

☐ American Indian   ☐ Alaska Native   ☐ Centralor South American Indian

Print, for example, Navajo Nation, Blackfeet Tribe, Mayan Aztec, Native Village of Barrow Inupiat Nome Eskimo Community, etc,

☐ **MIDDLE EASTERIN OR NORTH AFRICAN** – *Provide details below.*

☐ Lebanese   ☐ Iranian   ☐ Egyptian
☐ Syrian   ☐ Moroccan   ☐ Algerian

Print, for example, Israeli Iraqi, Tunisian, etc,

☐ **NATIVE HAWAIIAN OR OTHER PACIFIC ISLANDER** – *Provide details below.*

☐ Native Hawaiian   ☐ Samoan   ☐ Chamorro
☐ Tongan   ☐ Fijian   ☐ Marshallese

Print, for example, Palauan, Tahiaian Chuukese, etc,

☐ **SOME OTHER RACE, ETHNICITY, OR ORIGIN** – *Provide below.*

Source: "Federal Officials May Revamp How American Identify Race, Ethnicity on Census and Other Forms," Pew Research Center (October 2016), http://www.pewresearch.org/fact-tank/2016/10/04/federal-officials-may-revamp-how-americans-identify-race-ethnicity-on-census-and-other-forms/ft_16-10-04_censuschange_1-1/.

encounters were judged less important and less intimate. The researchers concluded that to ensure that interethnic contacts were harmonious, the communicators in their study limited the interactions to relatively superficial encounters.

Co-Culture

Whereas some define *subculture* as meaning "a part of the whole," in the same sense that a subdivision is part of—but no less important than—the whole city, other scholars reject the use of the prefix *sub* as applied to the term *culture* because it seems to imply being under or beneath and being inferior or secondary. As an alternative, the word co-culture is suggested to convey the idea that no one culture is inherently superior to other coexisting cultures (Orbe, 1998).

However, mutuality may not be easily established. Take the case of a homogeneous culture. One of the many elements of a culture is its system of laws. The system of laws in our hypothetical homogeneous culture, then, was derived from and reflects the values of that culture. Now assume immigration of another cultural group into the hypothetical culture. New immigrants may have different understandings of legal theory and the rights and responsibilities that individuals should have in a legal system. In the case of a true co-culture, both understandings of the law would be recognized.

See Focus on Culture 1.3 for a discussion of New Zealand struggling with the concept of co-culture. The Treaty of Waitangi, signed in 1840, was an attempt to define the relationship between the British and the Māori.

American Indians

The Census Bureau uses the term *American Indian*. That term is derived from a colonizer's worldview—that is, Columbus thought he was going to India—and the land was named for another Italian navigator. It is a label applied to people by someone other than themselves. During the civil rights movements of the 1960s and 1970s, the term *Native American* came into common use as it was considered to represent historical facts more accurately ("native" predated European colonization). Yet that term as well is a label applied by outsiders and for some has the pejorative meaning from the colonial era of "primitive."

To use the labels that people apply to themselves would be to use labels such as Cherokee, Seminole, and Navajo. However, in many cases these labels are actually derived from names created by the groups' neighbors or enemies. *Mohawk* is a Narraganset name meaning "flesh eaters." *Sioux* is a French corruption of an Anishinabe word for "enemy." *Navajo* is from the Spanish version of a Tewa word. A survey reported in 1997 showed that 96% of high school and college youth with American Indian or Native American heritage identified themselves with the nation name (e.g., Cherokee, Seminole).

In Canada, the term *Indian* is generally considered offensive. The term *First Nations* is now the preferred term. At the United Nations, the term *indigenous peoples* was first used in documents in 2002. Objections to this term include that it puts all peoples under one label.

In a 1977 resolution, the National Congress of American Indians and the National Tribal Chairmen's Association stated that in the absence of a specific tribal designation, the preferred term is American Indian and/or Alaska Native. In a 1995 survey, 50% preferred the term American Indian to

Focus on Culture 1.3

The Māori of New Zealand

Māori celebrate the signing of the Treaty of Waitangi, New Zealand's founding document, on a public holiday every February 6.

Hannah Peters/Getty Images News/Getty Images

The original inhabitants of what is today known as New Zealand were Polynesians who arrived in a series of migrations more than 1,000 years ago. They named the land Aotearoa, or land of the long white cloud. The original inhabitants' societies revolved around the *iwi* (tribe) or *hapu* (subtribe), which served to differentiate the many tribes of peoples. In 1642, the Dutch explorer Abel Janszoon Tasman sailed up the west coast and christened the land Niuew Zeeland after the Netherlands' province of Zeeland. Later, in 1769, Captain James Cook sailed around the islands and claimed the entire land for the British crown. It was only after the arrival of the Europeans that the term Māori was used to describe all the tribes on the land. Those labeled Māori do not necessarily regard themselves as a single people.

The history of the Māori parallels the decline of other indigenous peoples in colonized lands, except for the signing of the Treaty of Waitangi in 1840 by more than 500 chiefs. The treaty was recorded in Māori and in English. Differences between the two versions caused considerable misunderstandings in later years. The Māori and the English may have had different understandings of the terms *governance* and *sovereignty.* In exchange for granting sovereignty to Great Britain, the Māori were promised full exclusive and undisturbed possession of their lands, forests, fisheries, and other properties and the same rights and privileges enjoyed by British subjects. The terms of the treaty were largely ignored as Māori land was appropriated as settlers arrived.

Activism in the late 1960s brought a renaissance of Māori languages, literature, arts, and culture, and calls to address Māori land claims as the Treaty of Waitangi became the focus of grievances. In 1975, the government introduced the Waitangi Tribunal to investigate Māori land claims, which resulted in some return of Māori land. In 1994, the government proposed to settle all Māori land claims for $1 billion—a very small percentage of current value.

Today, New Zealand's population by descent is approximately 13% Māori and 78% Pakeha (European). New Zealand is governed under a parliamentary democracy system loosely modeled on that of Great Britain, except that there are two separate electoral rolls: one for the election of general members of parliament and one for the election of a small number of Māori members of parliament. Pakeha can enroll on the general roll only; people who consider themselves Māori must choose which one of the two rolls they wish to be on.

(Continued)

(Continued)

Map 1.1   New Zealand

The following article appeared in an August 1999 edition of the newspaper *The Dominion*.

What Makes a Māori?

The definition of Māori for voting purposes . . . is entirely one of self-definition. The 1956 Electoral Act defined a Māori as "a person belonging to the aboriginal race of New Zealand, and includes a half-caste and a person intermediate in blood between half-castes and persons of pure descent from that race."

   In 1975, the Labour government, prompted by then Māori affairs minister Matiu Rata, rewrote the act to define a Māori as "a person of the Māori race of New Zealand, and includes any descendant of such a person who elects to be considered as a Māori for the purposes of this act." Such a person could choose either the Māori roll or the general roll. So, if you are descended from a Māori, then you are Māori and can choose to vote on the Māori roll. Nigel Roberts, head of Victoria University's School of Political Science and International Relations, says such self-identification is appropriate: "I think that ethnicity is very largely, in the late 20th century, a matter of identification—it is a cultural matter. The world has moved on from classifying people by blood, which was a meaningless definition."

   What about Treaty of Waitangi settlements? How does one prove entitlement to the land, fisheries quota, shares, and cash that are being returned to Māori in compensation for successive Crown breaches?

   The definition is different again—and more stringently enforced. The South Island's Ngai Tahu iwi was awarded $170 million compensation [in 1998] after a gruelling process of Waitangi Tribunal hearings, mandating, and negotiations. Ngai Tahu *whakapapa* (genealogy) unit spokeswoman Tarlin Prendergast says the iwi is in the fortunate position of having good records from an 1848 census of Ngai Tahu members, just before the Crown's purchase of South Island land. And in 1920, a group of *kaumatua* had traveled around Ngai Tahu settlements recording the whakapapa of families. "Anyone who is Ngai Tahu must be able to show their lines of descent from a kaumatua alive in 1848.

   "That is the basis of our tribal membership," she says. "It is up to the individuals to align themselves with the *runanga* (area council) that they say they come from and to keep alive their connections. We call it *ahi kaa*—keeping the home fires burning."

Source: Milne (1999, p. 9). Reprinted with permission.

37% for Native American. Some activists such as Russell Means publicly are said to prefer American Indian to Native American ("People Labels," 1995, p. 28). In the belief that people should be referred to by the term they themselves prefer, this text uses the label of specific nations or, when referring to all nations within the United States, the term American Indian.

Can one nation have two legal systems? Can two legal systems coexist equally? Some 567 distinct nations exist by treaty within the territorial limits of the United States. One is the federal government in Washington, D.C. The remaining 566 are American Indian nations recognized by the U.S. Bureau of Indian Affairs that enjoy some areas of complete sovereignty and some areas of limited sovereignty. By treaty, the American Indian nations have their own territory, governmental structure, and laws; collect their own taxes; and are protected by U.S. federal law in the practice of their culture and religion (Dudley & Agard, 1993). The American Indian Religious Freedom Act of 1978 proclaimed "to protect and preserve for American Indians their inherent right to believe, express and exercise the traditional religions."

Recent Supreme Court decisions, however, have negated this law. In 1988, in *Lyng v. Northwest Indian Cemetery Protection Association,* the Supreme Court held that the U.S. Forest Service could build a road through an area sacred to three Indian tribes. And in 1990, in *Employment Division of Oregon v. Smith,* the Court held that the state could deny unemployment benefits to two men fired from their jobs because they ingested peyote as part of their religion. The *Smith* decision has now been cited in cases involving a Sikh wearing a turban on the job, a Hmong couple protesting their son's autopsy, and an Amish man refusing to post traffic signs. The Religious Freedom Restoration Act of 1993 attempted to restore those rights; however, the point being made here is that the U.S. government exercises ultimate dominance over all indigenous peoples within its boundaries.

When nations adopt one system of laws, that system reflects the cultural values of one culture. But when one is surrounded by a more powerful culture or exists within the culture of the other, the less powerful culture must accept the laws and legal system of the other, thus subordinating any other understanding of legal systems. At least in this one way, the groups are not mutually powerful. The case of American Indians supports the argument that the term *co-culture* does not accurately reflect reality in the United States. Just as the term *subculture* has undesired consequences, so too does *co-culture.* In an attempt to avoid misunderstandings, this text avoids using either word. Instead, as much as possible, it uses the terms *culture* or *microculture* except when the terms *subculture* and *subgroup* are necessary to communicate a specific meaning.

Subgroup

Just as cultures are regulators of human life and identity, so are subgroups. Let's look at the definition of the term subgroup and how subgroups can function in a similar manner to cultures.

Psychologists have long recognized that subgroups, or membership groups, have an important influence on the values and attitudes you hold. Like cultures, subgroups provide members with relatively complete sets of values and patterns of behavior, and in many ways pose similar communication problems as cultures. Subgroups exist within a dominant culture and are dependent on that culture. One important subgroup category is occupation. Think of large organizations and of occupations in which most people dress alike, share a common vocabulary and similar values, and are in frequent communication, as through magazines and Twitter. These subgroups include nurses and doctors, police officers, and employees of large organizations such as Microsoft. Subgroups usually do not involve the same large number of people as cultures and are not necessarily thought of as accumulating values and patterns of behavior over generations in the same way cultures do.

The term *subgroup* has at times been negatively linked to the word *deviant.* Actually, however, *deviant* simply means differing from the cultural norm, such as vegetarians in a meat-eating society. Unfortunately, in normal discourse, most people associate deviance with undesirable activities. To understand what is meant by subgroups, you must recognize that vegetarians are as deviant as prostitutes—both groups deviate from the norm, and both are considered subgroups.

Membership in some subgroups is temporary; that is, members may participate for a time and later become inactive or separate from it altogether. For example, there are organizations devoted to Ford cars and trucks. Some people are preoccupied with that for a while and then lose interest and relinquish membership in the group. Membership in other subgroups may be longer lasting. One person may be a firefighter for life and another gay.

However, it is a mistake to think of membership in a culture or subgroup as being so exclusive that it precludes participation in other groups. All of us are and have been members of a variety of subgroups. Think of times in your life when you were preoccupied with the concerns of a certain group. At those times, you were a subgroup member. Examples range from Girl Scouts to Alcoholics Anonymous to youth gangs to religious cults to the military.

Recognize, too, that individuals can adhere to values and attitudes and behaviors of groups of which they are not members. The term reference group refers to any group in which one aspires to attain membership (Sherif & Sherif, 1953). This behavior is identified in contemporary slang as the *wannabe,* an individual who imitates the behavior of a group he or she desires to belong to. Some people dress like and talk like gang members but are not members of any gang.

Just as each of us has a cultural identity and one or more subcultural identities, we may also have a subgroup identity. While that group membership may be short-lived, it can, for a while, provide some symbols, rituals, values, and myths that you acknowledge and share with others.

Microculture

We've seen that some believe the term *subculture* implies "less important." Others point out that the term *co-culture* doesn't seem to be a realistic term as history suggests that one culture will be dominant over the other. The term *subgroup* seems also to imply "not important." Others now advocate using the term *microculture,* which in biology referred to a small culture of microorganisms. Applied to human behavior, microculture refers to any identifiable smaller group bound together by shared symbol system, behaviors, and values.

Microculture, then, clearly communicates a smaller size, but national cultures can be large while others are so small that they may be smaller than some microcultures. Some scholars now suggest just using the term *culture* regardless of size or other factors.

Let's now begin to address the statement from the beginning of this chapter that "culture and communication can only be understood together."

Communication

From the perspective of the study of cultures, communication has two critical functions:

- Communication is the means by which individuals learn appropriate behaviors and the means by which those behaviors are regulated.

- Communication is the means by which individuals having one group identity interact with individuals with other group identities and on a more general level the means by which the groups interact with one another as formal groups.

As we saw above, the history of human interactions between groups has been fraught with suffering and death. Can there be a more critical time to study intercultural communication?

The remainder of this chapter is devoted to developing an understanding of communication. Our purpose is not to highlight any one definition or model of communication. Rather, the purpose here is to develop an understanding of how communication is defined and performed differently by diverse cultures.

Cultural Definitions of Communication

It has often been said that communication and culture are inseparable. As Alfred G. Smith (1966) wrote in his preface to *Communication and Culture*, culture is a code we learn and share, and learning and sharing require communication. Communication requires coding and symbols that must be learned and shared. Godwin C. Chu (1977) observed that every cultural pattern and every single act of social behavior involve communication. To be understood, the two must be studied together. Culture cannot be known without a study of communication, and communication can only be understood with an understanding of the culture it supports.

Focus on Theory 1.1

Anxiety/Uncertainty Management Theory

What are communication theories and who develops them? Foss, Foss, and Griffin (1999) define theory as "a way of framing an experience or event—an effort to understand and account for something and the way it functions in the world" (p. 8). All of us develop and test personal communication theories to guide our interactions with others. You may believe that people with degrees and offices have more knowledge. That's a personal communication theory. Life experiences may lead you to question that theory or refine it.

William B. Gudykunst first developed anxiety/uncertainty management (AUM) as a theory to define effective communication. In 1988, he applied his theory to intercultural communication. Gudykunst uses the terms *in group members* and *stranger*. In interpersonal communication with in group members, the stranger experiences both anxiety and uncertainty. When the communication is between people of different cultures, the stranger becomes hyperaware of the cultural differences. Gudykunst also introduced the concept of mindfulness. When we communicate mindlessly, we use stereotypes to predict behavior. With mindfulness, categories become more specific and accurate.

Gudykunst (2005, p. 299) developed a series of axioms with AUM theory. For example, one is that an increase in our understanding of similarities and differences between our groups and strangers' groups will produce a decrease in our anxiety and an increase in our ability to accurately predict their behavior. This axiom certainly presents an objective for learning more about cultures other than your own as you develop in your study of this textbook (for more information, see Gudykunst, 2005).

Note: Anxiety/Uncertainty Management Theory was based on Uncertainty Reduction Theory (see Focus on Theory 2.1).

Confucian Perspectives on Communication

That cultures define communication in diverse ways demonstrates that communication is an element of culture (Krippendorff, 1993). Definitions of communication from many Asian countries stress harmony (Chen & Starosta, 1996). This is most notable in cultures with a strong Confucian tradition. Societies heavily influenced today by Confucian history or tradition are China, North and South Korea, Singapore, and many East Asian countries with large Chinese communities.

The Chinese scholar K'ung-Fu-tzu, a title the Jesuits later Latinized as Confucius (550–478 BCE[1]), lived in a time when the feudal system in China was collapsing. Confucius proposed a government based less on heredity than on morality and merit.

Confucius set up an ethical-moral system intended ideally to govern all relationships in the family, community, and state. Confucius taught that society was made up of five relationships: those between ruler and subjects (the relation of righteousness), husband and wife (chaste conduct), father and son (love), elder brother and younger brother (order), and friend and friend (faithfulness). Three of these five bases of relations occur within the family. The regulating factors in family relationships

Map 1.2 Countries in Asia With Strong Confucian Influences

are extended to the whole community and state. The chief virtue is filial piety, a combination of loyalty and reverence, which demands that the son honor and respect his father and fulfill the demands of his elders.

Confucianism emphasizes virtue, selflessness, duty, patriotism, hard work, and respect for hierarchy, both familial and societal. Just as George Washington and the story of the cherry tree is used in the United States to teach the value of honesty, Confucianism reinforces its lessons with stories about people who represent particular virtues. For example, Chinese children learn about such heroes as Mu Lan, a woman of the 6th century who disguised herself as a man and served 12 years as a soldier so that her ill father would not be disgraced or punished because he could not report for military duty. Mu Lan teaches courage and filial devotion.

Confucianism guides social relationships: "To live in harmony with the universe and with your fellow man through proper behavior." Confucianism considers balance and harmony in human relationships to be the basis of society. June Yum (1988) describes five effects that Confucianism has on interpersonal communication:

1. *Particularism.* There is no universal pattern of rules governing relationships: No rules govern interaction with someone whose status is unknown. Instead of applying the same rule to everyone, such factors as status, intimacy, and context create different communication rules for diverse people. In fact, there are several patterns guiding interaction with others whose status is known. In the Confucian countries of North and South Korea, it's quite common for strangers to find out each other's age in the first few minutes of conversation and adjust their language to show respect. Koreans are friends (*chingu*) only with those whose age is within a few years of their own. If a male acquaintance is older than this "friendship age range," he must be addressed as *adjussi,* or if it is a female acquaintance, as *adjumoni*—terms that equate roughly to "uncle" and "aunt," respectively.

2. *Role of intermediaries.* Rituals should be followed in establishing relationships. In China, it's not unusual to use a third party to negotiate with future in-laws about wedding plans and, in general, to use a third party to avoid direct confrontations and resolve disputes (Gao & Ting-Toomey, 1998).

3. *Reciprocity.* Complementary obligations are the basis of relationships. Gratitude and indebtedness are important parts of Chinese culture. For example, a person feels uneasy to be indebted to someone, and payback is necessary to achieve balance in the relationship. Reciprocity is the basic rule of interpersonal relationships (Gao & Ting-Toomey, 1998). Obligations in relationships are contrary to Western ideas of individualism.

4. *In-group/out-group distinction.* Scollon and Scollon (1991) argue that the distinction between inside and outside influences every aspect of Chinese culture. In-group members engage in freer and deeper talk and may find it difficult to develop personal relationships with out-group members (Gao & Ting-Toomey, 1998). There can even be different language codes for in-group members.

5. *Overlap of personal and public relationships.* Business and pleasure are mixed. Frequent contacts lead to common experiences. This contrasts with Western patterns of keeping public and private lives separate. There are several Chinese terms for the English word *communication,* including *jiao liu* (to exchange), *chuan bo* (to disseminate), and *gou tong* (to connect among people). The Chinese term *he* denotes harmony, peace, unity, and kindness. Seeking harmony with family and others is the goal of communication in Chinese culture (Gao & Ting-Toomey, 1998).

As a consequence of the value placed on balance and social harmony, Chang and Holt (1991) explain how the Chinese have developed many verbal strategies such as compliments, greeting rituals, and so on to maintain good interpersonal relations. Fong (2000), for example, has described the "luck talk" (speech acts related to luck) during the celebration of the Chinese New Year.

Korea adopted Confucianism as a state religion for six centuries. Yum (1987) explains how the Korean language easily accommodates the Confucian rules of relationships. For example, a grammatical form of direct address, called an honorific, shows respect. English speakers might vary in how they ask a child, a friend, or a grandparent "to sit" by using a sentence, whereas Korean speakers would use different forms of the root *ahnta,* meaning "to sit or to take a seat":

- to a child, younger person, or person of lower rank: *ahnjo* or *ahnjara* (informal)
- to a friend or person of equal rank: *ahnjuseyo* (polite)
- to an elder, person of higher rank, or honored person: *ahnjushipshio* (more polite)

Korean has special vocabularies for each sex, for different degrees of social status and degrees of intimacy, and for formal occasions. When two people are introduced, they first engage in small talk to determine each other's social position so they know who should use common language and who should use honorific language. And ironically, because Confucianism does not consider relationships with strangers, Koreans are said to ignore—often to the point that some in other cultures would consider rude—anyone to whom they have not been introduced.

In modern Korea, a generation gap exists: Junior business associates may address seniors with familiar rather than honorific language. The collectivist values of Confucianism mandate a style of communication in which respecting the relationship through communication is more important than the information exchanged. Group harmony, avoidance of loss of face to others and oneself, and a modest presentation of oneself are means of respecting the relationship. One does not say what one actually thinks when it might hurt others in the group.

In some sense, the same ethic can be found in business dealings. Much of commercial life in China is lubricated by *guanxi,* a concept best translated as "connections" or "personal relationships." *Guanxi* is an alternative to the legal trappings of Western capitalism in that business is cemented by the informal relationships of trust and mutual obligation. Sometimes viewed as bribery, *guanxi* is less like using professional lobbyists than relying on mutual friends among whom trust can be maintained.

A Confucian perspective on communication would define it as an infinite interpretive process in which all parties are searching to develop and maintain a social relationship. Carey (1989) describes this as a ritual model of communication that "is directed not toward the extension of messages in space but toward the maintenance of society in time; not the act of imparting information but the representation of shared beliefs" (p. 18).

Western Perspectives on Communication

The study of communication in Western culture has a recorded history of some 2,500 years and is said to have begun in Greece with Aristotle's *Rhetoric and Poetics,* which described the process of communication as involving a speaker, the speech act, an audience, and a purpose. To demonstrate how a communication theory reflects Western culture, let's review one well-known theory made popular by David Berlo's (1960) *The Process of Communication.* There are many other models available, but we will use this one to highlight the components of communication and how communication models themselves reflect the culture within which they were developed.

Focus on Skills 1.2

Cultural Understandings of Gift-Giving Practices

Assume you work as an intake interviewer at a taxpayer-funded U.S. social service agency that helps low-income residents achieve self-sufficiency. Your agency provides employment services, English as a second language instruction, a clearinghouse for support services in the community, and immigration services. As a county employee you received a copy of the county ethics policy that prohibits "soliciting or accepting gifts of any value from persons or firms doing business with the county that could reasonably tend to influence you in the performance of your duties or give the appearance of influence."

At an interview with a Chinese couple and their children in early October, the mother offers you a wrapped gift. You say you cannot accept a gift. She insists, saying it is a mooncake. You bring the interview to a close and escort them out of your office, putting the gift back in her hand on the way out. That night you look up "mooncake" on the Internet and learn that in a Chinese family mooncakes are shared as a symbol of unity. But some also give them as part of the *guanxi* custom.

1. Should you violate laws to accommodate another's cultural behavior?
2. Should you have handled the situation differently?
3. The couple is coming in for another interview. Do you say or do anything about the gift?

Berlo was interested in using communication to solve problems such as finding more effective ways of communicating new agricultural technologies to farmers and communicating health information to the peoples of developing countries. He drew from engineering to conceptualize communication as a process of transmitting ideas to influence others to achieve the communicator's goals. Even though Berlo emphasized that communication is a dynamic process, as the variables in the process are interrelated and influence each other, overall his conceptualization of communication can be labeled machinelike or mechanistic. Communication was conceptualized as one-way, top-down, and suited for the transmission media of print, telephones, radio, and television.

Components of Communication. Because the transmission models of communication clearly identified components in the communication process, they are particularly useful in beginning a study of communication. You are better able to understand communication when you understand the components of the process (DeVito, 1986). The components of communication, shown in Figure 1.2, are source, encoding, message, channel, noise, receiver, decoding, receiver response, feedback, and context.

Source. The source is the person with an idea she or he desires to communicate. Examples are CBS, the White House, your instructor, and your mother.

Encoding. Unfortunately (or perhaps fortunately), humans cannot share thoughts directly. Your communication is in the form of a symbol representing the idea you desire to communicate. Encoding is the process of putting an idea into a symbol. The symbols into which you encode your thoughts vary. You can encode thoughts into words, and you also can encode thoughts into nonspoken symbols. Tobin and Dobard (1999), for example, have shown how messages were encoded in quilts made by slaves.

Figure 1.2   Ten Components of Communication

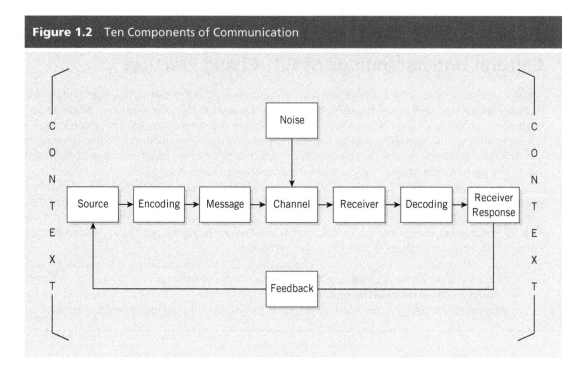

Message. The term message identifies the encoded thought. Encoding is the process, the verb; the message is the resulting object.

Channel. The term channel is used technically to refer to the means by which the encoded message is transmitted. Today, you might feel more comfortable using the word *media*. The channel or medium, then, may be print, electronic, or the light and sound waves of face-to-face communication.

Noise. The term noise technically refers to anything that distorts the message the source encodes. Noise can take many forms:

- External noise can be the sights, sounds, and other stimuli that draw your attention away from the message. Listening to an iPod while reading is an example of external noise.
- Internal noise refers to your thoughts and feelings that can interfere with the message. For example, being tired or hungry can distract you from paying complete attention to the message.
- Semantic noise refers to how alternative meanings of the source's message symbols can be distracting. For example, a speaker's use of uncalled-for profanity can cause us to wonder why the speaker used profanity and draw attention away from the message itself.

Receiver. The receiver is the person who attends to the message. Receivers may be intentional—that is, they may be the people the source desired to communicate with—or they may be any person who comes upon and attends to the message.

Decoding. Decoding is the opposite of encoding and just as much an active process. The receiver is actively involved in the communication process by assigning meaning to the symbols received.

Receiver Response. Receiver response refers to anything the receiver does after having attended to and decoded the message. That response can range from doing nothing to taking some action or actions that may or may not be the action desired by the source.

Feedback. Feedback refers to that portion of the receiver response of which the source has knowledge and to which the source attends and assigns meaning. You as a reader of this text may have many responses, but only when you respond to a survey or send an e-mail to the author does feedback occur. When a radio interview show host receives enthusiastic telephone calls and invites a guest back, feedback has occurred. Feedback makes communication a two-way or interactive process. Linear and interactive models seem to suggest that communication is an isolated single discrete act independent of events that preceded or might follow it.

Context. The final component of communication is context. Generally, context can be defined as the environment in which the communication takes place and helps define the communication. If you know the physical context, you can predict with a high degree of accuracy much of the communication. For example, you have certain knowledge and expectations of the communication that occurs within synagogues, mosques, and churches. At times, you intentionally plan a certain physical environment for your communication: You may want to locate your romantic communications in a quiet, dimly lit restaurant or on a secluded beach. The choice of the environment, the context, helps assign the desired meaning to the communicated words.

In social relationships as well, the relationship between the source and receiver may help define much of the meaning of the communication. Again, if you know the context, you can predict with a high degree of accuracy much of the communication. For example, knowing that a person is being stopped by a police officer for speeding is enough to predict much of the communication. Certain things are likely to be said and done; other things are very unlikely. Culture is also context. Every culture has its own worldview; its own way of thinking of activity, time, and human nature; its own way of perceiving self; and its own system of social organization. Knowing each of these helps you assign meaning to the symbols.

The component of context helps you recognize that the extent to which the source and receiver have similar meanings for the communicated symbols and similar understandings of the culture in which the communication takes place is critical to the success of the communication. From this perspective, communication is intentional, is symbolic, and involves at least two people. You might say that communication occurs when symbols are manipulated by one person to stimulate meaning in another person (Infante, Rancer, & Womack, 1993).

Not everyone agreed with the Berlo (1960) model. For example, semanticist S. I. Hayakawa (1978) noted that decoding—or listening—seems to give the receiver a subordinate role to the source. When someone speaks, others stop what they are doing to listen. Therefore, it would seem that the source is viewed as more active and as more important in the process. Hayakawa's observation makes it clear that cultural beliefs affect how the process of communication is defined.

The Berlo model can lead you to think of communication as consisting of an active source and a passive receiver. Speaking may be considered a more noble activity and may demand that others cease other activities to listen. Indeed, in many cultures, listening does place one in a subordinate role to that of the source. In other cultures, where the group's history and knowledge are told and retold verbally, the role of the listener who accurately remembers is critical. The story is told that the Puritans, believing themselves to have been called to save heathens, preached to the American Indians. The Indians affirmed conversions to Christianity to the delight of the early settlers. Then the Indians told the Puritans the Indian story of creation and asked the settlers to affirm it. The Indian communication style was not to disagree but to listen and affirm. The Puritans were disappointed that communication, in the Western understanding of communication, had failed. In the American Indian understanding of communication, it had not.

The Media of Intercultural Communication

One component of the communication process is the channel, or medium, by which the encoded message is transmitted. In past centuries, written letters carried by human couriers were the dominant media. In the Roman Empire of the first century BCE, letters and books were copied and distributed among friends that could reach Britain in 5 weeks and Syria in 7 weeks (Standage, 2013). In the 20th century, electronic mass media became dominant. Through today's social media, communicators create online communities to instantly share messages and images. The focus in this text is not on the form of media use but rather on how culture is reflected in media use.

Human Couriers and Intermediaries

One early form of intercultural communication still in widespread use today is human couriers. Another person can be used as a medium. You can easily imagine messages being entrusted to a courier to deliver to a faraway village.

In some cultures, intermediaries are used instead of face-to-face confrontation to reduce the risk of losing face or the value or standing one has in the eyes of others. Ting-Toomey (1985) has proposed that cultures like the United States with a greater concern for privacy and autonomy tend to use direct-face negotiation and express more self-face maintenance, whereas cultures such as China with a greater concern for interdependence and inclusion tend to use indirect-face negotiation and express more mutual-face and other-face maintenance. In a study conducted in central China, Ringo Ma (1992) confirmed that a friend or respected elder intervenes in interpersonal conflict situations, serving as a message carrier.

Telephone

It is estimated that as of 2015 there were 1.1 billion landlines in use. Alexander Graham Bell expected the telephone to be more of a broadcasting medium, more like what radio would become. Well into the 20th century, telephone executives believed the telephone was primarily a medium for business and actually discouraged "socializing" by telephone (see Figure 1.3).

Using the telephone in intercultural interactions has the barriers of the lack of contextual cues other than those related to voice. For this reason it may be the conversation openings that are significant in establishing the first impression from which the relationship develops. An opening sequence that violates a cultural expectation may lead the parties to develop negative views and attitudes toward each other (Pavlidou, 2006). Later language misunderstandings, such as the meanings of certain words, idioms, and humor, can exacerbate the problem.

Figure 1.3 Landline and Mobile Phones in Use

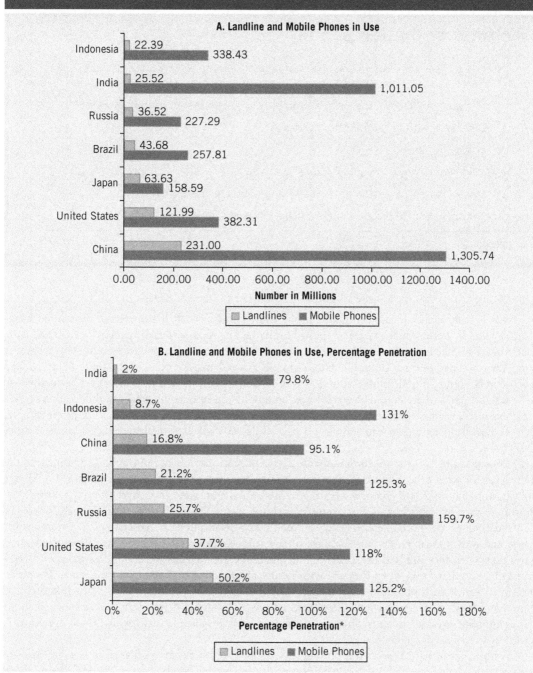

A. Landline and Mobile Phones in Use

- Indonesia: Landlines 22.39, Mobile Phones 338.43
- India: Landlines 25.52, Mobile Phones 1,011.05
- Russia: Landlines 36.52, Mobile Phones 227.29
- Brazil: Landlines 43.68, Mobile Phones 257.81
- Japan: Landlines 63.63, Mobile Phones 158.59
- United States: Landlines 121.99, Mobile Phones 382.31
- China: Landlines 231.00, Mobile Phones 1,305.74

Number in Millions

Landlines ■ Mobile Phones

B. Landline and Mobile Phones in Use, Percentage Penetration

- India: Landlines 2%, Mobile Phones 79.8%
- Indonesia: Landlines 8.7%, Mobile Phones 131%
- China: Landlines 16.8%, Mobile Phones 95.1%
- Brazil: Landlines 21.2%, Mobile Phones 125.3%
- Russia: Landlines 25.7%, Mobile Phones 159.7%
- United States: Landlines 37.7%, Mobile Phones 118%
- Japan: Landlines 50.2%, Mobile Phones 125.2%

Percentage Penetration*

Landlines ■ Mobile Phones

Source: Central Intelligence Agency (2017).

*Penetration is the percentage of the total population.

Focus on Culture 1.4

How We Answer the Telephone

France	"Allo." The French often add their name and the phrase "Qui est à l'appareil?" That is, "Who is on the phone?"
Italy	"Pronto" or "Ready." The caller may then ask, "Chi parla?" or "Who's speaking?"
Germany	Last name, such as "Schmidt" or "Mueller."
Spain	"Diga" or "Speak."
Mexico	"Diga" or "Bueno," meaning "Good" or "Well."
Southeast Asia	Most commonly a version of "Hello." Hong Kong Chinese say "Wei."
Japan	"Moshi moshi," the equivalent of "Hello," or perhaps "Hai," which is "Yes."

Source: Martin (2000).

What is commonly called a cell phone in the United States is called a mobile in the United Kingdom, cellular in Latin America, *keitai* (portable) in Japan, *shou-ji* (hand machine) in China, *nalle* (teddy bear) in Sweden, *Pelephone* (wonder phone) in Israel, and *handy* in Germany. By whatever name, the estimated number of mobile phones in 2015 was 7 billion. Because the United States relied heavily on landlines, mobile phone adoption was slower in the United States than in other countries. In Africa and Asia, where landlines were not as common, and in Europe, where mobile phone service is less expensive than landlines, mobile phone adoption was faster (Ling, 2005). In 2005, for example, 95% of European teenagers had mobile phones while 45% of U.S. teenagers did (Ling & Baron, 2007).

Text messaging is the more commonly used term in North America, the United Kingdom, and the Philippines for what other countries are more likely to refer to as short message service (SMS). Shuter and Chattopadhyay (2010) compared texting in the United States and India and found a definite relationship to each culture's norms. For example, consider where texting is done. Consistently, people in the United States are more likely to send and read messages in public social settings like restaurants, shops, and movie theaters. Perhaps because of the area where texting is done, people in the United States text when they are with strangers and acquaintances or friends but much less than with family members. Indians text when they are with family members or boyfriends or girlfriends. People in the United States are more likely to consider it impolite to text in a classroom, in a movie theater, at dinner, and while conversing with others, especially with loud text alerts. Indians are more likely to find as impolite swearing in texts. Shuter and Chattopadhyay conclude that the social use of texting is guided by forces deeply imbedded in each culture.

In sub-Saharan Africa, with the proliferation of mobile phone networks, countries are moving directly to the digital age without costly development of extensive landline networks. Household landline access is near zero. While in 2002 one in ten in Tanzania, Uganda, Kenya, and Ghana owned a mobile phone, today in some African countries, such as South Africa and Nigeria, mobile phones are as common as in the United States. The percentage of these that are smartphones with access to the Internet and apps, however, is lower.

Internet

The Internet can be defined as the worldwide interconnection of individual networks operated by government, industry, academia, and private parties. Since the mid-1990s, the Internet has grown to serve 3.17 billion users in every part of the world and has forever changed how we communicate. Figure 1.4 shows the 10 countries with the most Internet users.

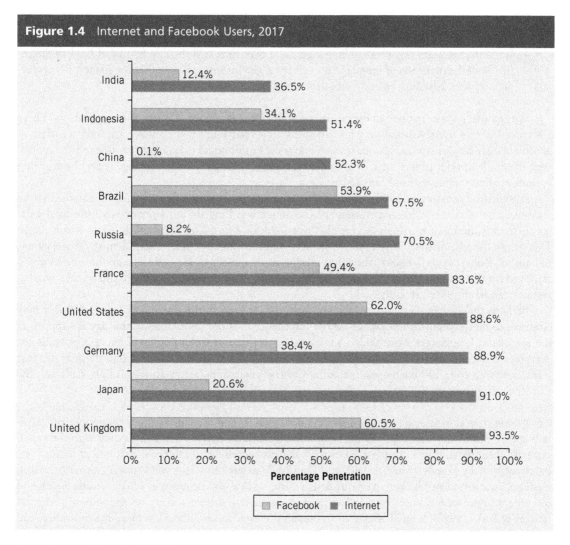

Figure 1.4 Internet and Facebook Users, 2017

Source: Internet World Stats (2017).

There are more than 2.5 times the number of Internet users in China as in the United States, and the United Kingdom has the highest percentage of Internet users. About one-half of the world's population now has Internet access.

Language Use. The Internet originated in the English-speaking world. Computers are English-oriented. Early computer systems were limited to the characters in the American Standard Code for Information Interchange (ASCII), making, for example, texts transmitted unaltered from Francophone keyboards appear as garbage on English-favoring keyboards; Netscape and Java are in English; search engines were developed in and for English. At its origin, the language of the Internet was English. But as Figure 1.4 shows, the Internet is now truly worldwide. That suggests two questions:

- Will the Internet encourage the worldwide dominance of English? Will the Internet, then, become a major force blending the world's population together?
- Will Internet users favor native languages, and over time will the dominance of English diminish? Will the divisions of language groups force the Internet to use other languages, perpetuating divisions based on existing language use lines?

We can't fully answer these questions by examining the language abilities of Internet users. There are more Internet users worldwide who can speak and read English than there are Internet users in predominantly English-speaking countries. While these multilingual users might be able to use English, they might also prefer to use their first language. Figure 1.5 shows the percentages of websites using various content languages as of late 2016.

A study first reported in 2000 examined the language use of young Egyptian professionals. For the reasons stated above, the dominant language use online was English, but a previously little-used written form of Romanized Egyptian Arabic also was used for expressing personal thoughts and feelings. This group used Romanized Egyptian Arabic as a reinforcement of their local identity (Warschauer, El Said, & Zohry, 2002). Today, though, with the development of Unicode, the computing industry standard for the consistent encoding, representation, and handling of text, most of the world's writing systems can be displayed reliably.

Perhaps the answer to the questions above is yes: At least in the immediate future, English may continue to be the dominant language on the Internet, but at the same time technology is supporting the use of local languages worldwide. Additionally, translation technology will make it possible for everyone to use any preferred language and be understood by anyone. Google Translate provides text translations for over 100 languages, including Chinese characters. Translations also are built into the Chrome web browser.

Design Elements. As you can see in the model of communication presented earlier, communication symbols can be verbal and nonverbal. While translation technology may deal to some extent with the verbal symbols, there remain the nonverbal. Research has demonstrated that culture is reflected in the nonverbal aspects of the Internet. Singh, Zhao, and Hu (2003) assert that "the web is not a culturally neutral medium," because websites contain unique design elements that give "country-specific websites a look and feel unique to the local culture" (p. 63). Design elements include different icons, colors, and site structures (Barber & Badre, 1998). Schmid-Isler (2000) compared Western and Chinese Internet news sites and found that their layout is different. She contended that this difference is related to culturally influenced perceptions of information storage and display. For example, Google has clean lines and uncluttered "negative

Figure 1.5 Language of Internet Content, 2017

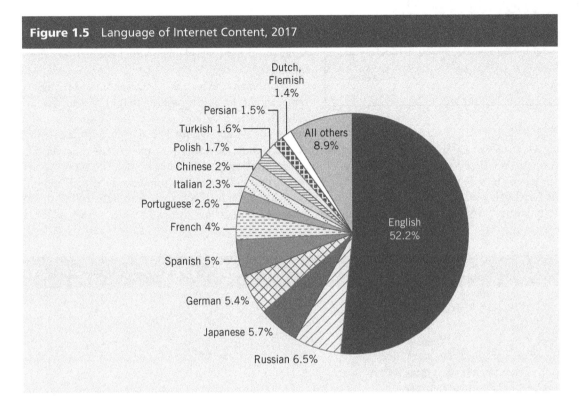

Dutch, Flemish 1.4%

Persian 1.5%

Turkish 1.6%

Polish 1.7%

Chinese 2%

Italian 2.3%

Portuguese 2.6%

French 4%

Spanish 5%

German 5.4%

Japanese 5.7%

Russian 6.5%

All others 8.9%

English 52.2%

Source: Q-Success (2017).

space." Chinese web users are accustomed to pop-ups and floating banner ads. Chinese webpages are "packed with information and multimedia graphics, requir[ing] many scroll-downs to see the whole page" (Clark, 2016, p. 166). In contrast, Google seems static and dull to Chinese web users.

Social Media

The term *social media* is used to describe a variety of Internet-based platforms, applications, and technologies, such as Facebook, Twitter, and YouTube, that enable people to socially interact with one another online. Social media sites are based on user participation and user-generated content. See Figure 1.4 for Facebook use worldwide. While Facebook has 1.7 billion users, it is not alone (see Figure 1.6 for leading social networks). Japan's Mixi had nearly 27 million members

Alex Robertson/Moment/Getty Images

Mobile phone use on Japanese public transport

Global Voices

> Facebook is where you lie to your friends, and Twitter is where you tell the truth to strangers.
>
> —Unknown

in 2010 (about 20% of the population; "Profiling the Facebooks of the World," 2010) and Russia has two local social network platforms that outperform Facebook.

For many Africans, smartphones became a replacement for technologies that, purchased individually, would be cost-prohibitive. A smart mobile device for African youth becomes a radio, a streaming video device, and a computer. Studies show that when Africans go online with their mobile phones, they spend much of their time on social media platforms. Facebook offers its free Internet service for mobile users in half the countries in Africa with a combined population of 635 million. As Facebook's service does not provide full access to all of the Internet, some have labeled it "digital colonialism." African companies are launching local social media platforms. In South Africa, MXit, a

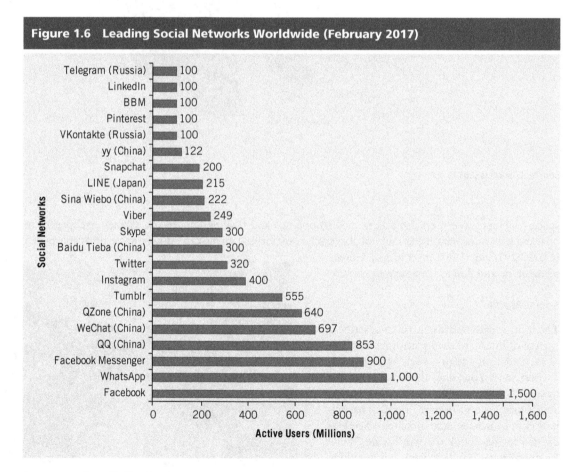

Figure 1.6   Leading Social Networks Worldwide (February 2017)

Source: Data from Chaffey (2017).

free instant messaging application, has an estimated 10 million users (Essoungou, 2010; Kalan, 2013; Pew Research Center, 2015b).

Yoojung Kim, Dongyoung Sohn, and Sejung Choi (2011) compared U.S. and Korean college student SMS use and found clear cultural connections. In both countries the reasons for using SMS were the same: seeking friends, social support, information, entertainment, and convenience. The difference was that, for students in the United States, socially close others (e.g., family members, close friends) were only a minor part of their online social networks, while families and close friends were 70% of the Koreans' networks. The researchers conclude that students in the United States tend to focus more on entertaining themselves by making new friends through SMS, while Korean students tend to focus more on existing relationships with socially close others from whom they can acquire useful information and social support. Abeele and Roe (2011) found a similar pattern comparing Flemish and U.S. new college students. Flemish students were more likely to text and instant message precollege friends, while U.S. students were more likely to text and instant message new friends.

Many countries limit or censor the Internet and social media. In 2015, Freedom House documented that 48 countries censored criticism of authorities on the Internet. Other types of content censored by a smaller number of countries include news on terrorism, accusations of corruption, political opposition, satire and ridicule commentary, content considered insulting to a religion, online petitions and campaigns, and information about minorities. For example, in the summer of 2012, Muslims and members of the Bodo tribal community in northeastern India clashed. Hate messages and altered photos of atrocities against Muslims were spread on social media sites. The government forced Twitter to block accounts and imposed a limit on the number of messages per day and forced Facebook and Google to block websites and user accounts. The Google Transparency report names India as one of the countries that routinely ask Internet firms to remove content. Freedom House documented only 14 countries with no Internet censorship (Freedom House, 2015).

Earlier you read that culture cannot be known without a study of communication, and communication can only be understood with an understanding of the culture it supports. Today's Internet and social media use demonstrates the continuing truth of that statement. Cultures communicate with the Internet and with social media in ways that reflect the values of that culture. You'll see this idea developed more in future chapters.

SUMMARY

Our culture provides regulation for life and provides individual identities. Six forms of regulators of human life and identity are religion, nation, class, gender, race, and civilization. Today, national identity has become synonymous with cultural identity. The term *culture* refers to the totality of a large group's thoughts, behaviors, and values that are socially transmitted as well as to members who consciously identify with the group.

Twentieth-century scientists have found no single race-defining gene. The sociohistorical concept of defining race explains that racial categories have varied over time and between cultures. Worldwide, skin color alone does not define race. Scholars from a variety of disciplines have argued that White people in countries such as the United States and South Africa are observed by other groups to be distinct, superior, and unapproachable, whereas Whites themselves are relatively unaware of their racial identity compared to people of color.

The term *subculture* refers to a group that exists within a culture, usually based on social class, ethnicity, or geographic region. As the prefix *sub* can mean "less than," some scholars prefer the term *co-culture* to indicate that no one culture is inherently superior to other coexisting cultures. Finally, the term *subgroup* refers to a group that provides members with a relatively complete set of values and patterns of behavior and in many ways poses similar communication problems as cultures. To avoid negative connotations with these words, the term *microculture* is becoming more commonly used.

A Confucian perspective on communication would define it as an infinite interpretive process in which all parties are searching to develop and maintain a social relationship. A Western perspective would define it as a process involving a speaker, the speech act, an audience, and a purpose. Components of communication can include source, encoding, message, channel, noise, receiver, decoding, receiver response, feedback, and context.

One component of the communication process is the channel or media by which the encoded message is transmitted. Today's new media use reflects significant aspects of culture. For example, people in the United States are more likely to send and read text messages in public social settings like restaurants, shops, and movie theaters; Indians text when they are with family members or boyfriends and girlfriends. And Western and Chinese Internet news sites have different layouts, which is related to culturally influenced perceptions of information storage and display.

DISCUSSION QUESTIONS

1. Damasio's thesis is that culture is a regulator of human life and identity. Give examples of what culture provides to its members. What is not a product of culture?

2. Cannadine posits six forms of regulators of human life and identity. Which have been major sources of conflict? How can that conflict be explained?

3. Why do you believe social class differences, ethnic identity, and skin color are uncomfortable for many people in the United States to discuss?

4. One study found that interactions between ethnically dissimilar people were judged to be relatively superficial encounters. The researchers concluded that communicators were trying to ensure that the interaction was harmonious. What do you believe could explain this?

5. Address the two questions presented in this chapter: Will the Internet encourage the worldwide dominance of English, or will native language use on the Internet weaken the dominance of English?

6. What could justify a nation censoring the Internet and social media?

KEY TERMS

channel	culture	heroes
co-culture	decoding	honorific
communication	encoding	message
Confucianism	ethnic identity	microculture
context	ethnicity	myths
cultural identity	feedback	noise

race   rituals   subgroup

receiver   social class   symbols

receiver response   source   values

reference group   subculture

1. Recently, BCE (before the common era or current era) and CE (common era or current era) have been used to avoid the more culturally limited BC (before Christ) and AD (*anno Domini*, in the year of the Lord).

All readings are from *Intercultural Communication: A Global Reader* (Jandt, 2004).

Claude Lévi-Strauss, "Race, History, and Culture" (p. 1)

Wally Penetito, "Research and Context for a Theory of Maori Schooling" (p. 173)

William J. Starosta, "On Intercultural Rhetoric" (p. 307)

ⓢSAGE edge™

Sharpen your skills with SAGE edge at edge.sagepub.com/jandt9e.

SAGE edge for Students provides a personalized approach to help you accomplish your coursework goals in an easy-to-use learning environment.

Chapter 2

©iStockphoto.com/itchySan

Barriers to Intercultural Communication

In Chapter 1, you read that every culture provides its members with rules specifying appropriate and inappropriate behavior. Were you to approach intercultural communication from the perspective of attempting to learn the norms of all cultures, it certainly would be an impossible task. There is no way that you could learn all the rules governing appropriate and inappropriate behavior for every culture with which you came into contact. You would always be doing something wrong; you would always be offending someone. In fact, you wouldn't even know if you were expected to conform to the other culture's norms or if you were expected to behave according to your own culture's norms while respecting those of the other. Your communication likely would suffer, as your violation of norms would be a form of noise limiting the effectiveness of your communication.

A better approach is to examine on a general level the barriers to intercultural communication. LaRay M. Barna (1997) has developed a list of six such barriers: anxiety, assuming similarity instead of difference, ethnocentrism, stereotypes and prejudice, nonverbal misinterpretations, and language. Her categories of barriers are used here when discussing problems that can arise in intercultural encounters. The first four kinds of barriers are discussed in this chapter. Nonverbal misinterpretations and language are discussed separately in following chapters. Taking these common mistakes into account can help you improve your intercultural communication skills.

Focus on Theory 2.1

Anxiety/Uncertainty Reduction Theory

The German sociologist Georg Simmel's (1858–1918) concepts of "the stranger" and "social distance" were precursors to C. R. Berger and Calabrese's (1975) anxiety/uncertainty reduction theory (Rogers, 1999). This theory assumes that during the initial phase of interaction with another person, your primary communication goal is to reduce your uncertainty about that person. Thus, you are attempting to discover information about the other person and to share information about yourself.

Gudykunst and his colleagues (see, e.g., Gudykunst, 1983, 1985) have applied this theory to intercultural communication by further developing the concept of the stranger. Strangers are people who are members of other groups who act in ways different from one's own culture. When encountering strangers, one experiences uncertainty and anxiety and is unsure how to behave. Uncertainty means not knowing what the reactions of strangers will be and not knowing how to explain the reactions of strangers. Anxiety arises when a person is apprehensive about initial interactions. When anxiety is high, we tend to avoid interactions, and when it is too low, we tend not to care what happens in the interaction.

Note: Anxiety/Uncertainty Reduction theory is the basis for Anxiety/Uncertainty Management Theory (see Focus on Theory 1.1).

This chapter concludes with an extended case study of communication barriers between China and the United States. At this critical time in the relationship between the two countries, misunderstandings have arisen over many issues, including the regulation of media and the Internet, the status of Tibet, human rights, the environment, and economic issues.

Anxiety

The first barrier is high anxiety. When you are anxious due to not knowing what you are expected to do, it's only natural to focus on that feeling and not be totally present in the communication transaction.

For example, you may have experienced anxiety on your very first day on a new college campus or in a new job. You may have been so conscious of being new—and out of place—and focused so much of your attention on that feeling that you made common mistakes and appeared awkward to others. Sugawara (1993) surveyed 168 Japanese employees of Japanese companies working in the United States and 135 of their U.S. coworkers. Only 8% of the U.S. coworkers felt impatient with the Japanese coworkers' English. While 19% of the Japanese employees felt their spoken English was poor or very poor and 20% reported feeling nervous when speaking English with U.S. coworkers, 30% of the Japanese employees felt the U.S. coworkers were impatient with their accent. Almost 60% believed that language was the problem in communicating with the U.S. coworkers. For some, anxiety over speaking English properly contributed to avoiding interactions with the U.S. coworkers and limiting interactions both on and off the job.

Assuming Similarity Instead of Difference

The second barrier is assuming similarity instead of difference. A middle-class Angolan teenager may purchase a CD of American music. Does that demonstrate that all teenagers like the same music? The cultural difference may be in how teenagers listen to that music: The Angolan teenager probably will play the music in communal fashion for several people to listen, dance, and sing along. Most probably in the United States, the teenager will listen to the music alone with ear buds. Four Spaniards may meet at a McDonald's in Madrid. They may order Big Macs, french fries, and milkshakes. Does that demonstrate that we all like the same food? The cultural difference may be in the rituals of dining together in Spain. Most probably they will not rush their meal, and the person who invited the others will pay as it is very unlikely each would pay for individual portions. When you assume similarity between cultures, you can be caught unaware of important differences.

When you have no information about a new culture, it might make sense to assume no differences exist, to behave as you would in your home culture. But making that assumption could result in miscommunication. In 1997, a Danish woman left her 14-month-old baby girl in a stroller outside a Manhattan restaurant while she was inside. Other diners at the restaurant became concerned and called the police. The woman was charged with endangering a child and was jailed for two nights. Her child was placed in foster care. The woman and the Danish consulate explained that leaving children unattended outside cafés is common in Denmark. Pictures were wired to the police showing numerous strollers parked outside cafés while parents were eating inside. The Danish woman had assumed that Copenhagen is similar to New York and that what is commonly done in Copenhagen is also commonly done in New York.

School districts in the United States have been accused of assuming similarity by groups such as the Council of American-Islamic Relations. Muslims pray five times a day and require space to unfurl a prayer rug, face Mecca, and touch the head to the floor. Muslim parents have asked schools to recognize difference and become more accommodating to Muslim students.

Each culture *is* different and unique to some degree. Boucher (1974), for example, has shown how cultures differ in terms of to whom it is appropriate to display emotions. If you assume that display of emotions is similar to your culture, you might see people of different cultures in certain circumstances as lacking emotion and people in other circumstances as displaying emotions inappropriately.

The inverse can be a barrier as well. Assuming difference instead of similarity can lead to one not recognizing important things that cultures share in common.

It's better to assume nothing. It's better to ask, "What are the customs?" rather than assuming they are the same—or different—everywhere.

Focus on Theory 2.2

The Fallacy of Stereotyping

Hamilton and Harwood (1997) note that while cultural differences may be the most visible among people, they may not be the differences most likely to cause conflict. The authors warn against treating people as members of a cultural group without recognizing their individuality and other identities that might be important to them.

Ethnocentrism

The third barrier to effective intercultural communication is ethnocentrism, or negatively judging aspects of another culture by the standards of one's own culture. To be ethnocentric is to believe in the superiority of one's own culture. Everything in a culture is consistent to that culture and makes sense if you understand that culture. For example, assume that climate change is a fact and, as a result, assume that summers in the United States average 43°C (109°F). It would be logical to make adjustments: Rather than air-conditioning buildings all day, you might close schools and businesses in the afternoons to conserve energy. Such adjustments would make sense. Why, then, do some people attribute sensible midday siestas in hot climates to laziness?

Focus on Culture 2.1

Benjamin Franklin's Remarks on American Indians

Savages we call them, because their Manners differ from ours, which we think the Perfection of Civility; they think the same of theirs.

Perhaps, if we could examine the Manners of different Nations with Impartiality, we should find no People so rude, as to be without any Rules of Politeness; nor any so polite, as not to have some Remains of Rudeness. The Indian Men, when young, are Hunters and Warriors; when old, Counsellors; for all their Government is by Counsel of the Sages; there is no Force, there are no Prisons, no Officers to compel Obedience, or inflict Punishment. Hence they generally study Oratory, the best Speaker having the most influence. The Indian Women till the Ground, dress the Food, nurse and bring up the Children, and preserve and hand down to Posterity the Memory of public Transactions. These Employments of Men and Women are accounted natural and honourable. Having few artificial Wants, they have an abundance of Leisure for Improvement by Conversation. Our laborious Manner of Life, compared with theirs, they esteem slavish and base; and the Learning, on which we value ourselves, they regard as frivolous and useless. An Instance of this occurred at the Treaty of Lancaster, in Pennsylvania, anno 1744, between the Government of Virginia and the Six Nations. After the principal Business was settled, the Commissioners from Virginia acquainted the Indians by a Speech that there was at Williamsburg a College, with a Fund for Educating Indian youth; and that, if the Six Nations would send down half a dozen of their young Lads to that College, the Government would take care that they should be well provided for, and instructed in all the Learning of the White People. It is one of the Indian Rules of Politeness not to answer a public Proposition the same day that it is made; they think it would be treating it as a light manner, and that they show it Respect by taking time to consider it, as of a Matter important. They therefor deferr'd their Answer till the Day following; when their Speaker began, by expressing their deep Sense of the kindness of the Virginia Government, in making them that Offer; "for we know," says he, "that you highly esteem the kind of Learning taught in those Colleges, and that the Maintenance of our young Men, while with you, would be very expensive to you. We are convinc'd, therefore, that you mean to do us Good by your Proposal; and we thank you heartily. But you, who are wise, must know that different Nations have different Conceptions of things; and you will therefore not take it amiss, if our Ideas of this kind of Education happen not to be the same with yours. We have had some Experience of it; Several of our young People were formerly brought up at the Colleges of the Northern Provinces; they were instructed in all your Sciences; but, when they came back to us, they were bad Runners, ignorant of every means of living in the Woods, unable to bear either Cold or Hunger, knew neither how to build a Cabin, take a Deer, or kill an Enemy, spoke our language imperfectly, were therefore neither fit for Hunters, Warriors, nor Counsellors; they were totally good for nothing. We are however not the less oblig'd by your kind Offer, tho' we decline accepting it; and, to show our grateful Sense of it, if the Gentlemen of Virginia will send us a Dozen of their Sons, we will take great Care of their Education, instruct them in all we know, and make Men of them."

Source: Quoted in Mott & Jorgenson (1939).

After reading the comments by Benjamin Franklin (see Focus on Culture 2.1), who do you think was being ethnocentric?

In contrast to ethnocentrism, cultural relativism refers to the view that an individual's beliefs and behaviors should be understood only in terms of that person's own culture. It does not mean that everything is equal. It does mean that we must try to understand other people's behavior in the context of their culture. It also means that we recognize the arbitrary nature of our own cultural behaviors and are willing to reexamine them by learning about behaviors in other cultures (M. N. Cohen, 1998).

Global Voices

The easiest idea to sell anyone is that he is better than someone else.

—Gordon Allport, *The Nature of Prejudice* (1954, p. 372)

A less extreme form of ethnocentrism can be labeled *cultural nearsightedness,* or taking one's own culture for granted and neglecting other cultures. For example, people in the United States often use the word *Americans* to refer to U.S. citizens, but actually that word is the correct designation of all people in North and South America. Its careless use is a form of ethnocentrism.

Cultural nearsightedness often results in making assumptions that simple things are the same everywhere. Designing forms for something as simple as a person's name is not that simple if you recognize how widely practices vary. For example, in Mexico, people may have two surnames, with the first from the father's first surname and the second from the mother's surname. Often, only the first surname is used and the second abbreviated. When a woman marries, she usually retains both of her surnames and adds her husband's first surname. Consider China, with 1.4 billion people and only about 4,000 surnames, with 85% of the population sharing 100 of them. According to the National Bureau of Statistics of China, nearly 95 million people share the name Wang—the most common surname in the world. Second most occurring is Li, with some 93 million Chinese. The most prevalent surname in the U.S., Smith, is shared by 2.4 million people.

Another example is Eurocentric ethnocentrism. This would include, for example, recognizing only Western holidays in schools or basing curriculum only on Western history, music, and art. The terms *the West* and *the East* themselves have been labeled Eurocentric ethnocentrism. Asia is east of Europe, but to call Asia "the East" makes its identity dependent on Europe.

Extreme ethnocentrism leads to a rejection of the richness and knowledge of other cultures. It impedes communication and blocks the exchange of ideas and skills among peoples. Because it excludes other points of view, an ethnocentric orientation is restrictive and limiting.

Stereotypes and Prejudice

Stereotypes and prejudice are a pernicious stumbling block to intercultural communication. The term stereotype is the broader term and is commonly used to refer to negative or positive judgments made about individuals based on any observable or believed group membership. Prejudice refers to the irrational suspicion or hatred of a particular group, race, religion, or sexual orientation. The terms are related in that they both refer to making judgments about individuals based on group membership. It's generally agreed that racism is prejudice with the exercise of power on or over the group through institutional, historical, and structural means (Hoyt, 2012).

Stereotypes

The word *stereotyping* was first used by journalist Walter Lippmann in 1922 to describe judgments made about others on the basis of their ethnic group membership. Today, the term is more broadly used to refer to judgments made on the basis of any group membership. Psychologists have attempted to explain stereotyping as mistakes our brains make in the perception of other people that are similar to those mistakes our brains make in the perception of visual illusions (Nisbett, 1980). When information is ambiguous, the brain often reaches the wrong conclusion. As illustrated in Figure 2.1, the moon appears to be much larger when it floats just above the horizon than when it shines overhead. The brain's estimation of distance changes, as does the apparent size of the moon.

What we see, the most readily available image, is what we expect to see. We can reject any information that challenges that expectation. In Figure 2.2, a sign appears to read "Paris in the spring," but it actually has an extra *the*. As we don't expect to see a double *the,* often we do not perceive it. In a like manner, if we expect that heads of corporations are tall, slender, White males, we don't see people with disabilities, women, and people of color in that group.

In Figure 2.3, a light green triangle appears to float in front of three darker green circles even though no triangle exists. Our brain constructs the triangle; we see something that doesn't exist. We do not so much believe what we see as see what we believe. We tend to discount any perceptions that do not conform to our beliefs.

In Figure 2.4, odds are you missed some of the *f*s that made a *v* sound and *s*s that sound like a *z*. The brain overlooks what it doesn't expect. (There are six *f*s in the first sentence and 14 *s*s in the second.)

Who stereotypes? And who is the target of stereotyping? The answer to both questions is that anyone can stereotype and anyone can be the target of stereotyping.

Identify the stereotypes in the following examples: Until recently, the sign for *Japanese* in American Sign Language was a twist of the little finger at the corner of the eye to denote a slanted eye. The new sign, taken from Japanese Sign Language, is a hand signal to show the shape of the Japanese islands (Costello, 1995). In Japanese Sign Language, the sign for *foreigner* is the index finger making a circular motion around the eye denoting "round eye."

Are American Indian logos and mascots stereotypes? Some say the stereotypes are positive; others find them demeaning. In 2001, the U.S. Commission on Civil Rights called for an end to the use of American Indian images and team names by non–American Indian schools. Beginning in 2006, the National Collegiate Athletic Association (NCAA) prohibited 18 colleges and universities from displaying their nicknames, logos, or mascots based on American Indian imagery or references at postseason games. By 2008, the ban also applied to the uniforms of cheerleaders, dance teams, and band members at NCAA championship sites. Central Michigan, Florida State, Midwestern State, Mississippi College, and the University of Utah retained their eligibility by receiving support from the eponymous tribe. Schools under this ban include the Florida State Seminoles, the Illinois Fighting Illini, and the Utah Utes. The University of North Dakota (UND) was one of the 18 schools with an American Indian mascot, the Fighting Sioux. UND sued the NCAA and reached a settlement permitting it to retain its mascot if both the Spirit Lake and Standing Rock Sioux reservations approved. One has; one hasn't. One said the name is a "source of pride"; the other said it "breeds prejudice." The state legislature passed a law prohibiting the university from changing its name. The law was repealed. Supporters of the name sued the NCAA. The suit failed. A statewide referendum voted to remove the name, and the university has done so.

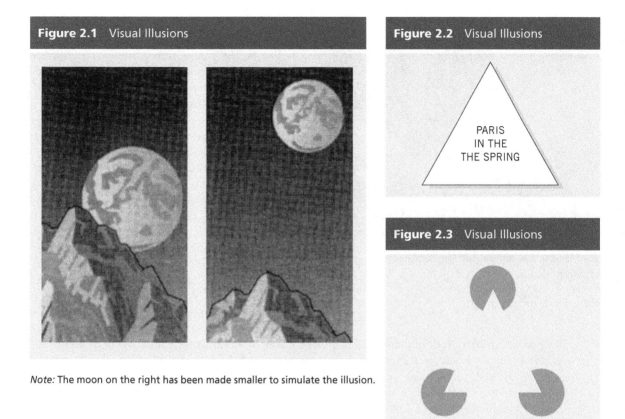

Figure 2.1 Visual Illusions

Note: The moon on the right has been made smaller to simulate the illusion.

Figure 2.2 Visual Illusions

PARIS
IN THE
THE SPRING

Figure 2.3 Visual Illusions

Figure 2.4 Visual Illusions

Count the number of times the letter *f* appears in the first sentence and the letter *s* in the second.

1. Finished files are the result of years of scientific study combined with the experience of years.

2. Sunday is shown after Wednesday, isn't it, inside those calendars he has made us paste together for our game days next season?

The National Congress of American Indians and other tribal organizations have protested the name Washington Redskins as perpetuating a demeaning stereotype. A U.S. historian has noted that Cleveland Indians, Kansas City Chiefs, and Atlanta Braves are not slurs, but Redskins has historically been an ethnic slur. The U.S. Patent and Trademark Office ruled that "redskins" cannot be registered as a trademark as it is derogatory. Former team owner Jack Kent Cooke (a Canadian) said that the Redskins name stands for bravery, courage, and a stalwart spirit. Current team owner Dan Snyder remains adamant that he will never change the name.

Washington Redskins' Chris Thompson and Niles Paul celebrate a touchdown. In 2014 the U.S. Patent and Trademark Office denied trademark protection for the team name and branding.

Jeff Zelevansky/Getty Images Sport/Getty Images

What is the difference between cultural sensitivity and ethnic stereotyping? In 1997, American Airlines was criticized for a flight manual that said Latin American customers like to drink before takeoff. Is that cultural information that makes it possible for the airline to provide better customer service, or is it a stereotype? That same flight manual also said that Latin American customers do not expect flights to depart on time and will even call in bomb threats if they are running late and want the flight to be delayed.

Is the practice of profiling stereotyping? Profiling refers to a law enforcement practice of scrutinizing certain individuals based on characteristics thought to indicate a likelihood of criminal behavior. For example, it's believed that a person traveling alone is more likely to engage in terrorist activity. Profiling also refers to, for example, conducting traffic stops based on the vehicle occupant's perceived race, ethnicity, gender, or economic status. Profiling can happen in commercial establishments as well. The department store Macy's recently settled claims for racial profiling minority customers at its flagship store in Manhattan. The September 11, 2001, attacks on the United States created a climate that gave law enforcement agencies wider latitude to engage in more intensive airport security checks of people who appear to be of Middle Eastern descent.

© Can Stock Photo Inc./monkeybusiness

In 2003 the federal government banned profiling on the basis of race or ethnicity and in 2014 extended that to religion, gender, national origin, sexual orientation, or gender identity. For the most part the policy does not apply to screening at borders and airports nor to local or state law enforcement.

Negative Effects on Communication

Does it matter who speaks the words? Don Imus lost his nationally distributed morning radio show after referring to the women of the Rutgers University basketball team as "nappy-headed hos." He later said he didn't realize the words would be offensive because he had heard Black rappers use the same language.

Some contend that ethnic sensitivity should be secondary to homeland security; others argue that increased racial profiling only raises ill feelings toward the United States.

Focus on Skills 2.1

Ethnic Stereotyping or Cultural Sensitivity?

You are a student counselor in your campus Ombuds office, which assists students, faculty, and staff in resolving conflicts on an informal basis. A complaint has been filed by a student group against the campus theater department. The theater group is selling Halloween costumes to raise money. Included in their costumes are sombreros. The complaint doesn't allege that sombreros are an offensive symbol but rather that their sale by the theater department as a costume is cultural appropriation and the misuse of a cultural symbol.

You call the president of the theater department student group, who is shocked by your call. She says their intention wasn't to diminish any culture with the costume sale. She asks how the department's sale is any different from a local Mexican restaurant that advertises with a man in a sombrero or from the Los Angeles Angels, which gave away thousands of sombreros at a recent Major League Baseball game. Then she asks, "Should the bakery on campus stop selling squaw bread?"

1. Is this an example of ethnic stereotyping or cultural insensitivity?
2. How might you help these two student groups resolve this conflict?
3. What about the squaw bread?

Stereotypes are harmful because they impede communication in at least four ways:

1. They cause us to assume that a widely held belief is true when it may not be. Research conducted by Gordon Allport (1954) showed, for example, that the prevalent stereotype of Armenians as dishonest was proved false when a credit-reporting association gave the group credit ratings as good as those given others. Although you may think of stereotypes as being negative judgments, they can be positive as well. Some people hold positive stereotypes of other individuals based on their professional group membership. For example, some people assume that all doctors are intelligent and wise.

2. Continued use of the stereotype reinforces the belief. Stereotypes of women as ornaments, people of color as stupid or licentious, and gay men as promiscuous reinforce a belief that places individual women, African-Americans, and gay men at risk. Popular television may reinforce those stereotypes. Shaheen (1984), for example, has cited the four Western myths about Arabs as shown on television: Arabs are wealthy, barbaric, sex maniacs, and terrorist minded.

3. Stereotypes also impede communication when they cause us to assume that a widely held belief is true of any one individual. For example, if a group is stereotyped as dishonest, that does not mean that any one individual in that group is dishonest. A classic psychology study in the 1970s had two groups of undergraduates read stories about a woman. The stories were identical, except that one had the sentence "Betty is now a lesbian." On a test one week later, individuals in the group who had read that Betty is a lesbian were much more likely than individuals in the other group to recall having read that Betty never dated men. In fact, the story that both groups had read stated that Betty dated men occasionally. The group's stereotype of a lesbian influenced what they recalled having read (Snyder & Uranowitz, 1978). Do you think that stereotype is commonly held today?

4. The stereotype can become a self-fulfilling prophecy for the person stereotyped. Research by psychologists Steele and Aronson (1995) has shown that a negative stereotype creates a threat that can distract the individual stereotyped and lower performance.

Case Study: Asian-Americans

Asian-American groups in the United States have experienced stereotyping, which, although often positive, has impeded communication. The term *Asian-American* was created by University of California, Los Angeles, historian Yuji Ichioka in the late 1960s to refer to all people of Asian descent in the belief that all Asians shared a common history and struggle in the United States. And up to the 1970s, Asian-Americans were largely born in the United States. The Immigration and Nationality Act amendments of 1965 abandoned the old policy of immigration quotas for each country and established a new system giving preference to relatives of U.S. residents. That change resulted in large numbers of Asians immigrating to the United States between 1981 and 1989. The label *Asian-American* includes more than 30 ethnicities, with family origins extending from East Asia and Southeast Asia to the Indian subcontinent as well as the Philippines and Indonesia. The continued use of the term *Asian-American* contributes to a stereotype of some 10 million people of Asian ancestry as a single community.

During the civil rights era of the 1960s, Asian-Americans became associated with the stereotype of the "model minority," who achieved success through hard work, perseverance, silent stoicism, strong family ties, and strong support for education. This stereotype seemed to continue the belief that any group can achieve the American Dream if its members "just work hard enough." Some 49% of Asian-Americans have a bachelor's degree, compared to 28% of the general population, and while Asian-Americans make up about 5.6% of the population, Asian-Americans account for 25% to 30% of National Merit Scholarships. Asian-Americans of all groups are most often portrayed in the press as industrious and intelligent; enterprising and polite, with strong values; and successful in schools and business and in science and engineering. The 2015 census data showed that Asian-Americans had the highest median annual income of $77,368 (compared to $59,698 for Whites). Asian-American high school students of all backgrounds complain that teachers often counsel Asian-Americans to go into math and sciences. Some teachers respond that this is done so that immigrants will not have to contend with language problems. Asian-Americans argue that some teachers continue to do this even to those who are fluent in English and that the reason why teachers do this is that Asians are perceived as not being free thinking or extroverted. California public universities are not allowed to use racial criteria in admissions. Berkeley's enrolments in 2014 were 41% Asian-American. Some allege that Ivy League universities limit the number of Asian-Americans they admit. A controversial study of admissions data from 10 unnamed selective colleges concluded that

Global Voices

Amy Chua and Jed Rubenfeld (2014) assume that some specific social habits communicated across group members and transmitted through generations may predispose those groups to success or failure. We might label these social habits as cultural traditions or traits. Chua and Rubenfeld contend in a controversial book that Asians, Cubans, Jews, Indians, Nigerians, Mormons, Iranians, and Lebanese are superior in succeeding in the United States because they share three cultural traits: a superiority complex, insecurity, and impulse control.

Calcutta-born journalism professor Suketu Mehta (2014) charges that such claims of superiority for "model minorities" is simply a new form of racism. The implication is that other cultures are inferior and unable to succeed. Mehta also contends that such claims now based on culture follow a century of discredited claims of superiority based on race, class, IQ, and religion.

Asian-Americans need 140 more SAT points than Whites for admission and Blacks need 310 fewer points for admission (Espenshade & Radford, 2009).

A recent study demonstrated that the model minority stereotype is very much accepted (Zhang, 2010). Using cultivation theory as a theoretical framework, Zhang (2010) showed that in the United States, Asians are perceived as most likely to achieve academic success, are most likely to be perceived as nerds, are perceived as most likely to be left out, and are one of two groups people are least likely to initiate friendship with.

Focus on Theory 2.3

Cultivation Theory

Cultivation theory links media content with the acquisition of stereotypes (Perse, 2001). Cultivation theory was developed by George Gerbner. Its proponents argue that television has long-term effects that are small, gradual, indirect, but cumulative and significant. Repeated exposure to media stereotypes leads to acceptance of the stereotype as a social reality (Gerbner, Gross, Morgan, & Signorielli, 1980). Gerbner believed that the mass media cultivate attitudes and values that are already present in a culture. Almost all cultivation theory studies have been U.S.-based.

Prejudice

Whereas stereotypes can be positive or negative, prejudice refers to the irrational dislike, suspicion, or hatred of a particular group, race, religion, or sexual orientation (Rothenberg, 1992). Persons within the group are viewed not in terms of their individual merit but according to the superficial characteristics that make them part of the group. Psychologists have identified the highly prejudiced individual as having an authoritarian personality (Adorno, Frenkel-Brunswick, Levinson, & Sanford, 1950). Such persons tend to overgeneralize and think in bipolar terms; they are highly conventional, moralistic, and uncritical of higher authority. Highly prejudiced people are unlikely to change their attitudes even when presented with new and conflicting information.

Focus on Technology 2.1

Can Technology Be Prejudiced?

Google Photos (in 2015) algorithmically identified Black people as gorillas. Snapchat (in 2016) provided a selfie-altering filter that showed users as an offensive Asian caricature. Software that coded gorillas as black in color may have resulted in machine algorithms that applied that label to people with black skin. One study demonstrated that if one did a Google search for a name more likely to be of African-American descent (DeShawn, Darnell, Jermaine), ads for companies that locate criminal records were more likely to be displayed than for names more commonly assigned to Whites (Geoffrey, Jill, Emma; Sweeney, 2013). Law professor Frank Pasquale (2015) contends that machine algorithms are learning our stereotypes.

Racism

White Privilege

Peggy McIntosh (1989) has written about White privilege, which describes how a dominant culture empowers some:

> As a white person, I have realized I had been taught about racism as something which puts others at a disadvantage, but had been taught not to see one of its corollary aspects, white privilege, which puts me at an advantage. I think whites are carefully taught not to recognize white privilege, as males are taught not to recognize male privilege. So I have begun in an untutored way to ask what it is like to have white privilege. I have come to see white privilege as an invisible package of unearned assets which I can count on cashing in on each and every day, but about which I was "meant" to remain oblivious. White privilege is like an invisible weightless knapsack of special provisions, maps, passports, code books, visas, clothes, tools and blank checks. (paras. 2–3)

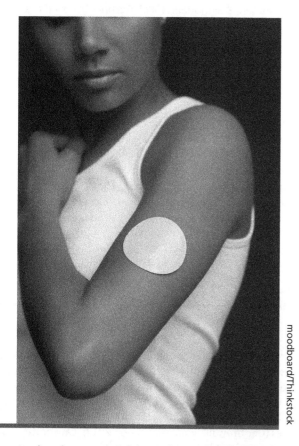

moodboard/Thinkstock

Are bandages racist? What color are flesh-colored bandages?

McIntosh (1994) uses a comparison to being right-handed. Pick up a pair of scissors, grasp a door handle, and sit at a student's desk. They are all designed for right-handed people. Yet right-handed people do not tend to recognize how the world favors right-handedness. White culture resulted from a synthesis of ideas, values, and beliefs inherited from European ethnic groups in the United States. As the dominant culture in the United States, White culture is the foundation of social norms and organizations.

White privilege exists in the United States as well as other nations, particularly South Africa (Drzewiecka & Steyn, 2009). Scholars from a variety of disciplines have argued that White people in the United States are observed by other groups to be distinct, superior, and unapproachable, whereas Whites themselves are relatively unaware of their racial identity compared to people of color (Bahk & Jandt, 2003, 2004; Dyer, 1997; Hayman & Levit, 1997; Katz & Ivey, 1977).

People of color are likely to be more aware of a racial identity and associate inferior traits with skin color. Racial categorization is prevalent, especially among people who live in a multiracial society. When given a list of racial categories, most people can identify their own racial group and those of others (Montepare & Opeyo, 2002). This perception of racial disparity can lead to socially constructed stereotypes and prejudice to influence interracial communication.

In one study conducted by Maddox and Gray (2002), participants were presented with photographs of Black discussants and statements made by the discussants. The skin tone (lightness and darkness) of discussants was varied in the photographs. The participants were asked to match each of the statements with the photograph of the discussant who they believed made the statement. The study found that both Black and White participants used race as an organizing principle in their perceptions—participants tended to associate positive traits with light-skinned Blacks and negative traits with dark-skinned Blacks. According to Ronald Jackson, Chang In Shin, and Keith Wilson (2000), through acknowledging the superiority and privilege of Whites in U.S. society, people of color can come to internalize their status as inferior and believe White interaction partners regard them as mediocre, unprivileged, and subordinate. While Whites may expect the privileges of being White, some may feel that they are being targeted as the "evil nemesis" when they do not feel personally responsible for racism (R. L. Jackson & Heckman, 2002).

It's important to note that both Whites and people of color are participants in this process. All people must challenge negative perceptions of race. Scholars such as McPhail (2002) argue that such perceptions must be engaged openly to remedy the communication patterns between racial groups.

Critics of the concept of White privilege point out that there is a wide diversity of peoples identified as White and argue that the concept ignores differences among White microcultures. Other critics reference intersectionality to explain that we have overlapping social identities of gender, race, and social class among others and can be privileged in some ways and not privileged in others.

Racism is not simply prejudice. Racism is the belief and practice of racial privilege or social advantages based on race. The term came into common usage in the 1930s to describe Nazi persecution of the Jews. Nazi belief was that humanity comprises biologically distinct subspecies and that some are inherently superior and others inherently inferior (Fredrickson, 2002).

One example today is found in the northeastern portion of India. Some people from there say they are the target of racism for having "Asian" facial features. Most northeastern Indians at some time have experienced culturally insensitive questions, such as "Is it true you eat snakes?" Many are on the receiving end of name calling and racial slurs, such as *chinki* and *chow-mein*. So widespread is this racism that in 2012 the Indian Ministry of Home Affairs determined that the use of the term *chinki* to refer to people in the northeast would be considered a criminal offense with a penalty of up to 5 years in jail. Activists in the region charge that the law is rarely enforced as police are as likely as anyone to participate in the harassment.

Hindustan Times/Hindustan Times/Getty Images

Candlelight vigil against racism and the beating and killing of a 19-year-old student in India's North East state.

Wherever it occurs, communication can play a role in either spreading prejudice and racism or stopping their spread. Prejudice and racism are commonly viewed as being rooted in a child's early socialization and fostered in communication with other people who are prejudiced or racist (Adorno et al., 1950). Just overhearing racist comments has been shown to negatively affect a listener's evaluation of the person being spoken about. Research studies have demonstrated this effect (Greenberg & Pyszczynski, 1985; Kirkland, Greenberg, & Pyszczynski, 1987). In the study conducted by Jeff Greenberg and Tom Pyszczynski (1985), groups of White college students observed a debate between a White student and an African-American student and were asked to evaluate the skill of the debaters. The debates were staged so that the African-American debater won half the time and lost half the time. Immediately after the debate and before the evaluations, a confederate made a derogatory ethnic slur against the African-American debater, criticized the African-American debater in a nonracist manner, or made no comment. Ethnic slurs cued prejudiced behavior. The study's results showed that when the audience overheard the derogatory ethnic slur, the rating given the African-American debater who lost was significantly lower but not so when the African-American debater won. The researchers' comment that evaluations of individual minority group members can be biased by overheard derogatory ethnic labels when the person's behavior is less than perfect.

Out of realizations that speech can cue prejudiced behavior in others, some have attempted to restrict that type of speech, often referred to as *hate speech*. Hate speech includes threats or verbal slurs directed against specific groups or physical acts such as burning crosses or spray-painting swastikas on public or private property (Walker, 1994). Some cities and colleges in the United States have adopted policies attempting to ban hate speech. Strong arguments have been raised that such prohibitions are in violation of the First Amendment, the right to protection from government abridgment of freedom of expression other than libel and obscenity. Others counter that hate speech is less like political expression and more like an action, such as a slap in the face (see Haiman, 1994), and that such regulations are necessary to protect equality. Internationally, the trend since World War II has been to protect individuals and groups from expressions of hatred, hostility, discrimination, and violence. In fact, Australia, Austria, Canada, France, Germany, Great Britain, India, Italy, the Netherlands, New Zealand, Norway, and Sweden all have statutes or constitutional provisions prohibiting forms of hate speech. The International Covenant on Civil and Political Rights, in Article 20(2), expressly

Asian American Resource Workshop

Abercrombie & Fitch (A&F) pulled a line of T-shirts after complaints. The T-shirts show Asian cartoon characters. Printed on the shirts were ads for hypothetical businesses: "Rick Shaw's Hoagies and Grinders. Order by the foot. Good meat. Quick feet" and "Wong Brothers Laundry Service— Two Wongs Can Make It White." A senior manager at A&F said, "These graphic T-shirts were designed with the sole purpose of adding humor and levity to our fashion line."

provides that "any advocacy of national, racial, or religious hatred that constitutes incitement to discrimination, hostility, or violence shall be prohibited by law." In 1992, when the U.S. Senate ratified this treaty, it stipulated that the United States would not be bound by this provision but would adhere to its own constitution.

Global Voices

"The notion of political correctness has ignited controversy across the land.... And although the movement arises from the laudable desire to sweep away the debris of racism and sexism and hatred, it replaces old prejudice with new ones."

—President George H. W. Bush, 1991 commencement speech at the University of Michigan

In 1996, the U.S. Congress passed the Communications Decency Act, which made it a federal crime to put obscene and indecent words or images on the Internet. The concern was to protect children from pornographic material. The next year, the U.S. Supreme Court invalidated a key provision of the law. The Court ruled that in seeking to protect children, the law violated the rights of adults. In that same year (1997), the Simon Wiesenthal Center identified more than 500 hate websites. The first federal prosecution of an Internet hate crime occurred in 1996. A 19-year-old former student at the University of California, Irvine, sent an e-mail message signed "Asian hater" to about 60 Asian students, accusing Asians of being responsible for all crimes on campus and ordering the students to leave the campus or be killed by him. He was convicted in 1998 of interfering with students' civil rights to attend a public university.

In 1997, Germany passed a law under which online providers can be prosecuted for offering a venue for content that is illegal in Germany, such as Nazi propaganda, if they do so knowingly and if it's technically possible to prevent it. The First Amendment would not permit such a restriction in the United States. Because laws banning hate speech may not be constitutional in the United States, there are other, more positive approaches to dealing with prejudice and racism. Establishing cultural norms against such behaviors may be more effective.

While hate speech refers to blatant threats or verbal slurs, microaggression refers to everyday slights and snubs, sometimes unintentional, which nevertheless inflict harm. Simple examples include "You're Chinese, right?" "You're really pretty for a dark-skinned girl," and "How come you sound White?" Studies have now documented that seemingly minor slights negatively impact psychological well-being by increasing anxiety, diminishing self-esteem, and diminishing self-efficacy (Wong, Derthick, David, Saw, & Okazaki, 2016). Some critics of these concerns label this a part of political correctness and a threat to free speech.

One research project demonstrated that hearing other people express strongly antiracist opinions influences both public and private expressions of racist opinions. In their study, Blanchard, Lilly, and Vaughn (1991) interviewed college students on the way to classes. In each interview, three people were involved: the White interviewer, a White confederate, and a naive White respondent. The interviewer asked the confederate and respondent questions about how their college should respond to anonymous racist notes. The confederate always answered first. The study compared how the respondents answered the questions when the confederate answered with the most antiracist statements to how they answered when the confederate answered with the least antiracist statements. The results showed that hearing the confederate express strongly antiracist opinions produced dramatically stronger antiracist opinions than hearing opinions more accepting of racism. In a second study, Blanchard and colleagues showed the same results when the respondents expressed their answers privately on paper. On the basis of this research, it can be argued that cultural norms can minimize the public expression of discriminatory or otherwise interracially insensitive behavior. Yum and Park

Global Voices

In an extraordinary soliloquy after the acquittal of George Zimmerman, who fatally shot Trayvon Martin, an unarmed African-American teenager, President Barack Obama spoke about his personal experiences:

> "When Trayvon Martin was first shot, I said that this could have been my son. And another way of saying that is Trayvon Martin could have been me 35 years ago.... When you think about why, in the African American community at least there's a lot of pain around what happened here. I think it's important to recognize that the African American community is looking at this issue through a set of experiences and a history that doesn't go away."

> "There are very few African American men in this country who haven't had the experiences of being followed when they were shopping in a department store. That includes me."

Source: Hennessey & Parsons (2013).

(1990), however, argue that for well-established stereotypes to change, more frequent information and stronger content are needed. What each of us says about racial discrimination really does matter. Your vocal opinions affect what others think and say.

Case Studies

Like stereotyping, anyone can be prejudiced and anyone can experience prejudice. Prejudice exists in cultures around the world, as can be seen in cases of the Roma and Japan and Korea.

The Roma

The Roma are believed to have migrated from India more than a millennium ago, settling first in Persia, then arriving in Europe in the 13th or 14th century. The name "Gypsy" was mistakenly applied by medieval Europeans, who thought all dark-skinned people came from Egypt. Leading a nomadic life, the Roma were often regarded as tramps and accused of thefts and robberies. From the beginning of the 17th century, attempts were made to forcibly assimilate the Roma people by requiring permanent settlement and banning the Romany language. The Roma were particularly persecuted by Nazi Germany. About 500,000 died in Nazi gas chambers and concentration camps. The Roma language and culture, including remembrance of the Holocaust (known in the Roma language as *porraimos,* or "the devouring"), are central to Roma identity throughout the world.

The Roma have no nation-state of their own and now number approximately 10 million in Europe, mainly in the Balkans and in Central and Eastern Europe, and about 2 million elsewhere, mainly in North and South America and North Africa. Romania has the largest number—about 500,000 according to census data but more reliably estimated at 2.5 million. For decades, Eastern European communist governments suppressed prejudice against the Roma and banned the nomadic life. As the countries shifted to market economies and many people lost jobs, the Roma have again experienced discrimination (Herakova, 2009).

The creation and expansion of the European Union made it possible for citizens to move freely across national boundaries. Italy, for example, had 210,937 foreign residents in 1981. That number grew to more than 4 million by 2006, with many migrating from Romania. In 2005 a councilman in a northern region of Italy appeared on television stating, "Nomads, they are animals," and suggested "a vaccine for Roma children which, with their saliva and spit, might 'infect' Italian children attending the same schools" (Nicolae, 2006, p. 138). On national television the president of the National Association of Sociologists of Italy claimed that the Roma stole children and then sold them "sometimes in parts" (Nicolae, 2006, p. 138). Graffiti appeared on walls: "Gypsies go away" and "Gypsies to the gas."

Map 2.1 Ten Highest European Roma Populations

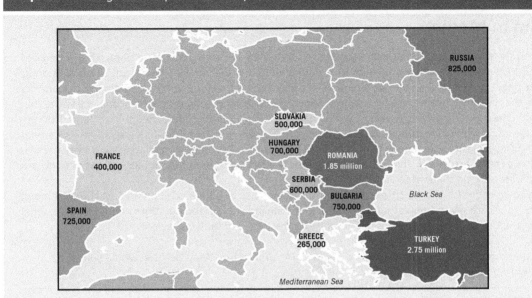

RUSSIA
825,000

SLOVAKIA
500,000

HUNGARY
700,000

FRANCE
400,000

ROMANIA
1.85 million

SERBIA
600,000

BULGARIA
750,000

Black Sea

SPAIN
725,000

GREECE
265,000

TURKEY
2.75 million

Mediterranean Sea

Source: Based on data from The Council of Europe's Roma and Travellers Division (2012).

Italian politicians proposed a census of the Roma in Italy as a first step to ending the discrimination. Yet, as Guillem (2011) explained, the census itself was a form of othering, reinforcing the belief that the Roma are uncivilized and inferior to European society (Kaneva & Popescu, 2014). As recently as 2010, France deported 1,000 Roma to Romania and Bulgaria, and bulldozed some 300 Roma camps. France's actions were called a "disgrace" by the European Commission and have been likened to ethnic cleansing (Bennhold & Castle, 2010).

The European Union states have made better treatment of the Roma a condition for new members. Critics charge that these efforts are for the purpose of reducing migration into the more prosperous Western European nations.

Japan and Korea

The relationship between Japan and Korea reflects deep-seated and longstanding prejudice. Historically, Korea had closer ties to China than did Japan, and both Korea and China tended to view Japan as a "troublemaking" state. This view was reinforced time and again by Japanese incursions into Korean territory and 35 years of Japan's colonial rule. It has only been in recent years that the South Korean and Japanese governments have signed mutual friendship treaties, established normal diplomatic relations, and entered into joint economic development agreements. In an act of historic symbolism, South Korea and Japan cohosted the 2002 World Cup soccer games. Despite economic ties, there remains a sense of *han,* or bitter resentment, that many Koreans feel toward the Japanese.

Focus on Skills 2.2

Racism in Media

You are on the town council for a small township. A local television station posted a photo of a young boy dressed in KKK regalia—floor-length white robe with a white hood—for Halloween trick or treating on its Facebook page. In an interview the boy's mother said that the costume was a family tradition—her brother had worn the costume when he was a young boy. Some Facebook users thought it was racism; one wrote that it is possible the boy thought it was a ghost costume. Later the boy's mother defended the costume: "It's supposed to be white with white, black with black, man with woman and all of that. That's what the KKK stands for. The KKK every year raises money to donate to the St. Jude's." The story immediately went viral and was picked up by media across the United States. Most media reports included the mother's statement without the last phrase about donations to St. Jude's.

At a town council meeting, citizens demand the town council take a position against racism. Among those who speak are several who argue for free speech. One individual, who identifies himself as an Imperial Wizard of the United Klans of America, says that today the KKK is unfairly ostracized.

1. You have studied the literature on communication and racism. What position would you take?
2. How would you explain your position?

Source: Gayle (2013).

After Japan's annexation of Korea in 1910, thousands of Koreans migrated into Japan seeking employment. Following the great 1923 Kanto earthquake in Japan, it was rumored that Koreans were poisoning water supplies. Mob violence left some 6,000 Koreans dead. Later, between 1939 and 1945, more Koreans were forced by the Japanese government to migrate to work in mines (Weiner, 1994). During World War II, the Koreans in Japan were forced to become Japanese nationals. Japan's surrender to the Allied Forces brought an end to the annexation of Korea, and the majority of Koreans who had been brought to Japan under forced immigration returned to Korea, but some 500,000 to 600,000 remained in Japan (Fukuoka, 1996).

When the San Francisco Peace Treaty came into effect in 1952, the government of Japan claimed that the Koreans then in Japan should not be granted Japanese nationality. The descendants of the Koreans who remained in Japan, who may never have been to Korea and who may not have spoken Korean, were legally foreigners.

Sipa USA via AP

Roma and other peoples demonstrate against discrimination of nomad people in Berlin in 2016.

Focus on Skills 2.3

Prejudice in a Place Name

Even international issues can become local issues. Assume you work in the governor's office in Virginia. The Virginia legislature passed a bipartisan bill that would require new public school textbooks in the state to note that the Sea of Japan is also referred to as the East Sea. You learn that New Jersey and New York are considering similar legislation.

The legislation was proposed by a Korean immigrant living in Virginia who saw that in his son's fifth-grade textbook, what he knew to be the East Sea was labeled as the Sea of Japan. Mark Keam, a Korean-American member of the Virginia House of Delegates, said that the labeling reminds Korean-Americans of Japan's 35-year colonial rule of the Korean peninsula. "When Virginia's kids are learning history and geography about that part of the world, they should be taught properly that there are two sides of the story."

Japan's government hired lobbyists to try to defeat the bill. Ambassador Kenichiro Sasae wrote to Virginia's governor that "positive cooperation and the strong economic ties between Japan and Virginia may be damaged" if the bill becomes law. After similar bills were introduced in New Jersey and New York, Japan's Chief Cabinet Secretary Yoshihide Suga called them "extremely regrettable" and pledged a "response through diplomatic channels." Both Korean and Japanese governments posted old maps and documents online. Korean arguments are that the name "East Sea" has been in use for hundreds of years and that "Sea of Japan" was used only when Korea was under Japanese rule. Japanese arguments state that "Sea of Japan" has been used on maps since 1602 and dismiss "East Sea" as only a name used locally in South Korea.

1. Now that you understand the relationship between Japan and Korea, how do you advise the governor?
2. What can you do to influence the course of centuries of misunderstanding in order to reduce this communication barrier?

Source: Simon (2014, p. A7).

As the largest minority group in Japan, Japanese-born Koreans are the victims of social, economic, and political prejudice. Japanese law provides little or no protection against the housing and employment discrimination many Japanese-born Koreans experience. In 1974, the National Council for Combating Discrimination Against Ethnic Minorities (*Mintohren*) was founded by Korean residents and concerned Japanese to fight for the human and civil rights of the Korean residents in Japan.

Extended Case Study of Intercultural Communication Barriers: China and the United States

A 2016 Pew survey of public opinion in China showed U.S. power and influence as the top international threat facing their country (Wike & Stokes, 2016). Neither country has especially positive views of the other. People in the United States were most concerned about the amount of U.S. debt held by

China, the loss of jobs to China, cyberattacks, and human rights. Most Chinese believed the United States was trying to hold their country back from becoming as powerful as the United States. In this extended case study, we'll use some of Barna's (1997) categories to examine the communication barriers between China and the United States.

Anxiety

You remember that anxiety referred to not knowing what you are expected to do in an intercultural encounter. Not knowing what you are expected to do is another way of saying that you need more information. How much information about China does the average U.S. citizen know? Reading the following information about China's history and people will better equip you to communicate interculturally.

History

Today's China represents 4,000 years of civilization. Its history was first recorded more than 1,500 years before the beginning of Christianity. For about half its history, China had multiple governments—at times both a southern and a northern regime. Until early in the 20th century, China was ruled by a series of dynasties and, through the centuries, was largely indifferent to the outside world in that from the Chinese perspective it dominated the world.

The Dowager Empress Cixi died in 1908 and was succeeded by the infant Pu-yi—China's last emperor. In 1911 military officers staged a successful revolt in Wuchang, which was followed by most of China's provinces proclaiming their independence. With the help of Chinese communities in Hawaii, Japan, the United States, and Europe, Dr. Sun Yat-sen led a nationalist movement. Frustrated with a lack of support from Western countries, Dr. Sun turned to Russian Communists for support. After his death in 1925, Sun Yat-sen was hailed as the father of modern China.

Chiang Kai-shek, who had been a Triad leader or warlord and at times felt alliance with the Russian Communists against foreign enemies, attempted to reunify the country. Chiang gained U.S. support partly due to the publicity Henry Luce provided through his *Time* magazine, the popularity of Pearl S. Buck's novels, and the images of Chiang as a convert to Methodism and of his Wellesley College–educated wife. Chiang reversed Dr. Sun's policy of working with the Communists, killing union leaders and Communist supporters. Meanwhile, Mao Zedong had been developing peasant revolts against landlords, establishing peasant-based soviets (Communist local governments). Mao took refuge in remote villages with thousands of Communist refugees and moved to organize the peasantry into a force to take power. Communist Party membership grew from 100,000 in 1937 to 1.2 million by 1945.

In the ensuing warfare the U.S.-backed Nationalists (Chiang) were no match for the Communists (Mao). In 1949, Chiang fled with his followers to the island of Taiwan, located about 161 kilometers (100 miles) off the coast of China. Taiwan, which had been occupied by Japan from 1895 until the end of World War II, when it was returned to China, is about the size of the states of Massachusetts and Connecticut combined. Only 15% of the island's population were 1949 immigrants, but they dominated Taiwan's government through martial law. The nationalist government of Taiwan (the Republic of China) considered itself the legal government of all China, whereas the mainland Chinese government claimed Taiwan as part of its territory. Chiang maintained an army of 600,000 in hopes of regaining the mainland. In 1955, the United States agreed to protect Taiwan in case of attack from mainland China.

For more than four decades, Mao was the dominant figure in Chinese life. In the 1950s, the country benefited from land redistribution, introduction of compulsory universal education, adoption of simplified Chinese characters that led to greater literacy, and the introduction of health and welfare reforms. In 1958, Mao launched the Great Leap Forward. This program forced farmers into communes, abolished private property, and set up backyard steel mills to speed China's entry into the industrial age. The program was a catastrophic failure and brought widespread starvation and the country to bankruptcy. President Liu Shaoqi and Deng Xiaoping, general secretary of the Communist Party, took over day-to-day control to restore the economy.

Beginning in 1966, Mao led the country through his infamous Cultural Revolution. In an attempt to destroy Liu's government and Deng's party, to purify the culture of all outside influences, and to build a new Marxist-Chinese culture, tens of thousands were executed. Millions were exiled to rural labor brigades. During my stays in China, I have spoken with people who were youths during that period. They angrily said their future was stolen from them by Mao. Their only education was Mao's *Red Book* (*The Thoughts of Chairman Mao*).

In 1971, the People's Republic of China (mainland China) was admitted to the United Nations in Taiwan's place despite U.S. objections. In that year, the U.S. national table tennis team was invited to China. They were among the first from the United States to visit the country since 1949. Later that year, President Richard Nixon hosted the Chinese national team in the White House. What became known as "ping-pong diplomacy" led to a breakthrough in U.S.-China relations in 1972, when President Nixon and his national security adviser, Henry Kissinger, established relations with the Chinese government.

On September 9, 1976, Mao died. Shortly after, the Communist Party officially declared Mao's concept of continuing class struggle an ideological mistake, and his call for cultural revolution was commonly believed to have been a terrible disaster. Post-Mao China was dominated by the leadership of Deng Xiaoping. In 1956, Deng had been fourth in power after Mao. By 1962, he had financial control of the country. Deng's economic approach was reflected in his comment to Mao during an argument over farming policies that became his trademark: "Whether a cat is black or white makes no difference. As long as it catches mice, it is a good cat." Deng replaced Marx and Lenin with a commodity economy and profit incentives, but in 1966, he was denounced as a "capitalist roader" and confined to his compound. At the urging of the dying Chou En-lai, Deng swore loyalty to Mao and was returned to power in 1973. Starting in 1978, Deng removed aging leaders and opponents and replaced them with younger, well-educated supporters. Later, in a highly significant move under President Jimmy Carter, on January 1, 1979, the United States normalized relations with the People's Republic of China and severed diplomatic relations with Taiwan, together with terminating the defense agreement protecting the island.

Economy

Deng's four modernizations—agriculture, industry, science, and technology—sought to remove the dogmas, irrationality, and inefficiencies of Mao's era and—at a deliberate speed—transformed China into a modern nation. Deng was credited with saying, "To get rich is glorious." The trademark of capitalism, a stock market, was established in 1990 in Shanghai, the most open and cosmopolitan of China's cities.

The post-Deng era has been one of state capital expenditure to expand the economy through production and exports. Exporting was promoted as the way to economic growth. In 25 years, China moved from a low-income, state-planned economy to a capitalistic, market-oriented economy with improved living standards for hundreds of millions of its people but at the cost of extreme environmental damage. China's challenge as it moves from a developing country to one with a large middle class is to manage that change economically and politically.

Perhaps in the long term, the village democracy program may prove to be the most important of Deng's modernizations. To the extent that democracy requires conflict between ideas, groups, and parties, some Chinese see it in opposition to Confucianism, which values harmony and cooperation. With the disbanding of the commune system, the village democracy program began in 1987 with the Organic Law on Village Committees as a way to make local leaders more accountable. A 1994 amendment to the law allowed secret ballots. By the end of 1997, 95% of China's 900,000 villages had implemented the program, and by 1998, district elections were held in the central province of Hubei. The program varies greatly from county to county, and some critics say it only transfers unpopular tasks such as tax collection and family planning to the local level. Nonetheless, millions of rural Chinese elect their local leadership, but there is no organized push for wholesale political changes.

Overall, China is the world's second largest economy (with $11.3 trillion nominal gross domestic product [GDP], compared to $18.5 GDP for the United States). The Chinese economy has had strong annual growth. Estimates vary, but the International Monetary Fund's projections in its World Economic Outlook are that China will soon become the world's largest economy. China is now the world's second largest importer and the largest exporter. Walmart is the largest single importer from China. In 2001, Walmart alone bought $14 billion in merchandise from China; by 2013, it was $49 billion.

Population

In terms of land area, China is slightly smaller than the United States. It's also the most populous country in the world. Its population was estimated to be 1.4 billion as of 2017, or about 4.2 times as many people as in the United States. China's population accounts for about one-fifth of the entire human race. Some estimates are that China has more than 160 cities whose population exceeds 1 million; the U.S. has 10. Over 90% of Chinese are of Han ethnicity. The government officially recognizes 55 other ethnic groups, and social harmony is one of the ideological underpinnings of the Chinese Communist Party. Yet ethnic unrest does exist. The northwestern-most region of China has seen frequent confrontations between the Uighurs, a Turkic-speaking Muslim people, and the Han Chinese who are perceived as a colonial power.

Largely due to its former one-child policy, China's population is aging. In 1980, the median age was 22.1. In 2013, it had risen to 35.4. One forecast is that by 2050, it will be 46.3. The consequence is that by

©iStockphoto.com/Tarzan9280

Beijing National Stadium (known as the Bird's Nest) was the site of the 2008 Summer Olympics and will be used again for the 2022 Winter Olympics.

mid-century China will have a smaller percentage of people in its workforce and a much larger percentage drawing pensions.

Regional Differences

China also has significant regional cultural differences. The north, including Beijing, is traditional and conservative. The ancestors of most Chinese in the south migrated from the north, overwhelming the original inhabitants and driving them into what is now Vietnam. Hong Kong, Macau, and Guangdong in the south have a distinctive history and culture.

Britain's 19th-century conflict with China enabled British traders to continue exchanging Indian opium for Chinese tea and silk, making huge profits while devastating China. Defeated in these wars, China was forced to open ports up and down the coast not only to the opium trade but also ultimately to foreign diplomats, residents, missionaries, and traders of every kind. Hong Kong island was ceded to Great Britain in perpetuity in 1841, the Kowloon peninsula in 1860, and another slice of the mainland leased in 1898.

Hong Kong is slightly smaller than Los Angeles and home to about 7 million people. It is one of the world's great cities, with the world's fourth largest containership port, one of the world's largest airports, the sixth largest stock exchange in the world, and an impressive trade and financial infrastructure. In 1997, this symbol of free enterprise was returned to China. In a critically important move, in 1990, China promised Hong Kong residents in the Sino-British document known as the Basic Law "one country, two systems." Hong Kong would be a special administrative region of China, with press freedom and continuance of its capitalist economic and social system guaranteed for at least 50 years after the takeover. The Basic Law specified that both Chinese and English would be official languages. In everyday life as well as de facto in government, Cantonese is most common. By 1998, most public schools had switched from teaching in English to Cantonese along with English. China has made it clear that Hong Kong was never a democracy under British rule. The colony's governor was appointed by the British government. It wasn't until 1991 that Great Britain allowed the first direct election of a portion of the seats in Hong Kong's legislature. Prior to the return, China wrote a new constitution for Hong Kong, reversing some of the civil and democratic rights legislation that was passed after the Basic Law agreement without China's consent. Hong Kong's first chief executive after the return was selected by Beijing through a process of indirect elections involving a campaign and vote by 400 businesspeople and community leaders selected by Beijing. Hong Kong's elected legislature was replaced by an appointed one. Currently, half of the legislature is directly elected by voters and the remainder by functional constituencies.

Some believe Hong Kong's leaders will be unable to maintain political distance from Beijing, as laws were changed in 2001 so that now the chief executive is chosen by a 1,200-member election committee largely composed of Beijing loyalists. So the committee essentially serves at the pleasure of the mainland government. And in 2007, China announced that Hong Kong would have to wait before it could directly elect its leader, and the choice would be among two or three candidates approved by a special nominating committee.

Local opposition continues to call for direct elections. In 2014, the "Umbrella Movement" brought tens of thousands of young pro-democracy protesters to the streets and demands for independence. Yet, economically, capitalism continues to thrive in Hong Kong. At least economically, China has become more like Hong Kong. In this way, China continues to change while Hong Kong has remained the same.

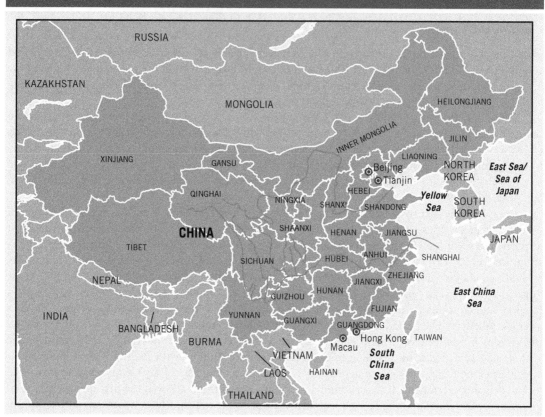

Map 2.2   China

Macau, the first European settlement in Asia and the last Portuguese-held colony, was returned to China in 1999 after 442 years under Portuguese control. Cantonese is the official language along with Portuguese for its 597,000 residents. Similar to Hong Kong, Macau is a special administrative district, with a chief executive chosen by a 300-member committee. Macau is the only place in China where casinos are permitted. It now surpasses Las Vegas in gambling revenue, with $45 billion annually compared to $6.5 in Las Vegas. China hopes that these colonies' return will be followed by the reunification of Taiwan and the mainland.

Assuming Similarity Instead of Difference

Remember that if we assume similarity between cultures, we can be unaware of important differences. Beginning with Marco Polo's sojourn in China in the late 13th century, there have been two "Chinas"—China as imaged by Westerners and the real China. Ironically, at times the China as imaged by Westerners was similar to Western countries in some ways rather than the real China. That today's China's relations with its neighbors and with the United States continue to be strained can at times be based in each country's assumptions of similarity.

In the three examples below, consider how assumptions of similarity have impeded intercultural communication.

Air Space

In 2013 China declared an air defense identification zone over islands that Japan administers in the East China Sea. China threatened to stop aircraft that had not filed flight plans in advance and refuse to maintain two-way radio communication when flying over the zone. The governments of Japan and

Focus on Culture 2.2

"Very Sorry" Proves to Be Key Phrase

In April 2001, a U.S. spy plane made an unauthorized emergency landing on Hainan island after colliding with a Chinese fighter jet, killing its pilot. China regards spy planes 8,000 kilometers from their home as unwarranted; the United States says it has a legal right to fly over international waters off China. China demanded an apology, which the United States refused to give. The wording of the U.S. letter of regret was thoroughly negotiated, yet each side offers a different Chinese translation.

When the U.S. declared itself not just "sorry" but "very sorry" for the loss of a Chinese fighter pilot, the government in Beijing finally had a phrase it could translate into a linguistically acceptable apology.

The nuance of language apparently paved the way for the release of the 24-member crew of the American spy plane detained since April 1. And it will go a long way toward determining how the Chinese people perceive the United States' intentions, spelled out in a key letter from U.S. Ambassador Joseph W. Prueher to Chinese Foreign Minister Tang Jiaxuan on Wednesday.

After days of diplomatic negotiations over the wording of the letter, the U.S. side agreed to insert the "very," breaking the stalemate that has kept the crew detained on Hainan island, according to a senior Bush administration official. The letter also said the Americans were "very sorry" that the U.S. Navy EP-3 intruded into Chinese airspace without verbal permission when it made an emergency landing after colliding with the Chinese jet.

But complicating matters, each side issued different Chinese translations of the document. The version prepared by the U.S. Embassy in Beijing offered feichang baoqian as a translation of "very sorry." But state-run Chinese media used shenbiao qianyi, a phrase that means "to express profound apology" but could suggest that the speaker is apologizing with some reservations.

Shenbiao qianyi is a "flexible fuzzy" phrase, according to a veteran Chinese language expert, speaking on condition of anonymity.

The word the Chinese wanted, but didn't get, was daoqian, which means "to apologize." "The American side ought to apologize to the Chinese people," Chinese President Jiang Zemin said last week, using the word daoqian. Government officials had dismissed as inadequate earlier official U.S. expressions of regret.

"Daoqian would be the word Chinese could accept most easily," the language expert said, but added, "Strictly speaking, there is no real difference between baoqian and daoqian."

"Anyway, without the character qian in there, I don't think there would have been a way out of the situation," he said.

(Continued)

(Continued)

The character qian comes from a classical Chinese character that means "bad harvest." The right half of the character means "to be inadequate" or "to owe something." In Chinese, qian implies that the person delivering the apology is at fault. It also implies that the apology is made sincerely and seriously, not just a casual "Sorry about that." "It's the sort of thing Japanese people would bow their heads when saying," the language expert said.

The political correctness of language has been serious business in China for millenniums, since the days when it was taboo to use the characters in an emperor's name. Lately, Chinese media have been careful to stick to the official description of the plane debacle, rendered as "the incident of an American military reconnaissance plane crashing into and destroying a Chinese military plane." After news of the apology broke, China's official media quickly began reporting that some Chinese citizens were not satisfied.

"I think the U.S. government's way of apologizing can't satisfy people," company manager Su Wei told the official *People's Daily* online edition. Su said U.S. leaders should compensate China for its losses and apologize not in a letter, but in a live, globally televised news conference.

Source: Kuhn (2001, p. A14). Reprinted with permission.

South Korea ordered their major airlines to refuse to comply, while the U.S. government encouraged U.S. carriers to file their flight plans in advance with China. Vice President Joe Biden asked China to avoid enforcement actions that could lead to a crisis. The Focus on Culture 2.2 reading from 2001 details a similar earlier misunderstanding.

South China Sea

China has embarked on a massive campaign of artificial island-building to assert its claims to disputed reefs and islets in the South China Sea. By dredging sand from the ocean bed, China now has reclaimed more than 1,214 hectares (3,000 acres) of land and built at least one military installation on the artificial islands. A case in the Permanent Court of Arbitration brought by the Philippines held that China's claims to the South China Sea had no legal basis. While the United States is not one of the six territorial claimants to the sea, it urged China to accept the ruling and has taken the position that China's actions threaten freedom of navigation in international waters. Chinese Foreign Minister Wang Yi has said that Vietnam and the Philippines started construction work 20 or 30 years ago on islands in the South China Sea they had illegally occupied. The U.S. Navy has flown and sailed close to the islands.

Broadcast Media and the Internet

Because today's media is worldwide, we might assume similarity instead of difference in today's media. Consider, though, the differences that follow:

All broadcast media in China are owned by, or affiliated with, the Communist Party of China or a government agency. The Publicity Department of the Communist Party enforces media censorship (Central Intelligence Agency, 2017). The first real Internet connection to China was established in 1994 when the Stanford Linear Accelerator Center connected with the Institute of High Energy

Physics in Beijing. The government encourages the Internet for education and business. Internet usage in China surged from 40 million in 2002 to 100 million in 2005 to 688 million in 2017—more than any other country—which is about 50% of the country's population.

But the Internet in China is not borderless. China's government promotes "Internet sovereignty," rejecting the idea that a nation's virtual borders should be less meaningful than its physical borders. China has unsuccessfully promoted its vision of Internet sovereignty to other countries.

China's regulation of the Internet has become commonly referred to as "the Great Firewall of China," which limits and censors the Internet. Google was first blocked in 2002. YouTube was blocked after unrest in Tibet in 2008. Facebook and Twitter were blocked after riots in Xinjiang in 2009. Yet the government permits a small window on the Internet through which a small number of largely elite English-speaking users can access the Internet through virtual private networks but at very slow browsing speed. China continues to block thousands of websites and monitor individuals' Internet access. Some contend the censorship is for economic protectionism as well as social control.

The three major "kingdoms" of China's Internet today are Baidu, Alibaba, and Tencent. Baidu (百度) is the world's largest Chinese Internet search engine, but it differs significantly from Google. Jiang (2014) compared the two search engines and demonstrated that there is minimal overlap and little ranking similarity between Baidu's and Google's results. Jiang argues that search engines can be designed to serve political regimes, shaping the perception of the world and arbitrarily creating social realities.

Focus on Culture 2.3

The date November 11 is represented by four single ones. In the early 1990s students at various Chinese universities began celebrating Singles' Day on that date. It started as a day for singles to party with other single friends. With the Internet it has evolved into the largest online shopping day in the world. Alibaba's one-day sales in 2016 were $17.9 billion.

Founded in 1999 by Jack Ma, Alibaba dominates Internet retailing and electronic payment services in China. It is the world's largest retailer. Its consumer-to-consumer portal Taobao (similar to eBay) lists nearly a billion products (Clark, 2016). Alibaba also has an interest in Sina Weibo, a Chinese version of Twitter, and an interest in Youku Tuduo, a video platform similar to YouTube. Tencent is China's gaming and social media company. It offers the instant messenger Tencent QQ and mobile chat service WeChat. Tencent's QQ PC-based instant messenger has almost 900 million accounts (users can have multiple accounts). Tencent's Weixin (pronounced way-shin), or WeChat, is its free social messaging app with over 1 billion accounts and 700 million active users by 2016. WeChat provides text messaging, hold-to-talk voice messaging, broadcast messaging, video conferencing, and other services. QQ and WeChat have changed the social lives of young Chinese. A 2008 survey reported that China was the only Asian country where young people reported having more online than offline friends (Hancock, 2013). In another study, two-thirds of Chinese Internet users said they felt that they are free to do and say things online that they would not do or say offline. That compares with just a third of U.S. respondents (Hancock, 2013).

Focus on Technology 2.2

Internet Censorship in China

The Tiananmen Square protests in spring 1989 ended on June 4 when troops with rifles and tanks advanced on unarmed students and other unarmed civilians. An estimated 400 to 800 civilians were killed. Student protester demands included freedom of the press, freedom of speech, and government accountability. The government arrested protesters and their supporters and controlled media coverage of the event.

On the 25th anniversary of the pro-democracy demonstrations in June 2014, Chinese authorities blocked most Google services in China, including search and Gmail. Greatfire.org, a site that monitors the Chinese net, characterized the restriction as an effort to prevent the dissemination of information about Tiananmen Square. After about a month, access was again possible, although social networks Facebook and Twitter and Google-owned video site YouTube continued to be blocked as they have been for years.

Source: Levin (2014).

Global Voices

The belief that non-Western peoples should adopt Western values, institutions, and culture is immoral because of what would be necessary to bring it about. . . . If non-Western societies are once again to be shaped by Western culture, it will happen only as a result of expansion, deployment, and impact of Western power. . . . As a maturing civilization, the West no longer has the economic or demographic dynamism required to impose its will on other societies and any effort to do so is also contrary to the Western values of self-determination and democracy.

—Samuel P. Huntington (1996, p. 310), conservative professor of political science, Harvard University

Former U.S. secretary of state Hillary Clinton (2010), in a major speech, drew an analogy between the Berlin Wall and restricted access to the Internet. Chinese reaction to her speech was that the United States uses the Internet as a means to create worldwide hegemony based on Western values. The *People's Daily* newspaper compared Google to the opium traders of the 19th century (Demick, 2011).

The United States has charged that many hacking attacks on U.S. companies and government sites originate in China. The personal data of millions of U.S. government employees have been hacked, and state-sponsored cybertheft has benefitted Chinese companies. Foreign Minister Wang Yi responded that Chinese websites have been hacked from the United States.

Ethnocentrism

Remember, ethnocentrism is negatively judging aspects of another culture by the standards of one's own culture. And this may be the barrier that is the greatest challenge for communication between China and the United States. Consider how the United States views China's positions on Taiwan and Tibet, human rights, and free speech and how China reacts to the U.S. positions.

Global Voices

We respect the uniqueness of other cultures and societies, but when it comes to expressing yourself freely and worshiping as you choose and having open access to information, we believe those universal rights—they are universal rights that are the birthright of every person on this planet.

—First Lady Michelle Obama, March 22, 2014, speech in Beijing (quoted in Demick, 2014, p. A6).

Status of Taiwan

Today, Taiwan is a technologically advanced island of 23 million people with a dynamic capitalist economy. In the past, Taiwan and the mainland disputed which was the legitimate government of one China. Taiwan's government has evolved from one-party rule under martial law into a full-fledged democracy. In 1996, Taiwan became the first government in the Chinese-speaking world to have a democratically elected president.

Taiwan has never declared formal independence. It has argued that China is one country with two governments, much like Germany before reunification. On that basis, Taiwan sought greater international recognition and readmission to the United Nations. U.S. presidents have recognized that Taiwan is part of China, yet the United States has sold jet fighters to the Taiwanese and dispatched aircraft carriers to the waters off Taiwan when China displayed military force near its shores. Under the current president, despite public protests, China and Taiwan have held talks on improved relations, launched regular direct flights between the two, and allowed more mainland tourists to visit the island.

Still, as recently as 2012, then Chinese vice president Xi Jinping (now president) voiced the demand that the United States view Taiwan and Tibet as parts of China.

Tibet

Chinese control over Tibet dates as far back as the 13th century. In the 1940s and 1950s, British and U.S. agents were seen to have been encouraging independence. Chinese troops occupied Tibet in 1950, waging war on the Dalai Lama and Tibetan Buddhism. In 1959, the Dalai Lama unsuccessfully tried to oust Chinese forces and was forced into exile, creating an exile community of some 145,000 around the world. The Dalai Lama has proposed autonomy—not independence—for Tibet, allowing China to retain control over defense and

©iStockphoto.com/hxdyl

The Potala Palace, the winter palace of the Dalai Lama since the 7th century until the 14th Dalai Lama fled to India during the 1959 Tibetan uprising. It symbolizes Tibetan Buddhism.

Global Voices

Such an act has grossly interfered in China's internal affairs, hurt the feelings of the Chinese people, and damaged Sino-American relations.

—Ma Zhaoxu, Chinese Foreign Ministry, on President Obama's meeting with the Dalai Lama, July 2011

foreign affairs. The major concern has been the elimination of the Tibetan culture, language, and faith as more Chinese move into the region. Tibetan exiles claim that more Chinese live in Tibet than Tibetans. Many young Tibetans now speak a pidgin of Chinese and Tibetan. No Western country challenges China's sovereignty, but the United States and others have protested the treatment of the people and culture of Tibet. China has responded that the Nobel Prize–winning Dalai Lama is trying to achieve political objectives of independence under the guise of religion. The Dalai Lama has since relinquished his political duties, and Lobsang Sangay was elected prime minister of the Tibetan government-in-exile. Chinese officials declared the election illegal.

Since 2011, a reported 140 Tibetans, many of them teenagers, have chosen self-immolation as a means of expressing their anger and desperation to China's repression. Among Tibetan Buddhists, self-immolation is most extreme as it is believed that suicide destroys not only the body but also the chance of being reincarnated as a human being (Demick, 2012). In a White House statement issued after President Obama's meeting with the Dalai Lama in February 2014, President Obama expressed his support for Tibet's "unique religious, cultural, and linguistic traditions, and the protection of human rights for Tibetans in the People's Republic of China."

Human Rights and Free Speech

In 1989, the death of former Communist Party General Secretary Hu Yaobang, whom many considered a political reformer, resulted in the student-led demonstration for democracy in Tiananmen Square in Beijing that June. The army crushed the protest, killing hundreds, perhaps even thousands, on orders believed to have come from Deng (Black & Munro, 1993). Ever since, the Chinese media have blamed the United States for siding with the protesters. Deng, who saw foreign influence in the uprising, dictated that severe measures, such as martial law, would again be taken in the event of future internal turmoil. Only by these means, he felt, would China's national sovereignty be protected from external interference.

China continues a hard line on dissent. Professor and human rights activist Liu Xiaobo advocated the end of communist single-party rule. He was arrested and tried for "inciting subversion of state power" and sentenced to 11 years of imprisonment and 2 years of deprivation of political rights on December 25, 2009. He was awarded the 2010 Nobel Peace Prize for "his long and non-violent struggle for fundamental human rights in China." Liu was diagnosed with liver cancer but not permitted to leave China for treatment. He died a prisoner in July 2017. Government censors deleted social media expressions of grief.

The United States, which has protested the imprisonment without trial of religious and democracy proponents and the use of prison and child labor in manufacturing, has insisted on human rights improvements in China. The United States has attempted repeatedly, but unsuccessfully, to gain censure for Chinese human rights policies from the United Nations Commission on Human Rights. Prior to the return of Hong Kong to China, the U.S. Congress passed legislation affirming the human rights of the people of Hong Kong. China censored references to communism on CCTV from President Obama's first inaugural address. In 2016, China issued a new law restricting the work of foreign nongovernmental organizations. The law requires that foreign groups must find an official Chinese partner and register with the police. U.S. Secretary of State John Kerry issued a statement that the law would "negatively impact ... the development of civil society in China."

China views these demands as attacks on its sovereignty, with the United States acting as a global judge of human rights. China also has charged that the U.S. human rights record includes huge prison populations, low voter turnout, and a history of slavery. Rather than viewing this only as a political clash, some would seek explanations based in cultural values. Chinese leaders place a higher premium on social order and a lesser one on individual expression. China emphasizes collective order, whereas Western cultures stress individual liberties (Wasserstrom, 1991).

Stereotypes and Prejudice

China's strong economy, growing military, and expanding role in international affairs threaten some in the United States and other countries. With fears can come negative stereotypes such as those of China as the world's polluter and as having a significant influence on others' economies.

Energy and Sustainability

China leads all nations in carbon dioxide emissions. Its pollutants cause acid rain in Seoul and Tokyo. China's proven oil reserves are about 25 billion barrels compared to Saudi Arabia's 268 billion. China's economic boom, which began in the late 1980s, has led to an increase in energy demand. Before 1993, China was self-sufficient in oil. Since the early 1990s, oil consumption has grown. In 2009, China consumed 8 million barrels a day, the third highest demand after the United States and the European Union. Its imports were 4.4 million barrels a day, fourth greatest after the United States, the European Union, and Japan. In September 2013, China became the world's leading oil importer, a demand driven in part by the country's booming auto sales. By 2015, 16.7% of all global crude oil imports went to China.

Along with energy consumption, other countries charge that China and its entrepreneurs disdain environmental concerns. China's rapid economic transformation has led to extensive environmental deterioration. Air pollution, soil erosion, and the steady fall of the water table will be long-term

Global Voices

Excerpts from Communiqué on the Current State of the Ideological Sphere
"A Notice from the Central Committee of the Communist Party of China's General Office"
April 22, 2013

Currently, the following false ideological trends, positions, and activities all deserve note:

1. Promoting Western Constitutional Democracy: An attempt to undermine the current leadership and the socialism with Chinese characteristics system of governance.

Western Constitutional Democracy has distinct political properties and aims.... Their goal is to use Western constitutional democracy to undermine the Party's leadership, abolish the People's Democracy, negate our country's constitution as well as our established system and principles, and bring about a change of allegiance by bringing Western political systems to China.

2. Promoting "universal values" in an attempt to weaken the theoretical foundations of the Party's leadership.

The goal of espousing "universal values" is to claim that the West's value system defies time and space, transcends nation and class, and applies to all humanity.

5. Promoting the West's idea of journalism, challenging China's principle that the media and publishing system should be subject to Party discipline.

Some people, under the pretext of espousing "freedom of the press," promote the West's idea of journalism ... by attacking the Marxist view of news and promoting the "free flow of information on the Internet."... The ultimate goal of advocating the West's view of the media is to ... gouge an opening through which to infiltrate our ideology.

Source: ChinaFile (2013).

Global Voices

> If you believe the consumer has some responsibility for the pollution caused to produce the goods they're consuming, then our study is showing that the folks in the U.S., Japan and other places have a role in that pollution coming from China.
>
> —Steve Davis, University of California, Irvine, Earth system scientist (quoted in Brenan, 2014, p. 8)

problems. Pollution levels considered unhealthy in the United States are classified as good by China. China argues that it is unfair to judge it as a developing country by U.S. standards. Resolution of the world's global environmental challenges will require China's full commitment and cooperation.

Air quality is a major problem in Chinese cities. One day in October 2013, in the city of Harbin, which has a population of 11 million, one index measuring particulate matter registered 1,000 on a scale that usually ranges from 0 to 500. The World Health Organization's recommended maximum is 25. Visibility dropped to 10 meters (33 feet). Several years ago, when the U.S. Embassy in Beijing began issuing pollution readings, Chinese media accused the U.S. ambassador of meddling in the country's internal affairs and attempting to embarrass the Communist Party.

Economic Issues

China's economic development continues at a fast pace. In 1999, the constitution was amended to include private industry as an "important component" of the nation's economy, and constitutional protection was expanded to private property. In 2000, the U.S. Congress granted China permanent normal trade status. And a year later, the Chinese Communist Party invited capitalist entrepreneurs to join its ranks. China was admitted to the World Trade Organization after agreeing to further open its economy.

China's currency remains undervalued. This has the effect of making Chinese products cheap, giving China's exporters an unfair competitive advantage, costing jobs in importing nations, and boosting China's trade surpluses with its trading partners. Former French president Nicolas Sarkozy urged China's leadership to let its currency rise before its trade imbalances become unmanageable. Growing trade deficits with countries such as the United States and France continue to increase at what some see as an alarming rate.

Of equal or greater concern to many in the United States is the amount of U.S. debt held by China. By 2011, China held about 11% of U.S. debt held outside the United States. The Chinese government expressed concerns about the size of U.S. budget deficits, which it contends has lowered the value of the dollar and caused global inflation in food and energy. In August 2011, when Standard & Poor's downgraded the U.S. government's credit rating, the New China News Agency commented, "China . . . has every right now to demand the United States address

VCG/Visual China Group/Getty Images

Air quality is a major problem in Chinese cities.

its structural debt problems and ensure the safety of China's dollar assets" (Olesen, 2011, para. 5). In 2015, China reduced its holdings while Japan increased its holdings. Today both hold between 6.5% and 7% of the U.S. debt.

China's leader, Xi Jinping, predicted in 2013 that China would become the chief military power in the Asia Pacific region by 2049. He spoke of the "China Dream" of a revival of the Chinese nation with a prosperous country and a strong military. Henry Kissinger was President Nixon's national security advisor and then secretary of state to Presidents Nixon and Ford. During that service his efforts contributed to formal diplomatic relations with China. Kissinger (2011) recently pointed out the critical importance of the United States and China remaining engaged, even if their interests diverge. Paraphrasing former General Secretary of the Chinese Communist Party Jiang Zemin, Kissinger said the two countries are "too large to be dominated, too special to be transformed and too necessary to each other to be able to afford isolation" (p. 487).

Focus on Skills 2.4

Adapting to Tourism From China

Due in part to China's thriving economy and new policies easing travel restrictions, Chinese travelers are the fastest-growing segment of the travel market. In 2014, 2.2 million Chinese travelers visited the United States. The average spending per visit for all tourists to the United States in 2012 was about $4,370. According to the U.S. Travel Association, the average spending per visit for Chinese tourists is $5,948. Luxury goods in the United States are far less expensive than in China, so shopping is the number one activity. Many first-time visitors focus their spending on gifts and souvenirs to take back home, and many leisure travelers stay at budget hotels. According to the 2013 China Rich List, about 40 of the 100 richest individuals in China made their fortunes in second- and third-tier cities and have had less contact with Western brands and fashion. Many higher-end U.S. hotel properties are planning to be more attractive to business and frequent leisure travelers.

Assume you are the director of training for a U.S. hotel that wants to be positioned to attract Chinese tourists.

1. How would you prepare the hotel staff to deal with the barriers discussed in this chapter?
2. How could you help employees deal with their anxiety when interacting with Chinese tourists for the first time? How would you deal with assumptions of similarity? Consider such things as using both hands when exchanging currency, language use, numbering system, coffee makers, and breakfast foods.
3. How would you deal with employees' ethnocentrism and stereotypes?
4. How would you use Weibo and WeChat or other social media with Chinese tourists before their trips?

SUMMARY

This chapter focuses on recognizing and avoiding breakdowns in intercultural communication. LaRay M. Barna developed a list of six such barriers: anxiety, assuming similarity instead of difference, ethnocentrism, stereotypes and prejudice, nonverbal misinterpretations, and language. The first four are discussed in this chapter. *Anxiety* refers to not being totally present in the communication transaction while focusing on one's feelings when one doesn't know what to do. *Assuming similarity instead of difference* refers to behaving as you would in your home culture. *Ethnocentrism* is negatively judging aspects of another culture by the standards of one's own culture. The term *stereotype* is used to refer to negative or positive judgments made about individuals based on any observable or believed group membership, whereas *prejudice* refers to the irrational suspicion or hatred of a particular group, race, religion, or sexual orientation.

This chapter applies Barna's categories to a discussion of the communication barriers between China and the United States. China is a country of 1.4 billion people and the world's second largest economy. Misunderstandings have arisen over air space, the South China Sea, broadcast media and the Internet, the status of Taiwan, Tibet, human rights and free speech, energy and sustainability, and economic issues.

DISCUSSION QUESTIONS

1. Identify nearby school and athletic team mascots. Would any be considered stereotypes? Why or why not?

2. What are possible consequences of using survey data, such as data on alcohol use, to conclude that a cultural group is superior to other groups?

3. It has been said that China's people both admire and resent the United States. Explain the possible reasons for that belief and its associated communication barriers.

4. China has been criticized for melamine-contaminated pet food and baby milk formula. International media reported the scandal as China's rather than as particular companies'. How does this contribute to communication barriers?

5. What are possible consequences to China's continuing control of access to a global Internet?

KEY TERMS

anxiety	Hong Kong	prejudice
authoritarian personality	Macau	profiling
Cantonese	microaggression	racism
cultural relativism	nominal gross domestic product (GDP)	Roma
Cultural Revolution		stereotype
cultural sensitivity	nongovernmental organizations	Taiwan
ethnocentrism		Tibet
four modernizations	othering	White privilege
hate speech	political correctness	

READINGS

All readings are from *Intercultural Communication: A Global Reader* (Jandt, 2004).

Rueyling Chuang, "An Examination of Taoist and Buddhist Perspectives on Interpersonal Conflicts, Emotions, and Adversities" (p. 38)

Jung-huel Becky Yeh and Long Chen, "Cultural Values and Argumentative Orientations for Chinese People in Taiwan, Hong Kong, and Mainland China" (p. 51)

Jonathan J. H. Zhu and Zhou He, "Information Accessibility, User Sophistication, and Source Credibility: The Impact of the Internet on Value Orientation in Mainland China" (p. 65)

STUDENT STUDY SITE

⑤SAGE edge™

Sharpen your skills with SAGE edge at edge.sagepub.com/jandt9e.

SAGE edge for Students provides a personalized approach to help you accomplish your coursework goals in an easy-to-use learning environment.

Part 2

Communication Variables

Chapter 3

Frank Bienewald/LightRocket/Getty Images

Context, Perception, and Competence

This chapter reviews three interrelated topics: high-context and low-context cultures, the process of perception, and intercultural communication competence. Our cultural identification affects how we perceive the world. What follows from this simple fact is that individuals can perceive differently and that can impede communication. This chapter begins with the concept of high- and low-context cultures developed by Edward T. Hall. Then it reviews the effect of culture on our perception of the world external to our minds. Finally, the chapter introduces the concepts of intercultural communication competence and intercultural communication ethics.

High Versus Low Context

The formal study of intercultural communication in the United States originated in 1946, when Congress passed the Foreign Service Act, which established the Foreign Service Institute to provide language and anthropological cultural training for foreign diplomats. Outside the Foreign Service Institute, the study of intercultural communication is generally associated with the publication of Edward T. Hall's book *The Silent Language* in 1959. While associated with the Foreign Service Institute, Hall applied abstract anthropological concepts to the practical world of foreign service and extended the anthropological view of culture to include communication (Leeds-Hurwitz, 1990). In his 1976 book, Hall focused attention on the communication of high-context and low-context cultures. Recall that context was defined in Chapter 1 as the environment in which the communication process takes place and that helps define the communication. Cultures in which little of the meaning is determined by the context because the message is encoded in the explicit code are labeled low context. Cultures in which less has to be said or written because more of the meaning is in the physical environment or already shared by people are labeled high context. Table 3.1 shows examples of both types.

Think of the difference this way: Upon meeting a stranger, your verbal communication with that person is highly explicit—or low context—simply because you have no shared experiences. You cannot assume anything. However, when you communicate with your sister or brother with whom you have shared a lifetime, your verbal communication is less explicit because you make use of your shared context. For example, the mention of a certain name can lead to laughter. With the stranger, you would have to explain in language the story that that name represented. Also, with your sister or brother, a certain facial expression can have a shared meaning, such as "There Mom goes again," but the stranger would have no idea what your facial expression communicated. Again, you would have to explain in words that your mother's specific behavior was characteristic, somewhat irritating, but so uniquely her.

In low-context cultures, verbal messages are elaborate and highly specific, and they tend to be highly detailed and redundant as well. Verbal abilities are highly valued. Logic and reasoning are expressed in verbal messages. In high-context cultures, most of the information is either in the physical context or internalized in the person. Very little is in the coded, explicit, transmitted part of the message. High-context cultures decrease the perception of self as separate from the group. High-context cultures are more sensitive to nonverbal messages; hence, they are more likely to provide a context and setting and let the point evolve.

It has been said that language separates people. When understood from the perspective of high and low context, that statement makes sense. In high-context cultures, people are brought closer by the importance of their shared context. Those meanings are often lost in low-context cultures. I have often shown films of the traditional Japanese tea ceremony to classes in the United States. The tea ceremony reflects the Zen and Taoist traditions celebrating the beauty in the mundane, the superiority

Table 3.1 Level of Context, by Culture

High	Low
China	Switzerland
Japan	Germany
Korea	North America, including the United States
American Indian	Nordic states
Most Latin American cultures	
Southern and eastern Mediterranean cultures, such as Greece, Turkey, and the Arab states	

of spirit over matter, and tranquility with busy lives. The ceremony unites the host and guest in a concert of harmony. Though not as commonly practiced as in the past, the tea ceremony is an excellent example of a high-context experience. Nothing is spoken; all the meanings are in the context of shared experience, the teahouse, the flower arrangement, the calligraphy scroll, and the ceramics. A typical response from a low-context observer is "Hurry up and drink the tea!" In contrast, your social experiences over coffee take little meaning from the context; rather it is the conversation—the words shared—that give meaning to the experience.

©iStockphoto.com/oluolu3

The Japanese tea ceremony, or *chanoyu,* is a revered tradition derived from Zen Buddhism and is approached with great respect and concentration. Adherence to time-honored rules is essential, both during the ceremony itself and in the construction of the tea house, or *cha-shitsi,* which should appear rustic, simple, and tranquil.

In some recent studies, European Americans and Japanese were shown scenes, each with a background scene and foreground objects (Miyamoto, Nisbett, & Masuda, 2006). These experiments compared perceptions of changes in the foreground with perceptions of changes in the background. European Americans were significantly better at detecting changes in the foreground, while the Japanese were significantly better at detecting changes in the background. These studies have argued that Europeans (low context) focus attention on objects independent of context (i.e., perceive analytically), whereas East Asians focus on the context (i.e., perceive holistically).

The concept of high and low context also applies to self-understanding. In low-context cultures, one speaks of a person as having attributes independent of circumstances or of personal relations. This self is a free agent who can move from group to group, from setting to setting, without significant changes. But in high-context cultures, the person is connected, fluid, and conditional. Participation in relationships makes it possible to act; completely independent behavior usually isn't possible, nor even desirable (Nisbett, 2003).

The Concept of Face

High-context cultures place great emphasis on relationships, and in those societies the concept of face is critical to understand. In Chinese culture, face is conceptualized in two ways: *lien* (face) and *mien* or *mien-tzd* (image). While these are often used interchangeably, they have different meanings. Hsien Hu (1944) defines *lien* as something that "represents the confidence of society in the integrity of ego's moral character, the loss of which makes it impossible to function properly with the community," whereas *mien* "stands for the kind of prestige that is emphasized in this country [United States], a reputation achieved through getting on in life, through success and ostentation" (p. 45). Masumoto, Oetzel, Takai, Ting-Toomey, and Yokochi (2000) define facework as the communicative strategies one uses to enact self-face and to uphold, support, or challenge another person's face.

Focus on Technology 3.1

Web Design in Low- and High-Context Countries

Heeman Kim, James Coyle, and Stephen Gould (2009) compared the design features of South Korean and U.S. websites. For example, the Dongsuh Corporation is a major food manufacturer and importer. Like many South Korean sites, the Dongsuh site (www.dongsuh.co.kr) at the time of their study included animation, streaming video, clickable images, rollover navigation bars, and pop-under windows. An embedded video of a man and woman enjoying a cup of coffee rotated continuously. Five animated circles grew larger when rolled over, and one of these circles included circles within it that also grew larger when rolled over. The navigation scheme included two navigation bars and two pop-under windows. Compared to the Dongsuh site, the Procter & Gamble (P&G) site (www.pg.com) at the time of their study had much less animation and the animation was much more subdued. Unlike the Dongsuh site, the P&G site relied on static navigation bars. The P&G site did not utilize pop-up windows, streaming audio, or streaming video.

After their analysis of 200 South Korean and U.S. corporate websites, Kim and colleagues concluded that low-context countries, such as the United States, relied more on less arbitrary textual formats and that high-context countries, such as South Korea, relied more on more ambiguous visual formats.

Raymond Cohen (1997) provides examples of ways one can lose face:

- a rebuffed overture
- exposure to personal insult
- exposure to a derogatory remark or disregard for one's status
- being forced to give up a cherished value
- making what may later be seen as an unnecessary concession
- failure to achieve goals
- revelation of personal inadequacy
- damage to a valued relationship

Global Voices

High-context cultures make greater distinction between the insiders and outsiders than low-context cultures do. People raised in high-context systems expect more of others than do the participants in low-context systems. When talking about something they have on their minds, a high-context individual will expect his interlocutor to know what's bothering him, so that he does not have to be specific. The result is that he will talk around and around the point, in effect putting all the pieces in place except the crucial one. Placing it properly—this keystone—is the role of his interlocutor.

—Edward T. Hall, *Beyond Culture* (1976, p. 98)

High-context societies tend to be more hierarchical and traditional societies in which the concepts of shame and honor are much more important than they are in low-context societies. High-context cultures thus avoid direct confrontation or use communication strategies to maintain harmony and reduce the possibility of conflict. Vargas-Urpi (2013) has shown in one study that Chinese communicators used forms of smiles and other nonverbal behaviors to avoid or to soften uncomfortable situations that would threaten a participant's face.

Communication in high-context cultures such as China is hence more indirect or implicit and is more likely to use intermediaries. Social harmony and face maintenance are crucial, so communication through intermediaries is especially functional because using intermediaries eliminates face-to-face confrontation and reduces the risk of losing face.

In interviews conducted in central China, Ringo Ma (1992) confirmed that unofficial mediation is common in situations involving interpersonal conflict. The mediator is usually a friend of the two parties in conflict or an elderly person respected by both. Intervention by the friend or respected elder is either self-initiated or in response to a request by a person not connected with the competing parties. Impartiality and face maintenance are considered the two key factors in successful mediation.

In low-context societies, individuals are guided more by personal responsibility rather than by shaming one's group. Ting-Toomey (1985) has proposed that low-context cultures, such as the United States, with a greater concern for privacy and autonomy, tend to use direct-face negotiation and

Focus on Skills 3.1

High-Context and Low-Context Cultures

At a 2016 G20 meeting in Hangzhou, Chinese officials welcomed British prime minister Theresa May, Brazil's president Michel Temer, South Korean president Park Geun-hye, Russian president Vladimir Putin, and other foreign leaders with "red carpet" treatment upon arrival. Only when U.S. president Barack Obama arrived was there no staircase provided to leave Air Force One. He was forced to disembark on a small stair through a little-used exit in the plane's belly normally reserved for high-security trips.

A Chinese foreign ministry official said that China provides a rolling staircase for every arriving state leader, but the U.S. side insisted they didn't need the airport staircase when they learned the driver didn't speak English and couldn't understand security instructions. Yet there was no apology.

One China expert observed, "The idea that they have been preparing for well over a year for the G20 but suddenly there be a malfunction with the ramp just for one president ... that really strains credulity.... It sure looks like a straight-up snub." Jorge Guajardo, Mexico's former ambassador to China, said, "These things do not happen by mistake. Not with the Chinese.... It's a snub.... It's part of the new Chinese arrogance.... It's part of saying: 'And by the way, you're just someone else to us.'" The ambassador added, "Just as the Chinese are about giving face they are also about not giving it and letting you know that they are not giving it to you.... They don't overlook these things by mistake. It's not who they are. It's not the way they do these things."

President Obama suggested that the Chinese hosts may have found the size of the U.S. delegation overwhelming, adding "I wouldn't over-crank the significance of it....[N]one of this detracts from the broader scope of the relationship."

Then Republican presidential candidate Donald Trump said that if it were him, he wouldn't have gotten off the plane. "I'd say, you know folks, I respect you a lot, but let's get out of here."

Assume you work with the Office of the Chief of Protocol responsible for advising the president on matters of national and international protocol.

1. How do high- and low-context concepts help you understand this incident?
2. How does the concept of face help you understand this incident?
3. What would you advise the chief of protocol to advise the president?

Sources: "Barack Obama 'Deliberately Snubbed'" (2016); Krauthammer (2016); Landler & Perlez (2016); "Trump Slams China" (2016).

express more self-face maintenance, whereas high-context cultures, such as China, with a greater concern for interdependence and inclusion, tend to use indirect-face negotiation and express more mutual-face or other-face maintenance.

Perception

As you read in the previous chapter, barriers to intercultural communication can arise particularly when individuals assume similarity rather than difference and negatively judge aspects of another culture by the standards of one's own culture. For example, a business person from a low-context culture who doesn't take time to inquire about family or other personal interests first before discussing business matters can be perceived by a high-context person as overly direct and offensive, and their communication suffers.

In this section you'll read in depth about perception, or the process whereby we sense, select, organize, and interpret our world. Perception begins with the reception of sensory data followed by selecting to attend to some of those sensations, organizing those sensations in some meaningful way, and then attaching meaning to them.

Sensing

Can we really say that there is a world external to our minds, that is, independent of our awareness of it? We do make that assumption. Early 20th-century quantum mechanics posited that on a sub-atomic level the observer is an active part of the observed. Wexler (2008) wants us to recognize how integrated our minds are with the external world: "The relationship between the individual and the environment is so extensive that it almost overstates the distinction between the two to speak of a relationship at all" (p. 39). Sensory input is a physical interaction; for example, cells in our mouths and noses have receptor molecules that combine with molecules from the environment to initiate electrical impulses. Our perception and thought processes are not independent of the cultural environment.

If our perception and thought processes are such a part of "what is out there," what, then, is the relationship between changes in the cultural environment and who we are? Wexler (2008) points out that we humans shape our environment and, hence, it could be said that the human brain shapes itself to a human-made environment. Our brain both is shaped by the external world and shapes our perception of the external world.

Sensation is the neurological process by which we become aware of our environment. Of the human senses, sight, hearing, smell, taste, and touch, including pain, temperature, and pressure, are the most studied (Gordon, 1971). The world appears quite different to other forms of life with different sensory ranges: A bat, for example, senses the world through ultrasound; a snake does so through infrared light; some fish sense distortions of electrical fields through receptors on the surface of their bodies—none of these are directly sensed by humans. But is there significant variation in sensation among individual humans? You need to remember that sensation is a neurological process. You are not directly aware of what is in the physical world but, rather, of your own internal sensations. When you report "seeing" a tree, what you are aware of is actually an electrochemical event. Much neural processing takes place between the receipt of a stimulus and your awareness of a sensation (Cherry, 1957). Is variation in human sensation attributable to culture? Pioneering psychologist William James explained that sensory data don't come to us "ready-made" but in an "unpackaged" state that we assemble into something coherent and meaningful from rules of perception we learn in our culture.

Nisbett (2003) has demonstrated that humans sense and perceive the world in ways unique to their upbringing by contrasting Eastern and Western cultures. Ancient Greeks had a strong sense of individual identity with a sense of personal agency, the sense that they were in charge of their own destinies. Greeks considered human and nonhuman objects as discrete and separate. And the Greeks made a clear distinction between the external world and our internal worlds. Thus, two individuals could have two different perceptions of the world because the world itself was static, unchanging, and independent of perception. It was through rhetorical persuasion that one could attempt to change another's perception. The attributes of individual objects are the basis of categorization of objects, and categories are subject to behavioral rules that could be discovered and understood by the human mind. Thus rocks and other objects are in the category of objects that have the property of gravity.

The Chinese counterpart to the Greek sense of personal agency was harmony. Every Chinese was a member of a family and a village. The Chinese were less concerned with controlling their own destinies but more concerned with self-control so as to minimize conflict with others in the family and village. For the Chinese, the world is constantly changing and every event is related to every other event. The Chinese understood the world as continuously interacting substances, so perception focused on the entire context or environment. Chinese thought is to see things in their context in which all the elements are constantly changing and rearranging themselves.

Effect of Culture on Sensing

How much alike, then, are two persons' sensations? Individuals raised in diverse cultures can actually sense the world differently. For example, Marshall Segall and his associates (Segall, Campbell, & Herskovits, 1966) found that people who live in forests or in rural areas can sense crooked and slanted lines more accurately than can people who live in urban areas. This demonstrates that the rural and urban groups sense the same event differently as a result of their diverse cultural learnings.

The term field dependence refers to the degree to which perception of an object is influenced by the background or environment in which it appears. Some people are less likely than others to separate an object from its surrounding environment. When adults in Japan and the United States were shown an animated underwater scene in which one large fish swims among small fish and other marine life, the Japanese described the scene and commented more about the relationships among the objects in the scene. The Americans were more likely to begin with a description of the big fish and make only half as many comments about the relationships among the objects. Not surprisingly, when showed a second scene with

Focus on Culture 3.1

The Greeks Had Aristotle and the Chinese Had Confucius

Much of the research on sensing and perception, and most of the examples in this chapter, contrast Eastern and Western cultures. Nisbett (2003) and others contend that Eastern and Western cultures literally perceive different worlds. Modern Eastern cultures are inclined to see a world of substances—continuous masses of matter. Modern Westerners see a world of objects—discrete and unconnected things. There is substantial evidence that Easterners have a holistic view, focusing on continuities in substances and relationships in the environment, while Westerners have an analytic view, focusing on objects and their attributes.

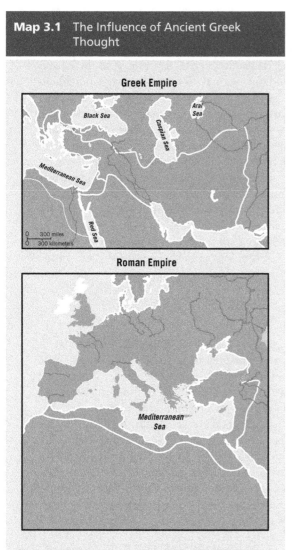

Map 3.1 The Influence of Ancient Greek Thought

Greek Empire

Roman Empire

Greek forms of sensing and perceiving were later carried forward in ancient Roman culture, as shown in the map above, where they were transmitted across Roman imperial holdings in much of modern Western, Central, and Eastern Europe. From the 17th century forward, European colonialism brought Western-style perception to the Americas, Africa, and Oceania.

Source: Adapted from Nau (2012, p. 77).

Note: Shaded regions represent the Roman and Greek Empires at their furthest extent.

the same big fish, the Americans were more likely to recognize the big fish as the same one as in the first scene (Nisbett, 2003).

More recently, Kitayama, Duffy, Kawamura, and Larsen (2003) showed Japanese and European Americans a picture of a square with a line inside it (see Figure 3.1). The participants were then given an empty square of a different size and asked to draw either a line the same length as the one they had seen or a line of the same relative length to the one they had seen. The European Americans were significantly more accurate in drawing the line of the same length, while the Japanese were significantly more accurate in drawing the line of relative length. Differences in the environment and culture affected sensation.

The researchers then compared Americans who had been living in Japan for a few years and Japanese who had been living in the United States for a few years. Given the same picture and task, the Americans who had been living in Japan were close to the Japanese in the original study, while the Japanese who had been living in the United States were virtually the same as the native-born Americans. While other explanations are possible, one strong suggestion is that even living for an extended time in a new culture can modify sensation and cognitive processes.

Perceiving

Culture also has a great effect on the perception process (Tajfel, 1969; Triandis, 1964). Human perception is usually thought of as a three-step process of selection, organization, and interpretation. Each of these steps is affected by culture.

Selection

The first step in the perception process is selection. Within your physiological limitations, you are exposed to more stimuli than you could possibly manage. To use sight as an example, you may feel that you are aware of all stimuli on your retinas, but most of the data from the retinas are handled on a subconscious level by a variety of specialized systems. Parts of our brains produce output from the retinas that we cannot "see." No amount of introspection can make us aware of those processes.

Figure 3.1 Stimulus for Culture's Effect on Sensation

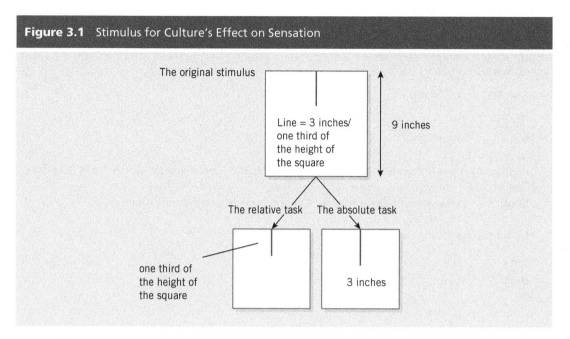

The original stimulus

Line = 3 inches/ one third of the height of the square

9 inches

The relative task   The absolute task

one third of the height of the square

3 inches

Source: Ishii & Kitayama (2003).

In an interesting study by Simons and Chabris (1999), participants viewed video of a basketball game. They were told to count the number of passes one team made. In the video, a woman dressed as a gorilla walks into the game, turns to face the camera, and beats her fists on her chest. Fifty percent of all people who watch the video don't see the gorilla. Mack and Rock (1998) argue that we don't consciously see any object unless we are paying direct, focused attention to that object. When we need something, have an interest in it, or want it, we are more likely to sense it out of competing stimuli. When we're hungry, we're more likely to attend to food advertisements.

Being in a busy airport terminal is another example. While there, you are confronted with many competing stimuli. You simply cannot attend to everything. However, if in the airport terminal an announcement is made asking you by name to report to the ticketing counter, you would probably hear your name even in that environment of competing stimuli. Just as you've learned to attend to the sound of your name, you've learned from your culture to select out other stimuli from the environment. A newborn child is a potential speaker of any language. Having heard only those sounds of one's own language and having learned to listen to and make only those differentiations necessary, anyone would find it difficult to hear crucial differences in speech sounds in another language.

Japanese/English Difficulties With Speech Sounds

If you grew up speaking English, certain aspects of the Japanese language are difficult for you to perceive. These aspects do not occur in English, so you never learned to listen for them and you literally do not hear them. For example, vowel length does not matter in English. You can say "Alabama" or "Alabaaama," and others would know you're referring to a southern U.S. state. Vowel length is important in Japanese. Japanese has short-duration vowels and long-duration vowels. Vowel length in the following pairs of Japanese words actually determines their meanings:

obasan	aunt
obaasan	grandmother
kita	came
kiita	heard

Because vowel length is not a critical attribute in English, perceiving the difference in sounds is a problem for those attempting to understand Japanese.

Other sounds that present difficulties for English speakers are the following:

Doubled consonants:

shita	did
shitta	new

Accent:

kaki	oyster
kaki	persimmon

Pitch:

hashi	bridge
hashi	chopsticks
hashi	edge of a table

If you grew up speaking Japanese, some aspects of the English language are difficult for you to perceive. English has some consonant sounds that do not exist in Japanese. If you grew up speaking Japanese, you didn't learn to listen for those consonant sounds. English uses the consonant sounds *f, v, th* as in *think, th* as in *breathe, z, zh* as in *treasure, j* as in the *dge* of *judge, r,* and *1.* Thus, if you grew up speaking Japanese, it is difficult to distinguish between the sounds *b* and *v, s* and *sh, r* and *1,* and so forth, with the result that *lice* and *rice* or *glamour* and *grammar* are frequently pronounced the same way.

Japanese has borrowed thousands of English words. But if you grew up speaking English, you would have difficulty recognizing them. In Japanese, syllables are basically a consonant sound followed by a vowel. Syllables can end only with a vowel sound or an *n.* For example, the Japanese word *iiau* (quarrel) has four syllables—each vowel is pronounced as a separate syllable. A native-born English speaker would not know to do that and would try to pronounce the word as an unsegmented single sound. An English speaker pronounces the word *thrill* as one syllable. In Japanese, consonant sounds do not exist without vowels, so a Japanese speaker would pronounce all three syllables, something like *sooriroo.* The Japanese *r,* by the way, is difficult for English speakers. It's similar to the Spanish *r* in *pero* or *Roberto.* From our first language, we learned what sounds are critical to listen for. Because languages can have different critical sounds, learning a new language means learning to attend to new sounds.

Organization

The second step in the perception process is organization. Along with selecting stimuli from the environment, you must organize them in some meaningful way. When you look at a building, you do not focus on the thousands of possible individual pieces; you focus on the unified whole, a building. Turning a picture upside down, for example, can trick you into focusing on individual components rather than your unified concept of the object in the picture.

How are perceptions categorized? One argument is that you somehow grasp some set of attributes that things have in common. On that basis they are grouped together in a category provided by language that gives the conceptual categories that influence how its speakers' perceptions are encoded and stored. The philosopher Ludwig Wittgenstein, however, concluded that there need be no such set of shared characteristics. Our language provides the symbol to group perceptions of any kind together.

Grouping Like Objects Together

"One of These Things" is a song used on *Sesame Street* when children are shown a group of four items, one of which is different from the other three. Children are asked to identify the item that does not belong with the others. Look at the three objects in Figure 3.2.

In this case, which two objects would you place together? The chicken and the grass? The chicken and the cow? Or the grass and the cow? Chiu (1972) showed such figures to children from China and the United States. Children from the United States grouped objects because they belonged to the same taxonomic category; that is, the same categorization term could be applied to both. The children from the United States would more likely group the chicken and cow together as "animals." The Chinese children preferred to group objects on the basis of relationships. The Chinese children would more likely group the cow and grass together because "cows eat grass" (Chiu, 1972).

In a similar study, Mutsumi Imai and Dedre Gentner (1994) showed objects to people of various ages from Japan and the United States and asked them to group them together. For example, one object was a pyramid made of cork, which they called a *dax,* a word that had no meaning to the participants. Then they showed the participants a pyramid made of white plastic and a different object made of cork. They then asked the participants to point to a dax. To which of these two later objects would you point?

People from the United States in the study chose the same shape, indicating that they were coding what they saw as an object. The Japanese were more likely to choose the same material, indicating that they were coding what they saw as a substance.

Interpretation

The third step in the perception process is interpretation. This refers to attaching meaning to sense data and is synonymous with decoding. University of Rochester researchers Netta Weinstein, Andrew Przybylski, and Richard Ryan (2009) showed participants computer images of either urban settings of buildings and roads or natural settings of landscapes and lakes. Participants were asked to study

Figure 3.2   Stimulus for Culture's Effect on Organization

a.

b.

c.

Source: Adapted from Nisbett (2003, p. 141).

the computer images, note colors and textures, and imagine the sounds and smells associated with the images. The researchers then asked the participants to complete questionnaires about various values, including wealth, fame, connectedness to community, relationships, and the betterment of society. Participants who studied the computer images of natural settings rated close relationships and community values higher than they had after observing the images of urban environments. Participants who studied the computer images of urban settings rated fame and wealth higher. This demonstrates that the same situation can be interpreted quite differently by diverse people. A police officer arriving at a crime scene can be experienced by the victim as calming and relief giving but by a person with an arrest record as fearsome and threatening. Here, too, the effect of culture is great. As you encounter people of your own culture, you constantly make judgments as to age, social status, educational background, and the like. The cues you

Global Voices

Language plays a large and significant role in the totality of culture. Far from being simply a technique of communication, it is itself a way of directing the perception of its speakers and it promotes for them habitual modes of analyzing experience into significant categories. And to the extent that languages differ markedly from each other, so should we expect to find significant and formidable barriers to cross-cultural communication and understanding.

—Harry Hoijer, *Language in Culture* (1954, p. 94)

use to make these decisions are so subtle that it's often difficult to explain how and why you reach a particular conclusion. Do people in the United States, for example, perceive tall men as more credible? Perhaps. Applying these same cues to someone from another culture may not work. People in the United States, for example, frequently err in guessing the age of Japanese individuals, such as judging a Japanese college student in her mid-20s to be only 14 or 15.

Dogs as Pets or as Food

The meanings you attach to your perceptions are greatly determined by your cultural background. Think of how speakers of English categorize life. Most probably use the categories of human life and animal life. Now think of how you typically categorize animal life— probably into wild animals and domesticated animals. Now think of how you typically categorize domesticated animal life—probably into animals used for food, animals used for sport and recreation, and pets. Look at the picture of the puppy and capture your feelings.

Many consider dogs as pets. (The author's first dog, Smokey.)

Most of us see this puppy in the category of pet, for which we have learned to relate warm, loving feelings. Puppies are cute, cuddly, warm, loving creatures. Now look at the next picture of dogs being rescued from a farm where they were raised to be eaten. Capture your feelings. Most of us who love dogs find this picture uncomfortable and disgusting. How can people eat dogs? They are pets, not food! It all depends on where you categorize them. Dogs are pets in some cultures and food in others. In the Arab world, dogs are acceptable as watchdogs and as hunting dogs but are not kept in the home as pets because they are seen as unclean and a low form of life. To call someone a dog is an insult among Arabs. People in most cultures have strong ideas about which foods are acceptable for human consumption and which are not. People in some countries think the custom in the United States of eating corn on the cob is disgusting because that food is fit only for pigs. Some Ukrainians like to eat *salo*, raw pig fat with black bread and vodka, which might cause nausea in some, as would knowing that horse meat from California is served in restaurants in Belgium, France, and Japan.

Dogs being rescued from South Korean dog meat farm. Can you explain your feelings about this photograph? Dogs were eaten to celebrate Liu Bang becoming emperor (202 BCE–195 BCE) in his hometown in Pei county in the eastern coastal province of Jiangsu. The practice was recognized as a provincial cultural heritage. Dog meat is also popular in Guangxi Zhuang Autonomous Region, in the south, Yanbian Korea Autonomous Prefecture, in northeastern China, and in neighboring North Korea. Urban Chinese today are more likely to have dogs as pampered companions. In 2009 China's first anti–animal cruelty legislation was proposed that would make eating dogs and cats illegal (Ying, 2010).

Your reaction of disgust to the picture is a culturally learned interpretation, and that interpretation can be quite strong. In 1989, California made it a misdemeanor for any person to sell, buy, or accept any animal traditionally kept as a pet with the intent of killing the animal for food. More recently, animal rights groups have protested the sale of live animals, such as turtles, frogs, lobsters, crabs, fish, and chicken, for food at Asian-American markets. Asian tradition is that fresh meat is tastier and more healthful, that the best meat "enters your house still breathing." Animal rights activists contend that the animals are treated inhumanely in the shops and are killed in ways that cause them unnecessary pain. Asian-American groups argue that eating dogs and cats is an extreme rarity among Southeast Asian immigrants and call the law and the animal rights activists racist.

In some cultures, parts of some animals are categorized as medicine. In other cultures, certain animals are considered sacred and definitely would not be eaten. The Hindu elephant-headed God[1] Ganesh is accompanied by a rat whenever he travels. Rats, like cows, are deified by Hindus in India. No Hindu worship is complete without an offering to Ganesh and his companion, the rat.

Weather Vane as Christian Cross

The examples so far have been of practices that could offend some English speakers. Let's turn that around with an example of what speakers of English do that could be offensive to others. Johnston

Johnston Pump poster

Pump Company, a U.S. company now based in Brookshire, Texas, has been doing business with Saudi Arabia for more than 70 years. By the 1930s, Johnston Pump was well established in California, its pumps having helped change California's arid lands into a leading agricultural area. Johnston's general manager at the time was a world traveler. During a trip to Saudi Arabia, he noted how similar the climate was to areas of California and convinced the Saudi government that vast wastelands could be turned into fertile farmland through the use of Johnston pumps. The first pump was installed in the king's palace.

Over the years, Johnston's success in the kingdom has largely been due to its respect for the country's strict religious customs. All personnel in its international division receive cultural training.

"Making the deserts bloom for 50 years" was Johnston's advertising campaign in 1986. Ads in English and Arabic began appearing in various Middle East publications early in the year. With the success of the campaign, Johnston made large posters of the ads to be distributed throughout the kingdom.

Focus on Technology 3.2

Using Social Media to Influence Perceptions

Perceptions of the status of animals vary across the world. However, people can use social media channels to influence those interpretations. The director of the International Fund for Animal Welfare has said that the use of social media in China has grown substantially to protest incidents of animal cruelty. Several animal rights groups amassed 11 million signatures on a petition calling for the cancellation of the dog meat festival in Yulin, China, and one anti-cruelty message was retweeted 34,000 times by users of Weibo. Celebrities support the protests as well. Actress Sun Li and singer-actress Yang Mi posted on Weibo. In one post, a dog sheds a red tear, saying, "Please don't eat us. We're your friends." Public opinion has turned against the festivals.

Sources: Kaiman (2017); Linshi (2016); Makinen (2013).

Study the Johnston Pump poster and see if you can tell why a Saudi customs inspector would not allow it into the country. Saudi Arabia allows no public worship of any religion other than Islam. No churches, temples, or any symbols of other religions are permitted. To the customs inspector, the weather vane in the poster (see circled area on the right side of the image) looked like a Christian cross and would therefore be prohibited from being displayed. It took intervention by the minister of customs to allow the posters into the country.

Years later, 10 million bags of potato chips from Thailand were confiscated by the Saudi Ministry of Commerce because toys inside each bag were adorned with crossed triangles that were perceived to be the Star of David. With the perception step of categorization comes a culture's values, and it is those differing categorizations that can so often impede communication, particularly when one group believes its perceptions are right and any other's wrong.

Case Study: Airport Security

People from nations and cultures around the globe pass through U.S. airports. In this case study, identify each of the steps of selection, organization, and interpretation. Identify the flawed assumptions.

In 2007 the U.S. Transportation Security Administration (TSA) launched a program called Screening of Passengers by Observation Techniques (SPOT) to identify potential terrorists at airports. The program was based on the Facial Action Coding System (Ekman & Friesen, 1978), which is a system of coding the movements of individual facial muscles. In the SPOT program, TSA behavior detection officers were trained to observe and interpret some 94 criteria that were assumed to be signs of stress, fear, or deception. According to a U.S. Government Accountability Office (GAO, 2013) publication, these were the steps:

1. Scan passengers in line and engage them in brief verbal exchanges while remaining mobile.
2. Identify passengers who exhibit clusters of behaviors indicative of stress, fear, or deception.
3. Identify passengers exhibiting behaviors that exceed SPOT point threshold for referral screening. (p. 10)

The TSA deployed thousands of behavior detection officers at about one-third of U.S. airports to scan security lines for certain behaviors. According to a document leaked by an anonymous source (Winter & Currier, 2015), these are some of the behaviors the officers were watching for:

- too much yawning (+1 point)
- whistling (+1 point)
- widely open staring eyes (+2 points)
- too much fidgeting (+1 point)
- cold stare (+2 points)
- rigid posture (+2 points)
- appears to be in disguise (+3 points)
- being a woman over the age of 55 (−1 point)
- being a man over the age of 65 (−1 point)

If a passenger was scored at 6 or more points, the passenger was sent to a pat-down and additional screening.

Behavior detection officers identified some 30,000 passengers each year for additional screening. Of those, only 1% were arrested for things such as drug possession or traveling with undeclared items. None was stopped for terrorism. The TSA has spent nearly $1 billion on the program.

In 2013, the Government Accountability Office review of over 400 studies on lie detection concluded that the average person can detect lying only 54% of the time. From that the GAO concluded there is not any scientific evidence to support that a TSA behavior detection officer could learn to detect a passenger who is "keeping a secret" and recommended limiting the SPOT program until the TSA could provide evidence that the program is useful.

The TSA responded that its SPOT technique uses a sequential combination of observation, situational awareness, logical analysis, and deception detection techniques to determine whether a passenger should receive additional screening and cited one study that indicates that SPOT is nine times more effective than randomly selecting individuals (L. Willis, 2011).

Intercultural Communication Competence

You've read how high-context and low-context cultures differ and how high and low context affects perception. Understanding this doesn't mean that we would automatically know how to communicate to be effective. Communicating effectively in intercultural settings is known as *intercultural communication effectiveness* or *intercultural communication competence*. For the purposes of this textbook, let's agree to define intercultural communication effectiveness as the degree of the source's success in accomplishing the goals set out for the interaction. (Review the Western model of communication in Chapter 1.) It would seem that one way to define intercultural communication competence places emphasis on the two behaviors of encoding and decoding (Monge, Bachman, Dillard, & Eisenberg, 1982). Encoding includes expressing ability, and decoding includes listening ability.

The term intercultural communication competence has a broader meaning. For the purposes of this textbook, let's agree to define this term as the ability to communicate effectively and appropriately with people of other cultures (Spitzberg, 2000). This concept adds to effectiveness consideration for appropriateness, that is, that relationship maintenance is valued. Intercultural communication

Focus on Skills 3.2

Christopher Lee/Getty Image Sport/Getty Images

Soccer player in London makes a gesture that some see as the quenelle.

Interpreting Gestures

Assume you work in public relations for the San Antonio Spurs. All-NBA point guard Tony Parker was harshly criticized in the media for making a gesture identified as a reverse Nazi salute. The Simon Wiesenthal Center, a major Jewish human rights organization in the United States, called on Parker to apologize for using the gesture.

You quickly do some background research and learn that the quenelle has been commonly used in France for many years. French comedian Dieudonné M'bala M'bala was said to have popularized the gesture (one hand pointing downward, the other touching the shoulder with an arm across the chest) to signify antiestablishment disdain. A native of France, Parker was photographed displaying the gesture with Dieudonné 3 years earlier.

Recently Dieudonné has been accused of using the gesture to connote anti-Semitism. Dieudonné has been convicted several times for inciting racial hatred or anti-Semitism. Photos on French news sites show a man doing the gesture in front of the Jewish school in Toulouse where three children and a rabbi were gunned down in 2012. Anti-Defamation League national director Albert Foxman issued a statement: "We recognize that its use is not always anti-Semitic. However, our concern is that French athletes and entertainers have now made the quenelle into a faddish element, which has the potential to be mimicked by other young fans and athletes around the world" (quoted in Monroe, 2013, p. A9).

1. Clearly, cultural background greatly influences perception. Is this a simple example of perceptual interpretation?
2. What would you say in a press release to be issued by Parker and the team?
3. Is the quenelle so offensive as to justify banning it?
4. Do professional athletes and entertainers have social responsibility for their communication?

competence requires understanding others' perceptions and values. There have been many attempts to identify the specific skills needed for intercultural communication competence. Chen (1989, 1990), for example, identifies four skill areas: personality strength, communication skills, psychological adjustment, and cultural awareness.

Personality Strength. The main personal traits that affect intercultural communication are self-concept, self-disclosure, self-monitoring, and social relaxation. *Self-concept* refers to the way in which a person views the self. *Self-disclosure* refers to the willingness of individuals to openly and appropriately reveal information about themselves to their counterparts. *Self-monitoring* refers to using social comparison information to control and modify one's self-presentation and expressive behavior. *Social relaxation* is the ability to reveal little anxiety in communication. Competent intercultural communicators must know themselves well and, through their self-awareness, initiate positive attitudes. Individuals must express a friendly personality to be competent in intercultural communication.

Communication Skills. Individuals must be competent in verbal and nonverbal behaviors. Intercultural communication skills require message skills, behavioral flexibility, interaction management, and social skills. Message skills encompass the ability to understand and use language and feedback. Behavioral flexibility is the ability to select an appropriate behavior in diverse contexts. Interaction management means handling the procedural aspects of conversation, such as the ability to initiate a conversation. Interaction management emphasizes a person's other-oriented ability to interact, such as attentiveness and responsiveness. Social skills are empathy and identity maintenance. Empathy is the ability to think the same thoughts and feel the same emotions as the other person. Identity maintenance is the ability to maintain a counterpart's identity by communicating back an accurate understanding of that person's identity. In other words, a competent communicator must be able to deal with diverse people in various situations.

Psychological Adjustment. Competent intercultural communicators must be able to acclimate to new environments. They must be able to handle the feelings of culture shock, such as frustration, stress, and alienation in ambiguous situations caused by new environments.

Cultural Awareness. To be competent in intercultural communication, individuals must understand the social customs and social system of the host culture. Understanding how a people think and behave is essential for communication with them.

Chen and Starosta's (1996) model of intercultural communication competence includes three perspectives:

1. *Affective or intercultural sensitivity*—to acknowledge and respect cultural differences
2. *Cognitive or intercultural awareness*—self-awareness of one's own personal cultural identity and understanding how cultures vary
3. *Behavioral or intercultural adroitness*—message skills, knowledge of appropriate self-disclosure, behavioral flexibility, interaction management, and social skills

There are other such lists of intercultural competence skills, but there is no agreement nor is there a coherent theoretical model (Paige, 2004; Yamazaki & Hayes, 2004).

In Chapter 1 you read that the definition of communication itself reflects the culture defining it. In a like manner, the understanding of intercultural communication competence reflects the culture defining it. Consider how it might be defined in high-context, collectivistic cultures. C. M. Chua (2004) showed that intercultural communication competence in collectivistic Malaysian culture differs from Western definitions in that in Malaysia there is more emphasis on relational issues. Komolsevin, Knutson, and Datthuyawat (2010) explain this by showing that people in high-context cultures are hesitant to engage in communication—that is, they are reserved and silent—until they have sufficient information to encode messages appropriate for the receiver. So being quiet and reserved in Malaysia and Thailand is a necessary first step for the competent intercultural communicator. But that same behavior might be evaluated negatively in more individualistic cultures.

Focus on Theory 3.1

The Theory of Rhetorical Sensitivity

The theory of rhetorical sensitivity describes three types of communicators:

1. Noble selves—display egotism and individualism communicating messages with regard to the effect on the receiver
2. Rhetorical reflectors—display behavior believed to be desirable by the receiver
3. Rhetorical sensitives—combine concern for self with concern for others to encourage engagement

Komolsevin, Knutson, and Datthuyawat (2010) use this theory to explain that Thais use rhetorical reflection to build rhetorical sensitivity. In high-context, collectivistic cultures the development of the relationship contributes to intercultural communication competence.

Focus on Skills 3.3

Assessing Intercultural Communication Competence

Read the following court transcript (Liberman, 1981):

Magistrate: Can you read and write?

Defendant: Yes.

Magistrate: Can you sign your name?

Defendant: Yes.

Magistrate: Did you say you cannot read?

Defendant: Hm.

Magistrate: Can you read or not?

Defendant: No.

Magistrate: [Reads statement.] Do you recall making that statement?

Defendant: Yes.

Magistrate: Is there anything else you want to add to the statement?

Defendant: [No answer.]

Magistrate: Did you want to say anything else?

(Continued)

(Continued)

Defendant:	No.
Magistrate:	Is there anything in the statement you want to change?
Defendant:	No.
Magistrate:	[Reads a second statement.] Do you recall making that statement?
Defendant:	Yes.
Magistrate:	Do you wish to add to the statement?
Defendant:	No.
Magistrate:	Do you want to alter the statement in any way?
Defendant:	[Slight nod.]
Magistrate:	What do you want to alter?
Defendant:	[No answer.]
Magistrate:	Do you want to change the statement?
Defendant:	No.

1. Assess the intercultural communication competence of the magistrate and the defendant from the transcript alone.
2. The defendant is an Aboriginal in an Australian court. Liberman (1990a, 1990b) describes the unique form of public discourse that evolved among the isolated Aboriginal people of central Australia: Consensus must be preserved through such strategies as unassertiveness, avoidance of direct argumentation, deferral of topics that would produce disharmony, and serial summaries so that the people think together and "speak with one voice." If any dissension is sensed, there are no attempts to force a decision and the discussion is abandoned. Western European discourse style is direct, confrontational, and individualistic. Thus, it can be said that the Aboriginal defendant in the example finds it difficult to communicate a defense by opposing what has been said and rather frequently concurs with any statement made to him (Liberman, 1990b). Now that you have this information, does the defendant's strategy of giving the answers "Yes," "No," or "Hm" to placate the magistrate demonstrate intercultural communication competence?
3. Obviously the magistrate knows the defendant is an Aboriginal. Does the magistrate's questioning demonstrate intercultural communication competence?

How does having multiple cultural identities affect intercultural communication competence? In the following sections we address how being competent in the communication skills of more than one culture affects intercultural communication competence. We'll look at third cultures, multiculturalism, and postethnic cultures.

Third Culture

John Useem, John Donahue, and Ruth Useem (1963) introduced the concept of *binational third culture*. Casmir and Asuncion-Lande (1989) refined the concept third culture to refer to a new culture that two or more individuals from different cultures can share that is not merely the fusion of the separate cultures but a new coherent whole. Think of a marriage between an individual raised in China and an individual raised in the United States. Imagine it might make a difference where the couple is living—China, the United States, or some other culture. In the relationship, one individual could attempt to adopt the culture of the other or both individuals could attempt to build a new culture beyond their original cultures. Using the rhetorical sensitivity theory, the individual who adopts the culture of the other may be a rhetorical reflector initially, but then probably uses that to build rhetorical sensitivity as the relationship continues to develop. The individuals who attempt to build a new culture may be rhetorical sensitives. Rhetorical sensitivity may be critical for intercultural marriages.

Five percent of marriages in Japan in 2008–2009 included a foreign spouse (with four times as many foreign wives as husbands). In South Korea, over 10% of marriages included a foreigner in 2010. In Taiwan, 13% of wives were foreigners in 2009. (Chinese citizens are not considered foreigners in Taiwan.) In France, the percentage of international marriage rose from about 10% in 1996 to 16% in 2009. In Germany, the rise was from roughly 11% in 1990 to 14% in 2010. Approximately one in five marriages in Sweden, Belgium, and Austria is with a foreign partner ("International Marriage," 2011).

Reliable data to determine the success of intercultural marriages are largely missing. If we define the success of an intercultural marriage by remaining together and not divorcing, one study in France demonstrated that intercultural marriages may be no more nor less likely to end in divorce than other marriages (Neyrand & M'Sili, 1996).

©iStockphoto.com/adamkaz

A wedding of a U.S. citizen and a Chinese citizen can combine cultural traditions.

Another use of the term *third culture* has been to refer to children in expatriate families who reside outside of their home culture for years at a time (R. Useem & Downie, 1976). Other terms that have been used are *global nomads, transnationals,* and *internationally mobile children* (Gerner, Perry, Moselle, & Archbold, 1992). Ruth Useem (1999) argues that these people integrate elements of their home culture and their various cultures of residence into a third, different and distinct culture and may experience cultural marginality because of no longer feeling comfortable in any specific culture. In some ways, President Obama is a third-culture kid. He was born in Honolulu to a mother from the United States and a father from Kenya. When Obama was 2 years old, his father returned to Kenya. His mother remarried and moved to her new husband's homeland, Indonesia. Obama attended public school in Indonesia until he was 10 and then returned to Honolulu to live with his maternal grandparents. *New York Times* columnist David Brooks (2008) described Obama as a "sojourner who lives apart" (p. A33).

While most research has been with children from the United States, studies have shown that third-culture kids have a high level of interest in travel and learning languages and feel accepting of cultures and diversity (Gerner et al., 1992). Iwama (1990) found third-culture kids to be more self-confident, flexible, active, and curious and to have greater bilingual ability.

Does biculturalism as represented by third-culture kids represent a way to transcend nationalism and ethnocentrism and a way to create diverse communities (D. B. Willis, 1994)? There are suggestions of difficulties: Third-culture kids may have difficulty in maintaining relationships and in direct problem solving (C. A. Smith, 1991).

Multiculturalism

Definitions of intercultural competence grounded in communication have tended to stress the development of skills that transform one from a monocultural person into a multicultural person. The multicultural person is one who respects cultures and has tolerance for differences (Belay, 1993; Chen & Starosta, 1996). Using rhetorical sensitivity theory, it could be argued that the multicultural person is more likely to be a rhetorical sensitive.

As you read in Chapter 1, nation-states have become the predominant form of cultural identification. Most Western nation-states developed a single national identity in the 18th and 19th centuries. Increasing immigration has been perceived as a challenge to those single national identities. Multiculturalism concerns "the general place of minorities, programs designed to foster equality, institutional structures created to provide better social services, and resources extended to ethnic minority organizations" (Vertovec, 1996, p. 222); these became the way to respond to cultural and religious differences.

The Canadian Royal Commission on Bilingualism and Biculturalism is often credited with developing the modern political awareness of multiculturalism beginning with a preliminary report in 1965 (R. L. Jackson, 2010). Initially a policy to protect indigenous cultures, multiculturalism became an official Canadian policy in 1971; soon Australia and most member states of the European Union followed.

In the United States the origins of multiculturalism date back as early as 1915 to philosopher Horace Kallen (1915, 1924/1970), who set forth the idea of cultural pluralism to describe the United States. He employed the metaphor of a symphony orchestra. Each instrument was an immigrant group that, together with other immigrant groups, created harmonious music. Kallen's opponents included John Dewey (Westbrook, 1991), who warned that cultural pluralism supported rigid segregation lines between groups. Hollinger (1995) has described the issue as a two-sided confrontation between those who advocate a uniform culture grounded in Western civilization and those who promote diversity.

Several European heads of state have denounced multicultural policies: Former British prime minister David Cameron, German chancellor Angela Merkel, former Australian prime minister John Howard, former Spanish prime minister Jose Maria Aznar, and former French president Nicolas Sarkozy have all challenged their countries' multicultural policies. Several European states—notably the Netherlands and Denmark—have returned to an official monoculturalism (Bissoondath, 2002). Chancellor Merkel, for example, announced that multiculturalism had "utterly failed" (Weaver, 2010).

The same concern that multiculturalism has failed exists in the United States. Increased immigration and international terrorism and domestic terrorism have led to renewed pressures against multiculturalism. In April 2013, three people were killed and 264 injured when two bombs exploded at the Boston Marathon. The FBI identified two suspects, brothers Tamerlan and Dzhokhar Tsarnaev. Although they had never lived in Chechnya, the brothers identified as Chechen. Their family emigrated in 2002 and applied for refugee status. Both spoke English well. Tamerlan enrolled in a community college and married a U.S. citizen. He was quoted as having said that he "didn't understand" Americans and had not a single American friend (Weigel, 2013). Dzhokhar became a naturalized U.S. citizen in 2012 and enrolled in a university program in marine biology. He was reported to be greatly influenced by his older brother. Some believe that the brothers were motivated by an anti-American, radical version of Islam that Tamerlan had learned in the Russian republic Dagestan or that they had learned in the United States.

Some columnists began to label the tragedy as an example of the failure of multiculturalism. Mike Gonzalez (2013), for example, asks how two refugee recipients of free education in the United States could not assimilate. Assimilation, Gonzalez asserts, does not connote coercion and loss of ancestral culture, but it does mean patriotism.

Postethnic Cultures

You read earlier in this chapter that John Dewey criticized cultural pluralism as encouraging people to identify themselves as members of one group. If a person is born female in Texas of immigrant parents from Mexico and then becomes an attorney, a Republican, and a Baptist and currently lives in Minneapolis, who is she? In the United States, can she identify herself as any one of these? As all of these? Will others most likely identify her first as Hispanic?

A postethnic perspective recognizes that each of us, like the Minneapolis attorney, lives in many diverse groups and so we aren't confined to only one group. Angela Davis (1992) used the image of "a rope attached to an anchor": While we may be anchored in one community, our "ropes" should be long enough to permit us to move into other communities.

A postethnic perspective does not assume that everyone is the same. Rather, it recognizes our interdependent future and stretches the boundaries of *we*; using the rhetorical sensitivity theory might be an example of noble selves.

Hollinger (1995) describes a postethnic perspective as a challenge to the "right" of our grandparents to establish our primary identity. Postethnicity "prefers voluntary to prescribed affiliations, appreciates multiple identities, pushes for communities of wide scope, recognizes the constructed character of ethno-racial groups, and accepts the formation of new groups as a part of the normal life of a democratic society" (p. 116). Postethnicity recognizes that groups based on affiliations are as substantive and authentic as groups based on blood and history.

In one sense, postethnicity is an idealistic attempt to redefine groups rigidly based on ethnicity into groups based on voluntary interests. However, if viewed from the perspective of dominant U.S. cultural values—particularly individualism—postethnicity is a reaffirmation of the individual's right to define herself or himself by individual interest and not by heritage. Postethnicity in the United States may be an extension of extreme individualism.

It's important to recognize the criticism of postethnicity: that it is idealistic to assume that others will not continue to label some people as members of a group and communicate with them as members of that group and not as individuals.

Intercultural Communication Ethics

Closely related to intercultural communication competence is ethics. We saw that the understandings of communication and of intercultural communication competence are specific to culture. Are there ethics

Focus on Culture 3.2

A Postethnic Identity Claim

In 2012 Elizabeth Warren (originally from Oklahoma of working-class upbringing) was elected the first woman to the U.S. Senate from Massachusetts. During her career as a Harvard Law School professor, she had listed herself as Native American in law school directories. Challenged to provide proof of her ancestry by her Republican opponent, Warren said her family lore was that she had an Indian ancestor. The New England Genealogy Association found indications, but not proof, that Warren had a Cherokee great-great-great-grandmother, which would make her 1/32 American Indian.

In an essay titled "Elizabeth Warren Says She's Native American. So She Is," David Treuer, an author and Ojibwe Indian from Leech Lake Reservation in Minnesota, wrote,

> An Indian identity is something someone claims for oneself; it is a matter of choice. It is not legally defined and entails no legal benefits. Being an enrolled member of a federally recognized tribe, however, is a legal status that has nothing to do with identity and everything to do with blood quantum.... (Elizabeth Warren is not enrolled in a tribe and doesn't seem to have sought such status. She doesn't claim an Indian identity, just Indian ancestry.)

Source: Treuer (2012).

that transcend all cultures or are all ethics, too, specific to culture? As a branch of philosophy, ethics addresses the question of how we ought to lead our lives. Kenneth E. Andersen (1991) makes clear that ethical theories tend to reflect the culture in which they were produced and, therefore, present challenges in intercultural communication. Western ethics tend to focus on the individual and individual freedoms and responsibilities (Fuse, Land, & Lambiase, 2010). Other ethics focus more on community.

As described in Chapter 1, Confucianism supports a just, orderly society with rituals for relationships that create a harmonious society. Interpersonal relationships and the concept of face are central to Confucianism. Confucian ethics revolve around the concept of *li,* or the social norms, rituals, and proprieties that characterize an orderly society. A recent study demonstrated that Confucian ethics guide people's lives today. Zhong (2008) found that U.S. students display a strong sense of individualism, while Chinese students tend toward collectivism. Confucianism is an example of ethics that privilege the community and society, as opposed to Western ethics that focus on individuals and rights.

What, though, guides the interactions of people from cultures with diverse ethical perspectives? Are there global values to guide intercultural interactions? Kale (1997) argues that peace is the fundamental human value. The use of peace applies not only to relationships among countries but to "the right of all people to live at peace with themselves and their surroundings" (p. 450). From this fundamental value, he developed four ethical principles to guide intercultural interactions:

1. Ethical communicators address people of other cultures with the same respect that they would like to receive themselves. Intercultural communicators should not demean or belittle the cultural identity of others through verbal or nonverbal communication.

2. Ethical communicators seek to describe the world as they perceive it as accurately as possible. What is perceived to be the truth may vary from one culture to another; truth is socially constructed. This principle means that ethical communicators do not deliberately mislead or deceive.

3. Ethical communicators encourage people of other cultures to express themselves in their uniqueness. This principle respects the right of expression regardless of how popular or unpopular a person's ideas may be.

4. Ethical communicators strive for identification with people of other cultures. Intercultural communicators should emphasize the commonalities of cultural beliefs and values rather than their differences.

Developing ethical principles to guide intercultural interactions is a difficult task. Even though Kale's (1997) principles may be more acceptable in some cultures than in others, they are certainly a beginning step.

Focus on Theory 3.2

Is the Academic Discipline of Intercultural Communication Intercultural?

Is the intercultural communication field of study truly intercultural? Is there an ethical issue applying a Western perspective to other cultures? As you read in this chapter, the discipline originated in the United States and has been developed in U.S. universities. Even scholars from the non-Western cultures have "failed to utilize the experiences of their own cultures... to demonstrate that they, too, have been able to see through the same eyes as those European and U.S. American scholars who have pioneered in this field" (Asante, Miike, & Yin, 2014, p. 4). Yoshitaka Miike (2003a) has raised the question about whether "the topics we pursue, the theories we build, the methods we employ, and the materials we read adequately reflect and respond to the diversity of our communicative experiences in a globalizing world" (pp. 243–244).

One major criticism of Eurocentric intercultural communication research has been that the discipline has facilitated the commercial interests of the dominant North American and European cultures with consumers in other cultures (see, for example, Chapter 13 in this text). Western theories of communication often begin with the expression of unique individuality and a means of demonstrating independence. From an Asiacentric perspective, then, communication is a process in which we remind ourselves of the interdependence and interrelatedness of the universe.

In a dialogue with Miike, Asante asserted, "The future of intercultural communication must reside in the courage of scholars to engage indigenous knowledge from all areas of the world.... We must learn to embrace new paradigms and their expert concepts that grow from the wisdom and teachings of diverse peoples" (Asante & Miike, 2013, p. 12).

For Additional Reading:

Miike, Y. (2007). An Asiacentric reflection on Eurocentric bias in communication theory. *Communication Monographs, 74,* 272–278.

SUMMARY

The concept of high-context and low-context cultures was popularized by Edward T. Hall (1976). Cultures in which little of the meaning is determined by the context because the message is encoded in the explicit code are labeled low context. Cultures in which less has to be said or written because more of the meaning is in the physical environment or already shared by people are labeled high context. Low-context cultures, such as the United States, with a greater concern for privacy and autonomy, tend to use direct-face negotiation and express more self-face maintenance, whereas high-context cultures, such as China, with a greater concern for interdependence and inclusion, tend to use indirect-face negotiation and express more mutual-face or other-face maintenance.

Individuals in high- and low-context cultures perceive the world differently. Perception and thought are not independent of the cultural environment; therefore, our brains both are shaped by the external world and shape our perception of the external world. Sensation is the neurological process of becoming aware of our environment and is affected by our cultures. The Greek idea of a strong individual identity and the Chinese idea of harmony affected both the sensation and perception process in each culture. Perception is usually thought of as having three steps—selection, organization, and interpretation—each affected by culture.

While we may recognize that we perceive the world differently, that alone does not guarantee effective intercultural communication. There have been many attempts to define the skills that make one an effective and competent intercultural communicator. The concept of intercultural communication competence is applied to individuals who have multiple cultural identities such as third cultures, multiculturalism, and postethnic cultures. Finally, ethics of intercultural communication are presented as a guide for intercultural interactions and intercultural communication studies.

DISCUSSION QUESTIONS

1. Consider specific countries that have diverse populations and those with fairly homogeneous populations. How does the concept of high and low context help explain political debate, dispute resolution processes, and other forms of public communication?

2. Describe how the concept of face can help explain dispute resolution. How might a student confront an instructor over a grading error? What might that interaction look like in a U.S. classroom versus a Chinese classroom?

3. My veterinarian once said that he wished he could be a cat just for a few minutes to experience how a cat senses the world. He speculated, though, that such an experience would forever change him. Explain in what ways the experience of *two realities* might be so disconcerting.

4. Even within one culture, subgroups may have diverse perceptions. Compare the diverse perceptions that hunters, vegetarians, and even political parties might have of a moose.

5. What are the most critical elements of intercultural communication competence?

6. Kale suggests that peace is a fundamental human value that could guide intercultural interactions. Evaluate this proposition.

KEY TERMS

Aboriginal

face

facework

field dependence

high context

intercultural communication competence

intercultural communication effectiveness

interpretation

low context

multiculturalism

organization

perception

postethnicity

selection

sensation

third culture

NOTE

1. The word *God* is capped throughout this text, but no endorsement of any religion is implied. The intent is to honor all religions.

READINGS

All readings are from *Intercultural Communication: A Global Reader* (Jandt, 2004).

Akira Miyahara, "Toward Theorizing Japanese Interpersonal Communication From a Non-Western Perspective" (p. 279)

Kiyoko Suedo, "Differences in the Perception of Face: Chinese Mien-Tzu and Japanese Metsu" (p. 292)

Ram Adhar Mall, "The Concept of an Intercultural Philosophy" (p. 315)

STUDENT STUDY SITE

$SAGE edge™

Sharpen your skills with SAGE edge at edge.sagepub.com/jandt9e.

SAGE edge for Students provides a personalized approach to help you accomplish your coursework goals in an easy-to-use learning environment.

Chapter 4

LEARNING OBJECTIVES

After studying this chapter, you will be able to:

- List the functions of nonverbal communication.
- Give examples of nonverbal misinterpretations for various types of nonverbal communication.
- Describe Edward Hall's work with proxemics.
- Give examples of gestures whose meaning varies by culture.
- Give examples of nonverbal communication behavior in one culture that reflects the values of that culture.
- Explain how nonverbal interpretations can be a barrier in intercultural communication.

Nonverbal Communication

In Chapter 1, you read about how communication as an element of culture is understood differently by diverse cultures. You read that in the Western transmission models of communication, sources encode ideas into symbols and that symbols can be words or nonspoken symbols. Messages sent without using words are nonverbal communication. Since misinterpretations of nonverbal communication are such a major barrier to intercultural communication, this whole chapter is devoted to this barrier.

Communication occurs when we intentionally use symbols—words or nonspoken symbols—to create meaning for others. This chapter first briefly describes those nonverbal behaviors, such as smiles, that appear to be universal. To better define nonverbal communication, the functions performed through nonverbal communication are identified. Then examples of nonverbal misinterpretations are described for each type of nonverbal communication. Finally, you'll read how nonverbal messages in a culture are consistent with other factors in that culture, using the Thai wai gesture as an example, and how nonverbal misinterpretations can be a barrier in intercultural communication, particularly in multicultural societies such as the United States.

Nonverbal Behaviors

Keep in mind that not all nonverbal behavior is nonverbal communication. Some nonverbal behaviors do seem to be perceptual cues as to a person's state of mind.

Focus on Theory 4.1

Approaches to the Study of Nonverbal Communication

Burgoon and Saine (1978) describe nonverbal behavior as analogic rather than digital. Whereas digital signals are discrete, like numbers, analogic signals are continuous, like the sound volume. In the same way, gestures and other nonverbal behaviors are continuous. We create an arbitrary meaning of that gesture, which may vary by the context of culture, relationship, or situation.

There have been three major approaches to the study of nonverbal behavior. Researchers from the nurture approach believe that nonverbal communication is learned. Traditionally, anthropologists and sociologists have used this approach. In contrast is the nature approach. In the tradition of Charles Darwin (1872/1969) in his classic book *The Expression of the Emotions in Man and Animals,* some researchers believe that nonverbal behavior is innate; that is, nonverbal behavior is believed to be genetically determined. Finally, the functional approach focuses on the types of nonverbal behaviors and the communication functions they perform. Burgoon (1986); Knapp (1990); McCroskey, Burroughs, Daun, and Richmond (1990); and Mehrabian (1981) are examples of researchers who have studied how nonverbal channels are used to accomplish communication functions.

Lovaas pointed out in 2003 that nonverbal communication research to that time had been largely limited to heterosexuals. It could also be argued that little nonverbal communication research has focused on ethnicities.

Darwin (1872/1969) wrote that our facial expressions, such as smiles and frowns, are not learned but are biologically determined. Studies of children born deaf and blind show that, despite the lack of social learning, they smile, laugh, and cry in ways virtually identical to infants who can hear and see adults. Most people worldwide correctly identify the facial expressions of anger, disgust, happiness, fear, sadness, and surprise (Ekman, Friesen, & Ellsworth, 1972; Ekman et al., 1987). Researchers

Stockbyte/Thinkstock

©iStockphoto.com/Britta Kasholm-Tengve

Stockbyte/Thinkstock

The smile is the near-universal gesture of friendliness. In parts of Southeast Asia, a person may mask embarrassment by smiling. In some Latin cultures, a smile may signal "Excuse me" or "Please."

have since found evidence for a seventh universal expression: contempt (Ekman & Heider, 1988). In every culture the researchers studied, a large majority of people correctly named the facial expression in pictures of people who were entirely foreign to them. However, in a more recent study of people in Japan and the United States (Shioiri, Someya, Helmeste, & Tang, 1999), the facial expressions of surprise and happiness were well understood by both groups, but those of anger, contempt, disgust, fear, and sadness were not always as well recognized by people in Japan. It was Darwin's idea that these expressions evolved because they allow us to know immediately the difference between strangers who are friendly and those who might attack.

These innate behaviors can change as we grow and learn our culture. For example, even though a smile is universally recognized as a sign of friendliness, it has other meanings that are specific to a culture. Germans smile less often than people from the United States, but this doesn't mean that Germans are less friendly. It means that people from Germany and the United States have different ideas of when a smile is appropriate. In a business meeting of people from Germany and the United States, the people from the United States complained that the Germans were cool and aloof; the Germans complained that the people from the United States were excessively cheerful and hid true feelings (E. T. Hall & Hall, 1990).

Japanese tradition favors reserved emotional expressions. In photographs, U.S. wives are usually shown smiling at their husbands; Japanese wives are rarely shown smiling. U.S. clerks greet strangers with a smile; Japanese clerks must learn to do so. On the other hand, to maintain reserve, it is said that the Japanese smile to disguise embarrassment, anger, and other negative emotions because the public display of these emotions is considered rude and incorrect in Japanese culture.

Nonverbal Communication Functions

Exactly what is meant by the term *nonverbal communication* must be specified. It can be narrowly defined to refer to intentional use such as when using a nonspoken symbol to communicate a specific message. In this case, nonverbal communication refers to a source's actions and attributes that are not purely verbal. For example, communication scholars Judee Burgoon and her colleagues (Burgoon, Boller, & Woodall, 1988) define nonverbal communication as those actions and attributes of humans that have socially shared meaning, are intentionally sent or interpreted as intentional, are consciously sent or consciously received, and have the potential for feedback from the receiver.

The term can also be more broadly defined to refer to elements of the environment that communicate by virtue of people's use of them. The color of the walls in the room in which you are interviewed for a job may in some way affect your performance and how you are perceived. Thus, from this perspective, wall color may legitimately be labeled a nonverbal element of communication (Hickson & Stacks, 1989).

One way to demonstrate how nonverbals can be used to intentionally communicate messages is to look at the functions typically performed through nonverbal communication.

Replacing Spoken Messages. In some situations words cannot be used. In a very noisy manufacturing facility, for example, communicators might use hand gestures to replace spoken messages. Another example is when communicators who do not share a language try to make themselves understood with gestures. Nonverbal symbols can also be used to communicate utilitarian messages (Knapp, 1990). For example, a police officer directing the flow of traffic uses nonverbal communication to replace spoken directions.

Focus on Technology 4.1

Replacing Words With Pictures in Social Media

Sergey Brin, Google's co-founder, was wearing Google Glass when he received a text message asking what he was doing. He snapped a picture with his glasses and replied with the photo of his surroundings. "It was fascinating to see that I could just reply to a text message with a photo," Mr. Brin said in an interview. He didn't need words; the image was enough.

Source: Bilton (2013).

Global Voices

The Original Recycling Symbol

©iStockphoto.com/airdone

In 1970, the year of the first Earth Day, the Container Corporation of America sponsored a competition on college campuses to design a graphic symbol to be used on recycled paper products. Gary Anderson submitted three variations of a design. His was chosen from the more than 500 that were submitted.

Anderson's basic idea was three arrows represented as strips of paper that curved and bent back upon themselves. Taken together as a continuous strip, they formed a Möbius strip. Anderson's design became one of the most recognizable symbols in the world.

Nordic Ecolabel Swan

In 1989 the Nordic Council of Ministers adopted the swan ecolabel as a symbol of a good environmental

http://www.svanen.se/

product choice. The Swan, a variation of the logo of the Nordic Council of Ministers, was selected as the symbol. Some 94% of people in the Nordic countries associate the symbol commonly known as "the Swan" with environmentally sound products. From a small start in the early 1990s, the Nordic Swan is now one of the world's most successful environmental symbols.

Sources: Infomancie (2008a, 2008b); www.nordic-ecolabel.org; http://www.svanen.se.

Signs and symbols can replace spoken messages when they are used to identify and to direct attention to the things they designate. Signs are sometimes arbitrary in character, sometimes based on a real or fancied analogy, and usually simpler than symbols. For example, arrows are used to point direction. Symbols frequently are based on likeness, metaphor, or comparison. In Japan, for example, the cherry blossom is a symbol of the samurai because it is beautiful, blooms early, and dies soon. Still, symbol use is arbitrary. For example, the color red is a symbol for Christian charity and for communism and class conflict.

As symbols are independent of language, they can be used to communicate across language barriers. For example, symbols were used along ancient roadways. More recently, international events such as the Olympics have made extensive use of symbols. In fact, Katzumie Masaru, the art director of the Tokyo 1964 Olympics, developed many of the symbols in use today (Modley, 1976). World travel is facilitated by symbols known to literate and illiterate people alike on highways; at airports; in hospitals, factories, and schools; and on packages and clothing. Almost anyone can function in any international airport. From the symbols, you can find restaurants, restrooms, and telephones.

Not all symbols, however, are universally accepted. What is commonly called the swastika in the United States and Europe has long been understood with other meanings in other parts of the world. The same symbol has been used as a Hindu sign of peace for 5,000 years. Hindus are protesting Germany's move to ban the use of the swastika in the European Union. The International Committee of the Red Cross faces the same challenge. The red cross symbol was adopted to identify medics and ambulances in war zones in 1864. The Ottoman empire unilaterally declared the use of the red crescent during the Russo-Turkish War of 1876 in the belief that the red cross would alienate its Muslim soldiers. The red crescent is still in use today in countries with majority Muslim populations. The international group recognized no other symbols, even though the Israeli first aid society insisted on using the Red Star of David. After years of criticism that its official symbols had religious meanings, in 2006 the International Committee of the Red Cross accepted a fourth symbol—the red crystal, a red square standing on one corner—as an officially recognized humanitarian symbol. One of these symbols must be used by medical staff in war zones.

Symbols continue to be invented. In 1992, at the televised Tony Awards, Jeremy Irons was the first celebrity to wear the red AIDS ribbon. It was the idea of a New York group, Visual AIDS, to bring attention to the AIDS epidemic. Later in 1992, during the Emmy Awards telecast, Jamie Lee Curtis explained the meaning of the symbol, and by the next year, the red AIDS ribbon had become one of the most recognized symbols worldwide. It was so successful as a symbol that soon there were pink ribbons for breast cancer, lavender ribbons for abused women, and so on. Its use then declined, but it raised the public's awareness of AIDS.

Sending Uncomfortable Messages. Some messages are awkward or difficult to express in words, but the meaning can be conveyed with nonverbals without hurt feelings or embarrassment. Imagine being on your way home and being stopped by an acquaintance who wants to talk. The message in your mind that you want to communicate is "Don't bother me. I don't have time for you now." You may not want to say those words, but you can communicate that meaning by slowly continuing to walk away. Your nonverbal communication, followed by the verbal message of "I really have to go," is received without bad feelings because it's clear you really do have to leave. Likewise, you may find it difficult or awkward to say, "I love you," but eye contact, touch, and close proximity deliver the message.

Forming Impressions That Guide Communication. We all attempt at times to manage the impressions that others have of us. Think about how you would give some thought to what you would wear to a job interview. You intentionally choose to wear certain clothes and groom in a certain way to send a message about who you are to the employer.

Making Relationships Clear. Communication messages have both content and relationship information. Content refers to the subject matter of the message. Relationship information refers to the relationship between the communicators. As relationship information might be uncomfortable if spoken, nonverbal communication removes the threat. For example, think of the nonverbal messages on the job that replace the spoken words "I am your boss and you do as I say even though you may not like it." In the United States, most nonverbal communication at work reinforces power. According to Mehrabian (1981), status manifests itself by a relaxed posture and way of interacting. Those of lower status display more rigidity.

Regulating Interaction. Have you ever considered how you know when it's your turn to talk in a conversation? If you didn't know when to start talking, you'd be interrupting others all the time. Directing turn taking is an example of how nonverbal communication regulates people's interaction.

Focus on Technology 4.2

Emoticon Symbols Vary From Culture to Culture

Emoticons are the graphic signs using keyboard letters and symbols in text messages. The smiley face :-) was first proposed by computer scientist Scott Fahlman in 1982 as a means to signal that something was a joke in messages posed to a computer science discussion forum. In 2000, Wolf reported that the smiley face was the most commonly used emoticon.

Thousands have been developed and are catalogued in dictionaries and websites. While the smiley face was developed in Western culture, other emoticons reflect other cultures, for example, Japanese emoticons, or *kaomoji* ("face marks"). The Japanese smiley ^-^ is viewed straight on. Not all emoticons translate as intended from one culture to another.

Emoticons are considered indicators of affective states to convey nonlinguistic information that in face-to-face communication would be conveyed through nonverbals such as facial expressions for sarcasm or happiness. Dresner and Herring (2010) argue that emoticons more likely function in the same manner as punctuation marks such as exclamation marks.

©iStockphoto.com/Todor Tsvetkov

In 1999 Shigetaka Kurita, a Japanese telecommunications planner, developed emoji as visual cues for emotions and ideas in mobile phone messages. (The word is derived by combining the Japanese words for picture, e, and character, *moji*.) Emoji are small images created by computer code. The Unicode Consortium standardizes digital code so text can be exchanged no matter the device or language. It tells companies like Apple that certain bits of code should show up as a smiley face, but it is up to the software manufacturer how the smiley face is displayed. Initially human faces were vaguely Caucasian.

Emoji became widespread in the United States when Apple included them in its 2011 system update. In 2015 Oxford Dictionaries named the "Face With Tears of Joy" emoji as the "Word of the Year." Emoji-only social networks have been built where words are not allowed (Steinmetz, 2014).

Hannah Miller (2016) reported a study showing that not only can an emoji be understood differently, but the different renderings of the same emoji by Apple, Google, Microsoft, Samsung, and LG could be interpreted differently. This becomes even more likely when an emoji is sent from one platform, such as an iPhone, to other platforms as that emoji will be displayed differently, creating the possibility for miscommunication.

In 2015 *Slate* reported that emojis may be less popular now in Japan as Western design departments have lost the unique style of Japanese emoji largely based on its cartoons and comic books. Increasing in popularity in Japan, Thailand, Taiwan, and Indonesia is Line, a free messaging app that allows users to send "stamps"—mascots and cartoon characters. While emoji differ from platform to platform, Line stamps are always the same. And just like spelling suggestions, stamps pop up in a window based on the text (Alt, 2015). Late in 2016, Apple updated its Messages app to include stamps.

Reinforcing and Modifying Verbal Messages. Nonverbal cues can be metamessages that affect the decoding of the spoken message. Nonverbal messages can reinforce the verbal message. You can use your hands to indicate how close another car came to hitting your car as you say the same message in words. Nonverbal messages also can modify—and even negate—the meaning of the verbal message.

Types of Nonverbal Communication

Another way to define nonverbal communication is by type. The types of nonverbal communication given the most attention by travelers and researchers alike are proxemics, territoriality, kinesics, chronemics, paralanguage, silence, haptics, artifactual communication, and olfactics. Examples of nonverbal misinterpretations resulting in intercultural communication barriers are used to describe each type of nonverbal communication below.

Proxemics

We use the space around our bodies to communicate messages. First is the physical distance between communicators and second is how space can be used to communicate ownership or occupancy of areas. The term given to the study of our use of personal space is proxemics. Edward T. Hall's (1959) work has demonstrated clearly that cultures differ substantially in their use of personal space. His general theory is that we exist inside an invisible "bubble," or personal space. How much space we each want between ourselves and others depends on our cultural learning, our upbringing in our families, the specific situation, and our relationship with the people to whom we're talking. Though the physical distance we want between ourselves and others does vary, Hall reports the range is fairly consistent for most people in North America (see Table 4.1).

Experience shows that these distances vary in diverse cultures. In India, there are elaborate rules about how closely members of each caste may approach other castes, and Arabs of the same sex stand much closer than North Americans. North Americans in an elevator maintain personal space if the physical space permits it. An Arab entering an elevator may stand right next to another person and be touching even though no one else is in the elevator.

Table 4.1   Proxemics

	Distance	Description	Voice
Intimate	Touching to 18 inches	Private situations with people who are emotionally close. If others invade this space, we feel threatened.	Whisper
Personal	18 inches to 4 feet	The lower end is handshake distance—the distance most couples stand in public.	Soft voice
Casual	4 feet to 12 feet	The lower end is the distance between salespeople and customers and between people who work together in business.	Full voice
Public	Greater than 12 feet	Situations such as teaching in a classroom or delivering a speech.	Loud voice

Source: Adapted from E. T. Hall (1959).

Queuing means how you form a line while waiting. The traditional first-come, first-served line was typical in 19th-century France, but today, along with the Italians and Spaniards, the French are among the least queue-conscious in Europe. Until recently, the British were known to stand in queues for taxis, for food, and for tickets. Even in shops and pubs, customers were served in order. The practice may be dying in Great Britain, but people in the United States still stand in line—usually—and have elaborate "rules of queuing" (e.g., "cutting in line," "saving places"). Some explain the absence of queues in Europe and in Mediterranean areas as a sign of feelings against unwarranted regulation and interference. Edward T. Hall (1959) argues that queues are more likely to be found in cultures whose people are treated as equals.

We learn how close to stand to another person in our culture. Standing too close or too far away from what we learn is appropriate can create an intercultural communication barrier.

©iStockphoto.com/asiseeit

Territoriality

Territory is the space that an individual claims, whether permanently or temporarily. Territoriality refers to how space can be used to communicate messages. Sennett (1999) has described how spaces can encourage democracy. From roughly 600 to 350 BCE, Athens used two very different spaces—the theater and the town square—for its democratic practices. The *Pnyx,* an open-air theater, focused attention on a single speaker at a time, yet it was still possible to gauge others' reactions. The space supported a verbal order, "the unfolding of argument." The *agora* was the town square used for many simultaneous activities. Rather than each group being isolated and segregated, the agora was the place in the city where citizens became accustomed to diversity.

Chinese geomancy, feng shui (pronounced fung SCHWAY), is the art of manipulating the physical environment to establish harmony with the natural environment and achieve happiness, prosperity, and health. It is used in site planning and design of buildings for the greatest compatibility with nature. Feng shui also has principles for designing homes and placing furniture. A home with good feng shui has a balance of comfort and style and radiates serenity. Location, room shape, color, plants, artwork, and furniture are arranged for positive energy and balance.

Kinesics

Gestures, body movements, facial expressions, and eye contact are behaviors termed kinesics. In his landmark book *Gestures,* Desmond Morris (1979) wrote that communication depends heavily on the actions, postures, movements, and expressions of our bodies. In a later book, *Bodytalk,* Morris (1995) explained that gestures can be intentional or unconscious. For example, lower classes in ancient Rome used four fingers and thumb to pick up food; upper classes used two fingers and thumb. The difference may have been unconscious, but it clearly communicated class distinctions. Morris and his colleagues studied the use of 20 of the most familiar European gestures to map their use across national boundaries. For example, they found the thumbs-up gesture commonly used in the United States by hitch-hikers to be more widely understood to mean "okay." But in Greece and Sardinia, it more accurately communicates the idea of "get stuffed." And in Australia, Iran, and Nigeria, it has similar obscene connotations.

©iStockphoto.com/Kylie088

The forefinger-to-thumb gesture forming a circle can mean "okay" in the United States. In France, it means zero or worthless. In Japan, the same gesture can mean change (coins), but in Brazil it is a symbol many times more offensive than the raised middle finger. Curling the middle three fingers into the palm, extending the thumb and little finger, and then twisting the hand back and forth from the wrist is the Hawaiian greeting "hang loose." To the University of Texas Longhorn fans, the pinkie and index finger raised up with the middle two fingers and thumb folded into the palm means "Hook 'em horns." But in parts of Africa, the same gesture is a curse, and to Italians, it is the *cornuto,* signaling that one's wife is being unfaithful. Extending one hand, palm forward, means "stop!" in the United States, but in Greece, it's the *moutza* or hand push, a sign of confrontation. In West Africa, the same gesture is more insulting than the upraised middle finger (Axtell, 1991).

In the United States a fist raised above the head was used by Martin Luther King Jr. and the Black Power movement of the 1960s as a gesture of defiance and unity. At the 1968 Olympics, when U.S. sprinters Tommie Smith and John Carlos accepted their medals they raised their black-gloved fists in solidarity with the struggle against racism, outraging the Olympics Committee, which evicted them from the Olympic Village. In later years the gesture, sometimes pumped, became used by athletes, politicians, and others throughout the world in a celebratory manner. Recently, though, the raised fist became associated with Black Lives Matters' antiracist activism (Joseph, 2016).

Morris (1979, 1995) and his colleagues found wide variations even with such universal rituals as nodding agreement and greeting friends. Although most cultures do indicate "yes" by an up-and-down head nod and "no" by shaking the head from side to side, there are variations: In Albania, Bulgaria, and parts of Greece, Turkey, Iran, and the former Yugoslavia, the yes-no gestures are reversed. In Ceylon, a yes answer to a specific question is indicated by a nod of the head, whereas general agreement is indicated by a slow sideways swaying of the head. For greetings, in the United States, a firm handshake with direct eye contact is appropriate. In France, where the traditional U.S. handshake is considered too rough and rude, a quick handshake with only slight pressure is preferred. In Southern Europe and Latin America, a hearty embrace is common among women and men alike, and men may follow it with a friendly slap on the back. In Ecuador, to greet a person without a handshake is a sign of special respect. In India, the handshake may be used by Westernized citizens, but the preferred greeting is the *namaste*—placing the palms together and bowing slightly. In Japan, the traditional form of greeting is a bow, with the depth and length conveying meanings of status. In Tibet, people sometimes stick their tongues out to greet one another.

Likewise, waving good-bye and beckoning vary among cultures. In Italy, Colombia, and China, people may wave good-bye by moving the palm and fingers back and forth with the palm face up, a gesture that more likely means "come here" in the United States. But in Malaysia, beckoning someone by moving the forefingers back and forth would be taken as an insult. In other regions of the world, the same gesture with the palm down can mean "come here," while in others "get out!" Even seemingly obvious gestures can be misunderstood. Using fingers to indicate numbers can vary. In the United States, most people would indicate 1 by holding up the forefinger. In parts of Europe, 1 is indicated by

Figure 4.1   V Gesture

The V gesture made by the palm facing away from the maker was first suggested in World War II because *V* is the first letter of the English word *victory*, the French word *victoire*, and the Dutch word *vrijheid* (freedom). The sign was popularized by British prime minister Winston Churchill and united millions in Europe during the war effort. In the United States in the late 1960s, the same gesture became a symbol for peace (Dresser, 1996). When former British prime minister Margaret Thatcher made a "V for victory" sign during an election campaign, she showed the back of her hand. In the United Kingdom, Australia, Ireland, New Zealand, and South Africa that gesture is equivalent to the middle finger gesture and extremely insulting.

Mistakes are easy to make. On a 1992 visit to Australia, President George H. W. Bush used the palm facing inward to a crowd. Justin Bieber is frequently photographed performing the gesture palm in. But be careful in Brazil, showing the back of the hand there means the same as showing the palm. Recently a sideways peace sign has become deuces, as in "chuck them deuces."

using the thumb and 2 by the thumb and forefinger.

And the list continues: Some Japanese point a forefinger to the face to indicate referring to self, whereas in the United States, people are more likely to point to the chest. In Brazil, people may add emphasis to statements by snapping the fingers with a whiplike motion of the hands. Scraping the sides of the chin with the thumb and forefinger as if stroking a beard is a sign of respect in Saudi Arabia (Armstrong & Wagner, 2003). Indians in Delhi may use hands to grasp the ears as a gesture meaning repentance or sincerity. Fijians may fold the arms as a sign of respect when talking to another person.

©iStockphoto.com/mikkelwilliam

Patterns of eye contact learned in childhood seem to be relatively unaffected by later experiences. One study showed that Arabs, Latin Americans, and Southern Europeans gaze on the eyes or face of conversational partners, whereas Asians, Indians and Pakistanis, and Northern Europeans tend to show peripheral gaze or no gaze at all (Harper, Wiens, & Matarazzo, 1978). Duration of eye contact varies in diverse cultures (Shuter, 1979). In the United States, the average length of time that two people gaze at each other is 1.18 seconds (Argyle, 1988; Argyle & Ingham, 1972). Any less than that and we may think the person is shy, uninterested, or preoccupied. Any more than that and we may think the person is communicating unusually high interest. A wink is improper in Australia and impolite in parts of Asia.

People from Asian, Latin American, Caribbean, and American Indian backgrounds may offer respect by avoiding eye contact. Looking someone directly in the eyes may be interpreted as a provocation that can lead to violence. Repeatedly blinking the eyes is considered impolite in Taiwan and Hong Kong (Armstrong & Wagner, 2003). In parts of the United States, such as Appalachia, more people have heard of the belief in the "evil eye"—the power attributed to certain persons of inflicting injury or bad luck by a look. One communication professor new to the area worked hard to maintain eye contact with students during lectures, only to be told that some students perceived him as having the evil eye. It is said that Spanish men even today in more rural areas may use eye contact to make "passes" toward women on the street. Returning the stare is accepted as a gesture indicating that the man may attempt conversation. It also is said that Spaniards snap the eyelids when angry or impatient. Psychologist Monica Moore (1995) has studied the nonverbals of heterosexual flirting. She says that in Western cultures, women control the process by making

©iStockphoto.com/GCShutter

@iStockphoto.com/iStock_Oles

the initial choice of the man. To attract men, Moore has noted that women most often smile, glance, primp, laugh, giggle, toss the head, flip the hair, and whisper.

Gestures continue to be developed. Some recently developed gestures in the United States are the high five, butt pat, raise the roof, loser, whatever, and sizzle.

Chronemics

Next is the study of chronemics, or the study of our use of time. But before considering how we use time, consider how time is closely tied to religious and cultural beliefs. Many American Indian peoples understood time to be cyclical, whereas Western cultures think of time in the linear sense of a flow from the past to the present to the future. Yet Western science accepts Einstein's and other physicists' concepts of quantum physics in which there is no definite past, present, or future but only possibilities of position, in which particles can move backward in time as well as forward and in which what happened in the past can be altered by energy events in the future. It is said that the idea of linear time became commonly accepted as we became more aware of change—that is, aware that things were different before change and after change. Acceptance of some religious beliefs necessitates the acceptance of the understanding of time as linear. For example, the Christian belief that Christ's birth and death were unrepeatable events necessitates the acceptance of the understanding of time as linear. It existed in the past of our present, and since it could only occur then, it could not be repeated in our future.

When does a day begin? That depends very much on religious beliefs. The Jewish and Islamic day begins at sunset as the creation story in Genesis begins with darkness followed by light. Hindu days begin and end at sunrise. Christian tradition follows the Roman tradition of midnight as the beginning of a new day. The sun was first used to measure time in a day. Some 5,000 years ago the Sumerians and Egyptians used sundials. The Egyptians divided the day into 10 hours with 2 hours each for dusk and dawn to account for the different length of days in summer and winter. The sexagesimal system based on the number 6 was developed in Mesopotamia. The Sumerians divided the time between sunrise and sunset into 12 and the whole day into 24 segments. Sundials in Europe were built into the walls of churches to divide the day into the seven canonical hours of matins, prime, tierce, sext, nones, vespers, and compline. The idea of using hours of equal length, however, wasn't developed until 1371 by the Muslim scholar Abul-Hasan Ibn al-Shatir.

Sundials, of course, have no use without the sun. By the 11th century, the Chinese scholar Su Sung and Muslim scholars had developed water-driven clocks. In the 13th century, English monasteries had mechanical clocks driven by weights. The bells on these devices were known as *cloks*. However, it wasn't until 1475 that clocks indicated minutes. Precision timekeeping came with the invention of the pendulum clock by Dutch scientist Christian Huygens. The clock introduced a new consciousness—the clock, rather than the sun, became the arbiter of time for everyone. Our technological world demands even more accurate timekeeping. Since 1948, we have used atomic clocks accurate to within

1 second in 300,000 years. Still, we have demanded more accurate marking of time: microsecond (one millionth of a second), nanosecond (one billionth of a second), picosecond (one trillionth of a second), and femtosecond (one thousandth of a picosecond). Consider this: There are more femtoseconds in 1 second than there are seconds in 31 million years.

Humans marked time with calendars based on the sun or the moon. Mayan astronomers determined that a year was precisely 365.24 days long. The Hijrah calendar divided the year into 354 days and 12 lunar months. The Sumerians divided the year into 360 days—12 lunar months of 30 days each. The Egyptians extended this calendar year by adding 5 days at the end of the year.

The original Roman calendar was composed of 10 months and 304 days. Two months and 1 day were added later. The Julian calendar, devised by Julius Caesar, became the basis for what is used today. Coming at the time of the Reformation, reforms instituted by Pope Gregory XIII in 1582 created the Gregorian calendar year in use today. Pope Gregory's reforms were not immediately adopted in Protestant countries: The Gregorian calendar was adopted in Germany in 1700, in Britain in 1752, in Sweden in 1753, in Russia in 1918, and in China in 1912 but not widely so until the communist victory in 1949 (Duncan, 1998).

How we use time varies from culture to culture. That cultures use time differently can be a barrier to intercultural communication. Edward T. Hall (1983) has provided a useful way of describing how cultures use time. One way is to do one thing at a time, which Hall labels monochronic time; this is characteristic of Northern Europe and the United States. These cultures tend to try to plan the order of their use of time.

Doing many things at once is called polychronic time and is characteristic of Latin America and the Middle East. Polychronic time stresses the involvement of people and completion of transactions rather than adherence to schedules. In polychronic cultures, nothing is firm; plans can be changed up to the last minute.

What time you are expected to arrive for an 8 p.m. party varies as to where the party is. How long you should be kept waiting—if at all—for a business appointment varies as well. And once a meeting has begun, it varies how much informal conversation takes place before the actual business discussion begins. Arabs, for example, engage in up to half an hour of informal conversation before turning to business.

Paralanguage

Early work by Trager (1961) defined paralanguage by categories. The main category is voice qualities (including pitch range and distribution, rhythm, and tempo). Another category is vocalizations, which include the following:

- vocal characterizers, such as laughter and sobs
- vocal qualifiers, such as intensity (loud/soft), pitch (high/low), and extent (drawl and clipping)
- vocal segregates, such as *uh, um,* and *uh-huh*

The sounds of *psst* and of whistling are examples of vocal characterizers. "Psst" is an acceptable way of calling a waiter in Spain. In India, whistling is considered offensive.

Thais speak in a very soft and gentle voice and manner. This is based on the cultural belief that speaking in a soft voice is how one shows good manners and an educated character. Voices are raised only to show the emotion of anger or in an argument or confrontation. When first hearing persons in the

United States speak, some Thais believe the speakers are rude or angry or even don't like Thais because people from the United States speak so loudly.

Paralanguage is addressed in the Qur'an. One demonstrates modesty and humility by modulating one's voice and being soft spoken (Zaharna, 2009).

Another example is tonal languages. Speakers of English use tone to some extent but most often to express emotion. Think of how you would say "thank you" to convey a degree of sarcasm. However, in true tonal languages such as Mandarin Chinese and Vietnamese, the denotative meaning of some words depends on the context and how the word is said. Japanese is replete with homophones, where the meanings of many words are distinguished only by stress and intonation, which in turn convey the emotional nuances of anger, surprise, sincerity, and displeasure.

Accents may be considered an aspect of paralanguage. British ears can detect a speaker's educational background in the accent. It can be said that everyone has an accent; it's just that some accents are more accepted than others. Accents may present problems and even lead to charges of racism (M. G. Ryan, 1974). One study in San Antonio, Texas, had employment interviewers listen to taped speech samples of males speaking with varying degrees of accents and make hiring predictions (de la Zerda & Hopper, 1979). Standard speakers were significantly favored for supervisory positions and accented speakers for semiskilled positions. Collier (1988) as well has shown that Whites note Hispanics' inability to speak English as socially inappropriate. In recalling conversations, Whites cite examples of Spanish language use and "broken English" as inappropriate and difficult to understand.

Midlevel Asian-American employees can find promotion to management closed, particularly if their spoken English is perceived as nonfluent. In Honolulu, a Filipino man was denied a job as a city clerk. He sued on the basis of racial discrimination. Attorneys for the city argued that his heavy Filipino accent would have kept him from working effectively as a clerk. The case was appealed to the Supreme Court, and in *Fragante v. City and County of Honolulu* (1989), the Court let stand a federal appeals court decision supporting the city.

In Massachusetts, parents petitioned their local school board to ban first-grade and second-grade teachers with pronounced accents. The opposition argued that such a ban would be discrimination based on national origin and would violate the Fourteenth Amendment, which provides equal protection for everyone under the law. In Anaheim, California, a radio station contest was based on telephoning convenience store clerks and asking listeners to identify the clerks' nationalities. Some refugee organizations charged the contest was racism disguised as humor.

Huh may be considered an example of a vocal segregate. Dingemanse, Torreira, and Enfield (2013) studied

RosalreneBetancourt 10/Alamy Stock Photo

Trains in Japan can get very crowded yet are generally quiet. Signs and public service announcements remind people not to talk on mobile phones on the train and to turn phones on "manner mode" (silent mode).

languages from around the world and found that all of them have a near-identical sound that functions as the English *huh?* They believe that *huh* is not an innate universal like sneezing or crying, but a sound that has to be learned because it has subtly different forms in each language.

Silence

Speech and silence have generally been defined in an either/or way. We are either communicating in speech or we are silent, which defines silence as simply the absence of speech (Acheson, 2008). To most people in the United States, silence means lack of attention and lack of initiative. A person must speak up to participate.

Silence can communicate agreement, apathy, awe, confusion, contemplation, disagreement, embarrassment, obligation, regret, repressed hostility, respect, sadness, thoughtfulness, or any number of meanings.

Traditionally, Eastern societies such as India, China, and Japan have valued silence more than Western societies have. Oliver (1971) observed that "silence in Asia has commonly been entirely acceptable, whereas in the West silence has generally been considered socially disagreeable" (p. 264). In India, on the individual level, silence can be viewed as a state of being, allowing you to experience the highest truth and bliss (Jain & Matukumalli, 1993). In the Confucian context, silence, not talking, is a virtue.

On the interpersonal level, silence is used to promote harmony, cooperation, and other collectivistic values; it is a sign of interpersonal sensitivity, mutual respect, personal dignity, affirmation, and wisdom. On the level of social movements, silence can be protest, as demonstrated by Mahatma Gandhi in his struggle for India's independence through nonviolence.

Silence can mean one is fearful of communicating. This form of silence is associated with the communication variable commonly studied in the United States and known as communication apprehension or, more commonly, stage fright. Communication apprehension refers to an individual's fear or anxiety associated with either real or anticipated communication with another person or persons. Studies of communication apprehension by James McCroskey and his colleagues (1990) led them to label that fear the most common handicap that people suffer from today. They also suggest that U.S. society stresses verbal performance so

Global Voices

Student A:	I have been to America.
Interviewer:	Oh. Can you tell me what the experience was like?
Student A:	The people and the country were very nice.
Interviewer:	Did you learn anything?
Student A:	No.
Interviewer:	Why not?
Student A:	Americans just talk all the time.
Interviewer:	Do you like Finland?
Student B:	Oh, yes, I like it a lot.
Interviewer:	How about the people?
Student B:	Sure, Finns are very nice.
Interviewer:	How long have you been at the university?
Student B:	About nine months already.
Interviewer:	Oh, have you learned anything?
Student B:	No. Not really.
Interviewer:	Why not?
Student B:	Finns do not say anything in class.

Source: Wilkins (2005).

Global Voices

Basso (1986) describes "speaking with names" among the Western Apache of Cibeque, Arizona. One speaker mentions the name of a local landmark followed by several minutes of silence, followed by another speaker mentioning the name of another landmark, and that again followed by several minutes of silence. Speakers may repeat or continue the cycle multiple times. The names conjure meanings in the minds of the listeners to communicate a drama and moral. Speaking with names can console and advise the listeners.

much that U.S. speakers may experience more pressure than those from other cultures. For example, they have shown that Swedish students consider themselves more competent communicators but are less prone to initiate communication than are U.S. students.

Haptics

Less well studied is haptics, or the study of our use of touch to communicate. Again, examples support that the use of touch to communicate varies from culture to culture. In Thailand and Laos, it is rude for a stranger or acquaintance to touch a child on the top of the head because the head is regarded as the home of the spirit or soul. It is believed that a child's spirit or soul isn't strong enough to be touched and has a tendency to become ill if patted (Smutkupt & Barna, 1976).

In Iraq, physical contact between adults—particularly between women and men—is governed by strict cultural mores. Postwar security concerns required body searches to help stabilize the country. The United States established the Facilities Protection Service, a security force of some 35,000 Iraqis to provide security checks at thousands of locations too numerous for U.S. soldiers to guard. Women are searched by women and men by men, yet running hands down limbs and patting torsos is an unfamiliar experience.

Compared with other cultures, people in the United States are touch deprived, having one of the lowest rates of casual touch in the world. If you are talking with a friend in a coffee shop in the United States, you might touch each other once or twice an hour. If you were British and in a London coffee shop, you probably won't touch each other at all. But if you were French and in a Parisian café, it is said that you might touch each other a hundred times in an hour.

In many cultures, adult male friends walk hand in hand—a behavior frequently misunderstood by people from the United States who assume the friends are gay. In other cultures, one does not offer anything to another with the left hand, as the left hand is used to clean oneself after using the toilet.

In the United States, more touching may take place in preschool or kindergarten than during any other period. Touching is lowest during the early to mid-teens. The first comprehensive study of communication and touch in the United States was conducted by Stanley Jones and Elaine Yarbrough (1985). Their study of students at a western U.S. university showed 12 meanings communicated with touch—affection, announcing a response, appreciation, attention getting, compliance, departures, greetings, inclusion, playful affection, playful aggression, sexual interest or intent, and support—as well as hybrid meanings such as departure/affection and greetings/affection.

©iStockphoto.com/StudioThreeDots

In his consulting with businesses, Stanley Jones (1993) says that employees are more aware of inappropriate touching and sexual harassment. At least in the United States, most touching has symbolic content, but contextual factors are critical to the meaning. What is appropriate touching in a four-person psychotherapy clinic may not be appropriate in a 200-person insurance office.

Artifactual Communication

Artifactual communication refers to messages conveyed through objects or arrangements of objects made by human hands (DeVito, 2014). It includes how we decorate our homes and offices as well as the clothing we wear and our physical appearance with jewelry, tattoos, and body piercings.

The *hongi*, the traditional greeting of the Māori of New Zealand, is the touching of noses to share the breath of life.

What we wear varies so much across the world, as does the meaning conveyed by the clothes. Clothing can reflect cultural heritage. Men in Saudi Arabia may wear a thawb, a loose-fitting, ankle-length, usually white shirt; the ghutrah, the white or red-and-white check cloth covering the head; and the iqual, or *agal*, the double ring of black rope or cord used to hold the ghutrah.

Muslim women may wear several different types of headscarves and veils generally referred to as hijab or covering. The burqa is a full-body covering with a small opening for the eyes worn by Muslim women over their clothing. The niqab veils a woman's face and hair down to the shoulder.

Focus on Skills 4.1

Touching as Nonverbal Communication

You are a young woman eager to learn more about the world. You sign up for a study tour of China. In the park you feel that people stare at you. Some people even come up to you, stop you, and take a photo of you and even try to touch your blond hair. You feel the staring is rude, and you find it frightening that people want to touch your hair.

Your faculty adviser explains that rural Chinese come to big cities to sightsee and that, especially in remote rural areas, many Chinese people have never seen a foreigner except on TV. Staring might be curiosity, not disrespect.

You want to avoid any misunderstandings, but even if it is curiosity, you still feel uncomfortable with people trying to touch your hair.

1. How would the competent intercultural communicator handle this situation?
2. In what ways can you respond to their nonverbal communication?
3. Do you smile, put your hands up in front of you, and shake your head no? Or do you smile and allow strangers to touch your hair? Something else?

The niqab does not cover the eyes. It was estimated that in 2011 about 1,900 women (out of a population of 5 million Muslims) in France wore the niqab. A French parliamentary committee found that women covering their faces was against the French republican principles of secularism and equality. France's former president Nicolas Sarkozy said to the country's Parliament, "In our country we cannot accept women prisoners behind a wire fence, cut off from all social life, deprived of all identity." France imposed a ban on wearing veils that cover the full face in public places such as parks, schools, and theaters. Anyone who violates the ban could be fined and required to take a citizenship course. Croucher (2008) contends that the ban is a response to a perceived threat to French sense of "nation" at a time of increased migration from non-Western and non-Christian countries to control Muslim identity and forcefully integrate this population. For many of the Muslim women in France, the hijab is a symbol of cultural uniqueness. Similar bans exist in Turkey and Belgium and have been proposed in the Netherlands, Italy, and Britain. In the United States, retailer Abercrombie & Fitch fired a Muslim worker for refusing to remove her hijab during work. In contrast to how events unfolded in Europe, the U.S. Equal Employment Opportunity Commission filed suit and Abercrombie & Fitch will now allow workers to wear head scarves.

Indian bride displays her gold jewelry before her wedding ceremony.

©iStockphoto.com/mantosh

India has a long cultural tradition with gold jewelry. Gold has spiritual meaning as well as practical meaning. For centuries gold was the safest currency in India. In some Hindu legends, Brahma, the god who created the universe, was born from a gold egg. Gold became a symbol of purity and prosperity. Today India is the world's biggest importer of gold and the largest hoarder of gold. In 2012 Indians imported about one-fifth of the world's gold at a cost of 2.5 trillion rupees (US$45 billion), second only to India's import expense for oil. Perhaps half of that gold is in jewelry for weddings. A bride's parents give gold as a symbol of their prosperity and as insurance against a bad marriage as gold jewelry belongs to the wife. Families begin buying gold jewelry for daughters several years in advance of their weddings.

To orthodox Sikhs throughout the world, the kirpan, or ceremonial dagger, is one of five sacred articles of faith and must be worn at all times by baptized Sikhs. (The other articles are the kesh, or turban; the kara, or steel bracelet symbolizing

The kirpan is an article of Sikh faith.

AAron Ontiveriz/Denver Post/Getty Images

strength and integrity; the kangha, or wooden comb symbolizing cleanliness; and the kachera, or undergarment symbolizing chastity and self-control.) The kirpan symbolizes readiness to protect the weak and defense against injustice and persecution. The U.S. Department of Homeland Security bans kirpans from airplanes, and as a result some Sikhs do not fly. Some U.S. school districts require that kirpans be sewn shut into a sheath. U.S. government attorneys argue that laws such as those that ban knives in schools and on airplanes are religious neutral and therefore do not violate a protected First Amendment right.

Clothing also can reflect subcultural and subgroup identity; medical professionals and members of the military, for example, often wear uniforms outside of work. Sometimes how an article of clothing is worn reflects subcultural or subgroup identity. Think of a baseball cap. A baseball cap with the brim curled worn straight on the head is a "jock look." But think of all the other ways a baseball cap can be worn to indicate other group identifications.

In Kenya, unlike most of West Africa, attire is generally conservative. In 2003, a legislator entered the nation's parliament dressed in the traditional cap and flowing *agbada* robes of West Africa. The parliament's speaker, dressed in the heavy black robes and white wig of the British parliamentary system, described the attire as "pajamas." This dispute over clothing is symbolic of Kenya's struggle to define an African identity.

One important aspect of clothing is color. The meaning of colors varies considerably by culture, as can be seen in Table 4.2. A garment chosen to communicate something in one culture might well communicate something contradictory in another.

AP Photo/Marcio Jose Sanchez

When he played for the San Francisco 49ers, quarterback Colin Kaepernick refused to stand for the national anthem to protest racism in American society. In 2016, India's Supreme Court ruled that movie theaters must play the national anthem before every screening and that everyone in the audience must "stand up to show respect."

Olfactics

The study of communication via smell is called olfactics. Smell remains one of the least understood senses. The amount of the human brain devoted to olfaction is very large. We do know that odor is first detected by the olfactory epithelium in the nose. This starts a chain of events that leads to an information flow to the olfactory bulb and limbic system of the brain, which plays a key role in regulating body functions and the emotions. Smell is the only sense linked directly into the limbic system, which may be evidence of its being our most basic, primitive sense. In all cultures, women can detect odors in lower concentrations, identify them more accurately, and remember them longer than men (Doty et al., 1984).

Scientists also have identified a tiny organ in the nasal cavity that responds to chemicals known as pheromones, natural substances believed to play a role in basic human emotions such as fear, hunger,

Table 4.2 Cultural Meanings of Colors

Color	Meaning for Different Cultures
Red	China: Good luck, prosperity, happiness, marriage
	Japan: Anger, danger
	Middle East: Purity, life
	Egypt: Death
	South Africa: Mourning
	United States and Western Europe: Danger, anger, stop
Blue	China: Immortality, heavens, depth, cleanliness
	Japan: Villainy
	India: Color of Krishna
	United States and Western Europe: Masculinity, calm, authority, peace
Yellow	East Asia: Sacred, imperial, royalty, honor
	Middle East: Happiness, prosperity
	India: Religious color (celebration), success
	Egypt: Mourning
	United States and Western Europe: Caution, cowardice
Green	Asia: Family, harmony, health, peace, life, youth, energy, growth
	Muslim countries: Religious color, fertility, strength
	Ireland: National color
	United States and Western Europe: Safe, go
White	Asia: Mourning, death, purity
	Middle East: Mourning, purity
	India: Death, purity
	United States and Western Europe: Purity, virtue
Black	Asia: Evil influences, knowledge, mourning
	Middle East: Mystery, evil
	United States and Western Europe: Mourning, elegance (black dress and tuxedo), death, evil
Brown	India: Mourning
Purple	Thailand: Mourning
	Catholics: Death
	Asia: Wealth, glamour
	Western Europe: Royalty
Orange	Ireland: Religious significance
	China: Light and warmth
	United States: Inexpensive goods

Source: Aykin & Milewski (2005).

Focus on Skills 4.2

Using Context to Help Interpret Artifactual Communication

You and three friends are on a spring break vacation in Puerto Rico. After a day on the beach, you are walking back to your residence hotel when you notice several locals shouting at you. None of you speak Spanish, so you quickly attempt to assess the situation. The four of you in beach clothes are walking across the lawn in front of what you assume is a Catholic church. One of your friends is carrying an open beer.

1. Is this an example of intentional nonverbal communication on your part? If so, what types of nonverbal communication are represented?
2. What perceptions of you might the locals have?
3. Have you violated a local cultural norm? Or might they be saying *piropos* (compliments) for you being good looking?
4. Assuming this is an example of a nonverbal misinterpretation, what should you do? Continue walking? Run? Attempt to communicate verbally with the locals?

Focus on Culture 4.1

You and I Are Close Friends

Every culture has its own polite fictions. Whenever we want to be polite, we must act out certain fictions, regardless of the facts. For example, when you meet someone, you may or may not like him, but either way, you must politely pretend to like him. In such a case, Americans and Japanese share the same polite fiction that "you and I like each other." But in many cases, Americans and Japanese are acting according to very different polite fictions.

The first time I was asked to appear as a guest speaker before a group of Japanese, the organizing committee very kindly arranged for two of the committee members to pick me up and drive me to the meeting place. They escorted me from my front door to their car, ushered me into the back seat, and then the two of them got into the front seat, leaving me to sit out the whole ride all alone in the back.

My first reaction was to feel rejected and lonely. "Why don't they want to sit next to me? Don't they like me? What's wrong with me?" Even after I realized that this must be their way of being polite to me, I still couldn't help feeling embarrassed and uncomfortable sitting all alone, separated from the others. In America, they would have put me in front with the member who was driving, and the other member would have sat alone in back.

The next time a welcoming committee arranged to pick me up, there were too many of them to fit into the front seat. "Good!" I thought. "Now someone will have to sit in back with me, and it won't be so embarrassing." But it was, if anything, even more embarrassing to have to listen to everyone trying to refuse to share the back seat with me. Once again, my initial reaction was, "Nobody wants to make friends with me; what's wrong with me?"

(Continued)

(Continued)

The same thing happened whenever my English students and I had a class party. All the students would cluster at the far side of the table. No one would sit next to me, or even near me. I felt very unpopular. By this time, of course, I knew that this reluctance to be near the guest of honor did not indicate personal dislike. It was simply an expression of the Japanese polite fiction, "I am in awe of you." Yet I still felt uncomfortable and embarrassed. Why? Because while I understood rationally, I couldn't help reacting emotionally, in terms of the very different American polite fiction, "you and I are close friends."

Source: Sakamoto & Naotsuka (1982, pp. 80–83).

and, most notably, those related to sex. Recently, scientists have uncovered evidence of human pheromones (Weller, 1998).

The ancient Romans were obsessed with roses. They were worn in garlands; used in pillows, medicines, and love potions; and displayed at banquets and orgies. In the 16th century, lovers exchanged "love apples," peeled apples kept in the armpit until they were saturated with sweat and then given to a lover to inhale. In ancient Hawai'i, when meeting, traditional Hawaiians inhaled one another's breath. Although many people today consider *haole* (outsider) a derogatory word, in Hawaiian, it originally meant "not of the same breath."

Aromatherapy is the use of oils of flowers, herbs, and plants to make people feel better. Aromatherapy was widely practiced in ancient Chinese, Egyptian, and Indian civilizations and is widely practiced today in Belgium, England, France, Germany, and Switzerland. In Japan, fragrance is used in the workplace. The architectural and construction firm Shimizu has developed computerized techniques to deliver scents through air-conditioning ducts to enhance efficiency and reduce stress among office workers.

Advertisers believe smell is important. Fragrance strips in magazines enable consumers to sample a perfume by pulling open a strip, releasing tiny fragrance capsules glued inside. British stores use smells such as freshly dried linen, chocolate, and musk in the air-conditioning system to put customers in the mood to buy their products.

Smell also refers to body odor. Some cultures are sensitive to any body odor; others mask body odor with perfumes and colognes; others find the odor of perfumes and colognes distasteful. Some say that body odor is affected by the food you eat and that meat eaters have a distinctive body odor.

Knowing Culture Through Nonverbal Messages

In Chapter 1, you read that Alfred G. Smith (1966) wrote that communication and culture are inseparable, that culture is a code we learn and share that requires communication, and that communication coding and symbols must be learned and shared. As some of those symbols are nonverbal, it is partially through nonverbal messages that we experience the culture.

Some nonverbal messages can be clearly identified with a culture. Min-Sun Kim (1992), for example, has demonstrated how the nonverbal messages shown in Korean and U.S. print media advertising clearly reflect the culture. Culture can be conceptualized as an interrelated system in which each aspect of culture is related to other aspects of that culture. For example, it is said that in Europe, body language is an important indicator of one's level of education and good manners, a relationship not seen as often in the United States. Many nonverbal messages used in a culture are related to and consistent with other aspects of the culture. In one sense, then, other aspects of a culture are revealed in the nonverbal code. In the following case study, consider how the nonverbal wai reflects other aspects of the Thai culture.

Case Study: The Wai in Thailand

In Thailand, the wai is a nonverbal gesture used to communicate greeting, bidding farewell, deep and sincere respect, and appreciation (Smutkupt & Barna, 1976). The palms of both hands are placed together and held vertically slightly under the chin followed by a slight head bow, chin toward the fingertips. There is no eye contact because the head is bowed. The wai is not accompanied by verbal communication. Usually the younger person or subordinate initiates the wai, and the older person or higher ranking person responds with a wai as well (Rojjanaprapayon, 1997).

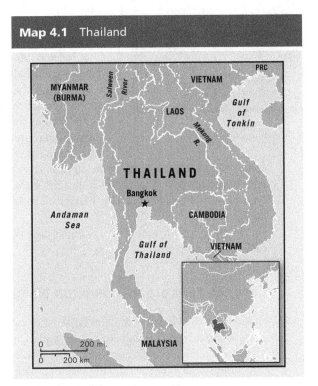

Map 4.1 Thailand

The wai is consistent with other elements of the Thai culture. Children absorb its nuances along with learning the Thai spoken language, which has a hierarchy of honorific titles and a special language of self-debasement to be used when speaking to royalty. The first nonverbal teaching the Thai child receives is this gesture of obeisance. The mother holds her infant, puts its palms together between her own, and raises the hands to the chin or the forehead—the higher the hands, the greater the degree of deference. Before the child is taken from the house, its hands will be put in the proper position to greet guests. When a mother takes her child to the temple, she raises its palms to pay homage to Buddha. The child is constantly directed to wai on every appropriate occasion until it becomes a regular component of behavior. Children never fail to wai parents and the family's elders before leaving for school in the morning. In the classroom, children stand and perform the wai upon the teacher's arrival. When school ends, the students wai to thank the teacher. On returning home, the children greet all parents and elders with the wai. The day ends with paying homage to Buddha by performing the wai in front of the family's altar. Thus, the wai is a representation of the cultural values, including respect for parents and elders, that the child learns while learning the nonverbal code. By understanding the wai, we also can understand part of the Thai culture.

The wai in Thailand

Nonverbal Misinterpretations as a Barrier

Chapter 3 identified *nonverbal misinterpretations* as a barrier in intercultural communication. While we expect languages to be different, we are less likely to expect and recognize how the nonverbal symbols are different. Often, when people don't share the same language, some resort to hand gestures to communicate. In such situations, people discover that the belief that hand signals and bodily expressions are universal is not true. Many nonverbal expressions vary from culture to culture, and it is just those variations that make nonverbal misinterpretation a barrier.

Judee Burgoon (1986) writes that nonverbal communication must have consensually recognized meanings and consistent usage within a culture. In the United States, for example, many gestures are commonly recognized across the country. But in a multicultural society, again such as the United States, the possibilities for nonverbal misunderstandings are great because subcultures may not completely understand each other's nonverbals. Burgoon contends that some nonverbal communication, even in the same culture, is so ambiguous that its interpretation is mediated by context. For example, in the United States, the meaning of a touch can often be ambiguous. The meanings conveyed by the same touching behavior can be quite different at a funeral than at a sports victory party.

In the following case study, consider how two subcultures in the United States can misunderstand each other's nonverbals.

Case Study: Korean-American Neighborhood Businesses

Communication barriers and racial tension can exist among groups within diverse cultures. One example has been African-American and Korean-American conflict. Today, about 85% of the Korean-American population are immigrants. Some African-Americans have viewed Korean-Americans in business as exploiters; the idea of a neighborhood business with no community commitment is unacceptable. Some Korean-Americans experiencing difficulty with English use words and phrases such as "Go" or "Come back later," which can be viewed as aggressive to customers expecting phrases like "Please come back later." Even how money is handled creates tension. Should cash be placed on the counter or placed in the other's hand? Some African-Americans feel the shopkeepers are trying to avoid touching; some Korean-American shopkeepers feel their customers "always want to touch." Since the 1992 riots in Los Angeles, Korean-American immigrants have received acculturation and U.S. business practices training to avoid the behaviors that have often been misinterpreted by those unfamiliar with Korean culture. Groups such as the Korean American Management Association advise shopkeepers to greet customers as visiting relatives rather than ignoring them.

Inappropriate smiles in the Korean culture are interpreted as shallow and thoughtless, so Korean-Americans accustomed to reserving smiles and small talk for friends and family are encouraged to smile and shake hands firmly.

An African-American entering a small store typically expects eye contact and some small talk. If the Korean-American storekeeper, reluctant to develop friendship with a stranger, doesn't engage in those behaviors, the African-American customer may think the store owner is disrespectful or rude. The Korean-American storekeeper, however, raised in a highly structured Confucian culture that stresses formality, sees the outgoing style of the African-American as inappropriate and threatening. Acculturation also involves learning U.S. values, such as the presumption of innocence until proven guilty. In Korea, a person caught shoplifting can be "roughed up" by anyone. Korean-American shopkeepers now learn that that same behavior could result in charges of battery and assault.

SUMMARY

This chapter examines nonverbal misinterpretations as a barrier to effective intercultural communication. Some nonverbals, such as smiles and frowns, are biologically determined but can develop culture-specific meanings. Other nonverbals can be used to intentionally communicate messages. Nonverbals can be used to replace spoken messages, to send uncomfortable messages, to form impressions that guide communication, to make relationships clear, to regulate interaction, and to reinforce and modify verbal messages.

Types of nonverbals include the following:

- *proxemics*—the use of personal space
- *territoriality*—the use of physical space to communicate messages
- *kinesics*—gestures, body movements, facial expressions, and eye contact
- *chronemics*—the use of time
- *paralanguge*—vocal characterizers, such as laughter; vocal qualifiers, such as pitch; and vocal segregates, such as *uh-huh*
- *silence*—when not talking can communicate meaning
- *haptics*—the use of touch to communicate
- *artifactual communication*—human-made objects and their arrangement as well as clothing and other aspects of personal appearance
- *olfactics*—the use of smell to communicate messages

Some nonverbals are specific to a culture and reflect other aspects of that culture. In Thailand, for example, the wai gesture is made by placing the palms of both hands together and holding them vertically slightly under the chin. The wai communicates greeting, farewell, sincere respect, and appreciation. Children learn the wai gesture as they learn other elements of the Thai culture.

While in homogeneous cultures the meanings of nonverbals are more likely to be commonly shared, in multicultural societies nonverbal misinterpretations are problematic. Misunderstandings can arise, for example, in interactions between some African-Americans and some Korean-Americans. Eye contact and smiles can have different meanings to each group, resulting in unfortunate misunderstandings.

DISCUSSION QUESTIONS

1. Reflecting on what you know about nonverbal symbols, should the European Union totally ban the use of the swastika symbol?

2. Create and evaluate the possible arguments in *Fragante v. City and County of Honolulu* (1989).

3. Evaluate France's ban on Muslim women wearing veils that cover the full face in public places.

4. Evaluate the U.S. Department of Homeland Security ban on Sikh kirpans on airplanes.

5. With increasing international travel and media, will nonverbal misinterpretations disappear or become more critical?

KEY TERMS

artifactual communication	hijab	polychronic time
burqa	Hijrah calendar	proxemics
chronemics	iqual	sign
communication apprehension	kinesics	silence
emoji	monochronic time	territoriality
feng shui	niqab	thawb
ghutrah	nonverbal communication	wai
Gregorian calendar	olfactics	
haptics	paralanguage	

STUDENT STUDY SITE

⑤SAGE edge™

Sharpen your skills with SAGE edge at edge.sagepub.com/jandt9e.

SAGE edge for Students provides a personalized approach to help you accomplish your coursework goals in an easy-to-use learning environment.

Chapter 5

LEARNING OBJECTIVES

After studying this chapter, you will be able to:

- Discuss the relationship between language and culture.
- Critique and apply the Sapir-Whorf hypothesis.
- Give examples of translation problems that impede intercultural communication.
- Give examples of how humans have communicated in language when there is no shared language.
- Explain the relationship between language and nationalism.
- Trace the development of English as the most widely spread language around the world.

Language as a Barrier

From Chapter 2, you know that language can be a barrier to intercultural communication. What, then, is meant by *language*? One definition of language is that it's a set of symbols shared by a community to communicate meaning and experience. The symbols may be sounds or gestures, as in American Sign Language. Of the estimated 7,100 languages spoken today, each has unique sounds, words, and structures.

In this chapter, as was done in the previous chapter with nonverbals, language will be shown to relate to other factors in culture in the discussion of the Sapir-Whorf hypothesis. You will learn about this hypothesis, which states that the world as we know it is predetermined by the language of our culture. Then you'll read criticisms of the Sapir-Whorf hypothesis and a more commonly accepted perspective of linguistic relativity.

This chapter also deals with two ways in which language affects intercultural communication: translation problems between languages and language as nationalism. Like nonverbals, words as symbols become barriers when their full meaning is not shared. Even speakers of the same language do not share exactly the same meaning for every word. That problem is compounded when you attempt translation between languages. The second way that language becomes a barrier is linguistic imperialism, that is, when the use of a particular language is forced on a people by those with more power.

Linguists study the words in languages and then look for similar-sounding words with similar meanings in different languages. In order to read Hindu legal texts, Sir William Jones, a judge in Calcutta at the end of the

Cat, chat, katze, katte, kot—all arbitrary words to refer to a furry domesticated carnivorous mammal with four legs and a tail noted for its skill at catching mice.

Fred E. Jandt

18th century, began to study Sanskrit, the ancient language of northern India. He found similarities between Sanskrit words and ancient Greek and Latin words and argued that the languages were derived from a common mother tongue. Scholars in the 19th century were inspired by this suggestion and began studying languages for their common ancestors.

Sapir-Whorf Hypothesis

Development of the Hypothesis

Many academic disciplines refer to the Sapir-Whorf hypothesis (also known as the Whorfian thesis) when accounting for the differences in languages across cultures (J. B. Carroll, 1956). Benjamin L. Whorf (1897–1941), a successful fire prevention engineer at the Hartford Fire Insurance Company, came into contact with the noted linguistic anthropologist Edward Sapir (1884–1939) through a course that Sapir (1921) was teaching at Yale. Largely self-taught, Whorf had studied ancient Hebraic, Aztec, and Mayan cultures, and in the 1930s he went to the U.S. Southwest to study the Hopi's Uto-Aztecan language. Among Whorf's observations were that the Hopi do not

- pluralize nouns referring to time, such as *days* and *years*. Instead, time is viewed as a duration.
- use words denoting phases of a cycle, such as *summer* as a phase of a year, as nouns. Whorf suggested that the Hopi view of time is the perpetual "getting later" of time.
- see time as linear in that there are no tenses in the language. Whorf observed that the Hopi have no words, grammatical forms, constructions, or expressions that refer to time.

Whorf's papers, written in the 1930s on the Hopi language, produced exact and documented expression of the Sapir-Whorf hypothesis that reality is embedded in culture's language and that language then controls thought and cultural norms. Each of us lives not in the midst of the whole world but only in that part of the world that our language permits us to know. Thus, the world as each of

Focus on Theory 5.1

Chomsky and Generative Grammar

Based on the observation that children learn their native languages so easily and quickly, major linguists, such as Noam Chomsky (1980), argue that all human brains have an innate set of linguistic principles, or Universal Grammar, that underlies the structure of all languages. This approach, known as *generative grammar,* studies grammar as innately possessed. Children need only learn the parochial features of their native languages. From this perspective, cultural differences in language are superficial.

us knows it is predetermined by the language of our culture. And the differences between languages represent basic differences in the worldview of diverse cultures.

Vocabulary

One level of the Sapir-Whorf hypothesis is vocabulary. You can assume that if a language has a particularly rich vocabulary for a thing or activity in comparison to other languages, that thing or activity is important in that culture. The most commonly used example is Eskimo and snow—although this example also has been challenged.

The name *Eskimo* was first applied to the peoples of the Arctic by a Jesuit who heard people using the word *eskimantsik,* which means "eaters of raw meat or fish." Alaska has three native groups: the Aleuts in the Alaska Peninsula and islands beyond; Indians such as the Athapaskan, Haida, and Tlingit; and Eskimo groups such as the Chugach, Koniag, Yupik, and Inupiat, known as the Inuit in Canada and the Inupik in Siberia. It was said that Eskimo languages have many words for different kinds of snow:

qana	falling snow; snowflakes
akilukak	fluffy fallen snow
aput	snow on the ground
kaguklaich	snow drifted in rows
piqsirpoq	drifting snow
qimuqsuq	snowdrift

Because the language has many separate single words to refer to different kinds of snow, then snow must be an important part of these groups' lives (Birke-Smith, 1959). Notice that other languages, such as English, may require several words to describe the same thing. Speakers of diverse languages can perceive all these different conditions of snow—it's just that the Eskimo peoples have more separate single words to refer to these different conditions. The challenge to this example contends that single English words such as *blizzard, dusting,* and *avalanche* exist as equivalents to the Eskimo words.

In a like way, the Hanunoo tribe of the Philippines has 92 separate single words to refer to rice. In fact, in most of the languages of Asia, one word means both *food* and *rice.* Using the Sapir-Whorf hypothesis, you can assume that rice is important in these cultures.

Speakers of Guguyimadjir in the Australian state of Queensland have no words for *right* or *left* but orient their world by the points of the compass, suggesting seeing things in relation to the world as a whole rather than to ourselves. In a similar way, you might assume that a language with a paucity of terms in comparison to other languages to refer to a thing or activity reflects a culture in which that thing or activity is absent or not important. The Yanomamo of southern Venezuela are one of the few societies in the world with a primitive technology. The Yanomamo language has only three numbers, which correspond to "one," "two," and "more than two" in English. The development of technology requires a language that can symbolize mathematics.

Compared to English, Japanese has a rich vocabulary of words to identify seasons of the year. The four seasons are divided into 24 subseasons according to the traditional lunar calendar. And each subseason is divided into the beginning, middle, and end.

Global Voices

The scientist Will Steger is working to establish the impact of climate change on the indigenous people of the Arctic. Hunters he has met on Baffin Island described to him newly arrived creatures in their environment that they have no words for in the Inuktitut language—robins, finches, and dolphins.

Source: Duff-Brown (2007)

Global Voices

It's said that when a Japanese writes a letter, it always begins with a remark on the weather and the season. It will say things like "It is already mid-May, and the young foliage is fresh and green."

Grammar and Syntax

The second level of the Sapir-Whorf hypothesis is grammar and syntax. Whorf felt that grammar had an even greater influence than vocabulary. For example, it has been observed that in the Eskimo language, there is a consistent use of the word *if* rather than *when* in reference to the future. Think of the difference between "When I graduate from college . . ." and "If I graduate from college . . . ." In this example, *when* seems to indicate more certainty than *if*. Linguists have associated the more common use of *if* in the Eskimo language with the harsh environment that Eskimos live in, where life is fragile and there is little control over nature (Chance, 1966).

English word order is typically subject-verb-object. English places emphasis on a doer, on an action taker. Only about a third of English sentences lack a subject. In contrast, 75% of Japanese sentences lack a subject. For example, you are more likely to hear, "I brought my textbook with me" in the United States and hear "Brought book" in Japan. The subject is known by context. Similarly, if you have hiked for a day into a deserted canyon, you might say to yourself, "I feel lonesome." A Japanese hiker would say only "*Samishii*," identifying the experience without the need to identify the subject. Yes, in English, we sometimes speak in abbreviated forms, but we're conscious of it being a shortened version of a more detailed statement. The Japanese speaker is not abbreviating; Japanese does not require the specification of a subject.

Criticisms of the Sapir-Whorf Hypothesis

There are many legitimate criticisms of the extreme linguistic determinism form of the Sapir-Whorf hypothesis (Fishman, 1972; Hoijer, 1954). One criticism has been Whorf's research methods. Whorf may not have even met a member of the Hopi, and his translations of the language seem to emphasize his conclusions when in fact subsequent research by Ekkehart Malotki (1983), a Northern Arizona University professor of languages who standardized a writing system for the Hopi, documented many references to *time* he had found in the Hopi language.

Linguist Steven Pinker presented a strong argument with the case of Idlefonso, an individual without a language who was still numerate and intelligent. When taught sign language, Idlefonso was completely able to communicate experiences and converse (Pinker, 1994). If language determines thought, then Idlefonso would not have been able to think, but he clearly did.

Another criticism is that of translatability. If language determines thought, then at least some concepts would be understandable only in the language in which they were first "thought." Pinker argues that just because it may take more words to translate a concept from one language to another, this is not evidence that the concept cannot be understood by speakers of different languages.

Focus on Theory 5.2

Pinker's Criticisms of Sapir-Whorf

Canadian-born Harvard professor Steven Pinker (1994) published *The Language Instinct* in which he popularized Noam Chomsky's theory that language is an innate faculty of mind and added the controversial idea that language evolved by Darwinian natural selection to solve the specific problem of communication among social hunter-gatherers. Pinker is a major critic of Sapir-Whorf:

> People who remember little else from their college education can rattle off the factoids: . . . the fundamentally different Hopi concept of time, the dozens of Eskimo words for snow. The implication is heavy: the foundational categories of reality are not "in" the world but are imposed by one's culture (and hence can be challenged, perhaps accounting for the perennial appeal of the hypothesis to undergraduate sensibilities).

> But it is wrong, all wrong. The idea that thought is the same thing as language is an example of what can be called a conventional absurdity: a statement that goes against all common sense but that everyone believes because they dimly recall having heard it somewhere and because it is so pregnant with implications.

Source: Pinker (1994, p. 57).

Linguistic Relativism

Very few today accept the extreme position of the Sapir-Whorf linguistic determinism that our thoughts and actions are determined by the language we speak; many more accept the view that language only somehow shapes our thinking and behavior. In this interpretation, linguistic characteristics and cultural norms influence each other. Steinfatt (1989), in an extensive review of the literature, argues that the basis of linguistic relativism is that the difference between languages is not what can be said but what is relatively easy to say.

There has been significant recent research to support the linguistic relativism position. One study demonstrated a relationship between culture and grammar. Dunn, Greenhill, Levinson, and Gray (2011) demonstrated cultural effects in language development. The research employed biological tools to construct evolutionary trees for four language families and showed that each followed its own idiosyncratic structural rules. This is evidence that even language rules are influenced by culture rather than innate rules.

Another study that demonstrated the interrelationship between language and culture was reported by Nisbett (2003). Remember the thesis that Westerners favor decontextualization and object emphasis and that Easterners favor integration and relationships in perception. If linguistic relativism is valid, then it should make a difference which language bilingual speakers are speaking. First, though, *bilingual speakers* should be defined. Coordinate bilingual speakers are people who learn a second language later in life and who typically use their second language in a limited number of contexts. Compound bilingual speakers are people who learned a second language early in life and use the

Global Voices

When you lose a culture, you're not losing a failed attempt at modernity. You're losing a unique set of answers to the question of what it means to be human.

—Edmund Wade Davis,
Light at the Edge of the World
(quoted in Hayden, 2003, para. 5).
Davis is a Canadian anthropologist,
ethnobotanist, and photographer whose
work has focused on indigenous cultures,
particularly in North and South America.

language in many different contexts. For example, many people from China and Taiwan learn English later in life, while people from Hong Kong and Singapore tend to learn English earlier and use it in many different contexts.

Mainland and Taiwanese Chinese tested in their native language were twice as likely to group on the basis of relationships, whether they were tested in their home country or in the United States. When tested in English, they were much less likely to group on the basis of relationships. The conclusion is that English served as a different way of representing the world than Chinese for this group.

While compound bilinguals from Hong Kong and Singapore grouped on the basis of relationships, the preference was much weaker than for the coordinate Chinese and Taiwanese speakers. And it made no difference for the compound speakers whether they were tested in Chinese or in English. The researchers concluded that

> there is an effect of culture on thought independent of language . . . because both the coordinate Chinese speakers and the compound Chinese speakers group words differently from Americans regardless of language of testing. The differences between coordinate and compound speakers also indicate a culture difference independent of language. The compound speakers from Westernized regions are shifted in a Western direction—and to the same extent regardless of language of testing. (Nisbett, 2003, pp. 161–162)

Case Study: Arabic and the Arab Culture

As a demonstration of the Sapir-Whorf hypothesis, you can use the following case study to learn about Arab culture from the characteristics of the Arabic language that are presented. As you read this section, identify elements of Arab culture that you see in the following description of the language.

Arabic is spoken in one form or another by more than 295 million first-language speakers. Because Arabic is strongly interconnected with the religion Islam, the Sapir-Whorf hypothesis explains the critical importance of the religion to the culture. The Qur'an is the ultimate standard for Arabic style and grammar. Islam has had major effects on both written and spoken Arabic. Classical Arabic, the language of the Qur'an, is the accepted standard for the written language (Asuncion-Lande, 1983). As Islam spread throughout the world, so too did spoken Arabic, as all Muslims, regardless of nationality, must use Arabic in their daily ritual prayers (*salat*).

Like any language, spoken Arabic continues to evolve and varies from country to country. In classical Arabic, the number 2 is *ithnayn,* but *tween* is used in Lebanon, *itneen* in Egypt, and *ithneen* in Kuwait. Perhaps because of the influences of the Qur'an, Arabic withstood Turkish-Ottoman occupation and colonial empires and changed less than would have been expected. Advocates of Arab unity continue to work to unify and purify the spoken language. Modern standard Arabic is used, for example, at Arab League meetings, in radio and television news broadcasts, and in books and newspapers. Nonetheless, English or French is still the second language in the region.

Arabic style attempts to go beyond reflecting human experience to transcending the human experience. As Merriam (1974) noted, Al-Sakkaki divided rhetoric into three parts: *al ma'ani* is the part dealing with grammatical forms and kinds of sentences, *al-bayan* refers to modes for achieving lucid style and clarity of expression, and *al-badi* (literally "the science of metaphors") refers to the beautification of style and the embellishment of speech. Skillful use of language commands prestige. Arabic vocabulary is rich. For example, there are 3,000 words for camel, 800 for sword, 500 for lion, and 200 for snake. Translated into English, Arabic statements often sound exaggerated. Instead of "We missed you," the statement may be "You made us desolate with your absence." It's said that because of the love of language, the Arab is swayed more by words than by ideas and more by ideas than by facts.

Global Voices

Learn a new language and get a new soul.

—Czech proverb

Human beings do not live in the objective world alone, nor alone in the world of social activity as ordinarily understood, but are very much at the mercy of the particular language which has become the medium of expression for their society.

—Edward Sapir, *Selected Writings in Language, Culture, and Personality* (1949, p. 162)

Arabic emphasizes creative artistry through repetition, metaphor, and simile in part because of the poetic influences of the Qur'an. The role that formal poetry, prose, and oratory play is missing today in Western culture. Westerners often find it difficult to locate the main idea of an Arabic message; Arabs often fault Westerners for being insensitive to linguistic artistry. Arabic makes more use of paralanguage—pitch, rhythm, intonation, and inflection—than other languages. The language rhythm can be magical and hypnotic. Higher pitch and greater emotional intonation are natural to Arabic speakers. Speakers of Arabic may talk with a lot of noise and emotion. The rhetoric of confrontation—verbal threats and flamboyant language—is common. What may appear to be a heated argument may just be two friends having a chat. A speaker of Arabic uses language as a mode of aggression. Such verbal aggression essentially diffuses and prevents actual violence.

It's said that when an Arab says yes, it means maybe. When an Arab says maybe, it means no. An Arab seldom says no because it may be considered impolite and close off options. Instead of no, an Arab may say *inshallah,* or "if God is willing." *Inshallah* is used when mentioning a future event of any kind as it is considered sacrilegious to presume to control future events. To mean yes, one must be both repetitive and emphatic.

Translation Problems

Assuming the Sapir-Whorf hypothesis is valid, then translation from one language to another is more than translating one word for another. Each word, each thought, carries with it important information about the culture. Even when cultures speak the same language—as do Australia and the United States—there can be vocabulary differences. Sechrest, Fay, and Zaidi (1972) have identified five translation problems that can become barriers to intercultural communication. Each of these is discussed below. Political leaders in particular want to avoid these translation problems. When President Jimmy Carter greeted the people of Poland on his 1977 trip there, the translator said, "The President says he is pleased to be here in Poland grasping your secret parts" (Axtell, 1994).

Focus on Theory 5.3

Muted Group Theory

Muted group theory (MGT) in communication studies developed as a feminist and intercultural theory. Cheris Kramarae (1981) contends that "the language of a particular culture does not serve all its speakers equally, for not all speakers contribute in an equal fashion to its formulation. Women (and members of other subordinate groups) are not as free or as able as men are to say what they wish, when and where they wish, because the words and the norms for their use have been formulated by the dominant group, men" (p. 1). Kramarae also contends that MGT exists on the Internet. Men dominated the technology fields that created the Internet and used masculine terms to describe it, which continue in use today.

Mark Orbe (1995, 1998) extended Kramarae's ideas to African-American and other co-cultures, subcultures, and subgroups. Dominant White European culture created the illusion that all African-Americans, regardless of gender, age, class, or sexual orientation, communicate in a similar manner. Instead, Orbe points out, muted groups may communicate in various ways, including downplaying differences or avoiding interaction with the dominant group.

Vocabulary Equivalence

First is the lack of *vocabulary equivalence*. Recall the discussions of the Sapir-Whorf hypothesis and the example given that Eskimo languages have many different words to refer to snow. Were you to translate on a word-for-word basis, you would translate all those different words into the one English word *snow*. Much of the meaning of the more specific and more descriptive words—for example, qualities of slushiness or hardness or newness—would be lost in a word-for-word translation. As another example, imagine having to translate all shades of pink, burgundy, orange-red, and so on into the one word *red*. As you might imagine, such a limitation would be frustrating to you if you were accustomed to using more descriptive words.

One frequently quoted example of the lack of vocabulary equivalence is from World War II. The Allies had issued the Potsdam Ultimatum, demanding the surrender of the Japanese military to end the war. At a press conference, Prime Minister Suzuki was asked for his opinion. He responded, "The government does not see much value in it. All we have to do is *mokusatsu* it." The Japanese cabinet had carefully chosen that word to convey their intended meaning. Later, Japanese cabinet officials said they had intended to convey a bland "no comment" at that time, as there was interest in negotiating a surrender and more time was required for discussions. Unfortunately, the word *mokusatsu* can mean anything from "ignore" to "treat with silent contempt." Western translators used the latter meaning, and the Potsdam Ultimatum was then considered to have been rejected. After-the-fact reasoning argues that that translation led to the continuation of the war and the first use of atomic weapons.

Languages that are different often lack words that are directly translatable. Consider the number of English words with different meanings: A U.S. businessperson might write a letter to be translated into Japanese with the sentence "We wonder if you would prepare an agenda for our meeting." The word *wonder* and the construction of this sentence may have been intended as a polite way of telling the Japanese counterpart to prepare the agenda. The word *wonder* could be translated with the Japanese word *gimon,* which most commonly means doubt. The translated sentence now would read,

"We doubt that you would prepare an agenda for our meeting" (Axtell, 1994).

Vocabulary equivalence is a major concern when translating book and movie titles. One of the Hunger Games titles is *The Hunger Games: Mockingjay*. English-speaking audiences can understand *mockingjay* as a bird. Publishers faced the challenges of translating a fictitious bird in English to other languages. The Brazil edition of the book uses the Portuguese work *esperança*, which translates in English as "hope" (Fleishman, 2016).

Global Voices

No one when he uses a word has in mind exactly the same thing that another has, and the difference, however tiny, sends its tremors throughout language. . . . All understanding, therefore, is always at the same time a misunderstanding . . . and all agreement of feelings and thoughts is at the same time a means for growing apart.

—Wilhelm von Humboldt (1767–1835; quoted in Cowan, 1963)

Idiomatic Equivalence

The second barrier to successful translation is the problem of *idiomatic equivalence*. The English language is particularly replete with idioms. Take the simple example of "the old man kicked the bucket." Native speakers know that this idiom means the old man died. If the sentence is translated word for word, the meaning conveyed would be literally that the old man kicked the bucket—quite different from the intended meaning. You can no doubt think of many other examples. Just think of how the idioms out to lunch and *toss your cookies* could cause communication problems!

It's easy to think of many idioms in common use in spoken U.S. English that can be misunderstood: *break a leg, read between the lines, hold your horses*, and *raining cats and dogs*. This is one reason why English is difficult to learn as a second language. However, learning the idioms of a language can be an effective way of learning the culture (W. S. Lee, 1994).

Focus on Technology 5.1

President Trump's Tweets Defy Translation

President Trump's tweets are a challenge for translators. According to former UCLA dean Alessandro Duranti, "He has a certain use of hyperbole. . . . He talks in a way that is not the typical political speech. When there's a choice, he goes for whatever is the most colloquial." Chinese translators struggle with the president's frequent use of hyperboles such as "huge," "enormous," and "tremendous." All translate into the same Mandarin word *da* or "big." Other troublesome words have been "bombed" and "nice."

The president's use of sarcasm in tweets is another challenge. For example, when he tweeted "Interesting how the U.S. sells Taiwan billions of dollars of military equipment, but I should not accept a congratulatory call"; to someone in the United States, that tweet seems to be sarcastic, but the Taiwan news agency interpreted it as expressing regret.

Duranti continued, "He's talking in a way that makes you feel that any person in the United States . . . can listen to him and talk to him." The problem is that his "American everyman language" gets lost in translation.

Source: Simmons (2017).

Grammatical-Syntactical Equivalence

Third is the problem of *grammatical-syntactical equivalence.* This simply means that languages don't necessarily have the same grammar. Often, you need to understand a language's grammar to understand the meaning of words. For example, words in English can be nouns or verbs or adjectives, depending on their position in a sentence. In English, you can say "plan a table" and "table a plan" or "book a place" and "place a book" or "lift a thumb" and "thumb a lift."

Experiential Equivalence

Fourth is the problem of *experiential equivalence.* If an object or experience does not exist in your culture, it's difficult to translate words referring to that object or experience into that language when no words may exist for them. Think of objects or experiences that exist in your culture and not in another. *Department store* and *shopping mall* may be as difficult to translate into some languages as *windsurfing* is into others. Navajo, for example, has no word for computer. Instead, the English word *computer* is translated as "thinking metal."

The experiential equivalence barrier can be seen when a country speaking one language is divided and kept separate for political reasons. One outcome of World War II was a divided Germany. For nearly 50 years the two Germanys were kept separate. During this period the German language in the East and West began to diverge to reflect changing experience. Communist East Germans used words meaning "year-end winged figure" for "Christmas angel," "waving element" (*Winkelement*) for "flag" (*Fahne*) because the people were expected to wave them at parades, and *der antifaschistische Schutzwall* ("antifascist protective wall") for the Berlin Wall, which divided the city of Berlin. The same barrier is developing in North and South Korea. Some estimates are that about a third of everyday words used in the two countries are different. For example, South Koreans have a word for "skin lotion." North Koreans have the word *salgyeolmul*, which translates literally as "skin water."

Table 5.1   Examples of Idioms Worldwide
Sha ji yan yong niu dao! Chinese (Mandarin)
"You moved house and forgot to take your wife!" (You've done something stupid.)
Hitori zumoo o totta! (Japanese)
"Like a one-man sumo match!" (Something that is impossible)
Har du røyka sokka dine? (Norwegian)
"Have you been smoking your socks?" (Are you mad?)
Vai pentear macacos! (Portuguese)
"Go comb a monkey's hair!" (Go do something else; don't bother me.)
Kak ob st'enku gorohk! (Russian)
"Like throwing peas against the wall!" (A useless, impossible task)

Source: Sacher (2012).

Conceptual Equivalence

Fifth, the problem of *conceptual equivalence* refers to abstract ideas that may not exist in the same fashion in different languages. For example, people in the United States have a unique meaning for the word *freedom*. That meaning is not universally shared. Speakers of other languages may say they are free and be correct in their culture, but the freedom they refer to isn't equivalent to what is experienced as freedom in the United States. The English word *corruption* translates as the Korean word *pup'ae*, but the words are not conceptually equivalent. For people in both the United States and Korea, the word connotes negative, bad, improper behavior, but in the United States, corruption is a crime and wrong on moral grounds, whereas in Korea, corruption is not morally wrong. It's wrong in the sense that it interferes with the proper functioning of government and is bad in its social consequences. Even though the word is negative and has similar interpretations, there are sufficient conceptual differences to create intercultural communication misunderstandings (Szalay, Moon, & Bryson, 1971).

A similar misunderstanding can occur with the word *democracy*. To people in both the United States and Korea, democracy means freedom and liberty. In the United States, the meaning of the word places strong emphasis on procedures such as elections, campaigning, and voting, whereas in Korea, the word *democracy* is an abstract ideal. Postcommunist Russians readily embraced the words *democracy, congress,* and *president,* but having just broken with the totalitarian tradition, many had trouble understanding the underlying concepts. In a 1994 interview, former president Jimmy Carter identified conceptual equivalence problems with the term *human rights*. According to Carter, each country defines the term by what it has. In the United States, human rights refers to the Bill of Rights (e.g., freedom of speech, right to a fair trial). In other countries, the term refers to adequate housing or universal health care.

One way to improve translation is to use back translation, which involves first translating into the second language, then translating back into the first language, and then comparing the result to the original. Often, the process can prevent amusing translation problems. For example, on a trip to see Hitler's Eagle's Nest, I was given a ticket for my return trip down the mountain. On the back of the ticket, I found this message translated into English: "The indicated return time must be strictly adhered to. A later return is determined by the disposable bus seats." The misuse of the word *disposable* would probably be caught if the sentence had been translated back into German and then compared to the original German sentence.

Human and Machine Translators

Machine translation dates back to the end of World War II, when coders recognized that cryptography and deciphering were basically math problems. In 1949 Warren Weaver developed the logic that paved the way for today's computation linguistics. One approach to machine translation is to first analyze the syntax of a sentence to identify subject, verb, object, and modifiers. Then, using a dictionary, the words are translated into another language. Finally, the program analyzes the result and generates an intelligible sentence in the new language based on the rules of that language's syntax.

By 1954 computer scientists developed a machine that could translate between Russian and English. The hope of the Georgetown-IBM experiment was that a future universal translator would promote world peace by eliminating language barriers (Li, 2015). We are not there yet, so the need for

Figure 5.1 Google Translate

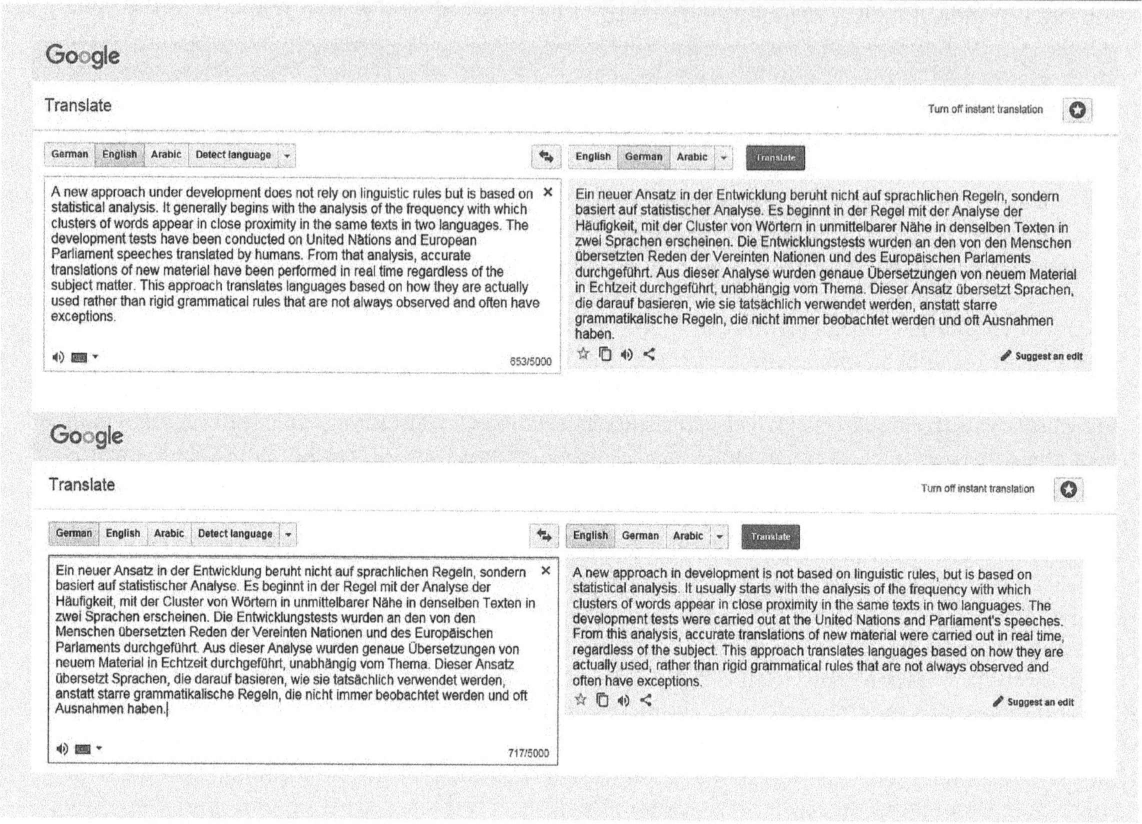

translated by Google

convenient translation has created a business opportunity. In the United States, companies offer live translation over the telephone and video translation to meet the demands of healthcare, insurance, financial services, communications, and government agencies. Language Line Solutions offers translators for over 240 languages. But can computer-translating programs be as accurate as human translators? A new approach under development does not rely on linguistic rules but is based on statistical analysis. It generally begins with the analysis of the frequency with which clusters of words appear in close proximity in the same texts in two languages. The development tests have been conducted on United Nations and European Parliament speeches translated by humans. From that analysis, accurate translations of new material have been performed in real time regardless of the subject matter. This approach translates languages based on how they are actually used rather than rigid grammatical rules that are not always observed and often have exceptions. Google Translate, the most popular machine translation tool, detects these patterns in texts already translated by humans, so the more human-translated documents and books are examined, the more accurate Google Translate is. While

Google Translate supports over 100 languages and translates over 100 billion words daily, the results do not yet approach human translation. A study at Matieland Language Centre compared documents translated between Afrikaans and English by Google Translate and professional human translators. Google Translate scored below average. Google Translate does, however, provide a "good enough" translation to determine what the source text was about.

Machine translation of the spoken voice is more difficult. In *The Hitchhiker's Guide to the Galaxy,* Douglas Adams envisioned for the future a translation device called the Babel Fish, a "small, yellow and leech-like" fish that one stuck in one's ear. One-way handheld voice translators were used by the U.S. military in Afghanistan in 2002. Two-way voice translators involving speech recognition, machine translation, and voice synthesis were developed for handheld devices for use between English and Iraqi Arabic.

Microsoft has developed apps that can translate voice to voice and voice to text as well as text to text. Skype Translator translates video chat into spoken or written translations initially available in seven languages. VoxOx Universal Translator comes close to being a Babel Fish. VoxOx provides real-time translation for text messages (SMS), chat (IM), e-mail, and two-way translated chat on Facebook. Users open their VoxOx Universal Messaging Window, select their language from dozens of major languages and their contact's language, and begin sending text and chat messages, e-mails, or Twitter replies to anyone in the world (Li, 2015).

Pidgins, Creoles, and Universal Languages

When cultures with no shared language came in contact, such as through international trade or during colonialism, one way to communicate without formal translation was through the development of pidgins and creoles. Once thought of as crude, nonstandard languages, they are now central to the study of linguistic development (Holm, 1989; Romaine, 1988).

Pidgins

A pidgin is the mixture of two or more languages to form a new language, originally used for restricted purposes such as trade. As a contact language between diverse language groups, pidgins have widespread use in West Africa. Cameroon used a pidgin drawn from English, German, French, and local words to facilitate communication among some 285 tribal languages. In the western Pacific, European traders, whalers, and missionaries and the hundreds of tribes there developed a pidgin based on English, German, and a local language with a distinctly Melanesian grammar and sentence structure. Melanesian Pidgin English is a pidgin language based on English. Use of Pidgin English became widespread when colonial European plantations were established in the 19th century in Samoa, Fiji, and other places using laborers from New Guinea and the Solomon Islands, an archipelago of several hundred islands spread over 1,000 miles and containing more than 50 languages. In the 20th century, Pidgin English died out in the monolingual communities of Samoa and Fiji but continued to be used in the multilingual communities of Papua New Guinea and the Solomons (Keesing, 1988).

The Papua New Guinea constitution recognizes three national languages: English, Hiri Motu, and Tok Pisin. English is the major language of education and written communication. Hiri Motu is the language of the southern provinces of the mainland. Its use is declining as the use of Tok Pisin expands. Tok Pisin is used in speeches and reports in the National Parliament and in social

Focus on Skills 5.1

Translation in Medical Emergencies

Assume you work in the technical resources department in a large regional privately owned hospital in the United States. The Emergency Department doctors have asked to speak with your department about a continuing problem. When non-English-speaking patients arrive in the Emergency Department with an acute problem, one of the staff's earliest and most emergent problems is rapidly finding and using an interpreter. If non-English-speaking patients bring along someone fluently bilingual in their native language who can be reasonably trusted to interpret objectively, then the immediate language-related problem is solved. However, frequently the bilingual people who come with the patients are children who are neither bilingually fluent nor necessarily objective. But given that the need for speed in making the diagnosis and administering treatment takes precedence over the need for full fluency and full objectivity, doctors often use children as young as 5 or 6 to quickly interpret for their parents. If patients come alone, doctors frequently grab anyone nearby who could help: nurses, delivery people, housekeepers, and so on. These are often "lifesavers" in the quest to save lives, but they may lack the ideal qualities of fluency, trustworthiness, and objectivity.

1. The doctors want you to recommend a non-human translation device that can deal with the vocabulary that speakers of various languages might use to describe their life-and-death medical concerns. Carefully research the latest technology available before making your recommendation.

2. What protocols would you recommend be put in place to ensure accurate translation?

interaction among people of diverse language backgrounds. It was spoken when Prince Charles of Great Britain opened Papua New Guinea's National Parliament during independence celebrations in 1975. And in 1984, Pope John Paul II celebrated Mass in New Guinea in pidgin (Romaine, 1992).

Pidgins are still being formed today. Ghana, Nigeria, and Singapore are developing versions of English. Singapore's Singlish combines English with Malay and the Chinese language Kokkien. "That's really very sayang lah" has no direct translation but conveys the feeling of "what a waste or pity."

Creoles

Today, a creole is defined as a new language developed from prolonged contact of two or more languages (Bickerton, 1981). Whereas a pidgin can be thought of as a second language, a creole is acquired by children as their first language. Creoles were largely the product of the colonial era. Creoles are concentrated in areas where slave labor was used—the Caribbean, the Indian Ocean, and the Pacific Islands. Typically, creoles incorporate the vocabulary of the dominant language with the grammar and some words from the subordinate language to become the new language of the subordinate group. The most well-known creoles are Jamaican Patois, a mixture of English and West African languages, with more than 2 million speakers, and French-based Haitian, with some 5 million speakers. These are used increasingly in newspapers and radio.

In Macao, a patois, or dialect, developed from Portuguese and Cantonese words in combinations such as *compra som,* meaning to buy groceries, from the Portuguese *compra* and the Cantonese *som,* and *avo gong,* which joins the Portuguese and Cantonese terms for grandfather.

Esperanto

Would communication between individuals of diverse cultures be improved if we all spoke one language? There have been attempts to construct such a universal language. The only moderately successful attempt was Esperanto, devised in 1887 by Polish oculist and philologist Lazarus Zamenhof when he was 19 years old. Zamenhof wrote under the name of Doktoro Esperanto, or "one who hopes."

Esperanto is a simplified, regular language with Latin-type grammar and European vocabulary. It is claimed that one can learn the language in 100 hours or less. Estimates of the number of speakers of Esperanto today range from 1 million to 2 million worldwide, with some 1,000 native speakers who learned the language as children. Vatican Radio, Cuba, and China broadcast programs in Esperanto, and on its 100th anniversary, an Esperanto version of the play *The Importance of Being Earnest* was presented in London.

When Esperanto was devised, English was the language of commerce, French of diplomacy, and German of science. Today, English, rather than Esperanto, has become the universal language of all three. Some see Esperanto as an alternative to the growing use of English as it is easier to learn than English.

Esperanto and other attempts at universal languages are not successful precisely for the reasons described earlier in this chapter as characteristics of language itself. Universal languages are artificial languages; they have no relationship to a culture—hence they are static and don't change and evolve as a culture changes and evolves. Nor do universal languages reflect the worldview of any culture. Any universal first language would probably begin to develop unique regional vocabularies and pronunciations over time and would then again begin to reflect cultural differences as the regional dialects grew further apart.

Language as Nationalism

Language is central to national identity. In 1846, Jacob Grimm, one of the Grimm brothers known for fairytales and a forerunner of modern comparative and historical linguistics, said that "a nation is the totality of people who speak the same language" (King, 1997). When Norway, Ireland, and Israel became independent states, each adopted a largely defunct language (Norse, Gaelic, and Hebrew, respectively) as an official language as necessary for national identity. Even Belgium is experiencing pressures along linguistic lines—the Dutch-speaking north and the French-speaking south. Citizens of the former Yugoslavia spoke roughly the same language, Serbo-Croat, with regional differences. Today, the nationalist regimes that rule Muslim, Serbian, and Croatian parts of Bosnia are adding new words and changing spellings and pronunciations to distinguish their language and national identity. In most post-Soviet countries, instruction at public universities is now almost exclusively in their native ethnic languages.

When a group with more power enforces the use of its language on another group, it also is making its culture dominant. The Brazilian Paulo Freire (1970) used the term cultural invasion to refer to one group penetrating the culture of another group to impose its own view of the world. Cultural invasion can be physical and overt as in war and political takeover, or it can be indirect or even in the form of assistance. The spread of a language to common use around a region also means the spreading influence of the culture native to that language.

We'll first look at an attempt to unify a region under a common language and then look in depth at the growing dominance of English worldwide.

Kiswahili in East Africa

There are various understandings of what countries make up the region known as East Africa. Tanzania, Kenya, Uganda, Burundi, and Rwanda are the members of the East African Community, but sometimes Burundi and Rwanda are considered part of Central Africa. Especially in English, the term *East Africa* refers to the three countries of Kenya, Tanzania, and Uganda (Ojwang, 2008).

Kenya is a country of 47 million composed of many ethnic groups: Kikuyu 22%, Luhya 14%, Luo 13%, Kalenjin 12%, Kamba 11%, Kisii 6%, Meru 6%, other African 15%, and non-African (Asian, European, and Arab) 1%. Kiswahili and English are the official languages. Tanzania is a country of 52 million. The population is 95% Bantu, consisting of more than 130 tribes. Kiswahili and English are the official languages. Uganda is a country of 38 million and also composed of many ethnic groups: Baganda 16.5%, Banyankole 9.6%, Basoga 8.8%, Bakiga 7.1%, Iteso 7.0%, Langi 6.3%, Bagisu 4.9%, Acholi 4.4%, Lugbara 3.3%, and other 32.1%. English is the official language. Ganda or Luganda, the most widely used of the Niger-Congo languages, is also used in publications and schools (Central Intelligence Agency, 2013). Today an estimated 5 million people speak Kiswahili as their native language and 135 million more worldwide are able to speak it as a second language. In Kenya and Tanzania, the majority of the population speak Kiswahili in addition to their first languages.

Kiswahili vocabulary includes many words of Arabic origin from contact with Arabic-speaking traders. It also includes many words of German, Portuguese, English, Hindi, and French origin, again due to contact with traders, slavers, and colonial officials. Kiswahili may have its soundest foundation in Tanzania. German colonial officials collected and translated Kiswahili manuscripts. Kiswahili is taught in several universities in Germany as well as other European and U.S. universities. In 1893

"Caution Children" sign in Gaelic in Ireland.

"Welcome to Serengeti National Park" in English and Kiswahili.

Tim Graham/Getty Images News/Getty Images

ullstein bild/ullstein bild/Getty Images

Map 5.1   The East African Community

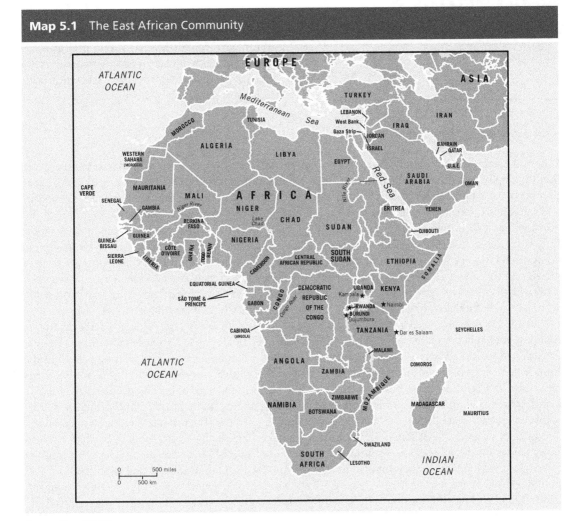

Source: Nau (2012).

the Germans established a school to train all middle-level officials in the language. When the British gained control of Tanzania, they allowed Kiswahili to continue to be taught along with English (King'ei, 2005).

The East African Community was formed in 1967 but dissolved in 1977. The union was revived in 2000. There are hopes for economic integration, a common currency, and a single government. The member states share a geography and a history. The question remains whether a common language can be adopted and serve to facilitate a shared identity.

In his complete analysis of the challenges, Ojwang (2008) identifies a few key considerations. Particularly in the rural areas of Kenya and Uganda, knowledge of Kiswahili is rudimentary. Non-regional languages are now finding growing support on radio stations and in popular music. And

Global Voices

The English language hasn't got where it is by being pure.

—Carl Sandburg

there is growing awareness of the need to maintain and develop the local vernacular languages in schools and government. Nonetheless, Kiswahili may grow to become the regional language of East Africa as it is the only language in Africa free from any association with an ethnicity-conscious tribe (Ojwang, 2008).

The Spread of English

Even though at one time it could not have been predicted, of particular concern today is the spread of English. English did not exist when Julius Caesar invaded Britain in 55 BCE. The Celts spoke languages that survive today as Welsh, Gaelic, and Breton. In the mid-5th century, the Jutes (modern Denmark) and the Saxons (Germany) migrated to the south of Britain, and the Angles (Germany) migrated to the north and east of Britain. The Germanic invaders intermarried with the existing population but took little from the language of the Celts. Place names and the language changed to those of the migrants. Soon assimilation of words from other languages began. First came Latin from Christian missionaries arriving in 597, then Old Norse from Danish invaders, then French from Norman rule (Stevenson, 1999). English kept its relatively simple Germanic structure while adding a huge vocabulary of French words. Even before Columbus, English had borrowed words from 50 languages.

In 1582, a scholar observed, "The English tongue is of small reach, stretching no further than this island of ours, nay not there over all" (quoted in Mencken, 1935, p. 541). In little more than 25 years, English had spread across the ocean and has not stopped expanding since. The printing press and the European Renaissance added thousands of words to the English vocabulary. In 1780, John Adams moved for the creation of an academy to keep the English language pure. His proposal died in the Continental Congress. The *Oxford English Dictionary* contains more than 750,000 English words. While comparisons are difficult to make, it is generally agreed that English has the largest vocabulary.

In early colonial days, some 5 million people spoke English. By 1930, the number had risen to 200 million. By the mid-1960s, counting those who used English as a second language, the number of people speaking English had doubled to 400 million. By 1990, that number had risen to about 750 million, or one of every seven people. Figure 5.2 shows the world's most widely spoken first languages. While Mandarin has the most speakers, with second language speakers English is the most widely spread around the world.

Today's estimate is that one-fifth to one-fourth of the world's population is familiar with English (Ostler, 2005). English is an official language in some 60 sovereign states and 28 nonsovereign states. Consider this: An Argentine pilot landing in Turkey speaks to the air traffic controller in English. English is the de facto language of aviation worldwide. Today, half of the world's published books are in English. A German physicist publishes findings in English-language journals. Japanese executives conduct business in Mexico in English. And in 2009, the Texas-bordering state of Tamaulipas declared itself the first Spanish and English bilingual state in Mexico. Its 320,000 public school students will learn conversational English. It's the most widely studied and most borrowed-from language in the world.

English has grown to dominate in the areas of science, technology, commerce, tourism, diplomacy, and pop culture. CNN International and MTV broadcast in English. Western companies today are outsourcing customers to call centers in southern India. The agents are trained in U.S. or British accents and popular culture such as sports teams and television shows. One Indian author and outspoken foe of globalization condemns the adoption of U.S. English accents for jobs in call centers as

Figure 5.2 Most Widely Spoken First Languages in the World

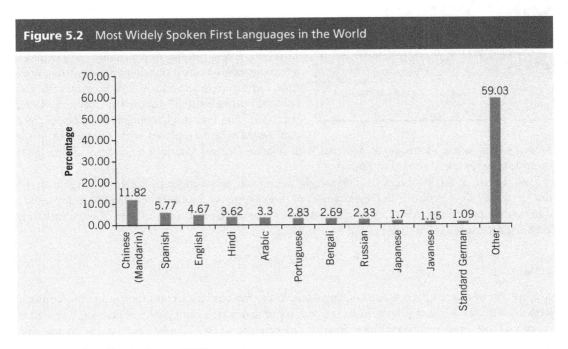

Source: Central Intelligence Agency (2017).

showing "how easily an ancient civilization can be made to abase itself completely" (quoted in Duff-Brown, 2001).

Academic discourse refers to the language used in research and in disseminating knowledge and ideas in university disciplines in lectures, dissertations, conference presentations, and research articles. English dominates the world of academic discourse. More than 90% of the journal articles in some sciences and 68% of the 58,698 periodicals indexed by Ulrich's Periodical Directory in 2007 were published in English (Hyland, 2009). Scholars worldwide are compelled to publish in English. If thinking and discourse cannot be separated, then it can be said that English dominates academic thought and practices.

The Internet was developed in the United States, and the overwhelming majority of websites, newsgroups, and chat rooms are based in the United States. Internet search engines are largely in English. Even computer keyboards are typically based on the English alphabet. Former French

Bloomberg/Bloomberg/Getty Images

Call center in Manila, the Philippines

Global Voices

The invasion of English words is a more "serious threat" to Gallic identity than the Nazi occupation of World War II.

—Avenir de la Langue Française

president Jacques Chirac told la Francophonie, a group formed in France to preserve the use of French in cyberspace, "If in this new medium our language, our programs, our creations don't have a strong presence, our future generations will be economically and culturally marginalized" (quoted in Romero, 1996, para. 10). The French government has since decreed that *e-mail* will be replaced with *courriel*, from the French words *courier electronique*, and *chat* with *eblabla*. General Charles De Gaulle made it a point of pride to never speak a word of English.

As the use of English becomes increasingly worldwide, more concerns are voiced that it carries the "baggage" of one culture. In the remainder of this chapter we'll look at how English has spread to dominate in India, South Africa, Australia and New Zealand, Canada, and the United States, including Hawai'i, American Indian nations, and Puerto Rico.

India

A more extreme case of the spread of English is India, the world's second most populous country, with more than 1.3 billion people. India is a country of diversity: a multiplicity of languages as well as religions, castes, and living conditions. Since its independence in 1947, India has struggled to maintain a society that values the country's diverse linguistic, religious, and historic groups.

India's people speak 20 major languages and hundreds of dialects. When India became an independent country in 1947, Hindi was slated to become the national language by 1965. But as 1965 approached, the use of Hindi had not spread. Today Hindi is the most widely spoken language, with 41% of the population. Hindi speakers concentrated in the north claim that English is elitist and a holdover from the colonial past. India is slowly eradicating the legacy of British colonial rule by renaming cities and streets. Madras is now Chennai, Calcutta is now Kolkata, and Bombay is now Mumbai. The new name of Mumbai is taken from the Marathi name for a Hindu goddess. As India's financial and entertainment center, Mumbai attracts migrants from across India who speak scores of languages in addition to English and Hindi. Store signs in the city were typically in English until a 1961 law made it mandatory to use local script. Even so, merchants displayed small Marathi signs next to large English ones.

From among India's officially recognized languages, individual states are free to adopt their own language of administration and education. Every citizen has the right to petition the government in any of the official languages. Yet English is India's most important language for national, political, and commercial communication. English speakers, largely in the south, argue that Hindi as an official language would exclude those who don't speak it.

India has 340 million Internet users. Currently, as the predominant language on the Internet in India is English, Facebook is the top social network in the country. The most popular local website in India, particularly among students, is Bharatstudent.com. The extent of social media use in India became known during the terrorist attacks in Mumbai in 2008. An estimated 80 eyewitness tweets were being sent via Twitter every 5 seconds. Mumbai-based bloggers turned their Metroblog into a news wire service, and the blog MumbaiHelp offered to help users get through to their family and friends in the city or to get information about them (Busari, 2008).

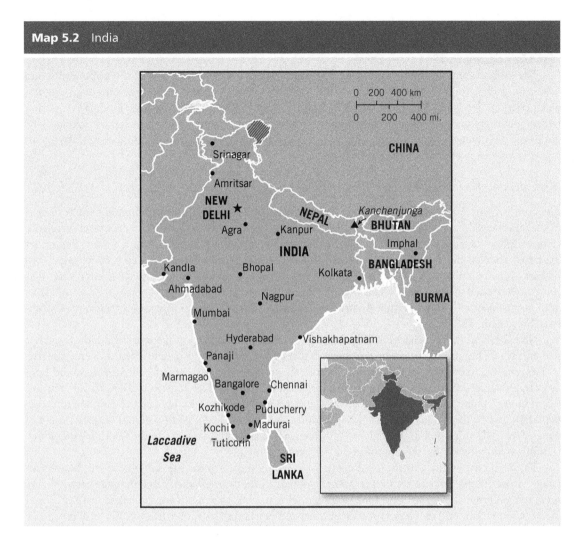

Map 5.2 India

South Africa

The first Dutch settlement on the southern tip of Africa dates back to 1652, followed by the arrival of Dutch, German, and French Huguenot immigrants (later known as Afrikaners or as Boers by the British). Dutch became the official language of that colony, but within 150 years, it had been replaced with Afrikaans, perhaps the world's youngest language and the only Germanic language born outside Europe.

Afrikaans was derived from 17th-century Dutch and reflects the influences of Malay, Portuguese, German, French, English, and native African languages. It represents a cultural tradition of self-sufficiency and Calvinist morality. For many years, speakers of Afrikaans were the oppressed under British colonial rule. But in 1925, Afrikaans joined English as one of the country's two official languages. From then on it earned the reputation among Blacks as the language of oppression. The most widely known word in the Afrikaans vocabulary is *apartheid*—literally "apart-hood" or separateness—the name for government-sanctioned segregation of racial and ethnic groups that ended with Nelson Mandela's election in 1994.

The most commonly spoken languages in South Africa are isiZulu (23% of the population) and isiXhosa (16%), followed by Afrikaans (14%), Sepedi, English (perceived as the language of colonial heritage), Setswani, Sesotho, Xitsonga, siSwati, Tshivenda, and isiNdebele. English is the first language for less than 10% of the population, but it is gaining popularity as the second language. The multitude of languages became a major factor in developing a new constitution. English and Afrikaans join nine others as official languages.

Australia and New Zealand

The continent of Australia, along with the island state of Tasmania, is approximately equal in area to the continental United States. The first English speakers to arrive in number in Australia were convicts and their guards, who put ashore in 1788 at the penal colony of Botany Bay. (Convicted under the penal code of the day, their offenses would be considered minor today.) The convict argot was known as flash and was so incomprehensible to speakers of Standard English that an interpreter was sometimes needed in the courts. Flash began to die out as former convicts joined new English and Irish immigrants in developing a unique Australian English with some words borrowed from the Aboriginals (Stevenson, 1999).

New Zealand English shares much with Australia's, but each has unique words and idioms. After seal and whale hunters came, other European traders and merchants, primarily British, were attracted by flax, forests, and trade with the Māori. Māori, the indigenous language of New Zealand, and English are recognized as official languages in New Zealand. The Māori constitute 14% of the nation's 4.5 million population. Māori is an Austronesian language similar to Hawaiian and Samoan and particularly close to the language of the Cook Islands and Tahiti. There were regional dialects, some of which diverged radically, but they have lost influence to a standard dialect. On the South Island, which is dominated by one tribe, the Southern dialect persists.

The final two decades of the 20th century saw an enthusiasm for the survival of the Māori language. Most notable were the efforts of Māori women to establish *kōhanga reo* (language nests), where preschool children are introduced to the language. The first *kōhanga reo* was established in 1982. There are now more than 460 that have provided immersion education for more than 60,000 children.

Canada

The situation in Canada is unique. More than 200 years ago, Canada's French settlers were defeated by the British Army on a Quebec field called the Plains of Abraham. New France then became British, but the French settlers were permitted to maintain their language (French) and religion (Roman Catholicism). By itself, Quebec would be the world's 18th largest country in size. Its population is about 8 million, roughly one-quarter of Canada's population.

Through the years, Quebec has maintained a vision of itself as a French-speaking society. Several generations chose to keep their language and culture. Canadian French has retained characteristics of the language of the 18th century. To the modern French, Canadian French has a somewhat monotonous intonation and lacks articulation (Stevenson, 1999). Colloquialism, slang, and accents differ widely. Quebec supports French-language artists, newspapers, radio, and television. More than 80% of its population speaks French as the first language.

Focus on Technology 5.2

Bilingual Social Media in Canada

Prime Minister Pierre Trudeau's government enacted Canada's two-language policy in 1969. All communication from or regulated by the federal government must appear in both French and English. Today's social media raise questions about federal ministers' use of Facebook, Instagram, Snapchat, and tweets. Prime Minister Justin Trudeau, son of Pierre Trudeau, makes a point of tweeting in both languages (Guly, 2015).

In the 1950s, Quebec began to protest the use of English. In response, the federal government appointed the Royal Commission on Bilingualism and Biculturalism. The commission first recommended that Canadians of French origin be brought into full participation in Canadian life and later included all other cultural groups. In 1971, the prime minister announced officially that Canada would be bilingual and multicultural. Officially a two-language country, Canada continues to deal with a strong separatist movement in Quebec. Quebec has never ratified the Canadian constitution because it is believed that it fails to protect the province's minority French language and culture. In 1977, Quebec established a French-only policy enforced by 400 "language police." Its inhabitants refer to the rest of Canada as "English Canada" and propose withdrawing from English-speaking Canada. The phrase *nous et les autres* (us and the others) united Quebecers against the English-speaking Canadians and the fast-growing immigrant population that claims neither French nor English as its first language.

©iStockphoto.com/BrookePierce

Canadian border sign in English and French.

United States

Whereas Canada has two official languages and India many, the United States has none. Nowhere does the U.S. Constitution provide for an official language. German, French, Greek, and Hebrew were suggested, and in 1795 Congress did consider a proposal to print federal laws in German as well as English. At the time of independence, the second language in the United States was a form of German known as Pennsylvania Dutch or Pennsylvania German. Half the population of Pennsylvania spoke German. Even an 1863 Pennsylvania law mandated that all official notices appear in German-language newspapers. German was the country's most common second language during the 19th century. Figure 5.3 shows the languages spoken at home today.

Since independence, there have been times when some have pressed to make English the official language of the United States. In the 1870s, faced with large numbers of Chinese immigrants, California considered English-only laws. Later, with the large number of central and southeastern European

Figure 5.3   Selected Languages Other Than English Spoken in U.S. Homes

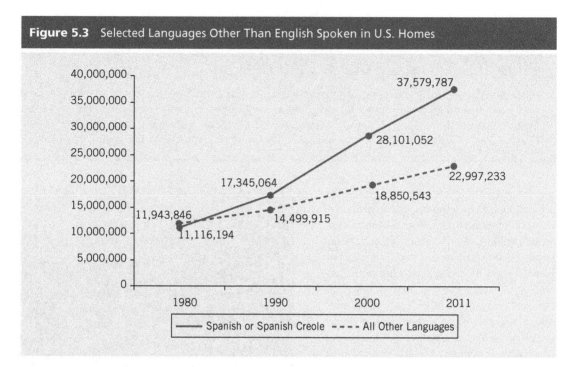

	1980	1990	2000	2011	Percentage change 1980–2011
Total	23,060,040	31,844,979	46,951,595	60,577,020	162.7
Vietnamese	197,588	507,069	1,009,627	1,419,539	618.4
Russian	173,226	241,798	706,242	905,843	422.9
Chinese	630,806	1,319,462	2,022,143	2,882,497	357.0
Korean	266,280	626,478	894,063	1,141,277	328.6
Spanish or Spanish Creole	11,116,194	17,345,064	28,101,052	37,579,787	238.1
Tagalog	474,150	843,251	1,224,241	1,594,413	236.3
Polish	820,647	723,483	667,414	607,531	minus 26.0
German	1,586,593	1,547,987	1,383,442	1,083,637	minus 31.7
Italian	1,618,344	1,308,648	1,008,370	723,632	minus 55.3

Sources: Ortman & Shin (2011); Ryan (2013).

Note: The Census Bureau collected language data in the 1980, 1990, and 2000 censuses. Beginning in 2010, the question was no longer asked but is now asked each year on the American Community Survey.

immigrants at the turn of the 20th century, the United States made oral English literacy a requirement for naturalization in 1906. Still later, during and after World War I, anti-German sentiment led some states to ban German, remove German-language books from libraries, and close German-language theaters (Crawford, 1992). Those laws were declared unconstitutional. During World War II, German-speaking residents of the United States experienced humiliation and insult because of their accents. Since 1950, the requirement for citizenship has been "to read, write, and speak words in ordinary English." Even so, the United States has had a long history of non-English-speaking immigrants. In 1848, Cincinnati, Ohio, had the first bilingual school, serving the German-American community. In the early 1900s, a dozen states had bilingual education, with at least 4% of students receiving all or part of their instruction in German. At one time, more than 4,100 schools taught German (Grosjean, 1982). By 1920, 75% of the population of some cities was foreign born. Several cities and states printed some official documents in languages other than English (Crawford, 1992).

By permission of Mike Thompson and Creators Syndicate, Inc.

Translated into English: "Welcome to Bosnia" . . . "Quebec separatists want to know what's wrong with dividing a nation along cultural boundaries."

Before 1980, only two states had official-English laws: Nebraska in 1920 and Illinois in 1923. By 2016, the number had grown to 32. By the 1950s, Spanish had effectively become the second language. In the 1980s, the official-English movement became active, due in large part to the high numbers of Hispanic immigrants, some of whom had not assimilated as quickly as earlier immigrants. Immigrant children have been taught the Pledge of Allegiance in foreign languages, and the Immigration and Naturalization Service has conducted citizenship ceremonies in Spanish.

Table 5.2 shows the U.S. metropolitan areas with the highest percentage of Spanish-speaking populations.

It is said that it's possible to live a full life in Miami without ever learning English. Miami has bilingual stores and restaurants, Spanish print and electronic media, and jobs for which only Spanish is required. Miami had an English-only ordinance but has since repealed it. In 2006 an ensemble of Latino pop music stars sang a Spanish-language version of "The Star Spangled Banner" called "Nuestro Himno" on Spanish-language radio stations to inspire solidarity for a protest over immigration reform. President George W. Bush voiced his opinion that the national anthem should be English-only.

In 1969, the federal government began providing funds for programs to help children with limited English. In 1974, the Supreme Court ruled in *Lau v. Nichols,* a class-action suit against the San Francisco Unified School District, that schools that don't provide special help for children with limited English are violating these students' civil rights. In the Court's language,

Table 5.2 U.S. Metropolitan Areas With the Highest Percentage of Spanish-Speaking Populations	
McAllen-Edinburg-Mission, TX	84.3%
El Paso, TX	72.4%
Miami-Fort Lauderdale-Pompano Beach, FL	39.8%
Los Angeles-Long Beach-Santa Ana, CA	36.7%
San Antonio-New Braunfels, TX	36.2%
Bakersfield-Delano, CA	35.9%
Riverside-San Bernardino-Ontario, CA	34.2%
Fresno, CA	32.4%
Modesto, CA	31.6%
Oxnard-Thousand Oaks-Ventura, CA	30.2%

Source: U.S. Census Bureau, 2010 American Community Survey.

The failure of the San Francisco school system to provide English language instruction to approximately 1,800 students of Chinese ancestry who do not speak English, or to provide them with other adequate instructional procedures, denies them a meaningful opportunity to participate in the public educational program and thus violates . . . the Civil Rights Act of 1964. (*Lau v. Nichols,* 1974)

In effect, the Court held that there was no equality of treatment of students who don't understand English.

As its ruling didn't specify what form this help should take, the Court did not require bilingual education. The Federal Bilingual Education Act of 1978 defined bilingual education as a program of instruction designed for children of limited English proficiency to achieve competence in English and to progress effectively through the education system.

Some arguments to make English the official language point to the millions spent on bilingual education, bilingual ballots, high school equivalency diploma tests, driving tests in foreign languages, and instant translation of court proceedings for defendants who don't speak English. Emergency and health care organizations would face a burden of providing information in all the languages spoken in the United States.

One of the organizations supporting official-English laws was founded with the guidance of former U.S. senator S. I. Hayakawa. U.S. English, a political lobbying organization, argues that because of the influx of Hispanic immigrants, the United States risks becoming divided linguistically and culturally like Canada. Between 1984 and 1988, 12 states passed

Global Voices

Until recent times, perhaps the U.S. has been the only country in which to speak two languages was a mark of low status.

—Edward C. Stewart, *American Cultural Patterns* (1972, p. 56)

Global Voices

As a nation built by immigrants, it is important that we share one vision and one official language.

—U.S. Senator Jim Inhofe (R.-Okla.) and U.S. Representative Steve King (R.-Iowa) reintroduced legislation in 2011 to make English the official language of the U.S. government

resolutions making English the official language. During the 1996 election campaign, the U.S. House of Representatives passed the English Language Empowerment Act, which would make English the official language. And in 2006, the U.S. Senate voted to declare English the "national language" in an amendment to an immigration bill. Neither of these measures became law. Generally, the laws don't affect what language is spoken in homes or in neighborhoods, but they do prohibit the states from printing documents, such as voter information pamphlets, in other languages.

So far, courts have shown a tendency to reverse restrictions from official-English ordinances. In 1988, Arizona voters approved by 50.5% an initiative that made English the official language of the state and the language of "all government functions and actions." A lawsuit was filed by a Spanish-speaking state employee saying the measure barred her from speaking Spanish to Spanish-speaking people. In 1990, a federal district court ruled that Arizona's English-only law violated First Amendment guarantees of free speech. The federal judge ruled that the law curtailed government employees' free speech rights by prohibiting them from using other languages when dealing with the non-English-speaking population. The citizens group that sponsored the initiative appealed the decision to the Ninth Circuit Court of Appeals, which affirmed the district court ruling. The case was then appealed to the Supreme Court, which ruled in 1997 on procedural problems. As the Arizona state employee who had originally sued had long since resigned, the U.S. Supreme Court said that the federal district court had no jurisdiction in the case (*Arizonans for Official English v. Arizona,* 1997), which had the effect of returning the issue to the Arizona state courts. Until that case, or another, reaches the U.S. Supreme Court, the state laws stand. The next year, the Arizona Supreme Court ruled that the 1988 voter-approved law provision requiring that official state and local business be conducted only in English violates constitutional free speech rights and the Fourteenth Amendment's equal protection clause (Crawford, 1992).

In private employment, though, the court has supported English-only job rules. Since 1970, the U.S. Equal Employment Opportunity Commission has told employers they may not enforce English-only rules except in cases of business necessity. This ruling was tested in 1991 when two employees sued their employer, a South San Francisco meat-processing plant, after having been accused of making racist remarks in Spanish about two coworkers. They alleged that their employer's English-only rule violated a federal law barring on-the-job bias based on national origin. A federal appeals court ruled in favor of the employer, and in 1994, the Supreme Court declined to hear the case, thus leaving the appeals court decision as binding law in nine western states. (First Amendment rights do not apply in this case. Remember, the First Amendment applies to the government, not to private employers. For example, a private employer can prohibit union slogans on T-shirts.)

The other side of the issue is the weakening and disappearance of languages. Hawaiian language and culture, for example, are on the verge of extinction. The same can be said of some indigenous American Indian languages.

The Situation in Hawai'i. The Hawaiians had no written language. Centuries of history, genealogies, legends, and religious teachings were passed from generation to generation orally. New England Christian missionaries who first arrived in 1820 devised a written language based on five vowels and seven consonants (*h, k, 1, m, n, p,* and *w*). The glottal stop, the short break between the pronunciation

Focus on Culture 5.1

Attempts to "Forge Unity From Diversity"
With Official Language Laws

In 1981, California senator S. I. Hayakawa introduced an amendment to the U.S. Constitution that would make English the official language of the United States. The new article would state the following:

Section 1. The English language shall be the official language of the United States.

Section 2. The Congress shall have the power to enforce this article by appropriate legislation.

The following comments were made by Hayakawa and quoted in a speech by Senator Steve Symms in the *Congressional Record,* January 22, 1985:

Language is a powerful tool. A common language can unify, separate languages can fracture and fragment a society. The American "melting pot" has succeeded in creating a vibrant new culture among peoples of many diverse cultural backgrounds largely because of the widespread use of common language, English.

The ability to force unity from diversity makes our society strong. We need all the elements. Germans, Hispanics, Hellenes, Italians, Chinese, all the cultures that make our Nation unique. Unless we have a common basis for communicating and sharing ideas, we all lose. The purpose of this proposal is to insure that American democracy always strives to include in its mainstream everyone who aspires to citizenship.

of two vowels, was acknowledged but not denoted. It later became marked with the apostrophe as in *u'ina,* the word for the glottal stop. The written language that was developed by the missionaries was not Hawaiian as the Hawaiians know it; it reflected what the New England English speakers perceived (Allen, 1982).

After the overthrow of the Hawaiian monarchy in 1893 by U.S. sugar planters and businessmen, Hawai'i became a republic and sought admission to the United States. The Hawaiian language was officially suppressed when the United States annexed the islands. In 1880, there were 150 schools teaching Hawaiian. A decade later, there were none. Public school regulations written at the turn of the 20th century prohibited the use of Hawaiian in the schools.

By 1990, only about 1,000 native Hawaiian speakers remained, and 200 of those lived on Ni'ihau, the privately owned island that is home to the last self-contained community of full-blooded Hawaiians. The language survived primarily through music and a few popular phrases. Nonetheless, at the 1978 constitutional convention, Hawaiian was made an official language of the state along with English and now is the only indigenous language in the United States that is an official state language.

Hawaiians indicating Indigenous Hawaiians and other Pacific Islands on census forms account for 10% of the state's population of 1.43 million. Recognizing that the loss of the language also means the loss of the culture, Hawaiians started a private preschool language immersion program in 1984. Inspired by the Māori of New Zealand and the Mohawks of Canada, a nonprofit foundation,

Focus on Skills 5.2

Official Language Laws

You work in human resources in a large regional privately owned hospital in the United States. One day you are at lunch in the cafeteria with several nurses. It's just friendly shop talk. One nurse starts laughing and says she has a funny story to tell. She says that the patient in Room 845 asked to speak with her. The patient said that earlier in the day two other nurses had been in his room taking his vitals. During that time they spoke in Spanish to each other. The patient explained to the nurse at your lunch table that he had been worried all day about what the nurses had been saying about him in Spanish. The patient was obviously anxious that the nurses were talking about his condition and that it must have been bad news or they wouldn't have spoken in a language he didn't understand. Everyone at the table, including you, enjoys the story and laughs.

Later that day, in your office you think back to that story and wonder if the hospital has a language policy. You find that your hospital does not. You can see now how the nurses' speaking in Spanish led to the patient feeling increased anxiety. But then you think about all the possible situations.

1. What about non-English-speaking patients? Should there be no English conversations in front of those patients?
2. Should the hospital provide translators for everything said in front of patients in languages the patient does not understand?
3. Review the section on English in the United States. If you believe language use should be regulated in the hospital for the best interests of the patients, draft a suggested policy.
4. Would the situation be different in a county-owned hospital?

Aha Punano Leo (which means "language nest" in Hawaiian), was established. In 1986, the state legislature lifted the century-old ban on schools teaching only in Hawaiian. The language immersion program then spread to the public school system. Words had to be created for concepts that hadn't existed before, such as *huna hohoki* for neutron and *wikio* for video.

The Hawai'i state constitution states that the state shall provide "for a Hawaiian education program consisting of language, culture and history in the public schools." In 1980, the state department of education created the Hawaiian Studies Program, which supports the study of ancient Hawaiian civilization, Hawaiian monarchy, and modern Hawaiian history. In 1986 it created the Hawaiian Language Immersion Program in which instruction is in the Hawaiian language with a culture-based curriculum and perspectives. Controversy surrounds the program. Some argue that the program is a chance to save the language and recapture a lost cultural identity; others argue that it is the first step toward a separated society like the French in Canada (Dudley & Agard, 1993).

Loss of American Indian Languages. Before the arrival of Europeans, it is estimated that 400 to 600 indigenous languages were spoken in North America. Today, only about 175 remain, with Navajo having the most speakers, approximately 169,471 (see Figure 5.4). From the 1860s until about the 1950s, federal policy and local practice combined to discourage and eliminate American Indian languages from schools and public settings. In the 1920s, students in federal boarding schools were

A public immersion school in Honolulu, where all instruction for students is in the Hawaiian language.

AP Photo/Lucy Pemoni

beaten for using their own language. Yet during World War II, U.S. Marines used Navajo "code talkers" at Guadalcanal and Iwo Jima; the Japanese never managed to decipher signals encoded in the Navajo language. Of the remaining languages, 155 are considered endangered.

In 1990, the U.S. Congress passed the Native American Language Act, legislation sponsored by Hawai'i senator Daniel Inouye. The act endorses the preservation of indigenous languages and encourages the use of American Indian languages as languages of instruction. Some tribes have received funding for language preservation. Yurok was predicted to soon be extinct. It is now taught in several Northern California schools. Other gaming tribes are funding

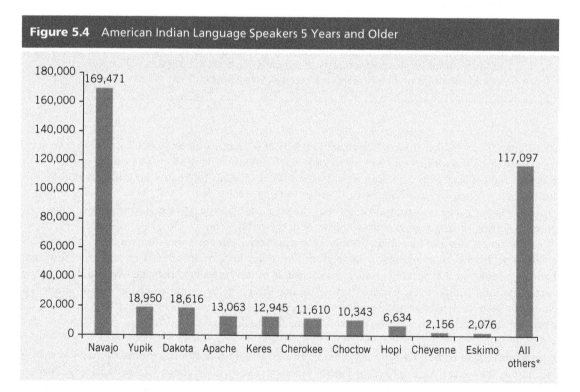

Figure 5.4   American Indian Language Speakers 5 Years and Older

Source: U.S. Census Bureau (2011).
*Fewer than 10,000 speakers each.

instruction in their languages themselves. It was said that movement to make English the official U.S. language mobilized many tribes to recognize that linguistic survival is the same as cultural or tribal survival.

Puerto Rico and Statehood. Another story is being played out in Puerto Rico, where the official language has been a part of the argument over statehood. Populated for centuries by aboriginal peoples, the island was claimed by the Spanish Crown after Columbus's second voyage to the Americas. Under colonial rule, the indigenous population was nearly exterminated and African slave labor introduced. The island was made a U.S. territory after Spain ceded it to the United States as a result of the Spanish-American War, in 1898. Residents became U.S. citizens in 1917, and in 1952 Puerto Rico became a commonwealth. Residents cannot vote, and they pay no federal income tax. A 1967 nonbinding plebiscite had 60.4% voting for commonwealth status, 39.0% for statehood, and 0.6% for independence.

New York Daily News Archive/New York Daily News Archive/Getty Images

During World Wars I and II, hundreds of American Indians joined the armed forces as "code talkers." They developed secret battle communications based on their languages. Their coded messages were never deciphered.

Map 5.3 Puerto Rico

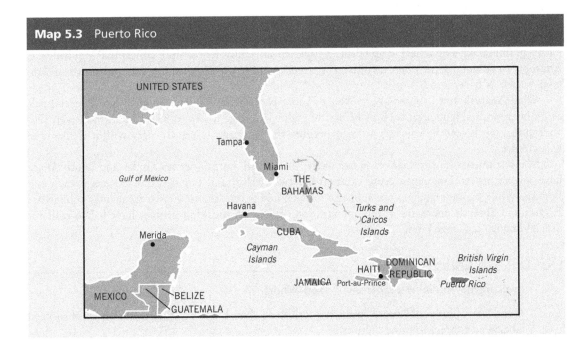

Spanish was made the island's official language in 1991 with the backing of statehood opponents. Proponents of statehood were successful in passing a new law in 1993 that made English and Spanish official languages of the territory. Yet Spanish predominates. U.S. Census Bureau (2009a) data show that for people at least 5 years old, 95% speak a language other than English at home. Governor Luis Fortuno proposed a plan to require all public schools to teach all courses in English instead of Spanish by 2022 to transform the island's populace into a true bilingual society better prepared for U.S. statehood.

A 1993 nonbinding plebiscite had 48.6% voting for commonwealth status, 46.3% for statehood, and 4.4% for independence. A third plebiscite, in 1998, had 46.5% voting for statehood and 50.2% voting "none of the above," which was the commonwealth option. A nonbinding plebiscite in 2012 saw 61% favoring statehood, the largest percentage and first majority to do so. Puerto Ricans voted on the issue for the fifth time in June 2017. Facing the largest local government bankruptcy in U.S. history, voters had the options of statehood, free association/independence, or remain a territory. Opposition parties urged boycotting the election, alleging that the options were framed to favor statehood. While turnout was only slightly above 20%, an overwhelming 97% favored statehood. Only the U.S. Congress has the authority to act on statehood.

SUMMARY

Language is a set of symbols shared by a community to communicate meaning and experience. New research has shown that our language choices are determined by culture rather than innate rules. The Sapir-Whorf hypothesis establishes the relationship between language and culture. Very few today accept the extreme position of the Sapir-Whorf linguistic determinism that our thoughts and actions are determined by the language we speak; many more accept the view that language only somehow shapes our thinking and behavior.

One way that language can be a barrier to effective intercultural communication is translation problems. Five possible translation problems are lack of vocabulary equivalence, idiomatic equivalence, grammatical-syntactical equivalence, experiential equivalence, and conceptual equivalence. Attempts to communicate when there is no shared language are pidgins, creoles, and universal languages such as Esperanto.

While Spanish and Chinese are spoken by more people than English, English has a special role as an international language, such as being the major language used on the Internet. However, that widespread use is seen by some as a threat because the language is seen to carry with it elements of U.S. culture.

Many countries have official language laws; the United States does not. India and South Africa have several official languages. New Zealand has two: Māori and English. Canada has French and English. While many languages are spoken in the United States, the two most frequently spoken are English and Spanish. Increases in the immigration of Spanish-speaking peoples have led to calls for official English language laws.

DISCUSSION QUESTIONS

1. Evaluate Steven Pinker's criticism of Sapir-Whorf.

2. Mandarin Chinese has more speakers worldwide than English. Why, then, has English been labeled as a threat to other cultures?

3. Can a strong nation exist when cultures within cultures each have a unique language?

4. Develop arguments for both sides of the *Lau v. Nichols* (1974) case.

5. What arguments can be raised for and against official language laws?

6. Should the U.S. Congress act to admit Puerto Rico as the nation's 51st state?

KEY TERMS

Arabic	Esperanto	patois
back translation	flash	pidgin
compound bilingual speakers	grammar	Qur'an
coordinate bilingual speakers	idiom	Sapir-Whorf hypothesis
creole	Islam	syntax
cultural invasion	language	
dialect	mother tongue	

READINGS

All readings are from *Intercultural Communication: A Global Reader* (Jandt, 2004).

Peter Mühlhäusler, "Babel Revisited" (p. 103)

Amadou Hampaté Bâ, "Africa: The Power of Speech" (p. 108)

Kil-Ho Kang, "Koreans' Politeness Strategies" (p. 131)

STUDENT STUDY SITE

⑤SAGE edge™

Sharpen your skills with SAGE edge at edge.sagepub.com/jandt9e.

SAGE edge for Students provides a personalized approach to help you accomplish your coursework goals in an easy-to-use learning environment.

Part 3

Cultural Values

Chapter 6

Dimensions of Nation-State Cultures

In Chapter 1 you read that national identity has become the primary identity for many people. If asked to identify their cultural identity, many people first respond with their national identity. Given this, the question becomes how to describe how national identity varies. In this chapter you will read how nation-state cultures differ in fundamental or underlying values. Approaches that focus on nation-state identity make the assumption that cultural boundaries match up with political boundaries. Thus to argue that nation-state is the major source of identity assumes that each nation-state represents a single cultural tradition.

You'll first read about cultural dimensions developed by Geert Hofstede. Hofstede initially developed his model in the 1960s and 1970s. His intercultural theory was one of the first that could be quantified and could be used to explain observed differences between cultures. It has become the major theory in intercultural communication research. Then a dimension of environmental sustainability is introduced and related to the Hofstede dimension. Next, you'll read about the dimensions developed by Alfonsus Trompenaars and Charles Hampden-Turner.

And finally, you will read a case study of Japan. Some have suggested that one way to better understand Japan is to study it as an example of a homogeneous society unlike most other nation-states.

The Hofstede Dimensions

In 1980, the Dutch management researcher Geert Hofstede first published the results of his study of more than 100,000 employees of the multinational IBM in 40 countries (Hofstede, 1980, 1983, 1984, 1991, 1997, 2001). Hofstede was attempting to locate value dimensions across which cultures vary. His dimensions have been used frequently to describe cultures.

Hofstede identified four dimensions that he labeled individualism-collectivism, masculinity-femininity, power distance, and uncertainty avoidance. His individualism-collectivism dimension describes cultures from loosely structured to tightly integrated. The masculinity-femininity dimension describes how a culture's dominant values are assertive or nurturing. Power distance refers to the distribution of influence within a culture. And uncertainty avoidance reflects a culture's tolerance of ambiguity and acceptance of risk.

Hofstede and Bond (1984; also see Chinese Culture Connection, 1987) identified a fifth dimension, a Confucian work dynamism, also labeled *long-term orientation versus short-term orientation to life.* The Confucian work dynamism dimension describes cultures that range from short-term values with respect for tradition and reciprocity in social relations to long-term values with persistence and ordering relationships by status.

In the 2010 edition of *Cultures and Organizations: Software of the Mind,* Hofstede, Hofstede, and Minkov added a sixth dimension: indulgence versus self-restraint.

When reading this chapter, and particularly when reading the rank-ordered lists of countries for each dimension, you might think of exceptions: individuals from a culture who do not act as might be implied by these lists. These lists reflect an overall average; no one person should be expected to fit that average exactly. Indeed, to expect so would be stereotyping.

Individualism Versus Collectivism

First is individualism versus collectivism. This dimension refers to how people define themselves and their relationships with others. In an individualist culture, the interest of the individual prevails over the interests of the group. Ties between individuals are loose. People look after themselves and their immediate families. Masakazu (1994) defines modern individualism as "a view of humanity that justifies inner beliefs and unilateral self-assertion, as well as competition based on these" (p. 127). In a

Focus on Theory 6.1

Individualism-Collectivism in Research

Young Yun Kim (2005) characterizes individualism-collectivism as top of the list of theories guiding cross-cultural research in communication, psychology, and anthropology. Individualist cultures stress self-direction and self-achievement; collectivist cultures stress in-group loyalty and conformity. This rich area of research has focused on competition and cooperation, conversational constraints, handling disagreements, silence, face work and conflict style, and in-group and out-group communication patterns.

Kim draws a relationship with individualism-collectivism and Edward T. Hall's (1976) theory of high-context and low-context cultures (see Chapter 3). Characterizations of high-context and low-context communication systems are closely associated with the characteristics of individualism and collectivism.

collectivist culture, the interest of the group prevails over the interest of the individual. People are integrated into strong, cohesive in-groups that continue throughout a lifetime to protect in exchange for unquestioning loyalty (Hofstede, 1997). One difference is reflected in who is taken into account when you set goals. In individualist cultures, goals are set with minimal consideration given to groups other than perhaps your immediate family. In collectivist cultures, other groups are taken into account in a major way when goals are set. Individualist cultures are loosely integrated; collectivist cultures are tightly integrated.

In individualist cultures such as the United States, for example, when meeting a new person, you want to know what that person does. You tend to define people by what they have done, their accomplishments, what kind of car they drive, or where they live. Individualist cultures are more remote and distant (see Table 6.1).

Table 6.1 Individualism Rankings for 76 Countries and Regions

1	United States	21	Switzerland (French)
2	Australia	22	Finland
3	Great Britain	23–26	Estonia
4–6	Canada total	23–26	Lithuania
4–6	Hungary	23–26	Luxembourg
4–6	Netherlands	23–26	Poland
7	New Zealand	27	Malta
8	Belgium and the Netherlands	28	Czech Republic
9	Italy	29	Austria
10	Denmark	30	Israel
11	Canada Quebec	31	Slovakia
12	Belgium (French)	32	Spain
13–14	France	33	India
13–14	Sweden	34	Suriname
15–16	Ireland	35–37	Argentina
15–16	Latvia	35–37	Japan
17–18	Norway	35–37	Morocco
17–18	Switzerland (German)	38	Iran
19	Germany	39–40	Jamaica
20	South Africa (White)	39–40	Russia

(Continued)

(Continued)

41–42	Arab countries	58–63	China
41–42	Brazil	58–63	Singapore
43	Turkey	58–63	Thailand
44	Uruguay	58–63	Vietnam
45	Greece	58–63	Africa West
46	Croatia	64	El Salvador
47	Philippines	65	South Korea
48–50	Bulgaria	66	Taiwan
48–50	Mexico	67–68	Peru
48–50	Romania	67–68	Trinidad
51–53	Africa East	69	Costa Rica
51–53	Portugal	70–71	Indonesia
51–53	Slovenia	70–71	Pakistan
54	Malaysia	72	Colombia
55–56	Hong Kong	73	Venezuela
55–56	Serbia	74	Panama
57	Chile	75	Ecuador
58–63	Bangladesh	76	Guatemala

Source: Hofstede, Hofstede, & Minkov (2010, pp. 95–97).

Cultures characterized by collectivism emphasize relationships among people to a greater degree. Collectivist cultures stress interdependent activities and suppressing individual aims for the group's welfare. Often, it is difficult for individuals from highly individualist cultures to understand collectivist values. This example may help: A student from Colombia may study in the United States and earn a PhD, teach at a distinguished university, and publish important books, but when he returns to visit Colombia, people to whom he is introduced will want to know to whom he is related. Colombians want to know who his family is because that places him in society much more so than any of his accomplishments in the United States.

In the United States, few family names—perhaps only Rockefeller, Kennedy, DuPont, and Bush—carry such defining meaning. You are not socially defined by your family name but by your individual accomplishments. A generation or two ago, people were introduced by family name, and a new acquaintance then asked permission to use one's given name. The asking and giving of permission was an important stage in the development of a friendship. Today's introduction by one's given name makes no reference to one's family. Individualism is so strong in the United States that you might even have difficulty appreciating how people might feel content in a collectivist culture. Contentment comes from knowing your place and from knowing you have a place.

In the workplace, in individualist cultures, the employer-employee relationship tends to be established by contract, and hiring and promotion decisions are based on skills and rules; in collectivist cultures, the employer-employee relationship is perceived in moral terms, like a family link, and hiring and promotion decisions take the employee's in-group into account. Hofstede's data revealed several associations with this dimension:

- *Wealth.* There is a strong relationship between a nation's wealth and individualism.
- *Geography.* Countries with moderate and cold climates tend to show more individualism.
- *Birth Rates.* Countries with higher birth rates tend to be collectivist.
- *History.* Confucian countries are collectivist. Migrants from Europe who populated North America, Australia, and New Zealand tended to be sufficiently individualist to leave their native countries.

Another interesting association with inheritance practices was developed by Knighton (1999). Those cultures that have rules for equal partition of parental property among all offspring tend to be collectivist; those that have rules permitting unequal partition and those that have historically allowed parents to have full freedom in deciding who will inherit tend to be individualist.

Individualism and collectivism have been associated with direct and indirect styles of communication—that is, the extent to which speakers reveal intentions through explicit verbal communication. In the direct style, associated with individualism, the wants, needs, and desires of the speaker are embodied in the spoken message. In the indirect style, associated with collectivism, the wants, needs, and goals of the speaker are not obvious in the spoken message. Rojjanaprapayon (1997), for example, demonstrated specific communication strategies in Thai communication: Thais do not use specific names when they express negative feelings. Thais tend to use words and phrases expressing probability, such as *maybe, probably, sometimes, likely,* and *I would say so, but I am not sure.* Thais do not show their feelings if doing so would make the other person feel bad.

Focus on Technology 6.1

Individualism and Collectivism Reflected in Webpage Design

In Chapter 1 you read that culture can be reflected in webpage design. Gennadi Gevorgyan and Naira Manucharova (2009) demonstrated that relationship using the Hofstede dimension of individualism. Webpages were categorized as individualistic if they had elements such as allowing users to selectively retrieve only that information of interest to them from a wide menu of available online information. Webpages were categorized as collectivistic if they had design elements that emphasized group membership and many-to-many forms of communication. Public chat rooms and message boards were among collectivism-oriented design features. The researchers found that the collectivistic Chinese participants preferred the websites with collectivistic features, and the individualistic U.S. participants favored the webpages with the elements that reflected individualistic values.

Focus on Culture 6.1

Apologies in SPAM Emails in Collectivist South Korea

E-MAIL MESSAGE

FROM: Happystudent Corporation

SUBJECT: Low price on books. Save 30–50% off!

Our sincere apologies for sending you this message without your prior approval. We hope that you find this message useful for you.

Hee Sun Park, Hye Eun Lee, and Jeong An Song (2005) found that in South Korea, as an example of a collectivist culture, spam emails were more likely to include an apology. They found that Koreans consider advertising messages with apologies more credible and normal and were more likely to model other people's apology messages.

And Thais also use indirect nonverbal communication by having less eye contact, or avoiding it altogether, and keeping greater personal distance.

Case Study: Singapore

Singapore is an island nation of 697 square kilometers, the smallest but one of the most prosperous countries in Southeast Asia. Various groups of people have migrated to Singapore. Its population of

Focus on Theory 6.2

Self-Construal Theory

Some researchers contend that the individualism-collectivism dimension does not have a direct relationship to communication behavior. These researchers turned to self-construal theory. Self-construal is an individual-level cultural orientation.

The concept of self-construal was introduced by Markus and Kitayama (1991) and was originally used to describe perceived cultural differences in the perception of the self. The theory assumes that we are influenced by the cultures we are raised in. This socialization that includes how we conceive of ourselves (self-construal) has a direct effect on communication behavior. Research based in this theory focuses on how individuals' selves differ across culture rather than Hofstede's abstract cultural dimensions.

Westerners were thought to have an *independent self-construal*, which is characterized by separateness from others; by attention to one's abilities, traits, preferences, and wishes; and by the primacy of one's individual goals over those of in-groups. East Asians were thought to have an *interdependent self-construal*, which is characterized by a sense of fundamental connectedness with others, by attention to one's role in in-groups, and by the primacy of group goals over one's individual goals (Cross, Hardin, & Swing, 2011). Later, *relational self-construal* was proposed to describe the ways people define themselves in terms of close, dyadic relationships.

Focus on Skills 6.1

Applying Individualism and Collectivism in Decision Making

You are in a project group with two other students in your intercultural communication class. You and one other student in the group, Tyler, are native to the United States. The third student, Nadya, is a visiting student from Indonesia studying at your university for one year. Everyone contributed to the project in some way.

Your instructor awards your group project 12 bonus points. Bonus points will be added to your course average at the end of the term. Each of you can use some of those bonus points. Your instructor requires that each project group allocate the bonus points among the members of the group.

When you meet to allocate the points, you start the discussion by saying, "Want to just divide them equally, 4 points each?" Tyler suggests allocating them based on the number of hours each person worked on the project. Nadya doesn't have a suggestion. Austin, who has been dating Nadya, texts you: "Nadya needs to bring up her grade to maintain her status as a visiting student."

Tyler then suggests using Hofstede's individualism versus collectivism dimension to evaluate the problem.

1. What insights does this give you?
2. How would you propose allocating the points?

5.7 million is 74% Chinese. Today, Singapore is a multiracial, multicultural society with a dynamic economy. Its government has been strict and paternalistic, steadily building the country into an economic and trade powerhouse that has education and income levels comparable to those in the United States. The island nation is clean, efficient, and law abiding. While on a trip there in 1987, I came across a newspaper editorial in which Confucianism was considered in juxtaposition to individualism (see Focus on Culture 6.2 on page 184).

Masculinity Versus Femininity

The second dimension across which cultures vary is masculinity versus femininity. Hofstede (1980) found that women's social role varied less from culture to culture than men's. He labeled as masculine cultures those that strive for maximal distinction between what women and men are expected to do. Cultures that place high values on masculine traits stress assertiveness, competition, and material success. Those labeled as feminine cultures are those that permit more overlapping social roles for the sexes. Cultures that place high value on feminine traits stress quality of life, interpersonal relationships, and concern for the weak. Table 6.2 shows examples of both types.

It is important to understand that these traits apply to both women and men; that is, both women and men learn to be ambitious and competitive in masculine cultures, and both women and men learn to be modest in feminine cultures. From his study of Thais in the United States, Rojjanaprapayon (1997) notes that masculinity in all cultures is not the same as Hofstede's Western concept of masculinity as assertiveness, aggressiveness, and goal orientation. Thais can be very aggressive and goal-oriented in some situations but are expected to be attentive, supportive, and yielding. Rojjanaprapayon suggests labeling this dimension more appropriately as affection.

Table 6.2   Masculinity Rankings for 76 Countries and Regions

1	Slovakia	31–32	Arab countries
2	Japan	31–32	Morocco
3	Hungary	33	Canada total
4	Austria	34–36	Luxembourg
5	Venezuela	34–36	Malaysia
6	Switzerland (German)	34–36	Pakistan
7	Italy	37	Brazil
8	Mexico	38	Singapore
9–10	Ireland	39–40	Israel
9–10	Jamaica	39–40	Malta
11–13	China	41–42	Indonesia
11–13	Germany	41–42	Africa West
11–13	Great Britain	43–45	Canada Quebec
14–16	Colombia	43–45	Taiwan
14–16	Philippines	43–45	Turkey
14–16	Poland	46	Panama
17–18	South Africa (White)	47–50	Belgium Netherlands
17–18	Ecuador	47–50	France
19	United States	47–50	Iran
20	Australia	47–50	Serbia
21	Belgium (French)	51–53	Peru
22–24	New Zealand	51–53	Romania
22–24	Switzerland (French)	51–53	Spain
22–24	Trinidad	54	Africa East
25–27	Czech Republic	55–58	Bulgaria
25–27	Greece	55–58	Croatia
25–27	Hong Kong	55–58	El Salvador
28–29	Argentina	55–58	Vietnam
28–29	India	59	South Korea
30	Bangladesh	60	Uruguay

(Continued)

(Continued)

61–62	Guatemala	69	Costa Rica
61–62	Suriname	70–71	Lithuania
63	Russia	70–71	Slovenia
64	Thailand	72	Denmark
65	Portugal	73	Netherlands
66	Estonia	74	Latvia
67	Chile	75	Norway
68	Finland	76	Sweden

Source: Hofstede, Hofstede, & Minkov (2010, pp. 141–143).

In the workplace, in masculine cultures, managers are expected to be decisive and assertive; in feminine cultures, managers use intuition and strive for consensus. Solidarity and quality of life are stressed. Hofstede's data revealed two associations with this dimension:

1. *Geography.* Feminine cultures are somewhat more likely in colder climates.
2. *Birth Rates.* In feminine cultures, the woman has a stronger say in the number of children. In masculine cultures, the man determines family size.

Power Distance

The third dimension is power distance, or the way the culture deals with inequalities. Hofstede (1997) defines power distance as "the extent to which less powerful members of institutions and organizations within a country expect and accept that power is distributed unequally" (p. 28). Table 6.3 shows countries' rankings on this dimension. Hofstede believes that power distance is learned early in families. In cultures with high power distance, children are expected to be obedient toward parents versus being treated more or less as equals. In these cultures, people are expected to display respect for those of higher status. For example, in countries such as Burma (Myanmar), Cambodia, Laos, and Thailand, people are expected to display respect for monks by greeting and taking leave of monks with ritualistic greetings, removing hats in the presence of a monk, dressing modestly, seating monks at a higher level, and using a vocabulary that shows respect.

Power distance also refers to the extent to which power, prestige, and wealth are distributed within a culture. Cultures with high power distance have power and influence concentrated in the hands of a few rather than distributed throughout the population. These countries tend to be more authoritarian and may communicate in a way to limit interaction and reinforce the differences between people.

One indicator of power distance is economic inequality. National comparisons of income inequality have been studied using the Gini coefficient scale that ranges from 0 (everyone in the country has the same income) to 1.00 (one person in the country has all the income). Data from selected countries are shown in Figure 6.1.

Of the 34 mostly developed economies of the Organisation for Economic Co-operation and Development, the United States ranked 10th in income inequality. After accounting for the redistributive impact

Table 6.3   Power Distance Rankings for 76 Countries and Regions

1–2	Malaysia	30–31	Colombia
1–2	Slovakia	32–33	El Salvador
3–4	Guatemala	32–33	Turkey
3–4	Panama	34–36	Africa East
5	Philippines	34–36	Peru
6	Russia	34–36	Thailand
7	Romania	37–38	Chile
8	Serbia	37–38	Portugal
9	Suriname	39–40	Belgium NL
10–11	Mexico	39–40	Uruguay
10–11	Venezuela	41–42	Greece
12–14	Arab countries	41–42	South Korea
12–14	Bangladesh	43–44	Iran
12–14	China	43–44	Taiwan
15–16	Ecuador	45–46	Czech Republic
15–16	Indonesia	45–46	Spain
17–18	Africa West	47	Malta
17–18	India	48	Pakistan
19	Singapore	49–50	Canada Quebec
20	Croatia	49–50	Japan
21	Slovenia	51	Italy
22–25	Bulgaria	52–53	Argentina
22–25	Morocco	52–53	South Africa (White)
22–25	Switzerland (French)	54	Trinidad
22–25	Vietnam	55	Hungary
26	Brazil	56	Jamaica
27–29	France	57	Latvia
27–29	Hong Kong	58	Lithuania
27–29	Poland	59–61	Estonia
30–31	Belgium (French)	59–61	Luxembourg

(Continued)

(Continued)

59–61	United States	69–70	Norway
62	Canada total	69–70	Sweden
63	Netherlands	71	Ireland
64	Australia	72	Switzerland (German)
65–67	Costa Rica	73	New Zealand
65–67	Germany	74	Denmark
65–67	Great Britain	75	Israel
68	Finland	76	Austria

Source: Hofstede, Hofstede, & Minkov (2010, pp. 57–59).

Figure 6.1 Income Inequality in Selected Organisation for Economic Co-operation and Development Countries

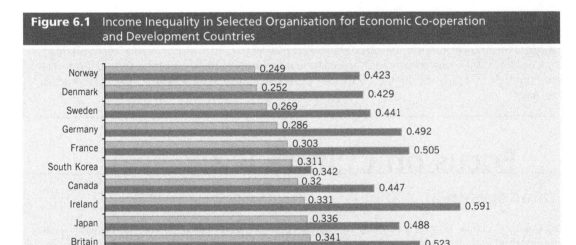

Source: Based on data from Organisation for Economic Co-operation and Development. (2016b). *OECD Income Distribution Database (IDD): Gini, poverty, income, methods and concepts.* Retrieved from http://www.oecd.org/els/soc/income-distribution-database.htm.

Note: Gini coefficient is a mathematical ratio that allows economists to put all countries on a scale with values that range (hypothetically) from 0 (everyone in the country has the same income) to 1 (one person in the country has all the income).

Global Voices

America now has more wealth and income inequality than any major developed country on earth, and the gap between the very rich and everyone else is wider than at any time since the 1920s.

—Senator Bernie Sanders, 2016 presidential campaign

of programs such as Social Security and unemployment insurance, the United States had the second-highest level of inequality. Before taking into account taxes and redistribution programs, the bottom 20% had 2.3% of all income, while the top 20% had 57.9%. After taxes and redistribution programs, the share of the bottom 20% rose to 9.3%, while that of the top 20% fell to 47.2% (Desilver, 2013).

Distribution of wealth is not necessarily the same as distribution of income. Table 6.4 shows selected national rankings.

Focus on Technology 6.2

Cultural Values in E-Commerce Sites

Singh and Baak (2004) compared Mexican and U.S. e-commerce sites for cultural values. The Mexican websites showed more content related to cultural values of collectivism, masculinity, and power distance—all characteristic of the Mexican culture. Pfeil, Zaphiris, and Ang (2006) studied contributions to French, German, Japanese, and Dutch Wikipedia pages and found cultural differences in the style of the contributions. The researchers conclude that "cultural differences that are observed in the physical world also exist in the virtual world" (p. 88).

Focus on Culture 6.2

Mitigated speech

Mitigated speech is a linguistic term describing deferential or indirect speech in communication between individuals of perceived high power distance (Ng & Bradac, 1993). The term was popularized in the book *Outliers* (Gladwell, 2008), where it is defined as "sugarcoating" the meaning of what is being said (p. 194). In a much-cited example, Gladwell gives one explanation of why Korean Air Lines (KAL) had one of the worst crash records from the late 1980s to the late 1990s. There was a higher chance for a crash when the most experienced pilots flew. As we saw in an earlier chapter, the Korean language has honorifics and deferential language that separates societal ranks. The culture reinforces power distance. What was happening was that the subordinate or lesser pilot would pay extreme deference to the senior captain and not overtly challenge the senior captain's stewardship of the plane. The subordinate pilot would only use deferential language that never directly challenged the captain nor changed the captain's mind about dangerous situations that should have been obvious. Korean Air instituted a major revision of pilot training. All KAL pilots must be fluent in English and train with U.S. pilots to help break down power distance behaviors. KAL has become one of the safest airlines today.

A 2013 blog post strongly criticized Gladwell's analysis (Ask a Korean, 2013). The blogger writes that Gladwell overlooked that status in Korean society is not so easily defined as by organizational title alone. Age, education, and other factors all contribute to one's status. Gladwell also didn't consider, or didn't report, that almost all of the cockpit conversation was in English. Finally, as is noted in the introduction to this chapter, to explain one specific incident by cultural information alone is an example of stereotyping.

A country can have highly concentrated wealth distribution and still have more equal distribution of income, such as is the case in Switzerland and Sweden. Compared to other industrialized democracies, in the United States both wealth and income distributions are highly concentrated (Domhoff, 2011).

In the workplace with high power distance, superiors and subordinates consider each other existentially unequal. Power is centralized, and a wide salary gap exists between the top and bottom of the organization. In cultures high in power distance, for example, corporate presidents' offices are more likely to be luxurious, with controlled access. Company bosses are "kings" and employees "loyal subjects" who don't speak out. In the workplace with low power distance, subordinates expect to be consulted, and ideal bosses are democratic. In more democratic organizations, leaders are physically more accessible. Marcus and Gould (2000) applied the power distance dimension to website design. They identified that the prominence given to leaders and the importance given to security and restrictions are related to the power distance of a country. Robbins and Stylianou (2002) analyzed commercial websites and found a relationship between the country of origin's power distance ranking and the frequency of organizational charts on websites.

Table 6.4 Percentage of Wealth Held by the Top 10% of the Adult Population in Various Countries, 2014

Country	Wealth Owned by Top 10%
Russia	84.8%
Turkey	77.7%
Hong Kong	77.5%
Indonesia	77.2%
Philippines	76.0%
Thailand	75.0%
United States	74.6%
India	74.0%
Peru	73.3%
Brazil	73.3%
Egypt	73.3%
Switzerland	71.9%

Source: Shorrocks, Davies, & Lluberas (2014).

Hofstede notes four interesting associations with power distance:

1. *Geographic Latitude.* Higher latitudes are associated with lower power distance.
2. *Population.* Large populations are associated with high power distance.
3. *Wealth.* National wealth is associated with lower power distance.
4. *History.* Countries with a Romance language (Spanish, Portuguese, Italian, French) score medium to high, as do Confucian cultural inheritance countries. Countries with a Germanic language (German, English, Dutch, Danish, Norwegian, Swedish) score low. Both the Romance language countries and the Confucian cultural inheritance countries were ruled from a single power center, whereas the Germanic language countries remained "barbaric" during Roman days.

Uncertainty Avoidance

Hofstede's (1980) fourth dimension is uncertainty avoidance, the extent to which people in a culture feel threatened by uncertain or unknown situations. Hofstede explains that this feeling is expressed through nervous stress and a need for predictability or a need for written and unwritten rules

Focus on Skills 6.2

Considering Power Distance:
Planning a University President's Office

You have been appointed to be the student body representative to the advisory committee planning the new campus administration building at your university in the United States. At an early meeting, the architects present a preliminary floor plan for committee comment. One of the faculty members comments on the university president's suite. It is large and prominent. There is even special security just for the president's office. One faculty member says it's bad enough that the president has a university car and driver and never goes anywhere without a vice president at his side to take care of his personal needs. The committee seems to be divided. Faculty members say the president's suite of offices is too elaborate and pretentious. Administrators on the committee side with the architect. In an attempt to reach a consensus, one of the architects says that the office should reflect the office and your university's president's total compensation is approaching a million dollars. The committee adjourns, postponing a recommendation until its next meeting.

During the next week you have the opportunity to ask your intercultural communication professor just how much the average faculty member makes. She explains that's not easy to answer because salary varies so much between public and private universities and so much by rank. Pushed for an answer, she says, "Maybe a range between $50,000 and $120,000." You're concerned about the university president's salary but have just studied Hofstede's power distance dimension. You've read that major corporate presidents in some countries have modest offices without all the trappings of status. That appeals to you personally.

1. At the next meeting of the advisory committee, do you side with the faculty or the administrators?
2. How do you explain your position?

(Hofstede, 1997). In these cultures, such situations are avoided by maintaining strict codes of behavior and a belief in absolute truths. Cultures strong in uncertainty avoidance are active, aggressive, emotional, compulsive, security seeking, and intolerant. Cultures weak in uncertainty avoidance are contemplative, less aggressive, unemotional, relaxed, accepting of personal risks, and relatively tolerant (see Table 6.5).

Table 6.5   Uncertainty Avoidance Rankings for 76 Countries and Regions

1	Greece	8	El Salvador
2	Portugal	9–10	Belgium (French)
3	Guatemala	9–10	Poland
4	Uruguay	11–13	Japan
5	Belgium (Netherlands)	11–13	Serbia
6	Malta	11–13	Suriname
7	Russia	14	Romania

(Continued)

(Continued)

15	Slovenia	46	Latvia
16	Peru	47–49	Bangladesh
17–22	Argentina	47–49	Canada Quebec
17–22	Chile	47–49	Estonia
17–22	Costa Rica	50–51	Finland
17–22	France	50–51	Iran
17–22	Panama	52	Switzerland (German)
17–22	Spain	53	Trinidad
23–25	Bulgaria	54	Africa West
23–25	South Korea	55	Netherlands
23–25	Turkey	56	Africa East
26–27	Hungary	57–58	Australia
26–27	Mexico	57–58	Slovakia
28	Israel	59	Norway
29–30	Colombia	60–61	New Zealand
29–30	Croatia	60–61	South Africa (White)
31–32	Brazil	62–63	Canada total
31–32	Venezuela	62–63	Indonesia
33	Italy	64	United States
34	Czech Republic	65	Philippines
35–38	Austria	66	India
35–38	Luxembourg	67	Malaysia
35–38	Pakistan	68–69	Great Britain
35–38	Switzerland (French)	68–69	Ireland
39	Taiwan	70–71	China
40–41	Arab countries	70–71	Vietnam
40–41	Morocco	72–73	Hong Kong
42	Ecuador	72–73	Sweden
43–44	Germany	74	Denmark
43–44	Lithuania	75	Jamaica
45	Thailand	76	Singapore

Source: Hofstede, Hofstede, & Minkov (2010, pp. 192–194).

Students from cultures with high uncertainty avoidance expect their teachers to be experts who have all the answers. And in the workplace, there is an inner need to work hard and a need for rules, precision, and punctuality. Students from cultures with low uncertainty avoidance accept teachers who admit to not knowing all the answers. And in the workplace, employees work hard only when needed, there are no more rules than are necessary, and precision and punctuality have to be learned. Hofstede notes two interesting associations with uncertainty avoidance:

1. *Religion.* Orthodox and Roman Catholic Christian cultures (except the Philippines and Ireland) score high. Judaic and Muslim cultures tend to score in the middle. Protestant Christian cultures score low. Eastern religion cultures score medium to very low (except Japan).
2. *History.* Cultures with a Romance language and history of Roman codified laws score high on uncertainty avoidance. Cultures with Chinese-speaking populations and Confucian tradition tend to score lower.

Long-Term Versus Short-Term Orientation

In 1987, the Chinese Culture Connection, composed of Michael H. Bond and others, extended Hofstede's work to include a new dimension they labeled Confucian work dynamism, now more commonly called long-term orientation versus short-term orientation to life. This dimension includes such values as thrift, persistence, having a sense of shame, and ordering relationships. Confucian work dynamism refers to dedicated, motivated, responsible, and educated individuals with a sense of commitment and organizational identity and loyalty.

Countries high in Confucian work dynamism are Hong Kong, Taiwan, Japan, South Korea, and Singapore—popularly referred to as the Five Economic Dragons. Long-term orientation encourages thrift, savings, perseverance toward results, and a willingness to subordinate oneself for a purpose. Short-term orientation is consistent with spending to keep up with social pressure, less savings, preference for quick results, and a concern with face (see Table 6.6).

Table 6.6	Long-Term Orientation Rankings for 24 Countries		
1	South Korea	13	Slovakia
2	Taiwan	14	Montenegro
3	Japan	15	Switzerland
4	China	16	Singapore
5	Ukraine	17	Moldova
6	Germany	18	Czech Republic
7	Estonia	19	Bosnia and Herzegovina
8	Belgium	20	Bulgaria
9	Lithuania	21	Latvia
10	Russia	22	Netherlands
11	Belarus	23	Kyrgyzstan
12	Former East Germany	24	Luxembourg

Source: Hofstede, Hofstede, & Minkov (2010, p. 240).

Indulgence Versus Self-Restraint

Another new dimension is indulgence versus restraint. "Indulgence... [is] a tendency to allow relatively free gratification of basic and natural human desires related to enjoying life and having fun.... [R]estraint, reflects a conviction that such gratification needs to be curbed and regulated by strict social norms" (Hofstede et al., 2010, p. 281). This dimension, as it is new, does not as of yet have sufficient data accumulated to be as significant in conclusions as the other dimensions. Indulgence scores are highest in Latin America, parts of Africa, the Anglo world and Nordic Europe; restraint is mostly found in East Asia, Eastern Europe, and the Muslim world. Table 6.7 shows the countries highest in indulgence and highest in restraint.

In indulgent cultures, there tends to be a higher percentage of very happy people, greater importance placed on leisure and having friends, more extroverted personalities, and lower death rate from cardiovascular diseases. In private life, there is more satisfying family life, more involvement in sports, and loosely prescribed gender roles. Indulgent cultures encourage enjoying life and having fun.

In restrained cultures, there tends to be a lower percentage of very happy people, a perception of helplessness, cynicism, more neurotic personalities, more pessimism, and higher death rates from cardiovascular diseases. Private life is characterized by family life being less satisfying, less involvement in

Table 6.7 Indulgence Versus Restraint	
High-Indulgence Countries	**High-Restraint Countries**
1. Venezuela	74. Morocco
2. Mexico	75. China
3. Puerto Rico	76. Azerbaijan
4. El Salvador	77–80. Russia
5. Nigeria	77–80. Montenegro
6. Colombia	77–80. Romania
7. Trinidad	77–80. Bangladesh
8. Sweden	81. Moldova
9. New Zealand	82. Burkina Faso
10. Ghana	83–84. Hong Kong
11. Australia	83–84. Iraq
12–13. Cyprus	85–87. Estonia
12–13. Denmark	85–87. Bulgaria
14. Great Britain	85–87. Lithuania
15–17. Canada	88–89. Belarus
15–17. Netherlands	88–89. Albania
15–17. United States	90. Ukraine
18. Iceland	91. Latvia
19–20. Switzerland	92. Egypt
19–20. Malta	93. Pakistan

Source: Hofstede, Hofstede, & Minkov (2010, pp. 282–285).

sports, more strictly prescribed gender roles, and priority given to maintaining order in the nation. Restrained cultures tend to enforce strict norms regulating gratification of human desires.

Environmental Sustainability

We will consider one additional dimension, environmental sustainability, which has relevance to the Hofstede dimensions.

Focus on Culture 6.3

Singapore Attempts to Balance Confucian Ethics and Individualism

Confucianism is once again in the news. Its role in Singapore's progress was the theme of the Prime Minister's recent interview with the *New York Times*. And several distinguished scholars are in Singapore this week to discuss the part Confucianism has played in the economic success of East Asian nations. At the heart of this debate is a fundamental question that has exercised the minds of philosophers and kings for ages: How should a society organize itself? The goal has always been to find an effective way to control the passions of people so they can live in harmony among themselves and in peace with their neighbors. The quest is not only for sound political systems but, more importantly, for better social and economic systems.

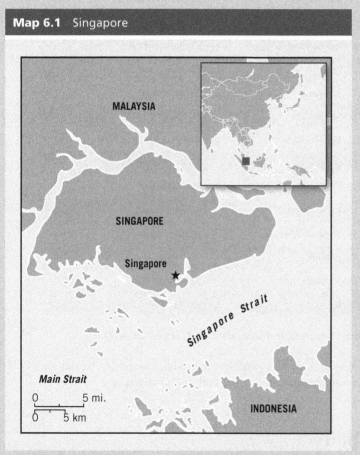

Map 6.1 Singapore

MALAYSIA

SINGAPORE

Singapore ★

Singapore Strait

Main Strait

0   5 mi.
0   5 km

INDONESIA

Whatever the arguments about the State and the individual, the Prime Minister was unequivocal about one of the driving forces behind Singapore's success, namely, the basic Confucian concept of placing the good of society above that of the individual. A related factor was social cohesion. Given Singapore's mix of races, cultures and religions, its fragile harmony cannot withstand what the Prime Minister called the "untrammeled individualism" of the West. There is good reason why these two concepts have been such a constant preoccupation of Singapore's leadership. For while Singaporeans may accept the notion of sacrificing individual interests for a larger common good and to preserve social harmony, several factors make this especially difficult to apply in real life.

One of these stems from the wrenching changes that cultures in Singapore have undergone, all in one generation. In many families now, children who are Western-educated and English-speaking find it difficult to accept the mores of their dialect-speaking and more traditional parents. As families are the basic units of Asian societies, the cultural strains that this imposes are enormous. Unfortunately, the individualist genie, once unloosed, cannot be easily coaxed back into the lamp. But on the other hand, some traditional social norms die hard no matter how badly changes are needed. Witness how even English-educated men in Singapore still have the Eastern preference for submissive wives.

An even bigger paradox arises when trying to preserve Confucian ethics and other Asian traditions within a modern capitalist economy. For capitalism is based essentially on the pursuit of individual gains. The political philosophers of Keynes' day justified capitalism on the grounds that moneymaking was less of an avarice than, and could in fact countervail, other more dangerous passions and vices. Individuals pursuing relentlessly their own interests will, in fact, further the common good. Or so the theory goes. Added to this, of course, is the colonial legacy of a democratic political system in which is enshrined each individual's right to vote.

So the task is to balance Confucian ethics, and its emphasis on the common good, with the individualism inherent in a capitalist economy and in a one-man, one-vote political system. Certainly selfish individualism and abrasive dissent have no place if there is to be order and harmony. Singapore has no margin for error. Still, room must be given for creativity and innovativeness. For Singapore cannot achieve the excellence it seeks as a society if there is no open-mindedness to new, and sometimes opposing, ideas. The government's important role is not so much to deliver the goods but more to inspire the people to accept what it takes to achieve the good life—and for them to work at getting there. Singaporeans must themselves find the golden mean that suits their circumstances for, in the end, they can only be their own selves.

Source: "Finding the Golden Mean" (1987, p. 24). Copyright © 1987 by The Straits Times Press. Reprinted with permission.

Sustainable development has been defined in many ways. The World Commission on Environment and Development (1987) defined the concept as "development which meets the needs of the present without compromising the ability of future generations to meet their own needs" (p. 8). In 2016 Pope Francis proposed that caring for the environment be added to the traditional seven works of mercy that Christians are called to perform.

Sustainability is a multidimensional construct. The World Economic Forum framed the dimensions in terms of the quality of environmental systems, stresses on those systems, the vulnerability of human populations to environmental degradation, the social and institutional capacity to respond to stresses, and global stewardship (Global Leaders, 2001). Yale University's Center for Environmental Law and Policy, in collaboration with Columbia University's Center for International Earth Science Information Network and the World Economic Forum, published the Environmental Sustainability Index (ESI) from 1999 to 2005. It was a composite index tracking 21 elements of environmental sustainability that cover natural resource endowments, past and present pollution levels, environmental management efforts, contributions to protect the global commons, and the society's capacity to improve its environmental performance over time. Finland, Norway, Uruguay, Sweden, and Iceland ranked highest. The United States ranked 45th, a high middle ranking that reflects high performance on issues such as water quality and environmental protection capacity and low performance on other issues such as waste generation and greenhouse gas emissions. North Korea, Taiwan, Turkmenistan, Iraq, Uzbekistan, and Haiti ranked lowest.

Husted (2005) studied the ESI elements related to Hofstede's dimensions. He concluded that countries with low levels of power distance, high levels of individualism, and low levels of masculinity have higher social and institutional capacity: "These egalitarian, individualist, and feminine values appear to constitute 'green' or 'sustainable' values" (p. 363). For example, Costa Rica is low in

Table 6.8 Environmental Performance Index, Selected Countries, 2016 Rankings

1.	Finland	13.	Australia
2.	Iceland	25.	Canada
3.	Sweden	26.	United States
4.	Denmark	39.	Japan
5.	Slovenia	67.	Mexico
6.	Spain	95.	Saudi Arabia
7.	Portugal	109.	China
8.	Estonia	176.	Afghanistan
9.	Malta	177.	Niger
10.	France	178.	Madagascar
11.	New Zealand	179.	Eritrea
12.	United Kingdom	180.	Somalia

Source: Hsu et al. (2016).

power distance and also quite low on masculinity. Even though it is quite collectivistic and relatively poor, it has invested considerable resources in its social and institutional capacity for sustainability. Husted then discusses ways that Hofstede's cultural dimensions can play a role in how sustainability programs can be successfully implemented. A similar study by Hoon Park, Clifford Russell, and Junsoo Lee (2007) showed a clear statistical link in a sample of 43 countries between two of Hofstede's dimensions and environmental sustainability, again measured by the ESI. Both power distance and masculinity are significantly negatively related to the ESI. The researchers also found that education was

Focus on Technology 6.3

What If the Social Web Reflected the Values of Cultures Other Than Those of the United States?

Most of the social web was developed in the highly individualistic U.S. culture. Gaurav Mishra's blog entry speculates as to what a social web developed in a more collectivist, paternalist, status-oriented, and relativist culture would be like:

- What if the social web subjugated individual profiles and activity streams (high individualism) to group affiliations (high collectivism)?

- What if the social web parsed and displayed relationships between two users based on their status relative to each other (high power distance) instead of treating everyone as a "friend" (low power distance)?

- What if the primary relationship on the social web was "becoming a fan" (long-term orientation) instead of "becoming a friend" (short-term orientation)?

- What if the complex relationships between users automatically changed over time and across context (low uncertainty avoidance) instead of staying the same until it is proactively changed (high uncertainty avoidance)?

Source: Mishra (2008).

positively related to the ESI. Peng and Lin (2009) reported the same relationship: Power distance and masculinity are effective and consistent predictors of environmental performance.

Later, a new measure, the Environmental Performance Index (EPI), was developed to use outcome-oriented indicators. Table 6.8 shows representative 2016 rankings. The EPI ranks 180 countries to show how close they are to established environmental policy goals.

The Trompenaars and Hampden-Turner Dimensions

Another attempt to identify cultural dimensions has been attempted by Alfonsus (Fons) Trompenaars and Charles Hampden-Turner. Fons Trompenaars worked with Shell in nine countries, including 7 years as the director of human resources. Taking the example of Geert Hofstede, Trompenaars worked with Charles Hampden-Turner to research the values of 46,000 managers in 40 countries. From their research they concluded that people from diverse cultures differ from one another in seven dimensions (Trompenaars & Hampden-Turner, 2012). Some of these value orientations are nearly identical to Hofstede's dimensions. Others offer a new perspective. Compare the Trompenaars dimensions to the Hofstede dimensions below.

Universalism versus particularism (rules versus relationships):

- In universalistic cultures people place importance on laws, rules, values, and obligations. To treat people fairly, one follows the accepted rules. Universalist cultures include the United States, Canada, the United Kingdom, the Netherlands, Germany, Scandinavia, New Zealand, Australia, and Switzerland.
- In particularist cultures people follow the dictates of each circumstance and relationship. Particularistic cultures include Russia, countries in Latin America, and China.

Individualism versus communitarianism (the individual versus the group):

- In individualistic cultures people believe they take care of themselves and make decisions for themselves. Freedom and personal achievement are values. Individualistic cultures include the United States, Canada, the United Kingdom, Scandinavia, New Zealand, Australia, and Switzerland.

Global Voices

Increasing environmental awareness in response to the export of hazardous toxic wastes in the 1980s to Africa, Eastern Europe, and other parts of the developing world where regulations and enforcement mechanisms were lacking, the Basel Convention on the Control of Transboundary Movements of Hazardous Wastes and Their Disposal was adopted in 1989. The objective was "to protect human health and the environment against the adverse effects of hazardous wastes." The United States has signed the convention but not ratified it.

It is legal to export discarded goods to poor countries if the goods can be reused or refurbished. But in 2013 *The Guardian* reported that Interpol, the international police organization, revealed that one in three shipping containers leaving the EU was found by its agents to contain illegal e-waste bound to developing countries in Africa and Asia. "Much is falsely classified as 'used goods' although in reality it is non-functional. It is often diverted to the black market and disguised as used goods to avoid the costs associated with legitimate recycling." The informal processing of the e-waste in these countries causes "significant environmental pollution and health risks for local populations."

Source: Vidal (2013).

- Communitarianistic cultures believe the group comes before the individual as the group is more important than the individual. The group provides safety and security for individuals. Communitarianistic cultures include Japan and countries in Latin America and Africa.

Specific versus diffuse:

- In specific cultures people keep their personal lives separate from their work lives. Additionally, there is the belief that relationships at work don't have a major impact on work and that people can work together without having a good relationship with each other. Specific cultures include the United States, the United Kingdom, Switzerland, Germany, Scandinavia, and the Netherlands.
- In diffuse cultures people see work and personal lives overlapping. Business people socialize with colleagues and clients. Diffuse cultures include Argentina, Spain, Russia, India, and China.

Focus on Theory 6.3

Criticisms of Hofstede

Hofstede has not gone without critics (McSweeney, 2002a, 2002b). Typical of the criticisms are the following:

- Nations are not the best units for studying cultures. Hofstede (2002) himself agrees, arguing that nations are the only kind of units available for comparison. However, Ladegaard (2007) demonstrated that in a large global corporation employing some 8,500 people in nearly 40 countries, employees perceive their nation-states as the frame of reference or identity.
- Hofstede's survey data are based on a small sample. Hofstede actually combined the results from two separate surveys from 1968–1969 and 1971–1973. The total of 117,000 questionnaires is the combined number for both surveys. Of that total, only data from 40 countries were used, and for only six of the included countries did the number of respondents exceed 1,000. In 15 countries, the number was less than 200.
- Hofstede's survey data are old and outdated. As Charles W. L. Hill (1998) points out, "Cultures do not stand still, they evolve over time, albeit slowly. What was a reasonable characterisation in the 1960s and 1970s may not be so reasonable today" (p. 89).
- Hofstede (2002) responds that the dimensions are assumed to have centuries-old roots, that recent replications show no changes, and that the dimensions have been validated against other measures.
- Hofstede's data are drawn from subsidiaries of only one company, which cannot provide information about entire national cultures. Hofstede (2002) responds that the dimensions are based on the differences between nations and that using the IBM data provides unusually well-matched samples from a large number of countries.

Despite such criticisms, Hofstede's work has become the dominant paradigm and framework for subsequent studies (Chapman, 1997).

Neutral versus emotional:

- In neutral cultures people take great care to control their emotions. Reason is valued over feelings. Neutral cultures include the United Kingdom, Sweden, the Netherlands, Finland, and Germany.
- In emotional cultures spontaneous emotional expressions are accepted and welcomed. Emotional cultures include Poland, Italy, France, Spain, and countries in Latin America.

Achievement versus ascription:

- In achievement-oriented cultures people believe you are what you do. An individual is judged accordingly. Performance is valued over identity. Achievement-oriented cultures include the United States, Canada, Australia, and Scandinavia.
- In ascription-oriented cultures title, position, and power influence how others view you. Your value is determined by who you are. Ascription-oriented cultures include France, Italy, Japan, and Saudi Arabia.

Sequential time versus synchronous time:

- In sequential time cultures people place a value on planning and staying on schedule. Punctuality and meeting deadlines are valued. Events should happen in the planned order. Sequential time cultures include Germany, the United Kingdom, and the United States.
- In synchronous time cultures people work on multiple projects at once. Commitments and plans are viewed as flexible. Synchronous time cultures include Japan, Argentina, and Mexico.

Internal direction versus outer direction:

- This dimension is also known as having an internal or external locus of control. In internally directed cultures people believe they can control their environment and nature in order to achieve their goals. Internally directed cultures include Israel, the United States, Australia, New Zealand, and the United Kingdom.
- In outer-directed cultures people believe they are highly influenced by their environment and must work with the environment to achieve their goals. People in outer-directed cultures tend to avoid conflict with others. Outer-directed cultures include China, Russia, and Saudi Arabia.

The Trompenaars and Hampden-Turner dimension of communitarianism-individualism seems to be virtually identical to Hofstede's collectivism-individualism. Their achievement-ascription value orientation appears to be somewhat related to Hofstede's power distance dimension; Hofstede's dimension is broader in that it includes how status is accorded but also how the culture accepts power distance. Their universalism-particularism dimension, which describes a preference for rules, could overlap with Hofstede's uncertainty avoidance dimension and the collectivism-individualism dimension. Trompenaars and Hampden-Turner's other dimensions don't have a clear relationship to Hofstede's.

Map 6.2   Japan

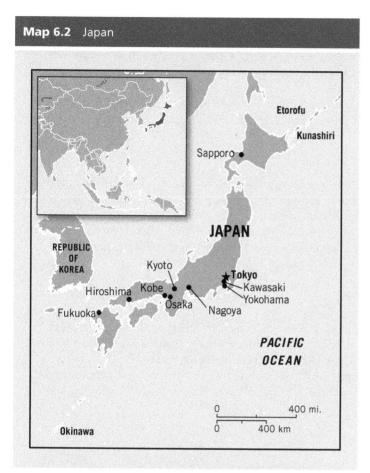

Mount Fuji is Japan's highest mountain and is frequently depicted in art and photographs as a symbol of Japan.

Case Study: Japan as a Homogeneous Culture

From Hofstede's (1983) research, Japan is placed about in the middle between individualism and collectivism. Yet Japan is popularly stereotyped as a group-oriented culture. In 1986, Prime Minister Yasuhiro Nakasone described Japan as being a "homogeneous" country—a widely held view in Japanese society at large. In this case study, look for ways that homogeneity may be a way to better understand Japan. In the discussions of Japan's geography and history, population and economy, and cultural patterns, identify specific ways that homogeneity affects communication.

Geography and History

Japan is an archipelago formed by four large islands and more than 3,000 small islands covering 377,915 square kilometers, roughly the size of California. Much of the land surface is hilly or mountainous, leaving only 12% arable land. Hence, Japan imports a large amount of its food and relies heavily on the ocean. Seafood is a staple in the Japanese diet, and Japan is the world's leading producer of fish. As an island nation, Japan will never be fully self-sufficient. It has virtually no energy natural resources. It must export in order to import materials it needs to survive.

Japan's origins are not clear. It is thought that Chinese culture as it passed through Korea was seminal. Japan is known as the Land of the Rising Sun, as is symbolized on its flag. Founded early in the Christian era, Japan has a parliamentary government with a constitutional monarchy. According to legend, all Japanese are genealogically related to the emperor at some distant point. In pre–World War II Japan, the emperor was worshiped as a living god. Hirohito was the emperor from 1926 until his death in 1989. Tradition dictated that a full year of mourning pass, followed by a full season to plant and harvest a crop of sacred rice, before his son Akihito could be formally enthroned as a symbolic constitutional monarch in 1990.

Japanese worldview is consistent with that of an isolated island. There is no differentiation: People from the United States, Europe, and other parts of Asia are foreigners. The world is divided into Japan and others: *gaikoku,* or outside nation, and gaijin, or outside person.

Population and Economy

Japan is one of the most homogeneous countries in the world: More than 98% of its population is Japanese; Koreans, Chinese, and native Ainu constitute most of the remaining 2%. In 1997, Japan's parliament, or *diet,* voted to replace a century-old law that forced the Ainu to assimilate. The Ainu were recognized by the United Nations as a native people in 1992 and the Japanese diet called for their recognition as an indigenous people in 2008, but the Ainu still face discrimination in Japan.

The population of Japan is approximately 127 million, equivalent to about 40% of the U.S. population, and inhabits only 4% of the U.S. land area, which translates to a population density of about 348 people per square kilometer; in the United States, the comparable density is 35. Japan is divided into 47 administrative units, or prefectures. More than 93% of Japan's population lives in urban areas, with approximately 45% of the population living in the two major metropolitan areas of Tokyo (the largest city in the world by total urban area population) and Osaka-Kobe. More than 25% of Japanese are over 65, compared to approximately 15% in the United States.

Because it is an island country and hence borders on no other countries, Japan was little affected by foreign influence until 1853. Japan's isolation means that its history is its own. Everyone shares the same ideas and, lacking outside influences, has no reason to doubt them. In addition, as a small, densely populated country, its ideas and information are easily shared. Even the tradition of rice growing contributes to a society based on minimizing conflict and enhanced cooperation, which, like the rice, are necessary for survival.

After Commodore Perry's arrival with battleships in 1853, Japan transformed itself from a feudal country into an industrialized nation by adapting Western technology. Later, from the mid-1920s to the mid-1930s, urban Japanese experienced U.S. fashions, movies, and music. The postwar constitution drafted by Allied occupation authorities and approved by the Japanese parliament made Japan a constitutional monarchy. The new constitution also renounced war and allowed military only for self-defense. Following World War II, Japan again adopted more Western culture.

Even after a decade of poor economic performance, Japan remains the world's third largest economy, with several world-class companies that are technological leaders and household names. Japan is a major foreign investor and a major foreign aid donor. Japanese life and language are Westernized. U.S. popular culture reaches Japan more quickly than it reaches some parts of the United States. English loan words in the Japanese language grow at a fast rate, and the Japan's Westernization has been criticized by some Asian countries.

In 2013 only 1% of its gross national product was spent on defense. (In the same period, the United States spent 4.4%.) By 2004, Japan was paying more than 70% of the cost of U.S. military bases in Japan. In response to criticism for not providing troops in the 1991 Gulf War, Japan approved providing troops for the United Nations peacekeeping operations in noncombat roles in East Timor, Cambodia, Afghanistan, and later Iraq. In 2015, over public opposition, the legislature interpreted the constitution to allow the military to operate overseas to participate with allies for collective self-defense.

Focus on Theory 6.4

Asian Perspectives

Miike (2004) believes that Asian scholars can "paint a number of wonderful portraits about humanity and communication." Miike's own portrait of communication is as "a process in which we remind ourselves of the interdependence and interrelatedness of the universe... [C]ommunication is a process in which we experience the oneness of the universe" (p. 74). In this portrait, we can transcend the illusion of separateness, of fragmentation, and gain a glimpse of the larger relationship of what often appear to be discrete aspects of life (Miike, 2003a, 2003b).

Cultural Patterns

Critical to understanding the cultural patterns of Japan is the homogeneity of its population, although some would argue that Japan is not all that homogeneous. However, the cultural myth of homogeneity is believed and therefore is an important cultural concept. A study by Hajime Nakamura (1964) of the National Institute of Science and Technology Policy in Japan asked citizens to name aspects of their country of which they were proudest. Topping that list was Japan's maintenance of social order, followed by its natural beauty, its history and traditions, the diligence and talent of its people, the high level of education, the country's prosperity, and its culture and arts.

Japan's homogeneity contributes to its social order and its people's "communication without language" (Tsujimura, 1968, 1987). It is said that being monolingual and monoracial makes it easy for the Japanese to understand each other with few words. The United States, with its high level of diversity, is verbose—more talking is required to overcome diverse languages, diverse lifestyles, and diverse ways of feeling and thinking. Japanese axioms teach that verbosity is dangerous: "Least said, soonest mended" and "Out of the mouth comes evil." Today, the education system maintains those same cultural values. All schools have the same curriculum. Schools have uniforms and encourage students to take part in after-school group activities.

Japan has often been described as a society in which conflict is avoided by emphasizing homogeneity and dismissing differentness as incidental. The Japanese do not have the same perception of self as an individual that is typical in the United States; instead, the Japanese feel most comfortable with others who empathize. To be completely understood, people have to cooperate in the same context, and in doing so, there can be no differentiation of individuals. In such an extremely homogeneous society, you are not seen as an individual, nor do you regard individualism as a positive trait. It has been said that group life is to the Japanese what individualism is to the United States. Homogeneity is the core value of society that substantially defines other values and permeates all areas of life. This social interdependence has been referred to by Takeo Doi (1956, 1973) as *amae* (a noun that comes from the verb *amaeru,* which means to look to others for support and affection). *Amae* is the feeling of nurturing for and dependence on another. *Amae* is a sense of complete dependence based on a wish to be loved and cared for unconditionally. It develops in the relationship between mother and child and later transfers to the child's teachers and others in positions of authority. *Amae* is a reciprocal relationship. Just as the child is dependent on the mother, the mother is dependent on the child, which arises from the need to be needed. *Amae,* with its emphasis on interdependence, contrasts sharply with individualism. (See Focus on Culture 6.3 for a description of how the game of baseball reflects Japanese cultural patterns.)

Focus on Culture 6.4

Baseball in Japan

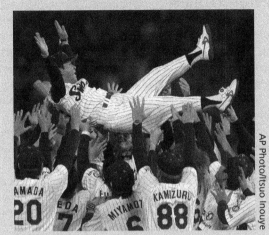

AP Photo/Itsuo Inouye

Yukult Swallows manager tossed in air by players in Tokyo's Jingu Stadium.

Japan began to adopt many modern Western ideas during the Meiji restoration (1867–1912). U.S. professors in Japan may have first organized baseball games with their students in 1872. The game became known as Yakkyu, or "field ball." The Japanese saw the psychology between the pitcher and batter as similar to the psychology in sumo and martial arts and appreciated the timing and mental and physical strength the game required (Whiting, 2009). Interest grew when the New York Giants and the Chicago White Sox came to Japan in 1910, and later Babe Ruth, Lou Gehrig, Jimmy Foxx, and numerous other stars played against Japanese college all-stars. Japan's first professional team, the Great Tokyo baseball club, was formed in December 1934.

After World War II, the Allied command official allowed the game to resume as a way to boost morale. By 1950, teams became supported by large corporations. Teams were organized into two leagues, the Central and Pacific, each with six teams.

According to Whiting (2009), a Japanese writer summed up his country's love for the game by saying, "Baseball is perfect for us, if the Americans hadn't invented it, we would have" (p. 51).

Yet there are cultural differences. "Everything from the way the players respectfully doff their caps when addressed by their coach to their strategy and philosophy of the game is infused with elements of Japanese culture" (Gillette, 1991).

For 20 years, the Yakult Swallows went to Yuma, Arizona, for training every February. (February is Japan's coldest month.) "To feed baseball frenzy, representatives of six Japanese TV stations, two radio stations, two news agencies, six all-sports dailies, and two general newspapers are on hand to record the Swallows' every move" (Gillette, 1991).

During training, the Swallows do everything as a team. "There is little room for individualism in Japanese baseball, as opposed to American baseball. The Americans like to do their own thing. Some observers say the stifling of initiative hampers Japanese baseball, but others say obedience, discipline, and respect for authority simply reflect their country's culture. American players have traditionally found it difficult to adjust to baseball in Japan. They face a different pitching style, different strike zones, inconsistent umpires, and a different philosophy and strategy" (Gillette, 1991).

One difference in strategy is that Japanese coaches believe it is easier to win while their team is ahead, so they press for runs in the early innings. But when a team is ahead, the team doesn't go for a big lead in order to allow the opposing team to save face.

Sources: Whiting (2009); Gillette (1991). Copyright © 1991, Automobile Club of Southern California. Reprinted by permission, courtesy of *Westways*.

Japan is changing: Its youth may hold significantly different cultural values and an aging and declining population may force an acceptance of immigration.

In a 1995 study of Japanese students using the original Hofstede questionnaires, Woodring found that students scored higher on individualism and lower on power distance than Hofstede's original sample. Woodring explained that the higher individualism and lower power distance score might be explained by age; that is, Japanese college students may value individualism and equality more than Japanese society does as a whole. Matsumoto (2002) concluded that "the stereotype of [Japanese being more collectivistic than Americans] is simply not congruent with contemporary Japanese culture and its younger generations" (p. 53). Matsumoto argues that today's Japanese parents have become less concerned with instilling collectivistic values in their children.

Hofstede's longitudinal study showed that national wealth and individualism were related. Around 1990, the term *shin jin rui* (literally "new human beings") was applied to youths 25 years old and younger, who were described by older Japanese as "selfish, self-centered, and disrespectful of elders and tradition." Hofstede's study suggested that the Japanese were group-oriented, hierarchical, and formal. There are reasons to suggest that at least younger Japanese prefer moderately egalitarian distribution of power and feel moderately independent of collective thought and action. This demonstrates that we should avoid allowing the Hofstede research to become a stereotype.

A second factor is Japan's aging population. Barring a baby boom or radical changes in its restrictive immigration policies, in 30 years 39% of the country's population will be over 65, and by 2060 its population will drop by one-third. Immigrants make up less than 2% of the population, and that number includes tens of thousands of ethnic Koreans born and raised in Japan who are not considered citizens. Whether Japan's immigration policy will change is yet to be seen.

Finally, perhaps Japan is beginning to recognize that it is not as homogeneous as the cultural myth suggests. Japan is beginning to identify itself more in terms of nationality rather than ethnicity. Traditional mores are becoming less important as Japan becomes more international. Many feel that modern Japan cannot continue to value the communication subtleties that are not easily understood by non-Japanese.

Yet there is evidence that the traditional mores are still deep seated. On March 11, 2011, a 9.0 earthquake and accompanying tsunami hit in northern Japan near Sendai, a city of 1 million people 304 kilometers north of Tokyo. News reports worldwide showed the massive damage to buildings and roadways and loss of life. They also showed people patiently waiting in lines for water and fuel and to enter supermarkets. There was a lack of looting and of egregious price gouging. Researcher Brigitte Steger recorded the daily lives of people displaced by the tsunami. She found that people were driven toward honest behavior by what she called social balance. In fact, by early fall, in Japan's culture of honesty and altruism, citizens had turned over to authorities more than $48 million in found loose cash in the area damaged by the tsunami (Coulton & Glionna, 2011).

Phillippe Lopez/AFP/Getty Images

Rather than looting or crowds, after the 2011 earthquake people in Japan waited patiently in line for food and water.

The term *Yamato-damashi*, or Japanese spirit, refers to group responsibility and collective consciousness. In that time of crisis, Japanese politesse and an ingrained instinct for orderliness and calm kept hold. In Tokyo, the earthquake temporarily closed the public transportation system. When trains appeared, there was no pushing—the queues were as orderly as on any other day.

The earthquake and tsunami also ravaged the Fukushima nuclear power plant. Fifty workers stayed behind to fight the fires and keep the reactors from melting down. They became known as the "Faceless Fifty." It was said that in watching news reports of

Global Voices

What must be admitted—very painfully—is that this [Fukushima meltdown] was a disaster "Made in Japan." Its fundamental causes are to be found in the ingrained conventions of Japanese culture: our reflexive obedience; our reluctance to question authority; our devotion to "sticking with the program"; our groupism; and our insularity.

—Nuclear Accident Independent Investigation Commission authorized by Japan's parliament (quoted in Beech, 2014, p. 36)

Focus on Technology 6.4

Japan's Top Mobile Messaging App

The social network Line was launched in 2011 by NHN Japan after the earthquake. The name refers to the lines that formed outside of public phones after the disaster. The app, which provides free instant messaging and calling via smartphones, tablets, and computers, became the world's fastest-growing social network, reaching 50 million followers in just 399 days.

Japan is the only market where Twitter is more popular than Facebook. Twitter grew quickly in Japan because in a culture where privacy is important, that Twitter allows users to fake names was valued. Also in Japanese you can communicate almost double what you can communicate in English with 140 characters. Japanese tend to tweet en masse during significant events. When the Japanese team scored a goal against Cameroon in the 2010 World Cup, Japanese users generated a record 2,940 tweets per second.

Facebook is growing in Japan as it is being adopted primarily for business and professional relationships and for business and commercial purposes.

©iStockphoto.com/Image_Source_

Japan is one of the world's most wired countries: In 2017, it had 67 million landline phones and 159 million mobile phones (eighth among the world's countries). At 118 million users, Internet use ranked fifth in the world. During the 2011 earthquake crisis, information distribution was constant and widespread. National television networks, newspapers, radio, and Internet sources provided information at local and national levels. The crisis called attention to the special needs of Japan's elderly: Tea kettles with wireless technology warn distant children if a parent doesn't use it every morning.

the Faceless Fifty risking their lives for the common good, the Japanese saw a quiet selflessness and recognized themselves. The group-first mentality remains in this essentially ethnically homogeneous society. While some say it is a sensitivity "bred" into the Japanese, it is really cultural learning from parents and teachers (Magnier, 2011).

SUMMARY

Dutch management researcher Geert Hofstede studied more than 100,000 IBM employees in 40 countries to determine the value dimensions across which cultures vary. His work continues to be widely used in a variety of disciplines and has been accepted by many as being helpful in understanding cultural values.

Hofstede identified four dimensions that he labeled individualism, masculinity, power distance, and uncertainty avoidance. The individualism-collectivism dimension describes relationships between the individual and the group. The masculinity-femininity dimension describes how a culture's dominant values are assertive or nurturing. Power distance refers to the distribution of influence within a culture. And uncertainty avoidance reflects a culture's tolerance of ambiguity and acceptance of risk.

Later, a fifth dimension was added: long-term orientation versus short-term orientation to life. This dimension describes cultures that range from short-term values with respect for tradition and reciprocity in social relations to long-term values with persistence and ordering relationships by status. And recently a sixth dimension was added: indulgence versus restraint, which deals with the gratification of human desires.

The Trompenaars and Hampden-Turner dimensions based on 46,000 managers in 40 countries are presented as a contrast to the Hofstede dimensions. Trompenaars and Hampden-Turner identified seven dimensions: universalism versus particularism (rules versus relationships), individualism versus communitarianism (the individual versus the group), specific versus diffuse, neutral versus emotional, achievement versus ascription, sequential time versus synchronous time, internal direction versus outer direction.

Recently, studies have attempted to correlate the Hofstede dimensions to environmental concerns. A relationship between power distance and masculinity has been shown to be a predictor of environmental performance. A new measure, the Environmental Performance Index, was developed to use environmental outcome-oriented indicators.

Japan is presented as a case study in this chapter. While some assume that Japan is a collectivist culture, it actually ranks near the middle on that dimension. Japan can be better understood as a homogeneous country. That belief is reflected in history, religion, cultural patterns, and communication style. A second case study presents Singapore as a culture that has balanced Confucian values with an individualistic capitalist economy.

DISCUSSION QUESTIONS

1. List and describe examples of each of the Hofstede dimensions at your university.
2. Explain how one can use the Hofstede dimensions without stereotyping.
3. What implications for environmental sustainability do the studies by Husted (2005), H. Park et al. (2007), and Peng and Lin (2009) suggest?
4. Compare the homogeneity in Japan with multicultural countries such as the United States. What important communication challenges become clear?
5. Explain how homogeneity can be related to the concept of high- and low-context cultures.

amae	gaijin	mitigated speech
collectivism	individualism	power distance
Confucian work dynamism	long-term orientation	short-term orientation
femininity	masculinity	uncertainty avoidance

READINGS

All readings are from *Intercultural Communication: A Global Reader* (Jandt, 2004).

Geert Hofstede, "Business Cultures" (p. 8)

Ashleigh C. Merritt and Robert L. Helmreich, "Human Factors on the Flight Deck: The Influence of National Culture" (p. 13)

STUDENT STUDY SITE

⑤SAGE edge™

Sharpen your skills with SAGE edge at edge.sagepub.com/jandt9e.

SAGE edge for Students provides a personalized approach to help you accomplish your coursework goals in an easy-to-use learning environment.

Chapter 7

LEARNING OBJECTIVES

After studying this chapter, you will be able to:

- Identify the five aspects of value orientation theory.
- Trace the origins of U.S. cultural patterns.
- Use value orientation theory to describe dominant U.S. cultural patterns.
- Use each aspect of value orientation theory to describe communication practices in the United States.
- Discuss whether U.S. cultural patterns vary by region and social class.

© iStockphoto.com/kreicher

Dominant U.S. Cultural Patterns Using Value Orientation Theory

As you read in Chapter 1, nation-state has become primary identity in many parts of the world, and it has become common practice to equate national identity with cultural identity. This chapter focuses on the United States—the third largest nation in the world by size and the third most populous. Its economy is the largest and most technologically powerful in the world. Since World War II, the United States has remained the world's most powerful nation-state.

If you are of the U.S. culture, you have learned values, what is competent, and what is desirable behavior from that culture. This type of learning is called emic knowledge, or knowledge of the culture learned from the inside. Emic knowledge constitutes the rules known from inside the culture and as such are seldom organized or consciously discussed (Stewart, 1982). It is not unusual, then, that you may find some of the descriptions in this chapter new concepts. If you are not of the U.S. culture, the theoretical and normative information you have learned about the United States is called etic knowledge. This chapter may help you understand some aspects of the culture that you have found puzzling.

Global Voices

For 500 years the West patented six killer applications that set it apart. The first to download them was Japan. Over the last century, one Asian country after another has downloaded these killer apps—competition, modern science, the rule of law and private property rights, modern medicine, the consumer society and the work ethic. Those six things are the secret sauce of Western civilization.

—Niall Ferguson, author of *Civilization: The West and the Rest* (2011; quoted in Zakaria, 2011, para. 5)

The first question to ask is "Is there now or has there ever been one dominant U.S. culture that everyone in the nation primarily identifies with?" In this chapter you'll first read about the origins of U.S. cultural patterns, and the forces that tended to shape a national character from several regional groups are described. Then, what have been labeled the dominant U.S. cultural patterns are described using Kluckhohn and Strodtbeck's (1961) value orientation theory. Finally, you'll read about challenges to a dominant cultural identity by new regional groups and by growing awareness of class identity.

Origins of U.S. Cultural Patterns

Pre-16th-Century Indigenous Americans

AP Photo/Kevin Rivoli

Iroquois flag at the Lafayette (New York) High School

Before Columbus arrived, North America was home to a diverse population of some 10 million people. Indigenous Americans spoke hundreds of languages. Arguably, though, the Iroquois were the most important indigenous group. Like many other indigenous groups, their name came from their enemies. The Algonquin called them the Iroqu (Irinakhoiw), or "rattlesnakes." The French added the Gallic suffix -ois. The Iroquois call themselves Haudenosaunee, meaning "people of the long house." The original homeland of the Iroquois was between the Adirondack Mountains and Niagara Falls, but at one time they controlled most of what is now the northeastern United States and eastern Canada. Surprisingly few in number, the Iroquois had an impact on North American history. Their number in 1600 has been estimated at 20,000. European epidemics and warfare reduced their population to about half that. Unlike other nations, the Iroquois assimilated conquered groups and grew in number.

The Iroquois political system, the Iroquois League (sometimes known as the Five Nations and later the Six Nations), was formed prior to any European contact and hence owed nothing to European influence. The league was founded to maintain peace and resolve disputes between its members. It had a written constitution with a system of checks, balances, and supreme law. Central authority was limited. By 1660, to deal with European powers as an equal, the Iroquois found it necessary to present a united front to Europeans.

Some argue that the Iroquois political organization was an influence on the U.S. Articles of Confederation and Constitution. Others strongly refute that. Nonetheless, in 1988 the U.S. Congress passed Senate Resolution 76 to recognize the influence of the Iroquois League on the Constitution and Bill of Rights.

European Enlightenment

The U.S. society that evolved and is dominant today grew from European roots. The scientific method, democracy, and capitalism are institutions of Western cultures (D'Souza, 2002). The dominant language, the system of representative government, the structure of law, and the emphasis on individual liberty all derive from the Enlightenment ideals formulated in England. Other important U.S. ideals, such as the separation of powers, derive from the French philosopher Montesquieu. These values, established early in U.S. history, remain strong.

Regional Differences Resulting From Immigration

The United States is a country of immigrants from all over the world, each person immigrating with his or her own cultural values. Many arrived in groups and tended to remain settled in the same area. Brandeis University historian David Hackett Fischer (1989) argues that the

Beinecke Rare Book & Manuscript Library, Yale University

De Tocqueville's *Democracy in America* is considered one of the most comprehensive and insightful books ever written about the United States.

early immigrants from England established distinctive regional cultures that remain today. He further argues that the United States has been a society of diversity—not homogeneity—from its very beginning.

The Puritans came from eastern England to Massachusetts between 1629 and 1641. A small number of Royalist elite and large numbers of indentured servants from southern and western England settled in the Chesapeake region between 1642 and 1675. Quakers from England's north midlands and Wales settled in the Delaware Valley between 1675 and 1725. The final group, from Northern Ireland, Scotland, and the border area of northern England, settled in Appalachia between 1717 and 1775. Each of these groups had diverse dialects and attitudes, and all retained a degree of separateness. Even Henry Adams's History of the United States had separate chapters on the "intellect" of New England, the Middle States, and the South in 1800. Zelinsky (1973) examined regional patterns in language, religion, food habits, architecture, place names, and the culture of the inhabitants who established the first effective settlements. He identified five regions: New England, the Midland, the Middle West, the South, and the West. More recently, Bigelow (1980) examined ethnicity, religion, party affiliation, and dialect and identified these regions: Northeast, Border South, Deep South, Midwest, Mexicano, Southwest, Colorado, Mormondom, Pacific Northwest, Northern California, and Southern California.

Map 7.1 The United States Circa 1800

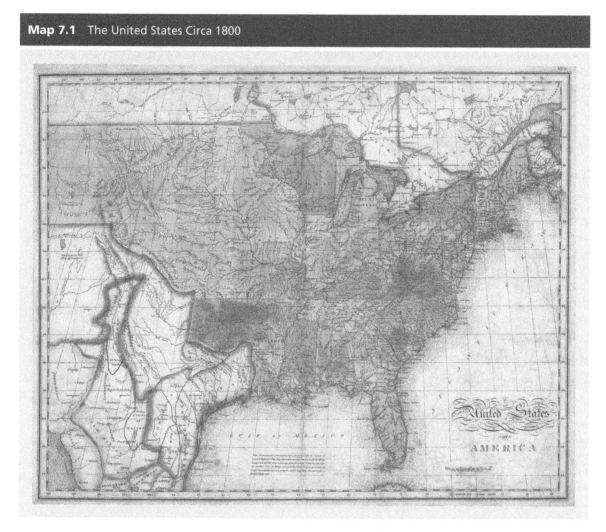

Source: John Melish map (1822), from Geographicus Antique Maps (http://en.wikipedia.org/).

These analyses clearly show that the United States may never have been a completely homogeneous culture. In 1831, then 26-year-old French aristocrat Alexis de Tocqueville (1805–1859) toured the United States and saw the country as composed of almost separate little nations (de Tocqueville, 1835/1945; see also Mayer, 1981).

Years later, communication researchers Peter Andersen, Myron Lustig, and Janis Andersen (1987) suggested that these regional differences continued to exist in three areas of communication behavior:

1. *Verbal Control and Dominance.* New Englanders were more likely to be introverts; those in the Mid-Atlantic region were characterized as not particularly talkative or verbally dominant.
2. *Affiliativeness and Immediacy.* People from Texas, Oklahoma, Arkansas, and Louisiana visited more neighbors and rated friends higher than did people in other regions. Pacific Coast

residents reported the most isolation from friends, least acquaintance with their neighbors, greatest distance from relatives, and lowest frequency of interactions with confidants.

3. *Arousal or Activation.* New Englanders employed a nondramatic and reserved communication style. The South and the Northwest were slow and relaxed compared to the fast pace of the urban Northeast.

Focus on Culture 7.1

The Frontier in U.S. Culture

In 1893, Frederick Jackson Turner published *The Frontier in American History* in which he argued that U.S. culture grew from and was nurtured by the ever-present frontier. The frontier provided resources, wildness, a place to test and build character. Survival challenges on the frontier produced a people of strong and durable character. The frontier symbolized economic opportunity, religious freedom, and relief from oppression. The continued promise of "greener pastures" produced a forward-looking people.

Forces Toward the Development of a Dominant Culture

De Tocqueville predicted that the United States would be a great power. The reasons he gave were the country's large geographic size, abundant natural resources, growing population, and vibrant national character. Historians have charted the series of events that resulted in a dominant national culture:

- opening of the Erie Canal in 1825 and emergence of New York as the financial and corporate capital of an integrated industrial complex stretching from the Northeast to the upper Midwest
- defeat of the South and passage of the Thirteenth, Fourteenth, and Fifteenth Amendments, which established national citizenship over state citizenship
- development of Theodore Roosevelt's "new nationalism," which provided the intellectual foundations for an activist national government
- passage of the Immigration Restriction Act of 1924, which permitted a degree of homogenization of the population
- development of radio and television, which nationalized politics and popular culture

Todd Plitt/Hulton Archive/Getty Images

News anchor Tom Brokaw reported on NBC—one of only three news networks for many years—from 1982 to 2004.

Global Voices

During the summer of 2013, the world turned its attention to Syria and its chemical weapons. President Barack Obama proposed U.S. airstrikes on the country, citing American exceptionalism. Russian president Vladimir Putin directly addressed the concept of American "exceptionalism" in an op-ed piece in the *New York Times*. President Putin wrote that he disagreed with the case for American exceptionalism President Obama had made: "It is extremely dangerous to encourage people to see themselves as exceptional, whatever the motivation." Putin continued that we are all different but created equal.

Source: Putin (2013).

- the automobile and interstate highway system, which made the country internally mobile
- the Great Depression, World War II, and the onset of the Cold War, all of which increased the need for a strong centralized national government

These forces contributed to an exceptional uniformity that characterized U.S. society in the early post–World War II period (Clough, 1997).

Yet, today, the United States is one of the most culturally diverse countries in the world. Nearly every region of the world has influenced the culture of the United States. As you read in Chapter 5, the United States does not have an official language nor an official national religion. Clothing styles vary by region and climate, occupation, and social status. Popular food varies as well by region, heritage, and social status. But are there values that are shared by everyone? One answer to this question is that it is possible to identify important underlying values that most people in the country share. You will read about these in the next section, on value orientation theory. Another answer to this question is that to talk about a dominant cultural pattern is to talk about the cultural patterns of the group that controls the society. In the last section of this chapter you'll read about groups with behaviors and values that differ in some ways from the dominant cultural pattern.

International opinion polls continue to show that U.S. residents have values different from those of other cultures. It was de Tocqueville who coined the phrase "American exceptionalism" to express the idea that the United States *is* different. Understanding these values and their development contributes to improved intercultural communication, for as you learn to understand and accept your own culture, your intercultural communication improves. As you go through this chapter, then, keep in mind that it is generalizing the values of an entire culture. You may find that you as an individual do not agree with all the values identified as typical in the United States, and you surely will know of others who would not agree. This chapter is about the dominant cultural values said to be characteristic of the majority of U.S. citizens.

As you examine these values, remember how everything that occurs in a culture is related to and consistent with other things in that culture. None of the values presented is discrete—all are related to and reinforce each other.

Value Orientation Theory

Kluckhohn and Strodtbeck (1961) argue that all human cultures are confronted with universally shared problems emerging from relationships with fellow beings, activities, time, and nature. These five basic problems are as follows:

1. What is a human being's relation to nature? (human being–nature orientation)
2. What is the modality of human activity? (activity orientation)

3. What is the temporal focus of human life? (time orientation)
4. What is the character of innate human nature? (human nature orientation)
5. What is the relationship of the individual to others? (relational orientation)

Kluckhohn and Strodtbeck's value orientation theory suggests that cultures develop unique positions in these five value orientations: human being–nature, activity, time, human nature, and relational. Human being–nature is described here as worldview (after Samovar, Porter, & Jain, 1981) and considers how humans dominate, live with, or are subjugated to nature. Activity orientation deals with people in the culture "being" (passively accepting), "being-in-becoming" (transforming), or "doing" (initiating action). Time orientation deals with the emphasis the culture places on the past, the present, or the future. Human nature orientation considers whether humans are primarily evil, primarily good, or a mixture of both. And relational orientation considers the way the culture organizes interpersonal relationships: linear hierarchy, group identification, or individualism.

There have been many excellent descriptions of U.S. cultural patterns (e.g., Kohls, 1984; Samovar et al., 1981; Stewart, 1972). The one used in this chapter is based on Kluckhohn and Strodtbeck's (1961) value orientations and modifies and adds to their categories as necessary to describe the cultural patterns that are characteristic of the majority of U.S. citizens and have an influence on communication.

The Kluckhohn and Strodtbeck value orientations can be used to describe other cultures and, therefore, provide a systematic way of comparing cultural values.

What Is a Human Being's Relation to Nature?

The term worldview deals with a culture's most fundamental beliefs about its place in the cosmos, beliefs about God, and beliefs about the nature of humanity and nature. Worldview refers to the philosophical ideas of being. Huntington (1993, 1996) has argued that the world can be divided into eight major *cultural zones* that have been shaped by religious tradition still powerful today: Western

Table 7.1 Religious Identifications, 2014

Self-Identification	U.S. Percentage	World Percentage
Christian	70.6	31.4
Jewish	1.9	0.2
Muslim	0.9	23.2
Buddhist	0.7	7.1
Hindu	0.7	15.0
Other/don't know/refused	2.4	6.7
Unaffiliated*	22.8	16.4

Sources: Pew Research Center (2015a); Central Intelligence Agency (2016).

*includes agnostic, atheist, nothing in particular.

Global Voices

There is no country in the world where the Christian religion retains a greater influence over the souls of men.

—Alexis de Tocqueville, *Democracy in America* (1835/1945)

[The United States] now has a greater diversity of religious groups than any country in recorded history.

—J. Gordon Melton, *Encyclopedia of American Religions* (1991)

Christianity; the Orthodox world; the Islamic world; and the Confucian, Japanese, Hindu, African, and Latin American zones.

Throughout the 19th century, religious discourse in the United States was dominated by White male Protestant conservatives of European heritage (Eck, 1993). In the 20th century, the United States became a meeting place for all the world's religions, yet it can be said that the European conservative Protestant worldview dominates U.S. culture.

The United States does have more Christians than any other country. Seven out of 10 identify with the Christian religion. However, the percentage of adults who describe themselves as Christian declined from 2007 to 2014 while those identified as unaffiliated (agnostic, atheist, and "nothing in particular") increased six percentage points over that same time period. A Pew Research Center (2015a) survey revealed clear regional differences: Those identified as unaffiliated varied from 19% in the South to 28% in the West, and while the numbers are small, the percentage identifying with religions other than Christianity grew from 4.7% in 2007 to 5.9% in 2014.

More than half (53%) of U.S. citizens say that religion is very important in their lives. This is slightly less than the global median of 55%. Generally, people in a number of countries in Africa, the Middle East, and Asia place more importance on religion. On the other hand, religion is more important to U.S. citizens than residents of many other Western and European countries as well as other advanced economy nations (China 3%, Japan 11%, France 14%, United Kingdom 21%, Germany 21%, Italy 26%, Israel 34%). The data show how the United States is unique: Overall, people in wealthier nations put less importance on religion than those in poorer nations; the exception to this is the United States. About twice as many people say religion is very important in their lives than do people in Australia, Germany, and Canada (Theodorou, 2015). Samovar et al. (1981) identified three parts to worldview: the individual-and-nature relationship, science and technology, and materialism.

The Individual-and-Nature Relationship

In the United States, people typically make a clear distinction between human life and nature, valuing nature but clearly placing a higher value on human life. This belief that humans have "dominion over nature" has made it possible for the United States to change the course of rivers, harvest forests for wood and paper, breed cattle for increased meat production, and destroy disease-causing bacteria. There can be little doubt that this belief has contributed to the material wealth of the United States. The environmental movement and the animal rights movement are not contradictory to this belief. Both movements share the basic assumption that humans have a responsibility to protect nature. For the most part, these activists agree that humans should act to protect nature—that is, that humans are different from the rest of nature and in some ways superior to it. Having a responsibility to protect nature implies a dominant role.

Other views are that humans are a part of nature and should attempt to live in harmony with it—not exploit or protect it—and that humans are subjugated by nature.

Science and Technology

People in the United States have a strong faith in the scientific method of solving problems. In the United States, it's a common belief that events have causes, that those causes can be discovered, and that humans can and should alter that relationship.

That events have causes rather than being random has a long tradition. The early colonists felt that nothing that occurred in the world was a random event but, rather, was the product of intent by some mover. A New England earthquake in 1727 "filled the houses of God" and contributed to the first Great Awakening. Pennsylvania's Johnstown Flood in 1889, the sinking of the *Titanic* in 1912, and the Great Depression of the 1930s were all attributed to the wrath of God.

Modern acceptance of the scientific method is reflected in much communication and logic. Objectivity, empirical evidence, and facts are valued. Consider the majority approach to the AIDS epidemic. Most people in the United States recognized that the disease had a viral cause and that the virus could be identified and eradicated, as polio had been.

The United States has strong faith in science and technology. The 1939 World's Fair celebrated technology in the United States. Also in 1939, the U.S. Army numbered 175,000 officers and men, 16th largest in the world, right behind Romania. World War II changed that. In 1945, Germany built 40,593 aircraft and Japan 28,180. The United States built 96,318. By 1945, half of all ships afloat in the world had been built in the United States. U.S. industry made the country's military the best equipped in the world.

Adoption of media has been far reaching in the United States. As of 2015, the country had 122 million landline telephones (third in the world, one for every 2.7 people), 382 million mobile phones (fifth in the world, 1.18 for every person), and 240 million Internet users (third in the world; Central Intelligence Agency, 2017).

Focus on Technology 7.1

Social Media Use in the United States

As of 2016, 79% of online people use Facebook—more than double that use Twitter, Pinterest, Instagram, or LinkedIn. For the entire population, that means 68% of all U.S. adults are Facebook users. Of Facebook users, 76% visit the site daily. Twitter is more popular among younger adults and the highly educated; Pinterest is used at a much higher rate by women; Instagram is used most by younger adults; LinkedIn is popular with college graduates and high income earners.

A majority of U.S. citizens now say they get news via social media, and half used social media to learn about the 2016 presidential campaign. Twitter figured prominently in that campaign:

@HillaryClinton had 11,918,590 followers with 9,837 tweets. Over 75% of the tweets were published using TweetDeck, a desktop tool used by social media professionals. Most retweeted: "To all the little girls watching … never doubt that you are valuable and powerful & deserving of every chance & opportunity in the world."

@realDonaldTrump had 18,992,296 followers with 34,253 tweets. Over 89% of the tweets were published directly from Android devices and iPhones. Most retweeted: "TODAY WE MAKE AMERICA GREAT AGAIN!"

Sources: Greenwood, Perrin, & Duggan (2016); Keegan (2017).

The United States has more self-storage units than the rest of the world.

Table 7.2 What the United States Buys Daily

50,051,507	12-oz. cans of Pepsi
35,079,448	12-oz. servings of Bud Light
8,179,726	20-oz. bottles of Aquafina water
2,400,000	Burger King Whoppers
500,000	Hostess Twinkies
300,000	Packs of Pampers
153,424	Lbs. of Starbucks coffee
150,000	Hot Wheels Basic Cars (small size)
125,000	Barbie dolls
123,287	Trojan Ultra Thin condoms
87,431	Slim-Fast Optima multipack shakes
14,100	First Response pregnancy tests
3,160	Men's Rogaine 5% Solution
34	Porsche 911s

Source: "America by the Numbers" (2007, p. 54).

Materialism

If there is one value that most of the rest of the world attributes to the United States, it is materialism, or the belief that possessions are important in life. In *Democracy in America,* de Tocqueville (1835/1945) wrote about how materialistic people in the United States were even in 1831. In 1872, Montgomery Ward printed the first merchandise catalog. Sears followed with a 500-page version two decades later. Soon after, department stores like Marshall Field's and Macy's offered those same products in one physical location. After World War II new appliances, furniture, and household goods became available. Television advertising and planned obsolescence triggered more consumption. By the mid-1980s, consumers were spending close to half of their annual expenditures on nonnecessities. In the past decade, due in part to low-cost overseas manufacturing, discount and online retailers could sell more products for less. Today, children in the United States make up 3% of the world's children but have more than 40% of the toys purchased globally. The average U.S. household has 248 garments and 29 pairs of shoes and purchases 64 garments and 7 pairs of shoes annually. (See Table 7.2 for a list of what people in the United States buy daily and Table 7.3 for total and per person municipal solid waste.) Materialism has given birth to two new industries: self-storage units (48,500 in the United States compared to 10,000 outside the United States) and professional organizers (Sanburn, 2015).

It's said that a man is a boy with more expensive toys. Others are judged by their possessions: Where do they live? What kind of car does she drive? What did he wear to the party? You can even express positive feelings about yourself by acquiring and showing things. The difference between clothes and designer clothes is price and how you feel about yourself when you wear them.

The annual survey conducted by the Higher Education Research Institute at the University of California, Los Angeles, shows that the number of college freshmen who said it was essential or very

Table 7.3 Total and Per Person Municipal Solid Waste, 2012

Region	Urban Waste Generation	
	Total (tons/day)	Per Capita (kg/capita/day)
United States	624,700	2.58
China	520,548	1.02
Brazil	149,096	1.03
Japan	144,466	1.71
Germany	127,816	2.11
India	109,589	0.34
Nigeria	40,959	0.56
Saudi Arabia	20,000	1.30

Source: Hoornweg & Bhada-Tata (2012).

important to be very well off financially grew from 41% in 1968 to 73% in 2001 to 82% in 2015 (Eagan et al., 2015; Sax, Lindholm, Astin, Korn, & Mahoney, 2001). During the same period, the number who said "developing a meaningful philosophy of life" was a top priority fell from 83% to 41% to 47%.

The desire to have possessions is also related to the high level of consumer debt in the United States. Borrowing money has a long history, but for the most part, in the past money was loaned only to start businesses because those businesses would generate profits to repay the loans. Consumer loans, which make instant gratification possible by using borrowed money to buy things, are a much more recent innovation.

Gasoline and store charge cards were the standard until 1950, when Diners Club established the first credit card. In 1986, the average cardholder debt was $900. By 1996, the average cardholder debt was $2,900; it's now estimated to be more than $9,600 per household with credit card debt. The typical U.S. cardholder has 3.7 credit cards. About 60% of college seniors have at least one credit card. Debt on these cards averages more than $900. That people are evaluated by their possessions can be seen in reactions to occasional stories of individuals who die in poor surroundings yet whose mattresses are stuffed with cash. The popular reaction is that these people must have been crazy.

Yet the genius of the U.S. economic system is that materialism makes high employment and a comfortable standard of living possible for a vast number of people and the huge middle class.

Global Voices

When do you have enough in America? Never! It's a culture of excess, a permanently nouveau riche mentality. We want the biggest, the most extreme of everything.

—G. Clotaire Rapaille, French anthropologist (quoted in Kiger, 2002, para. 5)

What Is the Modality of Human Activity?

The term activity orientation refers to the use of time for self-expression and play, self-improvement and development, and work. Most visitors to the United States find it a hectic, busy culture. You can see this in the following three aspects.

Activity and Work

It would seem from the preceding section that people in the United States work only to earn money to buy more things. Yet people in the United States have a special feeling about jobs, defining self and others by occupation. Work becomes part of one's identity. About half of U.S. citizens agree that a "feeling of accomplishment" is the most important aspect of work. This is about twice the agreement rate in other countries, where work is a means to get money and where self-identity and self-accomplishment come more from what one does outside work.

A series of studies first reported in a recent *Harvard Business Review* article argue that "busyness" is replacing conspicuous consumption as a status marker. When comparing someone who works long hours and has a full calendar with someone who has a leisurely lifestyle, people in the United States find the busy person to have higher status. Similarly, when comparing someone wearing a hands-free Bluetooth headset (a product associated with busyness and multitasking) with someone wearing a pair of headphones for music (a product associated with leisure and free time), people find the busy person of higher status (Bellezza, Paharia, & Keinan, 2016).

The United States is the only advanced economy that does not require employers to provide paid holidays or time off from work. (See Figure 7.1 for a comparative list of worker vacation time.) A survey showed that the average worker in the United States with access to vacation took 16 days of vacation excluding holidays but that more than half continued to work on their vacations, taking calls and e-mailing and texting (Dickey, 2015).

Work is taken very seriously in the United States. It's separated from play, which is something done outside work. To support that, a complex recreation industry has been developed to provide play away from work.

Efficiency and Practicality

People in the United States are perceived as placing such a high value on time that "efficiency experts," whose emphasis is on getting things done on time, cause lives to be organized for efficiency so that the most can be accomplished. How many people organize their lives according to lists? Or at least think about organizing the day to accomplish the most?

Global Voices

Democratic nations will habitually prefer the useful to the beautiful, and they will require that the beautiful should be useful.

—Alexis de Tocqueville, *Democracy in America* (1835/1945)

It's possible that the emphasis on efficiency results in losing sight of other values, such as contemplation and aesthetic values. For example, most people plan commutes for the shortest possible drive time. Rarely would a person think about going the scenic route—unless on vacation and with "time to kill."

Practicality refers here to a preference for short-term goals over long-term goals. This means planning for what works best for the short term—the most practical. As a culture, the United States is less likely

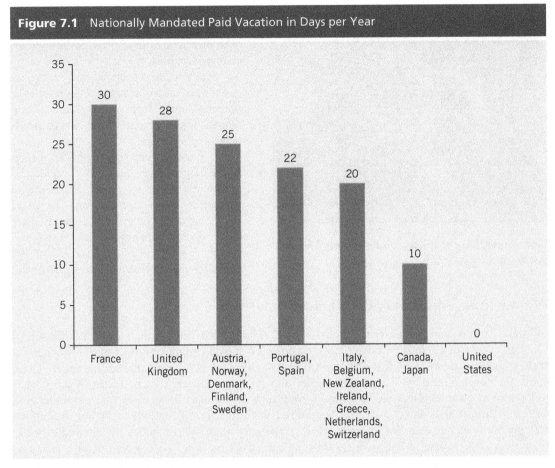

Figure 7.1 Nationally Mandated Paid Vacation in Days per Year

Source: Ray, Sanes, & Schmitt (2013).

to make short-term sacrifices for long-term gain because progress is judged so much by monthly and quarterly goals. Meaningful 10-year goals, much less 100-year goals, are very unlikely. It may appear that education is a long-term activity. However, a college education is divided into 40 or so courses. Education is viewed as a series of courses, each of which must be completed successfully. The focus on short-term practicality may appear shortsighted, but tomorrow is another day, with new problems and new opportunities.

Progress and Change

Related to practicality and to materialism is an unwavering fundamental faith in the future. The belief is that change is basically good, that the new is better than the old. For example, iPhone 6 is better than iPhone 5. Not only is the new viewed as better, but the new is often adopted without critically examining its effect on other aspects of the culture. For example, the microwave oven makes food preparation faster, but it also may lessen even more the time that families spend together. Such consequences usually are not considered in the adoption of the new. Perhaps the willingness to accept change also

Cell phones in the United States have a shorter replacement cycle than in other countries.

explains why the United States has one of the highest moving rates in the world. Each year, nearly one in eight U.S. households changes location.

The belief that progress and change are good is associated with technological developments. Some observers, however, contend that the faith in progress and change also is being applied to values.

U.S. values or standards of what is right and wrong change, and most would agree that these changes are proper. Public school integration is not that old, but you would agree that that change was right. Because social beliefs are changed so easily and so frequently in the United States, some say there are no longer any beliefs that are permanent.

What Is the Temporal Focus of Human Life?

Cultures differ widely in their conceptions of time, as was mentioned in the chronemics section of Chapter 4. First of all, in the United States, time is viewed as a commodity. Such phrases as *time is money, don't waste time, budget your time*, and *how much time do you have?* are common. Think about the conception of time as a commodity and the consequences of that belief. When time is thought of as a commodity, one needs to be constantly aware of it. Time clocks are everywhere: in homes, in cars, at work sites, on wrists, at organized play sites. Many people report feeling uncomfortable not knowing the time. Perhaps only when camping in the woods—without a tablet and a mobile phone—can one be free of time awareness in the United States. When time is considered a resource, it becomes something to be managed and used responsibly. It can become a master if one becomes a slave to it. How many people do you know who carry schedules of their day, week, or year?

Second, when time is viewed in a linear fashion, it obviously has a past, a present, and a future. Most will admit to being motivated by the future in how to act in the present: going to

Global Voices

[In the United States] they all consider society as a body in a state of improvement, humanity as a changing scene, in which nothing is, or ought to be, permanent; and they admit that what appears to them today to be good, may be superseded by something better tomorrow.

—Alexis de Tocqueville, *Democracy in America* (1835/1945)

school to get a degree and a satisfying job, working to provide for oneself and one's family in the future, dieting so as to have a better figure and more friends in the future, training so as to be better at sports in the future, and living the future in the present. Some would say that, because of living the future in the present, one is less aware of the present, having less time and appreciation for what is happening in the moment. Some would even say that living the future in the present is an illusion because the future is not yet here—it is unreal. In living for something that isn't real, one misses much of the reality of the present.

What Is the Character of Innate Human Nature?

What does it mean to be human? What is human nature? What are human rights and responsibilities? These are the types of questions meant by human nature orientation.

Goodness

This area refers to the question of the innate nature of humans. Are we born good? Evil? With the potential for both? It has been argued that the Puritan ancestry of the United States suggests a view that people are born evil but have the potential to be good. To achieve good in this view, one must control and discipline the self. Others argue that contemporary beliefs in the United States are that people are born with a mixture of or a potential for both good and evil.

Rationality

Related to the concept of the innate nature of humans is rationality. To believe that humans are rational is to believe that humans act on the basis of reason. In other words, if you believe that humans have the potential for both good and evil, you also believe that humans have free will and therefore responsibility for their actions. However, if you believe that humans are innately evil and lacking in rationality, you also believe that human evil is natural.

A belief in rationality, then, is consistent with a belief in the scientific method. Truth can be discovered through human reason. That being accepted, democracy, trial by jury, and a free enterprise system are all consistent beliefs because they assume that individuals can be trusted to make decisions for themselves.

It can be argued that the fundamental reason for the rise of the West was an extraordinary faith in reason. Christianity alone embraced reason and logic as the primary guide to religious truth. Christianity taught that reason was the supreme gift from God. Consequently, Christianity is oriented to the future while other religions assert the superiority of the past. Faith in the power of reason infused Western culture and stimulated the pursuit of science, democracy, and capitalism (Stark, 2005).

Global Voices

Every adult, no matter how unfortunate a childhood he had or how habit-ridden he may be, is free to make choices about his life. To say of Hitler, to say of the criminal, that he did not choose to be bad but was a victim of his upbringing is to make all morality, all discussion of right and wrong, impossible. It leaves unanswered the question of why people in similar circumstances did not all become Hitlers.

But worse, to say "It is not his fault; he was not free to choose" is to rob a person of his humanity, and reduce him to the level of an animal who is bound by instinct.

—Harold S. Kushner, *When Bad Things Happen to Good People* (1982)

Mutability

The term mutability means "subject to change." This, then, refers to the belief that human nature can be changed by society. This is reflected in the belief that education is a positive force in improving human nature. It's also fundamental to the belief that the prison system can rehabilitate wrongdoers, that although an individual chose to do evil, that individual can be changed by society to choose to do good. And if individuals are indeed determined to some extent by past experiences, observing punishment can act as a deterrent.

Through science, this belief is now open to renewed public debate. In studies linking biology and human behavior, some scientists believe they are finding a substantial genetic underpinning for human behavior, having now demonstrated a genetic role in intelligence and aggression, and the personality trait "novelty seeking." Genetic determinism diminishes the power of one's capacity to choose and accept responsibility for those choices. Is the alcoholic a helpless victim of biology or a willful agent with control over behavior?

Public debate also extends to whether unhealthy circumstances can lead individuals to do evil. Notice a contradiction here to the belief in rationality if you believe that a person who was abused as a child is more likely to abuse children and allow that fact in court to mitigate the individual's responsibility to have chosen rationally not to be abusive. These questions are not likely to change criminal justice in the United States as the overriding beliefs are that individuals are responsible for their actions and that we need to protect society from criminals.

What Is the Relationship of the Individual to Others?

This cultural pattern refers to perceptions of the self and the ways society is organized. Persons of diverse cultures tend to have differing perceptions of the self. In U.S. culture, people tend to define the self in terms of one's role and responsibilities in the society. Generally, people in the United States define self in terms of occupation rather than in terms of family or other relationships.

Individualism

Remember, as discussed in the preceding chapter, the United States is characterized to a high degree by individualism as opposed to collectivism. In fact, surveys conducted in industrialized nations during the 1980s clearly show that the most distinctive and perhaps permanent characteristics of the U.S. character are independence and individuality. Yet the word *individualism* did not enter the English vocabulary until 1835, when de Tocqueville used it to describe what he found in the United States. Those characteristics are echoes of constitutional guarantees of free speech and free press. Freedom for people in the United States is the freedom to be an individual. People in the United States have a passion for freedom. Patterson (1991) links this passion with the country's history of slavery. The concept of freedom that emerged from slave-holding Virginia was mass based and egalitarian.

This value is enforced early. According to a Chinese proverb, "You have to have the right name to do the right thing." In some cultures, names given to children have traditional or family meaning. Today, in the United States, names are more likely chosen by sound alone. Instead of tradition or family, children's names help reinforce individualism. Months-old infants are put in cribs in rooms separate from other people, and crying is tolerated because of the importance placed on learning to be an individual. In contrast, in virtually all preindustrial societies, mothers sleep with babies for many months—and might well consider the U.S. practice cruel, or certainly not attentive to the child's needs. Children in the United States are encouraged to be autonomous, make independent decisions, solve problems independently, and generally view the world from the point of view of the self.

Global Voices

I swear by my life and my love of it that I will never live for the sake of another man, nor ask another man to live for mine.

—Ayn Rand, *Atlas Shrugged* (2005)

Focus on Culture 7.2

Individualism Reflected in Language Use

Jean Twenge and her colleagues used Google Books Ngram Viewer to search 5 million books published between 1960 and 2008. They searched for individualistic words (*independent, individual, individually, unique, uniqueness, self, independence, oneself, soloist, identity, personalized, solo, solitary, personalize, loner, standout, single, personal, sole,* and *singularity*) and phrases (*all about me, captain of my ship, focus on the self, I am special, I am the greatest, I can do it myself, I come first, I get what I want, I have my own style, I love me, I'm the best, looking out for number one, me against the world, me first, my needs, self-love, self-reliance, self-sufficient,* and *there's only one you*) as well as communal words (*communal, community, commune, unity, communitarian, united, teamwork, team, collective, village, tribe, collectivization, group, collectivism, everyone, family, share, socialism, tribal,* and *union*) and phrases (*all in this together, band together, community spirit, common good, communal living, concern for the group, contribute to your community, it takes a village, sense of community, sharing of resources, strength through unity, the group is very important, the needs of all, together we are strong, united we stand, we are one, we can do it together, work as a team,* and *working for the whole*).

They found that both individualistic words and phrases increased significantly over time. The researchers interpret these changes as evidence that the U.S. culture has become increasingly focused on individualistic concerns since 1960.

Source: Twenge, Campbell, & Gentile (2013).

In the United States, adults maintain a separate self-concept when working in groups and organizations and are encouraged to accept responsibility as separate, independent individuals. Keep in mind, however, that independent individuals can cooperate—or compete—according to what maximizes benefits for the individual relative to costs.

A concern for individualism relates to views on love and marriage and life after death. In other cultures, marriage decisions are too important to be left to individuals because, where families are most important, marriages present opportunities for alliances between families. Love develops after the marriage. Only in cultures that value individualism is romantic love the reason for marriage. Individualism also is reflected in beliefs in an existence beyond death. Most people in the United States believe in an individual afterlife (Segal, 2004).

In contrast to some cultures, the emphasis on individuality may make it somewhat difficult to experience the comfort and security of association that other cultures experience. It also may explain a weaker family structure than is found in other cultures. In the 1960s, 73% of all children were living in a family with two married parents in their first marriage. By 1980 it was 61%, and by 2015 it was less than half (46%). By some estimates, less than 10% of households now are made up of career fathers, homemaker mothers, and school-age children, and one-fourth of all U.S. families are single-parent ones. De Tocqueville predicted that the United States would succumb to the excesses of individualism, which he called egoism. Glendon (1991) calls this hyperindividualism, a withdrawing into individual private shells.

Self-Motivation

The value of individualism in the United States is reflected in the belief that individuals should set their own goals and then pursue them independently. Motivation should originate in the individual; individuals have the power to determine their own destiny. Rather than favoring group decisions or having others decide for the person most affected, individual responsibility for decision making is favored.

A possible explanation for the emphasis on individualism and self-motivation can be seen in the history of Western religion and industrialization. What may appear to be an unlikely relationship has been clearly described by David McClelland (1976). In medieval Europe, society was rigidly structured. A person's place in society, or birthright, was defined by gender, social class, and lineage. The most holy life that one could aspire to on earth was to be a part of the church as a brother or nun and, in a sense, to be apart from the world. In medieval Catholicism, priests, nuns, saints, and rituals interceded with God for the masses. The Protestant Reformation changed this view. Protestant religious beliefs influenced attitudes toward work and relationships with God. Martin Luther taught that all forms of work are legitimate; that is, earthly work was not subordinate to spiritual work. Calvin and others taught that it was godly to be hardworking and that success was evidence of one's godliness. Within the Catholic Church, the

Time Life Pictures/The LIFE Picture Collection/Getty Images

In October 1517, Luther challenged the world to debate the 95 theses he posted on the Wittenberg church door. The Reformation diverted into secular life the energies that had been given in monastic life.

Council of Trent (1545–1563) eliminated the abuses identified by the Protestant Reformers. These actions represented a significant shift in attitude. Whereas in the distant past, a talented person might have found opportunity in the church apart from the world, after the Reformation, a talented person who worked hard might succeed in business. Success in the world became consistent with religious beliefs.

In addition, Protestantism of every kind argued for the private nature of religion. Protestantism sought to diminish the gap between people and God, thus supporting the growing individualism. Another influence was the Industrial Revolution. In the agricultural lifestyle, sons did what their fathers had done and daughters did what their mothers had done generation after generation. The Reformation and the Industrial Revolution made entrepreneurism, winning, personal ambition, and individualism a good thing.

McClelland (1976) labeled the consequences of this shift a need for achievement. Individuals in cultures with a high need for achievement want to excel because of the feeling of accomplishment that it brings. McClelland showed that economic development in the West was largely built by individuals so motivated.

A particularly interesting part of McClelland's 1976 study was that it used popular literature as an indicator of a culture's degree of need for achievement at any time. He studied the prevailing ideas and concerns in popular stories, songs, poems, plays, and speeches to index a culture's degree of need for achievement at any one time. He then correlated industrial activity in the culture to the presence of the achievement theme in popular literature. Not surprising was his finding that a peak in U.S. industrial activity was also a peak of this theme in popular literature, such as the Horatio Alger stories of the 1850s. Most of the 135 books that Horatio Alger wrote for boys in the 19th century stressed that a bright, self-reliant boy who works hard can go from "rags to riches."

The majority of the popular literature of the United States continues to stress the theme that an individual who works hard can succeed. The United States is called the land of opportunity, the country where people believe that if you work hard, you succeed. Many mistakenly believe that the saying "God helps those who help themselves" is from the Bible. Actually, the saying is attributed to Benjamin Franklin.

The class structure of the United States places strong emphasis on status-defining boundaries of power, money, and involvement in influential social circles. This contrasts sharply with the French, who define class boundaries based more on intelligence, cosmopolitanism, and refinement.

Closely related to individualism and self-motivation is the presence of competition. Competition is a part of life from early childhood. Children play games in which only one person can win. Video games are competitive. Schools are competitive. And that competition is carried into the workplace. The overwhelming presence of competition in U.S. society can be seen in the ever-present sports metaphor. Many human endeavors are spoken of in sports language: a playing field, competitors, scores, winners, rankings. A good book or a good movie is ranked "No. 1" by the newspapers. Presidential candidates are given daily scores by the media—one candidate is so many points ahead of the competition.

People in the United States subscribe to the cultural myth of self-motivation. In an international survey, 57% disagree with the statement "Success in life is pretty much determined by forces outside of our control." The international median of disagreement was 38%. Germany was 31% and India 27%. Similarly, people in the United States place great value on hard work. Some 73% believe it is very important to work hard in order to get ahead in life. The global median was 50%. Germany was 49%, India 38%, and Indonesia 28% (Pew Research Center, 2014a).

Surveys suggest that because of self-motivation values, U.S. citizens are less likely to vote on the basis of economic class. U.S. citizens are less likely to favor government redistributing income from rich to poor or providing jobs for all. In fact, surveys show that only 23% of U.S. citizens favor the state taking care of the poor. The next lowest in Europe is Germany at 50%. People in the United States, though, are far more likely to do volunteer work. More than 40% do. People in the United States prefer to help the needy independently. More than half of the people in the United States report donating to charities (see Figure 7.2).

Social Organization

This cultural pattern refers to the ways society is organized. For example, the United States separates religion and state. Other cultures integrate church and state. Two major social organization patterns—equality and conformity—may explain many other characteristics of the United States.

Equality. Equality is an important cultural myth in the United States, although beliefs may appear contradictory to actions.

Figure 7.2   World Giving Index: Top Six Countries, 5-Year Ranking

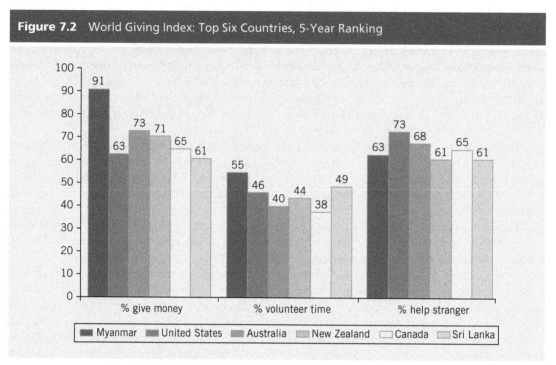

Source: Charities Aid Foundation (2011, 2012, 2015).

The word *equality* does not appear in the U.S. Constitution nor the Bill of Rights. The founders did not claim that all are equal in attributes, such as intelligence, nor that all should think and act in the same way. The founders did establish a government that would guarantee the rule of law equally to all, which became a hope for people of all backgrounds and religions. Yet that guarantee was contradicted by the existence of slavery. That guarantee was not made explicit until after the Civil War with the Thirteenth, Fourteenth, and Fifteenth Amendments, which are interpreted as saying that neither the federal nor state governments may classify people in ways that violate their rights under the Constitution, yet inequalities persisted for many.

Focus on Culture 7.3

The World Loves Football, Doesn't It?

You may have heard that 1 billion people watch the Super Bowl. That certainly demonstrates that the whole world loves NFL football. But that assertion has become a cultural myth. For this statement to be true, about one out of every seven people on the planet would have to view the game. The origin of the myth is that the Super Bowl is broadcast to about 225 countries with about 1 billion people who have access to the broadcast. This fact has gotten misconstrued to be that the Super Bowl is actually seen by over a billion people.

How many people actually view the broadcast? The 2014 Super Bowl audience in the United States was 111.5 million people. Outside of the United States, Canada, and Mexico, the audience was a couple million.

To most of the world, football refers to what in the United States is called soccer. The FIFA 2006 World Cup had an audience of 715.1 million worldwide. The 2014 World Cup had a U.S. audience of 26.5 million.

Students of culture have pointed out how U.S. football has become associated with patriotism and U.S. identity. "In 1986 Jack Kemp [former U.S. Congressman and professional football quarterback] took to the floor of Congress to contrast 'European socialist' soccer with 'democratic' and 'capitalist' American football. In 2003 a blogger even pointed out that a leading al-Qaeda terrorist had been a European soccer player: 'You don't see any former NFL players . . . joining al-Qaeda, do you?'" ("The Odd Man Out," 2006, p. 54).

Markovits and Hellerman (2001) point out that Europeans argue that the United States either has failed to embrace the "beautiful game" or, when it does, has gotten it wrong. And people in the United States insist on calling it soccer.

Sources: Bauder (2014); Markovits & Hellerman (2001); McLaughlin (2010); "The Odd Man Out" (2006).

Focus on Skills 7.1

Choosing Which Movies Best Represent Dominant U.S. Cultural Values

Assume you are a communication major at a U.S. university. Your College of Communication wants to gift to communication programs in several countries DVD copies of recent U.S. movies and television programs that represent dominant U.S. cultural values. You've been asked to be on the committee to recommend what DVDs to purchase.

A faculty member on the committee is concerned that while a cultural value may be evident in the movie, other aspects of the movie may lead to inaccurate perceptions. She points out that according to Eagleton (2013) people in the United States are admired for their friendliness, honesty, openness, inventiveness, courtesy, civic pride, ease of manner, generosity of spirit, and egalitarian manners, but at the same time are perceived as overly moral, idealistic, earnest, high-minded, and too often taking the position as "the finest country in the world."

1. What movies would you recommend to represent dominant U.S. cultural values?
2. What U.S. cultural value does each portray?
3. How do you respond to the faculty member's concern that the selections that demonstrate a cultural value might also show less desirable aspects of the United States?

Civil rights groups such as the NAACP achieved many legal victories for Black Americans under the equal protection amendments. Later, based on generations of discrimination, these organizations argued for affirmative action laws that gave preferential treatment to racial minorities in university admissions and access to jobs as the best way to alleviate the effects of past discrimination. The concept of affirmative action in university admissions continues to be tested and refined in the U.S. Supreme Court (Finkelman, 1991).

For generations, women in the United States could not vote nor serve on juries, and in the 1870s, Illinois refused to issue a woman a license to practice law based only on gender. The U.S. Supreme Court upheld the refusal. It wasn't until ratification of the Nineteenth Amendment that voting privileges were extended to women, and it wasn't until the 1970s that the Supreme Court extended the equal protection amendments to women. And by the 1980s, the Court supported an affirmative action plan that made it permissible to take gender into account in promotion decisions because women had been denied access in the past (*Johnson v. Transportation Agency of Santa Clara County*; Petrik, 1991).

Equal protection has only recently been extended to bisexuals, lesbians, and gay men. It has only been since 2003 that same-sex sexual activity has been legal nationwide (*Lawrence v. Texas*) and since 2015 that all states recognize same-sex marriage (*Obergefell v. Hodges*). Except for federal executive orders prohibiting discrimination by federal contractors in 2014, there is no federal law banning discrimination. While the cultural myth has long been a part of the culture, the reality has been slowly fought for by minority groups.

Conformity. Cultures differ in the content and type of conformity. Some emphasize conformity to traditional or past-oriented norms, whereas others exhibit conformity to modern or future-oriented norms. People in the United States tend to emphasize conformity to modern norms. U.S. citizens seem to conform to what is "in."

Global Voices

Civil rights for all Americans—black, white, red, yellow, the rich, poor, young, old, gay, straight, et cetera—is not a liberal or a conservative value. It's an American value that I would think that we pretty much all agree on.

—Conservative Southern Baptist evangelical pastor Jerry Falwell, speaking to commentator Tucker Carlson on MSNBC's *The Situation* (Wolff, 2005)

Global Voices

While de Tocqueville praised the United States, he also wrote that he knew of no other country with "less independence of mind and true freedom of discussion."

Though these fads may be short-lived, they involve much of the society in some way. Consider the following just from the 2000s: Crocs, energy drinks, fantasy leagues, flash mobs, Livestrong wristbands, MySpace, oversized sunglasses, PDAs, razor scooters, Texas hold 'em poker, and trucker hats.

Popular Acceptance of Dominant U.S. Cultural Patterns

U.S. citizens are also unusually patriotic. Some 52% of respondents to a June 2016 Gallup poll said they are extremely proud of their country. Another 29% said they are very proud and 13% moderately proud. Only 5% said they were "only a little proud," and 1% "not at all proud" (J. Jones, 2016). In fact, a 2015 study of 45,993 respondents in 36 countries, regions, and ethnic groups showed the United States to have the highest national pride (Fabrykant & Magun, 2015).

Figure 7.3 Qualities Associated With U.S. Citizens, 2016

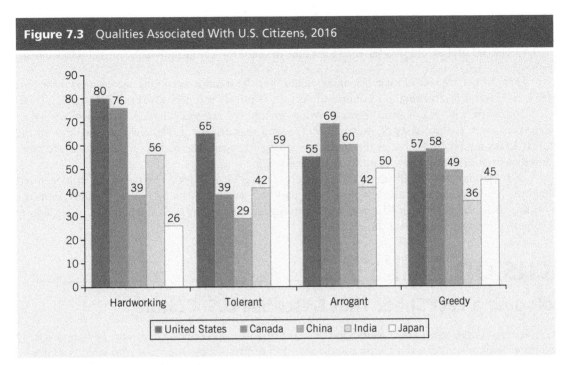

Sources: Wike, Poushter, & Zainulbhai (2016b); Pew Research Center, Spring 2016 Global Attitudes Survey.

Do others see the United States the same way U.S. residents do? Figure 7.3 compares perceptions of U.S. qualities from people in Canada, China, India, and Japan to perceptions from U.S. residents.

Given the high level of national pride, there may be significant forces weakening a strong nation-state identity. Just as the country developed from regional and social class identities, those identities still continue.

Forces Toward the Development of Regional Cultures

You've read about the various events that resulted in the development of a national culture during the early post–World War II period. Today, that national unity is fragmenting into new cultural regions. Let's look at the forces fragmenting the national culture:

- The old industrial heartland is being replaced with new regional economic centers in the south and west, while at the same time the United States is becoming part of an integrated global economy.
- Integration and equal rights have resulted in recognition and acceptance of social and cultural differences.
- Immigration has eroded the homogeneity of the U.S. population and created ties between U.S. society and other societies around the world.
- As national media have grown into global media, new forms of local, special interest, and multilanguage media have appeared.

- International air transportation makes it easier and less expensive to travel abroad than to rural U.S. locations.
- The end of the Cold War lessened for a time the need for a large national security establishment.

These forces are still in their beginning stages, but the trend is becoming increasingly clear that the United States is returning to a country of distinct, relatively independent regions (Clough, 1997).

Consistent with regionalism is the growing strength of regional dialects in the United States. Recent research (Labov, Ash, & Boberg, 1997) found that accents in Philadelphia, the cities of the Great Lakes region, and most of the south are getting stronger. The dialects of U.S. cities are more different from each other now than 50 or 100 years ago.

And regional words and sayings also are continuing in use, despite mass media homogenized English. If you know a "preacher's nose" is a part of a chicken's rump, you're probably from the south, and if you know that a "dropped egg" is an egg taken out of its shell and boiled in water, you're probably from New England (J. H. Hall, 2004).

Focus on Skills 7.2

Developing a Fact Sheet That Describes U.S. Culture

In this chapter you have learned about Kluckhohn and Strodtbeck's value orientation theory and applied it to U.S. culture. Think about how this theory could be used to describe another culture with which you are familiar. Developing the skill to better understand your own culture as well as others will facilitate more effective intercultural communication.

Assume you are a communication major at a U.S. university. Your College of Communication has had an increase in international students from India, South Korea, and Japan. You've been asked to be on the committee to develop a fact sheet on U.S. culture to send to these students before they arrive on campus. The committee has decided to focus on cultural variables relevant to the classroom and your local community.

1. Develop your version of the fact sheet on U.S. culture.
2. You begin to wonder if a similar fact sheet should be given to students on your campus reared in the United States in order to prepare them for the international students. What do your fellow U.S. students need to know?

The New Regions

About 35 years ago, Garreau (1981) described what he called the "nine nations" of North America. Today, it's possible to imagine even more. Some of the metropolitan areas that have taken on distinct cultures within the larger U.S. culture include the following:

- Atlanta, Georgia, site of leading global corporations Coca-Cola and Delta Air Lines, and CNN headquarters, has strong ties to developing countries from the presence of the Centers for Disease Control and Prevention and CARE, the world's largest relief organization, and interest in Africa by the city's African-American majority.
- Charlotte, North Carolina, the center of a new southern industrial belt dominated by manufacturing and banking, has close ties to Europe, especially Germany.

- Miami, Florida, is heavily linked to Cuba, Haiti, and Latin America and has diverse Hispanic and Caribbean immigrant populations.
- Houston, and the rest of Texas and the southwest, is an oil producer with increasing ties to Mexico as its culture and economic interests become ever more distinct from those of other parts of the United States.
- Los Angeles, and Southern California generally, with the nation's largest and most ethnically diverse immigrant community and global entertainment and tourist industries, is the leading entry port for trade with Asia.
- The San Francisco Bay Area is the capital of the world's high-tech industry.
- Seattle, Washington, home of Starbucks and Microsoft, has economic ties to Asia.

Evidence for the existence of distinct regions is the continuing existence of English dialects in the United States. Map 7.2 illustrates these regions.

Map 7.2   From Sea to See

Contrary to common perceptions that regional dialects are slowly disappearing into a homogenized stew, the dialects of North America are actually a dynamic mosaic of still-evolving pronunciation patterns, separated by unusually sharp boundaries.

Regional Dialects
The map illustrates dialect boundaries and pronunciation changes over the last century in their most extreme form. Texas accents are considered variants of southern American English. Texas accents include not only vocabulary but also pronunciation, cadence, and syntax and support a strong local identity perhaps weakened by pop culture and newcomers from other states, particularly California.

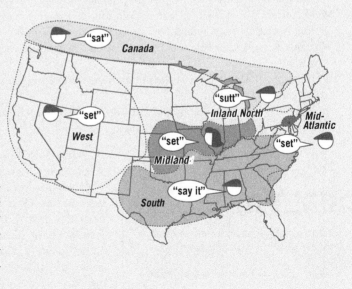

"set"	Old	New
South	set	say-it
Inland North	set	sutt
West	set	set
Midland	set	set
Mid-Atlantic	set	set
Canada	set	sat

"caught"	Old	New
South	caught	caught
Inland North	cot	cat
West	cot	cot
Midland	cot	cot
Mid-Atlantic	cot	cot
Canada	caught	caught

Source: Blakeslee (2002).

223

Focus on Technology 7.2

Regional Social Media

In 2013, 500 million messages were sent each day on Twitter. Found in these tweets are U.S. geographical variations. The term *suttin* (for "something") is associated with the New York area. The acronym *ikr* (for "I know, right?") is more likely to appear in Detroit.

A later study showed more regional social media use including *yinz* (second person pronoun) around the city of Pittsburgh, *yall* or *y'all* (second person pronoun) more common in the Southeast, and *hella* (an intensifier as in "i got hella nervous") more common in Northern California.

Sources: "Do You Have a Twitter 'Accent'?" (2013); Eisenstein (2014).

Social Class

In Chapter 1 you read that one of the forms of identity is class. Some argue that in the United States classes are based on wealth, education, occupation, and income. Taking those factors into consideration, Gilbert (2015) described U.S. social classes largely based on wealth, occupation, and income, which frequently result from education. Typical annual income for each is shown in 2015 U.S. dollars.

Capitalist class: The top 1% made up of executives who control large corporations, large investors, and heirs of extremely successful entrepreneurs—$2 million

Upper middle class: About 14% of the population, comprising high-ranking managers in large corporations, owners of medium-sized commercial interests, highly educated professionals in high-esteem occupations such as lawyers, doctors, and very successful accountants—$150,000

Middle class: About 30% of the population, comprising mid-level level managers, semiprofessionals, craftsmen, foremen, and nonretail sales—$70,000

Working class: About 30% of the population, comprising clerical, retail, and well-paid manual worker—$40,000

Working poor: About 13% of the population, comprising poorly paid manual, retail, and service workers—$25,000

An underclass of people (about 12% of the population) who are unemployed or work part time or rely on public support for sustenance—$15,000

Global Voices

To Americans, social status is all about money and power. To Brits it is all about birth and accent.

—Dr. Tim Stanley, U.S. historian

Others argue that U.S. society is stratified along a continuous gradation rather than into categories. They acknowledge that there is inequality, but that there are no clear lines separating one status group from the next. From a communication perspective, then, the basic question is to what extent people take on an identity along class divisions. Some would argue that at times people in the United States deny the existence of social class; at other times social class can be an important part of identity.

But it can be argued that indeed socioeconomic status or social class regulates human life and provides identity (Brislin, 1988). Hart and Risley (1995) demonstrate a relationship between social class and exposure to language. By the age of 3, children of professional parents in the United States have heard some 45 million words addressed to them. Children of working-class parents are exposed to 26 million, and children receiving welfare 13 million. Children of professional parents heard six times more encouragements per hour and half the number of prohibitions per hour as children in families receiving welfare. Earlier, Kohn (1977) demonstrated the effects of such differences. Middle-class parents emphasize self-control, intellectual curiosity, and consideration for others. The desired outcomes of self-direction and empathic understanding transfer easily to professional and managerial jobs that require intellectual curiosity and good social skills. Working-class parents emphasize obedience, neatness, and good manners. Gilbert and Kahl (1982) argue that this emphasis leads to a concern with external standards, such as obedience to authority, acceptance of what other people think, and hesitancy in expressing desires to authority figures. These working-class concerns can be a detriment in schools, with their emphasis on verbal skills. The resulting learned behaviors transfer more directly to supervised wage labor jobs. These observations, of course, do not apply to every working-class family. Working-class parents who encourage verbal skills through reading and conversation have children who are as successful in school. Although the United States does have social classes that have been shown to have different values, many people in the United States believe that the barriers of social class are easier to transcend in the United States than in other countries. That is the cultural myth of the American Dream.

Focus on Skills 7.3

Regional Word Use

Do you live east or west of the Mississippi? Which list of words is more familiar to you?

List 1: sneakers, yard sale, skillet, scrap paper, scallions, highway, lightning bugs
List 2: tennis shoes, garage sale, frying pan, scratch paper, green onions, freeway, fireflies

See note at the end of this chapter.

Source: Katz (2016).

The reality is that the American Dream is becoming increasingly elusive. Children born in 1940 had a 92% chance of making more money than their parents. Children born in 1984 have just a 50% chance of making more than their parents. Kitroeff and Etehad (2016) conclude that a major factor in this change is that in the past new income was more evenly spread across social classes, while today the disproportionate share goes to the very rich. In the fall of 2011, the Canadian anti-consumerist magazine *Adbusters* called for protests that became known as Occupy Wall Street, which was duplicated in cities across the United States. The slogan "We are the 99%" was used to call attention to the income and wealth inequality between the wealthiest 1% and the remainder of the population. And a Congressional Budget Office (2011) study showed that, from 1979 to 2007, after-tax income grew 275% for the top 1% of U.S. households, while it grew less than 40% for the 60% middle-income households and only 18% for the 20% poor households.

Global Voices

Working-class whites are the most pessimistic group in America. ... [T]he fact that hillbillies like me are more down about the future than many other groups ... suggests that something else is going on. ... We're more socially isolated than ever. ... Many of us have dropped out of the labor force or have chosen not to relocate for better opportunities. Our men suffer from a peculiar crisis of masculinity in which some of the very traits that our culture inculcates make it difficult to succeed in a changing world.

Source: Vance (2016, pp. 4–5).

The 2016 U.S. presidential election made social class an issue. Candidate Bernie Sanders gained a huge following with statements such as "America now has more wealth and income inequality than any major developed country on earth, and the gap between the very rich and everyone else is wider than at any time since the 1920s" ("Issues: Income and Wealth Inequality," n.d.).

During the campaign, historian Nancy Isenberg's (2016) book *White Trash: The 400-Year Untold History of Class in America* challenged the cultural myth that the United States is a class-free society where one achieves social mobility through hard work. She argues that the British sent their expendable "waste people" to the colonies and the poor then and now are disparaged by the upper and middle classes for being lazy and uncouth. In the United States the most important measure of class was land ownership; in 1990, the top 10% held equity in 90% of the land. And today, Isenberg argues, the best predictors of success are privileges and wealth from one's parents and ancestors. Not everyone starts with the same advantages. The United States celebrates equality but has never practiced genuine equality.

Global Voices

Bill Clinton called himself Bubba and played the saxophone.

Donald Trump wears a bright red Bubba cap and says, "I love the poorly educated."

Today there are 19.7 million people below the poverty line; 42% are White. The term *white trash* comes from the term *waste people*, which Isenberg says is associated with poverty and idleness, inferior kinds of land (e.g., hillbillies, rednecks), being landless (e.g., trailer trash), and inferior breeds of animals (e.g., briar hoppers). In the 2016 presidential campaign some journalists described Donald Trump's constituency as "white trash" and "trailer trash" and described their support of Trump as the "revenge of the lower classes."

Class unquestionably shapes identity. The issues to consider are whether real or perceived rigidity of class boundaries results in social conflict and whether social class identity weakens nation-state identity.

SUMMARY

The focus of this chapter is the fundamental values that people in the United States share. Alexis de Tocqueville's 1831 tour resulted in long-lasting insights into U.S. values.

Kluckhohn and Strodtbeck's value orientation theory provides a way to describe U.S. culture:

- *Human being–nature orientation.* The United States is the most religious of the world's industrialized states. People in the United States make a clear distinction between human life and nature, placing a higher value on human life, and have a strong faith in the scientific method. Much of the rest of the world attributes materialism, or the belief that possessions are important, to the United States.

- *Activity orientation.* In the United States, work becomes part of one's identity. Positive value is placed on change.
- *Time orientation.* Time is viewed as a commodity and viewed in a linear fashion.
- *Human nature orientation.* People are viewed as having the potential for good and evil, as having free choice, and as being able to change.
- *Relational orientation.* Perhaps the most defining value in the United States is the emphasis placed on individualism and self-motivation. The belief that everyone should have equal opportunity is an important cultural myth in the United States. And, finally, people in the United States tend to emphasize conformity to modern norms.

The early United States may have been fragmented into many groups, but over the years many pressures contributed to a single culture. More recently, there have been renewed pressures for regional cultures as well as growing social class identities.

DISCUSSION QUESTIONS

1. Discuss how unique cultural patterns developed in the United States, a country of immigrants from other nations.

2. Outline the positive and negative consequences on the environment that have resulted from the U.S. worldview.

3. Outline the positive and negative consequences that have resulted from each of the U.S. value orientations.

4. What do you believe is the most significant U.S. cultural pattern in the intercultural communication context?

5. Analyze the implications of the development of a dominant U.S. culture and of a fragmenting national culture.

KEY TERMS

activity orientation	etic	rationality
change	hyperindividualism	scientific method
conformity	materialism	worldview
emic	mutability	
equality	need for achievement	

NOTE

1. For Focus on Skills 7.3: List 1 contains words more commonly spoken east of the Mississippi. List 2, west.

READINGS

All readings are from *Intercultural Communication: A Global Reader* (Jandt, 2004).

M. Gene Aldridge, "What Is the Basis of American Culture?" (p. 84)

Ashis Nandy, "Consumerism: Its Hidden Beauties and Politics" (p. 400)

Mohan R. Limaye, "Five Ways to Reduce the Foreign Terrorist Threat to the United States" (p. 438)

STUDENT STUDY SITE

$SAGE edge™

Sharpen your skills with SAGE edge at edge.sagepub.com/jandt9e.

SAGE edge for Students provides a personalized approach to help you accomplish your coursework goals in an easy-to-use learning environment.

Chapter 8

Marco Di Lauro/Getty Images

Religion and Identity

In Chapter 1 you read that religion is the oldest source of human identity. Individuals who identify with the world's major religions have valued peace and played roles in resolving conflicts. And yet other individuals who identify with the world's major religions have engaged in intolerance, hatred, violence, and wars with other religions. Conflicts based on religious identity have a long history and continue today as leaders of nation-states adopt and proclaim religious identity as part of national identity. Sunni and Shia Muslim conflict is a major element in Middle East friction. Christian-Muslim tensions exist in Africa (such as with the Muslim Boko Haram in Nigeria), in the Middle East, in Europe (from the rise in Muslim immigration in the last several decades), and in the United States (beginning significantly with the 9/11 terrorist attack; J. Smith, 2015).

In the 2016 U.S. presidential campaign, Donald Trump charged that President Obama's refusal to use the term *radical Islam* represented a failure to see the real threat to the country. "Many of the principles of radical Islam are incompatible with Western values and institutions. Radical Islam is anti-woman, anti-gay and anti-American" (quoted in Beckwith, 2016). Communication scholar Martin Medhurst argued that words shape the world, so "by refusing to say 'radical Islamic terrorism,' Obama is trying to create a reality where all the world's great religions are on the same side" (quoted in Qiu, 2016).

The most recent estimates of the world's population show that we are 31.4% Christian, 23.2% Muslim, 15.0% Hindu, 7.1% Buddhist, 5.9% folk religions, 0.2% Jewish, 0.8% other, and 16.4% unaffiliated (Central

Intelligence Agency, 2016). In this chapter you'll briefly review Buddhism, Hinduism, and Christianity. Then you'll do an in-depth study of Islam and Arab culture and examine the critically important conservative Arab state Saudi Arabia.

Any two cultures could be compared as a way of learning more about both. In this chapter, the same categories used in the previous chapter to describe dominant U.S. cultural values are used to learn more about Arab culture. When reading this chapter keep two facts in mind: First, while it is true that religion, in part, defines Arab culture, it is important to remember that more Muslims live outside of the Arab states than in them. And, second, the Arab states are very diverse. Every attempt has been made to be accurate, yet remember that generalized information is only that. It may not accurately reflect individuals or smaller groups.

Throughout this chapter look for examples of when and where religious identity has become synonymous with nation-state identity.

Hinduism

Just as Europe is a land of many cultures (German, French, Spanish, etc.), India is as well, including Tamil, Maharashtran, Bengali, Rejasthani, Keralan, and others. It is in the land of India with its many cultures that Hinduism developed at least 3,500 years ago. Today there are over one billion believers. Hinduism evolved over the centuries as India's many cultures intertwined. Perhaps as a consequence, Hinduism includes the belief that there are many paths to the ultimate truth.

In Hindu belief God is one but cannot be fully defined as that would be limiting. God has many different attributes and functions, has many names, and is celebrated in many forms. The many names, symbols, and images of God enable people to discover God for themselves. This has led to the popular misconception that Hinduism has many gods.

In Hindu belief, the universe came out of Brahman, the Ultimate Reality or all-encompassing God, is sustained by it, and ultimately merges in it. Brahman is unique, pure, infinite, beyond time and space, and omnipresent. As God is revealed in any form of worship, Hinduism is a nonproselytizing religion.

Hinduism enables people to cope with life as it is given. Happiness and fulfillment come from discovering one's own dharma (duty) and carrying it out to the best of one's ability. Yet the ultimate goal of life is to be liberated from the world by uniting our true nature, or Atman, with the Brahman, or God. Life, then, is a journey of discovery in search of perfection. Each soul is potentially divine and destined to become perfect. As we are born many times, each life depends on what we did in the previous life, thus each of us is responsible for our own fate. Through many reincarnations we can achieve Moksha, or liberation from the cycle of birth and death (Bell, 1998).

Yoga is the Hindu ritual for uniting one's soul with God through meditation. Silence, then, is a central part of Hindu philosophy. In Chapter 4 you read about silence as a type of nonverbal communication and that Eastern societies value silence more than Western societies do. Jain and Matukumalli (2014) relate silence on the individual level in Hindu belief to the Hindu concept of yoga. Some kinds of yoga are practiced to unite the individual spirit or soul with God. Thus self-realization, salvation, wisdom, and peace can be "achieved in a state of meditation and introspection when the individual is communicating with himself or herself in silence" (p. 251). Speech directs us outward; silence helps us turn inward.

Buddhism

In one view Buddhism can be seen as a reaction to orthodox Hinduism, which tended to focus on the role of divine and supernatural powers in the affairs of human beings. In Buddhism human beings are seen more as the masters of their own destiny. The founder of Buddhism was the Indian prince Siddhartha Gautama, who lived in the 6th century BCE. He is not identified as a god nor as a prophet, but founded Buddhism as a spiritual tradition based on personal attainment of enlightenment. The word *Buddha* means "enlightened or awakened one." Today's global Buddhist population is about 490 million.

During the third century BCE, Buddhism divided into two main streams. Theravada is the more conservative stream, which preserves the earliest teachings of the Buddha. Sometimes known as Southern Buddhism, it is found in Sri Lanka, Myanmar (Burma), Laos, Cambodia, and Thailand. In Theravada it is believed that Nirvana (a state of pure being) can be reached only by a few who follow the way strictly and renounce the world. Mahayana, also known as Eastern Buddhism, is found in China, Japan, Korea, and Vietnam. In Mahayana Buddhism, the Buddha, Gautama, is treated as a Divine Being. Also in Mahayana Buddhism, ordinary Buddhists can attain Nirvana while continuing everyday life.

The most fundamental teachings in Buddhism are the Four Noble Truths:

1. The inevitability of sufferings and adversity: There is nothing truly satisfying in this world. Life is unhappiness and suffering.
2. The source of suffering: We suffer because we have desires. We are greedy and unsatisfied. This brings unhappiness and conflict.
3. Cessation of suffering: These feelings can be eradicated by not becoming attached to anything.
4. Paths to Nirvana: To achieve enlightenment, we can follow the eight right ways: right view, right thinking, right speech, right action, right livelihood, right diligence, right mindfulness, and right concentration. Together, the eight paths can prevent sufferings from happening (Bell, 1998).

Further, Mahayana Buddhist teachings offer advice to improve oneself based on six teachings:

1. Charity: By being charitable we gain something more intangible and valuable in return.
2. The Five Basic Moral Precepts: To abstain from taking life, to abstain from taking what is not freely given, to abstain from misuse of the senses, to abstain from speaking falsely, and to abstain from intoxicants that cloud the mind.
3. Inclusiveness, forbearance, and the capacity to receive and bear insults and sufferings: Inclusiveness teaches us to be compassionate and leads to love and acceptance.
4. Diligence or patience: Foster positive thoughts and actions through continuous effort and diligence.
5. Meditation and concentration: Meditation helps us relax and become more in touch with the core of our inner beings.
6. Profound wisdom and perfection of understanding: Profound wisdom is free from all knowledge, preconceived notions, habitual patterns, ideas, and perspectives (Chuang, 2002).

Chuang and Chen (2003) have carefully detailed the influence of Buddhism on communication behavior. First, in direct contrast to the Western linear or abstract thinking pattern, is an emphasis at intuitive communication to feel rather than to analyze or think about. Second, again in contrast to Western practice, silence is understood as an effective nonverbal expression for mutual understanding. Third is the importance of empathic communication. Thus, people should show concern for others' feelings and reactions and demonstrate reciprocity of affective displays to establish rapport. Finally, the concept of the *middle way* is manifest in emotional control and avoidance of aggressive behaviors.

Focus on Culture 8.1

The Buddhist Conception of the Individual

The Buddhist term for individual is *santana*, or "stream." It is intended to capture the idea of interconnectedness between people and their environment and between generations. Buddhist teaching places an emphasis on personal responsibility to achieve change in the world through change in personal behavior.

Source: United Nations Development Programme (2008, p. 61).

Japan

The majority of the Japanese population traditionally practices a syncretistic combination of Shinto and Buddhism. Shinto is exclusively nationalistic. It was the state religion from the Meiji Restoration of 1868 until the end of World War II. It is not so much a creed as it is a link to ancestors and Gods. Shinto means "the way of the Gods" and has three predominant ideas: worship of the Gods of Japan, loyalty to Japan, and cultivation of a pure Japanese spirit. Almost all Japanese are born Shinto. It is said that to be Japanese and to be a Shintoist are synonymous. There are two types of Shintoism: Popular Shinto, which has its strength in the home, and Sect Shinto, which believes in reincarnation and service to humanity as service to God. A third type, State Shinto, which taught that the Japanese were separate from other races, excelling in virtue, intelligence, and courage, was abolished by order of the Allies in 1945.

Except among the older people, religion is not a strong force in Japan. Officially, Japan is 66.8% Buddhist; however, because many people practice both Buddhism and Shintoism, the population is also 79.2% Shinto, 1.5% Christian, and 7.1% other.

Buddhism came to Japan from Korea in the mid-6th century. More than 200 sects of Buddhism exist in Japan, with wide differences in doctrines. Buddhism has been called the "adopted faith of Japan" and centers on the temple and the family altar. Most households observe some ceremonies of both religions, such as a Shinto wedding and a Buddhist funeral. Overall, though, religion is more a social tradition than a conviction. Some charge that due to a lack of religious beliefs, the Japanese have no principles. Meditation, aesthetic appreciation, ritual cleansing, and a respect for nature's beauty and humans' part in it are important cultural beliefs.

Christianity was brought to Japan by Jesuit missionaries in 1549. Though less than 2% of the population is Christian, Christian lifestyles, moral codes, and ethics have become part of Japanese life.

Christianity

Christianity is the world's largest religion, with some 2.17 billion followers. It began in Palestine, on the eastern Mediterranean Sea, which had been ruled by several foreign powers—Egypt and Assyria disputed the area for centuries, then Babylonians, Persians, Greeks, and Romans. The Persian Cyrus allowed the Jews to return to Palestine from exile. In the first century BCE, the region was a mix of beliefs: Judaism, the pagan religions of philosophies of the Roman state, mystery cults, and the Greek schools of philosophical thought. The Judaism of that time was strictly monotheistic with a strong sense of community and restlessness with foreign influences and with strong expectations of the coming of a messiah.

Christianity began in this context as a Jewish movement with Jesus of Nazareth. Around the age of 30 he was baptized by John the Baptist, receiving the blessing of God. He began his ministry of teaching and healing. His 12 disciples recognized him as the long-awaited Messiah. With opposition growing, he was crucified by the Romans. Three days later, women who went to anoint his body reported the tomb was empty and that an angel told them Jesus had risen from the dead. The disciples later revealed that Jesus appeared to them on several occasions and then ascended into heaven before their eyes.

In the remainder of the 1st century CE, the church grew rapidly, but in the 2nd and 3rd centuries, Christians were persecuted and doctrinal debates spread throughout the church. Then in the 4th century CE, the Roman emperor Constantine converted to Christianity. Persecution ceased as the religion became legal and many converted to the emperor's faith. Now allied with the Roman Empire, Christianity grew in influence and power. Later through alliance with Western European powers, it would encompass the entire Western world in the Middle Ages and Renaissance, and with 19th-century colonial and missionary movements spread worldwide, becoming increasingly multicultural.

Constantine moved the capital of the Roman Empire from Rome to Constantinople (Istanbul in modern Turkey). Upon his death, the empire was divided between his two sons. One ruled the Western half from Rome, while the other ruled from Constantinople. Over time, religious, cultural, and political differences grew between the Eastern and Western churches over a range of issues including the use of icons, the nature of the Holy Spirit, and when Easter should be celebrated. Finally, in 1054 CE, Pope Leo IX excommunicated the leader of the Eastern church, who condemned the Pope in return. Ever since, the church has been divided into Roman Catholic and Greek Orthodox.

After experiencing a personal conversion to the doctrine of justification by faith alone, German monk Martin Luther campaigned in 1517 against the Roman Catholic church's practice of selling indulgences. In the environment of growing German nationalism and the invention of the printing press, Luther's ideas spread quickly throughout Germany and similar reforming movements developed in England and Switzerland. Soon Protestant nationalists were fighting Catholic imperialists for religious and political freedom.

Today there are perhaps thousands of Christian denominations that differ in some doctrine issues and in practice but all of whom share the basic doctrines of the Council of Nicaea that Jesus is of "one substance" with the Father (J. L. González, 2014) and place a strong emphasis on rationality and individual choice and its consequences.

Focus on Culture 8.2

Orthodox Christianity

The Holy Mountain of Athos, a small peninsula in northern Greece into the Aegean Sea, has been governed by Orthodox Christian monks since the end of the 9th century CE. At the end of the 19th century, the Russian imperial court purchased land on Mount Athos and sent many Russian monks to live there as a symbol of its claim to being the global guardian of Orthodoxy. With the rise of communism, support for Mount Athos stopped. In the past decade, that support has returned. There are 20 monasteries on Mount Athos—17 Greek, one Serbian, one Bulgarian, and one built with funding from Russian billionaires and the Russian state.

Orthodox Christianity opposes the spread of Western liberalism, including gay rights and same-sex marriage. Russia's president Vladimir Putin has come to embrace the Orthodox faith as an opposing ideology to Western ideology. In 2011, faced with opposition, Putin called upon the monks for help, and they sent one of the holiest relics, a belt the Virgin Mary sewed for herself out of camel hair, for display in Russia to some 3 million worshippers. Millions more saw Putin helping to bring an important icon to Russia. Later, after the annexation of Crimea in 2014, Putin said in a national address that Russia had taken back a land of "sacred importance," where St. Vladimir the Great, a pagan ruler of ancient Russia, had been baptized after converting to Orthodox Christianity.

Sources: Fagan (2013); Shuster (2016b).

Islam

Islam is the second largest religion in the world after Christianity, with some 1.7 billion followers, or about 23% of the world's population. Figure 8.1 identifies the countries with the largest Muslim populations, and Figure 8.2 shows Muslim populations in selected Western countries. The Muslim religion extends far beyond the Arab world, from Africa to Europe to Asia, including republics of the former Soviet Union, which had experienced suppression of religion and language since the time of the Russian czars. Today, some 75 countries have large Muslim populations.

People who practice Islam are called Muslims (literally "submitters" to the will of God). Islam is a nonhierarchical religion; there is no priesthood. No one institution or individual speaks for all Muslims. Many Muslims stress the similarities between Islam and the principal Abrahamic faiths in the United States. (The three Abrahamic faiths are Judaism, Christianity, and Islam.) For example, Jewish and Islamic dietary laws resemble one another very closely. According to Islamic law, Muslims may not drink alcoholic beverages, eat pork, or gamble. Muslims honor Jesus as one of the prophets of the Bible but not as the son of God.

Muslims generally fall into either the Sunni or the Shiite branch. The Sunni, who account for about 90% of the world's Muslims, believe that Muslim leadership in the early years passed to a series of caliphs, whereas the Shiite Muslims believe that leadership should stay within the family

Figure 8.1 Largest Muslim Populations by Country, 2010 Estimates

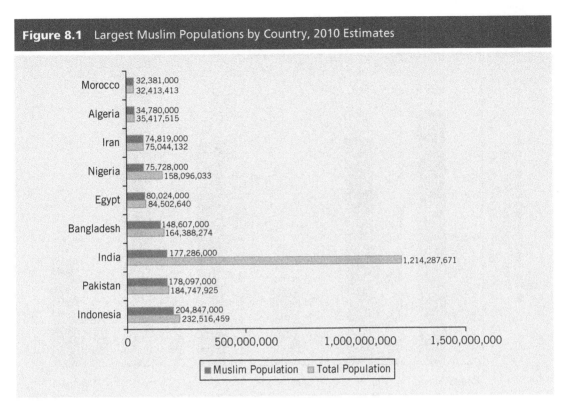

Morocco: 32,381,000 / 32,413,413
Algeria: 34,780,000 / 35,417,515
Iran: 74,819,000 / 75,044,132
Nigeria: 75,728,000 / 158,096,033
Egypt: 80,024,000 / 84,502,640
Bangladesh: 148,607,000 / 164,388,274
India: 177,286,000 / 1,214,287,671
Pakistan: 178,097,000 / 184,747,925
Indonesia: 204,847,000 / 232,516,459

■ Muslim Population   ▨ Total Population

Source: Based on data from Pew Research Center (2011).

of the Prophet, starting with his martyred cousin and son-in-law Ali and his descendants. Shiites tend to be more ecstatic in religious practice and have messianic expectations of a future imam who will bring justice to the world. Shiites form the majority in Iraq, Iran, Bahrain, Azerbaijan, and eastern Saudi Arabia, and most Shiite Muslims live in just four countries: Iraq, Iran, Pakistan, and India.

Salafism is an ultraconservative version of Islamic fundamentalism. Salafis are Sunni Muslims who regard the Shiites as infidels and nonbelievers. Salafis seek to follow the practices and beliefs of Islam as it was when it was founded. They believe most Islamic countries have fallen under Western influence and are not governed by Islamic practices and laws. Some Salafis are prepared to use violence to change nation-states into one Islamic empire or caliphate.

Sunni-Shiite differences continue in today's Iraq, where the Shiites, as the Islamic State of Iraq and the Levant (ISIL, also known as ISIS, for Islamic State of Iraq and Syria), are fighting to establish a caliphate in Iraq.

It is important to Muslims to preserve the family. Prohibitions against alcohol, smoking, and premarital sex are strict. To many Muslims, people in the United States don't care about families, abandon parents when they grow old, and have an epidemic of AIDS, pornography, pregnant teenagers, abortions, and illegitimate babies. These aspects of U.S. culture are not

Figure 8.2   Muslims and Mosques in the West

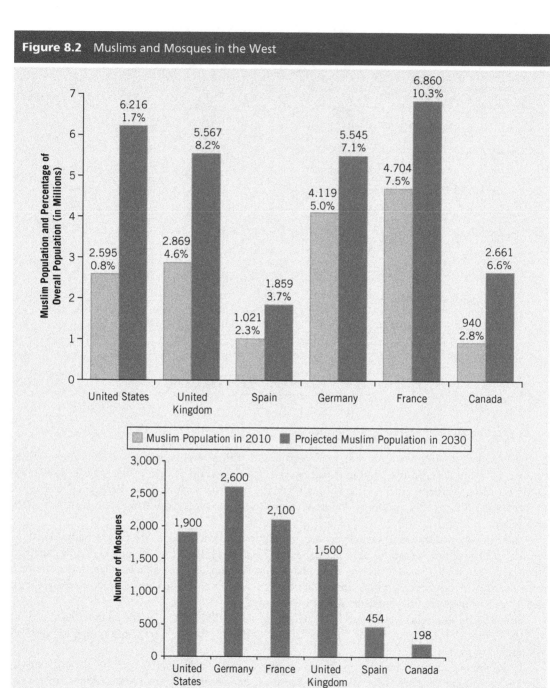

Sources: Based on data from Pew Research Center (2011); Ghosh (2010, p. 23); Central Intelligence Agency (2013).

Note: Muslim U.S. population percentage rose to 0.9% according to 2015 Pew data. See Table 7.1 in Chapter 7.

Focus on Theory 8.1

Views on Religion and Freedom of Thought

Christianity's New Testament makes no claims for religious orthodoxy, but in the 4th century, once it had been embraced by Emperor Constantine, its leaders began to demand it, converting some by the sword and burning alleged heretics at the stake. Achieving religious freedom without abandoning religious belief was the difficult challenge. The struggle for religious freedom paved the way for discussions of freedom of speech and of the press. Zagorin (2003) argues that a nation's progress depends on the creation and maintenance of human freedom, which in turn depends on religious freedom. Freedom in the modern sense of the term was introduced into the Arab culture through contact with Europe, particularly France. The scholar Ahmed bin Khalid al-Nasseri wrote, "The notion of freedom invented by the ferenja (foreigners or French) is, undoubtedly, the work of heretics. It requires disregard of the rights of God, the rights of parents and even the rights of humanity" (quoted in United Nations Development Programme, 2004, p. 54). On the other hand, the liberal Ahmed Lutfi al-Sayyid wrote, "Our freedom is our very being and our being is our freedom" (quoted in United Nations Development Programme, 2004, p. 55).

Between the 9th and 13th centuries, Muslim scholars improved and named algebra, refined techniques for surgery, advanced the study of optics, produced astronomical tables, proposed that the Earth turns on an axis, and proposed a sun-centered universe. Then the scientific spirit died (Masood, 2008). Today there are an average of 8.5 scientists per 1,000 population in Islamic countries, compared to 40.7 worldwide (Tolson, 2007). Nasr (2003) proposes that science in Islamic culture should not be seen as an extension of Western science but should be seen as an independent way of looking at nature. Rather than accepting that humans can know the world only through its quantifiable properties, Muslim scientists believe that full understanding requires seeing the world as signs of divine purpose. Lewis (2002) recognizes the argument that Islam was once the pioneer of freedom, science, and economic development yet also raises the same point that in modern times, it's the separation of church and state and the creation of societies governed by secular laws that have fostered freedom of thought and expression, which have made progress possible.

desired by Muslims as they bring shame on the family. To Muslims, God and family are most important. The dividing line between the Arab and Western worlds is religion. Islam is a religion, but also a way of life and the central force of Arab existence.

To better understand Islam, we will examine the prophet Muhammad, the Qur'an, and religious practices.

Muhammad, the Prophet

Muhammad (circa 570–632) founded the religion in the early 7th century in Arabia. Orphaned at an early age, Muhammad ibn Abdullah was a businessman when, in 610, it is said he received his first revelations

Global Voices

My Islam is a religion of tolerance and brotherhood.

—Sai'd Al-Ashmawy, former chief justice, Egypt's Supreme Court

Jews and Christians and whoever believes in God…and does what is right shall have nothing to fear or regret. Among his other signs are the creation of the heavens and the earth and the diversity of your tongues and colors. Surely there are signs in this for all mankind.

—Qur'an

through the angel Gabriel. These continued for another 20 years and formed the Qur'an, the holy book of Islam. Westerners once called Islam "Muhammadanism," but Muslims objected to the term because Muhammad is not regarded as divine. He is considered the last and most important prophet in a line that includes Abraham, Noah, Moses, and Jesus.

The Prophet Muhammad achieved victory as a military commander, state-builder, and political ruler. He intertwined religious and political functions. The state has been the instrument of Islam, and God was considered to be head of both the state and the religion. To argue for the separation of religion from politics is to argue against the model Muhammad established (Hamid, 2016). This is in sharp contrast to Western predominantly Christian countries, which separated church and state. Perhaps as a consequence, only three of the Arab states (Kuwait, Lebanon, and Morocco) are considered democratic; Egypt, Iraq, and Tunisia are sometimes considered partly democratic (Lexington, 2006). By the 8th century, a system of political-religious leadership that originated with the first successor to Muhammad held authority over parts of three continents, from what is now Pakistan across the Middle East and North Africa to Spain. Caliphate is the name given to a geographical area ruled by a chief Muslim civil and religious leader. The leader, known as the caliph, governed as a successor to Muhammad. By the 10th century, the office had become more political. Then, in 1924, the office was abolished by Kamal Ataturk, the founder of modern Turkey. Today some Muslims are campaigning for the restoration of the caliphate in a form resembling the Roman Catholic papacy as a means of restoring order. Today, any imam, or religious leader claiming descent from Muhammad, can assert authority.

The Qur'an

The Qur'an (often spelled Koran), which means "the recitation" in Arabic, was revealed by God to the Prophet Muhammad in Arabic and generally is considered to contain the verbatim words of Allah, or God. The Qur'an contains stories, admonitions, verse and prophetic segments, and social, political, and economic laws. It embraces all areas of human affairs, from the most personal to international relations. Not only is it unique in its completeness, but it also deals with human transactions in such a way as to make God's presence felt in every human interaction.

In Islam, there is no separation of church and state as in the United States. The Qur'an is a spiritual guide, a system of law, a code of ethics, and a way of life. Islam is the only world religion that offers rules by which to govern a state as well as a set of spiritual beliefs.

Focus on Culture 8.3

For Muslims, the Qur'an Is the Eternal and Indisputable Word of God

Muslims believe that every single letter and word in the Qur'an comes directly from God. As God is perfect and unchanging, so is God's speech. To question the divine origin of the Qur'an is to question God.

Source: Hamid (2016).

Dubai's ruler sponsors an annual competition for young men 21 and younger to recite the Qur'an from memory. This is to encourage young Muslims to better understand their faith. He provides nearly $700,000 in prize money. This competition is one of the most prestigious Qur'an recitation competitions in the world. The judges choose a section from the Qur'an at random, recite the beginning, and then the contestant is expected to pick up where the judges left off. The contestants must recite in Arabic in a melodic chant that follows rules known as *tajweed*. Tapes of the best reciters are sold across the Arab world.

The accounts of Muhammad's life and teachings are second only to the Qur'an as authoritative guidelines in Muslim faith and law. The *sunnah* are the traditions relating to the deeds and utterances of Muhammad. Together with the Qur'an, they are the basis of *sharia,* or canonic law. This legal system is different from Western models. The sharia system relies far less on physical evidence than on the accused's statements and answers to questions posed by judges. Cleric-scholars using the Qur'an and the acts of Muhammad as their guide get to the truth through patient questioning. If they err, they must answer to Allah. Anecdotal evidence indicates that the crime rate in the Arab states is low by Western standards. The Qur'an and *sunnah* dictate specific penalties for some crimes, such as amputating a thief's hand; however, contrary to popular belief, these are rarely carried out because the crimes are narrowly defined and proof is strict. For example, a shoplifter would not suffer amputation because shoplifting is not considered a theft as the goods were not locked up. Executions occur only if all heirs of the victim demand it. Judges often encourage the family to instead accept "blood money," traditionally the price of 100 camels. Punishment is often mild by Western standards. Some trials fall short of international standards—even "divine law must be carried out by mortals."

Religious Practices

The five religious obligations of Muslims begin with the public witness, or *shahadah:* "I testify that there is no God but God; I testify that Muhammad is the Messenger of God." Expressing this with conviction, it is said, is what makes one a Muslim. Short prayers, or *salah,* are recited by individuals five times daily at intervals from early morning to evening, each time after washing hands, arms, face, hair, and feet (although rubbing water lightly over socks is permissible). Facing toward Mecca, Muslims go through prescribed motions of standing, kneeling, and touching the floor with the forehead and palms. Congregational prayers at Friday noon are led by an imam, or spiritual leader. Alms giving, or *zakat,* is the duty of sharing with the poor a small percentage of the wealth beyond one's basic expenses.

©iStockphoto.com/Zurijeta

Entering the great Mosque in Mecca, pilgrims walk seven times around the Kaaba shrine in a counterclockwise direction, as part of the hajj, one of the pillars of Islam.

Fasting, or *sawm,* is central during Ramadan, the ninth month in Islam's lunar calendar. Ramadan commemorates the Prophet Muhammad receiving revelations from the angel Gabriel. Ramadan is a time to reflect on the meaning of Islam, to rejuvenate faith. Fasting Muslims abstain from food, drink, and sexual intercourse during the daylight hours. Nourishment is allowed only for the sick, the elderly, the pregnant, and the very young.

At least once in a Muslim's lifetime, a believer is expected to make a pilgrimage, or hajj, to Mecca. It's an elaborate series of rites requiring several days.

Focus on Culture 8.4

Islam in the United States

The first Muslims in the Americas were enslaved Africans brought over in the 17th century. African-Americans account for the majority of all converts to Islam in the United States. Among African-Americans, the Nation of Islam grew most rapidly in the 1960s. Most of its mosques underwent reforms after 1975 to join conventional Islam. Today, the Nation of Islam represents a small fraction of Muslims in the United States. Most South Asian and Arab Muslims' immigration dates to the 1960s and later. Today, Islam is one of the fastest-growing religions in the United States, and its presence is being felt in the country: Casio markets a watch that sounds an electronic call to prayer, some banks have set up "Islamic accounts" in response to the Muslim prohibition against paying or receiving interest, Warith Deen was the first Muslim to open the U.S. Senate with a prayer, and in 2006, Keith Ellison was the first Muslim elected to Congress. Minnesotan Ellison took the oath of office on a copy of the Qur'an owned by President Thomas Jefferson.

Sources: J. I. Smith (2000); Dannin (2002).

Katie Turley, Perrysburg, Ohio, Creative Commons Attribution-Share Alike 2.5 Generic

The Islamic Center of Greater Toledo is the third mosque ever built in the United States. It has been around since the early 1950s and, since 1981, has been located off of I-75 in its current iteration. It is perhaps the grandest and most beautiful mosque in the United States. Its unique design and structure lend it immediate recognition as a place of worship.

The Arab States

The Arab culture transcends time and space, particularly through its language and its Islamic faith. Arabs, the ethnic group that originally spread Islam, are now a minority in the religion. Just as the Muslim religion includes more than Arabs, not all Arabs are Muslim. The Arab world, however, is connected largely by a shared culture that developed in the Islamic faith. Of course, there is diversity within Islam, but it can be said that Islam is a "multidimensional system of beliefs that embraces the spiritual and the material, the divine and the earthly, the heavenly soul and mortal worldly deeds" (United Nations Development Programme, 2003, p. 118). In some countries, such as Egypt and Lebanon, many people identify themselves as Egyptians or Lebanese. But in much of the Arab world, people identify themselves as Arab or Muslim.

There is much diversity in the Arab world today, composed of 22 countries with a total population of 372 million. The population per country in 2016 ranged from 780,971 in Comoros to 88 million in Egypt. Iran is not considered an Arab country because its language is Persian (Farsi). Annual per capita gross domestic product (GDP) ranges from $400 in Somalia to more than $132,000 in Qatar (see Table 8.1).

Table 8.1 Overview of Arab Countries, as of 2016

Country	Population	Internet Users	Mobile Phones	GDP per Capita (US$)
Algeria	39,542,166	15,105,000	45,928,000	14,500
Bahrain	1,346,613	1,259,000	2,519,000	50,100
Comoros	780,971	58,000	422,000	1,500
Djibouti	828,324	99,000	312,000	3,200
Egypt	88,487,396	31,767,000	94,016,000	11,800
Iraq	37,056,169	6,381,000	33,559,000	15,500
Jordan	8,117,564	4,335,000	13,798,000	12,100
Kuwait	2,788,534	2,289,000	8,305,000	70,200
Lebanon	6,184,701	4,577,000	4,400,000	18,200
Libya	6,411,776	1,219,000	9,918,000	14,600
Mauritania	3,596,702	547,000	3,644,000	4,400
Morocco	33,322,699	19,021,000	43,080,000	8,200
Oman	3,286,936	2,438,000	6,647,000	44,600
Palestine (West Bank)*	2,785,366	2,673,000**	3,531,000**	4,300
Qatar	2,194,817	2,039,000	3,610,000	132,100
Saudi Arabia	27,752,316	19,320,000	52,796,000	53,600
Somalia	10,616,380	187,000	5,836,000	400
Sudan	36,108,853	9,610,000	27,939,000	4,300
Syria	17,064,854	5,116,000	13,904,000	5,100
Tunisia	11,037,225	5,355,000	14,598,000	11,400
United Arab Emirates	5,779,760	5,274,000	17,943,000	67,600
Yemen	26,737,317	6,711,000	17,359,000	2,700

Source: Compiled from Central Intelligence Agency (2017).

*The State of Palestine is recognized by many countries. Many of those that do not recognize the State of Palestine do recognize the Palestine Liberation Organization as the "representative of the Palestinian people."

**Including the Gaza Strip.

Map 8.1   Arab States

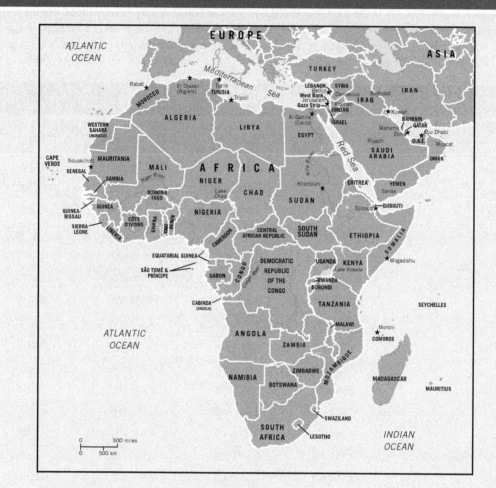

The Arab world's history spans more than 5,000 years. Yet from the time of Napoleon, who invaded Egypt in 1798, until the end of World War I, European countries conquered close to 90% of the Arab world by military force. After World War I, the European colonial powers began a slow retreat.

Saudi Arabia

Because of the political and economic importance of Saudi Arabia in the Arab world, we need to pay particular attention to this country. Its geography, oil wealth, ruling family, and conservative Wahhabism all enter into the country's control of media and relations with the United States. Increasingly, that relationship is one of shared interests rather than shared values.

Geography

Saudi Arabia occupies nearly 90% of the Arabian Peninsula and is the 13th-largest country in the world—2,149,690 square kilometers (830,000 square miles), or slightly more than one-fifth the size of the United States. As 98% of the land is desert, most cities are built on the coast and on oases. With an average of only 10 centimeters of rainfall a year, desertification, depletion of underground water resources, and lack of perennial rivers and permanent water bodies, Saudi Arabia has developed extensive seawater desalination facilities.

Discovery of Oil

In the 1940s, Saudi Arabia was mostly unknown to the rest of the world, and the rest of the world was unknown to most Saudis. Nomads outnumbered the settled. The economy was on a subsistence level. Illiteracy was high. In 1933, U.S. oil companies launched the California Arabian Standard Oil Company, which later became the Arabian-American Oil Company (ARAMCO). With monies from the oil discovered in the late 1930s, Saudi Arabia developed at a pace unparalleled in history. With 25%–30% of the world's proven oil reserves, Saudi Arabia became one of the strongest economies in the world. By 2015 oil accounted for roughly 90% of government revenue. The monarchy used its oil wealth to provide cheap energy and free education and healthcare to people in the country, and by 2015 had accumulated over $650 billion in currency reserves.

By 2007, the United States was importing nearly 1.5 million barrels of oil a day from Saudi Arabia. But with increased oil production in the United States and declining oil prices, the Saudi government posted a $96 billion deficit in 2015 and began raising prices of water, electricity, and fuel as it introduced new taxes. The oil era was ending.

Ruling Saud Family and Conservative Wahhabism

Today's Saudi Arabia is the third state created by the House of Saud. Two earlier kingdoms dating back to 1745 collapsed, in part, due to disputes over leadership succession. The Saud family gained power again in the 1920s. All three states have been based on an alliance between the Saud family and an ultraconservative brand of Islam, known as Wahhabism, that frowns on smoking, drinking, and virtually any contact between unmarried members of the opposite sex. As Saudi Arabia is guardian of the two holy Muslim mosques in Mecca and Medina, what happens in the country has global implications. It remains the most conservative Islamic country in the world.

By 2012 estimates, 85%–90% of citizens are Sunni Muslim and 10%–15% are Shiite Muslim. Non-Muslims are not allowed citizenship. Forms of religious expression inconsistent with the government interpretation of Sunni Islam are restricted or not permitted.

The Qur'an is part of Saudi Arabia's constitution. The country bases its legitimacy on its commitment to Islam and the implementation of *sharia* law. Anything that isn't allowed in Islam will not happen. Public morality committees called matawain, or the regional Societies for the Preservation of Virtue and the Prevention of Vice, ensure strict compliance with religious requirements. Salaried morals police patrol the public domain, making sure that businesses close at prayer times and that women are properly covered. Saudi Arabia has parallel legal systems—one civil and the other, more prominent sharia system, based on the Qur'an. Criminal cases are presided over by religiously conservative judges not bound by civil law. The religious judges hold power and are considered by some to be a check and balance on the monarchy.

While Saudi Arabia is a monarchy, it does honor an age-old practice of majlis, which provides any citizen access to the king and local governors. Also in Bedouin tradition are *diwaniyahs*, political meetings where men discuss community issues and debate politics. Perhaps in response to calls for change from both religious conservatives who resented the influx of Western forces during the Gulf War and liberals who saw the war as an impetus for opening the kingdom more to the West, early in 1992, King Fahd announced on national television a new administrative structure for the country. The king created a national consultative council that would review government policies and advise the Cabinet of Ministers, thus providing citizens with a voice in government, and he announced guarantees for personal liberties, such as freedom from unreasonable searches, for the first time in history.

From 2005 to 2015, King Abdallah introduced several social and economic initiatives to modernize the kingdom. He was widely regarded as a modernizer in a royal family balanced between those favoring changes and those who insist on maintaining a strict Wahhabi interpretation of Islam. In early 2009, he appointed the first woman to a ministerial post (a new post of deputy minister of women's education) and dismissed a leading fundamentalist cleric and the head of the nation's powerful religious police.

In 2005, municipal elections were held in Riyadh, Mecca, and Jeddah. These elected officials have some latitude in overseeing development in their cities. A second round of municipal elections was scheduled for 2009 but was repeatedly delayed until the fall of 2011. Only men were eligible to vote in these elections.

Before the second round of municipal elections, King Abdullah announced that women would be able to participate in future municipal elections, which occurred in 2015. For that election, some 130,000 women registered to vote, as did more than 1 million men. Some 1,000 women and 7,000 men ran for seats on 284 municipal councils. Nearly 80% of eligible women cast ballots and 21 women were elected.

-/AFP/Getty Images

Saudi women voted in municipal elections for the first time ever in 2015.

Since the death of ibn Saud in 1953, succession has moved only among his sons. King Abdullah was succeeded by Crown Prince Salman, who ascended to the throne in 2015. In 2017 he placed his 31-year-old son Mohammed bin Salman to be next in line to the throne. If he does succeed his father, he would be the first member of the third generation to rule the kingdom.

Media

Under Saudi Arabia's Basic Law, the role of media is to educate and inspire national unity. The government licenses all bookshops, printing presses, and public relations agencies to ensure that standards of taste are maintained. Most newspapers are privately owned but subsidized in varying degrees by the government. Editors patrol themselves, deferring to the government's Ministry of Information in questionable cases.

Television was introduced in the 1960s by the royal family as a propaganda tool. Clerics have a policymaking role and have imposed strict censorship rules (Boyd, 1999). State-controlled broadcast media emphasize religious programming. Satellite dishes are officially banned, but the government rarely enforces the ban. Channels from Beirut, Cairo, and Dubai, where Saudi censors do not control the media, target the wealthy Saudi audience and reflect more socially liberal programming, consumerism, and mixing of Arabic with French and English (Kraidy, 2009).

Social media is now a major force in Saudi culture. Facebook added an Arabic-language interface in 2009. By 2017, Facebook had over 14 million active users in the country and was the fourth most visited website in Saudi Arabia. The country has more than 2.4 million active Twitter users, who produce 40% of all tweets in the Arab world. Religious figures are the top Twitter users, with Mohammad al-Arefi at 17 million followers ("Facebook and Twitter Gain More Users," 2014; Socialbakers, n.d.). More than 90 million videos are watched daily on YouTube in Saudi Arabia (that's more than three a day for every citizen), making it the world's top YouTube nation per Internet user.

Focus on Technology 8.1

Saudi Election Campaigns Move Online

Saudi Arabia held municipal elections in 2005 and 2011 in which only men were eligible to vote. In September 2011, King Abdullah announced that women would be able to vote and run in the 2015 municipal elections.

In the 2005 elections, political parties and electoral blocs were banned. Instead, campaigners used Internet forums and SMS messages to promote their preferred candidates.

By the 2011 elections, with the expansion of social media, much of the election campaign moved online, with candidates using Facebook, Twitter, and SMS messages openly. The authorities tolerated this, probably because there was no sign of overt politics, sectarian campaigning, or electoral alliances.

In the 2015 elections women candidates were to be fined for speaking directly to male voters. Some resorted to social media to reach out to voters.

Sources: "Q&A: Saudi Municipal Elections" (2011); Linthicum (2015).

Perhaps recognizing the role social media had in Arab uprisings, the imam of Mecca's Grand Mosque called Twitter a threat to "national unity." Sheikh Abdul Latif Abdul Aziz al-Sheikh, the head of the religious police, was quoted as saying in 2013 that anyone using social media sites, particularly Twitter, "has lost this world and his afterlife." In the same year, Raif Badawi, the founder of a website known as Free Saudi Liberals, who had urged Saudis to share opinions about the role of religion in Saudi Arabia, was sentenced to 7 years in prison and 600 lashes.

In 2014, Reporters Without Borders described the Saudi government as "relentless in its censorship of the Saudi media and the Internet." In 2006, the government established the Communications and Information Technology Commission, which has become responsible for regulating the Internet in the country. It has censored thousands of websites deemed morally reprehensible or that present religious, human rights, or opposition viewpoints.

Regional Instability

Just weeks before his death, President Franklin Roosevelt hosted King Saud aboard a U.S. ship and gave the aging king his wheelchair. They formed a relationship that has continued between the two countries. President Harry S. Truman signed the first security agreement with Saudi Arabia in 1947. For years, American and Saudi peoples worked together, liked each other, but did not know much about each other. For example, the ARAMCO compound in Dhahran was originally built to house U.S. company employees in a Western environment separated from the restrictions of Saudi and Islamic laws.

Today, the United States is the world's second largest oil importer, and Saudi Arabia is the largest market for U.S. consumer products in the Middle East. For years, Saudi Arabia has worked with the United States to keep oil markets stable and advance common political goals. The 1991 war in the Persian Gulf (for which Saudi Arabia provided water, food, shelter, and fuel for coalition forces and made monetary payments to some coalition partners, including $15 billion to the United States) brought individuals from the two cultures into contact, and, as we have seen, neither will be the same in the future. A number of reform-minded Saudi businessmen, government officials, and academics used the 1991 war as an opportunity to advocate for expanded rights for women, a reliable court system, and an elected parliament. The conservatives, however, have worked to make Islamic Saudi Arabia even more fundamentalist, particularly in the areas of economic policies (e.g., eliminating Western-oriented banks), the parts of the legal system not fully based on sharia law, censorship of foreign media with secular ideas, and a heavy dependence on the West in foreign and defense policies (House, 2012).

ISIS originated in 1999 as an al-Qaeda splinter group. It proclaimed itself a worldwide caliphate and in 2014 claimed religious, political, and military authority over Muslims worldwide. Some understand that to include reclaiming the holiest sites in Islam, Mecca and Medina, thus taking over or dismembering the Saudi kingdom. The majority of ISIS's leadership has been dominated by Iraqis who adhere to the Wahhabi movement of Sunni Islam. ISIS leadership has been particularly effective in recruiting young Muslims on social media throughout the Middle East.

ISIS is believed to be operational in many countries across the world. It has been designated a terrorist organization by the United Nations, which, along with mainstream Muslim groups, rejects its claim of statehood.

In past years, Saudi Arabia relied on the United States for military support. With declining oil exports to the United States, the relationship has weakened as the Saudis felt the United States has become less attentive to their concerns in the region. That 15 of the 19 men who carried out the September 11 terrorist attacks in the United States also strained the relationship.

Iran and Saudi Arabia are the two most powerful nation-states in the Middle East. Each sees itself as the center of the Islamic world. Saudi Arabia is majority Sunni; Iran is majority Shiite. Iran, ruled by mullahs, has been expanding its influence with the Shiite Muslim crescent. Saudi Arabia's King Abdullah pushed President Obama to take a tougher stand against a potentially nuclear-armed Iran. To Saudi Arabia's north is Syria, a former Saudi ally now drawn under Iran's influence. Iran and Saudi Arabia have backed opposing sides in Syria's civil wars. Saudi Arabia has joined the United States in carrying out air strikes in Syria against ISIS. With the loss of held territory, ISIS may return to clandestine cells with no fixed territory.

To Saudi Arabia's south is Yemen, where Saudi Arabia has led an Arab coalition to fight the Iran-supported Shiite Huthi rebels. Saudi Arabia has built a concrete-filled security barrier along sections of the border with Yemen to stem cross-border activities.

While Saudi Arabia and the United States do share the objectives of regional stability and containment of Iran, significant differences, particularly relating to the political instability in the region, continue to strain the decades-long alliance.

Dominant Cultural Patterns

We will use the Kluckhohn and Strodtbeck (1961) universally shared problems, discussed in the previous chapter to describe U.S. cultural patterns, again here to describe mainstream Arab cultural patterns and to provide a useful comparison.

AP Photo/Evan Vucci

President Trump's first international trip was to Saudi Arabia. First daughter Ivanka Trump is admired as accomplished by Saudi women and men. Note that she did not cover her hair.

Human Being–Nature Orientation

As defined in Chapter 7, a worldview is the outlook that a culture has concerning the nature of the universe, the nature of humankind, the relationship between humanity and the universe, and other philosophical issues defining humans' place in the cosmos.

In virtually all aspects, the Arab worldview is derived from Islam and expressed in its language. Islam draws no distinction between religion and the temporal aspects of life. According to Islam, everything in the world except humans is administered by God-made laws. The physical world has no choice but obedience to God. Humans alone possess the qualities of intelligence and choice. Humans can choose to submit to the Law of God and, in so doing, will be in harmony with all other elements of nature.

Islam holds that the world is totally real. It is incumbent upon every Muslim to seek knowledge in the broadest sense from the created universe, as it reveals knowledge and truth. Though Islam demands faith in God as the basis of knowledge and research, it encourages all methods of gaining knowledge, whether rational or experimental. This overwhelming quest for knowledge gave birth to, among other things, the modern sciences of mathematics, physics, chemistry, and medicine and triggered the Renaissance in Europe (Haiek, 1992).

While Islam generally does not hinder private enterprise or condemn private possessions, it does not tolerate selfish and greedy capitalism. This is an expression of the general philosophy of Islam of a moderate and middle but positive and effective course between the individual and the state—yet among the most egregious violators of human rights are the authoritarian regimes in the Muslim world, such as Saddam Hussein's former Iraqi regime and ISIS.

Activity Orientation

Earning a living through labor is not only a duty but also a virtue. Islam respects all kinds of work as long as there is no indecency or wrong involved. Whatever a person makes is one's private possession that no one else may claim. Islam encourages Muslims to work, to engage in free enterprise, and to earn and possess, but the "owner" is God and the human is the trustee. This means Muslims have a responsibility to invest and spend wisely. Just as Islam provides the values for work, it also guides other aspects of human activity. Islam encourages practicality. It does not encourage wishful thinking but does encourage one to accept and deal with the reality within one's reach.

Adherence to Islam largely conflicts with uncritical acceptance of progress and change. Islam is conservative because of its adherence to the Qur'an.

Time Orientation

Saudi accounting of time shows a strong relationship to the cosmos. Saudi Arabia adheres to the traditional *Hijrah* (or *Hegirian*) calendar, which is based on the cycles of the moon. A lunar month is the time between two new moons. The Hijrah year contains 12 months and so is 11 days shorter than the solar year. As a result, the months shift gradually from one season to another. Months in the Hijrah calendar have no relation to the seasons. The first day of the first year of the Hijrah calendar corresponds to July 15, 622, the date on which Muhammad fled Mecca for Medina to escape persecution at the hands of the Quraish. The Western method of designating Islamic dates is AH (*anno Hegira*).

The traditional system of accounting time during the day is tied to the rising and setting of the sun. International communication, however, has forced Saudi Arabia to adopt Greenwich Mean Time.

Arab markets and stores appear to be in a state of mass confusion as customers all try to get the attention of a single clerk. Arab government offices may have large reception areas where groups of people are all conducting affairs at the same time. As a polychronic culture, Arabs can interact with several people at once and still be immersed in each other's business. Polychronic managers can supervise a large number of people. By their actions, polychronic cultures demonstrate that they are oriented to people, human relationships, and family.

Human Nature Orientation

Muslims believe that every person is born free of sin. It is said that when a person reaches the age of maturity, the individual becomes accountable for deeds and intentions. Thus, human nature is more good than evil, and the probability of positive change is greater than the probability of failure. God endowed only humans with intelligence and choice. The purpose of human life is to worship God by knowing, loving, and obeying him.

Relational Orientation

As we have seen, Arab culture is more group oriented. Social lives are traditionally organized around the family and tribal line. Loyalties are to family, clan, tribe, and government, in that order. Individuals subordinate personal needs to the family and the community.

Many Saudis live in large extended families, and devotion to the family is central. In contrast to Western culture, the concept of individuality is absent. There is a strong sense of identity with the family. Saudis see themselves in the context of family. Duty is not to oneself but to the group. Loyalty is first to the family. All family members suffer from the dishonorable act of any one of them. Honor is the collective property of the family. Islam unifies humanity on the basis of equality. There are no bounds of race, country, or wealth. All are born equal and should have equal civil, political, and spiritual rights. In this sense, Islam is an international religion. Central to the Arab culture's social organization is family and Islam. Generous hospitality is a matter of honor and a sacred duty.

A man is usually considered to be a descendant only of his father and his paternal grandfather. A man's honor resides in the number of sons he sires. A man belongs to his father's family. Decisions are made by the family patriarch, not by the individual.

Role of Women

Most Muslims would say that women in Arab cultures are equal to men. The Prophet Muhammad revolutionized life for women in the 7th century by granting women access to the mosque, full participation in public affairs, and the right to inherit property. The rights and responsibilities of women are equal to those of men but not identical to them. In Arab cultures, equality and sameness are two quite different things. It is said that women are deprived in some ways but are compensated in other ways. Thus, Arab women are equal as independent human beings, equal in the pursuit of knowledge, and equal in the freedom of expression. An Arab woman who is a wife and mother is entitled to complete provision and total maintenance by her husband. She may work and own property herself.

Patrick Baz/AFP/Getty Images

Saudi women order in the women's section of McDonald's in the Kingdom Mall. Most coffee shops and restaurants have a "family section" that women and children are allowed to frequent with or without their husbands.

Saudi women need the permission of a male relative to attend university, get married, or travel abroad. Public facilities are segregated by sex. Even the takeout counters at McDonald's and Häagen-Dazs have two sections split by plywood dividers. Women who work outside the home work in separate work spaces or in capacities with other women. Saudi society is structured to keep a woman within strictly defined limits to protect her chastity.

Wearing the *abaya* and the veil is an old tradition to safeguard women from the actions of strange men. A woman is not permitted to expose any part of her body before strangers. Thus, the abaya and the veil represent honor, dignity, chastity, purity, and integrity. The great majority of Saudi women are willing to accept this position in society in return for the guarantee of security that Arab traditions provide. Those who want change want it within the context of the Arab culture.

Communication Barriers

A challenge to intercultural communication between some people, both Christians and others, and Muslims in the United States has centered on the use of the term *radical Islam*. President Obama made a clear distinction between the religion Islam and the extremists who adhere to radical interpretations of the religion and who carry out acts of terror. In a February 2015 speech at the Summit on Countering Violent Extremism, the president said, "We are not at war with Islam. We are at war with people who have perverted Islam. … We must never accept the premise that they put forward, because it is a lie. Nor should we grant these terrorists the religious legitimacy that they seek. They are not religious leaders. They're terrorists" (quoted in Tau, 2015).

Then, as communication scholar Martin Medhurst contends, do words shape attitudes and intercultural communication? The major barrier to intercultural communication between U.S. and Arab peoples appears to be the stereotypes each holds of the other. Shaheen (2001) contends that U.S. media vilified Arab Muslims in the aftermath of the September 11 attacks.

A Pew Research Center (2014b) survey asked people in the United States to rate members of eight religious groups (Muslim, Jews, Catholics, evangelical Christians, Buddhists, Hindus, Mormons, and atheists) on a "feeling thermometer" from 0 to 100, where 0 represented cold, negative feelings and 100 represented warm, positive feelings. They rated Muslims lowest, at 40, atheists at 41, and the remainder more warmly. U.S. adults were closely divided on whether Islam is more likely than other religions to encourage violence. In a Pew Research Center (2016b) survey, about half thought that at least some U.S. Muslims are anti-American. More than half (59%) felt that there is a lot of discrimination against Muslims in the United States, and even more (76%) felt that discrimination against Muslims in the United States was rising.

Global Voices

Unfortunately, the term *jihad* has become synonymous with "terrorism" in the West. The 19th-century British author of *Historical Sketches of the South of India* introduced the term into English and defined it as a Muslim "holy war." The Oxford English Dictionary defined it as "a religious war of Muslims against unbelievers."

The term is derived from the Arabic word *juhd*, which translates as a struggle for the sake of a goal. The term is used some 30 times in the Qur'an and can mean a believer's inner spiritual struggle to fulfill religious duties (sometimes called the "greater" jihad) and an outer violent or nonviolent physical struggle against persecution and oppression by the enemies of Islam (sometimes called the "lesser" jihad). Because of the use of the term in the Qur'an, *jihad* has a positive meaning for the overwhelming majority of Muslims as the struggle to defend is noble.

In the 1980s, the radical Abdullah Azzam contended that it was the duty of *all* Muslims to fight non-Muslims invading or occupying Muslim territory, a claim not inconsistent with nationalist and religious struggles throughout history. Terrorists have claimed legitimacy of their killing of innocents, but this is explicitly forbidden by the Qur'an.

Source: Habeck (2006).

In an earlier Pew Research Center (2011b) survey of U.S., European, and Muslim countries, respondents were asked about characteristics they associate with one another. Across the Muslim-majority countries surveyed, a median of 68% viewed Westerners as selfish. Other highly rated characteristics were violent (median of 66%), greedy (64%), and immoral (61%). Fewer attributed positive characteristics such as respectful of women (44%), honest (33%), and tolerant (31%). Westerners' attitudes stood in contrast: Respondents from four Western European countries, Russia, and the United States viewed Muslims as fanatical (median of 58%), violent (50%), and respectful of women (22%). On the other hand, Westerners believed Muslims to be honest (51%) and generous (41%).

Over the course of 14 centuries, Christians and Muslims have at times lived together and interacted harmoniously and at other times been in conflict. There are many points of convergence between Christian and Islamic beliefs, such as an understanding of God as Creator, the centrality of prayer, and values such as justice and loving one's neighbor. But there are also real substantial differences in the faiths, such as Christian belief in the Trinity and Muslim denial of Jesus's crucifixion and resurrection. While it is a simplification to attribute all conflicts to differences in beliefs, those religious identities seem to be most threatened when nation-state and religious identities become one.

Focus on Culture 8.5

The Various Identity Labels Applied to Arabs in the United States

In Chapter 1 you read about the importance of the label applied to groups. Saskia Witteborn (2007) studied the various labels applied to Arabs living in the United States, showing that self-identification depended on situational factors such as the audience and the setting. People in the study identified as Arab in public settings where non-Arabs asked for their origin or imposed an identity that they did not accept for themselves.

The Arab-American label was used by some when addressing media and politicians to increase credibility and to contradict terrorist stereotypes. Others rejected the label, whether used by Arabs or non-Arabs, as contributing to othering.

The label Muslim was most likely to be used with people who were knowledgeable about Islam. In interactions with individuals perceived to be uneducated or prejudiced, other labels with a more positive connotation, such as Egyptian, were used.

The events of September 11, 2001, significantly influenced label use. Some believed September 11 increased responsibility to express an Arab identity for solidarity with other Arabs. Others avoided the label as they believed its use would create a risk to their personal well-being. And still others began using the label Arab-American to publicly identify as American.

Focus on Skills 8.1

Preparing to Conduct Business in Saudi Arabia

You work for a specialty food producer who wants to expand to Saudi Arabia. The company has partnered with a Western/Arab joint venture law firm, which has assisted in securing a required local partner and will register the business. Senior executives from your business are preparing to visit with the local partner in Saudi Arabia. You've been asked to brief them on what to expect.

Here are some of their concerns that you must address:

1. What is the best time of the year to visit?
2. What should they wear?
3. Should they bring gifts?
4. Will they be asked personal questions about family and religion? How should they answer?
5. How do Saudis conduct business meetings?
6. The CFO of your company is a woman. Should she participate in the meetings?
7. Should they plan on entertaining the Saudis at a dinner?
8. Is there anything else they need to know?

SUMMARY

Religion is the oldest source of human identity. The world's major religions are Christianity, Islam, Hinduism, Buddhism, folk religions, and Judaism. At times religious identity and nation-state identity have become synonymous, such as State Shinto, the state religion of Japan that was abolished by the Allies in 1945. Christianity grew in influence and power following the Roman emperor Constantine's conversion. Today, Russia's president Putin has embraced Orthodox Christianity as an opposing ideology to Western ideology.

Islam, the second largest religion in the world, was founded by Muhammad, who intertwined religion and political functions. The Qur'an, believed to come directly from God, is a spiritual guide as well as rules to govern a state.

Twenty-two countries with a combined population of 372 million make up the Arab world. It is characterized by the Islamic faith and Arabic language use. Saudi Arabia, the guardian of the two holy sites Mecca and Medina, is the most conservative Islamic country and has been ruled by the Saud family in alliance with the ultraconservative Wahhabism branch of Islam.

Today's instability in the Middle East pits ancient rivals Saudi Arabia and Iran against one another. Saudi Arabia is majority Sunni Muslim; Iran, majority Shiite Muslim. Each has backed opposing sides in Syria and Yemen as ISIS has proclaimed itself a worldwide caliphate, grows in influence, and threatens stability in Saudi Arabia.

The chapter focuses on values using the same Kluckhohn and Strodtbeck value orientation theory used in Chapter 7 to describe U.S. dominant cultural values.

Arab worldview is derived from Islam and expressed in its language. Islam respects all kinds of work as long as there is no indecency or wrong involved. Saudi accounting of time shows a strong relationship to the cosmos; Saudi Arabia adheres to the traditional *Hijrah* calendar, which is based on the cycles of the moon. Muslims believe God created only humans with intelligence and choice, and that the purpose of human life is to worship God. Arab culture is more group oriented, organized around the family and tribal line.

Communication barriers between Western and Arab peoples show that each holds significant negative attitudes of the other.

DISCUSSION QUESTIONS

1. Discuss the consequences that arise when religious and nation-state identities overlap.

2. Compare the relationship of Islam to Arab culture and Christianity to Western culture.

3. Explain how contemporary U.S. society can be seen from the perspective of fundamentalist Islam.

4. Of all the chapters in this textbook, the author has received the most e-mail about this one. About half complain that the chapter is anti-Muslim, about half that the chapter is pro-Muslim. Why do you think this chapter has generated the most feedback? How would you advise the author to respond?

KEY TERMS

Arabs	majlis	Shiite
caliph	matawain	Shinto
caliphate	Muhammad	Sunni
hajj	Muslim	
imam	Ramadan	

READINGS

All readings are from *Intercultural Communication: A Global Reader* (Jandt, 2004).

Mark Warschauer, Ghada R. El Said, and Ayman Zohry, "Language Choice Online: Globalization and Identity in Egypt" (p. 160)

George E. Irani, "Islamic Mediation Techniques for Middle East Conflicts" (p. 360)

STUDENT STUDY SITE

$SAGE edge™

Sharpen your skills with SAGE edge at edge.sagepub.com/jandt9e.

SAGE edge for Students provides a personalized approach to help you accomplish your coursework goals in an easy-to-use learning environment.

Chapter 9

Theo Wargo/Getty Images

Culture and Gender

In Chapter 1 you read that gender is one of Cannadine's forms of regulators of human life and identity. Perhaps the first and most influential label assigned to each of us is "It's a girl" or "It's a boy," an identity prescribed at birth based on genitalia. From antiquity to the end of the 17th century, there was no concept of gender. The female body was a variation of the male body (Laqueur, 1990). The recognition that there are only two sexes (female/male), two genders (feminine/masculine), and the understanding that sex is fixed before gender are products of the modern era in Western cultures. Actually, cultures around the world have long recognized three, four, five, or more genders. Today, beliefs about gender are evolving, as evidenced by the more than 50 terms Facebook provides users for their profiles.

At a minimum today, we recognize biological sex, gender identity, and gender expression. Biological sex is more frequently used to refer to features based on chromosomal evidence to categorize females and males (Brettell & Sargent, 1993). Yet perhaps 1% may be intersex, with a mix of female and male sexual characteristics. Gender identity is usually established by 3 years of age. It is a deeply felt sense of being a woman, a man, or a nonbinary identity that is both, fluid, or neither. The term *cisgender* refers to people who identify with the sex assigned at birth; the term *nonbinary* refers to the spectrum of gender identities based on rejection of the assumption that gender is a dichotomy. Gender as a dichotomy of either feminine or masculine has been most common in Western cultures, while other cultures have long acknowledged other possibilities. Whitehead (1981) described the Plains Indian berdache as a third gender. The berdache were men who dressed

Global Voices

Living in India was a revelation because I came to understand that there were old languages that didn't have gender—that didn't have "he" and "she." The more polarized the gender roles, the more violent the society. The less polarized the gender roles, the more peaceful the society.

—Gloria Steinem, one of the world's leading feminists since the 1960s ("Women Leaders," 2017, p. 3)

as women and performed women's tasks. Other examples are the nadle of the Navajo and Mojave, who were considered a combination of female and male. When performing tasks identified with women, the nadle dressed and acted as women. When performing tasks identified with men, the nadle dressed and acted as men. Nadles could marry either a woman or a man and were regarded as wise and accorded special privileges and deference (Olien, 1978). The Mohave, Lakota, and Chuckchee recognize four, five, and seven genders, respectively. In other parts of the world, the xaniths of Oman in Islamic societies and the Tahitian mahu are third genders in their respective cultures. Finally, transgender refers to a person whose gender identity does not match the biological sex they were assigned at birth.

Gender expression refers to how people express gender through language use, behavior, hairstyle, makeup, clothing, and other outward signs. Whether the expression is feminine, masculine, or androgynous varies among cultures. Gender conforming is expression consistent with cultural norms expected for that gender. Thus it is gender conforming for girls and women to be feminine and boys and men to be masculine. Gender nonconforming is gender expression that is inconsistent with cultural norms, for example, girls who are not feminine enough or are masculine.

In this chapter you will first study extensive data that show how the status of women varies considerably around the world. The major purpose of this chapter is to study how that variation can be at least partially explained by cultural values. For example, if in one culture women are almost equal to men, what in that culture's values supports that? If in another there is great inequity, what in that culture's values explains that? And how successful have countries been in attempting to reduce those inequities by political means?

You'll examine how those cultural values defining women continue into the practice of marriage and family units. You'll then read how various cultures deal with nonbinary gender identities. And finally, you'll read about examples of gender expression through language use.

Focus on Theory 9.1

Feminist Theories

Feminist theory is more of a variety of voices rather than a single theory. Feminist theorists contend that many aspects of life are experienced in terms of feminine and masculine. Furthermore, feminist theorists assume that gender is socially constructed and dominated by a male perspective that is oppressive to women in economic development, education, health care, family roles, and political participation (Foss & Foss, 1994). Feminist standpoint theories assume that women's experiences enable women to see privilege and power in ways that men cannot, not only in such things as wages and exclusion from power and decision making but also in the very way society itself is constructed (Hallstein, 1999). The relationship between language and power has been a focus in feminist theory. Muted-group theory contends that men created the meanings for a group through its language, which suppresses women. One result is that women develop unique forms of expression.

Status of Women

Many studies are now conducted on a regular basis detailing the status of women worldwide. Studies by the United Nations and the World Economic Forum serve as the foundation for our study of the cultural basis for the status of women. Note that these data assume a binary biological assumption of identity.

United Nations Studies

In 1990, the United Nations Development Programme (UNDP) first used the Human Development Index (HDI) as a measure of life expectancy at birth, educational attainment, and adjusted per capita income. These were selected as quantitative measures of leading a long life, being knowledgeable, and enjoying a decent standard of living. Over the past decades, all countries have made advancements in the education, health, and income dimensions of the HDI. Table 9.1 shows the 20 countries with the highest scores on the most recent HDI.

In its 1993 report, the UNDP calculated separate HDI scores for women in 33 countries from which comparable data were available. The report concluded that no country treated its women as well as it treated its men. In some cases, the gap was substantial. Japan had the world's highest HDI rating that year but fell to 17th on the female HDI scale. Sweden was 5th overall but 1st on the female version. Gender equality is not dependent on the income level of a country; several developing countries outperform much richer countries in the opportunities afforded women.

The HDI masks the differences in human development for women and men. In its 1995 report, the UNDP focused even more sharply on the status of women by using two new measures: the Gender-Related Development Index (GDI), to reflect gender imbalances in basic health, education, and income, and the Gender Empowerment Measure (GEM), to evaluate a country's progress in the political and economic advancement of women. The GEM ranked countries with data on women's representation in parliaments, share of positions classified as managerial or professional, participation in the active labor force, and share of national income. The GDI for every country remained lower than its HDI, implying that there continues to be gender inequality in every country.

Table 9.1	20 Highest-Scoring Countries on the Human Development Index, 2014
1.	Norway
2.	Australia
3.	Switzerland
4.	Denmark
5.	Netherlands
6.	Germany
7.	Ireland
8.	United States
9.	Canada
10.	New Zealand
11.	Singapore
12.	Hong Kong, China (SAR)
13.	Liechtenstein
14–15.	Sweden
14–15.	United Kingdom
16.	Iceland
17.	Korea (Republic of)
18.	Israel
19.	Luxembourg
20.	Japan

Source: United Nations Development Programme (2015, pp. 208–211).

Later, a new measure was introduced to better show the differences in the status of women and men across countries. The Gender Inequality Index is a composite measure of three dimensions: reproductive health (maternal mortality ratio and the adolescent fertility rate), empowerment (share of parliamentary seats held by each sex and secondary and higher education attainment levels), and labor (participation in the workforce). Over the past decade, reduction in gender inequality has been virtually universal, yet there remain significant gender gaps. Table 9.2 shows the countries with the lowest gender inequality, and Table 9.3 shows countries with the highest gender inequality. Generally, gender inequality is highest in South Asia, Sub-Saharan Africa, and the Arab states.

Table 9.2 Countries With the Lowest Gender Inequality, 2014	
1.	Slovenia
2.	Switzerland
3–4.	Germany
3–4.	Denmark
5.	Austria
6–7.	Sweden
6–7.	Netherlands
8.	Belgium
9.	Norway
10.	Italy
11.	Finland
12.	Iceland
13–14.	Singapore
13–14.	France
15.	Czech Republic
16.	Spain
17.	Luxembourg
18.	Israel
19.	Australia
20.	Portugal

Source: United Nations Development Programme (2015, pp. 224–227).

Note: The United States ranks 55th.

Table 9.3 Countries With the Highest Gender Inequality, 2014	
137.	Congo (Republic of the)
138.	Haiti
139.	Mauritania
140–141.	Malawi
140–141.	Papua New Guinea
142.	Benin
143.	Gambia
144.	Burkina Faso
145.	Sierra Leone
146.	Liberia
147.	Central African Republic
148.	Tonga
149.	Congo (Democratic Republic of the)
150.	Mali
151.	Côte d'Ivoire
152.	Afghanistan
153.	Chad
154.	Niger
155.	Yemen

Source: United Nations Development Programme (2015, pp. 224–227).

World Economic Forum Study

Independent of the United Nations, the World Economic Forum released its first annual report on world gender inequality in 2006. This study is based on health and survival, educational attainment, political empowerment, and economic participation and opportunity. Figure 9.1 shows the countries with the greatest and least gender equality from its 2016 report.

The 2016 World Economic Forum report shows that, on average, the 144 countries covered in the report have closed 96% of the gap in health outcomes between women and men, and more than 95% of the gap in educational attainment. However, the gaps between women and men on economic participation and political empowerment remain wide. The World Economic Forum report examines the relationship between economic performance and gender inequity. While correlation does not prove causality, the report cites evidence to show that empowering women means a more efficient use of a nation's human resources and that reducing gender inequality enhances productivity and economic growth (Hausmann, Tyson, & Zahidi, 2010). Let's look in more detail at the bases of these rankings.

Figure 9.1 The Global Gender Gap Index 2016 Rankings

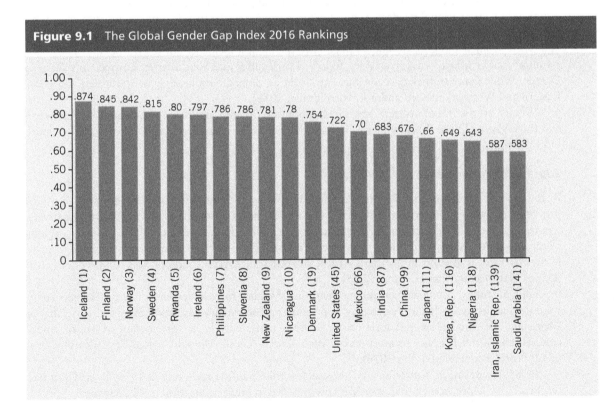

Source: World Economic Forum (2016).
Note: Highest possible score is 1.000 (equality); lowest possible score is 0 (inequality).

Health and Survival

This indicator of the differences between women's and men's health is based on sex ratio at birth and life expectancy. In the area of health, the World Economic Forum report examined the sex ratio at birth to measure infanticide. *The World Factbook* (Central Intelligence Agency, 2016) estimates sex ratio at birth worldwide at 1.03 males to 1 female. Countries with a sex ratio at birth greater than 1.1 males to 1 female include Vietnam, China, Hong Kong, and India. The high sex ratios at birth in some Asian countries can be attributed to sex-selective abortion and infanticide due to a strong preference for sons.

A lower than expected life expectancy refers to years lost to disease, malnutrition, violence, and other factors. In developing nations, adolescent girls' and young women's poor access to education, early marriage, and lack of decision-making power are linked to exposure to sexually transmitted infections, particularly HIV, and complications linked to pregnancy and childbirth. In industrial nations, maternal deaths are rare. Almost all births are attended by trained health personnel. In sub-Saharan Africa, only half of pregnant women receive adequate care during childbirth (United Nations Statistics Division, 2015).

Each year an estimated 800,000 women and girls are coerced or forced into sex trafficking servitude across international borders, and unknown numbers are trafficked within countries and in sex tourism for vacationing consumers. The poorest and most unstable countries with extreme poverty and where women and girls are undervalued have the highest incidences of sex trafficking. The greatest numbers of traffickers are from Asia, followed by Central and Southeastern Europe, and Western Europe. While many trafficking consumers are from developed nations, they are both rich and poor, Eastern and Western, married and not (Soroptimist, 2016).

Women are victims of neglect, rape, incest, domestic violence, political torture, abuses of refugees, and the ravages of war. Worldwide one in three women will experience some kind of sexual violence in her lifetime.

Educational Attainment

In the area of education, the World Economic Forum report examined literacy rate and access to primary, secondary, and tertiary education. The report shows 95% of the gap in education between women and men has been closed. Illiteracy among youth has largely been eradicated in most regions of the world. Yet nearly two-thirds of the world's 781 million illiterate people are women. Disparity in literacy rates is greatest in northern Africa, sub-Saharan Africa, southern Asia, and western Asia (United Nations Statistics Division, 2015).

Globally today, young women and men entering the labor force have almost identical levels of educational qualifications due to near parity in primary and secondary education except in sub-Saharan Africa and Oceania. However, girls do make up a marginally larger proportion of out-of-school children and a much larger proportion of youth not in school (United Nations Statistics Division, 2015; World Economic Forum, 2016).

In higher education, female enrollment was less than half the male rate in 1970. By 1990, it had reached 70%. More women than men are now enrolled in higher education in 32 countries.

Economic Participation and Opportunity

The reduction of the gender gap in education has not yet affected the gender gap in economic participation and opportunity. In the area of economics, the World Economic Forum report examined the differences in labor force participation, the ratio of female-to-male earned income, and the ratio of women to men employed as technical and professional workers, legislators, and senior officials and managers. Globally, 54% of working-age women are employed compared to 81% of men. Employed or not, women retain primary responsibility for caregiving and household chores. On average men do 34% of the unpaid work that women do.

In corporate leadership, global representation on boards is about 14%. The proportion of women in managerial and administrative positions worldwide is 14%, ranging from 28% in industrial countries to 3% in sub-Saharan Africa. In most of the Arab states and in South Asia, it is less than 10%. In the United States and Canada, women make up 46% and 42% of management, respectively; however, women in management tend to be concentrated in functions such as labor relations and personnel.

Wages for working women average about half those of men. The average global earned income for women and men is estimated at $10,778 and $19,873, respectively. In the United States in 2015, women earned 80% of what men earned—up from 59% in 1977 (Proctor, Semega, & Kollar, 2016). These statistics need to be interpreted carefully. The 1963 federal Equal Pay Act outlawed gender-based wage discrimination and requires employers to pay women and men the same wages for the same work. The difference in earnings results from women being available to work fewer hours than men, on average, and from lower salaries paid in fields traditionally held by women.

The majority of women in the workforce perform manual labor that requires minimal skills. As economies move toward greater use of technology, women are often the first unemployed by the changes. Of the estimated 1.3 billion people living in extreme poverty, more than 70% are women. In the United States in 1940, 40% of the poor were women; in 1980, it was 62%. Poverty has long been a women's issue. In the 1990s, two out of three poor adults were women, one in three female-headed families lived below the poverty line, and one in two poor families was headed by a woman.

Table 9.4 Women's Wages as Percentage of Men's Wages, Selected Countries

Country	Percentage
Mozambique	102
Burundi	99
Papua New Guinea	96
Norway	87
Sweden	87
Finland	86
Iceland	86
Canada	84
Denmark	84
China	83
New Zealand	82
United States	82
Australia	80
United Kingdom	80
Ireland	74
Japan	66
Spain	66
Italy	62
India	42
Turkey	36
Oman	28
Egypt	27
Saudi Arabia	22
Occupied Palestinian Territories	15

Source: United Nations Development Programme (2007).

Note: World average = 67%.

Figure 9.2   Year in Selected Countries That Women First Won the Right to Vote

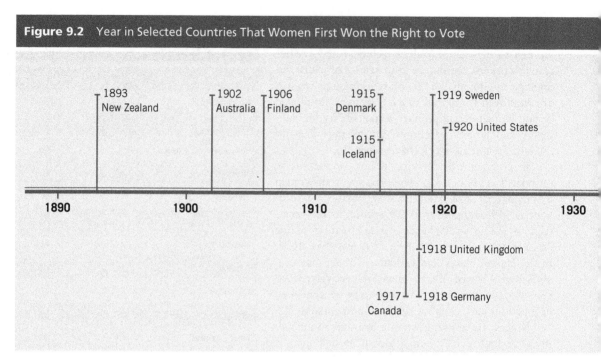

1893
New Zealand

1902
Australia

1906
Finland

1915
Denmark

1915
Iceland

1919 Sweden

1920 United States

1890   1900   1910   1920   1930

1918 United Kingdom

1917
Canada

1918 Germany

Source: United Nations Development Programme (2007).

Note: Vatican City remains the only country where women cannot vote.

Overall, the lowest-ranked countries on this indicator are from the Middle East and North Africa region.

Political Participation

In the area of political participation, the World Economic Forum report examined the ratio of women to men in parliamentary positions and in minister-level positions and the ratio of women to men in terms in countries' executive offices for the past 50 years. The report shows that only 20% of the gap in political participation between women and men has been closed.

In the ancient Roman era, women were not considered citizens. By the 1860s, middle-class women in Great Britain were organizing for voting rights. John Stuart Mill, who had recently been elected to the British Parliament, presented a women's petition for suffrage in 1866, initiating the first parliamentary debate on the subject. In 1869, Mill published *On the Subjection of Women,* in which he argued the feminist case in terms of liberal individualism. Particularly in Australia, New Zealand, and the United States, the women's suffrage movement gained strength from the temperance movement. In 1893, New Zealand became the first country in the world to grant women the vote. The state of South Australia followed the next year and Australia as a whole in 1902. Only in the 20th century did women gain the right to vote and to be elected to political office in almost all countries that have representative governments (see Figure 9.2). Until 1918, the Texas Constitution excluded "idiots, imbeciles, aliens, the insane, and women" from voting.

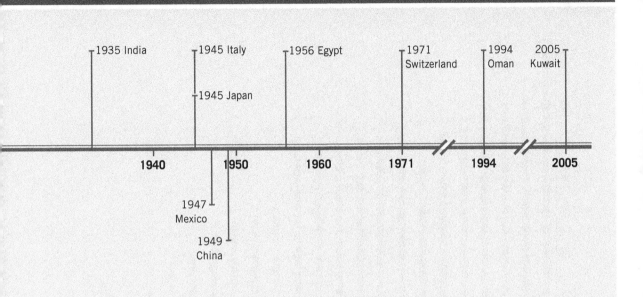

Worldwide, women's representation in national parliaments is about 22% (see Figure 9.3). In 33 countries, including Brazil, Iran, and Japan, women hold less than 10% of the seats in parliaments. In five countries there are no women in parliament; these include Qatar and Micronesia, Palau, Tonga, and Vanuatu in the Pacific region. By region, women's representation ranges from 15% in the Pacific and 19% in the Arab states to 42% in the Nordic countries. In 2017, 104 women served in the U.S. Congress (21 in the Senate and 83 in the House). This would seem to indicate that exclusion from politics is not as much a function of a country's level of development or the educational and income level of women as it is of social and cultural constraints.

In 2017, 25% of all U.S. state legislators were women—a percentage that has remained fairly constant for more than 10 years. The proportion of women legislators ranged from 39% in Arizona, Colorado, and Vermont to less than 14% in Oklahoma, Mississippi, South Carolina, and West Virginia. Also in 2017, the number of women in statewide elective executive posts was 75 (24%).

Representation will increase as more countries reserve seats for women. According to the United Nations Development Fund for Women, 32 countries have some kind of female quota for local or national assemblies. Beginning in 1994, India reserved a third of all *panchayat* (local council) seats for women, and in Uganda, by law a third of local council seats must go to women. Other countries have a quota for candidates. Germany's Christian Democratic Union (current chancellor Angela Merkel's party) reserved a third of party posts and election candidates for women beginning in 1995. And in Belgium, one gender cannot make up more than two-thirds of the candidates for the Chamber of Representatives and the Senate.

The effect of quotas is best demonstrated by Rwanda, the first country to have a majority of women in its legislature. After the period of Tutsi genocide, Security Council Resolution 1325 encouraged women to take part in the postconflict reconstruction, and the 2003 Rwandan Constitution included

Figure 9.3   Percentage of National Parliament Seats Held by Women as of 2015, Selected Countries

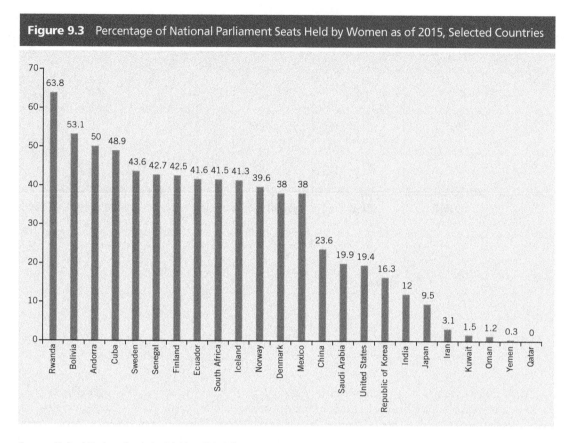

Source: United Nations Statistics Division (2016a).

Note: For countries with bicameral legislatures, percentages include both houses.

Global Voices

There is no occupation concerned with the management of social affairs which belongs either to women or to men, as such.

—Plato, *The Republic,* circa 390 BCE

a mandated quota of 30% women in the legislature. After the implementation of the quota in 2003, 24 women were elected. Today Rwanda has the world's highest percentage (nearly 64%) of women's representation. Although women in Rwanda still face discrimination, women legislators have worked for reforms in banking and property laws and to address gender-based violence (Hassim, 2009).

Worldwide, in 2015 women's representation in cabinets was 17%, many in areas such as social services and health. Leading countries include Finland (63%), Sweden (52%), Norway and the Netherlands (47% each), and Iceland (44%). In 1995, Sweden formed the world's first gender-balanced cabinet: 50% of the ministers were women. Canadian prime minister Justin Trudeau's 2015 cabinet was 15 women and 15 men. Worldwide, as of 2016, 10 women were serving as head of state and nine were serving as head of government.

With limited participation in political decision making, women worldwide are not treated as equal to men in laws governing travel, marriage and divorce, acquisition of nationality, property management, employment seeking, and property inheritance.

In 1979, the United Nations adopted the Convention on the Elimination of All Forms of Discrimination Against Women. Now sometimes referred to as the international bill of rights for women, only seven countries have not ratified or acceded to the convention: The Holy See, Iran, Somalia, Sudan, Tonga, and the United States and Palau (both of which signed without ratification).

Comparison of Individual Countries and Areas

As you study the following country-specific information, look for ways that the status of women and cultural values are linked in those countries.

Nordic Countries

According to the World Economic Forum, Iceland has closed more than 87% of its overall gender gap, the highest in the world. Finland at 85%, Norway at 84%, and Sweden at 82% are all in the top four in the world. Denmark is at 75%. Denmark, Finland, Iceland, Norway, and Sweden have a shared political, economic, and cultural development. Danish, Faroese, Icelandic, Norwegian, and Swedish are all North Germanic languages. A Dane, a Norwegian, and a Swede can understand each other with varying degrees of difficulty, but none will fully understand Faroese or Icelandic without studying the language. Finnish, however, is a Finno-Ugric language related to Estonian and Hungarian. The term *Nordic countries* is used to refer exclusively to these countries.

On Hofstede's dimension of masculinity versus femininity, the Nordic countries rank high in femininity and, as shown earlier in Table 9.2, rank the lowest in gender inequality. Hofstede (1997) argues that the concentration of feminine cultures in northwestern Europe (Denmark, Finland, the Netherlands, Norway, and Sweden) derives from shared historical factors. During major portions of their history, values associated with femininity were functional. A culture based on sailing and trading would value maintaining good interpersonal relationships and caring for ships and merchandise. During the Viking period, women managed the villages while men were away on long trips. And later, the association of trading towns of the Hanseatic League required feminine values to maintain such an association.

The Nordic countries have a strong value for personal freedom. One of the expressions of this freedom is that in Finland, Norway, and Sweden, all residents have free access to the forests, seas, and uncultivated land. The Nordic people were converted to Catholicism in the 10th to 12th centuries, but the Lutheran Reformation overcame most Catholic customs and memories in the 16th century. The Lutheran ideal of enabling everyone to read the Bible on her or his own encouraged strong education programs that, with a strong work ethic, contributed to decreasing social inequality.

A long tradition of egalitarianism and a strong women's movement contributed to the low degree of gender inequality in the Nordic countries. There has been a strong correlation between women's social movements and other forms of political participation. Women's movements since the beginning of the 20th century have had a politics-first strategy. As a result, women have had a prominent role in politics. In parliaments, there has been a marked equalization of the gender composition of

Map 9.1 Nordic Countries

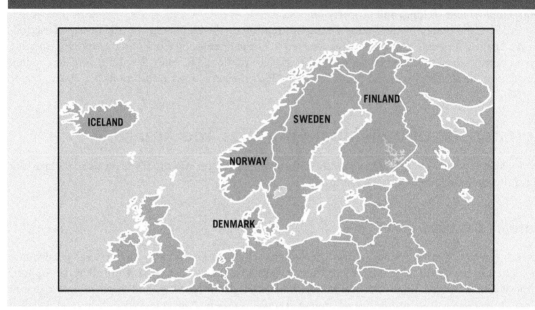

Canada's first gender-balanced cabinet. When asked why parity was important, Prime Minister Justin Trudeau said, "Because it's 2015."

GEOFF ROBINS/AFP/Getty Images

political posts within the democratic institutions. Since the mid-1970s, political parties have instituted quotas for women's representation. Women in political parties have used the slogan "women representing women." In 1999, Bergqvist and colleagues reported that women accounted for 11% in all parliaments across the world and 13% in Europe. In that year four Nordic parliaments were among the five national parliaments in the world with more than 30% participation by women. In 1981 (and again in 1986–1989 and 1990–1996), the head of Norway's Labour Party, Gro Harlem Brundtland, was Norway's first woman prime minister. In 2003, Finland became the first country in Europe to have women serving as prime minister and president at the same time. Social and gender equality in the Nordic countries has developed with increasing proportions of women in politics.

It is not surprising that these countries have adopted gender equality and women's empowerment as national policies. Consultative rather than confrontational politics focus political competition on issues. The Nordic countries have legislated equal rights, inexpensive childcare, free contraception and abortion, and parental leave policies. The women's movement now addresses the issues of wage differences, job segregation, violence against women, the environment, and peace (Borchorst, Christensen, & Raaum, 1999).

Figure 9.4 shows that the Nordic countries also rank high on foreign aid. In fact, only Sweden, Norway, and Denmark along with United Arab Emirates, Luxembourg, Netherlands, and the United Kingdom have reached the United Nations target for donor nations.

Mexico

Mexico has a history of male chauvinism. In 2007, Mexico's president, Felipe Calderon, said that despite antidiscrimination laws, millions of women suffer from workplace discrimination and physical

Focus on Culture 9.1

Gender Word Use in Swedish and U.S. English

Sweden

Gender neutrality is promoted by the Language Council of Sweden in its new official language policy for the country that includes the goal of minimizing sexist tendencies in official Swedish. One way this is accomplished is through the introduction of gender-neutral words. One example is the introduction of the word *hen* as an alternative to *hon* (she) and *han* (he). First used in the 1960s in the feminist and LGBT communities, the word received widespread use in 2012 when children's book author Jesper Lundqvist used it exclusively in his book *Kivi and the Monster Dog* (neither Kivi nor the dog are ever identified by gender). Now the word is included in the national encyclopedia and commonly used in major newspapers such as *Aftonbladet*.

Gender neutrality is promoted in other ways. Swedish toy catalogs show boys feeding baby dolls and girls firing Nerf guns. Legos and dinosaurs rather than dolls and trucks are more common in preschools. School libraries ensure that they stock the same number of books with female protagonists as those with male ones.

Source: Milles (2011).

United States

Jean Twenge and her colleagues (Twenge, Campbell, & Gentile, 2012) used the Google Books archive to analyze nearly 1.2 million books distributed in the United States for gender pronoun use. They found that from 1900 until 1950 the ratio of male to female pronouns was roughly 3.5 to 1. After World War II the gap began to widen, peaking at roughly 4.5 to 1 in the mid-1960s. By 1975 the ratio had declined to 3 to 1, and by 2005 to less than 2 to 1. The researchers interpret this trend as an increase in women's status since the late 1960s.

Source: Twenge, Campbell, & Gentile (2012).

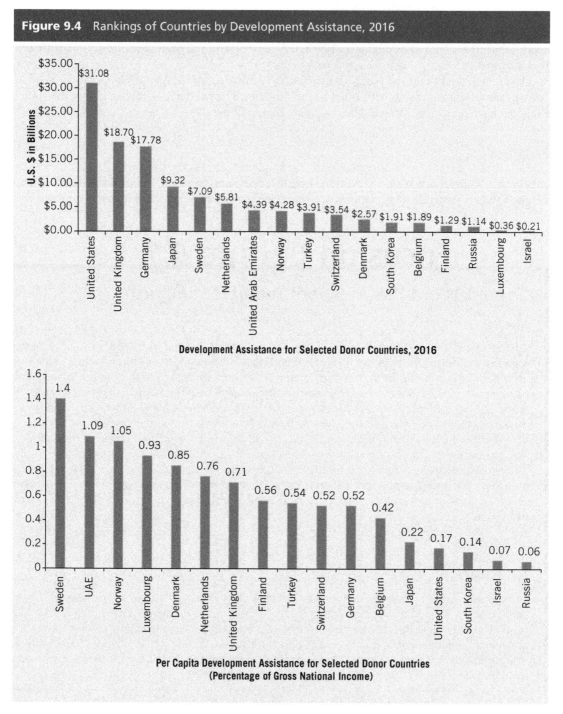

Figure 9.4   Rankings of Countries by Development Assistance, 2016

Development Assistance for Selected Donor Countries, 2016

Per Capita Development Assistance for Selected Donor Countries
(Percentage of Gross National Income)

Source: Organisation for Economic Co-operation and Development (2016a).

and psychological abuse due to Mexico's enduring cultural value of machismo and the cultural model for women of the Virgin of Guadalupe's suffering and sacrifice. In 2006, some 30 million Mexican women suffered some type of violence, and more than 80% of women who were murdered were killed in their own homes.

On the Hofstede ranking, Mexico ranks sixth highest in masculinity. It is reaching gender parity in educational attainment and health and survival but ranks much lower in economic participation and opportunity and political empowerment. Women and men both have a 13-year school life expectancy and 94% and 96% literacy rates, respectively. Life expectancy is 79 years for women and 73 for men. Some 80% of men participate in the labor market, compared to 45% of women. In government, the left-wing Democratic Revolution Party in 1998 announced that women would make up half of its candidates for high offices by 2000. The dominant Institutional Revolutionary Party set a quota of 30% for congressional candidates on the nationwide slate. Today, women account for 42% in the lower house and 34% in the upper house of the national legislature. Women in the legislature from different parties are working together to promote women's issues, such as laws punishing violence within the family and sexual harassment.

The status of women in Mexico, however, varies greatly from one region to another. In the southern states and central Mexico, around Mexico City, gender disparities are greatest. On the Yucatán, quality of life is lower but gender disparities are low. In the indigenous matriarchal Zapotec community of Juchitán, women play an important role in trading and decision making (Rhoda & Buton, 2010).

China

China ranks 40th on the Gender Inequality Index, ranking higher in educational attainment and health and survival than economic participation and opportunity and political empowerment. On the Hofstede dimensions, China ranks high in long-term orientation, high power distance, and masculinity.

Focus on Skills 9.1

Designing a Mediation Training Program for Women in a Border Community

You volunteer at a U.S.-Mexico border community center. Your special interest while you were a communication major at college was conflict resolution. You have been asked to develop a program to train volunteer mediators for the community. Mediators are neutral parties who help disputing parties resolve their own conflicts. You do some research and determine that in the United States the majority of community volunteer mediators are women. You're thinking about designing your training program for women.

1. Is this a culturally appropriate decision?
2. How would you design your program?
3. What intercultural communication barriers do you need to be prepared for?

Global Voices

In the traditional Confucian cultural tradition, the family comes before the individual, and boys are valued more than girls. Before the communist revolution, girls were subjected to feet-binding, and peasant girls were at risk of being kidnapped and sold into marriage. In the family, the respect for age exists, as does pride in sons. Women have lived by the Confucian ethic of serving fathers in their youth, husbands in marriage, and sons in old age. Confucian cultures consider not having children the greatest sin a son or daughter can commit against his or her parents.

Focus on Culture 9.2

China's One-Child Campaign

Louis Quail/Corbis Historical/Getty Images

Effects of China's one-child policy are the Little Emperor Syndrome and the 4-2-1 problem. Children receive sole attention from parents and grandparents. And there are too few young people to support a growing, aging population.

Family planning has been well established in China since 1956. Even so, as a family-oriented culture, it was not unusual for one couple to have as many as eight children. It was not until 1971 that a reduction in the fertility rate became a national priority. That year, the third family planning campaign, known as the *Wan, Xi, Shao* program, was initiated. These terms represent the three slogans of the campaign: late marriage, longer intervals between children, and fewer children. The total fertility rate fell from 5.4 children per woman in 1971 to 2.7 in 1979.

In 1979, the one-child campaign was introduced. The goals of the program were to eliminate all births above or equal to three per family and to encourage most families, particularly in urban areas, to have no more than one child. The Chinese government went to great lengths to ensure the success of the one-child policy. Couples were supposed to get a birth permit before conceiving. It was a familiar sight in China to see billboards advertising birth control and the one-child goals. It was not unusual to hear of coercion, abortions, and sterilizations being used to enforce the one-child policy. Over the years, though, many exceptions were permitted: Rural couples without boys and ethnic minorities were allowed more than one child. Hong Kong and Macau were exempt from the policy. Wealthy families avoided the law by going abroad to give birth or by paying large fines.

The one-child campaign was successful but had unplanned consequences: too few young people, too few young women, pampered only children, and concerns for care for the elderly. Sonogram technology contributed to abortions of female fetuses—a practice the government condemns. In 1999, China had a ratio at birth of 100 girls to 117 boys. As of 2016, the ratio at birth was 100 girls to 115 boys. In some provinces, the ratio may be as high as 100 girls to 130 boys. The World Economic Forum report ranks China as the world's lowest in birth rate ratio. It is estimated that by 2020, Chinese men between the ages of 20 and 44 will outnumber women by 24 million.

Many families now consist only of grandmothers, grandfathers, mother, father, and child. Implications for the society include pampered overweight children dubbed "Little Emperors"—four grandparents to spoil one child. A recent study of China's Little Emperors suggested the single-child family may have implications for China's culture beyond population control. The study compared people born in 1975 and 1978 before the one-child policy and people born in 1980 and 1983 after the policy was implemented. Compared with the adults born before the one-child policy, those born after grew up to be adults who were "significantly less trusting, less trustworthy, more risk-averse, less competitive, more pessimistic, and less conscientious" (Cameron, Erkal, Gangadharan, & Meng, 2013, p. 953). Their parents, who shared a culture of collectivism, hard work, and deprivation, created a relatively risk-averse generation that may hamper economic entrepreneurship and be less likely to embrace social institutions. Cameron et al. (2013) contend that the results should not be applied to single-child families in other cultures with different child-rearing practices.

Finally, China's one-child policy has created the world's largest elderly population no longer being able to rely on a large family to provide care in old age. By 2050, one in three Chinese will be older than 60—some 430 million elderly. The one-child program was undertaken to hold China's population at 1.3 billion by the end of the 20th century. And it can be said to have been successful: As of 2016, China's population was estimated at 1.37 billion, with a fertility rate of 1.6 (182nd out of 224 countries). In 2013 the one-child policy was changed to allow couples to have a second child if either of the parents is an only child. This one change permits an estimated 10 million couples to have a second child. In 2015 the policy was changed again to allow all couples to have two children. One rationale given for that change was that China's low birthrate was beginning to impair the country's economic growth, creating a population with too many elderly people and too few workers. State media today encourage women to return to the home and have babies (Fong, 2016).

Even though the improved status of women in China was state initiated, barriers such as Confucian traditions still remain (Wang, 1996). The very first law passed by the Chinese Communist Party abolished the holding of concubines and gave women the right to own property, choose husbands, sue for divorce, and use their own names. China's constitution states, "Women enjoy equal rights as men in all aspects, including politics, economy, culture, society, and family life."

In 2011, the school life expectancy for women and men in China was 14 years. China's literacy rate for women is 95% (98% for men). The average life expectancy of women in China climbed from 36 years in 1949 to 78 years in 2016, 4 years longer than the average life expectancy for men. Some 64% of women participate in the labor force compared to 78% of men. More than a fifth (24%) of parliamentary deputies are women. Since the 1980s, China's free market policies helped lift hundreds of millions of its people out of poverty, and economic conditions improved for many women. Women gained equality in education, marriage, rights, and freedoms, but in some villages and rural areas, the laws are ignored. Yet women are not included in leadership roles. Only two women sit on the powerful 25-member Politburo and only about 2% of Chinese women hold managerial roles.

Japan

The status of women has varied throughout Japanese history. In the 12th century, women could own and manage their own property, but the Meiji Civil Code of 1898 denied women legal rights and made women subject to the husbands.

Japan ranks 26th on the Gender Inequality Index. Japan approaches gender parity in educational attainment and health and survival, but like China ranks lower in economic participation and opportunity and political empowerment. Hofstede placed Japan highest in masculinity. In pre–World War II Japan, education was completely segregated by gender. Women were effectively forbidden from voting or going to 4-year colleges. In 1925, Japan's fertility rate averaged 5.1 children per woman. The Postwar Constitution of 1947 clearly stipulated equality under law and excluded discrimination on the basis of sex; however, in the 1993 HDI report, Japan had the world's highest HDI rating but fell to 17th on the HDI scale for women.

Japanese women and men have the same school life expectancy (15 years) and the same literacy rate (99%), but women have significantly greater life expectancy (89 years compared with 82 years for men). With high levels of education, health care, and income, Japanese women have more choices than ever before. Japanese women are postponing marriage; women's average age at first marriage is 29.3, and for men it is 30.9 (per 2014 data). (In the United States, the average age in 2008 was 27 for women and 29 for men.) The fertility rate has plummeted to a low of 1.41 in 2016 (210th out of 224 countries). During the 2005–2010 period, the population of Japan remained nearly stable. The decline in the marriage rate and the relatively older age at which couples now get married, on average, are considered to be two factors behind the downtrend in the birthrate.

The modern trend is away from traditional large multigenerational families and toward small families consisting of a husband and wife and one or two children. Some writers have described Japanese families today as like families in the United States in the 1950s—except the houses are much smaller. Most common are single family houses, but apartments in high-rise buildings are also common. The average home in Tokyo is a four-room condo of less than 95 square meters (1,023 square feet). Within the home, women control the household income and family life. It is the wife who handles the money and makes all of the family's financial decisions. In a country where serving men had been the long-accepted female role, some continue to want the woman inside the house all the time to serve her husband's needs day and night.

Women are increasingly active outside the home. A higher proportion of women than of men have voted in elections since 1980, but women constitute only about 12% of the Japanese legislature. Even though the national legislature and cabinet remain male dominated, women are a significant force in local government.

A 1986 equal employment opportunity law prevents discrimination against women in hiring. Some companies are using a two-track hiring system, which puts most women on career tracks to lower-paying positions. The traditional female role reappeared during Japan's economic slump in the mid-1990s, when there was a scarcity of jobs. Women job applicants and existing women employees

Global Voices

began to experience increased sexual harassment. Some accepted the harassment as normal in Japan's male-centered workplace. Today, approximately 49% of Japanese women participate in the labor force, compared with 70% of men (Central Intelligence Agency, 2016; Japanese Ministry of Internal Affairs & Communications, 2011).

Nonetheless, the most dramatic change in modern Japan is the changing role of women. Prescribed gender roles are breaking down. Japanese women are defining a unique interpretation of equality in gender relations in the home and in society. Along with changes affecting family structure, views on the proper relationship between women and men, student and teacher, and employee and employer are all changing. Yet concerns over Japan's royal family demonstrate the culture's continuation of male dominance. The current emperor, Akihoto, has two sons. Between them they have three daughters. For a time, the lack of a male heir may have become a catalyst for legal, cultural, and social change to redefine women's roles. The crisis was forestalled when, in 2006, Prince Akishino fathered a male heir, Hisahito.

South Korea

With a strong Confucian tradition, in South Korea a woman had a duty to her husband and her husband's family to provide a male heir. Korea's version of Confucianism is a "neo-Confucian" set of values devised as a formal state ideology in 1392 by Yi Seong-gye, the first king of the last Korean dynasty, imposed as a way to consolidate power. A Korean wife who did not produce a healthy son under Korean custom could be driven from the home and deprived of her status as a wife. Under the law, women were denied the right to become heads of household—a condition with implications for divorce, child custody, and communal property ownership.

South Korea's family law institutionalizes many elements of this traditional male-dominated family succession system. In many households, the eldest son is held in highest esteem to continue the lineage of an unbroken line of male-linked kin, perpetuate the family name, inherit the family property, and preside over ancestral rites. A bride was absorbed into her husband's household and was expected to adapt to its ways in everything from laundry methods to cooking styles. So deeply rooted and pervasive are these ethics that the average citizen does not think of them as Confucian.

Most of the Confucian-based discrimination against women in the nation's laws has been eliminated in recent years; however, in some ways Korea remains a patriarchal society.

South Korea (Republic of Korea) is an extremely homogeneous country (like Japan). About a million Chinese live in the country. South Korea ranks lower than China (116 compared to 99) and approximately the same as Japan on the World Economic Forum global gender gap (116 compared to 111), with, like Japan, the highest ranking for educational attainment and health and survival. Near Japan's rank of 26th on the Gender Inequality Index, South Korea's rank is 23rd. On Hofstede's masculinity scale, South Korea ranks 41st. Women's participation in parliament is only 17%.

India

India's population is now more than 1.27 billion, and it could become the world's most populous country by 2022. India today has a thriving economy, yet 300 million people live in desperate

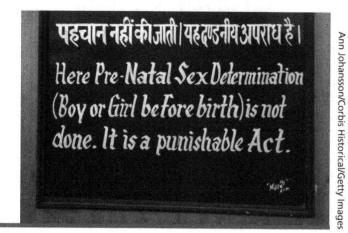

पहचान नहीं की जाती। यह दण्डनीय अपराध है।

Here Pre-Natal Sex Determination (Boy or Girl before birth) is not done. It is a punishable Act.

Ann Johansson/Corbis Historical/Getty Images

Clinics in India that perform ultrasounds display this sign in compliance with anti–sex selective abortion laws.

conditions. India's rank on the World Economic Forum global gender gap is similar to South Korea's. India's literacy rate for women is 63% compared to 81% for men; 28% of women participate in the labor force compared to 81% of men.

While China has slowed its birthrate with the one-child campaign, except for the years 1975–1977 India has relied on voluntary measures. Most Indian parents prefer to have boys because girls require a costly dowry at marriage and sons are the only ones permitted by the Hindu religion to perform last rites when their fathers die. In eastern Maharashtra state hundreds of girls were named Nakushi, a word that means "unwanted." The state has now allowed these women to choose new names. Women are trafficked into domestic work, agriculture, the garment industry, and street begging.

Similar to China, India has a history of female infanticide, which explains why there are upwards of 50 million girls "missing" over the past century. The advent of ultrasound and amniocentesis tests led to widespread abortions of unwanted females. India has passed a law preventing doctors from telling parents the sex of the fetus, but still, in 2011, there were 914 girls younger than 6 for every 1,000 boys, down from 927 girls to 1,000 boys a decade earlier. Some of the worst statistics come from the relatively wealthy northern states of Punjab and Haryana. Federal and state governments have programs to encourage parents to take care of their girls, ranging from free meals to free education. And India enacted a groundbreakingly progressive Domestic Violence Act in 2005 outlawing all forms of violence against women and girls. Yet Home Secretary G. K. Pillai said at announcing new census numbers in 2011, "Whatever measures that have been put in over the last 40 years have not had any impact."

A few Indian women have obtained some of the highest positions in politics (such as former prime minister Indira Gandhi) and business (such as PepsiCo CEO Indra Nooyi). India is one country with quotas for parliamentary seats held by women. India already had 50 years of a tradition of quotas for indigenous peoples, outcasts, and Indians of British descent in state and national parliaments. The idea of extending quotas to women was suggested by former prime minister Rajiv Gandhi, son of Indira Gandhi. At present, though, only 12% of members of parliament are women. India has not extended the quota for women to higher offices (French, 2011).

Sub-Saharan Africa

The countries of sub-Saharan Africa have a wide range of gender gap progress. Rwanda, Burundi, Namibia, and South Africa all score in the top and have closed at least 76% of their gender gaps. But other sub-Saharan countries are among many of the lowest-ranked. Much of that overall variance comes from greater differences on the educational attainment index as well as health and survival. Rwanda continues to rank in the world's top 10 countries and is one of only two countries worldwide that have more women in parliament than men.

African societies are largely patriarchal societies. In South Sudan young girls remain a commodity for marriage. Some families trade their daughters for cows. Despite constitutional guarantees of equality for women, Zimbabwe's Supreme Court issued a ruling in 1999 declaring that it is in "the nature of African society that women are not equal to men. Women should never be considered adults within the family, but only as a junior male or teenager." Under customary law in much of sub-Saharan Africa, women have fewer rights than men. In Kenya, women are taught that, other than to conceive children, the purpose of sex is to give pleasure to men. In the Democratic Republic of the Congo, over 1,000 women are raped every day (Peterman, Palermo, & Bredenkamp, 2011). The United Nations special representative on sexual violence in conflict called the Democratic Republic of the Congo the "rape capital of the world."

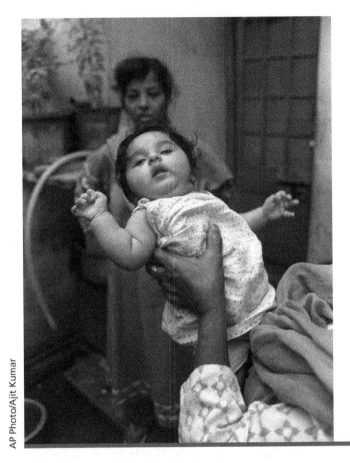

AP Photo/Ajit Kumar

Aastha Arura, India's one billionth child, was born in May 2000. By 2016, the country's population had increased to 1.26 billion. Aastha has become the face of India's population challenge. In the two months after her birth, 3.5 million more Indian babies were born.

Women have fared better in countries where there was participation in campaigns against colonialism, White minority rule, or authoritarian regimes. In Uganda, one-third of local council seats must, by law, go to women. Uganda's quotas grew out of the National Resistance Army's (NRA's) guerrilla war in the 1980s, when women fought side by side with men. In recognition, each of the rebel councils includes a secretary for women's affairs. After the NRA victory, the new president applied the same policy to national politics. The women in Uganda's parliament were successful in amending a land act to allow married women to share property ownership with husbands and in increasing women's access to education. South Africa's postapartheid constitution bars discrimination based on gender, marital status, sexual orientation, and pregnancy.

Every year 265,000 mothers and 4.4 million children, including 1.2 million newborns, die in sub-Saharan Africa. The region has half of the world's maternal, newborn, and child deaths resulting from pregnancy and childbirth complications, newborn illness, childhood infections, malnutrition, and HIV/AIDS (Kinney et al., 2010).

Arab States

The Middle East and North Africa ranks lowest on the overall World Economic Forum gender index. The region's best-performing countries are Qatar, Algeria, and the United Arab Emirates. The lowest are Syria and Yemen. In 7th-century pre-Islamic Arabia, girls were seen as having little value. Female infants could be buried alive. The Qur'an, which was revealed to the Prophet Muhammad, revolutionized life for women. In the Qur'an, all are equal in God's eyes—women and men, slave and master, subject and ruler. Against the status quo of the time, Islam gave women rights in marriage, divorce, property ownership, business, and inheritance. Muhammad welcomed women in the mosque as members of the community of believers.

Actual practices have not met Islam's ideal. Many Muslims contend, then, that the repressive practices against women ascribed to Islam are based on patriarchal cultural traditions, social considerations, and contested interpretations of the Qur'an. Women's education, though, has advanced in the Arab states. Princess Nourah bint Abdulrahman University, in Riyadh, Saudi Arabia, is one of the 10 largest universities in the world and the largest all-women university, enrolling over 60,000 women. In Saudi Arabia 60% of college students are women, but only 21% of its labor force consists of women, with most working in education and public health.

In Arab cultures, a man is considered a descendant only of his father and his paternal grandfather. A man's honor resides in the number of sons he sires. A man belongs to his father's family. A divorced woman may keep her children until they are 7 years old, but then they go to the father's family. Decisions are made by the family patriarch, not by the individual. Marriages in Saudi Arabia today may still be alliances between families. Islamic law gives the Saudi woman the right to approve or reject her family's choice.

Legally, a Muslim man can have four wives at once, if he can give each wife equal material goods and equal time, but a woman can marry only one man. Monogamy is the common practice today, however. "Strict disciplining" of women is openly encouraged. Divorce is discouraged, but marriage can be terminated by mutual consent, judicial ruling on the wife's request, or repudiation by the husband. He needs only to say "I divorce you" in front of a witness. He does not need to give a reason. If the woman does not want the divorce, she can claim her rights in court according to Islamic law.

Focus on Skills 9.2

Designing a Girl's Leadership Skills Group in South Africa

You have joined a youth outreach program to work with young women in South Africa. When you arrive you find that one of your duties will be to work with a girls group to develop leadership skills and networking and collaboration skills.

1. What ideas do you have for such a program that would be appropriate in South Africa's culture?
2. What intercultural communication barriers do you need to be prepared for?

While not true of all Islamic countries, Saudi Arabia enforces strict codes of behavior for women. Women may not vote except for chamber of commerce elections in two cities. No woman can sit on the kingdom's cabinet. Women are not allowed to register in hotels or leave the country without a male relative's or husband's written permission. Saudi Arabia is the only country in the world where women, including foreigners, were not permitted to drive cars. Since 1999, Saudi Arabian women who are married and over 35 years old have been allowed to drive cars during daylight hours, provided they have the husband's written permission; however, it is not clear that this change was ever enacted. Even Saudi-trained scholars agree that the restriction on women driving is not grounded in the Qur'an but is a modern social consideration

AP Photo/Hasan Jamali

Saudi women staged demonstrations defying the driving ban. Men argue that allowing women to drive will lead to greater mixing of genders, promote sex, and threaten the tradition of virgin brides.

to prevent women and men from being together in unsafe or unexpected circumstances. Families that can't afford a driver must rely on male relatives to drive women to school, work, or shopping. Challenges arose in 2011. June 17 of that year saw the first traffic ticket issued to a woman. Saudi religious authorities detained a Saudi woman who had posted a video of herself behind the wheel on Facebook and YouTube, where she hoped to encourage other women to copy her. Later a campaign waged on Twitter and Facebook led to a "driving demonstration." Amnesty International issued a statement calling for Saudi Arabia to stop treating women as second-class citizens and allow them to drive. Driving became a symbol. For some, it represented a change that could fundamentally alter Saudi society; for others, it represented the first step to other freedoms.

A traditional Saudi woman does not go out alone. She speaks to no man other than her husband or blood kin. All public facilities are segregated by sex. Women who work outside the home work in capacities in which the customers or clients are other women exclusively. Today's Saudi women may be teachers, computer technicians, social workers, laboratory technicians, physicists, engineers, bankers, or filmmakers, but most work in all-female facilities. Saudi society is structured to keep a woman within strictly defined limits to protect her chastity.

In Saudi Arabia, women must follow a rigid dress code. Observant Muslim women dress modestly and must be completely covered except for face and hands. Women walk the streets wearing a long black cloak called an abaya (also known by the Persian word *chador*). Most use veils to cover the face. Under the abaya, however, anything goes—from colorful cottons to blue jeans to haute couture.

The abaya and the veil represent an old tradition to safeguard women from advances by strange men. Women are not permitted to expose their bodies before strangers, thus the abaya and the veil represent honor, dignity, chastity, purity, and integrity. The majority of Saudi women are willing to accept women's position in society in return for the guarantee of security that Islamic traditions provide. Those who want change want it within the context of the Arab culture.

Marriage

Cultures regulate how many spouses a person can have, which partner has more authority and dominance in the union, and from what group a person can choose. Buss (1989, 1994) reported a study of criteria for selecting marriage partners in 37 countries. Mutual love, kindness, emotional stability, intelligence, and health were universally desired, but others varied by cultural dimensions. Brides in collectivist countries want age differences at marriage to be larger, and they want their husbands to be wealthy. Industriousness is a minor factor and chastity not at all. Bridegrooms in collectivist countries want age differences at marriage to be larger and put more stress on the bride being industrious, wealthy, and chaste. Grooms in masculine countries with high uncertainty avoidance place greater value on chastity. And in masculine countries, industriousness is deemed more important for women than for men; in feminine countries, it is equally important or unimportant.

Hofstede (1996) studied boyfriend and husband preferences of women in eight Asian cities. In the more masculine cultures, boyfriends should have more personality and more affection, intelligence, and sense of humor. Husbands should be more healthy, wealthy, and understanding. In the more feminine cultures, there was little or no difference between the preferred characteristics of boyfriends and husbands. Hofstede concludes, then, that in masculine countries, love and family life may be seen as separated, whereas in feminine countries, they are the same.

In Western countries, marriage as an institution has waned. More than a quarter of all children born in the United States, a third of those in France, and half of those in Sweden and Denmark are born outside marriage. With economic reforms and increasing Western influence, divorce rates in China have soared, particularly in urban areas. In 2003, the divorce process was simplified in China from a months-long ordeal to a 15-minute civil affair. Research by the Population Council found that between the early 1970s and mid-1980s, the number of single-parent households rose worldwide. In the United States, the figure rose from 13% to nearly 24%. In the United States, Australia, and Canada, more than half of all one-parent families are considered poor. In Great Britain and Germany, it is about one-third. In the industrialized world, only in the Nordic countries is the poverty rate below 10% for one-parent families.

Worldwide, with more women moving into the workforce, the parents' role in preparing children for adulthood is diminishing. A Population Council report found that in only 1 of 10 diverse nations—Indonesia—did both parents devote more than a combined average of 7.5 hours a week to direct child care (Bruce, Lloyd, & Leonard, 1995). In parts of Africa where the extended family had an important role in children's socialization, the decline of the kinship system has left children without their traditional direction. The Nordic countries with the greatest gender equity and the United States with strong individualism values may demonstrate that individual freedom and self-fulfillment affect the form and duration of the family. The authoritarian father rule has given way to democratization in these cultures, freeing many women and children from domestic tyrannies. Of course, families held together by duty and social responsibility still exist, but the trends demonstrate that cultural values affect the composition, size, and role of families.

Family Units

The family unit—however defined—remains the organization in which the majority of human beings continue to exist. Women's role in the family unit has a relationship to cultural values. Family could mean any one of several groupings. The nuclear family is composed of one married pair and their unmarried offspring. Anthropologist George P. Murdock (1949) found that in 92 of the 192 societies he studied, the extended family was predominant. The extended family is composed of two or more nuclear families joined by an extension of the parent-child relationship.

French social historian Emmanuel Todd (1985) developed a schema of family types in an attempt to link a country's prevailing family structure with its political ideology, arguing that why a country has a particular form of government is that it is consistent with the prevailing family structure. Todd based his schema on the work of 19th-century French political philosopher Le Play (1884), who identified two criteria: (1) whether sons continued to live with their parents after marriage (community family) or set up independent homes (nuclear family) and (2) whether inheritance was shared among all sons or whether only one son inherited.

Todd (1985) added the criteria of marriage partner choice. Exogamy refers to the practice of marrying outside a defined group. Endogamy refers to the practice of marrying within a defined group. Todd focused on whether marriage between first cousins was accepted. Using these criteria, he developed the following family types, which he related to the countries in which they were dominant:

- *Exogamous community family,* in which equality of brothers is defined by rules of inheritance, married sons cohabit with their parents, and cousins do not marry. Spouses are selected by custom. Typical in China, Vietnam, Russia, Hungary, and northern India.
- *Authoritarian family,* in which there is inequality of brothers as inheritance rules transfer patrimony to one of the sons, the married heir cohabits with his parents, and there is little or no marriage between the children of two brothers. Spouses are selected by parents. Typical in Japan, Korea, Germany, Austria, Sweden, Norway, Scotland, and Ireland.
- *Egalitarian nuclear family,* in which equality of brothers is laid down by inheritance rules, married children do not cohabit with their parents, and there is no marriage between the children of brothers. Spouses are selected by the individual with a strong exogamous obligation. Typical in northern France, northern Italy, central and southern Spain, central Portugal, Greece, Poland, and Latin America.
- *Absolute nuclear family,* in which there are no precise inheritance rules so there is frequent use of wills, married children do not cohabit with their parents, and there is no marriage between children of brothers. Spouses are selected by the individual with a strong exogamous obligation. Typical in Holland, Denmark, and the Anglo-Saxon world.
- *Endogamous community family,* in which there is equality between brothers established by inheritance rules, married children cohabit with their parents, and there is frequent marriage between children of brothers. Spouses are selected by custom. Typical in the Arab world, Turkey, Iran, Afghanistan, and Pakistan.
- *Asymmetrical community family,* in which equality between brothers is established by inheritance rules, married sons cohabit with their parents, and marriages between the children of brothers is prohibited, but there is a preference for marriages between the children of brothers and sisters. Spouses are selected by custom. Typical in southern India.
- *Anomie family,* in which there is uncertainty about equality between brothers since inheritance rules are egalitarian in theory but flexible in practice, cohabitation of married children with parents is rejected in theory but accepted in practice, and consanguine marriage is possible and sometimes frequent. Spouses are selected by the individual with a weak exogamous obligation. Typical in Cambodia, Laos, Thailand, Indonesia, the Philippines, and South American Indian cultures.

Knighton (1999) demonstrated a correlation between Hofstede's individualism dimension and Todd's family types. Countries with predominantly absolute nuclear families and with authoritarian families tend to be individualistic; those with egalitarian nuclear families tend to be collectivist. Countries that have rules regarding equal partition of parental property among all offspring tend to be collectivist. Countries that have rules prescribing unequal partition of inheritance and that have historically allowed parents (usually fathers) to have full freedom in deciding who will inherit tend to be individualist.

Nonbinary Gender Identities

As you read at the beginning of this chapter, nonbinary gender identity refers to the spectrum of gender identities based on the rejection of the assumption that gender is a feminine/masculine dichotomy. Throughout history there have always been cultures with people who do not identify with either category. In this section, we'll briefly review some contemporary examples of these cultures and then examine treatment of these genders in cultures today.

Examples

There are an estimated 500,000 transgender people in India. The Hijras are a third gender in India with a history of thousands of years in ancient Hindu texts and an important place in Indian history. Hijras are biological males who take on traditional female gender roles but have their own roles in society beyond that of male or female. Hijras bestow blessings and dance at weddings and play an important role with newborns. Despite this role, Hijras experience intense discrimination partly from India's colonial past that criminalizes sexual relations "against the order of nature."

Nonbinary identities have long been part of life in parts of Mexico from pre-Colombian times. The Zapotec in Oaxaca, in rural Mexico, recognize muxes as men who choose feminine appearances. One role of muxes is to care for their aging parents when their sisters and brothers have families of their own.

©iStockphoto.com/mrtom-uk

Perhaps most widely known are the kathoeys in Thailand. In today's Thailand, kathoeys range from occasional cross-dressers to transsexuals. While kathoeys have greater acceptance in Thailand than in other countries, they do not have legal recognition. Several popular singers and movie stars are kathoeys. Kathoeys may work in regular jobs, especially in fashion and entertainment industries where they may have leadership and management positions. Others, though, are often forced to be sex workers in Thailand's sex industry and otherwise experience discrimination. Nonetheless, Thai culture is one of the world's most tolerant toward third gender.

In the Balkan region of Albania, "sworn virgins" are women who live as virgins and take on more traditional males roles in society. Many appear as neither feminine nor masculine.

In pre-Cook Hawai'i there was a commonly accepted third gender of people known as mahu, who were neither feminine nor masculine. Mahus were respected as healers, teachers, and caretakers. Christian missionaries condemned the practice, but in recent years Hawai'i has become more accepting of mahu identity.

Finally, in recent times the term *genderqueer* has become a form of identity for people who reject binary gender identifications. The use of the term grew on the Internet and with pop culture star Miley Cyrus's declaration that she felt "like a third gender." Genderqueer has promoted gender-neutral alternative pronouns.

Cultural Status

In 2006, a group of human rights experts from diverse regions and backgrounds met in Yogyakarta, Indonesia, at Gadjah Mada University to clarify nation-states' human rights obligations concerning sexual orientation and gender identity. What have become known as the Yogyakarta Principles address issues of freedom of expression of identity and sexuality, nondiscrimination, freedom from violence, privacy, employment, accommodation, health, education, immigration and refugee issues, public participation, and a variety of other rights.

South Asian countries have led in making significant changes in their laws based on or similar to the Yogyakarta Principles. Bangladesh and Nepal now have legislation recognizing a third gender. Nepal's Supreme Court ordered the government to recognize a third gender category based on

Focus on Skills 9.3

Public Restroom

Your college is located in a small town. After the Trump administration suspended the guidance from the Obama administration that directed public schools to allow transgender students to use the restrooms corresponding to their gender identities, the town passed an ordinance requiring transgender people to use only public restrooms and shower facilities that matched the genders on their birth certificates. The ordinance resulted when a biological female high school student who identifies as a boy sought access to the boys bathroom at a city-run community center. One member of the city council was quoted as saying that the ordinance was necessary to protect the privacy of children using the town's restrooms and locker rooms. The town's mayor was quoted as saying that the town simply can't afford to build girls, boys, and unisex bathrooms at city facilities. A transgender advocate spoke at a city council meeting to argue that unisex bathrooms make transgender people feel discriminated against, while another town member said that "it will always be wrong for men to have access to women's showers and bathrooms."

A friend tells you that on her recent semester abroad in Berlin she saw toilets with signs for men, women, transgender, and intersex all on the same entry.

Your campus Associated Students wants to oppose the city ordinance. You would like to propose a culturally sensitive alternative that would be acceptable to all parties. What can you propose?

Emmy-nominated transgender actress Laverne Cox in the Netflix television series *Orange Is the New Black*. She is the first openly transgender person to appear on the cover of *Time* magazine.

Netflix/Photofest

an individual's "self-feeling." Nepal now includes the third gender category on voter rolls, federal census forms, citizenship documents, and passports.

Similarly, the Supreme Court in Pakistan called for the recognition of the third gender category. Following that, the country's cabinet issued a decree recognizing hijras as a legal gender, affirming "the right of every person to choose their gender" (Human Rights Watch, 2016).

In 2014, India's Supreme Court affirmed a person's right to identify as a man, woman, or transgender person. Later in 2016, legislation was introduced to guarantee third gender rights to education, employment, healthcare, and property ownership and reserved a number of government jobs for transgender persons, as India does for members of disadvantaged castes and tribes. The proposed law would require third gender people to obtain a certificate from a screening committee stating they are transgender. The proposed legislation was opposed as perpetuating the binary gender categories and having gender determined by a committee.

What is considered the most progressive legislation is a 2012 law in Argentina stating anyone over the age of 18 can simply choose their gender identity and revise official documents without judicial or medical approval. In the 3 years after that, Colombia, Denmark, Ireland, and Malta changed their laws permitting people to change their gender on documents simply by filing appropriate forms. Australia, New Zealand, and Canada's Ontario province now permit people to list their gender as "unspecified" on official documents with an X rather than male or female.

Gender Expression and Communication

You read at the beginning of this chapter that gender expression refers to how people express gender. That can be done through behavior, hairstyle, makeup, clothing, and other outward signs as well as, most importantly, language use.

Anthropologists have shown that women share some common communication behaviors across cultures. Women in completely different cultures are known to engage in ritual laments, spontaneously producing rhyming couplets that express pain, such as over the loss of a loved one. Men are more likely to use language to compete with one another by trading playful insults and put-downs. Women are pressured to be submissive and dependent, regardless of individual personality traits, and men are pressured to be assertive, competitive, and in control, regardless of individual personality traits. That pressure is reflected in the language that parents use with children: Girls are more likely to hear twice as many diminutives—affectionate words like *kitty* or *dolly* in place of *cat* or *doll*—than are boys.

Yet, in certain languages, great differences exist among the genders—so much so that speakers of other languages might think that the women and men in a given culture are speaking totally different languages. In isiZulu, for example, women and men use different words to refer to the same thing. In Japanese, the words for "it's beautiful" are *kirei dawa* if the speaker is a woman and *kirei dana* if the speaker is a man; the words for "(I) want to eat" are *tabetai wa* if the speaker is a woman and *tabetai na* if the speaker is a man. For the most part, women and men use the same nouns, but, as in these examples, the final particle indicates female or male speech. In general, *wa* is used by females and *na* by males. The resulting difference is one of tone rather than of meaning. Japanese male language sounds "stronger, less refined, more direct." Some members of the U.S. military who were taught Japanese by Japanese women learned the female style. To Japanese men, the language sounded "feminine, weak, sensitive." Within U.S. culture, Michael Miller, Rodney Reynolds, and Ronald Cambra (1987) have demonstrated that Japanese-American and Chinese-American males use more intense language than female counterparts.

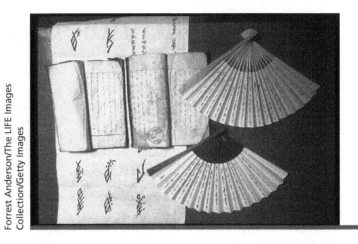

Forrest Anderson/The LIFE Images Collection/Getty Images

Nushu is a language in which women could communicate without men understanding them. Nushu when written is a series of strokes, dots, and horizontals and arcs similar to Chinese. The language is being documented and preserved by linguists in China.

A thousand years ago in rural China, women devised a secret language called Nushu, or woman's writing, to communicate with other women in male-dominated China. The women in Hunan province took characters from standard Chinese and gave them a new value corresponding to phonetic sounds in the local dialect. At its height, women in central China corresponded in the language. Nushu poems were common wedding gifts, and women often took Nushu books to the grave. Thousands of poems, songs, letters, and historical anecdotes were written in Nushu over the centuries. The language fell out of use when women were allowed to attend schools and learn written Chinese.

Focus on Culture 9.3

Gender-Sensitive Language

Language use has important consequences: How would you refer to a group of both sexes: "men and women" or "women and men"? Does the word order convey any message? Did you notice that this book uses "women and men"?

Focus on Technology 9.1

United Nations Efforts Toward Gender Equality

UN Women is the United Nations organization dedicated to gender equality and the empowerment of women. The HeForShe campaign actively engages boys and men by encouraging them to take action against inequalities faced by girls and women. Its website uses a geo-locator to record the number of boys and men around the world who have taken the HeForShe pledge.

Highlighting the severity of gender inequality from the World Economic Forum's Global Gender Gap Report in the political empowerment and workplace equality, the HeForShe IMPACT 10x10x10 campaign involves legislative bodies and corporations. Universities are the third part to engage youth in accelerating progress in gender equality and ending violence against women.

On International Women's Day, March 8, 2015, British actor and UN Women Global Goodwill Ambassador Emma Watson hosted a live Facebook conversation about gender equality viewed by millions around the world.

Source: http://www.heforshe.org/en.

SUMMARY

Gender is one important form of identity. Today we recognize biological identity, gender identity, and gender expression. This chapter first focuses on the status of women across cultures. The United Nations has developed a measure to assess the status of women in the world's countries. In 1990, the United Nations Development Programme first used the Human Development Index (HDI) as a measure of life expectancy at birth, educational attainment, and adjusted per capita income. In a 1993 report, separate HDI scores for women were calculated for 33 countries from which comparable data were available. The report concluded that no country treated its women as well as it treated its men. Consistent with the United Nations report, a 2016 World Economic Forum showed that 96% of the gap in health outcomes between women and men and more than 95% of the gap in educational attainment have been closed worldwide. However, the gaps between women and men on economic participation and political empowerment remain wide. The report also shows the Nordic countries to have the least gender inequality.

Individual countries are then compared: Nordic countries, Mexico, China, Japan, South Korea, India, sub-Saharan Africa, and the Arab states. Finally, family types are linked to cultural factors.

Gender identity has been thought of as feminine/masculine dichotomy. Worldwide recognition of third gender is growing following the Yogyakarta Principles, particularly in South Asia. Finally, examples of how gender is expressed are presented, such as the secret language called Nushu, or woman's writing, that was devised a thousand years ago in rural China for communicating with other women in the male-dominated society.

DISCUSSION QUESTIONS

1. What explanations can be given for why the Nordic countries have the least distinctions between women and men?

2. Describe the ways in which China's one-child campaign has changed the culture.

3. Project the future status of women in the Arab states.

4. In what ways does improving women's social, economic, and political opportunities enhance society at large?

5. Can gender equity be achieved by political means regardless of the cultural values of the country?

6. What possible cultural reasons can help explain the growing acceptance of third gender in South Asia?

KEY TERMS

abaya	gender expression	Nushu
biological sex	gender identity	one-child campaign
endogamy	infanticide	patriarchal society
exogamy	literacy rate	standard Chinese
extended family	machismo	sub-Saharan Africa
fertility rate	nuclear family	transgender

READINGS

All readings are from *Intercultural Communication: A Global Reader* (Jandt, 2004).

Becky Michele Mulvaney, "Gender Differences in Communication: An Intercultural Experience" (p. 221)

Berta Esperanza Hernandez-Truyol, "Women's Rights as Human Rights—Rules, Realities and the Role of Culture: A Formula for Reform" (p. 328)

STUDENT STUDY SITE

$SAGE edge™

Sharpen your skills with SAGE edge at edge.sagepub.com/jandt9e.

SAGE edge for Students provides a personalized approach to help you accomplish your coursework goals in an easy-to-use learning environment.

Part 4

Cultures Within Cultures

Chapter 10

SAUL LOEB/Getty Images

Immigration and Acculturation

Since humans first left Africa, we have been migrating around the planet. Some nation-states have attempted to secure their borders to either keep people out or keep people in. Perhaps the most famous wall, the barbed wire and concrete Berlin Wall, was torn down in 1989. At that time there were 16 border fences around world. But as governments reacted to immigration, more walls were built. During the 2016 U.S. presidential campaign, Donald Trump called for a great wall on the border with Mexico to be paid for by the Mexican government, adding to the 1,044 kilometers (649 miles) of fencing completed during the Obama administration. In fact, at the time of Trump's call, there were 65 border walls either completed or under construction worldwide by about one-third of the world's nations (Vallet, 2014). Turkey is building a wall along its southern border with Syria; Hungary has a fence along its border with Serbia and Croatia; India is building a 4,023-kilometer (2,500-mile) barbed-wire fence around Bangladesh; Saudi Arabia is building a 965-kilometer (600-mile) multilayer fence along its border with Iraq to add to its 1,170-kilometer (1,100-mile) barrier with Yemen; along the Moroccan border with Western Sahara is a sand wall second only in length to the Great Wall of China that is surrounded by mines. Walls have generally not stopped migration. People were able to cross even the heavily guarded Berlin Wall, but the symbolism of walls is dramatic.

In this chapter you'll first read about the originating and receiving countries of the world's immigrants. Then you'll read about the immigration experience of several individual countries.

A World of Migration

First, to clarify terminology: A tourist visits a country for a short time for such goals as relaxation and self-enlightenment. A sojourner lives in a country for a limited time, from as little as 6 months to as long as 5 years, with a specific and goal-oriented purpose, such as education. Both tourists and sojourners fully expect to return home and hence don't face the same challenges as migrants. Migrants are both emigrants and immigrants: One is an emigrant upon leaving the homeland country and an immigrant upon entering the destination country.

The word expatriate is more often used to refer to a noncitizen worker who lives in a country for an indeterminate length of time. Many people labeled "immigrants" in the United States and Europe are in fact expatriates whose intent is to work but not to become full-fledged members of the culture (Furnham, 1987). It is immigrants who relocate permanently to a new culture who face the greatest challenges. Immigrants include refugees and asylees. The words refugee and asylee are often confused. Generally, refugees are seeking safe haven because their home country is no longer safe due to natural disaster or war, while asylees are seeking refuge in another country for political reasons. In U.S. law, people seeking to become refugees must do so prior to their entry into the United States, while asylum seekers have already entered the United States.

The number of people counted as living outside their country of birth has grown dramatically: There were an estimated 84 million in 1975, 104 million in 1985, and 191 million in 2005 (United Nations, 2006a, 2006b). By 2016, 244 million people, or 3.3% of the world's population, lived outside their countries of birth. Countries losing the greatest number of people to migration are India (15.6 million), Mexico (12.3 million), Russia (10.6 million), China (9.5 million), and Bangladesh (7.2 million). Two major pathways for migration have been the Mexico-U.S. corridor and India–Persian Gulf countries. For both of these major pathways, economic opportunities are major.

Table 10.1 shows the countries receiving the largest number of immigrants and Table 10.2 shows countries with the highest percentage of immigrants in their population.

In the 19th and early 20th centuries, most of the world's migration was primarily people from European countries to the Americas. These immigrants were expected to adapt to the receiving countries' cultures, become citizens, and build the nation often by settling in frontier areas. In recent decades, countries have become more selective in deciding which immigrants are admitted and for how long (United Nations Department of Economic and Social Affairs, 2013). Migration impacts both origin and destination countries in many ways, including financial and demographics. As immigrants earn money, they send money back to relatives in

Global Voices

At this moment in human history, marked by great movements of migration, identity is not a secondary issue. Those who migrate are forced to change some of their most distinctive characteristics and, whether they like or not, even those who welcome them are also forced to change. How can we experience these changes not as obstacles to genuine development, rather as opportunities for genuine human, social and spiritual growth, a growth which respects and promotes those values which make us ever more humane and help us to live a balanced relationship with God, others and creation?

—Message of His Holiness Pope Francis for the World Day of Migrants and Refugees (2016)

Table 10.1 Countries With the Largest Number of Immigrants, 2015	
United States	46,630,000
Germany	12,010,000
Russia	11,640,000
Saudi Arabia	10,190,000
United Kingdom	8,540,000
United Arab Emirates	8,100,000
Canada	7,840,000
France	7,780,000
Australia	6,760,000
Spain	5,850,000
Italy	5,790,000
India	5,240,000

Source: Pew Research Center (2016a).

Note: In this table immigrants are people living 1 year or more in a country other than country of birth, which includes workers, students, and refugees and their descendants.

Table 10.2 Countries With the Highest Percentage of Immigrants in Their Population, 2015	
United Arab Emirates	88%
Qatar	75%
Kuwait	74%
Bahrain	51%
Singapore	45%
Jordan	41%
Oman	41%
Hong Kong	39%
Lebanon	34%
Saudi Arabia	32%
Switzerland	29%
Australia	28%
Israel	25%
New Zealand	23%
Canada	22%

Source: Pew Research Center (2016).

Notes: The number for the United States is 14%. The largest number of immigrants to the United Arab Emirates, Qatar, Kuwait, and Bahrain are from India, Bangladesh, and Pakistan. The foreign-born population in these countries grew from 1.3 million in 1990 to 7.8 million in 2013. In this table immigrants are people living 1 year or more in a country other than country of birth, which includes workers, students, and refugees and their descendants.

their home countries. In 2015 that was estimated at $600 billion annually and accounted for a quarter or more of some Central Asian countries' gross domestic product. Immigration can also alter the demographics of the destination countries, in some cases being perceived as a threat as potentially changing the country. Migrants' origin countries also experience demographic changes as migrants may be younger and more highly educated than the people who remain in the country.

Without immigration, most of the world's developed countries would experience a drop in population, with resulting challenges to their retirement and economic programs. With immigration, though, the countries may perceive challenges to their established nation-state cultural identity and values and place increased pressure on immigrants to assimilate into their new nation-state's culture (Aleinkoff & Klusmeyer, 2002). Some of the receiving nations, with the notable exception of the United States, use a point system based on education, occupation, age, language ability, and other criteria and adjust their system as needs change. Some countries consider religious and ethnic identity. Israel guarantees admission of persons of Jewish descent. Finland, Germany, Greece, Italy, and Japan give consideration to ethnic origin.

Immigration and National Identity

In the following sections, you'll study the intercultural communication challenges presented by immigration into Israel, Europe, Brazil, and the United States.

Israel

As you read about immigration into Israel, consider the implications of religious identity and nation-state identity.

Focus on Theory 10.1

Push-Pull Theory of Migration

The classical theory to explain migration is the push-pull theory. This theory originated with Ernest Ravenstein, who analyzed internal migration in England from 1871 to 1881, and was extended to a general theory of international migration by the U.S. demographer Everett Lee. Ravenstein believed pull factors were a more important factor than push factors; that is, people more often migrate to improve their lives rather than to escape unpleasant conditions. Pull factors include the perception of economic opportunities and better living conditions, political preferences and security, religious freedom, better education and medical services, and environmental advantages (seaside, warm climate, etc.). Push factors include natural disasters, population pressures, unemployment and economic hardships, political turmoil or disturbances, and environmental disadvantages such as famine and drought.

The push-pull theory has been criticized as being only descriptive; however, it remains widely used in immigration studies.

Source: E. S. Lee (1966).

Focus on Culture 10.1

Acquiring Citizenship

Citizenship in a country may be acquired in three ways: by birth, by blood, or by naturalization. By birth, or *jus soli,* means that one who is born within the borders of a country is automatically a citizen. By blood, or *jus sanguinis,* means that if one's parents are citizens of a country, no matter where one is born, one is a citizen of the parents' country. Naturalization requires a period of residency, an exam, an oath, or some combination of these.

Today, of the estimated 14.3 million Jewish people, 43% live in Israel. Proclaimed independent on May 14, 1948, Israel was a relatively poor, besieged nation in need of building the country's population. Citizenship may be acquired by birth, residence, naturalization, and the Law of Return. The Proclamation of the Establishment of the State of Israel stated,

> The State of Israel will be open for Jewish immigration and the ingathering of the exiles; it will foster the development of the country for all its inhabitants; it will be based on freedom, justice, and peace as envisaged by the prophets of Israel; it will ensure complete equality of social and political rights to all its inhabitants irrespective of religion, race or sex.

A fundamental aspiration of the State of Israel is *aliyah,* literally "ascending," the Hebrew word for immigration into Israel. The Law of Return, enacted in 1950, granted anyone with a Jewish mother or who had converted to Judaism the right to come to Israel as an oleh (a Jew immigrating to Israel) and become a citizen. By 1951, the number of immigrants more than doubled what the Jewish population of the country had been in 1948. The government devoted much effort to absorbing the immigrants through residence construction, job creation, Hebrew-language instruction, and educational expansion to meet the needs of children from diverse cultural backgrounds. (See Figure 10.1 for immigration into Israel by year.)

Since 1970, the right to immigrate under the Law of Return has been extended to include the child and the grandchild of a Jew, the spouse of a child of a Jew, and the spouse of the grandchild of a Jew. The purpose of the change was to ensure the unity of families where intermarriage had occurred, even though the Halakhah, or Jewish religious law, specifies that only those born to a Jewish mother and those who have converted are Jews. Since the establishment of Israel, more than 3.2 million people have immigrated, with the largest numbers from "countries of distress," places where Jews are unwelcome, harassed, or persecuted.

A fascinating part of Israel's immigration history is the descendants of the ancient Jewish community in Ethiopia known as the Falash Mura. Over generations, the community kept Shabbat and passed on the story of Jerusalem. Today, about 93,000 Ethiopians have been brought to Israel in organized immigration projects that began with a 1984–1985 airlift dubbed Operation Moses, 1991 Operation Solomon, and 2012 Operation Dove's Wings. The final group arrived in the summer of 2013, marking the end of the government's efforts to return Ethiopian Jews to Israel.

The Ethiopian Jews have faced the obstacles of immigration. The majority continue to speak Amharic and Tigrinya with family and friends but use Modern Hebrew for communication with other Israeli citizens. The Ethiopians were not prepared to move from a subsistence economy to a modern industrialized society. Many of the Beta Israel immigrants, especially those who came from remote villages in Ethiopia, had never used electricity, elevators, or televisions. In addition, adaptation to Israeli food was initially particularly difficult. Ethiopian Jews have a significant high school dropout rate and early discharge from mandatory military service. Many Ethiopian Israelis work in low-paying menial jobs. Some have charged that this group has experienced racist attitudes in Israel (Onolemhemhen & Gessesse, 2002). The Israeli government implemented programs to discourage discrimination.

Two other immigrant groups have met with resistance. Thousands of Africans have entered Israel as refugees. Roughly 50,000 people, many from Eritrea and Sudan, have crossed into Israel from

Figure 10.1   Immigration Into Israel, by Year

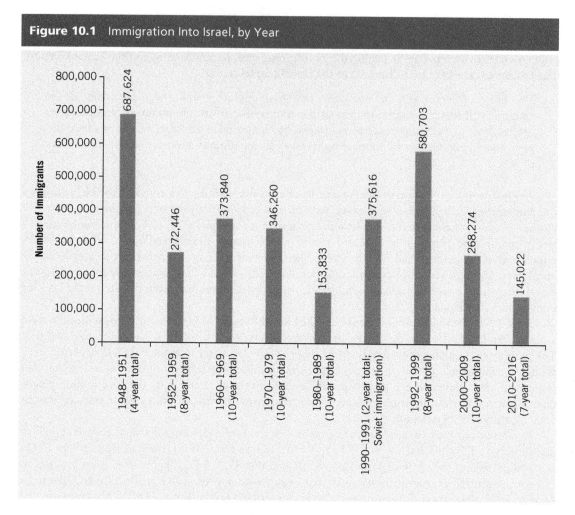

Source: State of Israel, Central Bureau of Statistics (2016).

Egypt to flee oppression. Israel has erected a fence to block more from entering the country. The second group came when Soviet Jews were permitted to leave the Soviet Union in large numbers in the late 1980s. The collapse of the Soviet Union in late 1991 brought more Soviet immigrants, many nonpracticing Jews. Some of these have a spouse, father, or grandparent who is Jewish but are not Jews themselves under Jewish religious law.

Today about 1.2 million of Israel's 8.1 million people are Russian by heritage. Israel has the world's third largest Russian-speaking community outside of the former Soviet Union. The Russian immigrants typically had job skills that Israel needed. One out of four employees in Israel's high-tech industries is Russian, one out of every two engineers is Russian, and about a third of Israel's Olympic coaches are Russian. This group of immigrants has strived to maintain a Russian identity.

In some areas signs are in Cyrillic; shop-keepers speak Russian with customers; grocery stories stock nonkosher pork, caviar, and vodka. Bars play Russian pop music. Russian bookshops, restaurants, television programs, and newspapers are evidence of a Russian identity.

Some Israelis fear that the country has become a preferred destination for non-Jews from the former Soviet Union who immigrated only for economic reasons; who brought prostitution, corruption, and crime; and who have no desire to become Jewish.

Today, Israel is a prosperous nation but with a mosaic of ultra-Orthodox Jewish immigrants who fled Europe and distinguish themselves from immigrants from

Oliver Weiken/EPA/Newscom

Ethiopian immigrants kiss Israeli ground at Ben Gurion airport in 2013.

North Africa and the Middle East. About 25% of the population is non-Jewish and mostly Arab. Some have proposed limiting immigration. The issue is no less than the character of Israel as a Jewish state.

Europe

Europe is not a continent of immigrants who can trace their ancestry to somewhere abroad, but a continent of discrete peoples with national identities. Created in 1993, the European Union is a political and economic union of 27 nations with a combined population of over 500 million. Its motto is "united in diversity." Its objectives include the passport-free movement of people and free movement of goods and services among its members. In 1995 the Schengen Agreement took effect, which enabled passport-free movement across most of the European Union's countries.

Immigration policies are not the same in every EU country. Most have both EU rules and their own national rules. Immigration has become one of the most controversial issues in Europe. Unlike in Australia, Canada, and the United States, immigration to Western Europe is a recent phenomenon. For example, in West Germany before 1960 and in Spain before 1990, the foreign-born population was below 1%. Beginning in the 1950s, European countries welcomed immigration for laborers in their economic expansion. Governments saw this immigration as temporary and expected the immigrants to return to their home countries. The economic reversal in 1973 brought an end to immigration. However, rather than returning home, the immigrants brought their family members to join them in fears that all immigration would be further curtailed. Later, the fall of the Berlin Wall and the collapse of the Soviet Union brought Eastern Europeans into Western European nations.

Today's challenge is immigration from Muslim countries, which was dramatically compounded by the greatest mass movement of people since World War II with the refugee immigration from war-torn and poverty stricken countries such as Syria, Iraq, and Afghanistan.

Muslim Immigration

Western Europe is challenged with increasing immigration, particularly from Muslim countries (see Table 10.3). The number of Muslims in Europe grew from 29.6 million in 1990 to 44.1 million in 2010. Europe's Muslim population is projected to exceed 58 million by 2030. In 2011, Muslims made up about 6% of Europe's total population, up from 4% in 1990. By 2030, Muslims are expected to make up 8% of Europe's population (Pew Research Center, 2011a).

In the Netherlands, where a half-century ago there were few foreigners, today there are about 1.2 million Muslims, the majority from Morocco and Turkey, which is equivalent to about 6% of the country's population. The Dutch welcomed guest workers in the 1960s and 1970s and accepted many seeking asylum from wars in Iraq, Kosovo, Africa, and Afghanistan. But that was before the September 11, 2001, attacks in the United States. In a 2003 poll, 61% of Dutch people felt that most societal tensions were between *allochtonen* ("not from here") and *autochtonen* ("from here"). Only 25% perceived tensions between rich and poor, 18% between old and young, and 9% between women and men. Throughout Western Europe a growing "us versus them" mentality grew.

Global Voices

Islam is threatening our future. . . . That faith belongs to a dark past, and its political aims are as destructive as Nazism was.

—Mogens Camre, member, Danish People's Party and the European Parliament

In 2011 the Netherlands officially abandoned its policy of multiculturalism. Immigrants are now required to learn the Dutch language and follow Dutch law. The government imposed a ban on face-covering burqas as of January 1, 2013. And the government stopped offering subsidies for Muslim immigrants.

Table 10.3 Muslims in the European Union, 2011

Country	Number	Percentage of Total, 2011	Percentage of Projected Population, 2030
France	4,704.000	7.5	10.3
Germany	4,119,000	5.0	7.1
United Kingdom	2,869,000	4.6	8.2
Italy	1,583,000	2.6	5.4
Spain	1,021,000	2.3	3.7
Netherlands	914,000	5.5	7.8
Belgium	638,000	6.0	10.2
Greece	527,000	4.7	6.9
Austria	475,000	5.7	9.3
Sweden	451,000	4.9	9.9

Source: Pew Research Center (2011a).

Focus on Culture 10.2

Test of Immigrant Readiness in the Netherlands

Would-be immigrants to the Netherlands must purchase and view a film that includes scenes of two gay men kissing in a park and a topless woman emerging from the sea walking onto a crowded beach. The film is a test of the immigrants' readiness to participate in the liberal Dutch culture.

Source: "Film Exposes Immigrants to Dutch Liberalism" (2006).

The same pressure is developing in the Nordic states. Norway is struggling to integrate 144,000 Muslims into its population of 5.3 million. Six of Norway's 10 most populous immigrant groups come from Muslim countries. Denmark, a Christian country for 1,000 years and a culture that prides itself on racial parity, has experienced growing Muslim immigration—currently at 226,000 in a country of 5.6 million people. Muslims in Denmark feel that, because of the country's fear of terrorism, pressure to assimilate is increasing. The summer of 2011 saw a lone terrorist kill some 93 people in Norway by a bombing in Oslo followed by a shooting spree at a youth camp. The accused terrorist had posed a manifesto advocating an armed campaign against Muslims it said were overrunning Europe. Sweden has given shelter to 100,000 Iraqis, 40,000 since the U.S. invasion in 2003. Sweden has gradually tightened its asylum rules, responding to fears that its generous welfare system cannot cope with the immigrant numbers.

European countries have adopted various policies to respond to growing Muslim immigration. Britain's approach allowed immigrants to keep distinctive cultural backgrounds and identities. Now there is fear that radical elements flourish in ethnic neighborhoods. France's Muslim population is expected to climb from 4.7 million in 2011 to 6.9 million in 2030, according to the Pew Research Center (2011a). France has encouraged immigrants to adopt all things French, a policy that has angered Muslims living in the slums outside of Paris. France does not compile statistics on foreign-born residents, and critics argue that this policy limits France's ability to recognize and treat the difficulties minorities face. The fall of 2005 and again in 2007 saw the worst civil unrest in France in nearly 40 years break out in the poor neighborhoods populated by immigrants, largely Black and Arab.

Refugees

Since the late 1980s, one of the ways to immigrate into a European Union country has been for asylum. People from Bosnia

Aris Messinis/Getty Images

Refugees arrive on an inflatable dinghy to the Greek island of Lesbos in 2015.

Global Voices

and Herzegovina, Kosovo, China, Somalia, Sri Lanka, Yugoslavia, Poland, and Afghanistan sought asylum in EU countries. And as the European Union permits nationals to move from one EU country to another, internal immigration within the EU countries grew (Ben-David, 2009). But it is the recent refugee crisis that has intensified the European Union's questions regarding public safety, assimilation, and national identity.

Civil war erupted in Syria in 2011 against the regime of President Assad. Two years into the conflict, it took on sectarian overtones, with the country's Sunni majority against the president's Shiite Alawite sect, which drew regional powers and the Islamic State of Iraq and Syria (ISIS) into the conflict. More than 4.8 million people fled Syria, one of the largest refugee exoduses in recent history. Nearly half fled to Turkey. Many of these left Turkey to cross the Aegean Sea to Greece. Lebanon took in over 1 million, almost a quarter of its own population. Jordan, Iraq, and Egypt each took in hundreds of thousands. About 1 million requested asylum in Europe in 2015 alone. Some crossed the Mediterranean from North Africa to Italy. By mid-2015, 500,000 refugees had made the sea voyage to Europe. More than 3,000 died trying.

Germany and Sweden were the top receiving countries in Western Europe. France and the United Kingdom accepted far fewer. With an aging population, without immigration Germany's population could drop from 81 million to 68 to 73 million by 2060. German industry lacks young skilled workers, and the country's welfare system is increasingly strained as its growing retiree population is supported by its shrinking working-age population. Initially, Chancellor Angela Merkel welcomed refugees and said there would be no limit on the number taken in. German citizens held up signs in German,

Table 10.4   Perception of Muslim Population

Country	Perception	Reality
France	31	7.5
India	28	14.2
South Africa	22	1.7
Germany	21	5.0
United States	17	1.0
United Kingdom	15	4.8

In answer to the question "Out of every 100 people in your country, how many do you think are Muslim?"

Source: Interviews conducted in 2016 by Ipsos MORI.

English, and Arabic welcoming the refugees. Attitudes changed as 2015 brought terrorist incidents as a far-right political party campaigned against refugees and won victories in three German state elections. And by 2016 Merkel had endorsed restrictions on full face-covering veils in public, similar to bans in France and Belgium, as not compatible with German cultural norms.

Sweden's population isn't declining, but historically Sweden has been one of the world's most accommodating countries for refugees. In 2015 some 163,000 migrants applied for asylum. Relative to its population of 9.8 million, Sweden took in the highest number of refugees per capita. Sweden has instituted near-automatic residency and programs for integration.

Britain has one of Europe's most diverse populations, with nearly one in eight U.K. residents foreign-born. In 1997, immigrants from EU countries totaled 18,000, about one-third of the total; in 2015, immigrants from other EU countries were nearly half of the total of 333,000. With immigration, Britain could grow to be Europe's most populous country by 2060. Britain has been reluctant to accept refugees. The country's anti-immigration sentiment was a major contributing factor in BREXIT, Britain's leaving the European Union. Only about 15% of Britain's population identifies with Europe, as the overwhelming majority see themselves as a separate nation with its unique history and culture (Shuster, 2016a).

With a high fertility rate and immigration, France has a growing population. But with terrorist attacks such as on the satirical magazine *Charlie Hebdo* and the Bataclan concert venue in Paris, both in 2015, and difficulties in assimilating its Muslim population, France has been reluctant to accept refugees.

Israel, Qatar, the United Arab Emirates, and Saudi Arabia took in no refugees. Hungary erected a border fence. In fiscal 2015 the United States admitted 12,587 Syrian refugees (second to 16,370 refugees from the Democratic Republic of the Congo). Canada accepted some 35,000 who had had health and criminal screenings and only as whole families, single women, and children. Single men were considered a possible security threat.

Brazil

The largest and most populous country in South America, Brazil is slightly smaller than the United States in area. It shares a border with every South American country except Chile and Ecuador.

Focus on Technology 10.1

Refugee Use of Social Media

The German Federal Office of Migration and Refugees posted a tweet stating that Syrians who could make it to Germany could apply for asylum.

When many refugees reached land on a Greek island, they raised their arms in thanks and then to take a selfie and message their families, their smartphones carefully protected in balloons and plastic bags and rubber bands. In refugee camps, UN workers distributed SIM cards and solar generators. Refugees used messaging apps such as WhatsApp, Viber, and Line to communicate with family members they had left behind. They navigated border crossings with Google Maps and Facebook Messenger. They documented their journey on Instagram. Many of the refugees carried only their smartphone with them.

Source: Witty (2015).

Its population is 206 million, fifth largest in the world. Its economy exceeds any other South American country. Brazil became one of the world's strongest emerging markets and hosted the 2014 FIFA World Cup and the 2016 Summer Olympic Games. Recently, Brazil has experienced a shrinking economy, growing unemployment, rising inflation, and political scandal.

Brazil was founded in 1500 by Portuguese colonists. From 1500 to 1822, some 700,000 Portuguese settled in Brazil, 600,000 of whom arrived in the 18th century alone. Portugal prohibited immigration from other countries to Brazil to prevent other European countries from establishing any claims to territory. On the other hand, Brazil was the major destination for slaves from Africa (see Figure 10.2). While the United States received some 500,000 slaves from Africa up to 1870, some 4 million were taken to Brazil to work on sugar cane plantations. Some estimates place that number as high as 6 million. An African slave in Brazil survived only about 7 years. Children of slaves remained as slaves, but most slaves were from the slave trade. While the African slave trade ended in the 1850s, Brazil was the last country in the Western Hemisphere to abolish slavery, in 1888. Today, Brazil has the largest African-heritage population outside of Africa and much of its culture is African.

As with other countries in the Americas, Brazil has a rich immigration history from many countries and became a melting pot. What is unique is that Brazil may have the highest degree of intermarriage in the world. Nonetheless, Brazilian society has social and economic class differences between European descendants (found more among the upper and middle classes) and African, indigenous, and multiracial descendants (found more among the lower classes). Portuguese is the official and most widely spoken language. Other languages in use that reflect the country's immigration history include Spanish, German, Italian, Japanese, English, and a large number of indigenous languages.

In the following sections, consider how immigration can be influenced by domestic and global economic factors.

First Wave

The first wave of mass immigration to Brazil occurred during the second half of the 19th century. Europeans were welcomed as a means to replace slave labor in coffee cultivation. From 1880 to 1903, 1.9 million Europeans arrived, mainly from Germany, Italy, Portugal, and Spain. People also came from Ukraine, Russia, Lithuania, Hungary, Armenia, China, and Korea (Lesser, 2013).

Following the U.S. Civil War, in the latter half of the 19th century thousands of people from all over the southern United States migrated to Mexico, Cuba, and Brazil. Ellsworths, Lees, McKnights, Stegalls, Yancys, and ancestors of former president Jimmy Carter were part of an estimated 10,000 to 40,000 Confederates who emigrated, many to Brazil, where the government promised cheap land in the hope that the immigrants would establish Brazil as a cotton-producing country where slavery was still legal.

The immigrants settled in several parts of Brazil: in an area 500 miles from the mouth of the Amazon River, which became the city of Santarem; in Rio Doce near the coast; and in settlements called Juquia, New Texas, Villa Americana, and Xiririca in southern Brazil near São Paulo. Only Villa Americana prospered.

Some of these immigrants failed and moved to the cities or returned to the United States. Others were successful and made fortunes in cotton and watermelons. The immigrants brought baseball, peaches, pecans, and various strains of rice to Brazil. The immigrants remained in cloistered communities and established schools, churches, and cemeteries because the Roman Catholic Church in Brazil

Map 10.1 Brazil and Other South American Countries

would not allow the Protestant Confederates to be buried with Catholics. Even years later, many spoke English exclusively in homes. But with time, more and more of the descendants moved to the cities and assimilated into the Brazilian culture.

Today, the descendants of the Confederates are attempting to recover this heritage by having picnics and celebrations where they wear antebellum gowns and Civil War uniforms, by flying the Confederate flag and sharing old photographs and stories, and by speaking Portuguese in a Southern

Japanese Brazilian fans watch Japan in an international soccer game. Liberdade is home of the largest Japanese community outside of Japan in the world.

Nelson Almeida/Getty Images

drawl. The experience of the Confederates in Brazil is not unlike the experiences of immigrants in the United States.

Second Wave

The second immigration wave was from 1904 to 1930. Another 2.1 million Europeans from Italy, Poland, Russia, and Romania immigrated, most arriving after World War I. Needing more workers, Brazil turned to Japan. In 1908, the first Japanese immigrants arrived in the country, settling mainly in the state of São Paulo and in the north of the state of Paraná to work on coffee plantations. Some built up large agricultural concerns.

Brazil has become home to the largest Japanese community outside Japan. Some 1.6 million people of Japanese origin now live in Brazil, mostly concentrated in São Paulo (Lesser, 2003).

By the 1920 census, 35% of São Paulo city's inhabitants were foreign born, compared to 36% in New York City at the time. The majority were from Italy, Portugal, and Spain. Some areas of the city remained almost exclusively Italian for many years.

Third Wave

Various factors limited immigration during Brazil's third wave (1930–1964): Demand for coffee declined in the Great Depression of the 1930s; new laws protected native workers, making it difficult for immigrants to find jobs; and the government initiated policies to encourage Europeans to assimilate into Brazilian culture. Learning Portuguese was encouraged, and classes in languages other than Portuguese were forbidden. Foreign language magazines and newspapers were forbidden. Europeans were prohibited from organizing their own political groups.

The immigrants of the 1930s came primarily from Japan. That immigration continued until World War II and was restarted in the 1950s. The Japanese immigrants worked primarily as agricultural workers (Lesser, 2003).

Recent Immigration

After the military coup d'état in 1964, Brazil largely ended policies to attract foreign migrants. The immigration law enacted by the military rulers treated foreigners as a security risk and a threat to Brazilian workers. It bars immigrants from taking part in political rallies, owning stakes in newspapers, or participating actively in trade unions. There were some exceptions. In 1962, South Korea and Brazil reached an agreement to ease unemployment in South Korea and to develop farmlands in Brazil. Tens of thousands of middle-class Koreans from South Korea and North Korea with little Portuguese language ability sailed for Brazil. Some did become farmers. Many others, however, sold their clothes from their trunks on arrival and became garment peddlers, replacing the Jewish and Armenian immigrants who had dominated the apparel trade in São Paulo and Buenos Aires. Thirty years later, some 50,000 Korean immigrants worked as entrepreneurs in the garment trade.

In the early 1990s Brazil began receiving asylum seekers from West Africa, particularly Angola and Sierra Leone and a decade later from Afghanistan. When its economy was strong, between 2008 and 2013, Brazil accepted immigrants from Haiti, Bolivia, Senegal, and other poverty-stricken countries. By 2009, Brazil's foreign-born population constituted only about 2.4% of the country's population. (Table 10.5 shows the country of origin of Brazil's immigrants based on the 2000 census.) Later, in 2015, Brazil began accepting refugees from Syria and announced plans to accept 100,000 but abandoned the plans when the economy weakened and the government changed. The interim president cited security as a top priority.

Table 10.5 Country of Origin of Brazilian Immigrants, 2000	
Country	**Percentage of Total Immigrants**
Portugal	31.2
Japan	10.4
Italy	8.0
Spain	6.4
Paraguay	4.2
Argentina	4.0

Source: 2000 Brazilian Census.

United States

The United States is host to more immigrants than any other nation. The first census to document country of birth was in 1850. At that time immigrants were 9.7% of the population. In 1970 the foreign-born population was 4.7% and increased to 12.9% in 2010 (see Table 10.6). Today, some 46.6 million (19%) of the world's 244 million immigrants reside in the United States (United Nations Population Division, 2013). As you read this section, compare how the United States has dealt with immigration to Israel, Europe, and Brazil.

Perhaps the least understood immigration into the Americas was the first one. The migration experiences of the groups now known as American Indians are lost in history, so this section begins with immigration to colonial America.

Colonial Policies on Immigration

In colonial America, three principal responses to immigration developed. Massachusetts wanted settlers who were "religiously pure." Virginia and Maryland recruited immigrants for cheap labor but did not allow full participation in government. Pennsylvania welcomed all European settlers on equal terms and as equal participants in the colony. Later, the Pennsylvania model largely prevailed in the

Global Voices

Uncontrolled immigration threatens to deconstruct the nation we grew up in. . . . Balkanization beckons.

—Patrick J. Buchanan, *The Death of the West* (2002, p. 3)

It's an act of love. It's an act of commitment to your family. I honestly think that that is a different kind of crime. There should be a price paid, but it shouldn't rile people up that people are actually coming to this country to provide for their families.

—Former Florida governor Jeb Bush (Fox News, April 6, 2014)

Once I thought to write a history of the immigrants in America. Then, I discovered that the immigrants were American history.

—Oscar Handlin, Pulitzer Prize–winning historian, *The Uprooted* (1952, p. 3)

Global Voices

An estimated 11.5 million unauthorized immigrants were living in the United States in January 2011. That number has remained steady since then as a drop in people coming from Mexico was offset by an increase from the rest of the world.

Sources: Hoefer, Rytina, & Baker (2012, p. 1); Passel & Cohn (2016)

new nation, which in its first 100 years encouraged immigration.

U.S. Policies on Immigration

In 1798, Congress passed the Act Concerning Aliens, which gave the president power to deport all immigrants deemed dangerous to national security. But it was the Fourteenth Amendment, ratified in 1868, that established an important foundation for U.S. immigration and citizenship laws even though it was not drafted in response to immigration. By stating that anyone born in the country was a citizen, it was drafted to establish that former slaves were citizens with all rights of citizens. The Supreme Court held in 1898 that someone born in California to noncitizen Chinese immigrants was a U.S. citizen under the Fourteenth Amendment. One result of the Fourteenth Amendment is that the United States is one of the last countries in the world to follow the principle of birthright citizenship, or *jus soli*.

Beginning in 1875, the first federal laws limiting immigration were enacted to bar convicts and prostitutes. Over the years, other laws excluded those who had "physical, mental, and moral defects"; those who advocated "subversive doctrines"; and those who had "economic disqualifications" or were illiterate (Carliner, 1977; Carliner, Guttentag, Helton, & Henderson, 1990).

Beginning in 1921, to prevent major changes in the country's racial and ethnic makeup, the U.S. Congress established country quotas based on the origins of the U.S. population using 1910 census data. Three years later, during the Prohibition era, Congress chose to use the 1890 census data, which had the effect of favoring immigration from northern and western Europe. In 1960, the United States was 85% White and 75% of U.S. immigrants came from Europe. The 1965 Hart-Celler Immigration Act liberalized the rules for immigration and permitted new citizens to sponsor relatives from their home countries. One result was that the new "immigration law quickly transformed the ethnic portrait of the United States" (FitzGerald & Cook-Martin, 2014, p. 121). By 2014, only 11% of immigrants came from Europe, about 50% came from Latin America, and more than 25% came from Asia.

The 2016 U.S. presidential campaign made immigration policy a major electorate concern. This attention has already resulted in changes in immigration law and practice. Many more changes are likely in the future.

Illegal immigrants who enter the United States come from all over the world. In 1997, the U.S. Immigration and Naturalization Service (now the Bureau of Citizenship

Family members in Tijuana visit with family in the United States at the border wall.

©iStockphoto.com/shakzu

and Immigration Services, part of the U.S. Department of Homeland Security) put the number of illegal immigrants at 5 million—half being in California. Half of these arrive with temporary visas, typically at airports. The remainder enter without valid documents, usually across the U.S.-Mexico border. About half of the total originate from Mexico.

Contributing Countries Prior to 1800

Prior to 1800, the number of immigrants from Europe to the New World was between 4 million and 5 million. In comparison, the largest migration was the involuntary movement of slaves from Africa, mainly to the New World. It is estimated that 12 million people were transported as slaves, with 10 million actually surviving the trip. Figure 10.2 shows where slaves were taken. This group was largely held in a state of separation and segregation.

Contributing Countries Since 1800

Between 1846 and 1932, 53 million people migrated to the Western Hemisphere, all but 2 million from Europe and more than three-quarters of that number from five areas: the British Isles, Italy, Austria-Hungary, Germany, and Spain. The United States received 60% of those.

Ellis Island, 8 kilometers (a half-mile) from the Statue of Liberty, processed its first immigrant in 1892 and its last in 1954. More than half of the immigrants entering the United States between 1892 and 1924 passed through its gates. In its peak year, 1907, 1 million immigrants were processed. The center handled 17 million newcomers from more than 90 countries. Of that total, 2.5 million were from Italy, 2.2 million from Austria-Hungary, 1.9 million from Russia, and 633,000 from Germany. Other important entry ports were Boston, Baltimore, and Philadelphia.

At one time, 35%–40% of the country's population could trace heritage to a family member who passed through the immigration processing station on Ellis Island.

Global Voices

In 1880, encouraged by the success of the Swiss settlers in Texas, a group of capitalists in Basel, Switzerland, organized a land company called the Basel Land Gesellschaft. The company provided the finances for the founding of a Swiss colony on the Guadalupe River approximately three miles south from Seguin. Around 1880, ten families left Switzerland and settled on the company's land. Each one was provided with sixty acres of land, a log cabin, a horse, a cow, chickens, hogs, and two hundred dollars per year to take care of the family needs.

Samuel Prabst was the first administrator of the colony. He was succeeded by Fredrick Wilhelm Naumann, who was given four hundred acres of land for his service. After a few years the colony failed and many of the original settlers moved to other parts of the state leaving only a few of the first settlers.

—Texas Institute of Cultures, San Antonio

Bismarck united Germany and in 1871 our father was on Germany's side against Napoleon III of France. He was in the reserves, and saw no fighting. He disliked militarism and the ungodly life of most soldiers. Therefore he moved to America before his oldest son, John, would be registered for service.

I am quite sure the ship's name was "Werra." We sailed on the Rhine River to the City of Köln (Cologne), then by rail to Bremen; on the "Werra" to New York; and by rail to New Braunfels, Comal County, Texas, March 9, 1885. I remember red hot pipes (too hot to sit on) on board ship; also the immigrants standing on deck singing:

"Noah's Arche schwankte/Lang of grauser Fluth, Wie das Schiff auch wankte/Ihm sank nicht der Muth."

—Phillip Herbold, German immigrant

Source: Personal archives of the author.

Global Voices

- Establish new immigration controls to boost wages and to ensure that open jobs are offered to American workers first.

- Protect the economic well-being of the lawful immigrants already living here by curbing uncontrolled foreign worker admissions.

  - Select immigrants based on their likelihood of success in the U.S. and their ability to be financially self-sufficient.

  - Vet applicants to ensure they support America's values, institutions and people, and temporarily suspend immigration from regions that export terrorism and where safe vetting cannot presently be ensured.

  - Enforce the immigration laws of the United States and restore the Constitutional rule of law upon which America's prosperity and security depend.

—"Donald J. Trump's Vision" (n.d.)

As you study the history of immigration presented in Table 10.6, identify the years with the least and most number of immigrants. What happened in those years that affected immigration? Identify the decades of significant shifts in the major contributing countries. What impacts did those shifts have on the United States?

Each major wave of immigrants experienced discrimination. In the 1850s, the Germans and Irish who were fleeing economic destitution were largely viewed as a "lower class of people." In the 1880s and 1890s, eastern and southern European immigrants were viewed with suspicion because of darker skin and the religion of Catholicism. The Irish were blamed for bringing cholera, the Italians for bringing polio, the Chinese for carrying bubonic plague, the Jews for spreading tuberculosis, and the Haitians for bringing AIDS (Kraut, 1994). President Theodore Roosevelt, who was in office from 1901 to 1909, urged "native Americans" (he didn't mean indigenous peoples) to have more children to combat the disintegration of racial purity that he said was threatening the American way of life. Charles Davenport, a leader of the eugenics movement, argued for protecting racial purity from eastern and southern European immigration. His lobby helped pass the Immigration Act of 1924, which is one of the most restrictive and discriminatory immigration statutes ever enacted in the United States.

Immigration from Mexico has largely been tied to labor needs in Mexico and the United States. Late 19th-century immigrants worked in agriculture in the Southwest, in building railroads, and in mining. Immigration accelerated in the 1920s following the economic tumult of the Mexican Revolution.

The Great Depression brought public outcry against illegal immigrants. Many illegal as well as legal immigrants and U.S. citizens were picked up for deportation. The changing labor market brought on by World War II saw the birth of the *bracero* program, a guest worker initiative for agriculture that lasted until the 1960s.

Library of Congress

The peak year for immigration at Ellis Island was 1907. More than 1 million immigrants were processed. In 1990 the facility was restored as a museum.

Figure 10.2 Slave Trade, 1450–1870

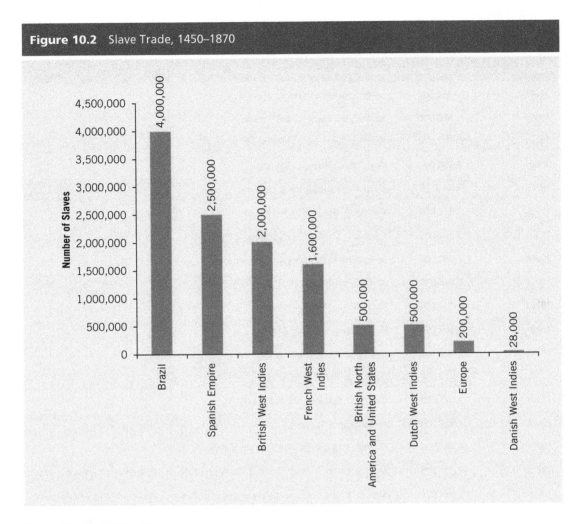

Source: Stauffer (2005, p. 61).

Note: The United States banned the importation of slaves in 1808.

In 1960, fewer than 600,000 Mexican-born people resided in the United States. By 1980, that number had grown to more than 2 million, and it further increased 50% from 1990 to 1996. This is the largest sustained mass migration of one group to the United States, far eclipsing earlier migrations of Irish and Italians. By 2007, for the first time, two Hispanic surnames, Garcia and Rodriguez, were among the top 10 most common names in the United States. Since 2005 greater numbers of Mexican nationals began to return

Global Voices

We find ourselves threatened by hordes of Yankee emigrants. What are we to do?

—Manuel Micheltorena, Mexican governor of California, 1846

Table 10.6	Immigration to the United States	
Decade	**Number**	**Major Contributing Countries**
1820s	152,000	Ireland, Great Britain, France
1830s	599,000	Ireland, Germany, Great Britain
1840s	1,713,000	Ireland, Germany, Great Britain
1850s	2,598,000	Germany, Ireland, Great Britain
1860s	2,315,000	Germany, Great Britain, Ireland
1870s	2,812,000	Germany, Great Britain, Ireland
1880s	5,247,000	Germany, Great Britain, Ireland
1890s	3,688,000	Italy, Austria-Hungary, Russia, Germany
1900s	8,795,000	Austria-Hungary, Italy, Russia
1910s	5,736,000	Italy, Russia, Austria-Hungary
1920s	4,107,000	Italy, Germany, Great Britain
1930s	528,000	Germany, Italy, Great Britain
1940s	1,035,000	Germany, Great Britain, Italy
1950s	2,515,000	Germany, Canada, Mexico, Italy
1960s	3,321,700	Mexico, Canada, Cuba
1970s	4,493,300	Mexico, Philippines, Cuba, South Korea
1980s	8,500,000[a,b]	Mexico, China (including Hong Kong and Taiwan), Philippines, Canada, Cuba
1990s	9,095,400[b]	Mexico, China (including Hong Kong and Taiwan), Philippines, India, Vietnam
2000s	13,900,000[b]	Mexico, China (including Hong Kong and Taiwan), India, Philippines, Vietnam

Sources: U.S. Bureau of the Census, *Statistical Abstract of the United States,* various editions, and 2010 American Community Survey.

a. Not including 2.3 million under the 1986 amnesty law.

b. The former Soviet Union would rank in the top 20 if it were still a country. By 2010 about 1 million immigrants from the Soviet Union were living in the United States.

to Mexico than at any time before. Table 10.7 shows this trend. A survey conducted in 2014 found that 60% of those who entered the United States and returned did so to reunite with their family or start a family of their own. Others returned to look for work (6%) or were deported (14%; Duara & Carcamo, 2015).

From 2000 to 2010, however, the fastest-growing group in the United States was people who identify as Asian. In that decade the number rose to more than 17 million, a 46% increase and four

Table 10.7 Profile of the U.S. Foreign-Born Population

Period	Number (in Millions)	Percentage of Population
1850	2.2	9.7
1860	4.1	13.2
1870	5.6	14.4
1880	6.7	13.3
1890	9.2	14.8
1900	10.3	13.6
1910	13.5	14.7
1920	13.9	13.2
1930	14.2	11.6
1940	11.6	8.8
1950	10.3	6.9
1960	9.7	5.4
1970	9.6	4.7
1980	14.1	6.2
1990	19.8	7.9
2000	31.1	11.1
2010	40.0	12.9

Countries of Birth of the U.S. Foreign-Born Population, 2010	Number (Percentage of Total)
Mexico	11,711,103 (29.3)
China (including Hong Kong and Taiwan)	2,166,526 (5.4)
India	1,780,322 (4.5)
Vietnam	1,240,542 (3.1)
El Salvador	1,214,049 (3.0)
Philippines	1,177,322 (2.9)
Cuba	1,104,679 (2.8)
Korea (North and South)	1,100,422 (2.8)

Sources: Decennial Census for 1900–2000 and American Community Survey for 2010.

Figure 10.3   Trends in Mexico-U.S. Immigration

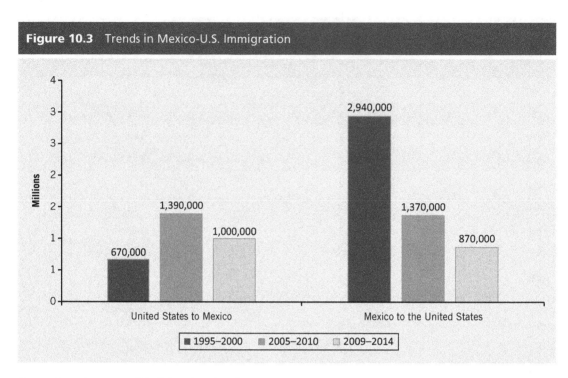

Source: Gonzalez-Barrera (2015), based on data from Pew Research Center.

Table 10.8   U.S. States With Highest Percentage of Foreign-Born Population, 2010

State	Immigrant Population	Percentage of Population
California	10,150,429	27.2
New York	4,297,612	22.2
New Jersey	1,844,581	21.0
Florida	3,658,043	19.4
Nevada	508,458	18.8
Hawai'i	248,213	18.2
Texas	4,142,031	16.4
Illinois	1,759,859	13.7
U.S. total	39,955,854	12.9

Source: U.S. Census Bureau (2010).

Focus on Culture 10.3

Emma Lazarus's "The New Colossus"

Not like the brazen giant of Greek fame,

With conquering limbs astride from land to land;

Here at our sea-washed, sunset gates shall stand

A mighty woman with a torch, whose flame

Is the imprisoned lightning, and her name Mother of Exiles.

From her beacon hand

Glows world-wide welcome;

her mild eyes command

The air-bridged harbor that twin cities frame.

"Keep, ancient lands, your storied pomp!" cries she

With silent lips. "Give me your tired, your poor,

Your huddled masses yearning to breathe free,

The wretched refuse of your teeming shore,

Send these, the homeless, tempest-tost to me,

I lift my lamp beside the golden door!"

Source: Poem written in 1883 by Emma Lazarus, a Sephardic Jew, mounted on the pedestal of the Statue of Liberty.

times the rate of growth of the U.S. population as a whole. This increase is accounted for mainly by immigration, and Asian immigration is expected to increase. In 2013, Asian immigrants outnumbered immigrants from Mexico.

Immigration and Individual Identity

One of the most researched areas in intercultural communication studies is that of individuals crossing cultural boundaries and adapting to a new culture (Y. Y. Kim, 2005). While many immigrants may relocate with their immediate family, everything else in their worlds changes. Most face the challenge of learning a new language; all are challenged with a new culture—everything from living arrangements to food, landscapes, social customs, government, education, popular culture, and more.

Focus on Culture 10.4

Successful Immigrants or Children of Immigrants

Sergey Brin, emigrated from Russia, co-founder of Google

Caterina Fake, daughter of Filipina immigrant, co-founder of Flickr

Elon Musk, emigrated from South Africa by way of Canada, founder of PayPal, SpaceX, and Tesla Motors

Indra Nooyi, emigrated from India, CEO of PepsiCo

Pierre Omidyar, son of Iranian immigrants, founder of eBay

Arnold Schwarzenegger, emigrated from Austria, former governor of California

Jerry Yang, emigrated from Taiwan, co-founder of Yahoo

Migrants are a disproportionately dynamic part of the labor force globally. Migrants are more entrepreneurial, create patents, start businesses, and found 40% of the Fortune 500 firms.

Source: Goldin, Cameron, & Balarajan (2011).

In this section, you'll first read about the experience of culture shock, the feelings one can experience upon introduction to a new culture. Then, you will read about the predictors of immigrants becoming fully functioning in a new culture. You will discover how modern media and transportation systems have significantly changed immigration and acculturation from what immigrants of a century ago experienced.

Culture Shock

Whether an individual enters a host culture as a sojourner or as an immigrant, culture shock is the first likely response (Furnham & Bochner, 1986). Unless you are prepared to function in the new culture, the situation can be highly stressful. Refer back to the intercultural barrier of anxiety identified in Chapter 2. This form of anxiety is called culture shock. Studies show that 30%–60% of expatriates suffer serious culture shock, whereas about 20% have no difficulty and enjoy the challenge.

The term *culture shock* was popularized by anthropologist Kalvero Oberg (1960) to describe the feelings of disorientation and anxiety that many people experience for a time while living in a foreign country. It results from an awareness that one's basic assumptions about life and one's familiar ways of behaving are no longer appropriate or functional.

Stages of Culture Shock

Adler (1975), Pedersen (1995), and others have described culture shock as a five-stage process. The first stage of initial contact, sometimes called the honeymoon stage or initial euphoria, is when everything is new and exciting. The person is effectively a tourist with her or his basic identity rooted in the home culture.

The second stage involves disintegration of familiar cues and irritation and hostility with the differences experienced in the new culture. For example, an international student in a U.S. grocery store may be asked, "Paper or plastic?" The student knows what paper is and what plastic is but doesn't understand the question. The student can experience feelings of inadequacy and can withdraw or become isolated.

The third stage involves a reintegration of new cues and an increased ability to function in the new culture. Perhaps surprisingly, though, the emotions experienced at this stage are typically anger and resentment toward the new culture for "being different."

In the fourth stage, gradual adjustment continues toward gradual autonomy and seeing "good" and "bad" elements in both the home and new cultures. The individual becomes more comfortable in the new culture as more things are predictable. Feelings of isolation are fewer, and people feel more in control and more comfortable.

The fifth and final stage is described as reciprocal interdependence, when the person has achieved biculturalism by developing the ability to cope comfortably in both the home and new cultures. Full adjustment can take years.

Symptoms

The symptoms of culture shock are pervasive and vary in intensity, duration, and severity among individuals. Individuals can experience both physical and psychological symptoms.

Physical symptoms are overconcern about cleanliness of food, bedding, and dishes; extreme stress on health and safety; fear of physical contact with anyone in the new country; great concern over minor pains and skin eruptions; craving "home cooking"; use of alcohol and drugs; and a decline in work quality.

Psychological symptoms are insomnia, fatigue, isolation and loneliness, disorientation, frustration, criticism of the new country, nervousness, self-doubt, irritability, depression, anger, and emotional and intellectual withdrawal. The effects of culture shock on intercultural communication are obvious: The immigrant's—or visitor's—intercultural communication becomes less effective.

Global Voices

Soon after arriving in the United States from Peru, I cried almost every day. I was so tense I heard without hearing, and this made me feel foolish. I also escaped into sleeping more than twelve hours at a time and dreamed of my life, family, and friends in Lima. After three months of isolating myself in the house and speaking to no one, I ventured out. I then began to criticize everything about this new culture: values, customs, climate, and its people. During this time I began to idealize my own homeland. I also began to have severe headaches. Finally I consulted a doctor, but she only gave me a lot of drugs to relieve the pain. Neither my doctor nor my teachers ever mentioned the two magic words that could have changed my life drastically during those times: culture shock! When I learned about this I began to see things from a new point of view and was better able to accept myself and my feelings.

I now realize most of the Americans I met in Lima before I came to the U.S. were also in one of the stages of culture shock. They demonstrated a somewhat hostile attitude toward Peru, making crude jokes and fun of the people and culture around them. Peruvians sensed this hostility and usually moved from an initially friendly attitude to a defensive, aggressive attitude or to avoidance as in my case. The Americans mostly stayed within the safe cultural familiarity of the embassy compound. Many seemed to feel that the difficulties they were experiencing in Peru were specially created by Peruvians to create discomfort for "gringos." In other words, they displaced their problem of adjustment and blamed everything on Peru for being an underdeveloped culture.

—R. Bimrose, quoted in *Handbook of Intercultural Training* (Landis & Brislin, 1983, p. 30)

Focus on Skills 10.1

Helping With Culture Shock

You are a student assistant in the international student office on campus. Your campus is hosting 50 young women from a private Japanese university for a 5-week intensive English and U.S. culture program. The women are all English majors and are highly motivated to improve their language skills with their U.S. host families and U.S. students on campus. You helped identify host families in the community and helped orient them for their hosting experience. Now that the Japanese students have arrived, you feel you have made a positive contribution and are having a wonderful time helping the instructors and students on campus.

You are taking roll in one class and notice that Misaki is absent. You ask her roommate Aiko if she knows where Misaki is. Aiko tells you she is so glad you asked. She says Misaki refuses to come out of her bedroom. The past few days when she gets home, she immediately goes into her room and doesn't come out for meals. Aiko says she believes she hears Misaki crying in her room. You go to the office and call Misaki's homestay parents. This is their first time as homestay parents and they were so enthusiastic at the orientation meetings. They confirm what Aiko says and ask for your help. They can't understand why Aiko is so well adjusted and social and such a delight and why Misaki is so upset and distant. They ask what they are doing wrong. The mother asks if she should go into Misaki's room and just hold her while she tells her how welcome she is in their home.

1. How do you help the homestay parents with the immediate situation?
2. How do you prepare to help Misaki?

For example, frustrations with the new culture may be interpreted by intercultural receivers as hostility toward them. Intercultural communication receivers need to be sensitive to the difficulties of culture shock that an individual may experience.

Reverse Culture Shock

If a person has adjusted exceptionally well to the host culture, reverse culture shock may occur upon return to the home country. This type of culture shock may cause greater distress and confusion than the original did. In reverse culture shock, the home culture is compared adversely to the admired aspects of the new culture.

Predictors of Acculturation

No immigrant, as long as livelihood needs are to be met in a new country, can escape acculturation. Individuals differ, however, in terms of the degree to which they become acculturated. Young Yun Kim (1986, 1988, 2001, 2005) proposed *cross-cultural adaptation theory* to describe the process an individual undergoes upon entering a new culture. It is an interplay of the individual himself or herself and the new environment. Kim describes the nature of the adaptation process as a stress-adaptation-growth dynamic. The new culture creates stress, which causes the individual to experience culture shock. The immigrant must overcome the challenges and develop new behaviors, but not all individuals adapt at the same rate. Kim has also identified the predictors of an immigrant's success in acculturation:

- *Host communication competence* refers to the capacity to communicate with the host culture's communication symbols and meaning systems. The ability to communicate skillfully in the host culture's dominant language is perhaps the most important factor in successful acculturation.
- *Participation in host social communication* refers to the time and skill devoted to participation in the host culture's mass media and in interpersonal communication with host culture members. The ability to interact successfully with individual host culture members is also a critical factor. Somani (2010) showed, for example, how Asian Indian immigrants in the United States watch U.S. television to learn not only U.S. English but how people think and act. Some reported watching U.S. football gave them something "U.S." to talk about with coworkers.
- *Participation in ethnic social communication* refers to the time devoted to communicating with fellow immigrants and time devoted to mass media targeted for the immigrant. Oftentimes this communication is in the immigrant's home language and is at the expense of time devoted to host social communication.
- *Host environment* refers to the relative strength of the immigrant group to maintain its culture and the relative strength of the new host culture to conform.
- *Predisposition* refers to how similar the home culture is to the new host culture. For example, an immigrant from Canada to the United States finds acculturation easier than a Vietnamese immigrant does. There can be differences among immigrants from the same country, depending on, for example, whether they grew up in a cosmopolitan urban center or in a rural area where they experienced relatively less outside influence. Predisposition also refers to adaptive personality attributes. Younger immigrants adapt more easily than older ones. Educational background and previous travel also are factors, and a person's personality (e.g., risk-taking, being gregarious and curious) can determine how readily she or he will desire to blend in with a new culture.

Effect of Media and Transportation Advances

It's useful to compare the immigration peaks of the early 1900s with today's. The European immigration of the early 1900s brought millions of people who at the time seemed just as alien to many native-born U.S. citizens as Salvadorans or Koreans do to some today. However, there are some important—and critical—differences in the intercultural communication context: Media and transportation advances contribute to the difference.

The immigrants of the 1900s left homes permanently, with little hope of returning even for a visit, and thus lost much of their original culture in assimilation. The immigrants of the 1900s had little contact with friends and families left behind. Letters and messages brought by friends were slow. Today the Internet provides easy and ongoing exposure to an immigrant's home mass media. Immigrants to the United States in the 20th century found newspapers and periodicals printed entirely or in part in languages other than English. These helped immigrants not only maintain contacts with each other but

Table 10.9 Ancestries in the United States, 2010

Ancestry	Population (in Millions)	Percentage of Total Population
German	42.8	15.2
Irish	30.5	10.8
African-American	24.9	8.8
English	24.5	8.7
American	20.2	7.2
Mexican	18.4	6.5
Italian	15.6	5.6
Polish	9.0	3.2
French	8.3	3.0
American Indian	7.9	2.8
Scottish	4.9	1.7
Dutch	4.5	1.6
Norwegian	4.5	1.6
Scotch-Irish	4.3	1.5
Swedish	4.0	1.4

Source: Based on 2010 U.S. Census.
Note: Based on responses to census question to identify national ancestry

Focus on Skills 10.2

Attitudes Toward Immigration

Your next-door neighbors are Tom and Phan. Over time you learn that they are in a long-term relationship. You also learn that Tom is a citizen of the United States. Phan, a citizen of Thailand, has lived in the United States since 1996, but is ineligible for permanent residency because he entered the United States with a non-immigrant tourist visa. Shortly after Phan's arrival in the United States, a local university issued him an I-20, the document needed to change visa status. Phan filed through the mail for a change of status and was granted an F-1 student visa, enabling him to remain in the United States as long as he made progress toward a legitimate degree. Phan has accumulated three college degrees since he was granted his F-1 visa.

Tom and Phan have been domestic partners in California since 1999, and in 2008 they were legally married. All is not well, however. Phan is not allowed to work in the United States and he has not been able to visit his family in Thailand. You are shocked to learn that if Phan left the United States, he would probably not be allowed to reenter the country, his home for the past 17 years. Although Tom and Phan seldom complain, they do allow that they suffer from the uncertainty of their life in the United States and feel that Tom's rights and responsibilities as a U.S. citizen are unconstitutionally denied. They also point out that they have been "cash hemorrhaging" due to legal expenses and Phan's inability to engage in legal employment.

Yesterday, Tom and Phan told you that they have an interview with the U.S. Customs and Immigration Service (USCIS) to petition for Phan's permanent residency. The U.S. Supreme Court ruled in June 2015 that same-sex married couples are entitled to the same rights and responsibilities as those extended to hetero-sexual married couples. Tom and Phan are eager and excited that they may soon be able to eliminate the con-fusion and uncertainty in their lives and visit Phan's family in Thailand without fear of being denied reentry into the United States. Phan tells you that he is very excited about the possibility of finding legal employment to help with their finances.

Earlier today, your brother Chad, who feels he has lost his job to what he calls "cheap immigrant labor," stopped by and asked you to sign a petition to restrict U.S. immigration. Chad also declared that the recent Supreme Court ruling will allow "thousands of faggots" to come live in the United States, thus jeopardizing the sanctity of marriage, damaging U.S. morality, and making it even more difficult for him to find a job. This evening, Tom and Phan dropped by with some Kao Niew Ma Muang, a Thai dish you have learned to love.

1. Do you sign your brother's petition? What do you say to your brother about the petition?
2. Do you say anything to Tom and Phan about your brother's petition?
3. What do you say to them about their upcoming interview with the USCIS?

Focus on Culture 10.5

Western Union Adapts to Meet Immigrants' Needs

Western Union was originally a telegraph company. But air travel, fax, and the Internet made telegraphs a thing of the past, and the company went bankrupt in 1992. The company emerged 2 years later as a money transfer company. Today the company has five times as many locations as McDonald's, Starbucks, Burger King, and Walmart combined and transfers some $150 billion annually for immigrants across the globe to their home countries.

From Western Union's homepage: "We proudly support migrants in their journey toward economic opportunity. These migrants are modern-day heroes."

also adjust to life in the United States. The non-English press was weakened by restrictive legislation in the 1920s and by a drop in the number of new immigrants. At the same time, members of the second generation were not interested in newspapers in the languages of their parents (Govorchin, 1961). According to the 1940 U.S. Census, there were nearly 8.4 million people in the United States whose native language was one other than English. At that time, about 1,000 newspapers and periodicals were printed entirely or in part in languages other than English (Chyz, 1945). In 1942, there were

Courtesy of Burleson County Chamber of Commerce

Czech immigrants founded dozens of communities in Texas, making the language the third most spoken in the state. Annual festivals renew ties to the culture with music and kolaches.

nearly 1,000 radio stations in the United States, 200 of which broadcast in some 26 languages. In fact, though, the media contributed to assimilation. Today, some 100 ethnic newspapers and magazines can be found in New York City, with a combined readership of 3 million. Research has consistently shown that as immigrants become acculturated, their use of host media increases and their use of native media decreases (Dalisay, 2012).

The U.S. Bureau of Citizenship and Immigration Services uses various social media platforms, including a blog, YouTube, and Twitter, to disseminate information to immigrants. Social media platforms also provide a way for those seeking citizenship to form online communities. During President Obama's administration, a youth-oriented group announced the mobile app Pocket DACA, which was designed to help take advantage of his nondeportation policy for childhood arrivals.

The platform LoonLounge, developed by a Canadian immigration attorney, is a social networking site where Canadian citizens and prospective Canadians can connect. The site eases the process of immigration to and settlement in Canada through the creation of personal and professional networks prior to and following arrival in the country. For today's immigrants, social media is taking the place of other forms of media that immigrants from the past relied on for information and support.

Today's immigrants can much more easily return to their home countries for visits. They can watch television programs from their home countries and be in easy telephone contact. The pressure to assimilate is not as great. It's quite possible to maintain their original cultural identity and participate in a meaningful way in the larger society.

A recent study compared the assimilation of immigrants into Austria, Canada, France, Greece, Italy, Portugal, Spain, Switzerland, and the United States (Vigdor, 2011). Canadian immigrants ranked first in overall assimilation. Canada has a 3-year residency requirement (compared to 5 in the United States and up to 12 in some European countries), accepts dual citizenship, and places priority

Focus on Technology 10.2

U.S. Immigrants and Official Social Media

The U.S. Citizenship and Immigration Service uses social media technologies and websites to communicate with immigrants—Instagram, Facebook, and Twitter for daily citizenship and immigration updates in English and Spanish, YouTube Videos, e-mail updates, and RSS data feeds.

Focus on Technology 10.3

Dreamers' Tweets

Deferred Action for Childhood Arrivals applies to immigrants between the ages of 15 and 30 who came to the United States as children and who are in school or have graduated from high school. Referred to as "Dreamers," as of June 2016, 728,000 had received approval. The program temporarily removes the chance of being deported for 2 years and makes it possible to get work permits, meaning that for the first time, driver's licenses and in-state college tuition are available to these individuals in many states. You can read tweets from dreamers at https://twitter.com/hashtag/WithDACA?src=hash.

on attracting skilled immigrants. The study showed that immigrants to the United States were more assimilated than those in European countries, with the exception of Portugal, where a large proportion of immigrants come from former Portuguese colonies. Muslim immigrants are most integrated in Canada, followed closely by the United States.

The next section presents a model for categorizing different degrees of immigrants' life in their new cultures.

Categories of Acculturation

Acculturation, or cultural adaptation, refers to an immigrant's learning and adopting the norms and values of the new host culture. Unlike a temporary visitor, the immigrant must find a new source of livelihood and build a new life. This adapting to a new host culture is called acculturation. Berry, Kim, and Boski (1987) have described acculturation in relation to two dimensions: the value placed on maintaining one's original cultural identity and the value given to maintaining relationships with other groups in one's new culture.

As shown in Table 10.10, marginalization refers to losing one's cultural identity and not having any psychological contact with the larger society. The person has feelings of "not belonging anywhere." Separation and segregation refer to maintaining one's original culture and not participating in the new culture. To some, segregation connotes a judgment of superiority and inferiority as well as prejudice and hatred between groups. Others use the term *insularity* to connote separation only. The person has a strong sense of ethnic identity.

Table 10.10 Dimensions of Acculturation			
		Value to Maintain Original Cultural Identity	
		Yes	No
Value to Build and Maintain Relationship With New Culture	Yes	Integration	Assimilation
	No	Separation (or segregation)	Marginalization

Focus on Technology 10.4

Social Media Usage by the Garifuna

The Garifuna people are descended from West African slaves and the Arawak. The British relocated the Garifuna to an island off the coast of Honduras. Now numbering some 600,000, the Garifuna live in Central America and as immigrant populations in the United States. With their own language, music, and religion, the Garifuna have strong ties to their culture.

Jared Johnson and Clark Callahan (2013) studied the Garifuna people's use of social media in today's global mass media with its homogenizing effect on culture and demonstrated that new forms of social media strengthened their culture. Garifuna take phones with them to events and upload images and video of these events, which are viewed by Garifuna living in the United States. One celebration in the village of Limon was shared with nearly two-thirds of the Garifuna involved in the study living in Los Angeles, New Orleans, and New York.

Source: Johnson & Callahan (2013).

Focus on Culture 10.6

Germans' Reminder of Home Lives On

Germans first arrived in large numbers in the 1720s, settling in Pennsylvania. A second and larger wave arrived between the 1830s and 1930s, with most going to the Midwest and the Upper Plains states. Today, about 23% of the U.S. population list German ancestry first on census forms. The German-born population was a record high 30% in 1890.

Immigrant farmers from the fertile lowlands of northern Germany—conquerors of Ohio's Great Black Swamp—turned Henry County into what some believe is a mirror image of their "fatherland."

Walter Delventhal, who recently shepherded the organization of the Low German Club through Napoleon and Henry County officials, said the majority of the German people in Henry County came from the Visselhovede area, a small community in the northern German lowlands generally between Bremen and Hamburg. And the majority of people in Henry County are of German descent. A sampling of ancestry of Henry County residents, taken from 1990 Census reports, showed that 18,832 residents claimed to be of German ancestry. The second-largest group, by ancestry, were the English, with a total of 1,518. . . .

Earlier this month, the county commissioners and Napoleon Mayor Don Strange signed an agreement establishing a sister city-county relationship with Visselhovede. They hope the relationship will encourage Henry County residents to seek their roots in Germany.

Mr. Delventhal and his wife, Lucia, have returned to their hometown of Visselhovede three times, in 1972, 1983, and 1984.

"It's just like going home," he said with a smile. "They talk just like we do." The Delventhals still speak "Low German" at home as their first language. Their children can understand it but do not speak it. The phrase "Low German" refers to the flat lowlands of northern Germany. The language is different from "High German," which is spoken in the southern highlands, including the Black Forest.

The Delventhals attend St. John Lutheran Church in Freedom Township, which until the 1960s had both German and English services. Germans traditionally had strong ties with their churches, and that continued when they came to the United States.

"What happened was that one family moved from Visselhovede or Walsrode, a village to the south, then wrote back to their relatives talking about how good things are in their new home," he explained. Soon, their relatives wanted to come too. Speeding the exodus was the German tradition that the oldest son always inherits the family farm. That left a lot of other family members disgruntled and anxious to move to the new world, he said.

Russell Patterson, a Napoleon druggist and grandson of a German immigrant, said his grandfather, Wilhelm Frederick Franz Bernicke, paid $30 for steerage passage to the United States. Like others, he arrived on the East Coast in 1893 to find that all of the farmland already was owned, so he used his money for a train ride west. He ultimately landed in Henry County. Hamler, once the hunting grounds of the Ottawa, Shawnee, Seneca, and Miami Indians, today is best known for its summer festival, when upwards of 25,000 or more polka lovers descend on the town.

Source: W. Ferguson (1997, pp. A11–A12). Reprinted with permission.

Assimilation results from giving up one's original cultural identity and moving into full participation in the new culture. The person identifies with the country and not the ethnic group. Assimilation is a long-term and sometimes multigenerational process.

True integration is maintaining important parts of one's original culture as well as becoming an integral part of the new culture. Integration ensures a continuity of culture. One contrast between assimilation and integration is that under assimilation policies, groups disappear through intermarriage but that in integration, groups continue to exist. The words *biculturalism* and *pluralism* also have been used to describe integration. The person feels as loyal to the country as to any ethnic group. Integration is supported by the dual-nationality trend, which allows expatriates from immigrant-sending nations to retain rights as nationals while taking on citizenship status in the United States or elsewhere. In a seeming paradox, new U.S. citizens must formally renounce allegiances to foreign governments as part of the naturalization process, but U.S. law still permits citizens to possess other nationalities. Keep these terms in mind as you read the next chapter, which describe various cultures within U.S. culture.

Focus on Skills 10.3

The Ethics of Immigration

This chapter raises some questions of ethics. In its history, the United States has at times opened its doors and offered shelter and opportunity to those fleeing persecution and, at other times, kept its doors tightly closed. Some point to humanitarian principles, to the need for laborers to do the work most citizens don't want to do, and to the talents that immigrants can bring to a new country. Some voice security concerns, fear of weakening cultural identity, demands for government assistance, and unemployment and economic concerns. In such debates, the competent intercultural communicator demonstrates respect for others and an appreciation of different points of view.

Explain your answers to the following three questions developed by Rabbi Nochum Mangel and Rabbi Shmuel Klatzkin (2013):

1. Does a country have the right to admit newcomers only under certain conditions?
2. Can a country make sure that the influx of immigrants will not disrupt its own labor market?
3. Does a country have the right to insist that its laws be respected and its culture honored?

SUMMARY

First, to study the effect of immigration on national identity, immigration into Israel, Europe, and Brazil are presented as examples of the challenges presented by immigration and as a comparison to the United States. U.S. immigration has come in distinct waves. In the 1850s, the Germans and Irish who were fleeing economic destitution were largely viewed as a "lower class of people." In the 1880s and 1890s, eastern and southern European immigrants were viewed with suspicion because of darker skin and the religion of Catholicism. The Irish were blamed for bringing cholera, the Italians for bringing polio, the Chinese for carrying bubonic plague, the Jews for spreading tuberculosis, and the Haitians for bringing AIDS. Recent immigration from Spanish-speaking countries has brought calls for official English language laws.

Second, immigration has effects on the individual. The term *culture shock* describes the feelings of disorientation and anxiety that many people experience for a time while living in a foreign country. It results from an awareness that one's basic assumptions about life and one's familiar ways of behaving are no longer appropriate or functional. Reverse culture shock also can occur upon returning home after a long stay outside one's home country. Predictors of an immigrant's success are host culture language skill, host culture interpersonal communication and mass media use, home culture interpersonal communication and mass media use, pressures to live separate or assimilate, and individual characteristics such as age, educational background, and personality (e.g., risk-taking, being gregarious). Categories of acculturation can be based on the value to maintain original cultural identity and value to maintain a relationship with a new culture.

DISCUSSION QUESTIONS

1. Describe what challenges and opportunities immigration presents to a country.

2. What comparisons and contrasts can be drawn among the immigration history and policies of Israel, Europe, Brazil, and the United States?

3. In what ways, if any, is immigration a threat to the national identities of European states?

4. How would you recommend revising U.S. immigration policies? Similar to policies in Australia and Canada, should the United States give preference to foreign applicants who speak English and have skills that contribute to the economy?

5. How could countries use predictors of an immigrant's success in acculturation in immigration policies or in facilitating acculturation?

6. Should immigrants be encouraged or mandated to give up their home cultures and to learn and participate in their new country's culture?

KEY TERMS

acculturation	emigrant	refugee
assimilation	expatriate	reverse culture shock
asylee	immigrant	segregation
biculturalism	integration	separation
cultural adaptation	marginalization	sojourner
culture shock	oleh	

READINGS

All readings are from *Intercultural Communication: A Global Reader* (Jandt, 2004).

Flora Keshishian, "Acculturation, Communication, and the U.S. Mass Media: The Experience of an Iranian Immigrant" (p. 230)

Tarla Rai Peterson, Susan J. Gilbertz, Kathi Groenendyk, Jay Todd, and Gary E. Varner, "Reconfiguring Borders: Health-Care Providers and Practical Environmentalism in Cameron County, Texas" (p. 243)

STUDENT STUDY SITE

$SAGE edge™

Sharpen your skills with SAGE edge at edge.sagepub.com/jandt9e.

SAGE edge for Students provides a personalized approach to help you accomplish your coursework goals in an easy-to-use learning environment.

Chapter 11

Jonathan Bachman/Getty Images

Cultures Within Cultures

You read in Chapter 1 about the controversy over the use of the words *subculture, co-culture,* and *microculture*. By whatever name, these "cultures within cultures" are most often based on geographic region, ethnicity, or economic or social class. These cultures can encompass a relatively large number of people and represent the accumulation of generations of human striving. Awareness of these cultures is a critical intercultural communication skill. Also in Chapter 1 you read that nation-state political boundaries do not necessarily reflect peoples' identities. For example, in Europe there are several examples of popular support for secessionist states. And in Chapter 10 you read about how immigration has created challenges for nation-states when large numbers of immigrants do not assimilate, preferring to maintain important aspects of their original identities. You should review the section "Categories of Acculturation" in Chapter 10, which identified the four categories of acculturation, before reading this chapter. Remember that *marginalization* refers to losing one's cultural identity and not having any psychological contact with the larger society. As an example of marginalization, this chapter discusses the Hmong, who were forced to leave Laos.

Remember that *separation* and *segregation* refer to maintaining one's cultural identity while not participating in the larger culture. Separation may be voluntary and reflect a strong cultural identity. As an example of separation, in this chapter you will read about the Koryo-saram in Russia and the Amish in the United States. As a culture with strongly defined and communicated values, the Amish have long resisted acculturation through voluntary separation. On the other hand, segregation connotes a forced condition involving power, prejudice, and hatred. As an example of segregation, you will read about the special case of indigenous cultures that continued to experience cultural domination.

Remember that *assimilation* refers to giving up one's original cultural identity and moving into full participation in the new culture, while *integration* refers to maintaining important parts of one's original culture as well as becoming an integral part of the new culture. This chapter briefly discusses the status of indigenous cultures and then looks in depth at when assimilation was more characteristic of the United States than it is today. You will see how Hispanic cultures are maintaining multiple cultural identities. What is called the Hispanic culture in the United States is a vast, dispersed, heterogeneous, multilingual multiclass with Mexican, Puerto Rican, Cuban, and Central American origins. You will read about specialized communication media and segmented marketing as forces against assimilation. As you saw in the previous chapter, modern transportation and communication technology have lessened immigrants' pressures to acculturate. In contrast to a century ago, specialized communication media and segmented marketing can have the effect of strengthening a culture's identity and lessening the pressures it feels to acculturate into the larger culture.

Marginalization: The Hmong

When you think of cultures within cultures, you probably think of immigrant groups. Scholars first used the word diaspora to refer to the experiences of Jews and, later, Armenians who were both forcibly exiled from their homelands. More recently, scholars have expanded that definition to include all groups that move from one part of the world to another, even if that migration was of free choice. Diaspora, of course, can have the effect of creating cultures within cultures in the country into which peoples move, as is the case with the Iu Mien and the Hmong, who left the villages of Laos, and the Montagnard, who left Vietnam (Kinefuchi, 2010). Many of the older Hmong immigrants lost their identity provided by their homeland and were unable to establish a new identity in the United States, and thus are an example of marginalization.

The Hmong (pronounced MONG and literally meaning "free men") are among recent immigrants who have been called the most ill-prepared people ever to immigrate to the United States. The extent of differences with dominant U.S. cultural patterns places these original immigrants in a state of marginalization. Tran Minh Tung (1990) described the groups within the Cambodian, Laotian, Hmong, and Vietnamese refugee cultures most at risk for marginalization:

Newcomers. Those who went through relocation camps experienced fear and humiliation in dehumanizing conditions, resulting in passivity, dependency, and learned helplessness. The first year of relocation to the United States can be a disappointment compared to what dreams had been. Newcomers see opportunities but also experience fear, uncertainty, and unhappiness.

Refugee teenagers. While the majority of refugee teenagers are well adjusted and do well in school, a significant number become involved in gang criminal behavior. Loss of traditional values and lack of support and guidance from parents who are themselves experiencing stress may be contributing factors.

Elderly refugees. Having minimal or nonexistent English language skills results in social isolation. Family structure changes as children and grandchildren begin to take places in the new culture and become strangers. The U.S. urban environment and the value placed on individualism reduce the need for interdependence traditionally provided by the family.

Rural refugees. Often less sophisticated than urban counterparts, rural refugees do not fare well in a capitalistic society, although their children progress economically and socially. The majority of refugee young adults have jobs, homes, and cordial, even if brief and infrequent, relations with U.S. colleagues and neighbors. Most of the refugees' social interactions occur within a small circle of relatives and friends in the numerous Little Saigons that have sprung up in several urban areas and recreate some feeling of home.

History

Worldwide, today's Hmong population is between 6 and 7 million. The Hmong are an ancient Asian hill tribe that has resisted assimilation for millennia (Geddes, 1976). A people long persecuted, the Hmong written language was destroyed centuries ago. The Hmong are thought to have originated in central China and to have been pushed out of China in the early 1800s for refusing to discard unique ways. The Hmong kept migrating south to the highlands of northern Laos. The term *Hmong* actually refers to a diverse group, including the Hmong Der (or White Hmong), Mong Leng (or Blue or Green Mong), Striped Hmong, Black Hmong, and Red Hmong—classifications based on dialect, clothing, and custom.

As mercenaries for the Central Intelligence Agency in the 1960s and 1970s, the Hmong fought the communists in Laos. More than 40,000 died in that war. After the U.S. withdrawal from Vietnam, Hmong villages in Laos were attacked by the Laotians and Vietnamese. Many Hmong fled to refugee camps in Thailand.

Hmong refugees migrated to Australia, Canada, France, the United States, and other parts of the world. Hmong immigration to the United States started in the late 1970s. Today, more than 260,000 Hmong reside in the United States, primarily in California, Minnesota, and Wisconsin. By metropolitan area, the largest population, with some 64,000, is in the Minneapolis-St. Paul area. The second largest concentration is the Fresno area, in California, with some 32,000. Other large populations are in Milwaukee, Wisconsin, and in Sacramento, Merced, and Stockton, California (Pfeifer, Sullivan, Yang, & Yang, 2012). The town of Wausau, Wisconsin, has the largest population of Hmong per capita in the United States. A small number have returned to Laos under United Nations–sponsored repatriation programs.

Cultural Patterns

Hmong culture is evident in the United States: grocery stores with familiar food, radio programs with familiar music and community news, Lao family centers and festivals, and traditional farming and funeral practices.

The Hmong brought with them religious practices that blend ancestor worship, animal sacrifice, and shaman healing. The killing of chickens, pigs, and an occasional dog inside the home of the ill was

Global Voices

When asked for her date of birth at a hospital, Foua gave the date October 6, 1944. "Foua is quite sure... that October is correct, since she was told by her parents that she was born during the season in which the opium fields are weeded for the second time.... She invented the precise day of the month, like the year, in order to satisfy the many Americans who have evinced an abhorrence of unfilled blanks on the innumerable forms the Lees have encountered since their admission to the United States.... Nao Kao Lee has a first cousin who told the immigration officials that all nine of his children were born on July 15, in nine consecutive years, and this information was duly recorded on their resident alien documents."

Source: Fadiman (1997/2012, p. 7).

practiced by shamans to placate evil spirits. Rites for the dead stretch some 72 hours and mix mourning, feasting, and woodwind music. The Hmong believe that any metal in and around the body prevents passage to the other life. Hence, gold and silver tooth fillings are removed. Instead of metal coffins, the Hmong use handmade oak Orthodox Jewish caskets. Red twine is strung from the casket to a cow outside the funeral chapel. The cow is sacrificed, and the meat is then cooked and brought back to the chapel, where it is eaten in honor of the deceased. In the United States, Hmong religious practices were misunderstood and a source of prejudice.

Hmong practices of early marriage age for females and fertility rates of 9.5 children per mother were continued by some. Between 50% and 70% of Hmong females are married before the age of 17—many at the age of 12, even though these marriages are not recognized by the state. The Hmong tribal tradition of "marriage by capture" was considered an acceptable form of elopement. Traditionally, the girl feigns resistance as the male takes his intended to his family's home. There the father performs a 30-second ceremony using a live chicken. The bride's parents are then notified, and the payment due from the bride's family is negotiated. In Fresno, California, a Hmong immigrant kidnapped and raped a Hmong woman. His defense for abuse was to claim that marriage by capture is a form of courtship in his native Laos. His cultural defense served to reduce the criminal charges against him to false imprisonment.

Ill-prepared for life in the United States and with few marketable skills, the poverty rate among Hmong is 24.2% (compared to 11.6% for the United States overall). Over 40% of Hmong in the United States speak English "less than very well." The Hmong have the highest welfare dependency rate of any refugee group in the United States. Family household size continues to be large at 5 (compared to 2.65 for the United States overall), with a median age of just over 22 compared to United States overall median of 37.5. While median household income is approximately the same as the United States overall, median income per person is less than half that of the United States overall (Pfeifer, 2014). Older adults who speak little English continue to exist in a state of marginalization—the homeland lost and the U.S. culture hostile and strange.

By 1990 about one-third of the Hmong were born in the United States. Today the number of Hmong who speak little or no Hmong is growing as any memory of life in Laos is declining. The children and grandchildren of the original Hmong have had access to education and jobs and are adopting U.S. culture. By 2013, 13.2% of Hmong earned a bachelor's degree, compared to 18.4% for the United States overall. Many Hmong have joined the U.S. military, and some have taken elected office in state governments.

Today many Hmong "live a dual lifestyle in a dual society: they follow the practices of the dominant culture while retaining Hmong customs and traditions" (Vang, 2016, p. 435). Hmong clans and tribes remain important, as do the cultural customs of marriages, funerals, and New Year's celebrations. The Hmong continue to live as close-knit communities and have taken steps to maintain their language and culture (Moua, 2002), though Hmong social media are in the early stages of development (Vang, 2016).

Separation: Koreans in Russia

The term *Koryo-saram* refers to ethnic Koreans in the post-Soviet states. Totaling some 470,000 people, the largest number are in Uzbekistan (198,000), Russia (125,000), and Kazakhstan (105,000). Koreans began migrating to Russia in the second half of the 19th century to escape famine, economic hardship, and Japanese imperialism in Korea. Prior to the construction of the Trans-Siberian Railway, Koreans actually outnumbered Russians in the Russian Far East. In the 1930s, Stalin's government relocated about 200,000 ethnic Koreans to central Russia under the pretense that the Koreans would act as spies for the Japanese.

The Koryo-saram lived in a state of separation from the Russian culture, interacting little with the nomadic peoples around them. They established rice farms and kept some Korean traditions: They maintained Korean food, adding only local ingredients, and maintained Korean birthday rituals. Rather than adopting the clothing of the peoples around them, they adopted Western-style clothing. The Koryo-saram maintained their own schools and colleges as well as print media with one large-circulation newspaper. And as would be predicted from the years of separation, language use changed. Those who continued to speak Korean had some difficulties conversing with today's South Koreans. About half of the Koryo-saram spoke Russian as a first language (Back, 2004).

Since the collapse of the Soviet Union, the Koryo-saram have faced marginalization, as in Uzbekistan, where there is a clash of ethnicity, religion, and language. Uzbekistan is Islamic and has adopted Uzbek as the official language of the country. The Koryo-saram are Russian-speaking ethnic Koreans and are either Russian Orthodox, Christian, or atheist.

Some Russian-speaking Koryo-saram have immigrated to the United States as refugees. In the United States, the Koryo-saram have found dealings with Korean-Americans to be difficult. The Koryo-saram lack fluency in Korean and tend to have become more expressive, emotional, and Western in their mannerisms and behavior. They experience older Korean-Americans as distant and reserved (Simmons, 2003).

Separation: The Amish

While the Hmong had little choice but to leave their homeland, the Amish left voluntarily and have voluntarily chosen to remain apart from the dominant U.S. culture and resist acculturation. The Amish immigrated to the United States as a religious community. Religion provides a complete defining cultural identity for the Amish. The Amish are an example of a culture within a culture that has attempted to maintain its original culture and to participate as little as possible in the dominant U.S. culture. That voluntary separation extends to not voting.

History

The Amish and Mennonites grew out of the Anabaptist movement that developed in Switzerland during the 1500s. The Mennonites took their name from the Dutch reformer Menno Simons and adhered to pacifism and a strict separation of church and state. The Amish were named after the leader Jacob Ammann, a Swiss Mennonite bishop. In the late 17th century, the Amish broke away from the Mennonites, who had begun taking a more liberal view of the policy of shunning the excommunicated.

As Anabaptists, the Amish believe in adult baptism and living apart from the world, preferring a simple, agrarian lifestyle. The Amish migrated from Switzerland in the 1720s to Pennsylvania, where they were welcomed by William Penn and found an abundance of land for farms and freedom to worship. About 5,000 Amish lived in the United States in 1900. Today, the Amish are one of the fastest-growing population groups in the United States and number about 300,000 in North America. They are concentrated in Lancaster County and other parts of Pennsylvania as well as in parts of Ohio, Indiana, Wisconsin, New York, and Michigan. Two and a half centuries later, the Amish remain basically the same (Aurand, 1938; Hostetler, 1980; Kraybill, 1989).

Diversity Among the Amish

An Amish settlement refers to a geographic area. Within each settlement, one or more affiliations of people share a set of theological rules and practices. Each affiliation makes its own decisions in meetings of members who, by consensus, develop their own set of rules. Each affiliation is made up of church districts or groups of 25 to 35 families. Each affiliation reacts to change from the same Amish religious value context but with seemingly contradictory results. Thus, the Dover affiliation prohibits the use of milking machines while others do not. The Lancaster affiliation permits the use of plows with two blades, while the Dover affiliation permits only the single-blade walking plow.

Map 11.1   States With the Highest Amish Population

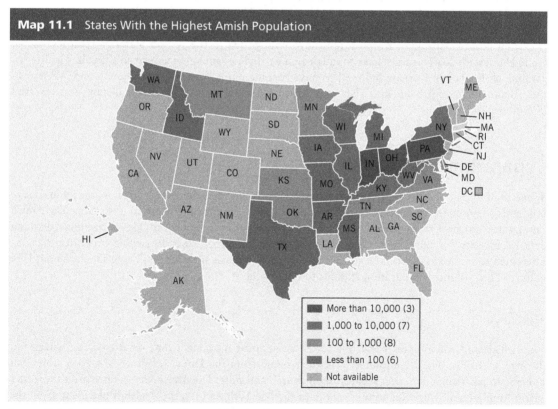

Source: Data from Religious Congregations and Membership Study.

Values

When Kluckhohn and Strodtbeck's (1961) value orientation theory is applied to the Amish culture, the contrasts with dominate U.S. cultural patterns stand out. Note particularly the areas of worldview and activity orientation.

Worldview

Gelassenheit is a common German word in Amish life. It means "submission." The Amish believe in complete submission to God and do not separate religion from other areas of life. The Amish home serves as the church. Every moment in Amish life is a religious one. The Ordnung contains the church rules and outlines the values of the community. Humility, obedience, simplicity, sharing, and community cooperation are valued. The Amish don't pay or accept Social Security; elderly Amish remain in the family's home.

Pride is a sin in the Amish community. Pride is the evil face of individualism that is believed to be the death of the community and of the family. This value is even reflected in clothing. Hooks and eyes replace buttons. Shirt pockets are prohibited as they can become a place to display fancy things and hence are prideful. Indeed, the Amish are often referred to as "plain people" because of dress and lifestyle.

The Amish do not condone technology unless it's clearly beneficial to the community by making it possible to continue as a community (Kraybill, 1989). The most conservative and strict, the Old Order Amish, avoid any use of electricity and automobiles. New Order Amish use telephones and powered farm equipment but use batteries and generators rather than public electricity. The Beachy Amish, named after the leader Moses Beachy, separated from the more conservative Amish in 1927 and use both automobiles and electricity.

Automobiles threaten the family, so horses and carriages are used. They symbolize the tradition of a slower pace and a closeness to nature. Some Amish have adopted automatic milking machines and refrigeration because that continues to make the family farm possible. Telephones and answering machines are not permitted in homes based on a prohibition of wires from the outside world into homes, but Amish may be found phoning inside wooden shanties (an outhouse-type version of the phone booth) across the road from an Amish home. Telephones in the home could lead to a change in values. The Amish are, however, currently debating mobile phone use. Internet pioneer Howard Rheingold (1999) visited the Amish to observe telephone use. He found that the Amish don't fear technology as such. Rather, they fear the ideas that technology is always beneficial, that individuality is a precious value, and that the goal of life is to get ahead. Rheingold asked, "If we decided that community came first, how would we use our tools differently?" (p. 131).

Activity Orientation

Work is important to Amish life. Work is preferred over idleness, which is believed to breed laziness, a trait of the outside world. Work also becomes a way to bring generations together on the farm; grandparents, parents, and children all work together. Also, work can bring the community together in projects such as barn raisings. A major source of income for the Amish is handicrafts, such as quilts, rugs, furniture, and other household products. Amish handicrafts, prized for their design and workmanship, are sold to the "English" world. (The Amish refer to anyone not Amish as English.)

In comparing Amish cultural patterns to dominant U.S. cultural patterns, major attention must be given to how the Amish control change. Each change is evaluated in terms of how it will affect the culture. Change does not come easily to the Amish. Many considerations must be examined before a change is adopted in the community. Any change that decreases the amount of family or community solidarity, increases visibility, promotes individualism, or threatens the values of the Amish in any way is rejected. If a change will better the life of the community without threatening the Amish society as a whole, it may be gradually adopted into Amish life.

The tradition of the Amish is farming, and the farms are profitable. Cultivating and nurturing the land is an important Amish value. But increasing population and land prices force change. Some Amish have emigrated to other areas to continue farming. Tobacco-growing Amish participated in growing genetically engineered tobacco. This change permits the farming culture to continue. Others have taken nonfarm employment to make it possible to remain near family and community. In the 1972 landmark Supreme Court ruling in *State of Wisconsin v. Jonas Yoder et al.*, Justice Burger wrote, "There can be no assumption that today's majority is right and the Amish and others like them are wrong. A way of life that is odd or even erratic but interferes with no rights or interests of others is not to be condemned because it is different." No matter how much the world changes, the Amish will strive to preserve the serenity of Amish culture.

Focus on Technology 11.1

©iStockphoto.com/Alija

Social media use is increasing among Amish and Mennonite adolescents.

Amish Youth Use of Social Media

A Lancaster, Pennsylvania, newspaper reported that the majority of Amish businesses have mobile phones. An Amish harness manufacturer was quoted to say that mobile phones "are here to stay."

There are no statistics on the number of Amish youth on Facebook, but it appears many youth of *rumspringa* age log on via mobile phones. Dr. Steve Nolt, author or co-author of nine books on Amish and Mennonite culture, notes that Amish youth may only "friend" other Amish youth. "In that sense, it serves [as] an insulating social network—one more way that Amish youth socialize only with other Amish youth—rather than a means of expanding Amish social circles."

The primary communication link among Amish communities across the country continues to be the small newspaper *The Budget*, published since 1890. Its reporters are hundreds of volunteers who send in handwritten dispatches. About 80% of its 19,000 subscribers do not have electricity or telephones.

Sources: Smart (2013); Huffstutter (2009).

Human Nature Orientation

The Amish have received a unique status in the U.S. educational system. A major factor in maintaining control of change was the dominant culture's allowing the Amish their own educational system. The practical skills of everyday life—spelling, English, German, mathematics, geography, and health—are taught in small private schools. Parents are involved in the curriculum, instruction, and administration of the schools. Religion is not taught in the schools as it is believed to be too important to be taught there instead of in the family and church. After the eighth grade, Amish children may continue education at home on the farm to learn the practical skills of providing for family and community. Further education is discouraged as it instills feelings of superiority that would lead to placing the needs of the self over those of the community.

© Can Stock Photo Inc./wico

What makes it possible for the Amish to remain a distinct culture separate from the culture around them?

Relational Orientation

Amish youth must choose to accept an Amish identity. During what is called "time out," or rumspringa, teenage Amish, beginning at the age of 16, are given quite a bit of freedom to investigate the outside world before deciding whether to rejoin the church for the rest of their lives. Young men may obtain driver's licenses, travel to large cities, and adopt contemporary clothing. Occasional instances of drug possession have even been reported. To marry an Amish woman, though, a man must agree to be baptized and take up the responsibilities of being an adult member of the Amish community. Some 80% to 90% make the decision to join the church and choose the Amish way of life (Shachtman, 2006). Amish society is male dominated. Women are respected and run the household, but the men have the final say.

Indigenous Cultures

Today there are 5,000 indigenous cultures worldwide totaling some 300 million people, or 5% of the world's population. At the same time that there are pressures on indigenous cultures brought on by contact with other cultures, individual indigenous peoples are asserting their cultural identities and claiming ancestral lands and the right to control their own destinies.

At different times in different countries, policies have ranged from forced assimilation to forced separation. In Canada, after the 1812 war, British colonists no longer required indigenous peoples as allies, explorers, or traders. Instead, they came to be seen as obstacles to Canadian settlement. From the early 19th century on, Canada rejected extermination

Global Voices

There were indigenous people living on this land [Taiwan] 400 years ago. Those people had their own life, their own languages, culture, customs and lands to live on. Then, without their permission, a different group of people [Chinese] suddenly came onto that land.

—Taiwanese President Tsai Ingwen's apology to her nation's 530,000 indigenous Austronesian people to mark the government's role in decades of forced cultural assimilation for its "Indian problem" but pursued a policy of absorbing the peoples by undermining the cultural distinctiveness of aboriginal society and subjecting the indigenous peoples to the rules and values of Euro-Canadian culture.

Focus on Theory 11.1

Nondominant Groups and Communication

Critical researchers focus on the politics of identity and the struggles of nondominant groups (Y. Y. Kim, 2005). Muted group theory posits that the leaders of culture determine the dominant communication system of the entire culture that supports their perception of the world. Orbe's (1998) theory of co-cultural communication argues that what are called co-cultures are in fact subordinate groups within the culture. People in co-cultures (as Orbe uses the term) when talking to people of the dominant group communicate using different strategies, such as working to build connections with the dominant group or trying to "pass" as members of the dominant group.

Mexico's indigenous peoples have been denied rights for centuries. It is estimated that by the 15th century, 40 million or more people lived in the Americas. These people varied greatly in physical appearance and culture. Different civilizations dominated at different times. Perhaps the most complex of these were the Maya, with a reliable agricultural base, a polytheistic religion, and developing mathematics, astronomy, and other sciences. As the Mayan culture declined, others arose, including the Aztecs, who, through military organization and trade, administered a large territory of some 10 million people. The Aztecs' special strength was synthesizing and using cultural elements from many conquered peoples. Its great city Tenochtitlán (Mexico City today) had a population of 100,000—four or five times that of contemporary London, Madrid, or Paris (Meier & Ribera, 1993).

The Aztecs were soon to meet the Spaniards, a people with a similar history of cultural synthesis. Spanish influence in the Americas was largely one of cultural blending rather than of cultural extinction, as occurred on the North American East Coast. Though the Spanish imposed government, religion, and technology, the basic Mesoamerican culture remained. While the heroes of Mexico's Aztec past are honored in monuments, the living descendants of the Aztecs are not allowed to eat in some of the country's finest restaurants. From the Spanish founding of Mexico, social class has been determined by racial purity (i.e., those born in Spain at the top and full-blooded Indians on the bottom).

In the United States, Congress passed the Indian Removal Act in 1820 to force American Indians west of the Mississippi River. Later, as colonists moved westward, the U.S. government sent many tribes to reservations and passed legislation intended to integrate American Indians into the rest of U.S. society. Only English-speaking teachers were employed to assimilate indigenous children into the dominant culture (Baron, 1990; Piatt, 1990).

Similar methods were widely used all over the world in an effort to assimilate indigenous peoples. In Taiwan, aboriginal tribes were dispossessed, forced to adopt Chinese names, and punished for speaking their languages. In Paraguay, the government banned Guaran from schools and required teachers to use only Spanish. The Sami people in Norway were prevented from renting or buying state-owned land by a 1902 law that required use of the Norwegian language in everyday life. In Australia, under a government policy that ran from 1910 until 1971, as many as 10% of all Aboriginal children were taken from their families to speed the process of assimilation. In countries all over the world, it was expected that the indigenous cultures and languages would eventually disappear naturally or by absorption into the population of an emerging national culture (Cobo, 1987).

Beginning in the second half of the 20th century, the situation began to shift. In the 1950s, Mexico was the scene of serious discussions, and by the middle of the 1960s, the policy had changed to early literacy in one's native language and teaching Spanish as a second language (Stavenhagen, 1990). The Zapatista rose up in the southern Mexican state of Chiapas in 1994 to protest the repression of Indians across the country. Mexico's army fought to contain the guerrilla movement. In 1996, the government of Mexico signed an agreement to amend the state's and nation's constitutions to guarantee respect for Indian languages and culture. This agreement marks the first time that the original peoples of Mexico were recognized as equals.

The situation is different in Brazil: Brazil's indigenous population was approaching near-extinction in the mid-20th century (100,000 people in the 1950s). Today, the population has grown to 350,000. Eleven percent of the landmass of the country (260 million acres) is now reserved for the Indians. On the other hand, under Brazil's constitution, the Indians are not full citizens. Instead, they are considered legal minors with the status of a protected species.

In Norway, Sami was allowed back as a language of instruction in schools in 1959. In 1969 and 1990, the right of indigenous children to be instructed in the indigenous language was legally formalized. Now, Norway, Finland, and Sweden have elected Sami consultative "parliaments." Finally, in New Zealand, numerous court decisions confirmed that the Māori language is protected under the Treaty of Waitangi as a *te reo Māori,* a valued Māori treasure. Thus, in 1987, Māori was made an official language.

Without question, early laws had as an objective the assimilation of indigenous peoples into national cultures as quickly as possible and at any human cost. The trend today is decidedly different. Indigenous peoples are encouraged or forced to learn a national official language but also are allowed to, and in some cases helped to, develop and promote indigenous languages and cultures.

Focus on Culture 11.1

Indigenous Cultures and Language

Koassaati naathihilka-wailiip aatko-aat-hommok iist-stilka-laho

We are told that as long as we can speak Koasati we will remain Indians

—The Coushatta Tribe of Louisiana

The United Nations Declaration on the Rights of Indigenous Peoples unequivocally suggests that indigenous peoples should occupy a privileged political and legal position. Indigenous peoples should have the right to autonomous governing and legal structures and institutions, including some power of taxation and control over resources and the right to use indigenous languages. In the cases where assimilation policies approached cultural genocide, such as in Australia and North America, the language of the declaration suggests that the governments could be obligated to assist in correcting past injustices and practices (Mikkelsen, 2010).

Assimilation: United States

Immigration and acculturation policies in the United States have included forced separation, most notably for slaves and their descendants, to assimilation for groups such as German immigrants, and now to acceptance of integration of subcultures, in which maintaining important aspects of one's original culture is accepted. The idea of the United States as one nation of peoples of many backgrounds has been a popular cultural myth. The United States proclaims the Latin phrase *E pluribus unum* ("from many, one") on its coins to symbolize the desire that the many will see themselves as one. Many wrote of the diversity of the country's creation. Ralph Waldo Emerson (1909–1914) wrote of a "new race" drawing "the energy of Irish, Germans, Swedes, Poles, and Cossacks, and all the European tribes—of the Africans, and the Polynesians" (p. 116). Herman Melville (1849/1976) wrote, "On this Western Hemisphere all tribes and peoples are forming into one federated whole" (p. 239). More recently, former British prime minister Margaret Thatcher said of the United States that "no other nation has so successfully combined people of different races and nations within a single culture."

Library of Congress

An extreme example of segregation occurred during World War II. After Japan attacked Pearl Harbor, President Franklin D. Roosevelt signed Executive Order 9066, which led to the forced evacuation of about 120,000 people of Japanese descent from the West Coast and their relocation to 10 internment centers. Approximately two-thirds of those relocated were U.S. citizens. This picture is of a Sunday school class at Manzanar Relocation Center in California. In 1998, President Bill Clinton apologized for the internment of more than 2,200 people of Japanese ancestry from 13 Latin American countries. One former internee said, "The worst part of camp was the psychological effect of being rejected by the public as an American citizen, an equal."

Melting Pot Concept

The phrase most often used to describe the assimilation of the early immigrants into the United States is *melting pot*, which comes from Israel Zangwill's popular 1908 play *The Melting Pot*. The melting pot of old included English, German, Irish, French, and Italian immigrants and encouraged ethnic uniformity. Patriotic significance was placed on learning English and becoming "American." You seldom think of those of English, German, Irish, French, and Italian descent as ethnic groups because throughout the generations, these groups have become assimilated into a somewhat homogenized society.

In the 1750s, Benjamin Franklin was worried that Pennsylvania German immigrants were not learning English nor adopting the new country's culture. Yet today, more than 42.8 million people in the United States claim German heritage, making German-Americans the largest ancestry group in the United States, and yet that culture isn't particularly evident today. Automaker Henry Ford established for his company the "English Melting Pot School." The graduation ceremony featured the automaker's foreign-born employees, dressed in Old World costumes and carrying signs noting their birthplace, marching into a large, kettle-shaped prop labeled "Melting Pot." Moments later, the same people would emerge dressed in neat business suits and waving small U.S. flags.

Immigration has made the United States home to many ethnic groups. U.S. citizenship is easy to acquire, is hard to lose, and imposes few duties.

Integration: United States

A century ago, there may have been greater consensus as to cultural norms, religion, and what it meant to be a "true American." The traditional melting pot assimilation theory held that ethnic identity largely disappeared in one or two generations after arriving in the United States. Today, there may no longer be a consensus as to the cultural norms, religion, and behavior that define a U.S. culture. More recent immigrants experience less pressure to immediately learn fluent English and otherwise become Americanized than did earlier immigrants.

U.S. residents today increasingly recognize their own immigrant roots. Acculturation is defined more in terms of integration than assimilation. Today's immigrants find a much more ethnically

Focus on Theory 11.2

Cultural Identity as Fixed or Evolving

Generally, self-identity theories share the concept of self-consciousness in a network of relations with others or a socially constructed "object." Cultural identity can provide a sense of historical connection and a sense of connection to others. Such an understanding tends to be a somewhat stable concept of the group that gives little recognition to individual variations within the group and the evolving nature of cultural identity throughout a person's life. Most researchers have conceived of cultural identity as an ascription-based, monolithic entity exclusive to a particular group of people (Y. Y. Kim, 2005). Collier and Thomas (1988) focused on identity negotiation as a key to intercultural communication competence.

Focus on Theory 11.3

Cultivation Theory

Gerbner, Morgan, and Signorielli (1986) identified television as having a homogenizing effect in a culture called *cultivation*. Television, it is believed, is a common experience of many and, therefore, provides a shared way of viewing the world. Cultivation analysis focuses on a totality communicated by television over a long period. Cultivation analysis contends that subcultures may retain their separate values, but the overriding images on television affect all social groups and subcultures. The contention is that culture becomes homogenized or mainstreamed through television. In other words, television is a stabilizing force for a culture.

In what ways do you believe today's media use has modified cultivation theory? Does social media have the same effect?

diversified country. In some areas, people of similar ethnic origin reside together in large communities. People in the United States today can maintain some original cultural identity and values and participate meaningfully in the larger society. Some argue that the melting pot myth was never true. Today, you are more likely to hear the salad analogy or stew analogy to suggest that the elements maintain their own taste or identity but exist together to create the whole.

English-Speaking Cultures

| Table 11.1 | People in United States Reporting Ancestry From English-Speaking Countries, 2015 |

Ancestry	Number
Irish	32,713,324
English	23,959,441
British	1,397,632
Jamaican	1,097,196
Canadian	673,137
Guyanese	251,101

Source: U.S. Census Bureau (2015).

Note: Other native English language countries represented fewer than 100,000 respondents each.

Let's look at an example of immigration and cultural identity. English is the native language in Great Britain, Ireland, Canada, the United States, Guyana, Australia, New Zealand, and the Caribbean countries of Bahamas, Barbados, Grenada, Jamaica, and Trinidad and Tobago. Table 11.1 shows the number of people in 2015 who identified their ancestry as from one of these countries.

That's a total of some 20% of the U.S. population in 2015 who shared an important part of their identity—that they claim an ancestry from an English-speaking country, yet we lack a label for them. Should they be called "English-speaking"? Other people living in the United States are English-speaking, so that label isn't descriptive. Should they be called "Americans"? Other people living in the United States would claim that label as well. How about "Amerienglish"? What other important cultural identifications do the Amerienglish share? Do they share ethnicity? Not necessarily. Do they share food or dress preferences? Not necessarily. We have created a term to describe a group based on ancestry and language use, but that term negates other important aspects of the peoples' cultures and is probably a term people in that group would reject if the Census Bureau were to classify them as such.

Were the Census Bureau to use the term *Amerienglish*, we might well consider that a form of othering as an identity imposed on a group by the powerful Census Bureau. Over time we might see the term becoming more commonly used and we might even begin to see media and advertising directed specifically to the Amerienglish. We might begin to see studies that break out data to show, for example, how alcohol consumption among the Amerienglish compares to other groups. Forty years after such common use, could we then say that the term identifies a culture within a culture? Questions to ask at this point are: Why did the English language become identified with the dominant culture of the United States? What are the consequences of labeling other groups by an ancestry and language use label other than English?

Spanish-Speaking Cultures

Spanish is the official or de facto official language in Spain, Mexico, Colombia, Peru, Venezuela, Ecuador, Guatemala, Cuba, Bolivia, Honduras, Paraguay, El Salvador, Costa Rica, Panama, Equatorial Guinea, Argentina, Chile, Dominican Republic, Nicaragua, and Uruguay. Figure 11.1 shows

Focus on Skills 11.1

The Immigrant Experience

It can be said for many of the world's countries that (almost) everyone living within the geographical boundaries of that country is an immigrant or descended from an immigrant, whether that immigrant arrived 1 year ago, 5 years ago, 50 years ago, 500 years ago, or 15,000 years ago. Determine what you can of your immigrant experience.

1. What were the originating country and the reasons for migration?
2. What were the receiving country and its immigration policy at that time?
3. Was language an issue?
4. What do you know of the acculturation experience?
5. If there have been generations of descendants, how has the experience of each generation been different?

Figure 11.1 Hispanic or Latino Population by Specific Origin, 2015

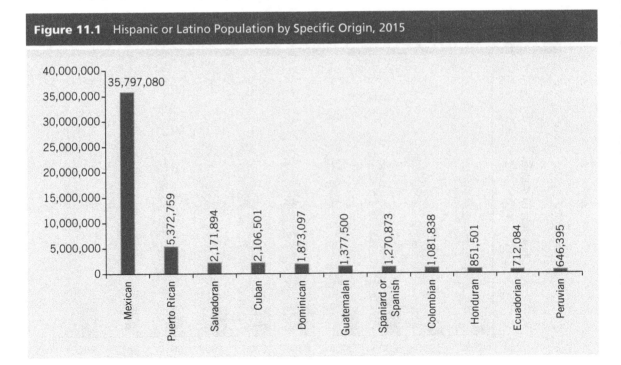

Source: U.S. Census Bureau (2015).

Note: Other Spanish-speaking countries represented fewer than 500,000 respondents each.

the number of people in the 2015 American Community Survey who identify their ancestry as from one of these countries.

That's a total of some 56 million or 18% of the U.S. population in 2015 who shared an important part of their identity—that they claim ancestry from a Spanish-speaking country. However, estimates of the number of people in the United States who speak Spanish regardless of claims of ancestry is much less, at 37 million or roughly 12% of the U.S. population.

The future of Spanish language use in the United States is still developing. The traditional pattern of other non-English languages such as Italian, German, and Polish was that the number of speakers declined while the number of people who traced their ancestry from those countries increased. The traditional pattern for these countries was that the first-generation immigrants preferred to speak their first language. The second generation was bilingual. The third generation was increasingly monolingual. It is possible that Spanish may have a different pattern. A 2012 survey showed that 95% of Hispanic adults said it is important that future generations speak Spanish (P. Taylor, Lopez, Martinez, & Velasco, 2012). However, as Figure 11.2 shows, the number of Hispanics who speak Spanish at home is declining, and the number who speak only English at home is increasing.

Overall, a declining share of Hispanics are speaking Spanish at home. In 2000, some 30% of Hispanics ages 5 to 17 grew up in homes where only English was spoken. That increased to 37% by

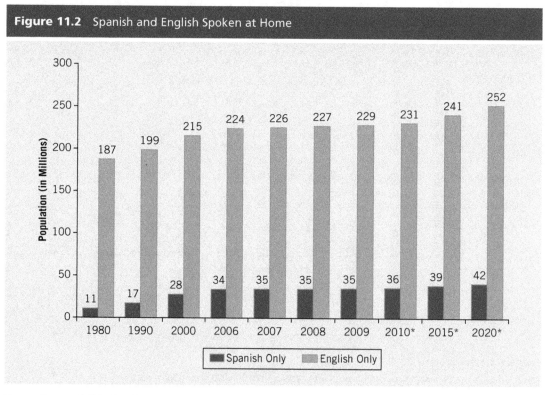

Figure 11.2   Spanish and English Spoken at Home

Source: Ortman & Shin (2011).

*projected numbers.

2014. That change is increasingly driven by the growth in the Hispanic population primarily by U.S. births rather than new immigrants. Of Hispanics born in the United States, 51% are English dominant (P. Taylor et al., 2012).

The evolving use of Spanish may impact identity and labeling. Labeling has a long history in the Americas. For example, Jose Vanegas, one of the original 46 settlers of Los Angeles, was first classified as an Indian in the Spanish census. Later, he was classified as mestizo. Similarly, Jose Navarro was first classified as mestizo in 1790 but later reclassified as Spanish. That fluidity continues today. Tanno (1994) and Mirandé and Tanno (1993) have called attention to the meaning and importance of ethnic labels. Remember from the discussion of othering the importance of labels imposed by an external, more powerful group or self-identified labels. For example, *Spanish speaking, Spanish surnamed, Spanish origin, Hispanic, Chicano, Latino,* and *Mexican-American* have all been used interchangeably to refer to that culture in the United States whose members originally came from a Spanish-speaking country. Antonio Guernica (1982) offers these distinctions:

- Spanish speaking refers to the population with the ability to speak and comprehend the Spanish language, whether as a primary or secondary language. This term encompasses non-Hispanics as well as Hispanics.
- Spanish surnamed refers to the population segment with last names that have been identified as Spanish by the U.S. Census Bureau.
- Spanish origin refers to that segment of the population that came from a Spanish-speaking country or that has ancestors who came from a Spanish-speaking country. This term does not indicate that the person is Spanish speaking or personally identifies with Hispanic cultures.
- Hispanic came into common use as a result of the 1980 census to identify various U.S. Spanish speakers' shared roots to Spain. It refers to that population segment with the capability of speaking and comprehending the Spanish language, with ancestry based in a Spanish-speaking country, and that identify with Hispanic cultures. The Census Bureau considers it an ethnicity rather than a race, so in the U.S. census, someone of any race can be Hispanic. The term has been rejected by some because its use was imposed by the government as a way to identify Spanish-speaking people in the census.
- Chicano most often refers to that segment of the population born in the United States but with ancestors who came from Mexico. The label Chicano has a political meaning and is often used to represent a nationalist or separatist identity and a commitment to disassimilation (Sedano, 1980).
- Latino most often refers to Spanish-speaking individuals who came from, or whose ancestors came from, anywhere in Latin America. The term is more commonly used in the U.S. Southwest.
- Mexican-American, a term similar to Irish-American, indicates a person from a specific country of origin who is in the assimilation process (Hurstfield, 1978).
- Tejano is a term in widespread use in Texas to refer to people born in Texas of Mexican ancestry.

As Tanno (1994) argues, none of these terms is accurate and yet all are. An individual could identify with one or more of these at different times in her or his life and be enriched by the opportunities each provides.

Map 11.2   Most Commonly Spoken Language Other Than English

Source: Data from the American Community Survey.

Any single label that includes Spaniards, Cubans, Mexican-Americans, Latinos, and Puerto Ricans groups together peoples with very diverse histories and cultures. A Black Cuban, a Uruguayan Jew, and a multiracial Peruvian all living in New York City share a heritage of language that originated in Spain. Is it accurate to say they are all Hispanic? Important differences are lost; for example, Cinco de Mayo is a Mexican holiday, not a Hispanic holiday.

The Pew Research Center (2014a) conducted a National Survey of Latinos, which focused on language use and identities. Overall, respondents saw Spanish as important, but they also believed being bilingual is important. Which label did the respondents accept?

- Half (51%) preferred to use their family's country of origin (i.e., Cuban or Salvadoran over the term *Hispanic* or *Latino*). One-quarter (24%) used the term *Hispanic* or *Latino* to describe their identity; one-fifth (21%) used the term *American* most often.
- When asked if the term *Hispanic* or *Latino* is preferred, half (51%) had no preference. Of those who had a preference, 33% preferred *Hispanic* versus 14% who preferred *Latino*.
- Most respondents did not believe Hispanics share a common culture. Most (69%) said Hispanics have many different cultures, while not quite a third (29%) agreed that Hispanics share a common culture (P. Taylor et al., 2012).

Generally, then, while the Spanish language is important, more than half would prefer to be identified by their country of origin as the majority believe the category Hispanic includes many different cultures.

Spanish has spread across the world for 500 years but has maintained an amazing coherence of grammar and vocabulary. Nonetheless, the interface of Spanish and English languages is producing Spanglish (or Tex-Mex or Cubonics)—a practice called code switching by linguists to refer to changing from one language to another for a single word, phrase, clause, or entire sentence (Eastman, 1992; Lipski, 1985). Spanglish used by Hispanics reflects both a knowledge of Spanish and an awareness of the U.S. culture. A teenage girl, for example, may admonish her mother by saying, "*No seas tan* old-fashioned!" Usually, the simpler word from either language is used. For example, "income tax" is used for *impuesto sobre la renta* and "*ir al* supermarket" replaces a longer explanation for leaving. Code switching goes both ways. In areas with a high concentration of Hispanics, Spanish words are used by those who do not speak Spanish. Examples are *gracias, bueno, amigo,* and *por favor.* Other words move into more general mainstream use through popular literature and music.

The major consequence of labeling is categorization, the act of setting those labeled peoples as separate and apart. Alberto Gonzalez (1990) has identified in labeling the themes of inclusion and separation. Inclusion is the desire for belonging on the basis of one's worth; separation is the fragmentation of not belonging, of being, for example, Mexican-American—not Mexican, not American, but somehow both. These themes can be seen in complex feelings about language use and in feelings about ethnic identity and assimilation.

Hispanic Culture Within the U.S. Culture

For the remainder of this chapter, the term *Hispanic* will be used, as a convenience, to refer to U.S. Spanish speakers with ancestry based in a Spanish-speaking country.

Global Voices

The interesting thing about Hispanics is that you will never meet us in Latin America. You may meet Chileans and Peruvians and Mexicans. You will not meet Hispanics. If you inquire in Lima or Bogotá about Hispanics, you will be referred to Dallas. For "Hispanic" is a gringo contrivance, a definition of the world according to European patterns of colonization.

—Richard Rodriguez (2003, p. 65), editor at Pacific News Service and essayist for PBS's *NewsHour* and *The Chronicle of Higher Education*

Global Voices

Mexicans have been the target of prejudice and racism. Arguing against the 1848 Peace Treaty of Guadalupe-Hidalgo, Senator John C. Calhoun (1848) of South Carolina said on the Senate floor,

"We have never dreamt of incorporating into our Union any but the Caucasian race—the free white race. To incorporate Mexico, would be the very first instance of the kind of incorporating an Indian race; for more than half of the Mexicans are Indians, and the other is composed chiefly of mixed tribes. I protest against such a union as that! Ours, sir, is the Government of a white race. The greatest misfortunes of Spanish America are to be traced to the fatal error of placing these colored races on an equality with the white race. That error destroyed the social arrangement which formed the basis of society. . . . Are we to overlook this fact? Are we to associate with ourselves as equals, companions, and fellow-citizens, the Indians and mixed race of Mexico? Sir, I should consider such a thing as fatal to our institutions."

Global Voices

I'm for making a cantonal system. The massive waves of Latinos sweeping across the border are quite correctly taking what they call "the occupied lands"—Southern California, Arizona, New Mexico, Texas. They're reoccupying it, and have no particular interest in the Anglo culture. . . . My theory is that, essentially, the thing is never going to integrate anymore. . . . We're going to end up with, if we're lucky, something like Switzerland with sort of Spanish cantons. . . . I like the diversity of it.

—Gore Vidal, novelist and grandson of Senator Thomas Gore (quoted in Scheer, 1991, p. M3)

[Samuel P. Huntington argues that] the continuing Latin American immigration could create a cultural clash between Hispanics and Anglos that would "replace the racial division between blacks and whites as the most serious cleavage in U.S. society." He warns that Mexicans, in particular, will increasingly refuse to assimilate into the mainstream and will create "an autonomous, culturally and linguistically distinct and economically self-reliant bloc." The U.S. would be divided into two peoples, two cultures, and two languages.

—Gregory Rodriguez (2004, p. 1)

The total U.S. Hispanic population of some 57 million (17% of U.S. residents as of 2015) is regionally concentrated according to national origin and exhibits differences (Szalay & Inn, 1987). States with over 1 million Hispanic inhabitants are California, Texas, Florida, New York, Illinois, Arizona, New Jersey, and Colorado. Since 2005 there are more Puerto Rican–origin Hispanics in the U.S. states than living on the island of Puerto Rico. More than 21% of the U.S. Puerto Rican population is found in New York. The Cuban population is primarily concentrated in Florida. The Central and South American population in the United States is dispersed geographically, with most centered in large urban centers such as New York, San Francisco, Los Angeles, Chicago, and Miami.

The Hispanic population in the United States became the subject of general-circulation media. The October 16, 1978, issue of *Time* magazine had "Hispanic Americans: Soon the Biggest Majority" emblazoned on the cover. *Newsweek* and *U.S. News & World Report* carried similar stories. In 1980, CBS-TV newscaster Walter Cronkite anchored a series of reports on the U.S. Hispanic population. Generally, these reports have taken the same approach as one would in writing about a foreign country and often present a stereotype of poverty.

Values

In the Pew Hispanic Center's National Survey of Latinos, it was reported that most of the respondents did not believe Hispanics share a common culture. Studies cited in this section argue that Hispanics do share some important cultural values.

Hispanics are often referred to as family and group-oriented compared to Anglo-Americans (Sabogal, Marín, Otero-Sabogal, Marín, & Perez-Stable, 1987). The extended family is often a major source of identity and source of emotional support (Clutter & Zubieta, 2009; Griffith & Villavicencio, 1985). Close relationships, cohesiveness, and cooperativeness with other family members are valued. This has been described as a collectivist culture with strong family values (*familismo*).

It is also contended that the cultural value of power distance or hierarchical relationships is important in that many Hispanics place value on *respecto,* or deferring to those who are viewed as authority figures. In the area of uncertainty avoidance, Hispanics have been described as accepting *fatalismo,* or taking each day as it comes, accepting the uncertainty inherent in life, that the individual can do little to alter fate. Consistent with that is a stress on relationship politeness, pleasantness, and avoidance of hostile confrontation (*simpatia*) with a flexible attitude to constraints of time.

And for many Hispanics, religion and spirituality play a critical role. Strong shared cultural values bind Hispanic individuals and families together into a larger community.

Cultural Identity and Media

Though many Spanish-origin individuals can neither read Spanish nor understand it when spoken, Hispanic cultures in the United States have a rich media—Spanish-language magazines, newspapers, radio, television, and social media. Hispanic media, like other forms of minority media, provide a forum where minority issues can be freely discussed (Downing, 1990). It is these media that help continue the culture and support an integrated status.

Print

In Mexico, well-read people patronize "libraries," which are bookstores, or pay a fee to take books from a lending library. It's frequently hypothesized that Hispanics in the United States have a reading tradition. Hispanic print media often appear in both Spanish and English to serve that portion of the culture who cannot read Spanish.

Only four other countries in the world buy more Spanish-language books than the United States. More than half of the books that Mexico exports are sent to the United States.

There are some 450 daily and weekly Hispanic newspapers in the United States—some English only, some Spanish only, and some bilingual—with a combined circulation of 12 million. As with daily English-language newspapers, circulation of the Spanish-language dailies has declined. The weeklies originate in regions with high Hispanic populations—Chicago, Sacramento, Los Angeles, Ft. Lauderdale, Riverside (California), San Francisco, and Orlando (Guskin & Mitchell, 2011).

There are myriad Hispanic magazines. Traditionally, the most successful Spanish-language magazines in national distribution have been geared toward Hispanic women and entertainment. *Vanidades* entered the U.S. market in 1961, making it the first Spanish-language women's magazine available nationally. Since then, the number of magazines has grown and diversified, although those for women retain prominence. The New York–based *Latina*, a bilingual quarterly for women, started publication in 1996, as did *People en Español* (the most widely read Spanish-language magazine). Others that lead in advertising revenue include *TV y Novelas*, *Ser Padres*, and *Siempre Mujer* (Guskin & Mitchell, 2011).

Global Voices

In 1800, if a reasonable person had asked which would be the dominant power in North America in 200 years, the logical answer would have been Mexico. It was far more developed and sophisticated.

There is a fundamentally geopolitical reason not to compare Mexican immigration with "immigration from distant countries." . . . Not only is Mexico adjacent to the United States, but in many cases the land the migrants are moving into is land that once belonged to Mexico. When Mexicans move northward, they are not necessarily breaking ties with their homeland. Indeed, within the borderland, which can extend hundreds of miles into both countries, the movement north can require minimal cultural adjustment. . . . Within the borderland, they have the option of retaining their language and their national identity, distinct from whatever legal identity they adopt. This state of affairs creates serious tension between the legal border and the cultural border.

—Excerpt(s) from *The Next Decade: Where We've Been ... and Where We're Going* by George Friedman, copyright © 2011 by George Friedman. Used by permission of Doubleday, an imprint of the Knopf Doubleday Publishing Group, a division of Penguin Random House LLC. All rights reserved.

Radio

While Spanish-language newspapers have been largely owned by members of the Hispanic community, radio stations that broadcast in Spanish were at first owned by majority-culture entrepreneurs (A. Rodriguez, 1999). In 2007, there were 872 Spanish-language radio stations, more than double the number from 10 years earlier (Arbitron, 2008), and by 2009, the count was 1,323 stations (Guskin & Mitchell, 2011). Local independent radio stations are being replaced with national network affiliates. Univision owns 70 stations, followed by Entravision with 48 stations. Historically, radio has been an important medium in Spanish-speaking communities as more people can speak Spanish than can read it. Spanish-language stations serve as a primary source of news and information for much of the audience. Spanish-language radio programming has been said to create a strong emotional tie to the Hispanic culture as Hispanics have higher-than-average station loyalty. Spanish-language radio stations frequently have close community involvement, providing information on voter registration, breast cancer screening, and the Better Business Bureau. A broadcast announcement about a family without housing or food because of fire or flood brings quick and generous responses.

Some stations have experimented with a bilingual format that attempts to bridge the two cultures by speaking both languages. These stations mix diverse musical styles with news and public affairs segments that focus on such issues as immigration, economic opportunities, and the problems related to growing up in two cultures. The bilingual announcers switch often and effortlessly from Spanish to English and back again—sometimes in midsentence. This is code switching in action. The changes are brief enough that a speaker of only one language never feels lost, and the context provided by the language one knows encourages learning the other language (Albarran & Hutton, 2009; Downing, 1990). "And when it comes to music, some 30% of third-generation Latino youths report that at least half of the songs they listen to are in Spanish" (Pew Hispanic Center, 2009, p. 4).

Television

Hispanic television now rivals non-Hispanic television in many of the larger cities. In 1961, Mexican mogul Emilio Azcárraga Vidaurreta bought KCOR-TV in San Antonio, the nation's first Spanish-language TV station. Spanish International Network (SIN) grew in one decade to nine stations and experimented with cable outlets, microwave and satellite interconnections, and repeater television stations (A. Rodriguez, 1999).

By early 1982, there were 12 Spanish-language television stations in the United States. Ten of them were SIN affiliates. SIN's programming was carried also by more than 100 cable systems and translators (low-power repeater stations). Hallmark Cards bought SIN in 1987, renaming it Univision, and then in 1992 announced its sale to an investment group linked with the huge Mexican media conglomerate Grupo Televisa, making it the dominant force in Spanish-language broadcasting in the United States. Univision has since gone private to become the fifth largest U.S. prime-time network. Univision, with some 2.8 million nightly viewers, now surpasses one or more of the English language networks in some age groups at some times, some weeks.

The second-place Spanish-language network, Telemundo, was created by Saul Steinberg and is based in Miami. In 2001, NBC purchased Telemundo for $2.7 billion (NBCUniversal is now Comcast). In addition to Univision and Telemundo, there are now several major Spanish-language broadcasters, including Estrella TV and Mega TV. To demonstrate to advertisers that people were watching Spanish-language television, Nielsen Media Research, with financing by Univision and Telemundo, began to develop a national Hispanic television rating service to help Spanish-language television compete for advertising revenue. One consequence of these efforts is the reinforcement of the label *Hispanic* to refer to a single culture within a culture (A. Rodriguez, 1999). By 2007, Nielsen ended separate rating services as Hispanic viewers were fully integrated into its sampling methodology.

In Los Angeles, Univision's Spanish-language 34 KMEX regularly wins news ratings over English-language stations. In New York, WXTV has more viewers younger than 49 for news than its English-language competitors. In Miami, Univision's WLTV in 1998 was the first Spanish-language station to get top ratings in both news and prime time. Spanish-language programming produced in the United States is, however, basically limited to local news

AP Photo/Wilfredo Lee

Hillary Clinton and Bernie Sanders debated on Univision in the 2016 presidential campaign.

programs, talk shows, and public affairs presentations. Imported programming offers *novelas* (which, unlike U.S. soap operas, usually come to a conclusion within a few months), news shows, movies, magazine-style shows, children's shows, talk shows, and variety. The Nielsen study of Hispanic television viewing showed that Hispanics watch very different TV shows than the general public does (A. Rodriguez, 1999). Adults prefer Univision and Telemundo to the English-language network shows three to one. Of English-language shows, only one in four of the top 10 shows preferred by the general public rated in the top 10 for Hispanics. The Nielsen study showed that Spanish language was the most important factor in reaching the Hispanic audience. It's no surprise, then, that the major English-language networks began to program for Hispanics.

Spanish-Language Internet and Social Media

In 2009, 76% of Hispanics owned a mobile phone. That increased to 86% by 2012 and is comparable to non-Hispanic Whites (84%) and African-American adults (90%). Mobile phone users are more likely to use English as their primary language or be bilingual. In 2009, 64% of Hispanics reported using the Internet at least occasionally. By 2012, that number was 78%. Again, the major factor was language use: Hispanic Internet users are more likely to be fluent in English than are Hispanic non-Internet users (Lopez, Gonzalez-Barrera, & Patten, 2013).

The same study reported that 76% of Hispanic Internet users access the Internet on a mobile phone, tablet, or other mobile handheld device at least occasionally (Lopez et al., 2013). An earlier Pew report showed that Hispanic mobile phone owners are more likely than non-Hispanic White mobile phone owners to access the Internet (40% vs. 34%), e-mail (36% vs. 31%), and instant messages (45% vs. 24%) from their mobile phone (Livingston, 2011). Again, language was a major factor. English-dominant and bilingual Hispanic Internet users are more likely to use a mobile phone or tablet to access the Internet.

In 2012 the bilingual multichannel network MiTu began producing original content for YouTube. By 2016 MiTu had more than 6,000 creators, 100 million global subscribers, and 2 billion monthly video views across YouTube, Facebook Video, and Vine. Former Univision executive Charlie Echeverry, then a senior advisor at MiTu, was quoted as saying that Hispanics lead the digital revolution and are the largest-growing demographic to consume media on multiple platforms.

Focus on Technology 11.2

Official U.S. Government Social Media

President Bill Clinton signed an executive order in 2000 that required federal agencies to provide Spanish-language versions of websites for people with limited English proficiency. That led to the creation of GobiernoUSA.gov, the official Spanish-language portal to federal government information and services.

The day Donald Trump became president, the Spanish language translation of the White House website went down. The White House director of media affairs said that removing the Spanish translation was not deliberate and that the page would be rebuilt. She directed people to the Twitter account @LaCasaBlanca, which publishes tweets in Spanish and English. Two months later a congressman from Southern California introduced legislation that would require the White House and all federal agencies to provide Spanish language versions of their websites.

Source: Wire & Bierman (2017).

Spanish Language and Marketing

Marketing in Spanish serves to continue and strengthen the language. Yet many attempts at marketing in Spanish have revealed translation errors. The story goes that one cigarette company advertising "low-tar" cigarettes used a phrase that translated to "low-asphalt." A Miller Lite slogan, translated, told readers that the beer was "Filling, and less delicious." And the Coors beer slogan "Get loose with Coors" became "Get the runs with Coors." As one restaurant chain learned, *nieve* means "ice cream" to some Mexican-Americans but "cocaine" to many Cuban-Americans. And in another ad, the word *point* was translated as *puta* (prostitute) instead of *punta*. An AOL Hispanic Cyberstudy concluded that Hispanics distrusted many Spanish language sites that were little more than literal translations of English content. Major advertisers moved from simple translations of their English language sites to separate sites for Hispanics. For example, the McDonald's website is www.meencanta.com, a play on its phrase "I'm lovin' it," which is memorable and sounds positive in Spanish. Advertisers discovered that marketing to the Hispanic community involves not only accurate language and images that mean something to the buyer but also cultural traditions and values. And the larger advertisers have learned that the Hispanic culture is not one culture within a culture but many, with diverse experiences, all of which are changing and evolving.

Budweiser was early to advertise in Spanish. In a 1979 print and television campaign, Budweiser advertised to three regional subgroups. In California, Texas, and the Southwest, advertisements aimed at Spanish speakers of Mexican heritage featured cowboys and cactus. In the Northeast, advertisements aimed at Puerto Ricans featured cityscapes and salsa music. And in Florida, advertisements aimed at Cubans featured palm trees, cigars, and bananas. Each advertisement featured differently accented Spanish and national origin–appropriate music. Other early advertisers, such as Procter & Gamble, Colgate-Palmolive, and Coca-Cola, used a similar strategy (A. Rodriguez, 1999). Miller Brewing,

Chevron, Nike, and Ford have all had Spanish-language ads with English subtitles on English-language television stations.

A truly national advertising campaign would need to be based on some shared culture. Coca-Cola was the first major corporation to systematize segmenting Hispanics in advertising. Coke directs its ads not to the consumer but to the Hispanic *community*, showing sensitivity toward such issues as job training and education. For the 1992 quincentenary celebration of Columbus's landing in America, Coke planned advertising recognizing Hispanic contributions to U.S. culture and featuring prominent Hispanic-Americans, such as actress Rita Moreno. To communicate an interest in the community, both Coca-Cola and PepsiCo sponsor ethnic festivals and concert tours and place special promotional displays in neighborhood stores. Pepsi sponsored the U.S. tour of Santo Domingo native Guerra and his group 4.40. Pepsi also designed a Hispanic version of its "Gotta Have It" ad campaign, featuring Guerra, tennis star Gabriela Sabatini, and comedian Paul Rodriguez.

Focus on Skills 11.2

Official Language Policies

Assume your father immigrated from Quebec to the United States in the early 1970s. At your state university you applied for a campus job in admissions. You were an active student leader on campus and feel you did well at the interview. You are surprised not to have received a job offer. You meet with the director of admissions to see how you could have done better in the interview. The director says, "You were a top candidate because of your knowledge of the campus, but we decided to go with the bilingual candidate who is fluent in Spanish." You say you understand. You go back and look at the job announcement and see that it stated, "Spanish speaking skills desired but not required."

Later your father asks you about the job. You tell him what happened and, to say the least, he is upset:

"I left Canada because if you didn't speak French you couldn't advance in Quebec and now the same thing is happening in the United States. Now there's French Canada and English Canada. Soon there will be Spanish United States and English United States. French is the official language of France and Spanish is the official language of Spain, but soon the United States will be just like Canada—two official languages and English speakers like our family will be discriminated against."

At first you don't know what to say. You recognize the struggle your father had in French-speaking Quebec. Then your father asks, "What are you going to do about this?"

1. What are your feelings about "one country, two languages"?
2. What action, if any, will you take about the job rejection?
3. What action, if any, will you take about U.S. immigration and language policies?

Budweiser and Bud Light beers sponsor Cinco de Mayo celebrations, U.S.-Mexican fiestas in honor of the 1862 Mexican victory over the French. In 1988, Budweiser began awarding about $1.5 million annually in college scholarships to Hispanic students. Because of these efforts, Anheuser-Busch has more than doubled the Hispanic market share of its nearest competitor. Appealing to similar values, Bank of America offers bilingual automated teller machines, envelopes, and checks. The check series, called *Im genes Familiares* ("Family Images"), portrays five Hispanic family scenes. The checks have "pay to the order of" and "dollars" in both English and Spanish. The message the bank wants to make is that it respects the Hispanic culture and wants to do business with Hispanics.

Burger chain Carl's Jr. simply wanted to translate its popular television ads into Spanish, but when it took its account to one of a growing number of Hispanic advertising agencies, the agency explained that the humor in the English-language ads directed at young males would confuse mothers in Hispanic households, who typically decide where families eat. The agency produced a series of highly successful ads for Carl's Jr. featuring Hispanic actors performing traditional dances. In 2001, Mattel introduced its first Hispanic-targeted brunette Barbie in the gown of the *quinceañera,* the traditional Mexican celebration marking a girl's 15th birthday.

Target's advertising campaign called "Sin Traducción," or "without translation," intentionally highlights Spanish terms and moments unique to Hispanic consumers that have no direct English translation. One television ad is called "Sobremesa," which depicts the time right after dinner when family and friends linger at dinner tables to spend quality time together. Target vice president Rick Gomez described the ad as "a way for Target to make a connection with our Hispanic guest on a deeper, more emotional level" (A. Rodriguez, 2015).

In 1989, Ford Motor Company introduced a Spanish-language version of its buying guide *Car and Truck Buying Made Easier.* Ford advertised its availability in cities with large Hispanic populations. Multilingual advertising is not new, of course, but now it seems that all types of businesses have discovered that "money talks, but it speaks many languages." Not everyone approves of the growing trend. One English-as-the-official-language organization is campaigning against multilingual customer service, arguing that it perpetuates linguistic divisiveness and separation rather than promoting assimilation.

SUMMARY

The Hmong have been called the most ill-prepared people ever to immigrate to the United States. The Hmong left the villages of Laos to resettle mainly in California, Minnesota, and Wisconsin. Many of the older Hmong immigrants lost their identity provided by their homeland and were unable to establish a new identity in the United States, and thus they are an example of marginalization. Examples of separation are the Koryo-saram, the ethnic Koreans in the post-Soviet states, and the Amish in the United States. Indigenous peoples across the world also have faced separation but at other times have faced forced assimilation.

Over the years, immigration policy in the United States has changed. The melting pot of old included English, German, Irish, French, and Italian immigrants and encouraged ethnic uniformity. Patriotic significance was placed on learning English and becoming "American." The major example today of integration in the United States is the Hispanic culture within a culture. Integration as an immigration status means maintaining aspects of one's original culture as well as becoming an integral part of the new culture.

DISCUSSION QUESTIONS

1. What reasons can you give for the Hmong integrating, assimilating, or remaining a separate culture?

2. Why do many young people who leave their Amish community return?

3. Discuss the consequences of labeling diverse peoples with terms such as *Latino* or *Hispanic*.

4. Will Spanish language use in the United States follow the same historical pattern as European language use?

5. In light of the official English movement, what are possible consequences of major political parties' candidates having Spanish-language websites?

KEY TERMS

Anabaptist	Latino	Spanglish
Beachy Amish	melting pot	Spanish origin
Chicano	Mexican-American	Spanish speaking
code switching	New Order Amish	Spanish surnamed
diaspora	Old Order Amish	stew analogy
Gelassenheit	Ordnung	Tejano
Hispanic	rumspringa	Telemundo
Hmong	salad analogy	Univision

READINGS

All readings are from *Intercultural Communication: A Global Reader* (Jandt, 2004).

Eric Aoki, "Mexican American Ethnicity in Biola, CA: An Ethnographic Account of Hard Work, Family, and Religion" (p. 112)

Richard D. Pineda, "Nuestro Espacio Cyber: The Internet as Expressive Space for Latina/os in the United States" (p. 252)

Paul Wehr and John Paul Lederach, "Mediating Conflict in Central America" (p. 345)

STUDENT STUDY SITE

ⓢSAGE edge™

Sharpen your skills with SAGE edge at edge.sagepub.com/jandt9e.

SAGE edge for Students provides a personalized approach to help you accomplish your coursework goals in an easy-to-use learning environment.

Chapter 12

©iStockphoto.com/kali9

Identity and Subgroups

In Chapter 1, you read that subgroups have similar communication dynamics as cultures and also are characterized by an identifiable distinction and by shared interests and values. Subgroups usually do not involve the same large numbers of people as cultures, and they are not necessarily thought of as transmitting values and patterns of behavior over generations in the same way as cultures. Existing within cultures, subgroups do provide members with patterns of behavior.

This chapter explains the importance of language in communicating a subgroup identity and offers the examples of British punk, corporations, and lesbians and gay men. These were chosen because they illustrate the unique intercultural communication challenges presented by all types of subgroups. Remember that each of us is a member of various subgroups throughout our lives. As you read this chapter, examine the ways your subgroups support an identity.

Argot

In previous chapters you learned about the importance of the study of a culture's language as a way to know that culture. The equivalent to learning about a subgroup is studying its specialized language, its vocabulary.

Specialized Vocabulary

According to the Sapir-Whorf hypothesis (discussed in Chapter 5), language provides the conceptual categories that influence how its speakers' perceptions are encoded and stored. That same concept is true for subgroups but on the level of vocabulary. The specialized vocabulary identifies the subgroup and establishes the group's boundaries. The specialized vocabulary of subgroups has been variously called *jargon, cant, argot,* and *slang,* sometimes depending on the perceived status of the group.

Jargon has been used to refer to the "shop talk" or technical language of an occupational subgroup, such as doctors, lawyers, and truck drivers. Jargon is the vocabulary that communicates the distinctions and specific meanings these professionals need to reference. Cant has been used to refer to the specialized vocabulary of created words or adopted words used by any nonprofessional subgroup. Argot has most often been used to refer to a jargon or cant that is primarily used as secret language among members of the subgroup only. Slang has been used to refer to the vocabulary of subgroups that has become known and accepted by the general public. As the term *argot* most clearly refers to subgroups' vocabularies that are unique and part of those groups' identities, it is used in this chapter to refer to the specialized vocabulary of subgroups regardless of how these subgroups are thought of by the dominant culture.

Argot and Subgroup Identity

The study of argot originated with the work of David Maurer (1981) in the 1930s. Before his work, observations of nonstandard language were limited to the study of regional dialects. Maurer, who had studied Sapir's work, was the first to gather, analyze, and present the speech of subgroups. He was also the first to observe that argots were not primarily secret communications used to deceive outsiders but, rather, were an important aspect of group identity.

In Maurer's (1981) studies of professional crime, he showed that individual criminals were not abnormalities but fully integrated and well-adjusted members of a subgroup. Professional crime is much more than individual identity and subgroups' lawbreaking; it's actually a way of life. Crime is not a mere facet of the life of some but is an entire way of life. Maurer's studies demonstrate that membership in the subgroup provides an identity and that the key to developing and understanding that identity is its language.

Argot and Subgroup Boundaries

Besides developing an identity, a subgroup's argot defines the boundaries of the subgroup. Because its argot can change rapidly, to be a member of the subgroup, you have to know the vocabulary. If you don't know the vocabulary, you're obviously not a member. Correct use of the argot, then, establishes the subgroup's boundary.

Gang argot, for example, serves several important functions. A special language can contribute to feeling special, to developing a group identity. Besides argot, there may be unique nonverbal symbols such as handshakes or clothing styles. The language and clothes say, "I'm somebody." Use of the argot and nonverbal codes establishes the boundaries of the gang.

A particular gang argot may appear in another part of the country when gang members move. It may die unnoticed when a gang dies out. Some argot may be absorbed into more mainstream language as slang. For example, *four-twenty* was once an obscure San Francisco Bay Area term related to marijuana. Later it began to show up nationally in advertising—420 Pale Ale, 420 Tours, and Highway 420 Radio.

Argot and Meaning

Argot has specific, unambiguous meaning for a subgroup. Air traffic controllers and seafaring radio operators have an argot that has specific, unambiguous meaning. Various scientific disciplines have developed specialized argot to express nuances of meaning precisely. That preciseness of meaning is clear only to the subgroup's members.

The medical professions have developed an argot for preciseness of meaning to avoid misunderstandings that can hurt a patient's health. A limited vocabulary has been devised to ensure that each word has a precise, unambiguous meaning.

Focus on Skills 12.1

The Misuse of Linguistic Privilege

Assume you are a gay man who assumes everyone knows you're gay. You don't go out of your way to announce it to everyone, but at the same time you don't hide it from others either. One day you are meeting with Greg, a manager from a different division than yours. The meeting is coming to an end and others have left. As the two of you are discussing what happened in the meeting, Greg says, "Just between us girls, I think. . . ." You're taken aback as you have no idea what he means, if anything, by that phrase. You don't say anything to Greg; you let it go. Several weeks pass and Greg uses the same phrase in conversation with you. This time you feel offended by his use of the phrase. Communication scholar Joseph DeVito (2013) calls this "misusing linguistic privilege" (p. 49). If one of your gay male friends had said that, you'd interpret it as a bonding behavior, an in-group phrase.

1. Using what you've read about argot, what do you think Greg was trying to communicate? Did he want to communicate to you that he is gay? Did he want to communicate to you that he knows you're gay? Did he want to communicate that he knows you're gay and he doesn't like gay people?
2. Should you say anything to Greg or let it go again?

Subgroup Media and Values

Besides argot, media use and values contribute to defining subgroup identity and boundaries. Media distributed only to members can vary widely from graffiti to newsletters, but the subgroup's argot and pictorial images will be used. To get an idea of the media of subgroups, simply visit a large newsstand. You'll find specialty magazines that appeal to a wide variety of subgroup interests. Social media have also become particularly important for most subgroups in helping maintain interaction and, hence, shared identity.

Most important, however, are common values or worldviews shared by members of the subgroup. For many subgroups, that common value may be a reaction to society's disapproval—that is, "because we're outcasts, we're together"—but for other subgroups, the shared values may grow to provide a member with a relatively complete set of guiding values and patterns of behavior.

Focus on Theory 12.1

Standpoint Theory

Each of us can have multiple group identities. Standpoint theory (Collins, 1990; Harding, 1991) focuses on how individuals understand and construct a social world. Rather than the belief that each of us must choose a single identity, standpoint theory contends that each of us can construct multiple identities. Standpoint theorists also incorporate the construct of power. Individuals whose identities include less powerful groups can see the world from that perspective as well as from the standpoint of those in power. However, those from more powerful groups never develop the need to see the world from the standpoint of the oppressed classes.

Examples of Subgroups

Just like with cultures, ethnographic and cultural approaches can be applied to subgroups. There are many reports of observations of subgroups that range in method from insider to participant observer. Insider reports can be most interesting and valuable; some have been written for self-justification or profit. Participant observer reports are based on the researcher's orderly and scientific study of a subgroup by actually becoming accepted as a member. In one sense, these reports can be viewed as self-reports of the acculturation process of learning the culture of the subgroup. Several fascinating reports of this kind are available that provide insight into the argot, nonverbal symbols, media, and values.

British Punk

A now-classic cultural studies analysis of a subgroup is Dick Hebdige's 1979 study of British punk youth culture. He described the use of random, mass-produced objects such as dog collars, safety pins, and school uniforms as a parody of consumerism.

Hebdige dates the origin of punk in the music press to the summer of 1976 as an alliance of diverse and superficially incompatible music traditions reproduced on the visual level in a clothing style. He interprets punk culture, in part, as a British White working-class "translation" of Black ethnicity and, in part, as the intentional self-construction of "otherness," which challenged, on a symbolic level, class and gender stereotypes.

Hebdige shows how subgroups develop a style through the intentional use of clothing, dance, argot, and music. Punks repositioned and recontextualized commodities by subverting the conventional uses and inventing new ones. It's how commodities are used in the subgroup that marks the subgroup off from the dominant culture. Lavatory chains became jewelry; school uniforms were covered with graffiti; sexual fetish clothing became street clothes; dance became robotic. What appeared as chaos was actually orderly.

Hebdige acknowledges that not all punks were aware of the signification on which the subgroup was based. The original or first wave of self-conscious innovators were aware and committed. The later "plastic punks" participated in the subgroup as a distraction from home, school, and work. Hebdige shows that the subgroup declined when punk's visual and verbal vocabulary became reassigned by the dominant culture as mass-produced commodities (clothing and music) and relabeled (boys wearing lipstick became "just kids dressing up" and girls in rubber dresses became "daughters just like ours").

Punk provides an interesting example of cultural diffusion. When record labels and music stores have surplus CDs, they often cut a little square notch out of the plastic case that then marks them as "remainder" products to be sold very cheaply. In China, punk was a rarity until Asian record labels and retailers trashed thousands of these surplus CDs, known in China as *dakou*. Through a network of scavengers and middlemen, these dakou CDs appeared in Chinese alternative record stores. The dakou CDs served as inspiration for launching a whole new generation of Chinese punk and Chinese punk rock bands who often sing in English to avoid Chinese censorship. And—just as in Britain—plastic punks now buy expensive punk clothing in Beijing.

Some bloggers suggest that social media is the punk of today. The mass market music industry of the 1970s was controlled and conservative. Punk of the 1970s was raw, confrontational, and passionate. It was about getting noticed and getting represented. Punk found niche audiences who listened and supported the artists. These bloggers' thesis is that today's social media has become the media for independent voices (Foster, 2011).

Corporate Cultures

One popular business buzz phrase of the 1980s was corporate culture. It has been defined as "the way we do things around here," or the set of values, goals, and priorities encouraged through the policies and procedures of the organization. Companies can act like cultures and present the same communication challenges (Deal & Kennedy, 1982; Pacanowsky & O'Donnell-Trujillo, 1982; L. Putnam & Pacanowsky, 1983; Sypher, 1985).

In Chapter 1, you read that Hofstede (1994) classified the elements of culture as symbols, heroes, rituals, and values. Organizations can have their own symbols: their own argot, their own dress codes, and status symbols recognized by insiders only. Organizational heroes are those people, dead or alive, who serve as models of the "ideal employee" or the "ideal manager" for behavior within the organization. Founders of organizations sometimes become mythical heroes later on, and incredible deeds are

©iStockphoto.com/Casarsa

Punk originated in London in the mid-1970s, recognizable by visual appearance and anarchic behavior. Scores of benefit punk concerts are held for social causes and medical research. Some punk bands run homeless shelters, mobilize youth to vote, and try to break down racial barriers.

ascribed to them: Thomas Watson Jr. at IBM, Ray Kroc at McDonald's, Walt Disney at Disney, and so on. Rituals in organizations include celebrations and also the many activities common to the organization, for example, meetings, memos, who may speak to whom, who can be late for meetings.

Focus on Skills 12.2

Subgroup Values

A close friend is an active member of an animal rights group that wants an end to all animal research regardless of the consequences. Some chapters of the group in the United Kingdom and the United States have been charged with using intimidation and harassment.

Your friend tells you that your campus has a program for middle school students to bring them on campus for tours to see what happens behind laboratory doors. The students are encouraged to examine a pig's heart on an operating table. She says that the group has secured a copy of the grant proposal that funds the program and that the only purpose of the program is to develop positive attitudes about medical research in youth to counter People for Ethical Treatment of Animals education programs that depict the use of animals in science as inhumane.

Her group is planning a protest on campus that includes a student boycott of all classes taught by professors known to conduct research using animals. You're taking a class from one of the professors who has been targeted for the boycott. Your friend asks you to join in the boycott and join the group. You say you are uncomfortable with her group's past strategies. She responds by asking what you think about your professor killing pigs just so "13-year-old boys can play with an animal's actual heart." It's clear from what she says that this is a critical incident—you're either with her or against her. You believe that animal rights has become an important part of her identity.

1. If you reject her subgroup and its values and tactics, will it be possible for your friendship to continue?
2. Do you boycott the class?
3. What do you tell your friend?

Chapter 1 also described cultures as having myths. Corporate rituals can take the form of myths within organizations. Ruth Smith and Eric Eisenberg (1987) have shown, for example, how "drama" and "family" are important myths at Disneyland.

Finally, organizations can have their own values. Hofstede (1994) makes it clear that we enter work organizations as adults with most of our values firmly entrenched, but we become socialized to the practices of the work environment. For many organizations, the value systems were established by the personality of the leader; these were value-shaping leaders with visions to excite thousands of employees.

IBM's Thomas J. Watson Jr. (1963) wrote an entire book about values in which he observed,

Consider any great organization—one that has lasted over the years—I think you will find that it owes its resiliency not to its form of organization or administrative skills, but to the power of what we call beliefs and the appeal these beliefs have for its people. This then is my thesis: I firmly believe that any organization, in order to survive and achieve success, must have a sound set of beliefs on which it premises all its policies and actions. (p. 5)

But does having clearly defined and communicated values affect the profitability of a business? The book *In Search of Excellence* (Peters, 1982) argues that the better performing companies all have a well-defined set of values. The poorly performing companies have either no explicit values or only quantified ones, such as a "percentage increase over last year." The book makes it clear that a well-defined set of values motivates and serves to direct the behavior of thousands of employees.

Corporate culture became a major factor in corporate mergers. Exxon, an otherwise low-profile company known for the *Valdez* oil spill, merged with Mobil, known for sponsoring *Masterpiece Theatre* and for full-page ads expressing views on various issues. Daimler-Benz and Chrysler formed a post-merger integration team to deal with issues as far-ranging as language, clothing, clashing values (quality vs. efficiency), labor-management relations, spending priorities, and even the German *vesper,* or employee beer break. And Time-Warner's suited executives met AOL's more casual dress style in what would prove to be an ill-fated merger that was to have brought Internet technology to Time-Warner.

Global Voices

When several workers at Disneyland's Jungle Cruise lost their jobs for telling their own jokes with contemporary references instead of following the company's official script, Disneyland issued a brief statement:

"Our philosophy is that Disneyland is very much a theatrical house or stage, which means we view our park as having both onstage and backstage presence. We entertain our guests with quality family entertainment and put on performances every day. Our goal is to deliver a consistent quality show daily."

—Disneyland spokeswoman, as quoted in the *Los Angeles Times* (Grad, 1997)

Case Study: Southwest Airlines

Herb Kelleher, an attorney in a San Antonio, Texas, law firm, along with Rollin King, developed the idea for Southwest Airlines in 1966. The meeting at which the idea was born is now part of the company's mythology, as the story is told and retold like a legend. The plan, penciled on a cocktail napkin, was to establish the airline as an intrastate carrier between the cities of Dallas, Houston, and San Antonio. It overcame overwhelming resistance from the major interstate carriers, but it was probably that resistance itself that helped shape the character of the company as reflecting efficiency, sound business decisions, and fun.

The Southwest corporate culture has evolved through the years, undoubtedly influenced by the gregarious, self-depreciating, chain-smoking, whiskey-drinking Kelleher, who was known to dress as Elvis and arrive at Southwest parties on a

Pam Francis/The LIFE Images Collection/Getty Images

Former Southwest Airlines CEO Herb Kelleher

Harley. Although no longer in a management role, Chairman Emeritus Kelleher still has the adulation of the Southwest workforce. Now, employees eagerly await the unveiling of current CEO Gary Kelly's Halloween costume every year. The strong Southwest corporate culture is carefully reinforced in its hiring policy. Recruiters look for a certain "Southwest Spirit" in every job candidate. Southwest rejects most job applicants to find those who will not only fit, but thrive, in the Southwest culture.

The Southwest story was turned into a children's book, *Gumwrappers and Goggles,* by Winifred Barnum (1982). In the story, a small jet, TJ Love, is sued by two larger jets to stop him from flying. It just so happens that TJ Love's colors are those of Southwest and the two larger jets' colors are those of Braniff and Continental (competing airlines). The attorney who helps TJ Love resembles Herb Kelleher. The book was adapted into a stage musical, *Show Your Spirit,* that played only in cities serviced by Southwest.

The airline has never laid off workers and its voluntary turnover rate has never topped 3%. Today it operates 719 aircraft, has 53,200 employees, and carries more passengers on U.S. domestic routes than any other. Its corporate culture has had to evolve but strives to continue to inspire its employees as through its purpose, values, and vision statements (see Focus on Culture 12.1).

Employees are evaluated against the company's values. Southwest celebrates its employees in an elaborate recognition program for all employees who are recognized by customers. They are lauded in newsletter features, on the intranet, by the CEO in videos that are played at staff meetings, and at dinners honoring them. In fact, the company capitalizes the E in Employee and the C in Customer to emphasize the importance of both.

Focus on Culture 12.1

On Southwest's Culture

Our Purpose: Connect people to what's important in their lives through friendly, reliable, low-cost air travel

Our Vision: To become the World's Most Loved, Most Flown, and Most Profitable Airline

Values: Live the Southwest Way

Warrior Spirit—Work hard, desire to be the best, and be fearless in terms of delivering the product

Servant's Heart—Follow the Golden Rule, treat others with respect, demonstrate proactive Customer Service, and embrace the SWA family

Fun-LUVing Attitude—Have FUN, don't take yourself too seriously, and be a passionate team player

Source: Southwest Airlines (2017).

Case Study: Google

Google was founded in 1998 by two Stanford graduate students, Larry Page and Sergey Brin. Just as it was Herb Kelleher at Southwest who established Southwest's corporate culture, it was Page and

Brin who established "how things are done at Google." In 2015 Page and Brin became president and CEO of a new holding company, Alphabet, which includes Google, with Sundar Pichai as its president.

Google is organized as a "flat" company with a small middle management and a hands-on upper management. The result is that Google's core employees have autonomy, but work with a single unifying philosophy. On corporate teams everyone has equal authority. In Google's early years, new product ideas moved forward without any formal process.

Even with 67,000 employees, Google continues to hold regular meetings at which employees are encouraged to present new ideas directly to Sundar Pichai, which are then broadcast live to offices around the world. TGIF includes a presentation about business strategy or a product area update, and then Googlers ask Sundar and other execs questions about company issues.

Sergey Brin and Larry Page, Google co-founders.

Google regularly ranks as one of the best companies to work for in the United States. Company perks include free breakfasts, lunches, beverages, and snacks; fitness classes and massage therapy; vehicle maintenance and car washes; hair salon services and dry cleaning; and banking and concierge services.

Focus on Culture 12.2

The Google Culture

It's really the people that make Google the kind of company it is. We hire people who are smart and determined, and we favor ability over experience. Although Googlers share common goals and visions for the company, we hail from all walks of life and speak dozens of languages, reflecting the global audience that we serve. And when not at work, Googlers pursue interests ranging from cycling to beekeeping, from frisbee to foxtrot.

We strive to maintain the open culture often associated with startups, in which everyone is a hands-on contributor and feels comfortable sharing ideas and opinions. In our weekly all-hands ("TGIF") meetings—not to mention over email or in the cafe—Googlers ask questions directly to Larry, Sergey and other execs about any number of company issues. Our offices and cafes are designed to encourage interactions between Googlers within and across teams, and to spark conversation about work as well as play.

Source: Google (n.d.).

Homosexuality Worldwide

In Chapter 9 you studied how the status of women varies considerably around the world. You read how that variation can be at least partially explained by cultural values. In this section you will study how the concept of homosexuality and attitudes toward homosexuality also vary considerably around the word by culture. In the first section the discussion is limited to men as many cultures exclude women from this discussion. In the following section you'll read about how sexual orientation for women and men in the United States can be the basis for a subgroup and consider how that subgroup may become assimilated.

Vocabulary presents a challenge in studying homosexuality worldwide. We need to distinguish between words describing behavior and words describing a self-accepted identity. In some non-Western cultures, men do not even regard sex with other men as sexual activity as by definition sex can only refer to relations with women. The term "men who have sex with men" includes men who do not see themselves as homosexual or gay. There are men in Africa and Latin America, for example, who engage in sexual relationships with other men and refer to themselves without question as heterosexual.

Some individuals may not accept the identity that their behavior would lead others to assume. Even in Western countries some men who have sex with men do not accept an identity associated by others with that behavior. The label *gay* came to refer in a positive way to individuals who form primary emotional attachments to members of the same sex and who value one another and who, as Halperin (2012) defines it, embody a way of being and a dedicated commitment to certain social or aesthetic values. One can be gay and not be sexual. Being gay means sharing certain beliefs and values with others. As Halperin defines it, "The same things later happened in other cultures, such as in Germany with the word *schwul* and in Sweden with the word *boeg*. However, it's impossible to fully reflect the worldwide diversity of labels and behaviors associated with gender identity and sexual orientation.

Attitudes About Homosexuality and Same-Sex Marriage

With the limitation of language in mind, let's first look at acceptance of homosexuality worldwide. A 2013 survey of people in 39 countries found wide variation in the answers to the question "Should society accept homosexuality?" (Pew Research Center, 2013b). A clear majority in the European Union believe that homosexuality should be accepted. Most accepting were Spain (88%), Germany (87%), Czech Republic (80%), France (77%), Britain (76%), and Italy (74%). Opinions are generally positive in North America and Latin America. Most accepting were Canada (80%), Argentina (74%), Chile (68%), Mexico (61%), and Brazil and the United States (both 60%, although both have experienced recent anti-gay violence).

Respondents were not accepting in Africa and in predominantly Muslim countries. Sub-Saharan

Global Voices

During a 2015 visit to Kenya, President Obama called for African countries to end state discrimination against gays and lesbians. President Uhuru Kenyatta replied gay rights is "really a non-issue" as the country needs to concentrate on other areas.

Source: "Obama in Kenya: Presidents Differ on Gay Rights" (2015)

African countries surveyed included Nigeria (98% negative), Senegal, Ghana, and Uganda (all at 96%), and Kenya (90%). As of 2015, 34 of 54 African nations criminalize homosexuality, with penalties ranging from years in prison to life imprisonment to the death penalty. The same overwhelming rejection came from predominantly Muslim countries such as Jordan (97%), Egypt (95%), Indonesia (93%), Pakistan (87%), and Malaysia (86%). In parts of Asia, attitudes are negative as well, including in South Korea (59%) and China (57%). Overall, 73 nations either outlaw same-sex sexual relations or have repressive regimes that functionally outlaw same-sex relations.

Nations with the death penalty for homosexuality include Saudi Arabia, Yemen, Sudan, Iran, Mauritania, and areas of Nigeria and Somalia. Nations with imprisonment from 14 years to life for homosexuality include India, Tanzania, Zambia, Bangladesh, Malaysia, and Guyana, and nations with imprisonment, no precise length of time, include Egypt, Libya, and Namibia (Carroll & Mendos, 2016).

Finally, countries where same-sex marriage is legal nationwide include Canada, the United States, Iceland, Scotland, England, Ireland, Greenland, Norway, France, Portugal, Spain, Brazil, Uruguay, Argentina, Colombia, Sweden, Finland, Denmark, the Netherlands, Belgium, Luxembourg, South Africa, and New Zealand (ILGA, 2014; Pew Research Center, 2015c). The only Western European country yet to recognize same-sex civil unions is Italy. Taiwan's Constitutional Court ruled that it is illegal to ban same-sex marriage and ordered the parliament to change the country's civil code, which would make Taiwan the first Asian country with a same-sex marriage law (Jennings, 2017).

Focus on Theory 12.2

Queer Theory

Queer theory was developed in Western culture. Queer theorists (Yep, Lovaas, & Elia, 2003) challenge the concepts of binary categories such as female or male and homosexual or heterosexual, arguing that identities are not as restricted as suggested by binary categories. The focus in queer theory, then, is on identity as voluntary or as choice. Queer theorists advocate for social change by incorporating race, ethnicity, social class, and personal experience into theory and discussion. Queer theory suggests that every part of our identity is fluid and mixed. The use of the term *queer* itself is an example of queer theory. The meaning of the term has evolved from shame, to bonding, to sanction.

Robert Reid-Pharr (2002) raised a question for queer scholars: "Specifically, I wonder what we might encounter if we shifted our inquiry away from the question of how we 'subalterns' can make ourselves heard within 'dominant society' to how all of us—all Americans, all members of the human family—can take up the task of fashioning that society; indeed, how we can talk to one another. That is the next step for queer studies to take" (p. B9).

Queer theorists today have questioned how these Western values are being imposed by choice or coercion on non-Western cultures. Have Western-style gay rights become the gay imperialistic standard by which other nations are evaluated? (Chávez, 2013).

In countries with no acceptance of homosexuality, even private media use can lead to prosecution. In Egypt in 2002 and 2003, gay men were arrested and tried after having agreed to meet other men whom they contacted through the Internet. The other men were security officers or police informants. The private Internet conversations were used as evidence against the gay men and their names were published in the media. In India in 2006, four men were arrested after the police traced a gay man's phone number that they got from a gay website. The police then forced him to call several of his friends, who were arrested on charges of operating a "gay racket" on the Internet, belonging to an "international gay club," and engaging in "unnatural" sex (Amnesty International, 2008). In 2017 the Russian newspaper *Novaya Gazeta* reported at least 100 gay men in Chechnya had been tortured in detention facilities. Chechnya's president denied that gay people existed in the Muslim-majority region (John, 2017).

Cultural Bases for Attitudes

Hofstede (1998) reports that the masculinity cultural dimension is negatively related to the acceptance of homosexuality. Those cultures with a high acceptance of masculinity tend to be less accepting of homosexuality. The irrational fear of gay men and lesbians is called homophobia, a term created in the United States (Pharr, 1988). It is related to heterosexism, the assumption that the world is and must be heterosexual, and patriarchy, the enforced belief in heterosexual male dominance and control. Homophobia is a learned attitude. Many historical studies have shown that homosexuals were not feared or despised in the past. Some point to 20th-century psychiatrists, who created the paradigm of thinking of various forms of sexualities as diseases, as creating negative stereotypes. Historian George Chauncey (1985) argues that the Cold War era of fear created the unfounded negative stereotype of homosexuals as subversive security risks.

Ross (1989) surveyed 600 gay men in Australia, Finland, Ireland, and Sweden. He reported that young gay men had more problems accepting a gay sexual orientation in Ireland and Australia, less in Finland, and least in Sweden. Ross ranks these societies in homophobia in the same order. His study tends to support Hofstede's hypothesis in that Ross's ranking on homophobia is also the order of these countries on Hofstede's masculinity dimension. Homosexuality tends to be perceived as a threat in masculine cultures (Bolton, 1994) and considered more as a fact of life in feminine cultures.

The survey of 39 countries cited earlier related acceptance of homosexuality to religion and affluence (Pew Research Center, 2013b). The survey showed a strong relationship between a country's religiosity and opinions about homosexuality. In countries where religion is considered to be very important, where it is believed that it is necessary to believe in God to be moral, and where people pray at least once a day, there is far less acceptance of homosexuality. One notable exception to this is Russia, which has low religiosity and low level of acceptance of homosexuality (16%). Homosexuality is more accepted in wealthy nations and less accepted in poorer countries with high levels of religiosity.

How do scholars explain the homophobia in much of Africa? Same-sex practices were widely practiced and accepted in Africa for thousands of years. Homosexuality wasn't banned until the era of colonization, when Europeans brought anti-gay attitudes and laws to Africa. While those same European countries have decriminalized homosexuality, the now independent African states continued and expanded laws against it. Homosexuality is seen by some as an unwanted legacy of colonialism and White culture (Zimmerman, 2013).

While South Africa's constitution guarantees gay and lesbian rights and legalizes same-sex marriage, 61% of South Africans believe homosexuality should be rejected.

Some Muslim scholars refer to the story in the Qur'an of the people of Lut (Sodom and Gomorrah) who were destroyed by Allah because they engaged in carnal acts between men. The Arabic word for homosexual behavior (*liwat*) and the derogatory word for a homosexual (*luti*) are both derived from the name Lut (Dynes, 1990). Islamic jurists and extremist groups have referenced the lesser-known *hadith* (sayings of Muhammad) and *akhbar* (accounts of his life), which are clear in their condemning of homosexual behavior (Dynes, 1990).

We can see more cultural relationships in attempts to guarantee human rights for homosexuals. Since the founding of the United Nations, the first discussion of sexual orientation did not occur until 2006, when Norway presented a joint statement on high rights violations on behalf of 54 states at the Commission on High Rights. That was followed in 2008 with the first declaration on gay rights read in the United Nations General Assembly. The nonbinding measure sought to decriminalize homosexuality and won the support of 66 countries in the General Assembly. An Arab League–backed statement was presented in opposition. Neither has been officially adopted by the General Assembly (Macfarquhar, 2008).

In June 2011, the United Nations endorsed the rights of gay, lesbian, and transgender people for the first time when the Human Rights Council adopted a resolution expressing "grave concern at acts of violence and discrimination, in all regions of the world, committed against individuals because of their sexual orientation and gender identity." The resolution established a formal UN process to document human rights abuses against gays, including discriminatory laws and acts of violence.

The resolution was put forward by South Africa, and the 23 states voting in favor included the United States, the European Union countries, Japan, South Korea, Brazil, and other Latin American countries. The 19 states voting against included Russia, Saudi Arabia, Qatar, Malaysia, Pakistan, Nigeria, and Uganda. China, Burkina Faso, and Zambia abstained. Most recently, in 2016, the United Nations Human Rights Council passed a resolution to authorize a study of the causes of discrimination based on gender identity and sexual orientation and to discuss with governments ways to protect the rights of people based on gender identity and sexual orientation.

Global Voices

In the former Soviet Union, homosexuality was considered a "foreign, bourgeois perversion that must be contained" (Essig, 1999).

Prior to the 2014 Sochi Olympics, Russian president Vladimir Putin said that gays should feel comfortable attending the Winter Games but warned them to "leave children in peace." His comment was in response to criticism of Russian legislation that criminalizes the promotion of "nontraditional sexual relations" in the presence of minors (Wharton, 2014).

While some world leaders boycotted the Olympics over Russia's anti-gay law, President Obama, who himself did not attend, included openly gay athletes in the U.S. delegation.

Opposition to Putin's stance on homosexuality appeared in social media, including YouTube, Facebook, and Twitter, and in corporate logos and diplomacy. Google created a logo depicting athletes performing in the rays of a rainbow and quoted parts of the Olympic Charter. AT&T posted a statement on its consumer blog voicing its opposition:

> "The Olympic Games in Sochi also allow us to shine a light on a subject that's important to all Americans: equality. As you may know, the lesbian, gay, bisexual and transgender (LGBT) community around the world is protesting a Russian anti-LGBT law that bans 'propaganda of non-traditional sexual relations.' To raise awareness of the issue, the Human Rights Campaign (HRC) has called on International Olympic Committee (IOC) sponsors to take action and stand up for LGBT equality (Hauser, 2014).

> "AT&T is not an IOC sponsor, so we did not receive the HRC request. However, we are a longstanding sponsor of the United States Olympic Committee (USOC), we support HRC's principles and we stand against Russia's anti-LGBT law."

Sources: Essig (1999); Hauser (2014); Wharton (2014)

Sexual Orientation as a Basis for Subgroups

In this section we first revisit the concept of othering, the consequences of othering for lesbians and gay men, and othering and media use. Then you'll read about how the gay subgroup may be moving away from a separate subgroup to an assimilated status, where some believe the subgroup will disappear.

Sexual Orientation and Othering

Othering applies to subgroups just as it does to subcultures. This is particularly true in the case of sexual orientation. The language people use to describe their and others' gender identity and sexual orientation varies widely by location and over time. It is easier to trace such a change over time in the United States. Words and symbols which at one time were used pejoratively by the dominant culture were claimed and embraced by the subgroup as an important part in the development of positive self-esteem. The turning point in gay male and lesbian identity was the June 28, 1969, riot at the Stonewall Inn, a gay bar located in New York's Greenwich Village, in which patrons fought back against the police raiding the bar. Prior to that event, people at a gay bar might have tried to hide or otherwise escape police recognition. After that event, with the birth of the gay liberation movement as an active political force, it became "OK to be gay" (Katz, 1976).

The words *dyke* and *faggot* now became symbols of gay pride. In a like manner, the word *lesbian* changed from a medical word to a label of pride. Queer Nation, a spin-off of ACT-UP (AIDS Coalition to Unleash Power), used the chant "We're here, we're queer, we're fabulous—get used to it." This self-labeling had a clear political utility (Epstein, 1990) in efforts to gain legal protections (D. H. Miller, 1998; R. R. Smith & Windes, 1997).

In the same way that word symbols are given positive meanings, nonverbal symbols facilitate group identification. For example, the pink triangle had its origin in Hitler's concentration camps to label homosexuals. (Lesbians, and other women, were not judged to have any decision-making power or sovereignty and so were forced to wear black triangles, which labeled them "antisocials.") The rainbow flag, which had its first use in gay parades in San Francisco, is often seen now to identify the gay community.

Global Voices

"Those who promote homosexuality want to put an end to human existence."

"It is becoming an epidemic and we Muslims and Africans will fight to end this behavior.

"Homosexuality in all its forms and manifestations which, though very evil, antihuman as well as anti-Allah, is being promoted as a human right by some powers."

—Gambian President Yahya Jammeh,
at the United Nations, September 27, 2013
(quoted in Nichols, 2013)

"Some have suggested that gay rights and human rights are separate and distinct; but, in fact, they are one and the same. . . .

"The . . . most challenging issue arises when people cite religious or cultural values as a reason to violate or not to protect the human rights of LGBT citizens. This is not unlike the justification offered for violent practices towards women like honor killings, widow burning, or female genital mutilation. . . . [W]e came to learn that no practice or tradition trumps the human rights that belong to all of us."

—Hillary Rodham Clinton, former U.S. Secretary of State, "Remarks in Recognition of International Human Rights Day," December 6, 2011

Consequences of Othering

Among the consequences of othering are the potential for emotional and physical harm to those being labeled. The emotional and physical harm to those labeled by sexual orientation has been studied in the United States as homophobia.

In 1969, the year of the Stonewall riot, there were no policies, laws, or ordinances prohibiting discrimination against lesbians and gay men. In fact, in 1967, the New York State Liquor Authority forbade bars to serve homosexuals, 49 states had laws banning sodomy, and there were no hate crime laws.

Isaac Kasamani/AFP/Getty Images

Demonstration against Uganda's court annulling the Anti-Gay law. Uganda's attorney general filed an appeal.

Media portrayal of gay men and lesbians contributed to stereotyping. The Motion Picture Production Code of 1930 banned all mention of homosexuality in U.S. films for more than 30 years. Russo (1987) has shown how the portrayal of lesbians and gay men in film has, until recently, been derisive and shown them as victims.

The early 1990s saw a nationwide rise in hate crimes against gay individuals, which has been attributed in part to increased visibility and activism in the gay community. These hate crimes include harassment, vandalism, assault, and police abuse: Lesbian and gay high school students are the targets of bullying, teasing, and violence.

Discrimination continues in employment. While federal government employees are protected from workplace discrimination based on sexual orientation, there are no federal laws that specifically outlaw workplace discrimination in the private sector. Only about half the states and the District of Columbia have laws that prohibit job discrimination against lesbians and gay men in both public and private companies. An increasing number of major U.S. corporations, such as Harley-Davidson, IBM, Kodak, Time-Warner, and 3M, have policies banning discrimination based on sexual orientation. Gay activists argue that discrimination based on sexual orientation is still widespread. Citing a 1991 corporate policy, Cracker Barrel Old Country Stores, a firm based in Lebanon, Tennessee, that runs restaurants along many southeast interstates, fired several employees for not conforming to "normal heterosexual values." The restaurant chain defended its actions by citing "traditional American values" and declared in a memo that it "is perceived to be inconsistent with those of our customer base to continue to employ individuals in our operating units whose sexual preferences fail to demonstrate normal heterosexual values which have been the foundation of families in our society" ("Decision to Fire Gays," 1991, para. 2). In late 2002 after protests and boycotts, the restaurant chain discontinued its practice, though gay activists say the rule still exists.

Problems that gay men and lesbians have faced in the workplace include being refused positions based on the perception of being gay, receiving anonymous harassing phone calls and letters, and not being promoted or retained when sexual orientation becomes known. Most discrimination against gays in employment in the 1990s was disguised. Employers who wanted to terminate a gay employee first found other reasons to disguise the termination. In early 2000, the Pentagon released a study of

72,000 troops. The results showed that 37% have witnessed or been targets of gay harassment. More than 80% reported hearing offensive speech, derogatory names, or jokes at least once over the past year, and more than 85% believed that antigay comments are tolerated at military installations or aboard ships (Richter, 2000). Under the "Don't Ask, Don't Tell" policy between 1993 and 2011, over 14,000 U.S. military men and women were discharged due to their sexual orientation. In September 2011, the United States ended the "Don't Ask, Don't Tell" policy, which restricted gays, lesbians, and bisexuals from openly serving in the military. For the first time in U.S. history, people of every sexual orientation could serve openly.

But just because homophobia is not public doesn't mean it isn't there. In 2011 a Southwest Airlines pilot accidently turned on his microphone and his true beliefs were broadcast over an air traffic control frequency. Referring to flight attendants he said: "Eleven f*****g over the top f*****g homosexuals and a granny. Eleven. I mean, think of the odds of that. I thought I was in Chicago, which was party-land. . . . After that, it was just a continuous stream of gays and granny" (quoted in R. Johnson, 2011, para. 7).

Media and Othering

In countries with a greater acceptance of homosexuality, traditional media and social media can reinforce subgroup identity. This can more easily be seen in the United States. Specialized print media have long existed for the U.S. gay community and serve to reinforce its existence, just as they do with other cultures and subgroups. Lesbian literature has been more prominent than other forms of lesbian media and has reflected a feminist perspective. Gay male literature of the 1960s and 1970s by such authors as James Baldwin, Truman Capote, Gore Vidal, and Tennessee Williams generally depicted gay men as social outsiders. Later writers, such as Andrew Holleran, Armistead Maupin, and Edmund White, created positive characters functioning within a gay community.

Local newspapers across the United States focused on community events and contributed to a shared identity, as did national magazines. More recently, gay men's magazines focused on human rights issues. They support responsibility, caring for and supporting one another, and maintaining identity in the face of AIDS in a largely indifferent society. It was the gay press—not the popular press or the medical community—that brought AIDS to the attention of gay men, and as a consequence, the spread of AIDS declined in the gay community while growing dramatically in other segments of society (Fejes & Petrich, 1993).

Gay magazines have drawn advertising from car companies such as Saab and Subaru. Subaru discovered that lesbians were one of its core demographics and actively cultivated its image as a car for lesbians. In the travel industry, Virgin Atlantic and American Express were major advertisers. Marriott used multiple channels such as #LoveTravels featuring openly gay NBA player Jason Collins and the transgender fashion model Geena Rocero. Others include liquor companies such as Absolut vodka and Tanqueray gin, and mainstream companies such as AT&T and MCI; Chase Bank, Chemical Bank, and Citibank; Evian and Perrier; Flowers Direct and Geffen records; and Quality Paperback Books and Viking/Penguin Press.

General-circulation magazines run "gay-vague" advertising as well as advertising using homosexuality as a means to draw attention. Seagram's once marketed Boodles gin with a bar mirror that featured "Six Famous Men of History" etched on it: Oscar Wilde, Lawrence of Arabia, Walt Whitman, Edgar Allan Poe, Ludwig van Beethoven, and Edgar Degas. Probably, most nonlesbians and nongay men did not recognize the six as homosexual, but the gay community did.

Rejecting All Labels

Non-White, non-middle-class lesbians and gay men and people of sexualities of all kinds began to challenge the idea of a single gay/lesbian identity (Lorde, 1984). The label, both externally applied and later redefined, categorized a group only on the basis of one dimension of sexual orientation. Identity politics imposed a unitary identity on gay men, lesbians, and bisexuals that "is alienating to those who do not fit into the mold constructed by the leaders of the movement" (Slagle, 1995, p. 86).

Queer theory challenges the idea of a single identity and rejects the categorization of heterosexuality and homosexuality. Queer theory argues that identities are multiple (sexual orientation and race and class and gender and so forth). Accepting such a label, even as an indicator of pride, can be restrictive in defining self (Fuss, 1991; Warner, 1993).

Focus on Theory 12.3

Gender Performativity

The term *gender performativity* was coined by Judith Butler. When gender is performed, it means taking on a role or acting in some way. Gender performativity means that the performance is what produces the individual identity it is purported to be. Thus gender and sexual orientation are always a doing, though not a doing by a subject who might be said to pre-exist the deed.

Source: Butler (1990).

From Separation to Assimilation

We have seen that the language people use to describe their and others' gender identity and sexual orientation varies widely by location and over time. We turn now to a consideration of how a subgroup's status within the dominant culture can change over time.

Some argue that some subgroups, particularly lesbians and gay men, can be studied as one would study an immigrant group in terms of acculturation. To apply this perspective, we will look first at the evidence of gay men and lesbians being treated as a separate or segregated group in the United States and then at how they are now becoming either an integrated or assimilated group.

Evidence of Separate Status

You read earlier in this chapter that argot is an indicator of a subgroup. A strong, secret argot is evidence of separate status. In 1976, Joseph J. Hayes described "gayspeak" as the language one acquires when entering the gay community. He identified three settings in which gayspeak is important: secret or threatening situations (i.e., in the presence of people who are not gay), social settings (i.e., in the presence of other gays), and radical gay activist settings.

Although not all lesbians and gay men recognize gayspeak, its acceptance by some suggests a dual persona, that is, using one language in the gay community and another language in the gay subgroup community.

A second indicator of separate status would be that subgroup members could hide their identity until they felt comfortable revealing their identity. Accepting the label *gay* for oneself is part of the communication process of coming out. Communication scholar Larry Gross (1993) wrote, "The preponderance of lesbian and gay political rhetoric, both within the community and externally, reflects an essentialist position, insisting that one doesn't 'choose' to be gay, but recognizes and 'accepts' that one is so" (p. 113). Before Stonewall, coming out meant taking a great risk as it could affect your career and family relationships. Today, coming out is a positive act of self-expression and identity. You might feel different from others, but with publicly disclosing the reason comes an acceptance of the label *homosexual* or *gay*. Now everyone knows, and some will treat you differently. That different treatment confirms your personal identification as a gay person.

Separate status is also demonstrated in that 20% of all LGBT youth are homeless and 40% of all homeless youth are LGBT, 58% of homeless LGBT youth have been sexually assaulted, and 62% of LGBT homeless youth have attempted suicide (Walmsley, 2016).

Focus on Culture 12.3

Gay and Lesbian Assimilation or Integration

The word *assimilation* is somewhat disingenuous if it's meant to imply that gays are thereby sacrificing something that is part of their natural character or essential nature. . . . Much the opposite, in fact. More and more gays are insisting that they be accepted for who they are wherever they happen to be and however they want to live.

Better words for this process might be *inclusion* or *integration*, words that suggest that a person is regarded and treated equally at the same time he or she remains fully himself or herself.

Source: Varnell (2000).

Integration or Assimilation of Subgroups

The change from separate or segregated status to integrated or assimilated status can be seen in today's discussions within the subgroup. When homophobia is a thing of the past and lesbians and gay men have equal rights, social recognition, and acceptance, that is when gay people are then fully assimilated into the dominant culture.

In a 1998 essay, Gabriel Rotello first framed the issue as similar to that of immigration, as one of assimilationists versus the radicals. Assimilationists argue that lesbians and gay men should be "just like everybody else," whereas radicals argue that gay men and lesbians should maintain a separate culture. Rotello contends that cultural separation occurs only when society stigmatizes a group. As long as society in some way stigmatizes gay men and lesbians, a separate culture will exist. Or, as Harris (1997) wrote, if gay men and lesbians become too mainstream, what it means to be gay will be lost. Martin Duberman, distinguished professor of history at the City University of New York and a pioneer in gay studies, also raises concerns about assimilation:

National organizations within the gay world are presenting themselves as just plain folks—"We're ordinary citizens. We're just like everybody else. So let us in. We're going to behave just the way you want us to behave." As a people we've had a different historical experience, just as Black people have. The mainstream needs to know what we know. (quoted in Ricci & Biederman, 2004, p. B1)

Gay novelist Edmund White also has commented on the shift from separate to integrated or assimilated: "You go to a pride march and it's just like every other civic parade with its crass commercialism" (quoted in Hallett, 2003, p. 38). Halperin (2012) raises the question: As long as homosexual children continue to be born into heterosexual families, will there continue to be sufficient support for a gay subgroup identity?

Focus on Technology 12.1

Coming Out on Facebook

Marginalized subgroups have used social and online media to disseminate information, support one another, and promote issues in countries tolerant and intolerant of LGBT rights. In the U.S. on June 26, 2015, the Supreme Court declared same-sex marriage a constitutional right. That same day, Facebook launched a tool for users to put a rainbow filter over their profile pictures. Within a few hours, more than 1 million people changed their profiles.

On National Coming Out Day on October 11 and #SpiritDay on October 15, 2016, Facebook published data on coming out. Facebook defined "coming out" as a person updating their profile expressing a same-gender attraction or specifying a custom gender. By that definition, more than 6 million people came out on Facebook. Its data also showed that 5.7 million users were fans of at least one of the 300 most popular LGBT pages such as Human Rights Campaign, GLADD, or Equality Now.

Source: Walgrove (2015).

SUMMARY

The Sapir-Whorf hypothesis establishes the relationship between cultures and languages, and the same can be true for subgroups, but on the level of vocabulary. The specialized vocabulary identifies the subgroup and establishes the group's boundaries. The specialized vocabulary of subgroups is known as *argot*. The British punk subgroup was about getting represented. Punk found niche audiences who listened and supported the artists.

Organizations can have their own symbols: their own argot, dress codes, and status symbols recognized by insiders only. And because of this, we can speak of organizations as corporate cultures. Herb Kelleher developed the Southwest Airlines corporate culture, which has been cited as one of the reasons for its success. Larry Page and Sergey Brin developed Google's corporate culture.

Subgroups based on sexual orientation have been examples of othering in many cultures. The Pew Global Attitudes Project reported responses to the question of whether homosexuality should be accepted or rejected. A clear majority in Western Europe believe that homosexuality should be accepted. In Africa, Asia, and the Middle East, attitudes toward homosexuals are negative. In eight of 10 African countries, less than 5% of the population feels society should accept homosexuality. Hofstede (1998) reports that the masculinity cultural dimension is negatively related to the acceptance of homosexuality. Homosexuality tends to be perceived as a threat in masculine cultures and considered a fact of life in feminine cultures. In the United States and some other cultures, lesbians and gay men have moved over time from separation to assimilation.

DISCUSSION QUESTIONS

1. Describe a subgroup you have identified with in terms of its argot, media use, and values.

2. Should corporations that want to build a strong corporate culture require employees to wear uniforms and use a corporate vocabulary? What if employees object for reasonable personal reasons?

3. How will social media be used by subgroups?

4. Should Western countries pressure African countries to repeal laws against homosexuality?

5. With growing acceptance of same-sex marriage, will the subgroup of lesbian and gay men continue to be a source of identity?

KEY TERMS

argot	corporate culture	jargon
cant	cultural studies	participant observer
coming out	homophobia	slang

READINGS

All readings are from *Intercultural Communication: A Global Reader* (Jandt, 2004).

Crispin Thurlow, "Naming the 'Outsider Within': Homophobic Pejoratives and the Verbal Abuse of Lesbian, Gay and Bisexual High-School Pupils" (p. 189)

STUDENT STUDY SITE

$SAGE edge™

Sharpen your skills with SAGE edge at edge.sagepub.com/jandt9e.

SAGE edge for Students provides a personalized approach to help you accomplish your coursework goals in an easy-to-use learning environment.

Part 5

Applications

Chapter 13

©iStockphoto.com/DannCardiff

Contact Between Cultures

In this chapter, you will examine what happens when people from diverse cultures interact with one another. First, we focus on colonialism and cultural imperialism. Then we'll focus on development communication and diffusion, the spread of practices from one culture to another. You will identify the roles in the diffusion process and the characteristics of those most likely to adopt new practices first. Then you will look at cultural icons such as Japanese instant ramen and U.S. cultural icons of Coca-Cola, Disney, McDonald's, and KFC. In contrast to other products, icons are minimally changed for the receiving culture. You'll also read about cultural hegemony, or the fear of the influence one culture can develop over another. And you will see through examples that key to successful diffusion is adapting the new practice to the receiving culture.

Colonialism

For hundreds of thousands of years, humans lived in isolated communities. Cultures developed largely independently and many were unaware of the others' existence. The initiation of contact among previously separate cultures has been the major world event of the past centuries. Mary Pratt (1992) coined the term contact zone to refer to "the space in which peoples geographically and historically separated come into contact with each other and establish ongoing relations, usually involving conditions of coercion, radical inequality, and intractable conflict" (p. 6). During the 16th, 17th, 18th, and 19th centuries, new contacts dominated the EuroAmerican cultures.

For a time, travel writings, explorer's lectures, exhibits of peoples from other cultures, and the proceedings of academic and scientific communities reporting on expeditions were major popular activities. Yet in the EuroAmerican cultures, the peoples and cultures from other lands were devalued and information from them ignored. The perception of difference lead to violence and extermination.

From the time of Columbus, Spain debated the rationality of the Indians—are the Indians rational humans with souls? The monarchy issued laws intended to regulate Indian-Spaniard relations, including the Laws of Burgos, which mandated that Spaniards who benefited from forced Indian labor must instruct their subjects in Christianity. A 1537 papal bull (announcement from the Pope to the Catholic world) proclaimed the Indians rational beings by confirming the Indians' capability to understand and receive the Christian faith. In 1539 Bartolomé de las Casas, in his *The Devastation of the Indies,* called attention to the actual treatment of the Indians, which was far from that of rational humans with souls. A disputation or debate resulted between Las Casas and Juan Ginés de Sepúlveda, a Dominican, in the city of Valladolid in 1550 and 1551, which, for a time, held the attention of Spain.

Sepúlveda made four arguments for enslaving the Indians: First, the state of their culture made them fit for slavery and it was the responsibility of the Spaniards to act as masters. Second, Spaniards were obligated to prevent Indians from engaging in cannibalism. Third, Spaniards were obligated to stop Indians from making human sacrifices to their Gods. Finally, slavery was an effective method of converting Indians to Christianity (Losada, 1971). Las Casas argued that the Indians were rational, free humans in the natural order, deserved the same treatment as others, and could be brought to Christianity without force.

The Valladolid disputation was not so much about the treatment of the Indians nor about Christianity as it was an enactment of European Spaniards believing they had the right to decide if the Indians were rational humans. If the decision was that they were not, then Spanish treatment of the Indians as slaves and property was justified.

Hawai'i

In chants, legends, and *mele* ("vocal music"), Hawaiians trace the origins of the culture to daring seafarers who discovered and colonized the islands. Sometime around 1000 CE, isolated from further outside influence, a unique culture emerged. Hawai'i's society was hereditary and composed of the *ali'i* ("ruling class"), *kahuna* ("priests" or "experts"), *maka'âinana* ("commoners"), and *kauwâ* ("slaves"). The society operated under a strict *kapu* ("restriction," "consequence," "separation," or "forbidden") system that dictated daily activity between the classes and between the people and nature and the Gods. A culture of about 1 million people had developed a harmony with its isolated island environment (Young, 1980).

British Captain James Cook departed on his third voyage in 1776, arriving in Hawai'i in 1778. Edward Said (1978, 1981) describes the contact and subsequent linguistic construction of non-Western cultures as "Orientalism," a process of labeling the peoples of "underdeveloped" cultures as insignificant "others." Captain Cook and his men, for example, wrote of the Hawaiians as "savage or animal-like or heathen." While the Hawaiians were labeled as savages, the Europeans interpreted the Hawaiians' actions as deifying Captain Cook. The ship's journals state that "[the Hawaiians] venerated [Cook] almost to adoration," looked upon him as "a kind of superior being," honored him "like a god," and "as far as related to the person of Captain Cook, they seemed close to adoration" (Obeyesekere, 1992, pp. 121, 142). The Europeans labeled the Hawaiians not by any uniqueness but

Focus on Theory 13.1

Cultural Studies

Cultural studies focus on the ways culture is formed through struggles among ideologies (Agger, 1992). Cultural studies scholars have as an objective to change Western cultures, in part through their scholarship, which helps people understand domination and pathways to reform. Media have been a focus for study as media are seen as tools of the powerful in disseminating information along with the social institutions of education, religion, and government. Cultural studies expose the ways that the ideology of powerful groups is established. Postcolonial theory refers to the study of cultures affected by colonization (Shome & Hegde, 2002). At its core is Edward Said's (1978) notion of "othering"—the stereotypic images of non-White populations. Postcolonial scholars study many of the same issues as cultural studies scholars.

on the basis of what the Hawaiians were not (i.e., not civilized by European standards). Shome (1996) calls this discursive imperialism (also see Tanno & Jandt, 1994).

The dehumanization of the Hawaiians into "others" contributed to near destruction of the Hawaiian culture. Native Hawaiians lost government, lands, and cultural identity with the U.S.-backed 1893 overthrow of the Hawaiian monarchy.

The current population of the state is approximately 1.4 million. The Hawai'i State Department of Health reported a Hawaiian population of 254,910 in 2000. In 1993, a U.S. congressional resolution apologized to Hawaiians for the 1893 overthrow, noting that economic and social changes since then have been devastating to the population and to the health and well-being of the Hawaiian people. In 2005, Senator Daniel Akaka sponsored a bill in the U.S. Senate that would have granted Native Hawaiians the same rights of self-government as American Indians and Native Alaskans and would have led to recognition of a native government entity. The bill was blocked by a Nevada senator out of fears that it would lead to legal gambling in Hawai'i.

Several native organizations claim sovereignty and are working for reparations and some form of self-government. The Native Hawaiian Government Reorganization Act, sponsored by Senator Daniel Akaka, would have created a "Native Hawaiian Governing Entity" that would exempt the entity from the First, Fifth, and Fourteenth Amendments and permit negotiations over land, natural resources, criminal and civil jurisdiction, and historical grievances. The act defines Native Hawaiians as direct lineal descendants of Indigenous people who lived on the islands before 1893. The legislation would, in effect, create a tribe. The bill was not enacted.

Australia

In a similar way, all that is known of European contact with Australia's Aboriginals is from the written journals and history of the Europeans. Eighteen years after Captain Cook first arrived off the eastern coast of Australia, Captain Arthur Phillip arrived with

Global Voices

What is Aboriginal? According to most white experts and the media, it's a black person who lives in a remote community, has social issues and claims benefits that are way above what they deserve. So being Aboriginal but white, fairly socially adjusted and living in an urban area, where do I fit in?

—Bindi Cole, Aboriginal artist (quoted in Korff, 2014)

Global Voices

The Declaration on the Rights of Indigenous Peoples was adopted by the UN General Assembly on Thursday September 13, 2007, by a vote of 144 states in favor, four against (Australia, Canada, New Zealand, and the United States), and 11 abstentions. Since its adoption, Australia, Canada, New Zealand, and the United States have all reversed their positions and now endorse the declaration.

Selected sections from the declaration:

Affirming that Indigenous peoples are equal to all other peoples, while recognizing the right of all peoples to be different, to consider themselves different, and to be respected as such,

Affirming further that all doctrines, policies and practices based on or advocating superiority of peoples or individuals on the basis of national origin or racial, religious, ethnic or cultural differences are racist, scientifically false, legally invalid, morally condemnable and socially unjust,

Concerned that Indigenous peoples have suffered from historic injustices as a result of, inter alia, their colonization and dispossession of their lands, territories and resources, thus preventing them from exercising, in particular, their right to development in accordance with their own needs and interests,

Recognizing that respect for Indigenous knowledge, cultures and traditional practices contributes to sustainable and equitable development and proper management of the environment,

Article 1

Indigenous peoples have the right to the full enjoyment, as a collective or as individuals, of all human rights and fundamental freedoms as recognized in the Charter of the United Nations, the Universal Declaration of Human Rights and international human rights law.

Article 8

1. Indigenous peoples and individuals have the right not to be subjected to forced assimilation or destruction of their culture.

11 ships and their cargo of prisoners, who established the British settlement on the shores of Sydney Harbor in January 1788.

Captain Phillip's view of the colonists as "guests" of the Indigenous inhabitants and his edict prohibiting molesting or killing Aboriginals was not long-lasting. The Europeans occupied coastal hunting grounds and disturbed sacred sites of local Aboriginals, not having learned of their existence, much less importance. There were no large-scale wars like those with American Indians and New Zealand's Māori. The Aboriginals resisted with spears and stone weapons in encounters that would later be called "guerrilla warfare."

In the book *Ancient Society*, published in 1877, the Australian Aboriginal was described as "the living representatives of that worldwide primeval culture from which all other cultures had evolved." The Aboriginal was labeled as not evolved, an oddity, or semihuman. As the Europeans moved further into the continent with farming and cattle raising, the Aboriginal population was decimated. Arsenic was mixed with the flour or inserted into the carcasses of sheep given to the Aboriginals for food. Numerous instances of large-scale slaughter have been documented, including the entire Aboriginal population of Tasmania (Isaacs, 1980).

Population size can only be rough estimates. At the time of the European settlements, the number of Aboriginal and Torres Strait Islanders may have been 700,000 speaking an estimated 250 to 300 spoken languages. By 1900, the number was estimated to have declined to around 93,000 people, a decrease of almost 87%.

The issue today is determining exactly who is Aboriginal. The popular image of an Aboriginal outside of Australia is a black-skinned individual standing with a spear. The truth is that from the time of the European settlements there has been interracial marriage and parenting. Aboriginals can trace heritage to Britain, Ireland, or Asian countries. By skin color, today's Aboriginals can be fair skinned. Thus, determining the Aboriginal population today is no simple task. Perhaps over a million Australians with Aboriginal ancestry do not identify themselves as Aboriginal on census forms.

In Australia, "reconciliation" refers to bringing together Aboriginal people and Torres Strait Islanders and other Australians. In practice it means working to overcome the inequality in health, income, living standards, and life expectancy between Aboriginal and non-Aboriginal people and eliminating forms of prejudice and racism. The reconciliation movement began with the 1967 referendum in which 90% of Australians voted to remove clauses in the Australian Constitution that discriminated against Indigenous Australians. In 2008, Labor Prime Minister Kevin Rudd issued a comprehensive apology for past wrongs and called for action to improve the lives of Australia's Aboriginals and Torres Strait Islanders. He particularly addressed the "Stolen Generations," the tens of thousands of Indigenous children who were removed from their families in a policy of forced assimilation that ended only in the 1970s.

In 2013, Australia's parliament passed the Aboriginal and Torres Strait Islander Peoples Recognition Act, which recognizes the Indigenous peoples of Australia and established a process to change the Constitution by a national referendum within 2 years. Reid, Gunter, and Smith (2005) contend that the ultimate resolution will depend on how Aboriginals identify themselves—as outcasts and separatists or as peoples within the bounds of Australian identity.

Cultural Imperialism

Is the age of colonialism past? Some argue that the cultural imperialism of colonialism continues in many ways today, including military occupation, corporate colonialism, and media.

Saddam Hussein's dictatorship kept satellite television, mobile phones, and the Internet out of Iraq. The U.S.-led invasion in 2003 and occupation through 2011 left behind a fledgling democracy as well as rap music and tattoos. Today nearly half of the population of Iraq is under 19 years of age. A quarter of the country's population was born after 2003. After years of contact with U.S. military, Iraqi youth have adopted what they saw and heard from soldiers on patrol, including Marine-style haircuts or

Iraqi teens rollerblade in Baghdad in 2011. While U.S. troops withdrew, U.S. cultural influences remained.

spiked hair, hoodie sweatshirts, Rollerblade runs through traffic, listening to 50 Cent and Eminem, watching vampire movies, and displaying tattoos regardless of Islam's strictures on baring the skin. Baghdad University sociologist Dr. Fawzia A. al-Attia has said teenagers

started to adopt the negative aspects of the American society because they think that by imitating the Americans, they obtain a higher status in society. . . . These young Iraqi people need to be instructed. They need to know about the positive aspects of the American society to imitate. (Juhi, 2011, para. 18)

Jacob Silberberg/Getty Images News/Getty Images

A worker subcontracted by Shell Oil Company cleans up an oil spill from an abandoned Shell Petroleum wellhead in the Nigerian town of Oloibiri. Wellhead 14 was closed in 1977 and has been leaking since. By June 2004, it had released more than 20,000 barrels of crude oil.

Entering the country now is U.S.-style food. One of the first restaurants to open was Lee's Famous Recipe Chicken (a Midwest and Southern U.S. chain). Iraqis used the word "Kentucky" for fried chicken regardless of where it's sold.

Another form of cultural imperialism is corporate colonialism, one example of which can be seen in Nigeria, Africa's most populous country. With proven oil reserves of 37.5 billion barrels, it has a petroleum-based economy. With 606 oilfields, the Niger delta supplies 40% of all the crude oil that the United States imports. The Niger delta is also the world capital of oil pollution. More oil is spilled in the Niger delta every year than was spilled in the Gulf of Mexico at BP's Deepwater Horizon site in 2010. Media coverage of the Gulf of Mexico spill was worldwide; little information is made available about the Niger delta.

Shell admits to spilling 14,000 tons of oil in the Niger delta in 2009. In 2010 ExxonMobil spilled more than a million gallons into the delta over the course of 7 days. The Nigerian government's national oil spill detection and response agency reported that between 1976 and 1996, more than 2.4 million barrels contaminated the environment. Oil spills have polluted drinking wells, forests, farming, and fishing areas. Nnimo Bassey, Nigerian head of Friends of the Earth International, has said that the oil companies "have been living above the law. They are now clearly a danger to the planet. The dangers of this happening again and again are high. They must be taken to the international court of justice" (quoted in Vidal, 2010, para. 29).

In addition to direct corporate colonialism, some contend that media themselves can contribute to colonialism. The cultural imperialist approach to communication recognizes that mass media are not value free—the media also carry important cultural values (Nordenstreng & Schiller, 1979; Schiller, 1976). In this theory, media that can capture and dominate international markets serve the originating country's intentions. The single largest export industry for the United States is not aircraft. It's entertainment. Hollywood films grossed more than $30 billion worldwide in 1997. Hollywood gets 50% of its revenues overseas (United Nations Development Programme, 1999).

Schiller (1976) points to the unrestricted flow of media from the United States having the effect of surreptitiously influencing other people's goals and aspirations. It was just that concern that led Canada to

Global Voices

Hollywood crystallizes to the world who we are as a nation, our exuberance, righteousness, desires, anxieties and our predilection, through the prism of action heroes and special effects, for freewheeling individualism and blowing things up.

—Jeffrey Fleishman (2014), foreign correspondent for 17 years require that radio stations devote at least 35% to 40% of their programming to Canadian music. Similar content quota laws exist in several other countries.

In Taiwan, some are talking about a "new colonialism," and one newspaper carried the headline "Be Careful! Your Kids Are Becoming Japanese." Japanese television reaches 75% of Taiwanese households on cable. Japanese comic books and trendy fashion magazines such as *Non-No* and *Check* are popular among teens, as are Japanese merchandise and pop singers. Teens say that Japanese popular culture is easy to relate to because the cultures are similar. Older people remember Japan's 50-year rule of Taiwan and have called for a boycott of Japanese products so as to preserve Chinese heritage.

Throughout history, ideas and technology have spread from one culture to another. Some of that was spontaneous and unplanned; some was carefully planned and managed. One result of contact between cultures is that through interaction, one culture may learn and adopt certain practices of the other culture. Perhaps the most significant example of adopting new practices resulted from Columbus's voyages linking two separate worlds into one. The Old World brought horses, cows, sheep, chickens, honeybees, coffee, wheat, cabbage, lettuce, bananas, olives, tulips, and daisies. The New World provided turkeys, sugarcane, corn, sweet potatoes, tomatoes, pumpkins, pineapples, petunias, poinsettias, and the practice of daily baths—a practice abhorred by Europeans.

The spread from one culture to another that is planned and managed can be from a developed country to a developing country with the intent of helping the developing country or can be marketing for the purpose of economic gain.

Global Voices

Gossip Girl was a U.S. teen television series on the CW from 2007 to 2012. The following quotes are from Chinese participants in a study of product placement in media (Shi, 2010):

> "*Gossip Girl* offers a sneak peek into the lives of Manhattan's Upper-East-Siders showing the mobile phones they use, the clothes they wear, the brands they prefer, the parties they go to."

> "All the girls around me are impressed by what Serena and Blair have—their cars, mobile phones, and dresses. . . . The dresses are designer products, some classic and some vintage. And the accessories! They are made in New York, right? That is why this show can keep me informed of the latest trend."

> "I love the new designs in *Gossip Girl*. . . . I would buy the entire wardrobe of Blair Waldorf. So cute!"

Development Communication

At least in Asia, the origin of the term *development communication* is attributed to Nora Quebral (1975), who defined it as the art and science of human communication applied to the speedy transformation of a country from poverty to a dynamic state of economic growth and that makes possible greater economic and social equality and the larger fulfilment of human potential. Development communication has been focused in the areas of agricultural practices, family planning, infant health, HIV/AIDS, nutrition, health education, and housing.

The field has been dominated by two conceptual models: diffusion and participatory. The diffusion model is attributed to Everett Rogers's (1962) diffusion of innovations theory. The basic model is known as KAP: *knowledge*, which leads to a change in *attitudes*, which in turn leads to *practice*. Diffusion projects tended to be media-based marketing projects, while some, particularly in the area of family health, relied more on interpersonal communication (N. Morris, 2003).

Global Voices

I do not want my house to be walled in on all sides and my windows stuffed. I want the cultures of all the lands to be blown about my house as freely as possible. But I refuse to be blown off my feet by any.

—Mahatma Gandhi (quoted in United Nations Development Programme, 1999)

This is the process of diffusion. Everett Rogers has studied the communication process by which innovations are spread to members of a social system (Rogers & Shoemarker, 1971). Since the early 1960s, communication researchers have investigated the agricultural, health, educational, and family planning innovations in developing nations. The communication model presented in Chapter 2 has been particularly robust in analyzing and planning innovation diffusion.

Opinion Leadership and Change Agents

Important roles in the diffusion process are opinion leadership and change agent. Opinion leadership is accomplished by individuals who can influence informally other individuals' attitudes or overt behavior in a desired way with relative frequency. A change agent is a person who influences innovation decisions in a direction deemed desirable by a change agency.

Adopters

The rate of adoption is the relative speed with which an innovation is adopted by members of a social system. Important to understanding the diffusion process are adoption categories or classifications of the members of a social system on the basis of innovativeness. In order of their adoption of a change are innovators, early adopters, early majority, late majority, and laggards.

The diffusion process also can be observed within a culture as it adopts new technologies. Everett Rogers (1986), in his book *Communication Technology,* recounts the introduction and adoption

Focus on Theory 13.2

Development Communication

Political scientist Daniel Lerner (1958) proposed that media helped transition from a traditional to a modernized country. Lerner argued that mass media expose people to events and ideas in other societies. That exposure would encourage them to reassess their current lifestyle and aspire to modern ways of life. Mass media at the societal level and interpersonal communication at the local level were seen as the paths to modernization. Studies from this perspective represent an area known as *development communication.* Development communication began as a Western political construct.

Non-Western scholars, particularly in Latin America, were critical of the imperialism of modernization in the dominant model (Beltran, 1976) and used cultural studies methods to focus more on the barriers that perpetuate inequalities. What is labeled as the *neomodernization* approach rejects the top-down perspective of the earlier modernization models and focuses on decentralized decision making and adopts a local, bottom-up view of modernization (Melkote, 2003).

of bank automated teller machines (ATMs). By 1985, only about one in three customers used them. The innovators, early adopters, and some of the early majority were users. As this 33% use seemed to be fairly stable, bankers began to speak of "smashing the wall"; that is, bankers began to try incentives to increase the percentage of customers using the ATM, or converting the late majority and laggards. Online banking has showed a similar adoption pattern. In 1994, the Stanford Credit Union offered the first online banking website. And by 2011, the majority of customers aged 55 and older preferred online banking to visiting a branch or an ATM. Now it is mobile phone banking that is in the early stages of the process.

Who are the innovators? Studies of adaptation potential, or an individual's possible success in adapting to a new culture, give us hints of likely innovators. Age and educational background are good predictors as innovators tend to be younger and better educated. Another characteristic of innovators is familiarity with the new technology or belief through previous contact, interpersonal contacts, and mass media. Personality factors, such as gregariousness, tolerance for ambiguity, risk taking, open-mindedness, and other related factors, are also good predictors of cultural adaptation and likely characteristics of innovators.

Change Agent Ethics

One final aspect of the diffusion process is change agent ethics. The introduction or rejection of an innovation has consequences for a society. It is important to recognize that the adoption—or rejection—of any innovation has consequences for the society. Introducing axes to the indigenous Australian tribes by missionaries (the change agents) resulted in an improved standard of living for the tribes but also contributed to the breakdown of the family structure, the rise of prostitution, and "misuse" of the axes themselves. Axes made hunting possible, which required men to live apart from their families, and axes could be used to kill humans as well as animals.

What are the consequences of providing birth control information and technology to a developing country? What might be the consequences for family size? The role of women? Support for the elderly? This fear of the consequences of culture contact is one reason why products are rejected.

The participatory model emerged in response to criticism of the diffusion model, including its heavy identification with mass media channels, but more particularly its basic assumption that information flows from the knowledgeable to the less knowledgeable. The participatory model stressed the dialogue as catalyst for individual and community empowerment adapted from the work of Paulo Freire (1970). The participatory model stresses that people should have control over decisions that affect them. Thus, groups should be involved in determining their needs and in designing and implementing programs to address these needs (N. Morris, 2003).

Rogers himself moved away from the diffusion model to what he called the convergence model. His model has been modified to treat communication as a process of convergence among members of interpersonal networks (Rogers & Kincaid, 1981). In the convergence model, communication is defined as a process in which information is shared by two or more individuals who converge over time toward a greater degree of mutual agreement. Whereas the diffusion model focuses on what one individual does to another, the convergence model focuses on the relationship between those who share information. Thus, the level of analysis shifts from the individual to the dyad or, on the macro level, to groups and cultures.

Focus on Skills 13.1

Philanthropy

As you have studied this chapter, you have seen not only ways to introduce new ideas, customs, and products into a culture but also that the introduction of those ideas, customs, and products can affect the receiving culture in many ways.

On one level, it is a skill to plan the introduction of a new product, for example, into a culture. Studying the receiving culture and finding ways to adapt the product to the receiving culture is an important skill. A more advanced skill level would be to attempt to anticipate the consequences of the introduction of that new product for the culture as a whole.

Philanthropy can be considered in the same way. As an exercise, assume you have $100 million to donate in a culture other than your own.

1. Look at several international charities, such as Heifer, Global Fund for Women, or U.S. Fund for UNICEF. Would you use an existing charity?
2. How would you apply what you have learned about development communication to this donation?
3. Based on what you have read in this chapter, develop criteria to assess the impact of the donation on the receiving culture as a whole.

Case Study: Quality Circles

In this case study, you will see an example of the diffusion of management concepts from the United States to Japan and then from Japan back to the United States.

After World War II, Japan's industry was destroyed. Japanese products of the time were popularly known as junk—they might last a day or two. "Made in Japan" meant the same thing as cheap and shoddy merchandise. General Douglas MacArthur asked Washington to send someone to help conduct a national census and assess Japan's ability to rebuild. Dr. W. Edward Deming, a relatively unknown statistician for the U.S. government, was sent.

Beginning in 1948, he gave lectures for the Union of Japanese Scientists and Engineers (JUSE), eventually lecturing to representatives of virtually every major Japanese corporation. Deming's message was that quality is the result of consistency, efficiency, and continual improvement. Deming believed that workers are intrinsically motivated to do well but that efforts are thwarted by incompetent, narrow-minded management. He stressed achieving uniform results during production rather than through inspection at the end of the production line. Deming's message was empowering workers with quality control decisions, monitoring the results statistically, and ensuring systematic cooperation with suppliers and buyers. In 1951, the JUSE honored his services by establishing the Deming Award for Quality. His portrait in Toyota headquarters is larger than that of the company's founder.

Later, Dr. Joseph Juran lectured in Japan on extending quality from just manufacturing to the entire process, from product design to product delivery to the customer. By 1956, there was a weekly radio series on quality, and in 1960, the government declared November "National Quality Month." From Deming's and Juran's work, by 1962 Japan developed the concept of the quality circle: a group of three to 10 employees who meet on the job to discuss and solve quality problems (Ingle, 1982).

By the 1970s, this and other efforts resulted in top-quality cameras, electronics, motorcycles, television sets, and radios.

Why did the quality circle as a concept succeed so well in Japan? The most important reason, as you have seen, is that the concept of working together in groups to benefit the organization matched with the Japanese cultural value placed on group affiliation, or homogeneity. But the story isn't over. In the 1960s, the United States was beginning to lose its lead in manufacturing. In the late 1960s, Juran published stories describing Japanese quality circles. Companies such as Lockheed and Honeywell started similar pilot programs. By 1973, Lockheed's programs were receiving wide publicity and wide imitation. Although many Fortune 500 companies began using quality circles, the programs did not have the same impact they had in Japan. Quality circles did not fit in well with the dominant U.S. value of individualism.

In the first part of this example, General MacArthur provided the opinion leadership and Deming was the change agent. In the second part, Juran provided the opinion leadership for the United States. As for the quality circles coming to the United States, the innovator was a corporation: Lockheed was the innovator in using Japanese quality circles in the United States.

Case Study: Vietnamese Nail Technicians

In the following case study, identify the diffusion process.

In the mid-1970s, Hope Village, outside Sacramento, California, was a holding place for Vietnamese refugees who had escaped the fall of Saigon. Actress Tippi Hedren (star of Alfred Hitchcock's *The Birds*) visited Hope Village every few days to mentor some of the women refugees. The women admired her glossy light pink fingernails, so she brought her manicurist in once a week to given the women lessons. Hedren then arranged for the women to receive free lessons at a nearby beauty school. The women passed their licensing exams and Hedren helped them find jobs in California.

As some opened their own beauty salons, the word spread. Vietnamese nail salons were opened all around Sacramento, then the rest of California, and then in other parts of the country. Today, 80% of manicurists in California and 40% nationwide are Vietnamese Americans (J. Berger, 2013).

Cultural Icons

Products can carry cultural values as well, and many products that are seen to represent a culture have been both widely popular and resisted. In his book *Mediamerica,* Edward Jay Whetmore (1987) writes of icons and artifacts as aspects of popular culture. An icon is a special symbol that tends to be idolized in a culture. (U.S. baseball is an example, with successes in Japan, South Korea, and Taiwan. See Focus on Culture 6.3 in Chapter 6.) An artifact is an object less widely recognized. English gardens, golf, English tea, Winnie the Pooh, Burberry, Laura Ashley, and the Body Shop represent British culture to many. Kangaroos, koalas, and boomerangs represent Australia to many. Louis Vuitton bags, France; and Ferragamo shoes, Italy. A global brand carries the same brand name or logo worldwide. Table 13.1 shows which ones are readily known worldwide.

Other examples of global brands are Braun, Budweiser, Canon, Cartier, Club Med, KFC, Levi's, Mercedes, Mitsubishi, Philips, and Sony. Most global brands are of U.S. origin, and to many they represent the U.S. lifestyle and culture (de Mooij, 2013). The positioning and values of global

Table 13.1 Twenty-Five Most Powerful Brand Names, 2016

Brand Name	Country of Origin
1. Google	United States
2. Apple	United States
3. Amazon.com	United States
4. AT&T	United States
5. Microsoft	United States
6. Samsung	Republic of Korea
7. Verizon	United States
8. Walmart	United States
9. Facebook	United States
10. ICBC	China
11. China Mobile	China
12. Toyota	Japan
13. Wells Fargo	United States
14. China Construction Bank	China
15. NTT Group	Japan
16. McDonald's	United States
17. BMW	Germany
18. Shell	United Kingdom
19. T (Deutsche Telekom)	Germany
20. IBM	United States
21. Mercedes-Benz	Germany
22. GE	United States
23. Alibaba	China
24. Walt Disney	United States
25. Chase	United States

Source: Brand Finance (2017).
Note: Ranking is based on Brand Finance's calculations using Royalty Relief methodology.

brands are identical in all countries, and they have brand loyalty in all countries in which they are marketed. Marlboro is an example. It is positioned worldwide as an urban premium brand appealing to the desire for freedom and open physical space symbolized by the "Marlboro man" and "Marlboro Country."

Cultural Hegemony

Some nations, like the United States, are major exporters of their own cultures. Though some societies are excellent markets for U.S. icons, other societies may resist adopting these ideas because they fear the changes that may accompany the new ideas. Some societies may perceive the increasing popularity of those icons as a form of cultural hegemony, or the fear of the predominant influence that one culture can develop over another. It is believed that what is being transmitted are the values of the culture. The receiving culture can unconsciously, or perhaps uncritically, absorb the values. *Cultural dependency* is the idea that a receiving culture becomes accustomed to cars from Japan or movies and TV from Great Britain and the United States, and that it's natural that they come from there, thus discouraging local businesses.

Japanese Icon in Mexico

In Japan, instant ramen was a post–World War II invention. The product soon became a cultural icon. Thousands visit a museum each year to see a replica of the workshop where instant ramen was developed.

Japanese fast-food noodles were first imported into Mexico in the 1980s. Today, Mexico is Latin American's largest per capita consumer of instant ramen—1 billion servings in 2004, a threefold increase since 1999. Instant ramen noodles, such as those marketed under the brand name Maruchan, which has an 85% share of the market, are supplanting beans and rice for many in Mexico. Convenience stores sell ramen, or *preparada,* with packets of salsa, and the Mexican government distributes it to remote rural areas. A cup of Maruchan costs 4 pesos (about U.S. 30 cents); a serving of beans costs much less, but Maruchan is ready to eat in minutes. Defenders of the nation's cuisine point to the relationship between food and culture. Ancient ancestors believed that humankind descended from corn. Mexican food traditionally has fresh ingredients, slow-cooked sauces, and hand-worked dough. Today's culture defenders see a threat to family and other traditional values.

Focus on Culture 13.1

South Korea's Cultural Exports

It's not only U.S. ideas that are spread by technology. Japan and Korea have a 2,000-year history of contact. In modern times, relations have been bitter, largely resulting from the Japanese occupation of Korea from 1910 to 1945, which included Japan conscripting Koreans into forced labor in Japan and conscripting some 200,000 Korean and Chinese young women to serve as "comfort women" at military instillations.

Against this backdrop, in 2002 came the South Korean television miniseries *Winter Sonata,* starring Choi Ji-woo and Bae Yong Joon, about first love, lost memory, and unknown family ties. In 2009 the series was adapted into an anime series. The series was broadcast on Japan's NHK and has had a major following in Japan and throughout Asia.

Bae Yong Joon became the most popular man in Japan. The actor was nicknamed "Yonsama" by the Japanese. *Sama* is an honorific usually reserved for royalty. In the series he plays "a sensitive, bespectacled architect with hair dyed brown and a scarf tied in a different way in each scene" (Onishi, 2004, para. 11). Older Japanese women said it reminded them of "simpler times at home." Yonsama represented qualities Japanese women found lacking in Japanese men. He was "sincere, pure, giving, passionate and soothing" (Onishi, 2004, para. 16).

After the series aired, Japanese tourism to South Korea grew by 40% in 2004. Japanese women took tours of the location where the series was filmed, others enrolled at his alma mater, others enrolled in Korean conversation classes. Total increased economic activity attributed to the series and Yonsama was estimated at $2.3 billion.

Media scholars have labeled Yonsama as one of the first *kkonminam* icons, young boyish male pop idols with style and fashion. Jung (2011) describes Bae Yong Joon's popularity with middle-aged Japanese women as an attraction to constructed "soft masculinity."

Yonsama's popularity in Japan continued long after the series. His 2009 book on Korean culture sold 50,000 copies in its first day of release in Japan. In the past, Koreans were discriminated against in Japan. *Winter Sonata* and Yonsama are examples of transborder popular media that have changed that prejudice (D. H. Ma, 2005).

In 2014, the South Korean soap opera *My Love From the Star* became as popular in China as *Winter Sonata* in Japan. When the female lead mentioned "beer and fried chicken" in an episode, restaurants in China started selling beer and fried chicken meals. By March 2014, the show had 25 billion views online.

U.S. Cultural Icons

Coca-Cola®

Without doubt, the most widely recognized U.S. icon worldwide is Coca-Cola. Coca-Cola products are sold in more countries than the United Nations has members, and it is claimed that *Coke* is the second most universally understood term in English after *okay*. The company has marketed internationally since 1900. Today, Coke sells 1.9 billion servings daily globally. The average human drinks 92 Coke products a year. Although U.S. residents drink 403 Coke products a year, 80% of the company's income comes from outside the United States.

Beginning in 1992, Coke began its first global marketing campaign: six commercials broadcast at the same time all over the world. So it's not all that surprising that Coca-Cola wanted Chinese characters that "sounded like" its name in English. That's what it was selling and why it has, on occasion, been met with opposition. China was one of Coca-Cola's first overseas markets when bottling plants were established in Shanghai and Tianjin in 1927. Forced to leave in 1949 by China's Communist Party as a symbol of U.S. imperialism, Coke returned in 1979. There have been new movements in China to limit the growing sales of U.S.-made Coke and Pepsi to protect local beverages. Coca-Cola was forced to leave India in 1977 after pressure from socialists, who labeled the soft drink a new form of colonialism pushing the U.S. culture. Coke returned to India in 1993.

The first U.S. factory to open in Vietnam since the United States restored diplomatic relations in 1995 was Coke's. Coke is seen as a status symbol. The Vietnamese paid 10% more for Coke than for a Vietnamese cola.

Coca-Cola is a registered trademark of the Coca-Cola Company. Permission for use granted by the company.

Coca-Cola markets an international T-shirt showing the various spellings of its name. Note that the trademark ribbon, part of Coke's logo, is always present.

Uriel Sinai/Getty Images News/Getty Images

The soft drink Mecca-Cola is part of anti-U.S. sentiment.

Some Arabs and other Muslims boycott U.S. products over the U.S. backing of Israel. Sales of the Iranian soft drink Zam Zam Cola, with its name taken from a holy spring in Saudi Arabia, increased in 2002. Another, Mecca-Cola, now sold in more than 60 countries, is marketed as a protest to U.S. foreign policy.

Disney

The first Disneyland outside the United States opened in 1983 in Tokyo and was totally owned by Japanese companies. Disney's $4.4 billion Euro Disney opened near Paris in April 1992. Some European intellectuals labeled the park a "cultural Chernobyl" (Chernobyl was the worst nuclear plant accident). Some were concerned how the park would affect French culture.

Disney made an attempt to "Europeanize" its attractions and products and downplayed the U.S. culture. Souvenir shops carried sweatshirts with small, discreet Disney logos. Rather than only fast-food restaurants, Euro Disney offered table-service restaurants. Disney's objective was to attract people from all over Europe and thus the company hired multilingual workers from throughout the continent.

The French have had little experience with theme parks. The French often dedicate Sunday—and only Sunday—to family outings. Most French do not snack and insist on eating at 12:30 p.m. This could create enormous and hostile bottlenecks at park restaurants. And French employees have an aversion to providing the smiles and friendly greetings so expected at any amusement park. Food, merchandise, and hotel business was weak: Europeans brought bag lunches and left early—not spending money at the park's gourmet restaurants and showcase hotels. Some European investors complained about a rigid, myopic U.S. management style.

At one point, the park was losing $1 million a day, forcing Disney to rename the park Disneyland Paris. Disney had discounted its own value as a U.S. icon, which is just what the French wanted to experience. Frontierland was just as popular as Discoveryland. French visitors to the park didn't want a leisurely, sit-down lunch; they wanted fast food. European visitors to the park didn't want discreet sweatshirts; they wanted sweatshirts with huge letters and big pictures of Mickey Mouse. After these changes, the park made its first small profit in the fiscal year ending in 1995. It became the most popular tourist attraction in France but was losing money again in 2002, attributed to a downturn in European travel, general economic conditions, and growing concerns about terrorism in France.

Disney had believed that the word *Euro* meant glamorous or exciting. To Europeans the word is associated with currency, commerce, and business. Disney conceded and changed the park's name. The park is now the most popular tourist destination in Europe.

VCG/Visual China Group/Getty Images

Opening day at Shanghai Disney in 2016.

In Asia, Disney opened the $3.5 billion Disneyland Hong Kong in 2005. Disney owns 48% and the Hong Kong government owns the remainder. In contrast to Europe, China, Taiwan, Singapore, Malaysia, and other countries close to Hong Kong don't have extensive acquaintance with the Disney culture and stories. Disney cartoons first appeared on Chinese television only in 1986. To counter that, Disney launched a Chinese television program called *The Magical World of Disneyland,* which had segments on the park; Disney merchandise appeared in more than 1,000 stores; and Disney used an alliance with an after-school program and the China Youth League to introduce Disney stories. Disney modeled this park closely after the original Disneyland, with only some features unique to Asian cultures. Guests meet the characters and take pictures with them in a large garden with five pavilions. Also, the vast majority of the food is Asian cuisine. The park has missed its attendance targets. The park is small and lacks the high-profile rides of other Disney parks, but Disney plans to expand the park with scores of new attractions.

Disney's $5.5 billion 390-hectare (963-acre) Shanghai Disneyland opened in June 2016. Built in partnership with the Shanghai Shendi Group, a government-controlled entity, Disney owns 43% of the park. The stated objective was to build a park that is "authentically Disney, distinctly Chinese." There is Starbucks and Cheesecake Factory, but also eel over rice and Peking duck pizza. There is no Main Street, USA, but a large garden featuring Disney versions of the Chinese zodiac animals. There are rigid barriers to encourage orderly queuing. Dialogue in performances is mainly in Mandarin with some Shanghainese. Song lyrics are a mix of Mandarin and English depending on the show. To prepare China for Disneyland (where Mickey Mouse is still known as Mi Lao Shu), Disney has partnered with China's two dominant online video sites to stream Disney's ABC primetime shows and is operating Disney English centers for children ages 2 to 12. The centers use learning materials filled with Disney images.

Disney has not been without its critics. Hom (2013) contends that the Disney brand outside the United States is a form of imperialism. Exhibits and performances often infuse non-Western folklore stories with notions of individualism and "the American Dream." The Jungle Cruise was eventually removed from Disneyland Paris after Europeans objected to its colonialism image (Spencer, 1995). Even in the film *Mulan,* the Chinese female longs to live in a society where individualism is promoted (Yin, 2011).

Focus on Theory 13.3

Stuart Hall's Concept of Articulation

The concept of articulation was developed by Stuart Hall and refers to the analysis of how a person or group with its own specific interests connects to other people, groups, ideas, and property to carry out their own interests. It shows how a person or group tries to force others to envision themselves as a group even though there are many differences.

Source: S. Hall, Morley, & Chen. (1996).

McDonald's

Restaurant chains have become cultural icons. Table 13.2 lists those most identified with the United States.

Most influential, by far, is McDonald's. The McDonald brothers operated a hamburger stand in San Bernardino, California, that offered a limited menu and used "assembly-line" procedures for cooking and serving food. Ray Kroc first visited it in 1954 and, the following year, in partnership with the McDonald brothers, opened the first restaurant (Ritzer, 1993). By 1998, McDonald's had about 25,000 restaurants in more than 110 countries. In a 1986 survey, 96% of the schoolchildren surveyed could identify Ronald McDonald—second only to Santa Claus in name recognition.

When McDonald's opened its first restaurant in Singapore in 1982, it quickly became the largest-selling McDonald's in the world. In early 1990, McDonald's opened its first restaurant in Moscow. One journalist described it as the "ultimate icon of Americana." Russians were unaccustomed to eating finger food, and Russian workers were unaccustomed to smiling and looking customers directly in the eye. McDonald's knew it was selling U.S. popular culture and kept much of the product the same. In 1992, in Beijing, McDonald's opened its largest restaurant at that time, with 700 seats, 29 cash registers, and nearly 1,000 employees. On its first day of business, it served about 40,000 customers (Ritzer, 1993). Today, McDonald's has some 2,200 restaurants in China and plans for more.

What "message" representing the United States does McDonald's communicate to the world? Ritzer (1993) identified the principles of the fast-food restaurant that are coming to dominate more and more sectors worldwide. He calls this the "McDonaldization of society."

- *Efficiency.* The McDonald's fast-food model offers an efficient method of satisfying many needs.
- *Quantification.* Time is quantified in terms of how quickly one is served, and quantity ("bigger is better") becomes more important than quality.
- *Predictability.* The food McDonald's serves in Baltimore is essentially identical to the food it serves in Houston. It offers no surprises.
- *Control.* Employees are trained to do a very limited number of things, and customers as well are controlled through limited options.

Table 13.2 Top U.S.-Based International Franchise Restaurant Chains, Ranked by 2011 International Sales

International Chain	Units Outside the United States	International (Non-U.S.) Sales (in Millions)
McDonald's	18,710	$44,985
KFC (Kentucky Fried Chicken)	11,798	$14,700
Burger King	4,998	$6,200
Pizza Hut	5,890	$4,800
Subway	10,109	$4,600
Domino's Pizza	4,422	$2,900
Starbucks	5,727	$2,289
Wendy's	693	$983
Dunkin' Donuts	3,005	$584
Dairy Queen	802	$433

Source: The Global 30 (2012).

Focus on Culture 13.2

Fast-Food Colonialism

When European germs wiped out Indians, at least that aspect of conquest was unintentional. Burger King has no such excuse.

The modern colonizers currently have an ad campaign called "Whopper Virgins." Commercials are running during televised sports events, and the company has a nearly 8-minute video on its website. In a bizarre parody of an actual documentary, Burger King sent a crew out to remote Hmong parts of Thailand, Inuit parts of Greenland, and a village in Romania where people have both never seen a hamburger nor ever heard of one through advertising. The narration starts, "The hamburger is a culinary culture and it's actually an American phenomenon" (as if we didn't know this).

The first part of the video involved plucking some villagers to come to a modern office in local and native dress to compare Burger King's signature burger with a McDonald's Big Mac. Villagers are shown fumbling with the burger, with a patronizing narrator saying, "It's been very interesting to see their reaction to the hamburger because they've never seen such a foreign piece of food before and they didn't even quite know how to pick it up and they didn't know how to—from what end to eat. It was really interesting. We were able to see these people's first bite of a hamburger."

Remarking on the villagers' awkwardness in handling the burger, the narrator added, "It took them awhile to understand the dynamics of it and so that was fascinating to see because we take it for granted 'cause we live in America where hamburgers are consumed like a staple."

After the guinea pig villagers decided (of course!) that the Whopper tasted better than the Big Mac, Burger King sent a production crew out to the villages to cook burgers. Under the guise of "sharing things about both our cultures" (Gee, where have we heard that before in sanitized colonial history?), shots of a burger broiler being airlifted and sledded in by dog are shown. The villagers, of course, like the burger, with the narrator saying, "They told us yesterday, 'No, we want to experience other things in this world, too. We want to taste other foods. We want to see other people. We want to see other things.'"

Right out of the most banal of Thanksgiving scripts, the narrator says, as one of the crew receives a coat, "And they've been extraordinarily gracious to us." Burger King defends the ads, saying it worked hard to respect cultural sensitivities.

All this, to spread disease to developing peoples. And Burger King knows it. The Westernization of the global diet, led by America's fast-food giants, is helping spread obesity and diabetes as it has never been seen before. It's not enough that those diseases are off the charts with Native Americans here at home. Now we want to seduce Inuits abroad. Even if levels of obesity stay what they are now, the number of people around the world with diabetes will explode from the 171 million people of 2000 to 366 million by 2030.

The numbers will more than triple in places ranging from the Democratic Republic of the Congo to Bangladesh to Guatemala. They will more than double or nearly triple in China, India, Brazil, and Mexico. According to WHO researchers, diabetes was already responsible in 2000 for nearly 3 million deaths around the world. "Given the increasing prevalence of obesity, it is likely that these figures provide an underestimate of future diabetes prevalence," those researchers said. Translated, even more people will die.

The WHO, not surprisingly, says, "Initiatives by the food industry to reduce the fat, sugar, and salt content of processed foods . . . could accelerate health gains worldwide."

But no, Burger King wants to colonize the farthest reaches with fat, sugar, and salt.

The irony was when the locals made the crew their native food in the video. The meal ladled out for them was smothered in vegetables. The crew yum-yummed "Nice," "Wonderful," "So good," and even, "Insane." That was the height of patronization given their mission. Burger King's violation of the "Whopper Virgins" is an insane reenactment of the worst of American colonial history.

Source: D. Z. Jackson (2008). © Globe Newspaper Company.

McDonald's as a U.S. cultural icon has not been welcome in Iran since the country's revolution in 1979. In 1994 an Iranian entrepreneur opened an official McDonald's franchise in Tehran. After 2 days the restaurant was burned down in protests. In fact, there are no U.S. chain restaurants in Iran today because of the government's hostility and sanctions that make such businesses impossible. Even though the relationship between the U.S and Iranian governments has been complex and tense, including U.S.-imposed sanctions, Iranians have launched their own spin-offs including one known as "Mash Donalds," complete with flashing logo that resembles McDonald's golden arches and posters of a clown in red jacket, yellow pants, and oversized red shoes waving to customers. In addition to Mash Donald's, Tehran also has a Kabooki Fried Chick, a Pizza Hat, and a Burger House. On its website, McDonald's does accept franchise applications for Iran but also states it has not set a firm date for the development of McDonald's restaurants in Iran.

KFC

Kentucky Fried Chicken, now simply known as KFC, was a leader in the international market. Today, it has more than 18,000 locations in 118 countries, including some 5,000 outlets in China. Its Original Recipe offerings are sold in every KFC restaurant around the world.

In 1987, KFC opened the first Western fast-food restaurant in China in Beijing's Tiananmen Square. KFC meals became a political statement at the prodemocracy demonstrations there. In 2007, KFC was opening a new restaurant every day. The target was 20,000 restaurants within two decades. KFC has adapted its menu to local tastes, including rice congee, egg custard tarts, and tree fungus salad. Chinese outlets are typically two to three times larger than elsewhere, and many are open 24 hours a day and provide home delivery. As a result, KFC is the most recognizable international icon of any kind in China, and today China is the largest source of revenue for the company.

HOANG DINH NAM/AFP/Getty Images

KFC in Ho Chi Minh City, Vietnam.

KFC remains popular in Muslim Indonesia despite less than favorable attitudes toward the U.S. government. In fact, in the world's largest Muslim nation, KFC is lucrative during Ramadan. Perhaps Muslims in Indonesia have divergent attitudes about the U.S. government and U.S. popular culture.

SPAM®

The "Miracle Meat in a Can" was launched in the United States in 1937. As it does not need to be refrigerated, it traveled easily with the U.S. military during World War II and the Korean War. Spam remains popular in the Philippines, Okinawa, Guam, and Saipan, all places with a history of U.S. military presence.

World War II brought thousands of U.S. military personnel to Hawai'i, and with them came mainland cultural influences that dominated and replaced existing traditions. One that remains a staple to this day is Spam, nearly 7 million cans of which are consumed annually in Hawai'i—even at McDonald's and Burger King.

Today, Spam is a luxury item in South Korea. *Chusok,* the Korean equivalent of U.S. Thanksgiving, is the biggest gift-giving occasion of the year. On this day alone, some 8 million cans of Spam are given as gifts, some in boxed sets.

Nike

Nike is one of the world's largest suppliers of athletic shoes and apparel. Nike employs some 44,000 people and grosses over $30 billion annually. Nike's marketing extends globally through its web operations. It uses Twitter for customer service, responding to product inquiries directly. It also launched a social media campaign during the 2012 Olympics. Nike localizes each website, including having subdomains for multiple languages spoken within one country.

Nike ties much of its advertising to well-known athletes, such as basketball star Michael Jordan, whose ad appearances contributed to billions in sales of sneakers and clothing. In 2015 Nike became the official apparel supplier for the entire NBA. But even Nike can foul. In China, Nike featured U.S. basketball player LeBron James battling a kung fu master as well as other cultural symbols. The Chinese government banned the commercial as violating regulations to uphold national dignity and respect for local culture (Fowler, 2004).

Later in China, Nike faced a challenge in marketing running shoes. In China, running is part of athletic drills. It's not something most people do in heavily polluted cities jammed with cars, bikes, and pedestrians. If someone is running on a crowded Chinese city street, it's most likely a Westerner. Rather than tell the Chinese consumer why running is good, Nike launched a campaign on Chinese social media networks and video-sharing sites featuring the few runners talking about why they run. Reasons included "I run to make the hidden visible" and "I run to get lost" ("Nike Faces Marketing Challenge in China," 2011).

Adapting the Message

As you have seen, key to the diffusion and convergence processes across cultures is adaptation of the message to the receiving culture. The key is to adapt to the local culture, localize thinking, localize the product, and localize the marketing strategy.

De Mooij (2014) has reviewed research and been able to relate advertising styles to Hofstede's dimensions. For instance, Japanese advertising reflects Confucian and collectivistic values. Concepts of face and harmony relate to an indirect communication style. It is said that the goal of Japanese advertising is to win the trust and respect of the consumer. Advertising is serene, mood creating, and subtle, with much symbolism. Dependency, nature, and respect for elders can be seen.

In commercials seen in the United States, the insurance company AFLAC makes use of an abrasive quacking duck. But for AFLAC's commercials in Japan, where the company earns about 70% of its income, the AFLAC duck has a more "smoothing" tone.

Taiwan advertising generally links the product to the consumer's traditional Chinese values, such as family relations and respect for authority. The advertising is indirect and promises an ideal that may be reached through the use of the product. Spanish advertising is less direct than the advertising style of northern European countries because Spain's culture is more collectivistic. People are depicted in family and other groups. Feminine aspects of the culture are seen in the softer approaches and relatively low use of celebrity endorsements. The use of art, color, and beauty is related to strong uncertainty avoidance.

U.S. advertising reflects assertiveness, the direct approach, and competitiveness, which de Mooij relates to a configuration of masculinity and individualism. Overstatement and hyperbole are typical, as are direct comparisons.

Two examples of message adaptation are the marketing of baby food worldwide and missionary work in New Guinea.

Case Study: Marketing Gerber Baby Foods Worldwide

Gerber Products first entered Australia in 1959, Japan in 1960, and the Philippines in 1972 under the assumption that the world would like and buy what was popularly used in the United States. The company discovered that each country not only likes different foods but also has different baby-feeding practices. Gerber then established advisory committees in those countries to determine what products would be acceptable. Out of that came "lamb stock stew" for Australia, "rice with young sardines" for Japan, and "strained mango" for the Philippines.

In Japan and South Korea, mothers are pressured to make meals for the family from scratch. In those countries, Gerber positions itself by marketing its products as part of a "scientifically based" feeding plan. The food containers are labeled as "lessons" to demonstrate that Gerber provides something that the mothers cannot make for babies.

Case Study: Religious Missionary Work in New Guinea

Before reading how missionaries took Christianity to the peoples of New Guinea, understand that missionaries look for what is called a redemptive analogy, or something in the culture that can be compared to the Christian gospel and hence makes the unknown knowable to the culture (Richardson, 1974). One missionary came upon the practice of peacemaking between two villages. A man from each village handed over to the other village one of each village's babies to live among the other people. The people in New Guinea called these children *tarop tim,* or "peace child." According to the tradition, everyone in the village must then touch the peace child as a symbol of accepting the peace. As long as the children were alive, no fighting was allowed to occur between the villages.

QUESTA NON TE L'ASPETTAVI.

Prova la nuova insalata di pasta con pasta Barilla

LE SORPRESE NON FINISCONO MAI, DA McDONALD'S.   ORA E SCOPRI LE TABELLE NUTRIZIONALI

© 2013 McDonald's

McDonald's no longer serves the same menu worldwide. It now caters to local tastes, but under the same golden arches. This placemat from 2013 pictures what is sold in Italy—a pasta salad. Pasta salads are popular in Italy.

The missionary built his message around the concept of the peace child. He explained how God gave his peace child to the world. In the local culture, fighting could begin again if the children died, but God's peace child is eternal because he rose from the dead and is still alive.

Adapting U.S. Icons

Initially, the marketing of U.S. icons required that they be the same as in the United States because what was being sold was the U.S. culture. Over time the focus has shifted to the value of the icon to local taste and customs.

By 1992, McDonald's had 882 outlets in Japan. These offer soup and fried rice to cater to Japanese eating habits, but the golden arches are there. McDonald's competitor in Japan is Japanese-owned MOS (Mountain, Ocean, Sea). Ironically, the MOS burger is based on the one made at Tommy's, a famous Los Angeles hamburger franchise.

In 1996, McDonald's opened in New Delhi, India, but without all-beef patties because 80% of the population is Hindu, a religion whose followers don't eat beef. The menu features the Maharaja Mac—"two all-mutton patties, special sauce, lettuce, cheese, pickles, onions on a sesame-seed bun." The restaurant opened with a traditional Hindu ceremony. In Jerusalem, McDonald's has

Table 13.3	How McDonald's Adapts to Local Tastes
Country	**Adaptation**
Brazil	Quiche de Queijo (cheese quiche)
France	M Burger (beef, cheese, lettuce, tomato, and natural Emmenthal cheese on a stone oven–baked Ciabatta-style roll)
Germany	Big Rösti (quarter-pound beef patty topped with Ementaler cheese, bacon, a crispy hash brown, and Big Rösti sauce)
Hong Kong	Red Bean Pie (red beans are commonly used in desserts)
India	Potato-patty McAloo Tikki burger and the Chicken Maharaja Mac (much of the population does not eat meat)
Italy	Parmigiano Reggiano burger
Portugal	Caldo Verde soup (made with cabbage, kale, onion, potato, and chorizo)

Source: McDonald's (2014).

nonkosher and kosher restaurants. As Jewish law forbids the cooking, serving, or eating of meat and milk products together, the kosher restaurants don't have cheeseburgers, milkshakes, or ice cream. The restaurants also are closed on Saturdays to observe the religious injunction against working on the Sabbath.

McDonald's in Great Britain, France, Germany, and Brazil serve beer and wine. McDonald's in Brazil has "happy hours" with salsa bands. But McDonald's has found that adaptations to local tastes can go too far: The McPloughman's sandwich, a version of the British pub staple featuring bread, cheese, and pickle, was not popular, nor was the forced "Thank you, please call again."

David Silverman/Getty Images News/ Getty Images

Israelis eat at kosher McDonald's. The word *kosher* is displayed in both Hebrew and English.

The same is true for KFC. In China, KFC offers breakfast of traditional Chinese foods like congee (a rice porridge). Kraft foods introduced Oreos in China in 1996. Oreos are a vanilla cream–filled chocolate cookie sandwich with a 100-year tradition that sells well in the United States. Kraft learned

Focus on Culture 13.3

Marketing to Local Cultures

Gillette wanted to increase its sales of razors in India. It wanted a razor that could displace the old-fashioned T-shaped double-edged razor used by some 500 million Indians. It developed the Vector, which had a plastic push bar that slid down to unclog the razor. Gillette was adapting its product to Indian men who generally have thicker hair and a higher hair density than many men in the United States. Indian men tend to shave less frequently, so they shave longer beards. Gillette tested a new product with Indian students attending MIT who reported liking the new product. But when the razor was launched in India, reception was much less positive. The difference: Gillette executives didn't realize that men in India use a cup of water to shave, whereas Indian students at MIT use running tap water. Without running water, Gillette's new razor stayed clogged.

Source: Proctor & Gamble (n.d.).

Panasonic had been receiving complaints from Indian consumers that its washing machines didn't fully get food stains off their clothes. After 2 years of analyzing what went into a typical Indian curry dish and testing water flow and temperatures, Panasonic introduced a "curry" button on its StainMaster washing machines. It plans similar machines for other Asian markets with settings for stains specific to those countries.

Source: "India Washing Machine Launched With 'Curry' Button" (2017).

Focus on Skills 13.2

Releasing a New High-Tech Product in the United States

Not all high-tech products are developed and sold in the United States. Because profit margins are slimmer and patent laws are more complex, many companies do not market their products in the United States at all. Many high-tech companies release products in South Korea first. The government in South Korea has policies to make the country the most wired nation on earth. South Korea is a more friendly country in which to introduce new innovative products.

Some high-tech products that may not yet be marketed in the United States include tobacco vending machines that verify a purchaser's age before dispensing the product, video glasses that turn iPods into a complete theater experience (Mikimoto Bean i-theater), mobile security robots for shopping malls (Reborg-Q Security Robot), and a device to detect liquid explosive threats at airport screening (Senicon).

Assume you are an intern at a marketing communications firm. You've been asked to study one of these products for possible release in the United States.

1. How would you recommend the product be marketed in the United States?
2. What U.S. cultural values might be relevant to the marketing of the product?

---

that Chinese don't like treats as big or as sweet as is typical in the United States. Kraft first adjusted to that. It then added green tea ice cream flavor and later other flavors popular in Asian desserts—raspberry, blueberry, mango, and orange. Oreos are now the top-selling cookie in China, surpassing a local product. Kraft is no longer so much selling a U.S. icon as a product that is desired by local tastes and customs.

The counterargument to cultural imperialism is that no surveys show that people are becoming more alike. While media flows globally, people receive and use the messages differently. Global marketing may symbolize the lifestyles that people aspire to, but evidence grows that local cultures have taken on a renewed significance as political movements promote local cultures and local identities. Finally, there is evidence that cultures do not flow in only one direction. Salsa music originated in the Caribbean but is now known worldwide, as are Ethiopian and Thai cuisines. German game shows and a Brazilian soap opera are popular on Cameroon television. And international students from Kenya are relieved to discover that KFC is available in the United States, too.

SUMMARY

Mary Pratt (1992) coined the term *contact zone* to refer to "the space in which peoples geographically and historically separated come into contact with each other and establish ongoing relations, usually involving conditions of coercion, radical inequality, and intractable conflict" (p. 6). Edward Said describes the contact and subsequent linguistic construction of non-Western cultures as Orientalism, a process of labeling the peoples of "underdeveloped" cultures, particularly Indigenous cultures, as insignificant "others." That cultural imperialism continues in the actions of multinational corporations. Products can carry cultural values, and many products that are seen to represent a culture have been both widely popular and resisted. A cultural icon is a special symbol that tends to be idolized in a culture. U.S. cultural icons include Coca-Cola, Disneyland, McDonald's, KFC, Spam, and Nike.

Diffusion is the communication process by which innovations are spread to members of a social system. Roles in the diffusion process include opinion leadership (individuals who can informally influence others), change agents (people who influence innovation decisions), and adopters (people who accept and use the innovation). Early adopters tend to be younger and more educated, have had previous contact with the innovation, and have personality characteristics such as gregariousness. The key to successful diffusion across cultures is adapting the message to the receiving culture.

DISCUSSION QUESTIONS

1. In what ways can it be said that colonialism is a continuing world theme today?

2. Can there be a balance between cultural imperialism and diffusion of cultural icons?

3. What are the arguments for and against anyone or any government introducing new ideas or technology into a culture?

4. Describe examples of advertising from countries that reflect those countries' cultural dimensions.

KEY TERMS

adaptation potential	convergence	icon
artifact	cultural imperialism	opinion leadership
change agent	diffusion	Orientalism
change agent ethics	discursive imperialism	quality circle
contact zone	hegemony	redemptive analogy

READINGS

All readings are from *Intercultural Communication: A Global Reader* (Jandt, 2004).

Fred E. Jandt and Dolores V. Tanno, "Decoding Domination, Encoding Self-Determination: Intercultural Communication Research Processes" (p. 205)

Ketra L. Armstrong, "Nike's Communication With Black Audiences" (p. 264)

STUDENT STUDY SITE

ⓈSAGE edge™

Sharpen your skills with SAGE edge at edge.sagepub.com/jandt9e.

SAGE edge for Students provides a personalized approach to help you accomplish your coursework goals in an easy-to-use learning environment.

Chapter 14

© iStockphoto.com/porcorex

Future Challenges

In Chapter 9 you read about the Human Development Index, the composite measure of indicators of life expectancy, educational attainment, and access to the resources needed for a decent living. Over the past decades all regions and groups in the world have demonstrated notable improvements in all Human Development Index indicators. From this evidence it can be said that on these indicators the improvement in the human condition worldwide in the past few decades has been unprecedented.

The United States remains the largest economy in the world and will remain so for the foreseeable future. Some of the world's largest countries have made significant advances in human development, notably Brazil, China, India, Indonesia, South Africa, and Turkey. Several smaller economies have made substantial progress as well, notably Bangladesh, Chile, Ghana, Mauritius, Rwanda, and Tunisia (United Nations Development Programme, 2013).

In centuries past, groups of people were separated by distance across oceans and land barriers. The physical distance heightened the perception of differences. The communication challenge was how to overcome those differences that we labeled as cultural. In today's world of over 7 billion people with modern transportation, we are not physically isolated. In today's world with modern communication, we recognize our interdependence. Our intercultural communication challenge today is how to better understand groups with unique cultural identities in order to work interdependently to meet global challenges.

In the previous chapter you read that Mary Pratt (1992) coined the term *contact zone* to refer to "the space in which peoples geographically and historically separated come into contact with each other and establish ongoing relations, usually involving conditions of coercion, radical inequality, and intractable conflict" (p. 6). You'll remember Captain Cook's sailing into the Hawaiian Islands as an unfortunate example. Today's contact zone, in contrast, is enacted on the Internet, in marketplaces, in the world economy, and in daily interactions in which important parts of people's identities clash.

In Chapter 1 you read about Cannadine's (2013) six forms of regulators of human life and identity: religion, nation, class, gender, race, and civilization. After studying the subsequent chapters, you may begin to recognize that not all peoples today identify with the same form of regulator of human life and identity. Consider the following that we have studied:

- *China and Japan.* To what extent do you believe ethnicity and nation-state identity have become coterminous (having the same boundaries)?
- *Israel.* To what extent do you believe religion, ethnicity, and nation-state identity have become coterminous?
- *Sub-Saharan Africa.* In many places, tribal identity, a form of ethnicity, is a much stronger identity than nation.
- *Arab world.* Can you identify countries where religion and nation-state identity have become coterminous?
- *Modern developed world in Europe, North America, Australia, and New Zealand.* Primary cultural identity has become nation-state identity, with other forms of identity recognized as microcultural identities.

Today's contact zones are not all among entities of the same type. For example, nation-states may interact with religious groups that transcend national boundaries or ethnic or tribal groups within a nation's boundaries.

In this final chapter you are invited to look ahead to the future and imagine the challenges for intercultural communication presented by the contact zones associated with each of Cannadine's regulators of human life and identity.

Religion

Cannadine (2013) argues that religion is the oldest source of human identity and conflict. In Chapter 1 only some examples of religious wars were listed. That wasn't to suggest that conflict based in religious identification is a thing of the past.

Conflict between Hindus and Muslims in the Indian subcontinent has a history that could date back to the 8th century. Today's conflict dates back to 1947, when Britain gave up control of the Indian subcontinent, splitting it into a predominantly Hindu India and a predominantly Muslim Pakistan. Hundreds of thousands from both groups were killed and millions were displaced. At least 14 million people migrated. Hindus and Sikhs were forced to leave Pakistan. Muslim families faced attacks as they tried to leave India. As many Muslims as there were in the new state of Pakistan stayed in India. About 80% of India's population is Hindu and about 14% is Muslim. The Muslims who remained in India were blamed for the division of the country.

In the split, the state of Kashmir initially remained independent. Pakistan later claimed Kashmir because most of its residents are Muslim. Its ruler agreed to join India if it sent the military to help him. The ensuing war divided Kashmir into Indian- and Pakistani-controlled portions. India and Pakistan went to war again in 1965 to a stalemate that ended in a 1972 cease-fire line. Since 1987 India and Pakistan have come to the brink of war four times.

Violence continues to break out today. In India's northern Uttar Pradesh state in 2013, a teenage Hindu girl complained to her family that she had been harassed by a Muslim boy. The girl's brother and cousin shot the boy. His family beat and killed the girl's brother and cousin. From that incident violence escalated: massive demonstrations, armed street battles, inflammatory speeches by local politicians, rumors spread by mobile phones and social media, and 13,000 security officers deployed.

Whether in Israel, the Arab world, the former Soviet Union, or any number of other places where religious identity is a central part of many individuals' identity, any threat to one's religious beliefs is a threat to one's identity. Oftentimes religious conflict becomes intertwined with ethic and nationalist causes, as with Catholics in Northern Ireland and Hindu nationalists in India.

Class

In Chapter 1 you read that Cannadine (2013) identified class, as developed by Marx, as a source of identity but that since the collapse of Communism, it is no longer pervasive nor an all-encompassing source of identity. Nonetheless, several studies have linked class, now defined as economic position in society, to important parts of one's identity, including child-rearing practices, career choices, and marriage choices.

In that modern economic perspective, is class a source of potential conflict? A Credit Suisse Research Institute study has shown that 1% of the world's population controls 46% of the world's money, property, and other material resources (Keating et al., 2013). The richest 10% control 86% of global wealth. The United States accounts for 46% of the super wealthy people worldwide, followed by China with 6%. In 2014 the British-based anti-poverty charity Oxfam released a report showing that the world's 85 richest individuals control the same wealth as half of the Earth's population—said another way, the poorest 3.5 billion people must live on an amount equal to what these 85 individuals possess. A particularly interesting part of the Credit Suisse study showed how much wealth stays in families. For example, in North America 10 generations or more have to pass before the wealth of an individual is completely unrelated to the wealth of her or his ancestors.

Two-thirds of the world's population controls no more than 3% of global wealth (Keating et al., 2013).

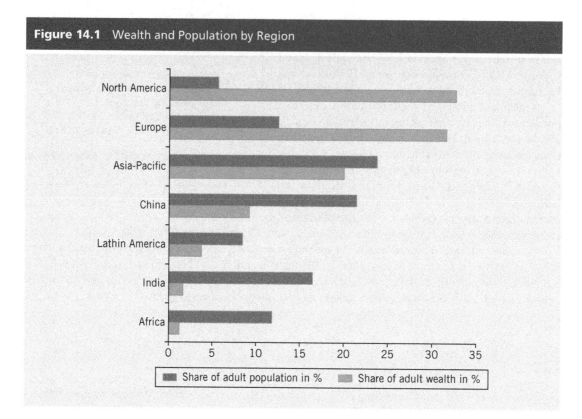

Figure 14.1   Wealth and Population by Region

Source: Keating et al. (2013).

Global Voices

Let me tell you about the very rich. They are different from you and me. They possess and enjoy early, and it does something to them, makes them soft where we are hard, and cynical where we are trustful, in a way that, unless you were born rich, it is very difficult to understand. They think, deep in their hearts, that they are better than we are because we had to discover the compensations and refuges of life for ourselves. Even when they enter deep into our world or sink below us, they still think that they are better than we are. They are different.

—F. Scott Fitzgerald, "Rich Boy," in *All the Sad Young Men* (1926)

India and Africa are disproportionately represented in this group; Europe and North America are underrepresented. Figure 14.1 shows the comparison of regions' population to wealth.

One consequence of this disparity of wealth is world hunger. In 1970 U.S. plant breeder Norman Borlaug was awarded the Nobel Peace Prize for his work in developing high-yield, disease-resistant varieties of wheat and other grains. Worldwide harvests tripled. Today, the world produces sufficient food to feed all 7 billion of us. Yet in sub-Saharan Africa, Central and Southeast Asia, and parts of Latin America and the Caribbean, millions live on the edge of starvation (see Figure 14.2).

Worldwide nearly 1 billion people can't afford to buy food and can't grow enough on their own. Poor transportation and storage facilities contribute to the problem. One consequence is that an estimated 8

Figure 14.2 Percentage of Population That Is Malnourished, 2015

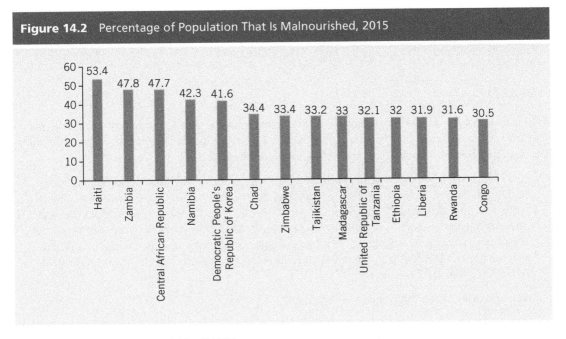

Source: United Nations Statistics Division (2016b).
Note: No available data for Somalia, Burundi, and Comoros, which in previous years have had more than 30%.

million people die each year of hunger-related diarrhea, pneumonia, and other illnesses—more than AIDS, malaria, and tuberculosis combined. A second consequence is mass migration across national boundaries.

Expanding middle classes tend to change their diets to consume more grain-fed beef and pork. Most of the world's best farmland is already cultivated and is being reduced by expanding cities and deserts. Creating more from remaining forests and grasslands would have major environmental consequences on wildlife and possibly on climate itself. Middle-class dietary change and an estimated additional 2 billion people by the middle of the 21st century will result in insufficient food supply.

China has 20% of the world's population and just 9% of the world's arable land. China has chronic droughts and desertification. Economic growth has taken arable land out of production, and pollution has made millions of acres unsuitable for farming. As a result, China is acquiring control of farmlands in the United States, Chile, Brazil, Russia, Ukraine, Bulgaria, and Australia.

Bloomberg/Bloomberg/Getty Images

Some of the products from China's largest pork producer, Shuanghui International Holdings, are displayed. The group paid $4.7 billion for Smithfield Foods and acquired more than 40,468 hectares (100,000 acres) of farmland in Missouri, Texas, and North Carolina.

Yet we don't see large-scale conflicts based solely on economic class. The pressures of income disparity are more likely to result in migration, which then can become a source of conflict.

Gender

As you read in Chapter 1, Cannadine (2013) dismisses gender as a major source of group identity as he contends it is difficult to substantiate that there is a unifying identity solidarity among all women. You read in Chapter 9 that cultures treat the genders differently.

In 1979, the UN General Assembly adopted the Convention on the Elimination of All Forms of Discrimination Against Women. According to the convention, discrimination against women is any distinction, exclusion or restriction made on the basis of sex which has the effect or purpose of impairing or nullifying the recognition, enjoyment or exercise by women, irrespective of their marital status, on a basis of equality of men and women, of human rights and fundamental freedoms in the political, economic, social, cultural, civil or any other field. (United Nations, 1979, para. 4)

The measures to end discrimination included

- incorporating the principle of equality of men and women in their legal systems, abolishing all discriminatory laws, and adopting appropriate ones prohibiting discrimination against women;
- establishing tribunals and other public institutions to ensure the effective protection of women against discrimination; and
- ensuring elimination of all acts of discrimination against women by persons, organizations, or enterprises.

In July 2010, the UN General Assembly voted unanimously to create a single UN body tasked with accelerating progress in achieving gender equality and women's empowerment. These are its objectives:

- promoting gender equality and empowering women as essential to the achievement of development goals
- strengthening the full integration of women into the formal economy
- boosting national and international efforts to prevent and eliminate all forms of violence against women and girls
- improving access to health systems for women and girls
- creating a new vision for conserving earth's biological diversity that must encompass gender ("In Historic Move," 2010)

Women's economic status is related to fertility rate. Areas of high income disparity also tend to be areas with high fertility rates. A fertility rate of 2.1 children per woman is the replacement rate for a population. The current global fertility rate is now 2.5 children per woman. Tables 14.1 and 14.2 show the world's highest and lowest fertility rates. In 1970–1975 half of the top 10 were in sub-Saharan Africa. This increased to eight countries in 1990–1995 and nine countries in 2010–2015. The top 10 lowest fertility countries or areas are no longer primarily in Europe. In 1970–1975, eight of the 10 countries were in Europe. By 1990–1995, there were three in Asia, and by 2020–2015, five of them were in Asia.

One potential indirect consequence of high fertility rates and a large young population in a nation is the potential for violence. One way to better study a country's population is by the percentage of total population by age, such as displayed in population pyramids (see Figure 14.3). When countries' populations are compared in this fashion, a significant trend is noted: About 80% of the world's civil conflicts since the 1970s have occurred in countries with young populations.

Does the association with violence result from youth or other related factors? A youth boom was associated with the rise of the Nazis in Germany, Japan's militarization, U.S. activism of the 1960s and 1970s, and China's 1989 Tiananmen Square protests. Typically, though, countries with young populations also tend to experience poverty, unemployment, and unstable governments.

Table 14.1	Countries or Areas With the Highest Total Fertility, 2010–2015
Niger	7.6
Somalia	6.6
Mali	6.4
Chad	6.3
Angola	6.2
Democratic Republic of the Congo	6.2
Burundi	6.1
Uganda	5.9
Timor-Leste	5.0
Gambia	4.2

Source: United Nations (2015).

Race, Skin Color, and Ethnicity

Some would argue that race (however defined), skin color, and ethnicity are major regulators of human life and of identity creation for some. The 1904 World's Fair in St. Louis included an exhibit of living "foreign people." The head anthropologist at the fair wrote in an essay titled "The Trend of Human Progress" that humans "are conveniently grouped in the four culture grades of savagery, barbarism, civilization, and enlightenment. . . . The two higher culture-grades [are] especially the Caucasian race, and . . . the budded enlightenment of Britain and full-blown enlightenment of America" (quoted in Wexler, 2008, p. 204). The human "exhibits" at the fair were grouped to illustrate this progression.

As you have seen, this historic ranking of individuals has resulted in othering, or the labeling and degrading of cultures and groups outside of one's own (Riggins, 1997). While many groups have been

Table 14.2	Countries or Areas With the Lowest Total Fertility, 2010–2015
Taiwan	1.1
Macao	1.2
Hong Kong	1.2
Singapore	1.2
Republic of Korea	1.3
Republic of Moldova	1.3
Bosnia and Herzegovina	1.3
Portugal	1.3
Spain	1.3
Hungary	1.3

Source: United Nations (2015).

the subject of othering, racial and ethnic groups have been particularly subjected to othering in language. One common way is to represent the Other as the binary opposite. For example, "White colonists were hard-working; dark-skinned natives were lazy" (Jandt & Tanno, 2001).

Figure 14.3   Egypt, Japan, United States, and Yemen Population Pyramids

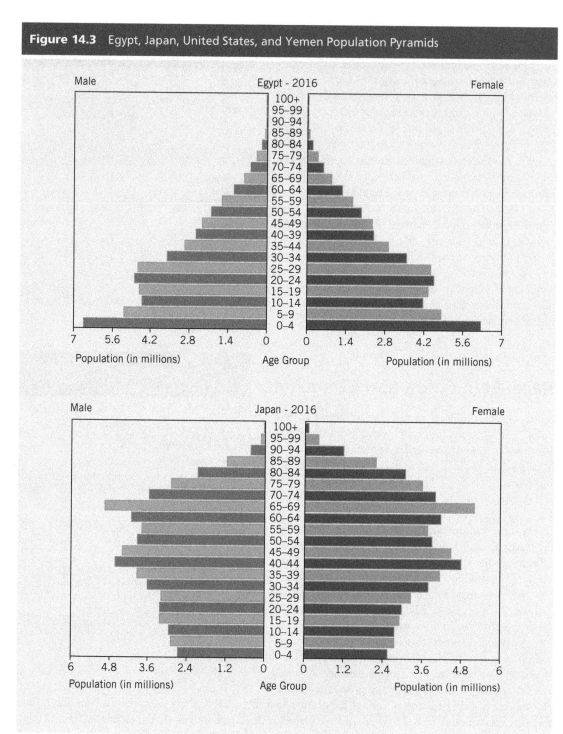

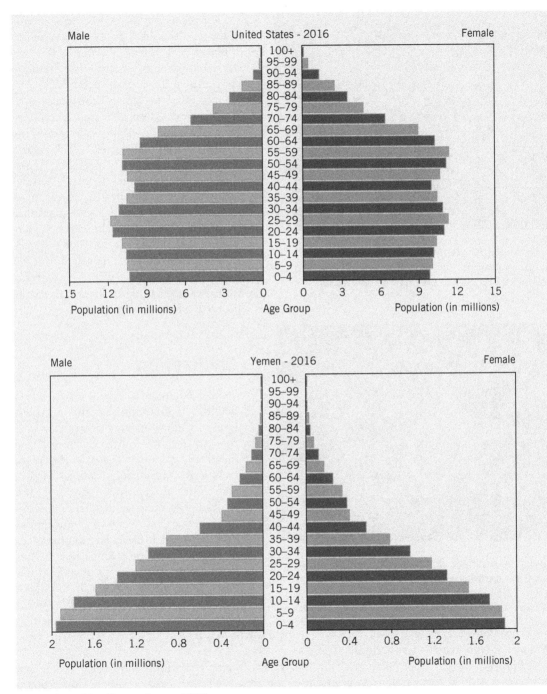

Source: Central Intelligence Agency (2016).

It seems that as people create a category called "us," another category of "not us" or "them" is created. The collective pronouns *us* and *them* become powerful influences on perception. The names given to "them" can be used to justify suppression and even extermination. Bosmajian (1983) calls this "the language of oppression." The Nazis labeled Jews "bacilli," "parasites," "disease," "demon," and "plague." Why do the words used to refer to "them" matter? It's because although killing another human being may be unthinkable, "exterminating a disease" is not. The subjugation of American Indians was defensible when the word *savage* was used. Segregation was justified when Blacks were considered "chattel" or property.

Saudi writer and activist Raif Badawi was arrested for "insulting Islam through electronic channels." In 2015 he was sentenced to 10 years in prison and 1,000 lashes.

Jenny Matthews/Corbis News/Getty Images

Civilization

Samuel Huntington (1993, 1996, 2004) defined civilizations as the broadest level of cultural identity people can have that are distinct from one another. He identified eight civilizations: Western, Confucian, Japanese, Islamic, Hindu, Slavic-Orthodox, Latin American, and African. His thesis is that these civilizations interact but remain separate entities that could and do clash. Huntington is not without critics. Some argue that he has oversimplified the concept of civilizations and that modern conflicts are ideological in nature rather than based in such a broad level of identity. Others argue that

The Rwandan government, dominated by the Tutsi tribe, overthrew the old government dominated by the Hutu tribe. Before losing power, the Hutu militia massacred over half a million people.

Chio Somodevila/Getty Images News/Getty Images

modern nation-states include within their borders people who may have some identification with more than one of Huntington's civilizations.

Huntington asserts that Western civilization versus Islamic civilization dates back for the last 1,300 years and has become more virulent due to the 1990 Gulf War. Tensions in the United States date back more than 200 years: Some of the Founding Fathers suspected presidential candidate Thomas Jefferson of supporting Islam, and piracy along the North African coast drew the United

Map 14.1 Civilizations

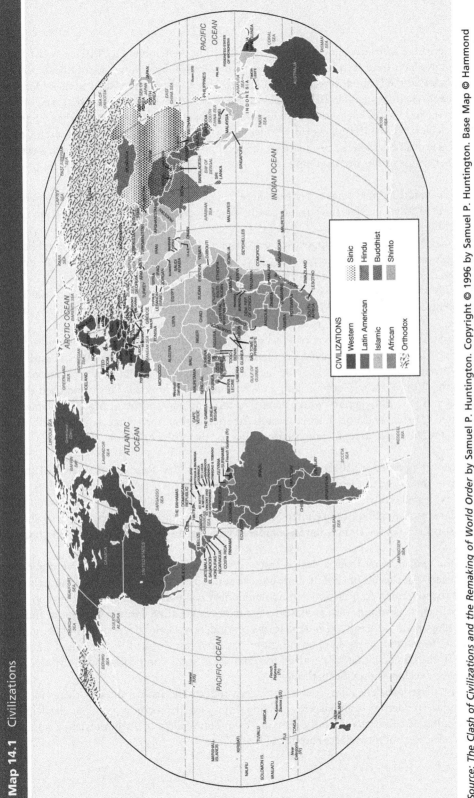

Source: *The Clash of Civilizations and the Remaking of World Order* by Samuel P. Huntington. Copyright © 1996 by Samuel P. Huntington. Base Map © Hammond World Atlas Corp. All rights reserved. Reprinted by permission of Georges Borchardt, Inc., for the Estate of Samuel P. Huntington.

States into battle with a Muslim country (Spellberg, 2013). The September 11, 2001, terrorist attacks on the United States have been seen by some as a battle in the Western-Islamic war. Others have tried to make it explicit that the U.S. nation-state is not at war with a religion. President Barack Obama, in a weekly radio address in September 2012, stated his position: "I have always said that America is at war with al Qaeda and its affiliates—and we will never be at war with Islam or any other religion."

There are elements in the Islamic world who would disagree. In 2006 the Pew Research Center's Global Attitudes Project released the results of studies that investigated how Muslims and Westerners regard each other. Some results are troubling:

- "The war on terrorism . . . has never been accepted as legitimate by Muslims. It has been seen as the United States picking on Muslim countries, protecting Israel, and attempting to control the world" (para. 7).
- "There has been substantial support for terrorism and terrorists among Muslim publics. Sizable minorities in many Muslim countries have said that suicide bombings that target civilians can often or sometimes be justified in defense of Islam" (para. 8).
- "Each side has a mostly negative image of the other people. Westerners see Muslims as fanatical, violent, and not tolerant. Muslims see Westerners as selfish, immoral, and greedy, as well as violent and fanatical" (para. 17).
- "Western publics . . . do not think of Muslims as respectful of women. But half or more in four of the five Muslim publics surveyed say the same thing about people in the West" (para. 18).
- "Both Muslims and Westerners are convinced that relations between the peoples are generally bad. In the West, 70% of Germans and 55% of Americans think so. This is matched by 64% of Turks and 58% of Egyptians who believe this, too. Large majorities of Muslims blame Westerners for the problem. Many Europeans and Americans point their fingers at the Muslims, but many in the West also accept some responsibility for the problem" (para. 16).

The survey was updated in 2012, and little had changed (Pew Research Center, 2012b). For example, in Egypt the image of the United States remained roughly where it had been 4 years earlier. In 2008, 22% expressed a favorable opinion of the United States; in 2012, it was 19%. Among Pakistanis and Jordanians, the rating of the United States had declined further; in both countries in 2008, 19% held a positive view of the United States, compared with just 12% in 2012 (Pew Research Center, 2012b).

To move the debate away from a nation-state versus religion conflict, some have argued that today's conflicts are not clashes of civilizations, but clashes and competitions between modernity and forces opposed to modernity. At least 50 years ago modernity was viewed as a unitary concept. Therefore, as nation-states modernized, they would become increasingly alike. However, as more and more states attained degrees of modernity, different forms of modern societies developed. In fact, it would be more accurate to say that every state on the globe has been transformed in some significant ways by modernity. So the outcome that modernized societies are in some competition with those rejecting modernity did not develop as previously thought.

In fact, how diverse societies have become modern reflects the basic values of their culture. In Western countries, modernity emphasized individualism and democratic popular participation. In some other cultures, communal identity (ranging from nationalism to authoritarian communism) and centralized-efficient authority were emphasized.

Nation

Nation-state is considered last because, as stated in Chapter 1, nation-state identity has superseded other sources as the primary identity in most of the world. Nation-state identity is strongest in modern developed nations. As these groups are more easily surveyed, we have good data on what contact zone threats nation-state groups perceive. A 2007 Pew Research Center worldwide survey found increasing concerns about threats to culture, threats to the environment, and threats posed by immigration. In nearly every country surveyed, people expressed concerns about losing their traditional culture and national identities and felt their way of life needed protection against foreign influences.

Focus on Skills 14.1

A Friend Converts to Islam

Your friend Matt grew up in a Methodist family in Raleigh. He went to church with his father and participated in youth fellowship and Bible study. In college he took a world religions course and first learned about Islam. He became friends with some Muslim students in the class and grew to love their faith as he questioned his own. He discussed his feelings with his parents, who expressed their concerns but supported his independence to make his own decisions. He started attending meetings of the Muslim Student Association, and after about 6 months he went with his Muslim friends to a Raleigh mosque to convert. He did the *shahada,* or oath to Allah, before witnesses. He was only sorry that his parents and you weren't there. He no longer dates nor drinks. Since learning some Arabic, he prays the *isha'a* every night and follows the five pillars. He says he likes the boundaries his new faith provides.

You and your friends from high school don't understand his faith. You are with Matt and Alex, who was a friend to both of you in high school. Alex says that at his college he learned that both militant and nonviolent Muslims share the same goal of instituting the rule of sharia globally. He believes that Islam is trying to create a global Islamic state governed by sharia, or Islamic law based on the Qur'an and the sunnah of the Prophet. He asks Matt why he has turned against the United States.

1. Should you express your opinion?
2. What should you say?

Threats to Culture

As you read in the previous chapter, cultures feel threatened by the spread of products and ideas from one culture to another when those products and ideas are perceived as weakening the receiving culture. The imperialism of nations a century ago is today seen as the imperialism of modern multinational corporations.

Frank (2000) argues that "the corporation [is] the most powerful institution on earth" (p. xv). Global corporations such as Monsanto, Time Warner, and McDonald's are seen as undermining local cultures. Technology has made it possible for Mexico to have Frappuccinos at Starbucks and for the United States to have the novels of Carlos Fuentes (Cowen, 2002). Because the United States has promoted both free markets and democracy throughout the world, technology is perceived as reinforcing

U.S. wealth and dominance. Between July and October 2002, the Pew Research Center surveyed some 38,000 people speaking 46 languages around the world. In country after country where people liked U.S. technology and popular culture, they were displeased with the spread of U.S. ideas and cultural values (see Figure 14.4), which are seen as embedded in U.S. technology.

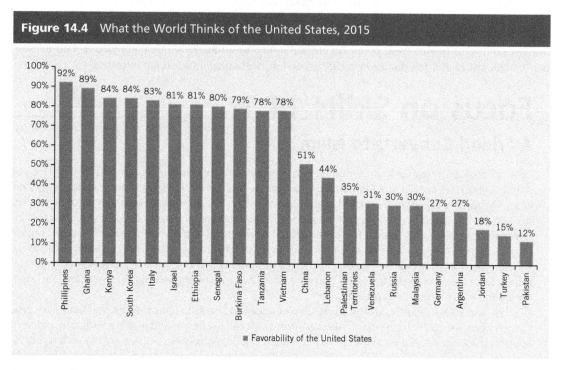

Figure 14.4 What the World Thinks of the United States, 2015

Source: Based on data from Wike, Stokes, & Poushter (2015).

The few countries with negative attitudes shown in Figure 14.4 notwithstanding, overall global attitudes toward the United States are positive. In the 2016 Pew survey, 63% in Europe viewed the United States favorably (Wike, Poushter, & Zainulbhai, 2016a). Of the countries in that survey, only in Greece did the majority view the United States unfavorably. The survey's authors concluded that U.S. image is linked to impressions of the people. People in the United States are perceived as optimistic and hardworking, but also arrogant, greedy, and violent. In Chapter 7 you read about science and technology as an important cultural pattern in the United States; the country's achievements in science and technology are a particularly strong aspect of the international image of the United States. Also extremely popular was U.S. popular culture—music, movies and television. Yet as you read in Chapter 13, even in the United States there are concerns about the influence of U.S. ideas and customs.

Threats to the Environment

Easter Island in the Pacific Ocean is one of the most remote locations on Earth. The gigantic stone statues located in the Rono Raraku volcanic crater are all that remain of what was a complex civilization. The civilization disappeared because of the overexploitation of environmental resources. Competition between rival clans led to rapid deforestation, soil erosion, and the destruction of bird populations, undermining the food and agricultural systems that sustained human life (Diamond, 2005). The Easter Island story is a case study of the consequences of failure to manage shared ecological resources.

The World Commission on Environment and Development (1987), also known as the Brundtland Commission, defined sustainable development as development that "meets the needs of the present without compromising the ability of the future generations to meet their own needs."

One revision of this definition is attributed to the state of Oregon: Sustainability means "using, developing and protecting resources at a rate and in a manner that enables people to meet their current needs and also provides that future generations can meet their own needs" ("What Is Sustainability," n.d., para. 1), and "sustainability requires simultaneously meeting environmental, economic and community needs" (Office of the Governor, 2000, p. 2). Such definitions have become the basis of significant international policy.

Spencer Platt/Getty Images News/Getty Images

Secretary of State John Kerry holds his granddaughter as he signs the Paris Agreement on climate change at the United Nations in 2016.

Focus on Culture 14.1

Disposing of Electronic Waste

How long will you use your current mobile phone? How will you dispose of it when you get a new one? One estimate is that four mobile phones per second end up in landfills.

Since mobile phones first came on the market, there have been at least 5 billion in existence. While the ecological impact of one mobile phone may be small, the cumulative effect is a major problem. Mobile phones contain heavy metals such as mercury, lead, and cadmium, as well as brominated flame retardants in the printed circuit boards and casings. These substances can have a devastating impact if they are released into the environment.

The UN Environment Programme (UNEP) estimates that up to 50 million tons of waste from discarded electronic goods is generated annually. The majority is shipped from the West to Asian countries such as China and India, but tighter regulations means more and more is ending up in Africa where there are few facilities to safely deal with it.

The EU law, the Waste Electrical and Electronic Equipment (WEEE) Directive, requires producers to bear the cost of the collection, recovery, and disposal of "e-waste." NEC has developed a handset that uses plant-derived bioplastics and emits 50% less carbon dioxide than conventional approaches.

Source: Kinver (2006).

People fill every ecological niche on the planet, from icy tundra to rainforests to deserts. In some locations, societies have outstripped the carrying capacity of the land, resulting in chronic hunger, environmental degradation, and a large-scale exodus of desperate populations.

The exact impact of greenhouse gas emission is not easy to forecast. In 2016, the United States, with nearly 5% of the world's population, accounted for 16% of the world's carbon emissions. China, with 20% of the world's population, accounted for 28% of carbon emissions. India accounted for 6%, Russia almost 5%, and Japan approximately 4%. People have unequal incomes and wealth across the world, and climate change will thus affect regions very differently. Climate change is already starting to affect some of the poorest and most vulnerable communities around the world, threatening food supplies, coastlines, health, and the survival of countless species.

Agriculture accounts for more than 90% of all the fresh water used by humans. Demand is so great that many of the world's mightiest rivers no longer reach the sea year-round. Grain farmers in the top three cereal-producing countries—China, India, and the United States—are pumping water from aquifers faster than rainfall can replace it.

Arab countries score below average on 17 of the Environmental Sustainability Index's 20 indicators. The Arab states are, in general, far below average on measures of environmental systems (e.g., air and water quality) and on measures of social and institutional capacity and global stewardship. Water shortages are serious in many Arab countries. With 10% of the world's land, the Arab states control only about 1% of global water reserves and rely on imports from outside the region for 60% of their needs. Arab countries generally exhibit higher levels of air emissions than other countries, particularly of oxides of nitrogen and volatile organic compounds. For example, the United Arab Emirates has almost double the per capita carbon dioxide emissions of the United States. Representative of a pattern of environmental disengagement is that not a single Arab League member contributes payments to the Global Environmental Facility (Esty, Levy, & Winston, 2002, 2003).

Environmental concerns become a source of tension between groups when developed countries that are able to reduce their sources of emissions are compared with developing countries that are dependent on high emissions to develop their economies. The term *ecoimperialism* refers to global governance that protects the existing power structure at the expense of poor countries.

Fundamentally, ecoimperialism undermines the capacity of people to escape poverty. Ecoimperialists impose a set of beliefs on people in poor countries through environmental regulations, restrictions on trade, and the fundamental belief that they should make decisions for everyone else. People in poor countries need more development, more technology, more resource consumption, and more energy consumption—and they should reject ecoimperialism, just as they rejected imperialism. People everywhere should be empowered to make choices for their own lives, and not be prevented from doing so by people and governments in wealthy countries.

For example, should a worldwide ban on the use of DDT (dichlorodiphenyltrichloroethane, a pesticide widely used in the past in the United States and later banned as a carcinogen and threat to wildlife) take priority over a poor country's attempt to deal with immediate problems of human suffering from malaria (Elliott, 1998, p. 118)?

China is the best example. Economic development in China is a severe threat to the environment:

- Sixteen of China's cities rank among the 20 most polluted in the world.
- In major cities, much of the water is too toxic to drink; only 1% of the surface water in Shanghai is safe.

- Some 700 million Chinese people drink water contaminated with animal and human waste.
- The Gobi Desert is growing by about 4,900 square kilometers (1,900 square miles) annually, resulting in millions of refugees.
- Within 15 years, almost 130 million cars will be on China's roads.
- In 2009, coal-dependent China emitted 50% more greenhouse gases than the United States (Zuckerman, 2008, p. 94). However, with growing public backlash, since 2011 China has become a world leader in renewable energy investments and pollution control plans. By 2014, China's coal consumption dropped.

On Earth Day in April 2016, China, the United States, and 173 other countries signed a global climate agreement reached in Paris the previous December to hold the increase in the global average temperature below 2 degrees Celsius (3.6 degrees Fahrenheit) and pursue efforts to limit that increase to 1.5 degrees Celsius above pre-industrial levels. That followed Obama administration efforts in alternative energy and auto emissions and China's new efforts. The agreement would become international law when the governments of 55 countries representing at least 55% of global emissions formally accepted the accord, which could have taken until 2020. But the threshold was reached in October 2016. President Obama's negotiators helped shape the agreement so that it is not defined as a treaty requiring U.S. Senate approval. Instead it is an executive agreement and was accepted by both the United States and China on September 3, 2016.

In the United States, political and public opinion on climate change have polarized. President Trump campaigned against Obama's climate plans and for bringing back jobs in the coal industry. After his election he signed an executive order rolling back several climate change initiatives. The Chinese Foreign Ministry announced later that China would still uphold the Paris climate change accord despite President Trump's overturning climate change regulations.

Threats From Immigration

In both poor and rich countries, people are concerned about immigration. Large majorities in nearly every country express the view that there should be greater restriction of immigration and tighter control of their country's borders. Figure 14.5 shows the percentage of citizens in selected countries who favor restricting immigration.

Immigration issues in Europe and the United States are quite distinct. In Europe, the issues focus more on concerns over Islam and cultural differences. Historically, Europe is a continent of nations with aging populations and falling birthrates. The Muslim population in Europe increased from 4% in 1990 to 6% in 2010. It is projected that it could increase to 8% by 2030. Some see the religious head scarves, arranged marriages, and conservative imams as challenges to equality and democracy.

Consider the challenge that Sweden, a country of 9.8 million, is facing. As you read in Chapter 10, a large number of refugees have settled in Sweden because for decades the country has offered refugees and asylum seekers government aid and generous family reunification plans. At the peak of the 2015 migrant crisis, more than 160,000 people arrived in Sweden requesting asylum. Refugees must then apply for asylum and learn Swedish, with its many sounds for the letter g, adapt to Swedish culture without the familiar calls to prayer, eat meat that was not slaughtered according to Islamic tradition, and drink hot tea in a land of lattes and espressos.

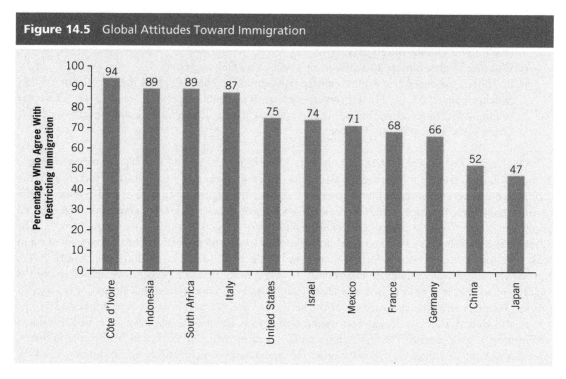

Figure 14.5   Global Attitudes Toward Immigration

Source: Pew Research Center (2007).

Consider also France: For more than 200 years since the French Revolution, France has declared that distinctions of race or creed must be submerged for the good of La France. Everyone is French, so no politician campaigns for the votes of ethnic groups. The French are so committed to the idea of equality that it is against the law to survey the population by race, ethnicity, or religion.

Despite the burgeoning population of immigrants from North African and Muslim countries, France has no Black or Arab mayors and no minorities representing mainland France in the National Assembly. Philippe Maniere, director of the Montaigne Institute, a nonpartisan think tank, said, "In France, we still believe in this completely idealistic principle born during our revolution that you should not talk about your community [of origin] because it gives the impression you will favor it, which is unacceptable" (quoted in Baum, 2008, p. A3).

North Americans are generally more welcoming to immigrants than Western Europeans are, and the issues in the United States focus more on Hispanic immigrants and employment.

Consider the United States: Immigrants accounted for 43 million people, or 13.5% of the U.S. population in 2015. The leading country of origin was India, followed by China, Mexico, the Philippines, and Canada. In 2013, India and China overtook Mexico as the top countries of origin. In that year, of the immigrants in the United States, 27% were from Mexico, followed by India at 6%. The challenge that immigration presents was identified by Robert Putnam (2007) in a study based on 30,000 interviews in the United States. The greater the diversity in a community, the less civic engagement it shows; fewer people vote, fewer volunteer, less is given to charities, and less cooperative work is done on community projects. In addition, the greater the diversity in a community, the less people

Focus on Theory 14.1

Environmental Ethics

The field of environmental ethics concerns human beings' ethical relationship with the natural environment. While numerous philosophers have written on this topic throughout history, environmental ethics in the United States only developed into a specific philosophical discipline only in the 1970s. This emergence was no doubt due to the increasing awareness in the 1960s of the effects that technology, industry, economic expansion, and population growth were having on the environment. The development of such awareness was aided by the publication of two important books at this time. Rachel Carson's *Silent Spring,* first published in 1962, alerted readers to how the widespread use of chemical pesticides was posing a serious threat to public health and leading to the destruction of wildlife. Of similar significance was Paul Ehrlich's 1968 book, *The Population Bomb,* which warned of the devastating effects the spiraling human population has on the planet's resources. Of course, pollution and the depletion of natural resources have not been the only environmental concerns since that time: Dwindling plant and animal biodiversity, the loss of wilderness, the degradation of ecosystems, and climate change are all part of a raft of "green" issues that have implanted themselves into both public consciousness and public policy over subsequent years. The job of environmental ethics is to outline our moral obligations in the face of such concerns. In a nutshell, the two fundamental questions that environmental ethics must address are as follows: What duties do humans have with respect to the environment, and why? The latter question usually needs to be considered prior to the former. In order to tackle just what our obligations are, it is usually thought necessary to consider first *why* we have them. For example, do we have environmental obligations for the sake of human beings living in the world today, for humans living in the future, or for the sake of entities within the environment itself, irrespective of any human benefits?

Source: Cochrane (2007, para. 1).

trust each other, not only across ethnic lines but also within the lines. In other words, people in the most ethnically mixed neighborhoods show the least trust not only of other ethnicities but also of people of their own ethnicity.

Putnam (2007) was concerned that his research would be used to argue against immigration, affirmative action, and multiculturalism, and that has occurred. His research, in total, argues the following:

- Increased immigration and diversity not only are inevitable in modern societies but over the long term are desirable. The history of the United States demonstrates that over the long run, ethnic diversity is an important social asset.
- In the short to medium run, immigration and ethnic diversity challenge social solidarity and inhibit the strength of relationships that bond similar people together and bridge people of diversity.
- In the medium to long run, successful immigrant societies create new forms of social solidarity and dampen the negative effects of diversity by constructing new, more encompassing identities.

Global Voices

Putnam's research findings are consistent with conflict studies that show that the challenge of modern immigrant societies is to create new broader definitions of the sense of "we"—that is, to create a larger, more inclusive sense of identity.

Consider India's approach. On August 15, 1947, the new independent state of India was born on a subcontinent with a history of bloody divisions. Its very survival was in doubt. No other nation-state has ever had such diversity of ethnic groups, mutually incomprehensible language (35 languages spoken by more than a million people each), variety of topography and climate, and diversity of religions and cultural practices. Six decades later, India is the world's largest democracy, with years of rapid economic growth.

In stark contrast to the U.S. motto of *e pluribus unum*, India embraced *e pluribus pluribum*—one land embracing many. If the United States is a melting pot, India is a *thali,* a selection of dishes in different bowls on one plate to make one meal. Instead of suppressing diversity in the name of a single national identity, India acknowledges pluralism. All groups, faiths, tastes, and ideologies were to participate in the new system. It wasn't easy. India suffered caste conflicts, clashes over the rights of different linguistic groups, religious riots between Hindus and Muslims, and threats of separation from various ethnicities.

India permits all religions to flourish while ensuring none is privileged by the state. Muslims have their own "personal law" to govern their marriages, divorces, and deaths distinct from the common civil code. No one identity has triumphed in India; the country saw a Roman Catholic political leader replaced by a Sikh sworn in as prime minister by a Muslim in a country that is 81% Hindu (Tharoor, 2006, 2007).

The Promise of New Media

The November 2011 issue of the *Journal of International and Intercultural Communication* was devoted to the prospect and promise of new media across cultures. E-mail, mobile phones, text messaging, and social media are now enabling individuals to connect across cultures in ways that were not possible only a couple of decades ago. Throughout this book you have read about some of the ways new media are being used in various cultures and how cultures may be impacted by this.

Hamdy and Gomaa (2012) compared the use of semiofficial newspapers, independent newspapers, and social media postings in the January and February 2011 uprisings in Egypt. Social media postings depended on the activists themselves for information, and these people were more likely to be believers. Social media were more likely to focus on the "suffering and resiliency of ordinary Egyptians in the face of a repressive regime" (p. 207) and label the uprisings as a revolution calling for Mubarak's resignation and the end of government controls on the Internet.

Communication scholar Guo-Ming Chen (2012) argues that new media "provides a space in which people of different cultures can freely express their opinions and establish relationships" (p. 7). New media may facilitate the development of new cultural values. New media may challenge the traditional definition of cultural identity by weakening or strengthening the importance of the relationships between people and communities. New identities may be forged in virtual communities.

Focus on Culture 14.2

Country/Region	Practice	Comment
Japan	Announcements remind train commuters to put their mobile phones on vibrate or silent mode. Bus drivers will not allow someone to board a bus who is using a mobile phone. In movie theaters, light from phone screens is not allowed.	Social harmony valued; social disturbance sanctioned
Spain and Italy	It is acceptable to take calls in restaurants, during meetings, and during concerts. It is acceptable to discuss personal matters on mobile phones in public places. There is little use of voice mail.	Obligation to be available to friends, colleagues, and customers
India and parts of Africa	It is acceptable to take calls inside a movie theater and at official functions. There is little use of voice mail.	Communal societies with traditions of tolerance in public space

Source: Canton (2012).

A Final Word

You have come to the end of this book. You have studied how culture affects perception, how language and nonverbal communication are part of culture, and how language and nonverbal communication

Focus on Skills 14.2

Choosing a Guest Speaker for Improving Intercultural Communication

You are a student representative on your university's Intellectual Life Committee charged with sponsoring speakers on campus. You've been asked to develop a list of possible speakers on the topic of improving intercultural communication in today's world. Assume there are no limitations—anyone is available to you. In each of the areas below, who would you invite and what would you ask them to address?

1. Government and politics
2. Religion
3. Social media

Photodisc/Thinkstock

along with other factors can be barriers to effective intercultural communication. You have studied cultural values, including how they affect the role of women in societies. You have studied what happens when cultures come in contact and when people emigrate from one country to another.

The world has changed dramatically since 1405, when the Chinese eunuch admiral Cheng Ho commanded 62 ships and explored Vietnam, Java, and Malacca, and then headed west across the Indian Ocean to cities on the southwest coast of India. And the world has changed dramatically since 1768, when the British captain James Cook sailed in the *Endeavour* to Tahiti, New Zealand, Australia, and the Dutch East Indies. Both explorers encountered cultures with languages and behaviors that may have seemed new and strange to them.

Have the centuries of contact among cultures reduced the challenges presented to Cheng Ho and James Cook? Has our understanding of the planet changed over the centuries?

In the capsule on humanity's first voyage to the moon, looking back at the earth Neil Armstrong realized he could extend his arm and block his vision of the earth with his thumb. He was later asked if that made him feel like a giant. Armstrong responded, "No, it made me feel really, really small." Other astronauts who followed Armstrong made similar observations. Bill Anders described the earth as "very delicate." Stu Roosa said, "It's the abject smallness of the Earth that gets you." John Swigert said, "Everything that I know, my family, my possessions, my friends, and my country, it's all down there on that little thing. And it's so insignificant in this great big vastness of space" (all quoted in Nelson, 2009, p. 274).

Later Neil Armstrong observed,

From our position on the Earth it is difficult to observe where the Earth is and where it's going, or what its future course might be. Hopefully, we'll be able to make some people step back and reconsider their mission in the Universe, to think of themselves as a group of people who constitute the crew of a spaceship going through the universe. If you're going to run a spaceship, you've got to be pretty cautious about how you use your resources, how you use your crew, and how you treat your spacecraft. (Nelson, 2009, p. 327)

Perhaps our modern-day explorers have helped set the objective for intercultural communication studies.

SUMMARY

The term *contact zone* refers to the space in which cultures come into contact and establish ongoing relations, usually involving coercion, inequality, and conflict. In this chapter you read about how Cannadine's six forms of regulators of human life and identity can also be seen as today's contact zones. Conflicts over religion continue, as do conflicts over race, skin color, and ethnicity. Some would deny conflict exists between civilizations, preferring to consider these conflicts over degrees of modernity. Others contend that the concept of civilizations is not a useful concept today, preferring again the national state as the primary source of individual identity. Economic disparities and differential treatment of the genders may not themselves be sources of conflict, but may enter into other conflicts.

Finally, tensions between nation-states currently focus on threats of cultural identity from multinational corporate imperialism, threats to the environment, and threats from immigration. Astronaut Neil Armstrong, who had the opportunity to observe the planet from space, once questioned whether it would be possible for humanity to think of ourselves as one group of people.

DISCUSSION QUESTIONS

1. How do identities from the world's religions lead to conflicts?

2. From the perspective of "think globally, act locally," how could your food choices affect income disparities?

3. What measures, if any, should a developing country employ to reduce the fertility rate?

4. *Identity politics* refers to political positions taken on the basis of self-identified groups such as race, ethnicity, sexual orientation, or any other subculture or subgroup. Do identity politics pose a challenge to nation-state identity?

5. Should developed countries that in the past damaged the environment prohibit developing countries from using those same practices in order to raise their standard of living?

6. Is the United States on the path to becoming another India, with many strong cultures within the dominant culture?

7. How can people begin to develop a world identity? Is that something to be desired? Are there dangers to a world identity?

READINGS

All readings are from *Intercultural Communication: A Global Reader* (Jandt, 2004).

Lalita Rajasingham, "The Impact of Universities on Globalisation" (p. 413)

Randy Kluver, "Globalization, Informatization, and Intercultural Communication" (p. 425)

STUDENT STUDY SITE

⑤SAGE edge™

Sharpen your skills with SAGE edge at edge.sagepub.com/jandt9e.

SAGE edge for Students provides a personalized approach to help you accomplish your coursework goals in an easy-to-use learning environment.

Coventry University London

Glossary

Abaya: A long black cloak worn in public by Muslim women

Aboriginal: The indigenous peoples of Australia (often applied to indigenous peoples in other countries)

Acculturation: An immigrant's learning and adopting the norms and values of the new host culture (*see also* Cultural adaptation)

Activity orientation: Use of time for self-expression and play, self-improvement and development, and work

Adaptation potential: An individual's possible success in adapting to a new culture

Amae: Japanese for a nurturing concern for and dependence on another

Anabaptist: A 16th-century Reformation movement that insisted that only adult baptism was valid and held that true Christians should not bear arms, use force, or hold government office

Anxiety: A diffuse state of being uneasy or worried about what may happen

Arabic: The literary language of the Qur'an; the language and culture of the Arabs

Arabs: Ethnic group that originally spread Islam; the Semitic peoples originally from Arabia and now living throughout the Near East, North Africa, and the Arabian peninsula

Argot: Traditionally refers to the specialized vocabulary of subgroups primarily used as secret language among members of the subgroup only

Artifact: An object from a culture

Artifactual communication: Messages conveyed through human-made objects, including clothing and the ways space is decorated

Assimilation: An immigrant's giving up the original culture identity and moving into full participation in the new culture

Asylee: A person seeking refuge in another country for political reasons (*see also* Refugee)

Authoritarian personality: An individual who tends to overgeneralize and think in bipolar terms and who is highly conventional, moralistic, and uncritical of higher authority

Back translation: Translating from one language into another and then translating back into the original to compare the result to avoid errors in translation

Beachy Amish: A group that separated from the more conservative Amish over the use of automobiles and modern farm equipment

Biculturalism: The ability to function in two cultures

Biological sex: Categories based on genitals, chromosomes, gonads, and hormones labeling most people as female or male, with about one in a hundred placed in between

Burqa: A loose garment worn by some Muslim women covering the entire body, with a veiled opening for the eyes

Caliph: The secular and religious head of a Muslim state

Caliphate: The office, jurisdiction, or reign of a caliph

Cant: Specialized vocabulary of created words or adopted words by any nonprofessional subgroup

Cantonese: A form of Chinese spoken mainly in southeastern China (including Hong Kong)

Change: Substitution of the new for existing; an aspect of a culture's activity orientation

Change agent: A person who influences innovation decisions

Change agent ethics: Concern for the unanticipated consequences of introducing a new idea or product into a culture

Channel: The means by which a message is transmitted

Chicano: Refers to people born in the United States whose ancestors came from Mexico; often used to represent a nationalist identity and a commitment to disassimilation

Chronemics: The study of our use of time

Co-culture: An interdependent and equal subculture within a society

Code switching: Going from one language to another in the same sentence, as from Spanish to English and then back to Spanish

Collectivism: A dimension of culture; refers to interdependence, groupness, and social cohesion

Coming out: One's public disclosure of being gay

Communication: Intentionally stimulating meaning in other humans through the use of symbols

Communication apprehension: Fear or anxiety associated with either real or anticipated communication with another person or persons

Compound bilingual speakers: People who learn a second language relatively late in life and who use it in a limited number of settings

Conformity: Compliance or acquiescence

Confucian work dynamism: A dimension of culture; persistence, commitment, and organizational identity and loyalty; relabeled by Hofstede as *long-term* versus *short-term orientation* (*see also* Long-term orientation, Short-term orientation)

Confucianism: An ethical system based on the teaching of Confucius, emphasizing personal virtue and devotion to family and society

Contact zone: The space in which geographically and historically separate peoples come into contact, usually establishing relations involving coercion, radical inequality, and intractable conflict

Context: The physical and social environment in which communication takes place

Convergence: A process in which information is shared by individuals who come together over time to a greater degree of agreement

Coordinate bilingual speakers: People who learn a second language relatively early in life and who use it in a variety of settings

Corporate culture: Thinking of an organization as a culture; the values, goals, and priorities that guide policies and procedures of an organization

Creole: Language that develops from prolonged contact of two or more languages and is acquired by children as their first language

Cultural adaptation: An immigrant's learning and adopting the norms and values of the new host culture (*see also* Acculturation)

Cultural identity: Identification with and perceived acceptance into a culture

Cultural imperialism: The practice of a more powerful nation to impose its culture over less powerful societies

Cultural invasion: One group penetrating the culture of another group to impose its own view of the world

Cultural relativism: A theory from anthropology that the differences in peoples are the results of historical, social, and geographic conditions and that all populations have complete and equally developed cultures

Cultural Revolution: Mao Zedong's attempt to purify China of outside influences and build a Marxist-Chinese culture

Cultural sensitivity: Making no value judgments based on one's own cultural values about other cultures' practices or artifacts (i.e., better or worse, right or wrong)

Cultural studies: An approach that attempts to develop an ideal personification of the culture, which is then used to explain the actions of individuals in the culture

Culture: Sum total of ways of living, including behavioral norms, linguistic expression, styles of communication, patterns of thinking, and beliefs and values of a group large enough to be self-sustaining and transmitted over the course of generations

Culture shock: Anxiety, disorientation, and stress that one experiences when in a new culture

Decoding: The process of assigning meaning to symbols

Dialect: A variety of speech differing from the standard

Diaspora: Dispersion of an originally homogeneous people

Diffusion: The spread of innovations into a culture

Discursive imperialism: Labeling of a group as a dehumanized "other," which facilitates actions taken against it

Emic: Knowledge learned from the inside; that is, the norms of culture known by its members (*see also* Etic)

Emigrant: Term used to refer to a migrant upon leaving homeland (*see also* Immigrant)

Emoji: Any small image used to communicate an emotion or an idea in electronic messages

Encoding: The process of putting the communication source's ideas into symbols

Endogamy: Marriage in which the partners must be members of the same group (e.g., a religious community)

Equality: Being alike or the same in some rank, ability, quantity, and so forth

Esperanto: A widely used universal language devised in 1887, based on European vocabularies and Latin grammar

Ethnic identity: Identification with and perceived acceptance into an ethnic group

Ethnicity: Subculture or subgroup identified by shared descent and heritage

Ethnocentrism: Negatively judging aspects of another culture by the standards of one's own culture

Etic: Knowledge learned by an outsider; that is, theoretical information about a culture developed by a researcher who is not a member of the culture (*see also* Emic)

Exogamy: Marriage in which the partner must be chosen from outside a defined group (e.g., members of the same extended family lineage may not marry)

Expatriate: A noncitizen worker in a foreign country

Extended family: A family group that includes parents and their married children

Face: In collectivist cultures, public image or reputation that one has achieved (*mien* in Chinese culture); also, the community's confidence in the integrity of one's moral character (*lien* in Chinese culture)

Facework: In communication studies, the communicative strategies that can be used to enact self-face and to support or challenge another person's face

Feedback: The portion of receiver response that a source attends to

Femininity: A dimension of culture; both women and men being concerned with quality of life, interpersonal relationships, and concern for the weak

Feng shui: The Chinese art of manipulating the physical environment, such as homes and offices, to establish harmony with nature and achieve happiness, prosperity, and health

Fertility rate: The average number of children born alive to a woman in her lifetime; a fertility rate of 2.1 children per woman would eventually result in zero population growth

Field dependence: The degree to which perception is affected by the surrounding perceptual or contextual field

Flash: The cant originally brought to Australia by thieves and convicts from London

Four modernizations: Deng Xiaoping's economic programs in China in agriculture, industry, science, and technology

Gaijin: Japanese for foreigner or "outside person"

Gelassenheit: A German word used by the Amish to mean submission to God

Gender expression: A person's outward gender presentation through clothing, hairstyle, makeup, jewelry, and other nonverbal expressions typically categorized as feminine, masculine, or androgynous

Gender identity: A person's internal sense of who they are as a gendered being, the gender with which they identify themselves

Ghutrah: A cloth worn by men in Saudi Arabia and some other Arab countries to cover the head

Grammar: Linguistic rules governing sounds (or gestures in sign languages), meanings, and syntax of a language

Gregorian calendar: A calendar based on the cycles of the sun

Hajj: The pilgrimage to Mecca that every Muslim is expected to undertake at least once

Haptics: Study of the use of touch to communicate

Hate speech: Threats or verbal slurs directed against specific groups or physical acts such as burning crosses or placing swastikas on public or private property

Hegemony: Predominant influence by one culture over another

Heroes: Real or imaginary persons who serve as behavior models within a culture

High context: A dimension of culture; holds that much of the meaning of messages is determined by the context or environment

Hijab: A general term referring to any of several different types of headscarves and veils worn by Muslim women

Hijrah calendar: A calendar based on the cycles of the moon

Hispanic: Refers to people with the capability of speaking and comprehending the Spanish language whose ancestry is based on a Spanish-speaking country and who identify with the subculture

Hmong: A people living in Laos who sided with the United States in the Vietnam War and now have resettled in the United States

Homophobia: Irrational fear of lesbians and gay men

Hong Kong: A British Crown Colony returned to China in 1997

Honorific: Form of direct address used in some languages to show respect

Hyperindividualism: Excesses of individualism, disregard for others, and withdrawing into individual private shells

Icon: A popular symbol that represents a culture

Idiom: An expression whose meaning is not predictable from the usual meanings of its words

Imam: One of the leaders regarded by the Shiites as successors of Muhammad; any religious leader claiming descent from Muhammad

Immigrant: Term used to refer to a migrant upon arriving at the destination country (*see also* Emigrant)

Individualism: A dimension of culture; refers to the rights and independent action of the individual

Infanticide: The termination of the life of an infant

Integration: Maintaining important parts of one's original culture as well as participating fully in a new culture

Intercultural communication: Communication between people and groups of diverse culture, subculture, or subgroup identifications

Intercultural communication competence: The ability to communicate effectively and appropriately with people of cultures other than one's own

Intercultural communication effectiveness: The ability to accomplish one's goals when communicating with people of cultures other than one's own

Interpretation: The step in the perception process referring to attaching meaning to sense data

Iqual: Also known as *agal,* the double ring of black rope or cord used to hold the *ghutrah* worn by men in Saudi Arabia and some other Arab countries

Islam: The world's second largest religion, with nearly 1 billion followers, based on the teachings of the prophet Muhammad, believing in one God, and having a body of law put forth in the Qur'an and the *sunnah*

Jargon: Technical language of an occupational professional subgroup

Kinesics: Gestures, body movements, facial expressions, and eye contact

Language: A set of symbols shared by a community to communicate meaning and experience

Latino: Spanish-speaking individuals who themselves or whose ancestors came from anywhere in Latin America

Literacy rate: Percentage of people age 15 and older who can, with understanding, both read and write a short, simple statement on their everyday life

Long-term orientation: Fostering of virtues, particularly perseverance and thrift, oriented toward future rewards

Low context: A dimension of culture; holds that little of the meaning of messages is determined by the context or environment

Macau: A Portuguese colony returned to China in 1999

Machismo: Exaggerated aggressiveness and intransigence in male-to-male interpersonal relationships and arrogance and sexual aggression in male-to-female relationships (Stevens, 1973)

Majlis: The practice in Saudi Arabia of allowing any citizen access to the king and local governors

Marginalization: Losing one's cultural identity and not having any psychological contact with society

Masculinity: A dimension of culture; refers to distinct traits of being assertive, tough, and focused on material success

Matawain: Public morality committees in Saudi Arabia that ensure compliance with religious requirements

Materialism: Emphasis on material objects, needs, and considerations over spiritual values

Melting pot: Metaphor for the assimilation of early immigrants into a homogenized United States

Message: Encoded ideas of the communication source

Mexican-American: Someone from Mexico undergoing the assimilation process

Microaggression: Brief everyday communications that send unintentional denigrating messages to individuals because of their group membership; the communication source often intends no offense and is unaware of any harm of their message

Microculture: Specialized groups that can be considered cultures but may comprise fewer people than most cultures; to avoid the negative connotations of the terms *subculture, co-culture,* and *subgroup,* this term is used

Mitigated speech: Deferential or indirect speech between individuals of perceived high power distance

Monochronic time: In the use of time, doing one thing at a time in an orderly fashion

Mother tongue: The parent language of other languages or a person's first learned language

Muhammad: The founder of Islam; born circa 570, died 632

Multiculturalism: Understanding, acceptance, and constructive relations among people of many different cultures and subcultures

Muslim: Literally, one who submits to the will of God; one who practices the religion of Islam

Mutability: A state of changeability or variability

Myths: Stories and images representing a culture's values, handed down from generation to generation as a guide for living

Need for achievement: The desire to excel because of the feeling of accomplishment it brings

New Order Amish: A moderate group of the Amish, accepting some modern conveniences

Niqab: A veil worn by some Muslim women that covers all of the face except for the eyes

Noise: External, internal, or semantic limitations on the effectiveness of communication

Gross domestic product (GDP): The total value of all goods and services produced within a country's borders at current prices in its currency

Nongovernmental organization: Not-for-profit organization independent of national and international governmental organizations usually funded by donations and run by volunteers

Nonverbal communication: Actions and attributes with a socially shared meaning intentionally sent and received

Nuclear family: A family group including only parents and children

Nushu: Women's writing developed in rural China as a secret language to communicate with other women

Old Order Amish: The most conservative and strict of the Amish

Oleh: A Jew immigrating into Israel under the Law of Return; plural is *olim*

Olfactics: Communication by smells

One-child campaign: China's birth control program introduced in 1979 to encourage most families to have no more than one child

Opinion leadership: Individuals who can influence others' attitudes and behaviors

Ordnung: Church rules and values of the Amish

Organization: The step in the perception process referring to organizing sense data in some meaningful way

Orientalism: Since the publication of Edward Said's book *Orientalism,* the term has been used to refer to the patronizing Western attitude toward Middle Eastern, Asian, and North African societies

Othering: The degrading of cultures and groups outside of one's own and creating artificial divisions between cultures and groups by labeling language that emphasizes power relations and domination

Paralanguage: Nonverbal elements of the voice, including intensity, pitch, laughter, and so forth

Participant observer: A researcher's orderly and scientific study of a subgroup by actually participating in the group

Patois: Any language that is considered nonstandard, including pidgins, creoles, and dialects, but not commonly jargon or slang; implies a class distinction compared to those who speak the standard or dominant language

Patriarchal society: A social structure in which men hold power in families, social groups, work groups, and government

Perception: Becoming aware of, knowing, or identifying by means of the senses

Pidgin: A mixture of two or more languages to form a new language

Political correctness: The avoidance of language and practices that can be perceived to offend particular groups of people; the term has become used as a pejorative implying that these actions are excessive

Polychronic time: In the use of time, placing stress on the involvement of people and completion of transactions rather than on adherence to schedules

Postethnicity: Belief that associations or group memberships can be voluntary rather than determined by birth

Power distance: A dimension of culture; the extent to which the less powerful members of a culture expect and accept that power, prestige, and wealth are distributed unequally

Prejudice: Irrational suspicion or hatred of a particular group, race, religion, or sexual orientation

Profiling: A law enforcement practice of scrutinizing certain individuals based on characteristics thought to indicate the likelihood of criminal behavior

Proxemics: Use of fixed space, territoriality, and personal space

Quality circle: An employee group working to improve quality during the production process

Qur'an: The holy book of Islam, considered to contain the literal words of Allah, or God; the Arabic text includes stories, admonitions, verse, and prophetic segments (also spelled *Koran*)

Race: Biologically defined as groups who share some hereditary physical characteristics; sociohistorically defined by unstable social meanings constantly being transformed by debate

Racism: The belief that races, however defined, can be ranked as inherently superior or inferior to others, accompanied with actions to accord privilege and social advantages based on race

Ramadan: The month of the lunar Islamic calendar during which Muslims abstain from food and drink from sunrise to sunset in commemoration of God's revealing the Qur'an to Muhammad

Rationality: Mental powers to form conclusions and sound judgments; intelligent and dispassionate thought

Receiver: Someone who attends to a communication message

Receiver response: Anything the receiver of a communication message does after having decoded the message

Redemptive analogy: Something in a culture that can be compared to the Christian gospel

Reference group: A group to which one aspires to attain membership

Refugee: A person seeking safe haven because his or her home country is no longer safe due to natural disaster or war (*see also* Asylee)

Reverse culture shock: Anxiety, disorientation, and stress that one can experience upon return to one's home country

Ritual: A socially essential collective activity within a culture

Roma: A widely dispersed ethnic group now concentrated in Europe; one of the ethnic groups targeted for genocide by the Nazis; under Communist regimes, the Roma were subject to forced sterilization

Rumspringa: Pennsylvania Dutch term usually translated as "running around"; late teenage years not subject to the Amish church's rules and ending with the decision to be baptized into the church and become an adult member of the community

Salad analogy: In contrast to the melting pot analogy, a description of a culture in which individuals may retain elements of their original culture and still exist together without assimilating

Sapir-Whorf hypothesis: A useful way of thinking about the relationship between language and culture (also known as *Whorfian thesis* and *linguistic relativity*)

Scientific method: Identifying a problem, gathering data, and formulating and testing a hypothesis

Segregation: Maintaining one's original culture and not participating in the new culture

Selection: The step in the perception process referring to limiting attention only to part of the available sense data

Sensation: Neurological process of becoming aware through the senses of stimuli in the environment

Separation: Maintaining one's original culture and not participating in the new culture (*see also* Segregation)

Shiite: The smaller branch of Islam that has messianic expectations of world justice

Shinto: The former state religion of Japan linking the people to ancestors and gods

Short-term orientation: A dimension of culture; the fostering of virtues related to the past and present, in particular respect for tradition, preservation of face, and fulfilling social obligations

Sign: Something that signifies a place, object, event, and so on (e.g., graphic representations in international airports to guide people to departure gates, baggage claim, and other areas)

Silence: Absence of verbal communication that can communicate messages nonverbally

Slang: The vocabulary of subgroups that has become known and accepted by the general public

Social class: A term used to refer to horizontal stratification of people; commonly used today to refer to a group of people of similar wealth, income, and power acquired by factors such as education, occupational success, and social connections rather than birth

Sojourner: One who lives in a country for a specific time for a specific purpose, such as employment, and expects to return home

Source: Someone with an idea he or she desires to communicate

Spanglish: Spanish and English words mixed in one sentence

Spanish origin: Coming from or having ancestors from a Spanish-speaking country

Spanish speaking: Speaking and comprehending the Spanish language as a primary or secondary language

Spanish surnamed: Having a last name identified as Spanish by the U.S. Census Bureau

Standard Chinese: Mandarin dialect spoken by the majority of people in China

Stereotype: Judgment made about another solely on the basis of ethnic or other group membership

Stew analogy: Similar to the concept of the melting pot, though the degree of cultural distinctiveness is higher

Subculture: A group within a larger society that shares distinctive cultural characteristics to distinguish it from others

Subgroup: A group based on vocation, avocation, or special skills that, like cultures, provide patterns of behavior and values

Sub-Saharan Africa: Countries on the African continent south of the Sahara Desert

Sunni: The largest branch of Islam

Symbol: A person, place, action, word, or thing that is used to represent something other than itself (e.g., the five intertwined rings that represent the Olympics); in models of communication, verbal and nonverbal language that is used to communicate the idea of a communication source

Syntax: Grammatical rules governing the way that words combine to form sentences

Taiwan: Republic of China, located on the island of Formosa off the southeastern coast of China

Tejano: A person born in Texas of Mexican ancestry

Telemundo: A Spanish-language television network

Territoriality: How space can be used to communicate messages

Thawb: Loose-fitting, ankle-length, usually white shirt worn by men in Saudi Arabia and some other Arab countries

Third culture: An adaptation of the term *third culture kids,* which refers to people who as children spent a significant period of time in one or more cultures other than their own original home culture and who integrate elements of those cultures and their own birth culture into a third culture

Tibet: A country in South Asia north of the Himalayas under the suzerainty, or overlordship, of China

Transgender: A person whose gender identity does not match their birth biological sex

Uncertainty avoidance: A dimension of culture; the extent to which people are made nervous by unstructured or unpredictable situations

Univision: A Spanish-language television network

Value: A central organizing belief or belief system that shapes a person's goals and motivations

Wai: A nonverbal gesture used in Thailand to communicate greeting, farewell, respect, and appreciation

White privilege: Advantages that Whites have living in a White culture

Worldview: Philosophical ideas of being; a culture's beliefs about its place in the cosmos and the nature of humanity

References

Abeele, M. V., & Roe, K. (2011). New life, old friends: A cross-cultural comparison of the use of communication technologies in the social life of college freshmen. *Young: Nordic Journal of Youth Research, 19*, 219–240.

Acheson, K. (2008). Silence as gesture: Rethinking the nature of communicative silences. *Communication Theory, 18*, 535–555.

Adler, P. S. (1975). The transitional experience: An alternative view of culture shock. *Journal of Humanistic Psychology, 15*(4), 13–23.

Adorno, T. W., Frenkel-Brunswick, E., Levinson, D. J., & Sanford, R. N. (1950). *The authoritarian personality.* New York, NY: Harper.

Agger, B. (1992). *Cultural studies as critical theory.* London, UK: Falmer.

Albarran, A. B., & Hutton, B. (2009). *A history of Spanish language radio in the United States.* Denton: University of North Texas, Center for Spanish Language Media.

Aleinkoff, T. A., & Klusmeyer, D. B. (2002). *Citizenship policies for an age of migration.* Washington, DC: Carnegie Endowment for International Peace.

Allen, H. G. (1982). *The betrayal of Liliuokalani: Last queen of Hawaii, 1838–1917.* Honolulu, HI: Mutual.

Allport, G. W. (1954). *The nature of prejudice.* Reading, MA: Addison-Wesley.

Alt, M. (2015, December 7). Why Japan got over emojis. *Slate.* Retrieved from http://www.slate.com

America by the numbers. (2007). *Time, 170*(21), 54.

Amnesty International. (2008). *Love, hate and the law: Decriminalizing homosexuality.* London, UK: Author.

Andersen, K. E. (1991). A history of communication ethics. In K. J. Greenberg (Ed.), *Conversations on communication ethics* (pp. 3–19). Norwood, NJ: Ablex.

Andersen, P. A., Lustig, M. W., & Andersen, J. F. (1987). Regional patterns of communication in the United States: A theoretical perspective. *Communication Monographs, 54*(2), 128–144.

Arbitron. (2008). *Hispanic radio today: 2008 edition.* Retrieved from http://www.americanradiohistory.com/Archive-Arbitron-Radio-Today/HispanicRadioToday-2008.pdf

Argyle, M. (1988). *Bodily communication* (2nd ed.). New York, NY: Methuen.

Argyle, M., & Ingham, R. (1972). Gaze, mutual gaze, and distance. *Semiotica, 6*(1), 32–49.

Arizonans for Official English v. Arizona, 520 U.S. 43 (1997).

Armstrong, N., & Wagner, M. (2003). *Field guide to gestures: How to identify and interpret virtually every gesture known to man.* Philadelphia, PA: Quirk.

Asante, M., & Miike, Y. (2013). Paradigmatic issues in intercultural communication studies: An Afrocentric-Asiacentric dialogue. *China Media Research, 9*(3), 1–19.

Asante, M. K., Miike, Y., & Yin, J. (2014). Introduction: New directions for intercultural communication research. In M. K. Asante, Y. Miike, & J. Yin (Eds.), *The global intercultural communication reader* (2nd ed., pp. 1–14). New York, NY: Routledge.

Ask a Korean. (2013, July 11). *Culturalism, Gladwell, and airplane crashes.* Retrieved from http://askakorean.blogspot.com/2013/07/culturalism-gladwell-and-airplane.html

Asuncion-Lande, N. (1983). Language theory and linguistic principles. In W. B. Gudykunst (Ed.), *International and intercultural communication annual* (Vol. 7, pp. 253–257). Beverly Hills, CA: Sage.

Aurand, A. M., Jr. (1938). *Little known facts about the Amish and the Mennonites.* Harrisburg, PA: Aurand Press.

Axtell, R. E. (1991). *Gestures: The do's and taboos of body language around the world.* New York, NY: John Wiley.

Axtell, R. E. (1994). *The do's and taboos of international trade.* New York, NY: John Wiley.

Aykin, N., & Milewski, A. E. (2005). Practical issues and guidelines for international information display. In N. Aykin (Ed.), *Usability and internationalization of information technology* (pp. 21–50). Mahwah, NJ: Lawrence Erlbaum.

Back, T.-H. (2004). The social reality faced by ethnic Koreans in Central Asia. *Korean and Korean American Studies Bulletin, 12*(2–3), 45–88.

Bahk, C. M., & Jandt, F. E. (2003). The perception of whiteness and interracial communication anxiety among Koreans in the United States. *Journal of Intercultural Communication Research, 32,* 97–115.

Bahk, C. M., & Jandt, F. E. (2004). Being white in America: Development of a scale. *Howard Journal of Communications, 15,* 57–68.

Barack Obama "deliberately snubbed' by Chinese in chaotic arrival at G20. (2016, September 4). *Guardian.* Retrieved from https://www.theguardian.com

Barber, W., & Badre, A. (1998, June). Culturability: The merging of culture and usability. In *Proceedings of the Fourth Conference on Human Factors and the Web.* Retrieved from http://zing.ncsl.nist.gov/hfweb/att4/proceedings/barber/

Barna, L. M. (1997). Stumbling blocks in intercultural communication. In L. A. Samovar & R. E. Porter (Eds.), *Intercultural communication: A reader* (8th ed., pp. 337–346). Belmont, CA: Wadsworth.

Barnum, W. (1982). *Gumwrappers and goggles: The tale of a jet.* San Antonio, TX: Summit.

Baron, D. (1990). *The English-only question: An official language for Americans?* New Haven, CT: Yale University Press.

Basso, K. H. (1986). *Wisdom sits in places: Landscape and language among the "Western" Apache.* Albuquerque: University of New Mexico Press.

Bauder, D. (2014, July 14). The World Cup final was the most watched soccer game in U.S. history. *Huffington Post.* Retrieved from http://www.huffingtonpost.com

Baum, G. (2008, March 9). Paris politician introduces ethnicity into municipal race. *Los Angeles Times,* p. A3.

Beckwith, R. T. (2016, June 13). Read Donald Trump's speech on the Orlando shooting. *Time.* Retrieved from http://time.com/

Beech, H. (2014, September 1). The world's most dangerous room. *Time,* pp. 32–39.

Belay, G. (1993). Toward a paradigm shift for intercultural and international communication: New research directions. In S. A. Deetz (Ed.), *Communication yearbook 16* (pp. 437–457). Newbury Park, CA: Sage.

Bell, D. (1998). *Ethnic New Zealand: Towards cultural understanding.* Hamilton, New Zealand: Ethnic NZ Trust.

Bellezza, S., Paharia, N., & Keinan, A. (2016, December 15). Research: Why Americans are so impressed by busyness. *Harvard Business Review.* Retrieved from https://hbr.org

Beltran, L. R. S. (1976). Alien premises, objects, and methods in Latin American communication research. *Communication Research, 3*(2), 107–134.

Ben-David, E. (2009). Europe's shifting immigration dynamic. *Middle East Quarterly, 16,* 15–24.

Bennhold, K., & Castle, S. (2010, September 14). E.U. calls France's Roma expulsions a "disgrace." *New York Times.* Retrieved from http://www.nytimes.com

Berger, C. R., & Calabrese, R. J. (1975). Some explorations in initial interaction and beyond: Toward a developmental theory of interpersonal communication. *Human Communication Research, 1*(2), 99–112.

Berger, J. (2013). *Contagious: Why things catch on.* New York, NY: Simon & Schuster Paperbacks.

Bergqvist, C., Borchorst, A., Christensen, A.-D., Ramstedt-Silén, V., Raaum, N. C., & Styrkársdottir, A. (Eds.). (1999). *Equal democracies? Gender and politics in the Nordic countries.* Oslo, Norway: Scandinavian University Press.

Berlo, D. K. (1960). *The process of communication.* New York, NY: Holt, Rinehart & Winston.

Berman, P. (2003). *Terror and liberalism.* New York, NY: W. W. Norton.

Berry, J. W., Kim, U., & Boski, P. (1987). Psychological acculturation of immigrants. In Y. Y. Kim & W. B. Gundykunst (Eds.), *International and intercultural communication annual* (Vol. 11, pp. 62–89). Newbury Park, CA: Sage.

Bickerton, D. (1981). *Roots of language.* Ann Arbor, MI: Karoma.

Bigelow, B. (1980). Roots and regions: A summary definition of the cultural geography of America. *Journal of Geography, 79*(6), 218–229.

Bilton, N. (2013, June 30). Disruptions: Social media images form a new language online. *New York Times.* Retrieved from http://www.nytimes.com

Birke-Smith, K. (1959). *The Eskimos.* London, UK: Methuen.

Bissoondath, N. (2002). *Selling illusions: The myth of multiculturalism.* Toronto, Ontario, Canada: Penguin.

Black, G., & Munro, R. (1993). *Black hands of Beijing: Lives in defiance in China's democracy movement.* New York, NY: John Wiley.

Blakeslee, M. (2002, June 24). Speech's utter dynamics. *Los Angeles Times,* p. A12.

Blanchard, F. A., Lilly, T., & Vaughn, L. A. (1991). Reducing the expression of racial prejudice. *Psychological Science, 2*(2), 101–105.

Bolton, R. (1994). Sex, science, and social responsibility: Cross-cultural research on same-sex eroticism and sexual intolerance. *Cross-Cultural Research, 28*(2), 134–190.

Borchorst, A., Christensen, A., & Raaum, N. (1999). Equal democracies? Conclusions and perspectives. In C. Berqvist, A. Borchorst, A.-D. Christensen, V. Ramstedt-Silén, N. C. Raaum, & A. Styrkársdottir (Eds.), *Equal democracies? Gender and politics in the Nordic countries* (pp. 227–289). Oslo, Norway: Scandinavian University Press.

Bosmajian, H. A. (1983). *The language of oppression.* Lanham, MD: University Press of America.

Boucher, J. D. (1974). Culture and the expression of emotion. In F. R. Casmir (Ed.), *International and intercultural communication annual* (Vol. 1, pp. 82–86). New York, NY: Speech Communication Association.

Boyd, D. A. (1999). *Broadcasting in the Arab world: A survey of the electronic media in the Middle East* (2nd ed.). Ames: Iowa State University Press.

Brand Finance. (2017, February 1). Global 500 2017: The most valuable brands of 2017. Retrieved from http://brandirectory.com/league_tables/table/global-500-2017

Brenan, P. (2014, January 22). Study points to yet another import from China: Smog. *Inland SoCal Register*, p. 8.

Brenner, J., & Smith, A. (2013). *72% of online adults are social networking site users.* Washington, DC: Pew Research Center. Retrieved from http://www.pewinternet.org/files/old-media/Files/Reports/2013/PIP_Social_networking_sites_update_PDF.pdf

Brettell, C. B., & Sargent, C. F. (Eds.). (1993). *Gender in cross-cultural perspective.* Englewood Cliffs, NJ: Prentice Hall.

Brislin, R. W. (1988). Increasing awareness of class, ethnicity, culture, and race by expanding on students' own experiences. In I. Cohen (Ed.), *The G. Stanley Hall lecture series* (Vol. 8, pp. 137–180). Washington, DC: American Psychological Association.

Brooks, D. (2008, October 17). Thinking about Obama. *New York Times*, p. A33.

Bruce, J., Lloyd, C. B., & Leonard A. (with P. L. Engle & N. Duffy). (1995). *Families in focus: New perspectives on mothers, fathers, and children.* New York, NY: Population Council.

Buchanan, P. J. (2002). *The death of the west: How dying populations and immigrant invasions imperil our country and civilization.* New York, NY: Thomas Dunne/St. Martin's.

Burgoon, J. K. (1986). Communication effects of gaze behavior: A test of two contrasting explanations. *Human Communication Research, 12*, 495–524.

Burgoon, J. K., Boller, D. B., & Woodall, W. G. (1988). *Non-verbal communication: The unspoken dialog.* New York, NY: Harper & Row.

Burgoon, J. K., & Saine, T. J. (1978). *The unspoken dialogue: An introduction to nonverbal communication.* Boston, MA: Houghton Mifflin.

Busari, S. (2008). Tweeting the terror: How social media reacted to Mumbai. *CNN.* Retrieved from http://edition.cnn.com

Buss, D. M. (1989). Sex differences in human mate preferences: Evolutionary hypotheses tested in 37 cultures. *Behavioral and Brain Sciences, 12*, 1–14.

Buss, D. M. (1994). Mate preferences in 37 cultures. In W. Lonner & R. Malpass (Eds.), *Psychology and culture* (pp. 197–201). Needham Heights, MA: Allyn & Bacon.

Butler, J. (1990). *Gender trouble: Feminism and the subversion of identity.* New York, NY: Routledge.

Calhoun, J. C. (1848). *Conquest of Mexico.* Retrieved from http://teachingamericanhistory.org/library/index.asp?document=478

Cameron, L., Erkal, N., Gangadharan, L., & Meng, X. (2013). Little emperors: Behavioral impacts of China's one-child policy. *Science, 339*, 953–957.

Campbell, B. G. (1976). *Human-kind emerging.* Boston, MA: Little, Brown.

Canale, M., & Swain, M. (1980). Theoretical bases of communicative approaches to second language teaching and testing. *Applied Linguistics, 1*, 1–47.

Cann, R. L., Stoneking, M., & Wilson, A. C. (1987). Mitochondrial DNA and human evolution. *Nature, 325*, 31–36.

Cannadine, D. (2013). *The undivided past: Humanity beyond our differences.* New York, NY: Alfred A. Knopf.

Canton, N. (2012, September 28). Cell phone culture: How cultural differences affect mobile use. *CNN.* Retrieved from http://www.cnn.com

Carey, J. W. (1989). *Communication as culture: Essays on media and society.* Boston, MA: Unwin Hyman.

Carliner, D. (1977). *The rights of aliens: The basic ACLU guide to an alien's rights.* New York, NY: Avon.

Carliner, D., Guttentag, L., Helton, A. C., & Henderson, W. J. (1990). *The rights of aliens and refugees: The basic ACLU guide to alien and refugee rights* (2nd ed.). Carbondale: Southern Illinois University Press.

Carroll, A., & Mendos, L. R. (2016, May). *State sponsored homophobia 2016: A world survey of sexual orientation laws: Criminalisation, protection and recognition.* Geneva, Switzerland: ILGA.

Carroll, J. B. (Ed.). (1956). *Language, thought, and reality: Selected writings of Benjamin Lee Whorf.* New York, NY: John Wiley.

Carson, R. (1962). *Silent spring.* New York, NY: Houghton Mifflin.

Casmir, F. L., & Asuncion-Lande, N. C. (1989). Intercultural communication revisited: Conceptualization, paradigm building, and methodological approaches. In J. A. Anderson (Ed.), *Communication yearbook 12* (pp. 278–309). Newbury Park, CA: Sage.

Cavalli-Sforza, L., Menozzi, P., & Piazza, A. (1994). *The history and geography of human genes.* Princeton, NJ: Princeton University Press.

Cavalli-Sforza, L. L., Piazza, A., Menozzi, P., & Mountain, J. L. (1988). Reconstruction of human evolution: Bringing together genetic, archaeological and linguistic data. *Proceedings of the National Academy of Science USA, 85*, 6002–6006.

Central Intelligence Agency. (2011). *The world factbook.* Washington, DC: Author.

Central Intelligence Agency. (2013). *The world factbook.* Washington, DC: Author.

Central Intelligence Agency. (2014). *The world factbook*. Washington, DC: Author.

Central Intelligence Agency. (2016). *The world factbook*. Washington, DC: Author.

Central Intelligence Agency. (2017). *The world factbook*. Retrieved from https://www.cia.gov/library/publications/the-world-factbook

Chaffey, D. (2017). Global social media research summary 2017. *Smart Insights*. Retrieved from http://www.smartinsights.com/social-media-marketing/social-media-strategy/new-global-social-media-research/

Chance, N. A. (1966). *The Eskimo of north Alaska*. New York, NY: Holt, Rinehart & Winston.

Chang, H.-C., & Holt, G. R. (1991). More than relationship: Chinese interaction and the principle of Kuan-Hsi. *Communication Quarterly, 39*, 251–271.

Chapman, M. (1997). Preface: Social anthropology, business studies, and cultural issues. *International Studies of Management & Organization, 26*(4), 3–29.

Charities Aid Foundation. (2011). *World giving index 2011: A global view of giving trends*. Retrieved from https://www.cafonline.org/docs/default-source/about-us-publications/world_giving_index_2011_191211.pdf?sfvrsn=4.pdf

Charities Aid Foundation. (2012). *World giving index 2012: A global view of giving trends*. Retrieved from https://www.cafonline.org/docs/default-source/about-us-publications/worldgivingindex2012web.pdf?sfvrsn=4.pdf

Charities Aid Foundation. (2015). *CAF world giving index 2015: A global view of giving trends*. Retrieved from https://www.cafonline.org/docs/default-source/about-us-publications/caf_worldgivingindex2015_report.pdf?sfvrsn=2

Chauncey, G., Jr. (1985). Christian brotherhood or sexual perversion? Homosexual identities and the construction of sexual boundaries in the World War One era. *Journal of Social History, 19*(2), 189–211.

Chávez, K. R. (2013). Pushing boundaries: Queer intercultural communication. *Journal of International and Intercultural Communication, 6*, 83–95.

Chen, G.-M. (1989). Relationships of the dimensions of intercultural communication competence. *Communication Quarterly, 37*(2), 118–133.

Chen, G.-M. (1990). Intercultural communication competence: Some perspectives of research. *Howard Journal of Communications, 2*, 243–261.

Chen, G.-M. (2012). The impact of new media on intercultural communication in global context. *China Media Research, 8*(2), 1–10.

Chen, G.-M., & Starosta, W. J. (1996). Intercultural communication competence: A synthesis. In B. R. Burleson (Ed.), *Communication yearbook 19* (pp. 353–383). Thousand Oaks, CA: Sage.

Cherry, C. (1957). *On human communication*. Cambridge, MA: Technology Press of MIT.

ChinaFile. (2013). *Document 9: A ChinaFile translation*. Retrieved from http://www.chinafile.com/document-9-chinafile-translation

Chinese Culture Connection. (1987). Chinese values and the search for culture-free dimensions of culture. *Journal of Cross-Cultural Psychology, 18*(2), 143–164.

Chiu, L.-H. (1972). A cross-cultural comparison of cognitive styles in Chinese and American children. *International Journal of Psychology, 7*, 235–242.

Chomsky, N. (1980). *Rules and representations*. New York, NY: Columbia University Press.

Chu, G. C. (1977). *Radical change through communication in Mao's China*. Honolulu: University Press of Hawai'i.

Chua, A., & Rubenfeld, J. (2014). *The triple package: How three unlikely traits explain the rise and fall of cultural groups in America*. New York, NY: Penguin Press.

Chua, C. M. (2004). The Malaysian communication competence construct. *Journal of Intercultural Communication Research, 33*, 131–146.

Chuang, R. (2002). An examination of Taoist and Buddhist perspectives on interpersonal conflicts, emotions, and adversities. *Intercultural Communication Studies, 11*, 23–40.

Chuang, R., & Chen, G.-H. (2003). Buddhist perspectives and human communication. *Intercultural Communication Studies, 12*(4), 65–80.

Chyz, Y. J. (1945, October 13). Number, distribution, and circulation of the foreign language press in the United States. *Interpreter Releases, 20*, 290.

Clark, D. (2016). *Alibaba: The house that Jack Ma built*. New York, NY: HarperCollins.

Clinton, H. R. (2010, March). *Remarks on Internet freedom*. Speech at Newseum, Washington, DC.

Clinton, H. R. (2011, December 6). *Remarks in recognition of International Human Rights Day*. Palais des Nations, Geneva, Switzerland.

Clough, M. (1997, July 27). Birth of nations. *Los Angeles Times*, pp. M1, M6.

Clutter, A. W., & Zubieta, A. C. (2009). *Understanding the Latino culture*. Columbus: Ohio State University Extension.

Cobo, J. R. M. (1987). *Study of the problem of discrimination against indigenous populations*. New York, NY: United Nations.

Cochrane, A. (2007). Environmental ethics. In *Internet encyclopedia of philosophy*. Retrieved from http://www.iep.utm.edu/e/envi-eth.htm

Cohen, M. N. (1998). *Culture of intolerance: Chauvinism, class, and racism in the United States*. New Haven, CT: Yale University Press.

Cohen, R. (1997). *Negotiating across cultures: Communications obstacles in international diplomacy*. Washington, DC: U.S. Institute of Peace Press.

Cole, M. (1996). *Cultural psychology*. Cambridge, MA: Belknap Press.

Collier, M. J. (1988). A comparison of conversations among and between domestic culture groups: How intra- and intercultural competencies vary. *Communication Quarterly, 36*(2), 122–144.

Collier, M. J., & Thomas, M. (1988). Cultural identity: An interpretive perspective. In Y. Y. Kim & W. B. Gudykunst (Eds.), *Theories in intercultural communication* (*International and Intercultural Communication Annual,* Vol. 12, pp. 99–120). Newbury Park, CA: Sage.

Collins, P. H. (1990). *Black feminist thought: Knowledge, consciousness and the politics of empowerment.* Boston, MA: Unwin Hyman.

Congressional Budget Office. (2011). *Trends in the distribution of household income between 1979 and 2007.* Washington, DC: Author. Retrieved from https://www.cbo.gov/publication/42729

Connaughton, S. L., & Jarvis, S. E. (2004). Invitations for partisan identification: Attempts to court Latino voters through televised Latino-oriented political advertisements, 1984–2000. *Journal of Communication, 54,* 38–54.

Costello, E. (1995). *Signing: How to speak with your hands.* New York, NY: Bantam.

Coulton, T. M., & Glionna, J. M. (2011, September 23). In Japan, finders not keepers. *Los Angeles Times,* pp. A1, A7.

The Council of Europe's Roma and Travellers Division. (2012). *Who are the Roma people?* Retrieved from http://www.euronews.com/2012/04/30/who-are-the-roma-people-

Cowan, M. (Ed. & Trans.). (1963). *Humanist without portfolio: An anthology of the writing of Wilhelm von Humboldt.* Detroit, MI: Wayne State University Press.

Cowen, T. (2002). *Creative destruction: How globalization is changing the world's cultures.* Princeton, NJ: Princeton University Press.

Crawford, J. (1992). *Hold your tongue: Bilingualism and the politics of English-only.* Reading, MA: Addison-Wesley.

Cross, S. E., Hardin, E. E., & Swing, B. G. (2011). The what, how, why, and where of self-construal. *Personality and Social Psychology Review, 15,* 142–179.

Croucher, S. M. (2008). French-Muslims and the hijab: An analysis of identity and the Islamic veil in France. *Journal of Intercultural Communication Research, 37,* 199–213.

Crystal, D. (1997). *English as a global language.* Cambridge, UK: Cambridge University Press.

Dalisay, F. (2012). Media use and acculturation of new immigrants in the United States. *Communication Research Reports, 29*(2), 148–160.

Damasio, A. R. (2010). *Self comes to mind: Constructing the conscious mind.* New York, NY: Pantheon.

Dannin, R. (2002). *Black pilgrimage to Islam.* Oxford, UK: Oxford University Press.

Darnell, D., & Brockriede, W. (1976). *Persons communicating.* Englewood Cliffs, NJ: Prentice Hall.

Darwin, C. (1969). *The expression of the emotions in man and animals.* Westport, CT: Greenwood. (Original work published 1872)

Davin, D. (2000). Migrants and the media: Concerns about rural migration in the Chinese press. In L. S. West & Y. H. Zhao (Eds.), *Rural labor flows in China* (pp. 278–291). Berkeley: University of California at Berkeley, Institute of East Asian Studies.

Davis, A. (1992, May 24). Rope. *New York Times,* Sec. 4, p. 11.

Davis, E. W. (2007). *Light at the edge of the world: A journey through the realm of vanishing cultures.* Vancouver, British Columbia, Canada: Douglas & McIntyre.

de la Zerda, N., & Hopper, R. (1979). Employment interviewers' reactions to Mexican American speech. *Communication Monographs, 46*(2), 126–134.

de Mooij, M. (2014). *Global marketing and advertising: Understanding cultural paradoxes* (4th ed.). Thousand Oaks, CA: Sage.

de Tocqueville, A. (1945). *Democracy in America.* New York, NY: Vintage. (Original work published 1835)

Deal, T. E., & Kennedy, A. A. (1982). *Corporate cultures: The rites and rituals of corporate life.* Reading, MA: Addison-Wesley.

Decision to fire gays stirs anger. (1991, February 28). *Los Angeles Times.* Retrieved from http://articles.latimes.com

Deetz, S. (1973). An understanding of science and a hermeneutic science of understanding. *Journal of Communication, 23*(2), 139–159.

Demick, B. (2009, September 20). Chinese babies stolen by officials for adoption fees. *Los Angeles Times,* p. A1ff.

Demick, B. (2011, April 2). Wary of unrest, China cracks down on dissent. *Los Angeles Times,* p. A9.

Demick, B. (2012, November 9). Tibetan protests cloud China party congress. *Los Angeles Times,* p. A3.

Demick, B. (2014, March 23). In China, first lady extols free speech. *Los Angeles Times,* p. A6.

Desilver, D. (2013, December 19). Global inequality: How the U.S. compares. Retrieved from http://www.pewresearch.org/fact-tank/2013/12/19/global-inequality-how-the-u-s-compares/

Deutscher, G. (2010). *Through the language glass: Why the world looks different in other languages.* New York, NY: Metropolitan Books/Henry Holt.

DeVito, J. A. (1986). *The communication handbook: A dictionary.* New York, NY: Harper & Row.

DeVito, J. A. (2013). *The interpersonal communication book* (13th ed.). Boston, MA: Pearson.

DeVito, J. A. (2014). *The nonverbal communication book.* Dubuque, IA: Kendall Hunt.

Diamond, J. (2005). *Collapse: How societies choose to fail or succeed.* New York, NY: Viking Press.

Dickey, J. (2015, June 1). Save our vacation. *Time,* pp. 44–49.

Dingemanse, M., Torreira, F., & Enfield, N. J. (2013). Is "huh?" a universal word? Conversational infrastructure and the convergent evolution of linguistic items. *PLoS ONE, 8*(11), e78273.

Do You Have a Twitter "Accent"? (2013, September 4). *WBUR*. Retrieved from http://hereandnow.wbur.org

Doi, L. T. (1956). Japanese language as an expression of Japanese psychology. *Western Speech, 20*(2), 90–96.

Doi, L. T. (1973). The Japanese patterns of communication and the concept of *amae*. *Quarterly Journal of Speech, 59*(2), 180–185.

Domhoff, G. W. (2011). Wealth, income and power. *Who rules America?* Retrieved from http://sociology.ucsc.edu/whorulesamerica/power/wealth.html

Donald J. Trump's vision. (n.d.). Retrieved from https://law.yale.edu/system/files/documents/pdf/Faculty/immigrationtalk_trumpimmigrationstatement_11-15-16.pdf

Doty, R. L., Shaman, P., Applebaum, S. L., Giberson, R., Siksorski, L., & Rosenberg, L. (1984). Smell identification ability: Changes with age. *Science, 226*, 1441–1443.

Downing, J. D. H. (1990). Ethnic minority radio in the United States. *Howard Journal of Communications, 2*(2), 135–148.

Dresner, E., & Herring, S. C. (2010). Functions of the nonverbal in CMC: Emoticons and illocutionary force. *Communication Theory, 20*, 249–268.

Dresser, N. (1996). *Multicultural manners*. New York, NY: John Wiley.

Drzewiecka, J. A., & Steyn, M. (2009). Discourses of exoneration in intercultural translation: Polish immigrants in South Africa. *Communication Theory, 19*, 188–218.

D'Souza, D. (2002, May 10). Two cheers for colonialism. *Chronicle of Higher Education*. Retrieved from http://chronicle.com

Duara, N., & Carcamo, C. (2015, November 20). Balance tips as more exit U.S. for Mexico, survey finds. *Los Angeles Times*, pp. A1, A16.

Dudley, M. K., & Agard, K. K. (1993). *A call for Hawaiian sovereignty*. Honolulu, HI: Na Kane O Ka Malo Press.

Duff-Brown, B. (2001, June 17). Service over fiber-optic miles—to India. *Los Angeles Times*. Retrieved from http://articles.latimes.com

Duff-Brown, B. (2007, April 15). Those at home on the ice watch it slowly vanish. *Los Angeles Times*. Retrieved from http://articles.latimes.com

Duggan, M. (2013, September 12). It's a woman's (social media) world. Retrieved from http://www.pewresearch.org/fact-tank/2013/09/12/its-a-womans-social-media-world

Duncan, D. E. (1998). *Calendar: Humanity's epic struggle to determine a true and accurate year*. New York, NY: Avon.

Dunn, M., Greenhill, S. J., Levinson, S. C., & Gray, R. D. (2011). Evolved structure of language shows lineage-specific trends in word-order "universals." *Nature, 473*, 79–82.

Dyer, R. (1997). *White*. New York, NY: Routledge.

Dynes, W. (1990). *Encyclopedia of homosexuality*. New York, NY: Garland.

Eagan, K., Stolzenberg, E. B., Bates, A. K., Aragon, M. C., Suchard, M. R., & Rios-Aguilar, C. (2015). *The American freshman: National norms full 2015*. Los Angeles: University of California, Los Angeles, Higher Education Research Institute.

Eagleton, T. (2013). *Across the pond: An Englishman's view of America*. New York, NY: W. W. Norton.

Eastman, C. (Ed.). (1992). *Code switching*. Avon, UK: Clevedon.

Eck, D. L. (1993). *Encountering God: A spiritual journey from Bozeman to Banaras*. Boston, MA: Beacon.

Ehrlich, P. (1968). *The population bomb*. New York, NY: Ballantine.

Eisenstein, J. (2014, August 6). Identifying regional dialects in online social media. Retrieved from http://www.cc.gatech.edu/~jeisenst/papers/dialectology-chapter.pdf

Ekman, P., & Friesen, W. V. (1978). *Facial Action Coding System: A technique for the measurement of facial movement*. Palo Alto, CA: Consulting Psychologists Press.

Ekman, P., Friesen, W. V., & Ellsworth, P. (1972). *Emotion in the human face: Guidelines for research and an integration of findings*. New York, NY: Pergamon Press.

Ekman, P., Friesen, W. V., O'Sullivan, M., Chan, A., Diacoyanni-Tarlatzis, I., Heider, K., . . . Tzavaras, A. (1987). Universals and cultural differences in the judgments of facial expression of emotion. *Journal of Personality and Social Psychology, 53*, 712–717.

Ekman, P., & Heider, K. G. (1988). The universality of a contempt expression: A replication. *Motivation and Emotion, 12*, 303–308.

Elliott, L. (1998). *The global politics of the environment*. New York, NY: New York University Press.

Emerson, R. W. (1909–1914). *Journals of Ralph Waldo Emerson* (Vol. 7). Boston, MA: Houghton Mifflin.

Employment Division of Oregon v. Smith, 494 U.S. 872 (1990).

Epstein, S. (1990). Gay politics, ethnic identity: The limits of social construction. In E. Stein (Ed.), *Forms of desire: Sexual orientation and the social constructionist controversy* (pp. 239–293). New York, NY: Garland.

Espenshade, T. J., & Radford, A. W. (2009). *No longer separate, not yet equal: Race and class in elite college admission and campus life*. Princeton, NJ: Princeton University Press.

Essig, L. (1999). *Queer in Russia: A story of sex, self, and the other*. Durham, NC: Duke University Press.

Essoungou, A.-M. (2010). A social media boom begins in Africa: Using mobile phones, Africans join the global conversation. *Africa Renewal, 24*(4), 3. Retrieved from http://www.un.org/africarenewal/magazine

Esty, D. C., Levy, M. A., & Winston, A. (2002). *Environmental Sustainability Index (ESI)*. New Haven, CT: Yale Center for Environmental Law & Policy.

Esty, D. C., Levy, M. A., & Winston, A. (2003). *Environmental sustainability in the Arab world*. In K. Schwab (Ed.), *Arab world competitiveness report 2002–2003* (pp. 236–248). Oxford, UK: Oxford University Press.

Fabrykant, M., & Magun, V. (2015). *Grounded and normative dimensions of national pride in comparative perspective*. Retrieved from https://www.hse.ru/data/2015/04/28/1098372529/62SOC2015.pdf

Facebook and Twitter gain more users in Saudi Arabia. (2014, January 9). *Al Arabiya News*. Retrieved from http://english.alarabiya.net

Fadiman, A. (2012). *The spirit catches you and you fall down: A Hmong child, her American doctors, and the collision of two cultures*. New York, NY: Farrar, Straus and Giroux. (Original work published 1997)

Fagan, G. (2013). *Believing in Russia: Religious policy after communism*. New York, NY: Routledge.

Fejes, F., & Petrich, K. (1993). Invisibility, homophobia and heterosexism: Lesbians, gays and the media. *Critical Studies in Mass Communication, 10*, 395–422.

Ferguson, N. (2011). *Civilization: The West and the rest*. London, UK: Penguin Press.

Ferguson, W. (1997, May 25). Germans' reminder of home lives on. *The Blade*, pp. A11–A12.

Film exposes immigrants to Dutch liberalism. (2006, March 16). *NBC News*. Retrieved from http://www.nbcnews.com/

Finding the golden mean. (1987, January 9). *The Straits Times*, p. 24.

Finkelman, P. (1991). Race and the constitution. In K. L. Hall (Ed.), *By and for the people: Constitutional rights in American history* (pp. 149–162). Arlington Heights, IL: Harlan Davidson.

Fischer, D. H. (1989). *Albion's seed: Four British folkways in America*. New York, NY: Oxford University Press.

Fishman, J. A. (1972). *The sociology of language*. Rowley, MA: Newbury House.

FitzGerald, D. S., & Cook-Martin, D. (2014). *Culling the masses: The democratic origins of racist immigration policy in the Americas*. Cambridge, MA: Harvard University Press.

Fitzgerald, F. S. (1926). *All the sad young men*. New York, NY: Scribners.

Fleishman, J. (2014, January 19). How U.S. films translate abroad. *Los Angeles Times*, pp. D1, D8.

Fleishman, J. (2016, April 17). Global accent. *Los Angeles Times*, pp. E1, E4–E5.

Fong, M. (2000). "Luck talk" in celebrating the Chinese New Year. *Journal of Pragmatics, 32*, 219–237.

Fong, M. (2016). *One child: The story of China's most radical experiment*. Boston, MA: Houghton Mifflin Harcourt.

Foss, K. A., & Foss, S. K. (1994). Personal experience as evidence in feminist scholarship. *Western Journal of Communication, 58*(1), 39–43.

Foss, K. A., Foss, S. K., & Griffin, C. L. (1999). *Feminist rhetorical theories*. Thousand Oaks, CA: Sage.

Foster, R. (2011, March 9). Social media = punk rock? *Is this binding* [Web log post]. Retrieved from http://www.musicalfoster.com/blog/?p=675

Fowler, G. A. (2004, December 7). China bans Nike's LeBron ad as offensive to nation's dignity. *Wall Street Journal*. Retrieved from http://online.wsj.com

Fragante v. City and County of Honolulu, 888 F.2d 591 (9th Cir. 1989).

Frank, T. (2000). *One market under God: Extreme capitalism, market populism, and the end of economic democracy*. Garden City, NY: Doubleday.

Fredrickson, G. M. (2002). *Racism: A short history*. Princeton, NJ: Princeton University Press.

Freedom House. (2015). *Freedom on the net 2015*. Retrieved fromhttps://freedomhouse.org/report/freedom-net/freedom-net-2015

Freedom to Marry. (2016). *The freedom to marry internationally*. Retrieved from http://www.freedomtomarry.org/pages/the-freedom-to-marry-internationally

Freire, P. (1970). *Pedagogy of the oppressed* (M. B. Ramos, Trans.). New York, NY: Continuum.

French, P. (2011). *India: A portrait*. New York, NY: Knopf.

Friedman, G. (2011). *The next decade: Where we've been . . . and where we're going*. New York, NY: Doubleday.

Fukuoka, Y. (1996). Koreans in Japan: Past and present. *Saitama University Review, 31*(1), 1–15.

Furnham, A. (1987). The adjustment of sojourners. In Y. Y. Kim & W. B. Gundykunst (Eds.), *International and intercultural communication annual* (Vol. 11, pp. 42–61). Newbury Park, CA: Sage.

Furnham, A., & Bochner, S. (1986). *Culture shock: Psychological reactions to unfamiliar environments*. New York, NY: Methuen.

Fuse, K., Land, M., & Lambiase, J. J. (2010). Expanding the philosophical base for ethical public relations practice: Cross-cultural case application of non-Western ethical philosophies. *Western Journal of Communication, 74*, 436–455.

Fuss, D. (Ed.). (1991). *Inside/out*. New York, NY: Routledge.

Gao, G., & Ting-Toomey, S. (1998). *Communicating effectively with the Chinese*. Thousand Oaks, CA: Sage.

Garreau, J. (1981). *The nine nations of North America*. Boston, MA: Houghton Mifflin.

Gayle, A.-L. (2013, November 4). Mother responds to controversy after son dresses as Klansman for Halloween. *WHSV3*. Retrieved from http://www.whsv.com/

Geddes, R. W. (1976). *Migrants of the mountains: The cultural ecology of the Blue Miau (Hmong) of Thailand*. Oxford, UK: Clarendon.

Gendered Innovations in Science, Health & Medicine, Engineering, and Environment. (n.d.). Machine translation: Analyzing gender. http://genderedinnovations.stanford.edu/case-studies/nlp.html

Gerbner, G., Gross, L., Morgan, M., & Signorielli, N. (1980). The mainstreaming of America: Violence profile no. 11. *Journal of Communication, 30*, 10–29.

Gerbner, G., Morgan, M., & Signorielli, N. (1986). Living with television: The dynamics of the cultivation process. In J. Bryant & D. Zillmann (Eds.), *Perspectives on media effects* (pp. 17–40). Hillsdale, NJ: Lawrence Erlbaum.

Gerner, M., Perry, F., Moselle, M. A., & Archbold, M. (1992). Moving between cultures: Recent research on the characteristics of internationally mobile adolescents. *Global Nomad Quarterly, 1*(2), 2–3, 8.

Gevorgyan, G., & Manucharova, N. (2009). Does culturally adapted online communication work? A study of American and Chinese Internet users' attitudes and preferences toward culturally customized web design elements. *Journal of Computer-Mediated Communication, 14*, 393–413.

Ghosh, B. (2010). Muslims and mosques in the west. *Time, 176*(9), 23.

Gibson, C., & Jung, K. (2002). *Historical census statistics on population totals by race, 1790 to 1990, and by Hispanic origin, 1970 to 1990, for the United States, regions, divisions, and states* (Working Paper Series No. 56). Retrieved from https://www.census.gov/content/dam/Census/library/working-papers/2002/demo/POP-twps0056.pdf

Gilbert, D. (2015). *The American class structure in an age of growing inequality* (9th ed.). Thousand Oaks, CA: Sage.

Gilbert, D., & Kahl, J. A. (1982). *The American class structure: A new synthesis.* Homewood, IL: Dorsey.

Gillette, J. (1991). Sporty Japanese import. *Westways.*

Gladwell, M. (2008). *Outliers: The story of success.* New York, NY: Little, Brown.

Glendon, M. A. (1991). *Rights talk: The impoverishment of political discourse.* New York, NY: Free Press.

The global 30. (2012). *QSR.* Retrieved from http://www.qsr-magazine.com/

Global Leaders. (2001). *Pilot environmental sustainability index.* Davos, Switzerland: World Economic Forum.

Goh, B. (2009, September 8). Asian social networking sites profit from virtual money. *Reuters.* Retrieved from http://www.reuters.com

Goldin, I., Cameron, G., & Balarajan, M. (2011). *Exceptional people: How migration shaped our world and will define our future.* Princeton, NJ: Princeton University Press.

Gonzalez, A. (1990). Mexican "otherness" in the rhetoric of Mexican Americans. *Southern Communication Journal, 55*, 276–291.

González, J. L. (2014). *A history of Christian thought.* Nashville, TN: Abingdon Press.

Gonzalez, M. (2013, May 1). *Wrong message on assimilation.* Retrieved from http://www.heritage.org/research/commentary/2013/4/wrong-message-on-assimilation

Gonzalez-Barrera, A. (2015). Migration flows between the U.S. and Mexico have slowed—and turned toward Mexico. Retrieved from http://www.pewhispanic.org/2015/11/19/chapter-1-migration-flows-between-the-u-s-and-mexico-have-slowed-and-turned-toward-mexico/

Google. (n.d.). Our culture. Retrieved from http://www.google.com/about/company/facts/culture/

Gordon, D. R. (1971). *The new literacy.* Toronto, Ontario, Canada: University of Toronto Press.

Govorchin, G. G. (1961). *Americans from Yugoslavia.* Gainesville: University of Florida Press.

Grad, S. (1997, October 12). Disney tells jungle cruise jokers to take a ride. *Los Angeles Times.* Retrieved from http://articles.latimes.com/1997/oct/12/local/me-42072

Greenberg, J., & Pyszczynski, T. (1985). The effect of an overheard ethnic slur on evaluations of the target: How to spread a social disease. *Journal of Experimental Social Psychology, 21*, 61–72.

Greenwood, S., Perrin, A., & Duggan, M. (2016, November 11). Social media update 2016. Retrieved from http://www.pewinternet.org/2016/11/11/social-media-update-2016/

Greer, G. (1999). *The whole woman.* New York, NY: Anchor.

Griffith, J. E., & Villavicencio, S. (1985). Relationships among acculturation, sociodemographic characteristics and social supports in Mexican American adults. *Hispanic Journal of Behavioral Sciences, 7*(1), 75–92.

Grosjean, F. (1982). *Life with two languages: An introduction to bilingualism.* Cambridge, MA: Harvard University Press.

Gross, L. (1993). *Contested closets: The politics and ethics of outing.* Minneapolis: University of Minnesota Press.

Gudykunst, W. B. (1983). Toward a typology of stranger-host relationships. *International Journal of Intercultural Relations, 7*, 401–413.

Gudykunst, W. B. (1985). The influence of cultural similarity, type of relationship, and self-monitoring on uncertainty reduction processes. *Communication Monographs, 52*, 203–217.

Gudykunst, W. B. (2005). *Theorizing about intercultural communication.* Thousand Oaks, CA: Sage.

Guernica, A. (1982). *Reaching the Hispanic market effectively: The media, the market, the methods.* New York, NY: McGraw-Hill.

Guillem, S. M. (2011). European identity: Across which lines? Defining Europe through public discourses on the Roma. *Journal of International and Intercultural Communication, 4*, 23–41.

Guly, C. (2015, December 19). In Canada, law applies to *les tweets. Los Angeles Times*, p. A3.

Guskin, E. & Mitchell, A. (2011). Hispanic media: Faring better than the mainstream media. Retrieved from http://www.stateofthemedia.org/2011/hispanic-media-fairing-better-than-the-mainstream-media/

Habeck, M. R. (2006). *Knowing the enemy: Jihadist ideology and the war on terror*. New Haven, CT: Yale University Press.

Haiek, J. R. (1992). *Arab-American almanac* (4th ed.). Glendale, CA: News Circle.

Haiman, F. S. (1994). *"Speech acts" and the First Amendment*. Carbondale: Southern Illinois University Press.

Hall, E. T. (1959). *The silent language*. Greenwich, CT: Fawcett.

Hall, E. T. (1976). *Beyond culture*. New York, NY: Anchor.

Hall, E. T. (1983). *The dance of life: The other dimension of time*. New York, NY: Doubleday.

Hall, E. T., & Hall, M. (1990). *Understanding cultural differences*. Yarmouth, ME: Intercultural Press.

Hall, J. H. (Ed.). (2004). *Dictionary of American regional English* (Vol. 4). Cambridge, MA: Harvard University Press.

Hall, S., Morley, D., & Chen, K.-H. (1996). *Stuart Hall: Critical dialogues in cultural studies*. London, UK: Routledge.

Hallett, V. (2003, July 14). Who do you love? *U.S. News & World Report*, p. 38.

Hallstein, L. O. (1999). A postmodern caring: Feminist standpoint theories, revisioning caring, and communication ethics. *Western Journal of Communication, 63*(1), 32–56.

Halperin, D. M. (2012). *How to be gay*. Cambridge, MA: Belknap Press.

Hamdy, N., & Gomaa, E. H. (2012). Framing the Egyptian uprising in Arabic language newspapers and social media. *Journal of Communication, 62*, 195–211.

Hamid, S. (2016). *Islamic exceptionalism: How the struggle over Islam is reshaping the world*. New York, NY: St. Martin's Press.

Hamid, S. (2016, September 11). Why Islam isn't like other faiths. *Los Angeles Times*, p. A19.

Hamilton, S., & Harwood, J. (1997). Cultural and structural differences in communication-related work values: The potential for conflict. In C. D. Brown, C. C. Snedecker, & B. Sykes (Eds.), *Conflict and diversity* (pp. 139–156). Cresskill, NJ: Hampton Press.

Hancock, T. (2013, January 13). March of the QQ penguin. *The World of Chinese*. http://www.theworldofchinese. com/2013/01/march-of-the-qq-penguin

Handlin, O. (1952). *The uprooted*. Boston, MA: Little, Brown.

Hanson, G. (2009). *The economics and policy of illegal immigration in the United States*. Washington, DC: Migration Policy Institute.

Harding, S. (1991). *Whose science? Whose knowledge? Thinking from women's lives*. Ithaca, NY: Cornell University Press.

Harper, R. G., Wiens, A. N., & Matarazzo, J. D. (1978). *Nonverbal communication: The state of the art*. New York, NY: John Wiley.

Harris, D. (1997). *The rise and fall of gay culture*. New York, NY: Hyperion.

Hart, B., & Risley, T. (1995). *Meaningful differences in the everyday experiences of young American children*. Baltimore, MD: Paul H. Brookes.

Hassim, S. (2009). Perverse consequences? The impact of quotas for women on democratization in Africa. In I. Shapiro, S. C. Stokes, E. J. Wood, & A. S. Kirshner (Eds.), *Political representation* (pp. 211–235). Cambridge, UK: Cambridge University Press.

Hauser, C. (2014, February 7). As Olympics open, social media is a prism for protests against Russia's anti-gay law. *The Lede*. Retrieved from http://thelede.blogs. nytimes.com

Hausmann, R., Tyson, L. D., Bekhouche, Y., & Zahidi, S. (2013). *The global gender gap report 2013*. Geneva, Switzerland: World Economic Forum.

Hausmann, R., Tyson, L. D., & Zahidi, S. (2010). *The global gender gap report 2010*. Geneva, Switzerland: World Economic Forum.

Hayakawa, S. I. (1978). *Through the communication barrier*. New York, NY: Harper & Row.

Hayden, T. (2003, May 18). Losing our voices: Too many languages are speaking last words. *U.S. News & World Report*. Retrieved from http://www.usnews.com

Hayes, J. J. (1976). Gayspeak. *Quarterly Journal of Speech, 62*, 256–266.

Hayes-Bautista, D. E., Hurtado, A., & Valdez, R. B. (1992). *No longer a minority: Latinos and social policy in California*. Los Angeles: University of California, Los Angeles, Chicano Studies Research Center.

Hayman, R. L., Jr., & Levit, N. (1997). The constitutional ghetto. In R. Delgado & J. Stefancie (Eds.), *Critical white studies: Looking behind the mirror* (pp. 239–247). Philadelphia, PA: Temple University Press.

Hebdige, D. (1979). *Subculture: The meaning of style*. London, UK: Methuen.

Hennessey, K., & Parsons, C. (2013, July 20). A president reflects on race. *Los Angeles Times*, pp. A1, A9.

Herakova, L. L. (2009). Identity, communication, inclusion: The Roma and (new) Europe. *Journal of International and Intercultural Communication, 2*, 279–297.

Hickson, M. L., III, & Stacks, D. W. (1989). *NVC, nonverbal communication: Studies and applications* (2nd ed.). Dubuque, IA: William C. Brown.

Hill, C. W. L. (1998). *International business: Competing in the global marketplace* (2nd ed.). Boston, MA: Irwin/ McGraw-Hill.

Hill, S. (2013, November 30). Is it bonjour or hola? These apps will help you translate languages wherever you are. *Digital Trends*. Retrieved from http://www.digitaltrends.com

Hoefer, M., Rytina, N., & Baker, B. (2012). *Estimates of the unauthorized immigrant population residing in the United States: January 2011*. Retrieved from http:// www.dhs.gov/xlibrary/assets/statistics/publications/ois_ ill_pe_2011.pdf

Hofstede, G. (1980). *Culture's consequences*. Beverly Hills, CA: Sage.

Hofstede, G. (1983). Dimensions of national cultures in fifty countries and three regions. In J. B. Deregowski, S. Dziurawiec, & R. C. Annis (Eds.), *Expectations in cross-cultural psychology* (pp. 335–355). Lisse, Netherlands: Swets & Zeitlinger.

Hofstede, G. (1984). The cultural relativity of the quality of life concept. *Academy of Management Review, 9,* 389–398.

Hofstede, G. (1991). *Cultures and organizations: Software of the mind.* New York, NY: McGraw-Hill.

Hofstede, G. (1994). Business cultures. *UNESCO Courier, 47*(4), 12–16.

Hofstede, G. (1996). Gender stereotypes and partner preferences of Asian women in masculine and feminine cultures. *Journal of Cross-Cultural Psychology, 27,* 533–546.

Hofstede, G. (1997). *Cultures and organizations: Software of the mind* (Rev. ed.). New York, NY: McGraw-Hill.

Hofstede, G. (1998). Comparative studies of sexual behavior: Sex as achievement or as relationship? In G. Hofstede (Ed.), *Masculinity and femininity: The taboo dimension of national cultures* (pp. 153–178). Thousand Oaks, CA: Sage.

Hofstede, G. (2001). *Culture's consequences: Comparing values, behaviors, institutions, and organizations across nations* (2nd ed.). Thousand Oaks, CA: Sage.

Hofstede, G. (2002). Dimensions do not exist: A reply to Brendan McSweeney. *Human Relations, 55,* 1355–1361.

Hofstede, G., & Bond, M. H. (1984). Hofstede's culture dimensions: An independent validation using Rokeach's value survey. *Journal of Cross-Cultural Psychology, 15,* 417–433.

Hofstede, G., Hofstede, G. J., & Minkov, M. (2010). *Cultures and organizations: Software of the mind* (3rd ed.). New York, NY: McGraw-Hill.

Hoijer, H. (1954). The Sapir-Whorf hypothesis. In H. Hoijer (Ed.), *Language in culture* (pp. 92–105). Chicago, IL: University of Chicago Press.

Hollinger, D. A. (1995). *Post-ethnic America: Beyond multiculturalism.* New York, NY: Basic Books.

Holm, J. A. (1989). *Pidgins and creoles* (2 vols.). Cambridge, UK: Cambridge University Press.

Hom, S. (2013). Simulated imperialism. *Traditional Dwellings and Settlements Review. 25*(1), 25–44.

Hoornweg, D., & Bhada-Tata, P. (2012). *What a waste: A global review of solid waste management* (Knowledge papers no. 15). Washington, DC: World Bank. Retrieved from https://openknowledge.worldbank.org/handle/10986/17388

Hostetler, J. A. (1980). *Amish society* (3rd ed.). Baltimore, MD: Johns Hopkins University Press.

Hotz, R. L. (1995, April 15). Official racial definitions have shifted sharply and often. *Los Angeles Times,* p. A14.

House, K. E. (2012). *On Saudi Arabia: Its people, past, religion, fault lines—and future.* New York, NY: Knopf.

Hoyt, C., Jr. (2012). The pedagogy of the meaning of racism: Reconciling a discordant discourse. *Social Work, 57,* 225–254.

Hsu, A., et al. (2016). *2016 Environmental Performance Index.* New Haven, CT: Yale University. Retrieved from http://epi.yale.edu/sites/default/files/2016EPI_Full_Report_opt.pdf

Hu, H. C. (1944). The Chinese concepts of "face." *American Anthropologist, 46*(1), 45–64.

Hu, X. B., Wang, G. T., & Zou, Y. M. (2002). Political economy of the floating Chinese population. *Journal of Contemporary Asia, 32,* 536–552.

Huffstutter, P. J. (2009, September 20). The news from Amish country. *Los Angeles Times,* p. A3.

Human Rights Watch. (2016). World report 2016: Rights in transition. Retrieved from https://www.hrw.org/world-report/2016/rights-in-transition

Huntington, S. P. (1993). The clash of civilizations? *Foreign Affairs, 72*(3), 22–49.

Huntington, S. P. (1996). *The clash of civilizations and the remaking of world order.* New York, NY: Simon & Schuster.

Huntington, S. P. (2004). *Who are we? The challenges to America's national identity.* New York, NY: Simon & Schuster.

Hurstfield, J. (1978). Internal colonialism: White, black and Chicano self-conceptions. *Ethnic and Racial Studies, 1*(1), 60–79.

Hurtado, A., Hayes-Bautista, D. E., Valdez, R. B., & Hernandez, A. C. R. (1992). *Redefining California: Latino social engagement in a multicultural society.* Los Angeles: University of California, Los Angeles, Chicano Studies Research Center.

Husted, B. W. (2005). Culture and ecology: A cross-national study of the determinants of environmental sustainability. *Management International Review, 45,* 349–371.

Hyland, K. (2009). *Academic discourse: English in a global context.* London, UK: Continuum.

ILGA. (2014). *Lesbian and gay rights in the world.* Retrieved from http://old.ilga.org/Statehomophobia/ILGA_Map_2014_ENG.pdf

Imai, M., & Gentner, D. (1994). A cross-linguistic study of early word meaning: Universal ontology and linguistic influence. *Cognition, 62*(2), 169–200.

In historic move, UN creates single entity to promote women's empowerment. (2010, July 2). *UN News Centre.* Retrieved from http://www.un.org/apps/news/story.asp?NewsID=35224

Issues: Income and wealth inequality. (n.d.). Retrieved from https://berniesanders.com/issues/income-and-wealth-inequality/

India washing machine launched with "curry" button. (2017, March 10). *BBC News.* Retrieved from http://www.bbc.com/news/business-39176358

Infante, D. A., Rancer, A. S., & Womack, D. F. (1993). *Building communication theory* (2nd ed.). Prospect Heights, IL: Waveland.

Infomancie. (2008a, January 30). Nordic Ecolabel swan: Scandanavian co-operation. *Infomancy.* Retrieved from http://infomancie.wordpress.com/2008/01/30/nordic-ecolabel-swan-scandinavian-co-operation

Infomancie. (2008b, March 10). The original recycling symbol. *Infomancy*. Retrieved from http://infomancie.wordpress.com/2008/03/10/the-original-recycling-symbol

Ingle, S. (1982). *Quality circles master guide: Increasing productivity with people power*. Englewood Cliffs, NJ: Prentice Hall.

International marriage: Herr and Madame, Señor and Mrs. (2011, November 12). *The Economist*. Retrieved from http://www.economist.com

Internet World Stats. (2017). *Internet world stats: Usage and population statistics*. Retrieved from http://www.internetworldstats.com/stats.htm

Ipsos MORI. (2016, December 14). Perceptions are not reality: What the world gets wrong. *Ipsos Perils of Perception Survey 2016*. Retrieved from https://www.ipsos-mori.com/researchpublications/researcharchive/3817/Perceptions-are-not-reality-what-the-world-gets-wrong.aspx

Isaacs, J. (1980). *Australian dreaming: 40,000 years of aboriginal history*. Sydney, Australia: Lansdowne.

Isenberg, N. (2016). *White trash: The 400-year untold history of class in America*. New York, NY: Viking.

Ishii, K., & Kitayama, S. (2003, July–August). *Selective attention to contextual information in Japan*. Poster presented at the 25th annual meeting of Cognitive Science Society, Boston, MA.

Iwama, H. F. (1990). *Factors influencing transculturation of Japanese overseas teenagers* (Unpublished doctoral dissertation). Pennsylvania State University, University Park, PA.

Jablonski, N., & Chaplin, G. (2000). The evolution of human skin color. *Journal of Human Evolution, 39*(1), 57–106.

Jackson, D. Z. (2008, December 9). Burger King's greasy campaign. *Boston Globe*. Retrieved from http://www.boston.com

Jackson, R. L. (Ed.). (2010). *Encyclopedia of identity*. Thousand Oaks, CA: Sage.

Jackson, R. L., II, & Heckman, S. M. (2002). Perceptions of white identity and white liability: An analysis of white student responses to a college campus racial hate crime. *Journal of Communication, 52*, 434–450.

Jackson, R. L., II, Shin, C. I., & Wilson, K. B. (2000). The meaning of whiteness: Critical implications of communicating and negotiating race. *World Communication, 29*(1), 69–86.

Jacoby, R. (2011). Bloodlust. *Chronicle Review, 57*(30), B8.

Jain, N. C., & Matumkamalli, A. (2014). The functions of silence in India: Implications for intercultural communication research. In M. K. Asante, Y. Miike, & J. Yin (Eds.), *The global intercultural communication reader* (2nd ed., pp. 248–254). New York, NY: Routledge.

Jandt, F. (2004). *Intercultural communication: A global reader*. Thousand Oaks, CA: Sage.

Jandt, F. E., & Tanno, D. V. (2001). Decoding domination, encoding self-determination: Intercultural communication research process. *Howard Journal of Communications, 12*(3), 119–135.

Japanese Ministry of Internal Affairs & Communications. (2011). *Labour force survey*. Retrieved from http://www.stat.go.jp/english/data/roudou/index.htm

Jeb Bush says decision on 2016 run coming before year's end, says immigration can be "act of love." (2014, April 7). *Fox News*. Retrieved from http://www.foxnews.com/

Jennings, R. (2017, May 25). A boost for gay unions in Taiwan. *Los Angeles Times*, p. A3.

Jiang, M. (2014). The business and politics of search engines: A comparative study of Baidu and Google's search results of Internet events in China. *New Media & Society, 16*, 212–233.

John, T. (2017, May 31). The world won't ignore Chechnya's purge of gay men. *Time*. Retrieved from http://time.com/

Johnson, J. L., & Callahan, C. (2013). Minority cultures and social media: Magnifying Garifuna. *Journal of Intercultural Communication Research, 42*, 319–339.

Johnson, R. (2011). Listen: Southwest pilot goes on homophobic sexist rant on an open frequency. *Business Insider*. Retrieved from http://www.businessinsider.com

Jones, J. (2016, July 1). New low of 52% "extremely proud" to be Americans. Retrieved from http://www.gallup.com/poll/193379/new-low-extremely-proud-americans.aspx

Jones, S. (1993). *The right touch: Understanding and using the language of physical contact*. Cresskill, NJ: Hampton Press.

Jones, S. E., & Yarbrough, A. E. (1985). A naturalistic study of the meanings of touch. *Communication Monographs, 52*(1), 19–56.

Joseph, P. E. (2016, May 27). The many meanings of a fist. *Chronicle of Higher Education*, pp. B4–B5.

Juhi, B. (2011, November 24). U.S. military legacy rubs off on Iraqi youth. *Washington Times*. Retrieved from http://www.washingtontimes.com

Jung, S. (2011). *Korean masculinities and transcultural consumption: Yonsama, Rain, Oldboy, K-Pop Idols*. Hong Kong: Hong Kong University Press.

Kaiman, J. (2017, May 19). No dog meat sales at festival. *Los Angeles Times*, p. A3.

Kalan, J. (2013). African youth hungry for connectivity. *Africa Renewal, 27*(1). http://www.un.org/africarenewal/magazine

Kale, D. W. (1997). Peace as an ethic for intercultural communication. In L. A. Samovar & R. E. Porter (Eds.), *Intercultural communication: A reader* (8th ed., pp. 448–452). Belmont, CA: Wadsworth.

Kallen, H. (1915, February 18–25). Democracy versus the melting pot. *Nation*, pp. 190–194, 217–220.

Kallen, H. M. (1970). *Culture and democracy in the United States*. New York, NY: Arno Press. (Original work published 1924)

Kaneva, N. & Popescu, D. (2014). "We are Romanian, not Roma": Nation branding and postsocialist discourses of alterity. *Communication, Culture & Critique, 7,* 506–523.

Katz, J. (Ed.). (1976). *Gay American history: Lesbians and gay men in the USA.* New York, NY: Thomas Y. Crowell.

Katz, J. (2016). *Speaking American: How y'all, youse, and you guys talk: A visual guide.* New York, NY: Houghton Mifflin Harcourt.

Katz, J. H., & Ivey, A. (1977). White awareness: The frontier of racism awareness training. *Personnel and Guidance Journal, 55,* 484–489.

Keating, G., O'Sullivan, M., Shorrocks, A., Davies J. B., Lluberas, R., & Koutsoukis, A. (2013). *Global wealth report 2013.* Zurich, Switzerland: Credit Suisse AG.

Keegan, J. (2017, June 5). Clinton vs. Trump: How they used Twitter. *Wall Street Journal.* Retrieved from http://graphics.wsj.com/clinton-trump-twitter/

Keesing, R. M. (1988). *Melanesian pidgin and the oceanic substrate.* Stanford, CA: Stanford University Press.

Kelly, G. (2013, October). Living the Southwest way. *Spirit,* p. 14. Retrieved from http://www.southwestthemagazine.com

Kelly, N., & Zetzsche, J. (2012). *Found in translation: How language shapes our lives and transforms the world.* NY: Perigee.

Kern, S. (2011). *The Netherlands to abandon multiculturalism.* Retrieved from http://www.gatestoneinstitute.org/2219/netherlands-abandons-multiculturalism

Kiger, P. J. (2002, June 9). Living ever larger: How wretched excess became a way of life in Southern California. *Los Angeles Times.* Retrieved from http://articles.latimes.com

Kim, H., Coyle, J. R., & Gould, S. J. (2009). Collectivist and individualist influences on website design in South Korea and the U.S.: A cross-cultural content analysis. *Journal of Computer-Mediated Communication, 14,* 581–601.

Kim, M.-S. (1992). A comparative analysis of nonverbal expressions as portrayed by Korean and American print-media advertising. *Howard Journal of Communications, 3,* 317–339.

Kim, Y., Sohn, D., & Choi, S. (2011). Cultural difference in motivations for using social network sites: A comparative study of American and Korean college students. *Computers in Human Behavior, 27,* 365–372.

Kim, Y. Y. (1986). *Interethnic communication: Current research.* Beverly Hills, CA: Sage.

Kim, Y. Y. (1988). *Cross-cultural adaptation: Current approaches.* Newbury Park, CA: Sage.

Kim, Y. Y. (2001). *Becoming intercultural: An integrative theory of communication and cross-cultural adaptation.* Thousand Oaks, CA: Sage.

Kim, Y. Y. (2005). Inquiry in intercultural and development communication. *Journal of Communication, 55,* 554–577.

Kinefuchi, E. (2010). Finding home in migration: Montagnard refugees and post-migration identity. *Journal of International and Intercultural Communication, 3,* 228–248.

King, R. D. (1997). Should English be the law? *Atlantic Monthly, 279*(4), 55–64.

King'ei, K. (2005). The globalization of Kiswahili. In *Proceedings of the DAAD conference on benefitting from cultural differences* (pp. 278–286). Nairobi, Kenya: German Academic Exchange Services.

Kinney, M. V., Kerber, K. J., Black, R. E., Cohen, B., Nkrumah, F., Coovadia, H., . . . Lawn, J. E. (2010). Sub-Saharan Africa's mothers, newborns, and children: Where and why do they die? *PLoS Medicine, 7*(6).

Kinver, M. (2006, December 1). Do mobile phones cost the earth? *BBC News.* Retrieved from http://news.bbc.co.uk

Kirkland, S. L., Greenberg, J., & Pyszczynski, T. (1987). Further evidence of the deleterious effects of overheard derogatory ethnic labels: Derogation beyond the target. *Personality and Social Psychology Bulletin, 13,* 216–227.

Kissinger, H. (2011). *On China.* New York, NY: Penguin Press.

Kitayama, S., Duffy, S., Kawamura, T., & Larsen, J. T. (2003). Perceiving an object and its context in different cultures: A cultural look at new look. *Psychological Science, 14,* 201–206.

Kitroeff, N. & Etehad, M. (2016, December 9). The fading American dream. *Los Angeles Times,* pp. C1, C4.

Kluckhohn, F. R., & Strodtbeck, F. L. (1961). *Variations in value orientations.* Evanston, IL: Row, Peterson.

Knapp, M. L. (1990). Nonverbal communication. In G. L. Dahnke & G. W. Clatterbuck (Eds.), *Human communication: Theory and research* (pp. 50–69). Belmont, CA: Wadsworth.

Knighton, J. (1999). *Intergenerational transfer and the rise of individualism* (Unpublished manuscript). Victoria University of Wellington, New Zealand.

Kohls, L. R. (1984). *The values Americans live by.* New York, NY: Meridian House International.

Kohn, M. L. (1977). *Class and conformity* (2nd ed.). Chicago, IL: University of Chicago Press.

Komolsevin, R., Knutson, T. J., & Datthuyawat, P. (2010). Effective intercultural communication: Research contributions from Thailand. *Journal of Asian Pacific Communication, 20,* 90–100.

Korff, J. (2014). Aboriginal identity: Who is "Aboriginal"? Retrieved from http://www.creativespirits.info/aboriginalculture/people/aboriginal-identity-who-is-aboriginal

Kraidy, M. (2009). Reality television, gender, and authenticity in Saudi Arabia. *Journal of Communication, 59,* 345–366.

Kramarae, C. (1981). *Women and men speaking: Frameworks for analysis.* Rowley, MA: Newbury House.

Kraut, A. H. (1994). *Silent travelers: Germs, genes, and the immigrant menace.* New York, NY: Basic Books.

Krauthammer, C. (2016, September 8). Incident in Hangzhou. *Washington Post.* Retrieved from https://www.washingtonpost.com/

Kraybill, D. B. (1989). *The riddle of Amish culture.* Baltimore, MD: Johns Hopkins University Press.

Krippendorff, K. (1993). Conversation or intellectual imperialism in comparing communication (theories). *Communication Theory, 3*, 252–266.

Kuhn, A. (2001, April 12). "Very sorry" proves to be the key phrase. *Los Angeles Times,* p. A14.

Kushner, H. S. (1982). *When bad things happen to good people.* Boston, MA: G. K. Hall.

Labaree, L. W. (Ed.). (1959). *The papers of Benjamin Franklin. Vol. 4.* New Haven, CT: Yale University Press.

Labov, W., Ash, S., & Boberg, C. (1997). *A national map of the regional dialects of American English.* Retrieved from http://www.ling.upenn.edu/phono_atlas/National-Map/NationalMap.html

Ladegaard, H. J. (2007). Global culture—Myth or reality? Perception of "national cultures" in a global corporation. *Journal of Intercultural Communication Research, 36*, 139–163.

Landis, D., & Brislin, R. (Eds.). (1983). *Handbook of intercultural training* (Vol. 2). Elmsford, NY: Pergamon Press.

Landler, M., & Perlez, J. (2016, September 5). Obama plays down confrontation with China over his plane's stairs. *New York Times.* Retrieved from https://www.nytimes.com/

Laqueur, T. (1990). *Making sex: Body and gender from the Greeks to Freud.* Cambridge, MA: Harvard University Press.

Lau v. Nichols, 414 U.S. 563, 39 L. Ed. 2d 1, 94 S. Ct. 786 (1974).

Le Play, F. (1884). *L'Organization de la famille* [The organization of the family]. Paris, France: Dentu Libre.

Lee, E. S. (1966). A theory of migration. *Demography, 3*, 47–57.

Lee, W. S. (1994). On not missing the boat: A processual method for intercultural understanding of idioms and lifeworld. *Journal of Applied Communication Research, 22*(2), 141–161.

Leeds-Hurwitz, W. (1990). Notes in the history of intercultural communication: The Foreign Service Institute and the mandate for intercultural training. *Quarterly Journal of Speech, 76*, 262–281.

Lerner, D. (1958). *The passing of traditional society: Modernizing the Middle East.* New York, NY: Free Press.

Lesser, J. (Ed.). (2003). *Searching for home abroad: Japanese Brazilians and transnationalism.* Durham, NC: Duke University Press.

Lesser, J. (2013). *Immigration, ethnicity, and national identity in Brazil, 1808 to the present.* Cambridge, UK: Cambridge University Press.

Levin, D. (2014, June 3). China escalating attack on Google. *New York Times* (New York edition), p. B1.

Lewis, B. (2002). *What went wrong? The clash between Islam and modernity in the Middle East.* New York, NY: Oxford University Press.

Lexington. (2006, June 8). The odd man out. *The Economist.* Retrieved from http://www.economist.com

Li, A. (2015, December 24). Machines, lost in translation: The dream of universal understanding. *NPR.* Retrieved from http://www.npr.org/

Liberman, K. (1981). Understanding Aborigines in Australian courts of law. *Human Organization, 40*, 247–255.

Liberman, K. (1990a). An ethnomethodological agenda in the study of intercultural communication. In D. Carbaugh (Ed.), *Cultural communication and intercultural contact* (pp. 185–192). Hillsdale, NJ: Lawrence Erlbaum.

Liberman, K. (1990b). Intercultural communication in central Australia. In D. Carbaugh (Ed.), *Cultural communication and intercultural contact* (pp. 177–183). Hillsdale, NJ: Lawrence Erlbaum.

Lieblier, C. A., Rastogi, S., Fernandez, L. E., Noon, J. M., & Ennis, S. R. (2014). *America's churning races: Race and ethnic response changes between Census 2000 and the 2010 Census.* Washington, DC: U.S. Census Bureau. Retrieved from https://www.census.gov/library/working-papers/2014/adrm/carra-wp-2014-09.html

Ling, R. (2005). The socio-linguistics of SMS: An analysis of SMS use by a random sample of Norwegians. In R. Ling & P. Pedersen (Eds.), *Mobile communications: Re-negotiation of the social sphere* (pp. 335–349). London, UK: Springer.

Ling, R., & Baron, N. S. (2007). Text messaging and IM linguistic comparison of American college data. *Journal of Language & Social Psychology, 26*, 291–298.

Linshi, J. (2016, May 19). 6 things you need to know about China's dog-eating Yulin festival. *Time.* Retrieved from http://time.com/

Linthicum, K. (2015, December 13). For the first time, women vote in Saudi Arabia. *Los Angeles Times,* p. A3.

Lipski, J. (1985). *Linguistic aspects of Spanish-English language switching.* Tempe: Arizona State University, Center for Latin American Studies.

Livingston, G. (2011). *Latinos and digital technology, 2010.* Retrieved from http://pewresearch.org/pubs/1887/latinos-digital-technology-internet-broadband-cell-phone-use

Lopez, M. H., Gonzalez-Barrera, A., & Patten, E. (2013). *Closing the digital divide: Latinos and technology adoption.* Washington, DC: Pew Hispanic Center. Retrieved from http://www.pewhispanic.org/files/2013/03/Latinos_Social_Media_and_Mobile_Tech_03-2013_final.pdf

Lorde, A. (1984). *Sister outsider.* Freedom, CA: Crossing Press.

Losada, A. (1971). *Bartolome de las Casas in history: Toward an understanding of the man and his work.* DeKalb: Northern Illinois University Press.

Lovaas, K. A. (2003). Speaking to silence. Toward queering nonverbal communication. *Journal of Homosexuality, 45*(2/3/4), 87–107.

Lyng v. Northwest Indian Cemetery Protection Association, 485 U.S. 439 (1988).

Ma, D. H. (2005). A new northeast Asian community? The experience of "Winter Sonata" in Japan. *Asian Communication Research, 9*, 43–64.

Ma, R. (1992). The role of unofficial intermediaries in interpersonal conflicts in the Chinese culture. *Communication Quarterly, 40*, 269–278.

Macfarquhar, N. (2008, December 18). In a first, gay rights are pressed at the U.N. *New York Times*. Retrieved from http://www.nytimes.com/

Mack, A., & Rock, I. (1998). *Inattentional blindness: An overview*. Cambridge, MA: MIT Press.

Maddox, K. B., & Gray, S. A. (2002). Cognitive representations of black Americans: Reexploring the role of skin tone. *Personality & Social Psychology Bulletin, 28*, 250–259.

Magistad, M. K. (2012). How Weibo is changing China. http://yaleglobal.yale.edu/content/how-weibo-changing-china

Magnier, M. (2011, March 18). In Japan, it's about the group. *Los Angeles Times*, p. A1ff.

Makinen, J. (2013, June 22). China animal lovers raise voices. *Los Angeles Times*, p. A3.

Malotki, E. (1983). *Hopi time: A linguistic analysis of the temporal concepts in the Hopi language*. Berlin, Germany: Mouton.

Mangel, N., & Klatzkin, S. (2013). *A Torah perspective on national borders and illegal immigration*. Retrieved from http://www.chabad.org/library/article_cdo/aid/1898474/jewish/A-Torah-Perspective-on-National-Borders-and-Illegal-Immigration.htm

Marcus, A., & Gould, E. W. (2000). Crosscurrents: Cultural dimensions and global web user-interface design. *Interactions, 7*(4), 32–46.

Markovits, A. S., & Hellerman, S. L. (2001). *Offside: Soccer and American exceptionalism*. Princeton, NJ: Princeton University Press.

Markus, H. R., & Kitayama, S. (1991). Culture and the self: Implications for cognition, emotion, and motivation. *Psychological Review, 98*, 224–253.

Martin, J. (2000). *World telephone cultures*. Retrieved from http://www.netjeff.com/humor/item.cgi?file=HelloOnTelephoneWorldwide

Marx, K., & Engels, F. (1850). *Manifest der kommunistischen partei* [The communist manifesto] (H. Macfarlane, Trans.).

Masakazu, Y. (1994). *Individualism and the Japanese: An alternative approach to cultural comparison* (B. Sugihara, Trans.). Tokyo: Japan Echo.

Masood, E. (2008). *Science and Islam: A history*. London, UK: Icon Books.

Masumoto, T., Oetzel, J. G., Takai, J., Ting-Toomey, S., & Yokochi, Y. (2000). A typology of facework behaviors in conflicts with best friends and relative strangers. *Communication Quarterly, 4*, 397–419.

Matsumoto, D. (2002). *The new Japan: Debunking seven cultural stereotypes*. Boston, MA: Intercultural Press.

Maurer, D. W. (1981). *Language of the underworld*. Lexington: University Press of Kentucky.

Mayer, J. P. (with A. P. Kerr). (1981). *Journey to America by Alexis de Tocqueville* (G. Lawrence, Trans.). Westport, CT: Greenwood.

McClelland, D. C. (1976). *The achieving society*. New York, NY: Irvington.

McCroskey, J. C., Burroughs, N. F., Daun, A., & Richmond, V. P. (1990). Correlates of quietness: Swedish and American perspectives. *Communication Quarterly, 38*(2), 127–137.

McDonald's. (2014). Catering to local tastes. Retrieved September 23, 2014, from http://www.aboutmcdonalds.com/mcd/our_company/amazing_stories/food/catering_to_local_tastes.html

McIntosh, P. (1989, July/August). White privilege: Unpacking the invisible knapsack. *Peace and Freedom Magazine*. Retrieved from https://nationalseedproject.org/white-privilege-unpacking-the-invisible-knapsack

McIntosh, P. (1994, Fall). White privilege: Unpacking the invisible knapsack. *Hungry Mind Review*, pp. 12–13.

McLaughlin, E. C. (2010, February 5). Super Bowl is king at home but struggles on world stage. *CNN*. Retrieved from http://www.cnn.com

McPhail, M. L. (2002). *Rhetoric of race revisited: Reparation or separation?* Lanham, MD: Rowman & Littlefield.

McSweeney, B. (2002a). The essentials of scholarship: A reply to Geert Hofstede. *Human Relations, 55*, 1363–1372.

McSweeney, B. (2002b). Hofstede's model of national cultural differences and their consequences: A triumph of faith—a failure of analysis. *Human Relations, 55*, 89–118.

Mehrabian, A. (1981). *Silent messages: Implicit communication of emotions and attitudes* (2nd ed.). Belmont, CA: Wadsworth.

Mehta, S. (2014, February 3). The superiority complex. *Time, 183*(4), 34–39.

Meier, M. S., & Ribera, F. (1993). *Mexican Americans/American Mexicans: From conquistadors to Chicanos* (Rev. ed.). New York, NY: Hill & Wang.

Melkote, S. (2003). Theories of development communication. In B. Mody (Ed.), *International and development communication: A 21st-century perspective* (pp. 129–146). Thousand Oaks, CA: Sage.

Melton, J. G. (Ed.). (1991). *Encyclopedia of American religions: A comprehensive study of the major religious groups in the United States*. New York, NY: Triumph.

Melville, H. (1976). *Redburn*. London, UK: Harmondsworth. (Original work published 1849)

Mencken, H. L. (1935, April). The future of English. *Harper's*, pp. 541–548. Retrieved from http://www.harpers.org

Merriam, A. H. (1974). Rhetoric and the Islamic tradition. *Today's Speech, 22*(1), 43–49.

Message of His Holiness Pope Francis for the World Day of Migrants and Refugees 2016. (2016, January 17). Retrieved from https://w2.vatican.va/content/francesco/en/messages/migration/documents/papa-francesco_20150912_world-migrants-day-2016.html

Meyer v. Nebraska, 262 U.S. 390 (1923).

Miike, Y. (2003a). Beyond Eurocentrism in the intercultural field: Searching for an Asiacentric paradigm. In W. J. Starosta & G.-M. Chen (Eds.), *Ferment in the intercultural field: Axiology/value/praxis (International and Intercultural Communication Annual,* Vol. 26, pp. 243–276). Thousand Oaks, CA: Sage.

Miike, Y. (2003b). Toward an alternative metatheory of human communication: An Asiacentric vision. *Intercultural Communication Studies, 12*(4), 39–63.

Miike, Y. (2004). Rethinking humanity, culture, and communication: Asiacentric critiques and contributions. *Human Communication, 7*(1), 69–82.

Miike, Y. (2007). An Asiacentric reflection on Eurocentric bias in communication theory. *Communication Monographs, 74,* 272–278.

Mikkelsen, C. (Ed.). (2010). *The indigenous world 2010.* Copenhagen, Denmark: International Work Group for Indigenous Affairs.

Miller, D. H. (1998). *Freedom to differ: The shaping of the gay and lesbian struggle for civil rights.* New York, NY: New York University Press.

Miller, H. (2016, April 5). Investigating the potential for miscommunication using emoji. http://grouplens.org/blog/investigating-the-potential-for-miscommunication-using-emoji/

Miller, M. D., Reynolds, R. A., & Cambra, R. E. (1987). The influence of gender and culture on language intensity. *Communication Monographs, 54*(1), 101–105.

Miller, T. (2012). *China's urban billion.* London, UK: Zed Books.

Milles, K. (2011). Feminist language planning in Sweden. *Current Issues in Language Planning, 12*(1), 21–33.

Milne, J. (1999, August 6). What makes a Maori? *The Dominion,* p. 9.

Mirandé, A., & Tanno, D. V. (1993). Labels, researcher perspective, and contextual validation: A commentary. *International Journal of Intercultural Relations, 17*(1), 149–155.

Mishra, G. (2008, September 1). Using Geert Hofstede cultural dimensions to study social media usage in BRIC countries. *International Values and Communications Technologies.* Retrieved from https://blogs.commons.georgetown.edu/isdyahoofellow/using-geert-hofstede-cultural-dimensions-to-study-social-media-usage-in-bric-countries

Miyamoto, Y., Nisbett, R. E., & Masuda, T. (2006). Culture and the physical environment: Holistic versus analytic perceptual affordances. *Psychological Science, 17*(2), 113–119.

Modley, R. (1976). *Handbook of pictorial symbols.* New York, NY: Dover.

Monge, P. R., Bachman, S. G., Dillard, J. P., & Eisenberg, E. M. (1982). Communicator competence in the workplace: Model testing and scale development. In M. Burgoon (Ed.), *Communication yearbook 5* (pp. 505–527). New Brunswick, NJ: Transaction.

Monroe, M. (2013, December 31). Parker apologizes for gesture seen as anti-Semitic. *San Antonio Express-News,* pp. A1, A9.

Montepare, J. M., & Opeyo, A. (2002). The relative salience of physiognomic cues in differentiating faces: A methodological tool. *Journal of Nonverbal Behavior, 26*(1), 43–59.

Moore, M. M. (1995). Courtship signaling and adolescents: "Girls just wanna have fun." *Journal of Sex Research, 32,* 319–328.

Morris, D. (1979). *Gestures.* Briarcliff Manor, NY: Stein & Day.

Morris, D. (1995). *Bodytalk: The meaning of human gestures.* New York, NY: Crown Trade Paperbacks.

Morris, N. (2003). A comparative analysis of the diffusion and participatory models in development communication. *Communication Theory, 13,* 225–248.

Mott, F. L., & Jorgenson, C. E. (Eds.). (1939). *Benjamin Franklin: Representative selections, with introduction, bibliography, and notes.* New York, NY: American Book.

Moua, M. N. (Ed.). (2002). *Bamboo among the oaks: Contemporary writing by Hmong Americans.* St. Paul, MN: Borealis Books.

Murdock, G. P. (1949). *Social structures.* New York, NY: Macmillan.

Murphy, D. (2011, September 25). Saudi women to vote . . . *Christian Science Monitor.* Retrieved from http://www.csmonitor.com

Nakamura, H. (1964). *Ways of thinking of Eastern peoples: India-China-Tibet-Japan.* Honolulu, HI: East-West Center.

Nasr, S. H. (2003). *Science and civilization in Islam.* Cambridge, UK: Islamic Texts Society.

Nau, H. R. (2012). *Perspectives on international relations: Power, institutions, and ideas* (3rd ed.). Washington, DC: CQ Press.

Nelson, C. (2009). *Rocket men: The epic story of the first men on the moon.* New York, NY: Viking Press.

Neyrand, G., & M'Sili, M. (1996). *Les couples mixtes et le divorce* [Mixed couples and divorce]. Paris, France: Editions l'Harmattan.

Ng, S. H., & Bradac, J. J. (1993). *Power in language: Verbal communication and social influence.* Newbury Park, CA: Sage.

Nichols, M. (2013, February 27). Gambian president says gays a threat to human existence. *Reuters.* Retrieved from http://www.reuters.com

Nicolae, V. (2006). Words that kill. *Index on Censorship, 35,* 137–141.

Nike faces marketing challenge in China: Make running cool. (2011, October 31). *Ad Age.* Retrieved from http://adage.com

Nisbett, R. E. (1980). *Human inference: Strategies and shortcomings of social judgment.* Englewood Cliffs, NJ: Prentice Hall.

Nisbett, R. E. (2003). *The geography of thought: How Asians and Westerners think differently*. New York, NY: Free Press.

Nordenstreng, K., & Schiller, H. I. (Eds.). (1979). *National sovereignty and international communication*. Honolulu, HI: East-West Center.

Obama in Kenya: Presidents differ on gay rights. (2015, July 25). *BBC News*. Retrieved from http://www.bbc.com/

Oberg, K. (1960). Cultural shock: Adjustment to new cultural environments. *Practical Anthropology, 7*, 177–182.

Obeyesekere, G. (1992). *The apotheosis of Captain Cook*. Princeton, NJ: Princeton University Press.

The odd man out. (2006, June 10). *The Economist*, p. 54.

Office of the governor. (2000). Executive order no. EO-00-07. Retrieved from http://archivedwebsites.sos.state.or.us/Governor_Kitzhaber_2003/governor/legal/execords/eo00-07.pdf

Ojwang, B. O. (2008). Prospects of Kiswahili as a regional language in a socioculturally heterogeneous East Africa. *Journal of International and Intercultural Communication, 1*, 327–347.

Olesen, A. (2011, August 6). China blasts U.S. over credit rating downgrade. *Associated Press*. Retrieved from http://www.huffingtonpost.com

Olien, M. (1978). *The human myth*. New York, NY: Harper & Row.

Oliver, R. T. (1971). *Communication and culture in ancient India and China*. Syracuse, NY: Syracuse University Press.

Omi, M., & Winant, H. (1986). *Racial formations in the United States from the 1960s to the 1980s*. New York, NY: Routledge & Kegan Paul.

Onishi, N. (2004, December 23). What's Korean for "real man"? Ask Japanese women. *New York Times*. Retrieved from http://www.nytimes.com

Onolemhemhen, D. N., & Gessesse, K. (2002). *The black Jews of Ethiopia: The last exodus*. Lanham, MD: Scarecrow Press.

Orbe, M. P. (1995). African American communication research: Toward a deeper understanding of interethnic communication. *Western Journal of Communication, 59*, 61–78.

Orbe, M. P. (1998). *Constructing co-cultural theory: An explication of culture, power, and communication*. Thousand Oaks, CA: Sage.

Organisation for Economic Co-operation and Development. (2016a). *Development aid rises again in 2015, spending on refugees doubles*. Retrieved from http://www.oecd.org/dac/development-aid-rises-again-in-2015-spending-on-refugees-doubles.htm

Organisation for Economic Co-operation and Development. (2016b). *OECD Income Distribution Database (IDD): Gini, poverty, income, methods and concepts*. Retrieved from http://www.oecd.org/els/soc/income-distribution-database.htm

Ortman, J. M., & Shin, H. B. (2011, August). *Language projections 2010–2020*. Paper presented at the annual meeting of the American Sociological Association, Las Vegas, NV. Retrieved from http://www.census.gov/hhes/socdemo/language/data/acs/Ortman_Shin_ASA2011_paper.pdf

Ostler, N. (2005). *Empires of the word: A language history of the world*. New York, NY: HarperCollins.

Owens, K., & King, M. C. (1999). Genomic views of human history. *Science, 286*, 451–453.

Oxfam. (2014). *Working for the few: Political capture and economic inequality*. http://www.oxfam.org/sites/www.oxfam.org/files/bp-working-for-few-political-capture-economic-inequality-200114-en.pdf

Paabo, S. (2001). Genomics and society: The human genome and our view of ourselves. *Science, 291*, 1219–1220.

Pacanowsky, M. E., & O'Donnell-Trujillo, N. (1982). Communication and organizational cultures. *Western Journal of Speech Communication, 46*, 115–130.

Paige, R. M. (2004). Instrumentation in intercultural training. In D. Landis, J. M. Bennett, & M. J. Bennett (Eds.), *Handbook of intercultural training* (3rd ed., pp. 85–128). Thousand Oaks, CA: Sage.

Park, H., Russell, C., & Lee, J. (2007). National culture and environmental sustainability: A cross-national analysis. *Journal of Economics and Finance, 31*(1), 104–121.

Park, H. S., Lee, H. E., & Song, J. A. (2005). "I am sorry to send you SPAM": Cross-cultural differences in use of apologies in email advertising in Korea and the U.S. *Human Communication Research, 31*, 365–398.

Pasquale, F. (2015). *The black box society: The secret algorithms that control money and information*. Cambridge, MA: Harvard University Press.

Passel, J. S., & Cohn, D. (2016, September 20). *Overall number of U.S. unauthorized immigrants holds steady since 2009*. Retrieved from http://www.pewhispanic.org/2016/09/20/overall-number-of-u-s-unauthorized-immigrants-holds-steady-since-2009/

Patterson, O. (1991). *Freedom: Freedom in the making of Western culture* (Vol. 1). New York, NY: Basic Books.

Pavlidou, T. S. (2006). Telephone talk. In J. L. Mey (Ed.), *Concise encyclopedia of pragmatics* (2nd ed., pp. 1072–1075). Oxford, UK: Elsevier.

Pedersen, P. (1995). *The five stages of culture shock: Critical incidents around the world*. Westport, CT: Greenwood.

Peng, Y.-S., & Lin, S. (2009). National culture, economic development, population growth and environmental performance: The mediating role of education. *Journal of Business Ethics, 90*, 203–219.

Penn, M. J. (2011). The pessimism index. *Time, 178*(2), 36–37.

People labels. (1995, November 20). *U.S. News & World Report*, p. 28.

Perse, E. M. (2001). *Media effects and society*. Mahwah, NJ: Lawrence Erlbaum.

Peterman, A., Palermo, T., & Bredenkamp, C. (2011). Estimates and determinants of sexual violence in the

Democratic Republic of the Congo. *American Journal of Public Health, 101,* 1060–1067.

Peters, T. J. (1982). *In search of excellence: Lessons from America's best-run companies.* New York, NY: Harper & Row.

Petrik, P. (1991). Women and the Bill of Rights. In K. L. Hall (Ed.), *By and for the people: Constitutional rights in American history* (pp. 133–148). Arlington Heights, IL: Harlan Davidson.

Pew Hispanic Center. (2009). Between two worlds: How young Latinos come of age in America. Retrieved from http://pewhispanic.org/reports/report.php?ReportID=117

Pew Research Center. (2002). What the world thinks in 2002. Retrieved from http://people-press.org/2002/12/04/what-the-world-thinks-in-2002

Pew Research Center. (2006). Islam and the West: Searching for common ground. Retrieved from http://www.pewglobal.org/2006/07/18/islam-and-the-west-searching-for-common-ground/

Pew Research Center. (2007). *World publics welcome global trade—but not immigration.* Washington, DC: Author.

Pew Research Center. (2008). *The Pew global attitudes project: Unfavorable views of Jews and Muslims on the increase in Europe.* Washington, DC: Author.

Pew Research Center. (2011a). The future of the global Muslim population: Region: Europe. Retrieved from http://www.pewforum.org/2011/01/27/future-of-the-global-muslim-population-regional-europe

Pew Research Center. (2011b). Muslim-Western tensions persist. Retrieved from http://www.pewglobal.org/2011/07/21/muslim-western-tensions-persist/

Pew Research Center (2011c, January 27). Table: Muslim population by country. Retrieved from http://www.pewforum.org/2011/01/27/table-muslim-population-by-country/

Pew Research Center. (2012a). *Social networking popular across globe.* Washington, DC: Author.

Pew Research Center. (2012b). Wait, you still don't like us? Retrieved from http://www.pewglobal.org/2012/09/19/wait-you-still-dont-like-us

Pew Research Center. (2012c). Why most Facebook users get more than they give. Retrieved from http://www.pewinternet.org/2012/02/03/why-most-facebook-users-get-more-than-they-give-2

Pew Research Center. (2013a). *America's global image remains more positive than China's.* Washington, DC: Author.

Pew Research Center. (2013b). *The global divide on homosexuality.* Washington, DC: Author.

Pew Research Center. (2014a). 2012 National Survey of Latinos. Retrieved from http://www.pewhispanic.org/2014/04/18/2012-national-survey-of-latinos/

Pew Research Center. (2014b, October 7). Americans stand out on individualism. http://www.pewglobal.org/2014/10/09/emerging-and-developing-economies-much-more-optimistic-than-rich-countries-about-the-future/pg_14-09-04_usindividualism_640-px/

Pew Research Center. (2014c). How Americans feel about religious groups. Retrieved from http://www.pewforum.org/2014/07/16/how-americans-feel-about-religious-groups/

Pew Research Center (2015a, May 12). America's changing religious landscape. Retrieved from http://www.pewforum.org/2015/05/12/americas-changing-religious-landscape/

Pew Research Center. (2015b, April 15). Cell phones in Africa: Communication lifeline. http://www.pewglobal.org/2015/04/15/cell-phones-in-africa-communication-lifeline/

Pew Research Center. (2015c, June 26). Gay marriage around the world. Retrieved from http://www.pewforum.org/2015/06/26/gay-marriage-around-the-world-2013/

Pew Research Center. (2016a). International migrants by country. Retrieved from http://www.pewglobal.org/interactives/migration-tables/

Pew Research Center. (2016b). Republicans prefer blunt talk about Islamic extremism, Democrats favor caution. http://www.pewforum.org/2016/02/03/republicans-prefer-blunt-talk-about-islamic-extremism-democrats-favor-caution/

Pew Research Internet Project. (2012). *Why most Facebook users get more than they give.* Retrieved from http://www.pewinternet.org/2012/02/03/why-most-facebook-users-get-more-than-they-give-2

Pfeifer, M. E. (2014, November). Hmong Americans in the 2013 American Community Survey. Retrieved from http://www.hmongstudiesjournal.org/uploads/4/5/8/7/4587788/2013_acs_hmong_analysis_article_for_website.pdf

Pfeifer, M. E., Sullivan, J., Yang, K., & Yang, W. (2012). Hmong population and demographic trends in the 2010 census and 2010 American Community Survey. *Hmong Studies Journal, 13*(2), 1–31.

Pfeil, U., Zaphiris, P., & Ang, C. S. (2006). Cultural differences in collaborative authoring of Wikipedia. *Journal of Computer-Mediated Communication, 12*(1). Retrieved from http://jcmc.indiana.edu

Pharr, S. (1988). *Homophobia: A weapon of sexism.* Inverness, CA: Chardon.

Piatt, B. (1990). *Only English? Law and language policy in the United States.* Albuquerque: University of New Mexico Press.

Pinker, S. (1994). *The language instinct.* New York, NY: William Morrow.

Plyler v. Doe, 457 U.S. 202 (1982).

Pratt, M. L. (1992). *Imperial eyes: Travel writing and transculturation.* London, UK: Routledge.

Proctor, B. D., Semega, J. L., & Kollar, M. A. (2016). *Income and poverty in the United States: 2015.* Washington, DC: U.S. Government Printing Office.

Proctor & Gamble. (n.d.). *Latest innovations: Gillette Guard.* Retrieved from http://www.pg.com/en_US/downloads/innovation/factsheet_final_Gillette_Guard.pdf

Profiling the Facebooks of the world. (2010, June 14). *Advertising Age*. Retrieved from http://adage.com

Putin, V. V. (2013, September 12). A plea for caution from Russia. *New York Times*, p. A31.

Putnam, L., & Pacanowsky, M. (Eds.). (1983). *Communication and organizations: An interpretive approach*. Beverly Hills, CA: Sage.

Putnam, R. E. (2007). E pluribus unum: Diversity and community in the twenty-first century—The 2006 Johan Skytte prize lecture. *Scandinavian Political Studies*, 30(2), 137–174.

Q&A: Saudi municipal elections. (2011, September 28). *BBC News*. Retrieved from http://www.bbc.co.uk

Q-Success. (2017). *Usage of content languages for websites.* Retrieved from http://w3techs.com/technologies/overview/content_language/all

Qiu, L. (2016, June 14). Obama vs. Trump on the phrase "radical Islam." *Politifact*. Retrieved from http://www.politifact.com

Quebral, N. C. (1975). Development communication: Where does it stand today? *Media Asia*, 2(4), 197–202.

Rand, A. (2005). *Atlas shrugged*. New York, NY: Plume.

Ray, R., Sanes, M., & Schmitt, J. (2013). *No-vacation nation revisited*. Washington, DC: Center for Economic and Policy Research. Retrieved from http://www.cepr.net/documents/publications/no-vacation-update-2013-05.pdf

Recycling advocates. (2004, June 28). *U.S. News & World Report*, p. 41.

Reid, S. A., Gunter, H. N., & Smith, J. R. (2005). Aboriginal self-determination in Australia: The effects of minority-majority frames and target universalism on majority collective guilt and compensation attitudes. *Human Communication Research*, 31, 189–211.

Reid-Pharr, R. (2002, August 16). Extending queer theory to race and ethnicity. *Chronicle of Higher Education*, pp. B7–B9.

Rheingold, H. (1999). Look who's talking. *Wired*, 7(1), 128–131.

Rhoda, R., & Buton, T. (2010). *Geo-Mexico: The geography of dynamics of modern Mexico*. Ladysmith, British Columbia, Canada: Sombrero Books.

Ricci, J., & Biederman, P. W. (2004, March 30). Acceptance of gays on rise, polls show. *Los Angeles Times*, p. B1.

Richardson, D. (1974). *Peace child*. Glendale, CA: GL Regal Books.

Richter, P. (2000, March 25). Armed forces find "disturbing" level of gay harassment. *Los Angeles Times*. Retrieved from http://articles.latimes.com

Riggins, S. H. (Ed.). (1997). *The language and politics of exclusion*. Thousand Oaks, CA: Sage.

Ritzer, G. (1993). *The McDonaldization of society*. Newbury Park, CA: Pine Forge.

Robbins, S. S., & Stylianou, A. C. (2002). A study of cultural differences in global corporate websites. *Journal of Computer Information Systems*, 42(2), 3–9.

Robinson, E. (1999). *Cool to cream: A black man's journey beyond color to an affirmation of race*. New York, NY: Free Press.

Rodriguez, A. (1999). *Making Latino news: Race, language, class*. Thousand Oaks, CA: Sage.

Rodriguez, A. (2015, March 3). There's no direct translation for Target's latest effort aimed at Hispanics. *Advertising Age*. Retrieved from http://adage.com

Rodriguez, G. (2004, February 20). Mexican Americans are building no walls. *Los Angeles Times*. Retrieved from http://articles.latimes.com

Rodriguez, R. (2003). The North American. In J. Roden & S. P. Steinberg (Eds.), *Public discourse in America* (pp. 60–70). Philadelphia: University of Pennsylvania Press.

Rogers, E. M. (1962). *Diffusion of innovations*. New York, NY: Free Press.

Rogers, E. M. (1986). *Communication technology*. New York, NY: Free Press.

Rogers, E. M. (1999). Georg Simmel's concept of the stranger and intercultural communication research. *Communication Theory*, 9(1), 58–74.

Rogers, E. M., & Kincaid, D. L. (1981). *Communication networks: A new paradigm for research*. New York, NY: Free Press.

Rogers, E. M., & Shoemarker, F. F. (1971). *Communication of innovations: A crosscultural approach* (2nd ed.). New York, NY: Free Press.

Rojas, R. (2011, March 27). When students' words go viral, schools react. *Los Angeles Times*, pp. A29, A33.

Rojjanaprapayon, W. (1997). *Communication patterns of Thai people in a non-Thai context* (Unpublished doctoral dissertation). Purdue University, West Lafayette, IN.

Romaine, S. (1988). *Pidgin and creole languages*. London, UK: Longman.

Romaine, S. (1992). *Language, education and development: Urban and rural Tok Pisin in Papua New Guinea*. Oxford, UK: Oxford University Press.

Romano, L. (2013, May 27). Latinos push immigration reform on social media. *Politico*. Retrieved from http://www.politico.com/

Romero, D. (1996, March 3). Most signposts are in English along the info superhighway. *Los Angeles Times*. Retrieved from http://articles.latimes.com

Ross, M. W. (1989). Gay youth in four cultures: A comparative study. *Journal of Homosexuality*, 17, 299–314.

Rotello, G. (1998, January 20). Last word: Inside the circle. *The Advocate*, p. 112.

Rothenberg, P. S. (Ed.). (1992). *Race, class, and gender in the United States: An integrated study* (2nd ed.). New York, NY: St. Martin's.

Roy, A. (2001). *Power politics*. Cambridge, MA: South End.

Rushing, J. H. (1983). The rhetoric of the American western myth. *Communication Monographs*, 50, 15–32.

Rushing, J. H., & Frentz, T. S. (1978). The rhetoric of "Rocky": A social value model of criticism. *Western Journal of Speech Communication*, 42(2), 63–72.

Russo, V. (1987). *The celluloid closet: Homosexuality in the movies* (Rev. ed.). New York, NY: Harper & Row.

Ryan, C. (2013). Language use in the United States: 2011. American Community Survey Reports.

Ryan, M. G. (1974). The influence of speaker dialect and sex on stereotypic attribution. In F. L. Casmir (Ed.), *International and intercultural communication annual* (Vol. 1, pp. 87–101). New York, NY: Speech Communication Association.

Sabogal, F., Marín, G., Otero-Sabogal, R., Marín, B. V., & Perez-Stable, P. (1987). Hispanic familism and acculturation: What changes and what doesn't. *Hispanic Journal of Behavioral Sciences, 9*, 397–412.

Sacher, J. (2012). *How to swear around the world.* San Francisco, CA: Chronicle Books.

Said, E. (1978). *Orientalism.* New York, NY: Pantheon.

Said, E. (1981). *Covering Islam: How the media and the experts determine how we see the rest of the world.* New York, NY: Pantheon.

Sakamoto, N., & Naotsuka, R. (1982). *Polite fictions: Why Japanese and Americans seem rude to each other.* Tokyo, Japan: Kinseido.

Samovar, L. A., Porter, R. E., & Jain, N. C. (1981). *Understanding intercultural communication.* Belmont, CA: Wadsworth.

Sanburn, J. (2015, March 23). The joy of less. *Time,* pp. 44–50.

Sapir, E. (1921). *Language: An introduction to the study of speech.* New York, NY: Harcourt Brace Jovanovich.

Sapir, E. (1949). *Selected writings in language, culture, and personality.* Berkeley: University of California Press.

Sax, L. J., Lindholm, J. A., Astin, A. W., Korn, W. S., & Mahoney, K. M. (2001). *The American freshman: National norms for fall 2001.* Los Angeles: University of California, Los Angeles, Higher Education Research Institute.

Scheer, R. (1991, December 15). Gore Vidal: Novelist of U.S. past sees an empire replacing republic he so admired. *Los Angeles Times.* Retrieved from http://articles.latimes.com

Schiller, H. I. (1976). *Communication and cultural domination.* White Plains, NY: International Arts and Science Press.

Schmid-Isler, S. (2000, January). The language of digital genres—A semiotic investigation of style and iconology on the world wide web. In *Proceedings of the 33rd Hawaii International Conference on System Sciences.* Retrieved from http://www.computer.org/csdl/proceedings/hicss/2000/0493/03/04933012.pdf

Scollon, R., & Scollon, S. W. (1991). Mass and count nouns in Chinese and English: A few further Whorfian considerations. In R. Blust (Ed.), *Currents in Pacific linguistics: Papers on Austronesian languages and ethnolinguistics in honor of George W. Grace* (pp. 465–475). Canberra, Australia: Pacific Linguistics.

Sechrest, L., Fay, T. L., & Zaidi, S. M. (1972). Problems of translation in cross-cultural communication. *Journal of Cross-Cultural Psychology, 3*(1), 41–56.

Sedano, M. V. (1980). Chicanismo: A rhetorical analysis of themes and images of selected poetry from the Chicano movement. *Western Journal of Speech Communication, 44*(3), 177–190.

Segal, A. F. (2004). *Life after death: A history of the afterlife in Western religion.* Garden City, NY: Doubleday.

Segall, M. H., Campbell, D. T., & Herskovits, M. J. (1966). *The influence of culture on visual perception.* Indianapolis, IN: Bobbs-Merrill.

Sennett, R. (1999, Summer). The spaces of democracy. *Harvard Design Magazine,* pp. 68–72.

Shachtman, T. (2006). *Rumspringa: To be or not to be Amish.* New York, NY: North Point Press.

Shaheen, J. G. (1984). *The TV Arab.* Bowling Green, OH: Bowling Green State University Popular Press.

Shaheen, J. G. (2001). *Reel bad Arabs: How Hollywood vilifies a people.* New York, NY: Olive Branch.

Sherif, M., & Sherif, C. W. (1953). *Groups in harmony and tension.* New York, NY: Harper.

Shi, Y. (2010). Product placement and digital piracy: How young Chinese viewers react to the unconventional method of corporate cultural globalization. *Communication, Culture & Critique, 3*, 435–463.

Shin, H. B., & Bruno, R. A. (2003). *Language use and English-speaking ability: 2000.* Washington, DC: U.S. Census Bureau.

Shin, H. B., & Kominski, R. A. (2010). *Language use in the United States: 2007* (American Community Survey Reports, ACS-12). Washington, DC: U.S. Census Bureau.

Shioiri, T., Someya, T., Helmeste, D., & Tang, S. W. (1999). Misinterpretation of facial expression: A cross-cultural study. *Psychiatry and Clinical Neurosciences, 53*(1), 45–50.

Shome, R. (1996). Postcolonial interventions in the rhetorical canon: An "other" view. *Communication Theory, 6*(1), 40–59.

Shome, R., & Hegde, R. S. (2002). Postcolonial approaches to communication: Charting the terrain, engaging the intersections. *Communication Theory, 12*, 249–270.

Shorrocks, A., Davies, J., & Lluberas, R. (2014). *Global wealth report, 2014.* Zurich, Switzerland: Credit Suisse.

Shuster, S. (2016a, July 11). Europe's crisis of faith. *Time,* pp. 11–16.

Shuster, S. (2016b, September 12). Putin's pilgrimage. *Time.*

Shuter, R. (1979). Gaze behavior in interracial and intraracial interactions. In N. C. Jain (Ed.), *International and intercultural communication annual* (Vol. 5, pp. 48–54). Falls Church, VA: Speech Communication Association.

Shuter, R., & Chattopadhyay, S. (2010). Emerging interpersonal norms of text messaging in India and the United States. *Journal of Intercultural Communication Research, 39*(2), 123–147.

Simmons, A. M. (2003, December 21). Minority within a minority. *Los Angeles Times*, pp. B1, B12.

Simmons, A. M. (2017, February 8). His tweets defy translation. *Los Angeles Times*, p. A2.

Simon, R. (2014, February 24). Textbooks caught in a global clash. *Los Angeles Times*, p. A7.

Simon Wiesenthal Center. (2009). *Facebook, YouTube+: How social media outlets impact digital terrorism and hate*. Los Angeles, CA: Author.

Simons, D. J., & Chabris, C. F. (1999). Gorillas in our midst: Sustained inattentional blindness for dynamic events. *Perception, 28*, 1059–1074.

Singh, N., & Baak, D. W. (2004). Web site adaptation: A cross-cultural comparison of U.S. and Mexican web sites. *Journal of Computer-Mediated Communication, 9*(4). Retrieved from http://jcmc.indiana.edu

Singh, N., Zhao, H., & Hu, X. (2003). Cultural adaptation on the web: A study of American companies' domestic and Chinese websites. *International Journal of Global Information Management, 11*(3), 63–80.

Slagle, A. (1995). In defense of Queer Nation: From identity politics to a politics of difference. *Western Journal of Communication, 59*(2), 85–102.

Smart, G. (2013, September 12). Amish youth hitchin' up to Facebook. *LancasterOnline*. Retrieved from http://lancasteronline.com

Smith, A. G. (1966). *Communication and culture: Readings in the codes of human interaction*. New York, NY: Holt, Rinehart & Winston.

Smith, C. A. (1991). *The absentee American*. New York, NY: Praeger.

Smith, J. (2015). Muslim-Christian relations: Historical and contemporary realities. *Oxford Research Encyclopedia of Religion*. Retrieved from http://religion.oxfordre.com/

Smith, J. I. (2000). *Islam in America*. New York, NY: Columbia University Press.

Smith, R. C., & Eisenberg, E. (1987). Conflict at Disneyland: A root-metaphor analysis. *Communication Monographs, 54*, 367–380.

Smith, R. R., & Windes, R. R. (1997). The progay and antigay issue culture: Interpretation, influence, and dissent. *Quarterly Journal of Speech, 83*(1), 28–48.

Smutkupt, S., & Barna, L. M. (1976). Impact of nonverbal communication in an intercultural setting: Thailand. In F. Casmir (Ed.), *International and intercultural communication annual* (Vol. 3, pp. 130–138). Falls Church, VA: Speech Communication Association.

Snyder, M., & Uranowitz, S. W. (1978). Reconstructing the past: Some cognitive consequences of person perception. *Journal of Personality & Social Psychology, 36*, 941–950.

Socialbakers. (n.d.). Twitter statistics for Saudi Arabia. https://www.socialbakers.com/statistics/twitter/profiles/saudi-arabia/

Somani, I. S. (2010). Becoming American. *Journal of International and Intercultural Communication, 3*, 59–81.

Soroptimist. (2016). Sex slavery/trafficking: Frequently asked questions. Retrieved from http://www.soroptimist.org/trafficking/faq.html

Southwest Airlines. (2017). *Culture*. Retrieved from https://www.southwest.com/html/about-southwest/careers/culture.html

Spellberg, D. A. (2013). *Thomas Jefferson's Qur'an: Islam and the founders*. New York, NY: Alfred A. Knopf.

Spencer, E. P. (1995). Educator insights: Euro Disney—What happened? What next? *Journal of International Marketing, 3*(3), 103–114.

Spitzberg, B. H. (2000). A model of intercultural communication competence. In L. A. Samovar & R. E. Porter (Eds.), *Intercultural communication: A reader* (pp. 375–387). Belmont, CA: Wadsworth.

Standage, T. (2013). *Writing on the wall: Social media—The first 2,000 years*. New York, NY: Bloomsbury.

Stark, R. (2005). *The victory of reason: How Christianity led to freedom, capitalism, and Western success*. New York, NY: Random House.

State of Israel, Central Bureau of Statistics. (2016). Table 1—Immigrants, by period of immigration (1948-2016). Retrieved from http://www.cbs.gov.il/hodaot2017n/21_17_156t1.pdf

State of Wisconsin v. Jonas Yoder et al., 406 U.S. 205 (1972).

Stauffer, J. (2005). Across the great divide. *Time, 166*(1), 58–65.

Stavenhagen, R. (1986). *Problems and prospects of multiethnic states*. Tokyo, Japan: United Nations University Press.

Stavenhagen, R. (1990). Linguistic minorities and language policy in Latin America: The case of Mexico. In F. Coulmas (Ed.), *Linguistic minorities and literacy: Language policy issues in developing countries* (pp. 56–62). Berlin, Germany: Mouton.

Steele, C. M., & Aronson, J. (1995). Stereotype threat and the intellectual test performance of African Americans. *Journal of Personality & Social Psychology, 69*, 797–811.

Steinfatt, T. M. (1989). Linguistic relativity: Toward a broader view. In S. Ting-Toomey & F. Korzenny (Eds.), *International and intercultural communication annual* (Vol. 13, pp. 35–75). Newbury Park, CA: Sage.

Steinmetz, K. (2014, July 28). Not just a smiley face. *Time*, pp. 52–53.

Stevens, E. P. (1973). *Marianismo*: The other face of machismo in Latin America. In A. Pescatelo (Ed.), *Female and male in Latin America* (pp. 89–102). Pittsburgh, PA: University of Pittsburgh Press.

Stevenson, V. (1999). *The world of words: An illustrated history of Western languages* (Rev. ed.). New York, NY: Sterling.

Stewart, E. C. (1972). *American cultural patterns: A cross-cultural perspective*. Chicago, IL: Intercultural Press.

Stewart, E. C. (1982). Applications of intercultural communication in Japan. *Speech Education, 9*, 4–7.

Sugawara, Y. (1993). *Silence and avoidance: Japanese expatriate adjustment* (Unpublished master's thesis). California State University, San Bernardino.

Sweeney, L. (2013). Discrimination in online ad delivery. *Communications of the ACM, 56*(5), 44–54.

Sypher, B. D. (1985). Culture and communication in organizations. In W. Gudykunst (Ed.), *International and intercultural communication annual* (Vol. 9, pp. 13–29). Newbury Park, CA: Sage.

Szalay, L. B., & Inn, A. (1987). Cross-cultural adaptation and diversity: Hispanic Americans. In Y. Y. Kim & W. B. Gundykunst (Eds.), *International and intercultural communication annual* (Vol. 11, pp. 212–232). Newbury Park, CA: Sage.

Szalay, L. B., Moon, W. T., & Bryson, J. A. (1971). *Communication lexicon on three South Korean audiences: Social, national, and motivational domains.* Kensington, MD: American Institutes for Research.

Tajfel, H. (1969). Social and cultural factors in perception. In G. Lindzey & E. Aronson (Eds.), *The handbook of social psychology* (Vol. 3, 2nd ed., pp. 315–394). Reading, MA: Addison-Wesley.

Tanno, D. V. (1994). Names, narratives, and the evolution of ethnic identity. In A. Gonzalez, M. Houston, & V. Chen (Eds.), *Our voices: Essays in culture, ethnicity, and communication* (pp. 28–32). Los Angeles, CA: Roxbury.

Tanno, D. V., & Jandt, F. E. (1994). Redefining the "other" in multicultural research. *Howard Journal of Communications, 5*(1–2), 36–45.

Tau, B. (2015, February 18). Obama: U.S., West at war with extremists, not Muslims. *Wall Street Journal.* Retrieved from http://www.wsj.com

Taylor, D., Dubé, L., & Bellerose, J. (1986). Intergroup contact in Quebec. In M. Hewstone & R. Brown (Eds.), *Contact and conflict in intergroup encounters* (pp. 107–118). Oxford, UK: Basil Blackwell.

Taylor, P., Lopez, M. H., Martinez, J. H., & Velasco, G. (2012, April 4). *When labels don't fit: Hispanics and their views of identity.* Washington, DC: Pew Hispanic Center. Retrieved from http://www.pewhispanic.org/files/2012/04/PHC-Hispanic-Identity.pdf

Tharoor, S. (2006). *India: From midnight to the millennium and beyond.* New York, NY: Arcade.

Tharoor, S. (Ed.). (2007). *The elephant, the tiger and the cell phone: Reflections on India, the emerging 21st century power.* New York, NY: Arcade.

Theodorou, A. E. (2015, December 23). Americans are in the middle of the pack globally when it comes to importance of religion. Retrieved from http://www.pewresearch.org/fact-tank/2015/12/23/americans-are-in-the-middle-of-the-pack-globally-when-it-comes-to-importance-of-religion/

Ting-Toomey, S. (1985). Toward a theory of conflict and culture. In W. Gudykunst (Ed.), *Communication, culture, and organizational processes* (International and intercultural communication annual, Vol. 9, pp. 71–86). Newbury Park, CA: Sage.

Tobin, J., & Dobard, R. G. (1999). *Hidden in plain view: The secret story of quilts and the underground.* Garden City, NY: Doubleday.

Todd, E. (1985). *The explanation of ideology: Family structures and social systems* (D. Garrioch, Trans.). Oxford, UK: Basil Blackwell.

Tolson, J. (2007). Islam vs. science. *U.S. News & World Report, 143*(8), 48–49.

Trager, G. L. (1961). The typology of paralanguage. *Anthropological Linguistics, 3*(1), 17–21.

Treuer, D. (2012, May 4). Elizabeth Warren says she's Native American. So she is. *Washington Post.*

Triandis, H. C. (1964). Cultural influences upon cognitive processes. In L. Berkowitz (Ed.), *Advances in experimental psychology* (Vol. 2, pp. 1–48). New York, NY: Academic Press.

Trompenaars, A., & Hampden-Turner, C. (2012). *Riding the waves of culture: Understanding diversity in global business* (Rev. and updated 3rd ed.). New York, NY: McGraw-Hill.

Trump slams China over Air Force One stairs incident. (2016, September 6). *The Week.*

Tsujimura, A. (1968). *Japanese culture and communication.* Tokyo, Japan: NHK Books.

Tsujimura, A. (1987). Some characteristics of the Japanese way of communication. In D. L. Kincaid (Ed.), *Communication theory: Eastern and Western perspectives* (pp. 115–126). San Diego, CA: Academic Press.

Tung, T. M. (1990). Southeast Asia refugee mental health: Fourteen years later. *Journal of Vietnamese Studies, 1*(3), 56–64.

Twenge, J. M., Campbell, W. K., & Gentile, B. (2012). Pronoun use in U.S. books reflects women's status, 1900–2008. *Sex Roles, 67,* 488–493.

Twenge, J. M., Campbell, W. K., & Gentile, B. (2013). Changes in pronoun use in American books and the rise of individualism. *Journal of Cross-Cultural Psychology, 44,* 406–415.

Tylor, E. B. (1871). *Primitive culture: Researches into the development of mythology, philosophy, religion, art, and custom.* London, UK: J. Murray.

United Nations. (1979). Convention on the Elimination of All Forms of Discrimination Against Women. Retrieved from http://www.un.org/womenwatch/daw/cedaw/text/econvention.htm

United Nations. (2000). *The world's women 2000: Trends and statistics.* New York, NY: Author.

United Nations. (2006a). *Trends in total migrant stock.* New York, NY: United Nations, Department of Economic and Social Affairs, Population Division.

United Nations. (2006b). *World population monitoring, focusing on international migration and development: Report of the Secretary-General* (E/CN.9/2006/3). New York, NY: Author.

United Nations. (2015). World fertility patterns 2015. Retrieved from http://www.un.org/en/development/desa/population/publications/pdf/fertility/world-fertility-patterns-2015.pdf

United Nations Department of Economic and Social Affairs. (2013). *International migration policies: Government views and priorities.* New York, NY: United Nations.

United Nations Development Programme. (1990). *Human development report.* New York, NY: Oxford University Press.

United Nations Development Programme. (1993). *Human development report.* New York, NY: Oxford University Press.

United Nations Development Programme. (1995). *Human development report.* New York, NY: Oxford University Press.

United Nations Development Programme. (1999). *Human development report.* New York, NY: Oxford University Press.

United Nations Development Programme. (2003). *Arab human development report 2003: Building a knowledge society.* New York, NY: Author.

United Nations Development Programme. (2004). *Arab human development report 2004: Towards freedom in the Arab world.* New York, NY: Author.

United Nations Development Programme. (2007). *Human development report.* New York, NY: Oxford University Press.

United Nations Development Programme. (2008). *Human development report 2007/2008.* New York, NY: Oxford University Press.

United Nations Development Programme. (2013). *Human development report.* New York, NY: Author.

United Nations Development Programme. (2015). *Human development report.* New York, NY: Author.

United Nations Population Division. (2013). *Trends in international migrant stock: The 2013 revision—Migrants by age and sex.* Retrieved from http://www.un.org/en/development/desa/population/publications/pdf/migration/migrant-stock-age-2013.pdf

United Nations Statistics Division. (2015). The world's women 2015: Trends and statistics. Retrieved from http://unstats.un.org/unsd/gender/worldswomen.html

United Nations Statistics Division. (2016a). Millennium Development Goals gender chart 2015. Retrieved from https://mdgs.un.org/unsd/mdg/Resources/Static/Products/Progress2015/Gender_Chart_Web.pdf

United Nations Statistics Division. (2016b). Population undernourished, percentage. Retrieved from http://data.un.org/Data.aspx?d=MDG&f=seriesRowID%3A566

United States v. Sandoval, 231 U.S. 28 (1913).

U.S. Census Bureau. (2009a). *2005–2009 population and housing narrative profile for Puerto Rico.* Washington, DC: Author.

U.S. Census Bureau. (2009b). *American community survey.* Washington, DC: Author.

U.S. Census Bureau. (2010). Selected population profile in the United States: 2010 American Community Survey 1-year estimates. Retrieved from https://factfinder.census.gov/faces/tableservices/jsf/pages/productview.xhtml?src=bkmk

U.S. Census Bureau. (2011). *Native North American languages spoken at home in the United States and Puerto Rico: 2006–2010.* Retrieved from http://www.census.gov/prod/2011pubs/acsbr10-10.pdf

U.S. Census Bureau. (2015). 2015 American Community Survey 1-year estimates. Retrieved from https://factfinder.census.gov/faces/tableservices/jsf/pages/productview.xhtml?src=bkmk

U.S. Government Accountability Office. (2013, November). *Aviation security: TSA should limit future funding for behavior detection activities.* Washington, DC: Author.

Useem, J., Donahue, J. D., & Useem, R. H. (1963). Men in the middle of the third culture: The roles of American and non-Western people in cross-cultural administration. *Human Organization, 22,* 169–179.

Useem, R. H. (1999). *Third culture kids: Focus of major study.* Retrieved from http://www.tckworld.com/useem/art1.html

Useem, R. H., & Downie, R. D. (1976). Third-culture kids. *Today's Education, 65*(3), 103–105.

Vallet, E. (Ed.). (2014). *Borders, fences and walls: State of insecurity?* Abingdon, UK: Routledge.

Vance, J. D. (2016). *Hillbilly elegy: A memoir of a family and culture in crisis.* New York, NY: HarperCollins.

Vang, C. T. (2016). *Hmong refugees in the new world: Culture, community and opportunity.* Jefferson, NC: McFarland.

Vargas-Urpi, M. (2013). Coping with nonverbal communication in public service interpreting with Chinese immigrants. *Journal of Intercultural Communication Research, 42,* 340–360.

Varnell, P. (2000, June 20). The threat of assimilation. *Chicago Free Press.* Retrieved from http://igfculturewatch.com/2000/06/28/the-threat-of-assimilation

Vertovec, S. (1996). Multiculturalism, culturalism, and public incorporation. In S. Vertovec (Ed.), *Migration and social cohesion* (pp. 222–240). Northampton, MA: Edward Elgar.

Vidal, J. (2010, May 29). Nigeria's agony dwarfs the Gulf oil spill: The US and Europe ignore it. *The Observer.* Retrieved from http://www.guardian.co.uk

Vidal, J. (2013, December 14). Toxic "e-waste" dumped in poor nations, says United Nations. *The Observer.* Retrieved from http://www.theguardian.com

Vigdor, J. L. (2011). *Comparing immigrant assimilation in North America and Europe.* Retrieved from http://www.manhattan-institute.org/html/cr_64.htm

Vin, J. (2011). Popular culture and public imaginary: Disney vs. Chinese stories of Mulan. *Javnost-The Public. 18*(1). Retrieved from http://javnost-thepublic.org/

Walgrove, A. (2015, October 21). How Facebook changed LGBT culture, in 3 charts. *Contently.* Retrieved from https://contently.com/strategist/2015/10/21/facebook-changed-culture-3-charts/

Walker, S. (1994). *Hate speech: The history of an American controversy.* Lincoln: University of Nebraska Press.

Walmsley, C. (2016, July 21). The queers left behind: How LGBT assimilation is hurting our community's most vulnerable. *Huffington Post.* Retrieved from http://www.huffingtonpost.com

Wang, X. (1996). Conflict over the role of women in contemporary China: Prospects for liberation and resolution. In F. E. Jandt & P. B. Pedersen (Eds.), *Constructive conflict management: Asia-Pacific cases* (pp. 97–111). Thousand Oaks, CA: Sage.

Warner, M. (Ed.). (1993). *Fear of a queer planet.* Minneapolis: University of Minnesota Press.

Warschauer, M., El Said, G. R., & Zohry, A. (2002). Language choice online: Globalization and identity in Egypt. *Journal of Computer Mediated Communication, 7*(4). Retrieved from http://onlinelibrary.wiley.com/journal/10.1111/(ISSN)1083-6101

Wasserstrom, J. N. (1991). *Student protests in twentieth-century China: The view from Shanghai.* Stanford, CA: Stanford University Press.

Watson, T. J., Jr. (1963). *A business and its beliefs.* New York, NY: McGraw-Hill.

Weaver, M. (2010, October 17). Angela Merkel: German multiculturalism has "utterly failed." *Guardian.* Retrieved from http://www.guardian.co.uk

Weigel, D. (2013, April 19). Tamerlan Tsarnaev, dead bombing suspect: "I don't have a single American friend." *Slate.* Retrieved from http://www.slate.com

Weiner, M. (1994). *Race and migration in imperial Japan.* London, UK: Routledge.

Weinstein, N., Przybylski, A. K., & Ryan, R. M. (2009). Can nature make us more caring? Effects of immersion in nature on intrinsic aspirations and generosity. *Personality and Social Psychology Bulletin, 35,* 1315–1329.

Weller, A. (1998). Human pheromones: Communication through body odour. *Nature, 392,* 126–127.

Wells, S. (2002). *The journey of man: A genetic odyssey.* Princeton, NJ: Princeton University Press.

Westbrook, R. B. (1991). *John Dewey and American democracy.* Ithaca, NY: Cornell University Press.

Wexler, B. E. (2008). *Brain and culture.* Cambridge, MA: MIT Press.

Wharton, D. (2014, January 17). Putin to gays going to the Sochi Olympics: "Leave children in peace." *Los Angeles Times.* Retrieved from http://articles.latimes.com/

What is sustainability? (n.d.). Retrieved from https://www.oregon.gov/ODOT/SUS/pages/what_is_sustainability.aspx

Whetmore, E. J. (1987). *Mediamerica: Form, content, and consequence of mass communication* (3rd ed.). Belmont, CA: Wadsworth.

Whitehead, H. (1981). The bow and the burden strap: A new look at institutionalized homosexuality in Native North America. In S. B. Ortner & H. Whitehead (Eds.), *Sexual meanings: The cultural construction of gender and sexuality* (pp. 80–115). Cambridge: Cambridge University Press.

Whiting, R. (2009). *You gotta have wa* (2nd ed.). New York, NY: Vintage.

Wike, R., Poushter, J., & Zainulbhai, H. (2016a, June 28). America's international image. Retrieved from http://www.pewglobal.org/2016/06/28/americas-international-image/

Wike, R., Poushter, J., & Zainulbhai, H. (2016b, June 29). As Obama years draw to close, president and U.S. seen favorably in Europe and Asia. Retrieved from http://www.pewglobal.org/2016/06/29/as-obama-years-draw-to-close-president-and-u-s-seen-favorably-in-europe-and-asia/

Wike, R., & Stokes, B. (2016, October 5). Chinese public sees more powerful role in world, names U.S. as top threat. Retrieved from http://www.pewglobal.org/2016/10/05/chinese-public-sees-more-powerful-role-in-world-names-u-s-as-top-threat/

Wike, R., Stokes, B., & Poushter, J. (2015, June 23). America's global image. Retrieved from http://www.pewglobal.org/2015/06/23/1-americas-global-image/

Wilkins, R. (2005). The optimal form: Inadequacies and excessiveness within the *asiallinen* [matter of fact] nonverbal style in public and civic settings in Finland. *Journal of Communication, 55,* 383–401.

Willis, D. B. (1994). Transculturals, transnationals: The new diaspora. *International Schools Journal, 14*(1), 29–42.

Willis, L. (2011). Statement. "Behavioral Science and Security: Evaluating TSA's SPOT (Screening of Passengers by Observational Techniques) Program." U.S. House of Representatives, Committee on Science and Technology Subcommittee on Investigations and Oversight, 111th Cong. Retrieved from http://www.dhs.gov/news/2011/04/05/testimony-mr-larry-willis-program-manager-science-and-technology-directorate

Winter, J., & Currier, C. (2015, March 27). Exclusive: TSA's secret behavior checklist to spot terrorists. *The Intercept.* Retrieved from https://theintercept.com/

Wire, S. D., & Bierman, N. (2017, March 22). Still no Espanol on WhiteHouse.gov. *Los Angeles Times,* p. B2.

Witteborn, S. (2007). The situated expression of Arab collective identities in the United States. *Journal of Communication, 57,* 556–575.

Witty, P. (2015, October 8). Searching for signal: The smartphone is the refugee's best friend. *Time,* pp. 56–57.

Wolf, A. (2000). Emotional expression online: Gender differences in emoticon use. *CyberPsychology and Behavior, 3*, 827–833.

Wolff, B. (Producer). (2005, August 5). *The situation* [Television broadcast]. New York, NY: MSNBC.

Women leaders, relying on their peers' power and their own. (2017, January). *National Geographic, 231*(1). Retrieved from http://www.nationalgeographic.com/

Wong, D. F. K., Li, C. Y., & Song, H. X. (2007). Rural migrant workers in urban China: Living a marginalised life. *International Journal of Social Welfare, 16*(1), 32–40.

Wong, G., Derthick, A. O., David, E. J. R., Saw, A., & Okazaki, S. (2016). The *what*, the *why*, and the *how*: A review of racial microaggressions research in psychology. *Race and Social Problems 6*(2), 181–200.

Woodring, A. A. (1995). Power distance and individualism among Japanese university students. *Hiroshima Shudo University Research Review, 11*, 61–75.

World Commission on Environment and Development. (1987). *Our common future*. Oxford, UK: Oxford University Press.

World Economic Forum. (2014). *Global risks 2014* (9th ed.). Geneva, Switzerland: Author. Retrieved from http://www3.weforum.org/docs/WEF_GlobalRisks_Report_2014.pdf

World Economic Forum. (2016). *Global Gender Gap Index 2016*. Retrieved from http://reports.weforum.org/global-gender-gap-report-2016/rankings/

World Economic Forum. (2017). *Top 5 global risks in terms of likelihood. Global Risks Report 2017*. Retrieved from http://reports.weforum.org/globalrisks-2017/the-matrix-of-top-5-risks-from-2007-to-2017/

World Health Organization. (2016). Female genital mutilation: Fact sheet. http://www.who.int/mediacentre/factsheets/fs241/en/

The world's most valuable brands. (2013). *Forbes*. Retrieved from http://www.forbes.com

Yale Center for Environmental Law & Policy. (2012). *2012 EPI*. Retrieved from http://epi.yale.edu/files/2012_epi_report.pdf

Yamazaki, Y., & Hayes, D. C. (2004). An experiential approach to cross-cultural learning: A review and integration of competencies for successful expatriate adaptation. *Academy of Management Learning and Education, 3*, 362–379.

Yep, G. A., Lovaas, K. E., & Elia, J. P. (2003). *Queer theory and communication: From disciplining queers to queering the discipline(s)*. Binghamton, NY: Harrington Park Press.

Yin, J. (2014). Popular culture and public imaginary: Disney vs. Chinese stories of Mulan. *Javnost—The Public, 18*(1), 53–74.

Ying, X. (2010, March 5). No more dog soup? *News China, 20*, 31.

York, J. (2011). How much does internet access matter? *Global Voices Advocacy*. Retrieved from http://advocacy.globalvoicesonline.org/2011/03/10/how-much-does-internet-access-matter

Young, B. B. C. (1980). The Hawaiians. In J. F. McDermott Jr., W.-S. Tseng, & T. W. Maretzki (Eds.), *People and cultures of Hawaii: A psycho-cultural profile* (pp. 5–24). Honolulu: University Press of Hawai'i.

Yum, J. O. (1987). Korean philosophy and communication. In D. L. Kincaid (Ed.), *Communication theory: Eastern and Western perspectives* (pp. 71–86). San Diego, CA: Academic Press.

Yum, J. O. (1988). The impact of Confucianism on interpersonal relationships and communications patterns in East Asia. *Communication Monographs, 55*, 374–388.

Yum, J. O., & Park, H. W. (1990). The effects of disconfirming information on stereotype change. *Howard Journal of Communication, 2*, 357–367.

Zagorin, P. (2003). *How the idea of religious toleration came to the West*. Princeton, NJ: Princeton University Press.

Zaharna, R. S. (2009). An associative approach to intercultural communication competence in the Arab world. In D. K. Deardorff (Ed.), *The SAGE handbook of intercultural competence* (pp. 179–195). Thousand Oaks, CA: Sage.

Zakaria, F. (2011, March 3). Are America's best days behind us? *Time*. Retrieved from http://www.time.com

Zelinsky, W. (1973). *The cultural geography of the United States*. Englewood Cliffs, NJ: Prentice-Hall.

Zenner, W. (1996). Ethnicity. In D. Levinson & M. Ember (Eds.), *Encyclopedia of cultural anthropology* (pp. 393–395). New York, NY: Holt.

Zhang, Q. (2010). Asian Americans beyond the model minority stereotype: The nerdy and the left out. *Journal of International and Intercultural Communication, 3*, 20–37.

Zhao, Y. H. (2000). Rural-to-urban labor migration in China: The past and the present. In L. A. West & Y. H. Zhao (Eds.), *Rural labor flows in China* (pp. 231–250). Berkeley: University of California, Berkeley, Institute of East Asian Studies.

Zhong, B. (2008). Thinking along the cultural line: A cross-cultural inquiry of ethical decision making among U.S. and Chinese journalism students. *Journalism & Mass Communication Educator, 63*, 110–126.

Zimmerman, J. (2013, June 30). An African epidemic of homophobia. *Los Angeles Times*, p. A26.

Zuckerman, M. B. (2008). China's gold-medal moment. *U.S. News & World Report, 145*(5), 94–96.

Index